THE CHRISTIAN MOSES

STUDIES IN CHRISTIANITY AND JUDAISM
Series editor: Terence L. Donaldson

The Studies in Christianity and Judaism series publishes volumes dealing with Christianity and Judaism in their formative periods, with special interest in studies of the relationships between them and of the cultural and social contexts within which they developed.

The series is sponsored by the Canadian Corporation for Studies in Religion whose constituent societies include the Canadian Society of Biblical Studies, Canadian Society for the Study of Religion, Canadian Society of Patristic Studies, Canadian Theological Society, Société canadienne de théologie, and Société québécoise pour l'étude de la religion.

I SACRED RITUAL, PROFANE SPACE
The Roman House as Early Christian Meeting Place
Jenn Cianca

2 THE CHRISTIAN MOSES
Vision, Authority, and the Limits of Humanity in the New Testament and Early Christianity
Jared C. Calaway

The Christian Moses

*Vision, Authority, and the Limits of Humanity
in the New Testament and Early Christianity*

JARED C. CALAWAY

McGill-Queen's University Press
Montreal & Kingston · London · Chicago

© McGill-Queen's University Press 2019

ISBN 978-0-7735-5863-2 (cloth)
ISBN 978-0-7735-5864-9 (paper)
ISBN 978-0-7735-5979-0 (EPDF)
ISBN 978-0-7735-5980-6 (EPUB)

Legal deposit fourth quarter 2019
Bibliothèque nationale du Québec

Printed in Canada on acid-free paper that is 100% ancient forest free
(100% post-consumer recycled), processed chlorine free.

We acknowledge the support of the Canada Council for the Arts.

Nous remercions le Conseil des arts du Canada de son soutien.

Library and Archives Canada Cataloguing in Publication

Title: The Christian Moses : vision, authority, and the limits of humanity
    in the New Testament and early Christianity / Jared C. Calaway.
Names: Calaway, Jared, author.
Series: Studies in Christianity and Judaism ; 2.
Description: Series statement: Studies in Christianity and Judaism ; 2
    | Includes bibliographical references and index.
Identifiers: Canadiana (print) 20190149353 | Canadiana (ebook)
    20190149396 | ISBN 9780773558649 (paper) | ISBN 9780773558632
    (cloth) | ISBN 9780773559790 (EPDF) | ISBN 9780773559806 (EPUB)
Subjects: LCSH: Moses (Biblical leader)—In the New Testament. | LCSH:
    Bible. New Testament—Criticism, interpretation, etc. | LCSH: Visions
    in the Bible. | LCSH: God (Christianity) | LCSH: Christianity and
    other religions—Judaism. | LCSH: Judaism—Relations—Christianity.

Classification: LCC BS580.M6 C35 2019 | DDC 222/.1092—dc23

This book was typeset by True to Type in 10.5/13 Sabon

For Ben and Xander

Contents

Acknowledgments   ix

Abbreviations to Ancient Sources   xiii

1 Introduction: Moses, Vision, and Human Limits   3

2 To See God and Live in the Hebrew Bible and Ancient
   Judaism   22

3 Moses' and Humanity's Limitations in the New Testament   64

4 Justin Martyr of Flavia Neapolis (c. 100–165 CE):
   Theophany Is Christophany   86

5 Theophilus to Autolycus: The Son's Masquerade   105

6 Ireneaus of Lyons (c. 140–202 CE):
   Progressive Dispensational Visions of Purification   111

7 Clement of Alexandria (c. 150–215 CE):
   Moses as the Model Gnostic Visionary   132

8 Tertullian of Carthage (c. 160–220 CE):
   Theophany as Incarnation Training   154

9 Origen (c. 185–254 CE): Purifying the Eye of the Mind   169

10 Moses, Vision, and Episcopal Authority in Late-Antique
    Christianity   191

11 "Show Me Yourself": Corporeal, Spiritual, and Intellectual Vision
    in Augustine of Hippo (354–430 CE)   213

12 Conclusion: The Agonies and the Ecstasies of Moses' Visions   235

Notes   265
Bibliography   359
Index   381

Acknowledgments

This project has multiple roots. At an annual meeting of the Society of Biblical Literature and the American Academy of Religion several years ago, after I had finished my dissertation, I had several chats with some of my mentors, colleagues, and friends as I was searching out my next project. I occasionally threw out the idea of a history of the interpretation of Moses on the mountaintop, and, though they may not remember it, I received early encouragement from two very different scholars to pursue this idea: David Carr and April DeConick.

Even before I started working on my dissertation, I had worked out some of the themes and portions of this book in a paper written for John Anthony McGuckin concerning how Philo, Clement of Alexandria, Origen of Alexandria, Gregory of Nyssa, Pseudo-Dionysius the Areopagite, and Maximus the Confessor interpreted the dark cloud Moses entered in Exodus 19 and 24. Just after I finished my dissertation, I quickly wrote an essay for John McGuckin and Jeff Pettis, who convened a conference at Union Theological Seminary on divine visions in various parts of antiquity. I was assigned ancient Judaism, and, using the method of the history of interpretation, I worked through how ancient and late-ancient Jews handled the problems of the competing verses of Exodus 33:20 and Numbers 12:8, among others, concerning divine vision. This essay was then published as "To See God and Live in Late Antique Judaism" in a volume edited by Jeff Pettis and published by Gorgias Press, and now serves as the basis for Chapter 2. I would like to thank Gorgias Press for the permission to reprint an updated version of that essay.

This project additionally combines these streams of thought with some of the concerns I laid out in my dissertation, which became my first monograph, of how ancient writers discussed who can access the sacred and divine – as well as when and how. In that monograph, I focused on accessing sacred space and sacred time; in this study, I turn to ancient histories of interpretations of Moses' encounters with God to demarcate the boundaries of that encounter, which lead to questions of how others can also have such an encounter, including who, when, and who gets to decide these questions.

As I was the last student that Alan Segal ever saw to completion before his untimely death, one might expect to see his influence in my work most overtly in my dissertation and first monograph; it turns out that my research has taken the opposite direction. As strange as this may seem, there is not a single reference to any of his works in my earliest publications. By contrast, one can see his work liberally cited throughout this current volume, as our interests finally intersected at several points, especially his own dissertation-turned-monograph, *Two Powers in Heaven*.

There are many people and institutions to thank for their support. I taught at Illinois Wesleyan University twice while doing research for this project. I would like to thank the Religion Department – Carole Myscofski, Kevin Sullivan, Bob Erlewine, Tao Jin, and Nawaraj Chaulagain – for giving me both space and time to do massive amounts of reading. The IWU religion program also invited me to give a public presentation on this book at the Illinois Wesleyan Religion Colloquium in October 2014. I would like to thank the program for the invitation, and the faculty and students for their feedback.

I started writing this book in earnest while teaching at the University of Mississippi, Desoto. Many of my initial readings of ancient sources occurred during that very productive year. I presented some material that did not make it into the final manuscript on the "gnostic Moses" at the University of Mississippi Religious Studies Colloquium in September 2013. I would like to thank the religion and philosophy faculty and students for their questions at this early stage of my project, and the Outreach Program for providing support.

The bulk of the writing occurred, however, during my time teaching at Illinois College. I would like to thank my colleagues at Illinois College, especially Adam Porter, Caryn Riswold, Paul Spalding, John Laumakis, and, more recently, Jenny Barker-Devine, for their support, giving me a place to teach, read, and write.

I would also like to thank everyone at McGill-Queen's University Press. Firstly, Kyla Madden, senior editor extraordinaire, sat with me at the SBL/AAR conference in 2017, patiently listening to me discuss my book at great length, and encouraged me to submit it to the press. She has made each stage of the publishing process as painless as possible. I would also like to thank Terry Donaldson for accepting my manuscript into his series – as well as the board for officially accepting it. Patricia Kennedy's astute eyes have saved me from several grammatical and stylistic problems.

In addition to the colleagues and students who have asked questions and made comments on my many Moses presentations, I want to thank Jeff Pettis for reading and commenting on portions of the manuscript, and Celia Deutsch for offering detailed critical feedback on the entire manuscript, often persistently asking difficult questions, particularly on social contexts and relations of the ancient figures studied here. These were often questions that I still cannot answer, but they have led me to create thicker descriptions of interrelations of biblical interpretation and social contexts. One could not ask for a more generous and critical reader. I would like to thank April DeConick, who outed herself as one of my blind reviewers with a twinkle in her eye, and the other blind reviewer for offering substantial feedback, especially leading to greater clarity in my introduction and conclusion, and in the introductions and conclusions to each chapter.

Finally, I have been working on this book in earnest since 2013. I want to thank my family – especially my wife, Stacy – for not only putting up with my long absences at the office working on this book, but for actively encouraging me to work on it. I started on this the summer before my first son, Benjamin (Ben), was born. Since then, we have moved four times and had another son, Alexander (Xander). I would not have been able to read and write as much as I have if my mother-in-law, Norma Camacho, were not around as much as she is to look after the boys. I have also used my parents – Gerald and Jane Calaway – as sounding boards for some of my ideas. Ultimately, I decided to dedicate this book to my boys, Benjamin and Alexander, whose lives thus far have been entwined with its production.

Abbreviations to Ancient Sources

1 Apoc. Jas.	*First Apocalypse of James*
1 Clem.	*1 Clement*
1 Cor.	1 Corinthians
1 En.	*1 Enoch*
1 Kgs.	1 Kings
1 Pet.	1 Peter
1 Tim.	1 Timothy
2 Cor.	2 Corinthians
2 En.	*2 Enoch*
2 Kgs.	2 Kings
3 En.	*3 Enoch*
Acts	Acts of the Apostles
Abot. R. Nat.	*Abot de Rabbi Nathan*
Ambrose of Milan, *Expos. Luke*	*Exposition on the Gospel of Luke*
Anastasius I of Antioch, *Hom. Transf.*	*Homilies on the Transfiguration*
ANF	*Ante-Nicene Fathers*, 10 Volumes
Apoc. Ab.	*Apocalypse of Abraham*
Apoc. John	*Apocryphon of John*
Apoc. Pet.	*Apocalypse of Peter*
Apoc. Zeph.	*Apocalypse of Zephaniah*
Apost. Const.	*Apostolic Constitutions*
Asc. Isa.	*Ascension of Isaiah*
Augustine of Hippo, *Conf.*	*Confessions*
– City of God	*City of God against the Pagans*

– *Hom.*	*Homilies*
– *Hom. Ps.*	*Homilies on the Psalms*
– *Literal Genesis*	*Literal Interpretation of Genesis*
– *Retr.*	*Retractiones*
– *Teaching*	*On Christian Teaching*
– *Trinity*	*On the Trinity*
b. B. Metz.	*Bavli* (Babylonian Talmud), *Baba Metzi'a*
b. Ber.	*Bavli, Berakot*
b. Hag.	*Bavli, Hagigah*
b. Meg.	*Bavli, Megillah*
b. Men.	*Bavli, Menachot*
b. San.	*Bavli, Sanhedrin*
b. Shab.	*Bavli, Shabbat*
b. Sotah	*Bavli, Sotah*
b. Yev.	*Bavli, Yevamot*
b. Yoma	*Bavli, Yoma*
Barn.	*Epistle of Barnabas*
Basil of Caesarea, *Adol.*	*To Adolescents*
– *Hom. Hex.*	*Homilies on the Hexaemeron*
Clement of Alexandria, *Adum.*	*Adumbrationes / Sketches*
– *Ecl.*	*Eclogae Propheticae / Selections of the Prophets*
– *Exc.*	*Excerpta ex Theodoto / Excerpts from Theodotus*
– *Paed.*	*Paedagogus / Instructor*
– *Prot.*	*Protrepticus / Exhortation to the Greeks*
– *Strom.*	*Stromateis / Miscellanies*
Col.	Colossians
Cyril of Alexandria, *Hom.*	*Homilies*
Dan.	Daniel
Deut.	Deuteronomy
Deut. Rab.	*Deuteronomy Rabbah*
Did. Apost.	*Didascalia Apostolorum*
Eccl. Rab.	*Ecclesiastes Rabbah / Kohelet Rabbah*
Eusebius of Caesarea, *Constantine*	*Life of Constantine*
– *Hist. Ch.*	*History of the Church*

Exod.	Exodus
Exod. Rab.	*Exodus Rabbah*
Ezek.	Ezekiel
Ezekiel the Tragedian, *Exag.*	*Exagoge*
Gal.	Galatians
Gen.	Genesis
Gen. Rab.	*Genesis Rabbah*
Gos. Phil.	*Gospel of Philip*
Gregory of Nazianzus, *Or.*	*Orations*
Gregory of Nyssa, *Ag. Eun.*	*Against Eunomius*
– *Comm. Song*	*Commentary on the Song of Songs*
– *Hom. Beat.*	*Homilies on the Beatitudes*
– *Inscr. Ps.*	*Treatise on the Inscription of the Psalms*
– *Moses*	*Life of Moses*
– *Thaum.*	*Life of Gregory the Wonder worker / Thaumaturgus*
Heb.	Hebrews
Hekh. Rab.	*Hekhalot Rabbati*
Hekh. Zut.	*Hekhalot Zutarti*
Ignatius of Antioch, *Phil.*	*To the Philadelphians*
– *Smyrn.*	*To the Smyrnians*
Irenaeus, *A.H.*	*Against Heresies / Refutation and Over-throw of the Knowledge Falsely So Called*
– *Dem.*	*Demonstration of Apostolic Teaching*
Isa.	Isaiah
Jer.	Jeremiah
Jerome, *Comm. Isa.*	*Commentary on Isaiah*
– *Comm. Matt.*	*Commentary on Matthew*
– *Ep.*	*Epistles / Letters*
John of Damascus, *Or. Transf.*	*Orations on the Transfiguration*
Josephus, *Ag. Ap.*	*Against Apion*
– *Ant.*	*Antiquities of the Jews*
– *War*	*Jewish War*
Jub.	*Jubilees*
Judg.	Judges

Justin, *Apol.*	*Apology*
– *Dial.*	*Dialogue with Trypho the Jew*
Leo I, *Hom.*	*Homilies*
Lev.	Leviticus
Lev. Rab.	*Leviticus Rabbah*
LXX	Septuagint
m. Avot	*Mishnah, Avot*
Maʿas. Merk.	*Maʿaseh Merkavah*
Matt.	Matthew
Mek.	*Mekhilta de Rabbi Ishmael*
Mek. R. Shim. b. Yoh.	*Mekhilta de Rabbi Shimeon bar Yohai*
Methodius, *Or. Simeon and Anna*	*Oration on Simeon and Anna*
– *Resurrection*	*On the Resurrection*
Mid. Prov.	*Midrash Proverbs*
Mid. Ps.	*Midrash Psalms / Tehillim*
Neofiti	*Targum Neofiti 1*
Num.	Numbers
Num. Rab.	*Numbers Rabbah*
Origen, *Ag. Cels.*	*Against Celsus*
– *Comm. Eph.*	*Commentary on Ephesians*
– *Comm. John*	*Commentary on John*
– *Comm. Luke*	*Commentary on Luke*
– *Comm. Matt.*	*Commentary on Matthew*
– *Comm. Ps.*	*Commentary on the Psalms*
– *Comm. Song*	*Commentary on the Song of Songs*
– *Frag. Gen.*	*Fragments on Genesis*
– *Hom. 2 Sam.*	*Homilies on 2 Samuel*
– *Hom. Exod.*	*Homilies on Exodus*
– *Hom. Gen.*	*Homilies on Genesis*
– *Hom. Jer.*	*Homilies on Jeremiah*
– *Hom. Num.*	*Homilies on Numbers*
– *Hom. Song*	*Homilies on the Song of Songs*
– *Martyrdom*	*Exhortation to Martyrdom*
– *Princ.*	*On First Principles*
Pesiq. Rab.	*Pesiqta Rabbati*
Pesiq. Rab Kah.	*Pesiqta de Rab Kahana*
PG	J.P. Migne, *Patrologiae Graecae*
Phil.	Philippians

Philo, *Abraham*	*On the Life of Abraham*
– *Agriculture*	*On Agriculture*
– *Alleg. Int.*	*Allegorical Interpretation*
– *Cherubim*	*On the Cherubim*
– *Confusion*	*On the Confusion of Tongues*
– *Contemplative Life*	*On the Contemplative Life*
– *Creation*	*On the Creation of the World*
– *Decalogue*	*On the Decalogue*
– *Dreams*	*On Dreams*
– *Eternity*	*On the Eternity of the World*
– *Flight*	*On Flight and Finding*
– *Giants*	*On Giants*
– *Good Person*	*That Every Good Person Is Free*
– *Heir*	*Who Is the Heir of Divine Things?*
– *Migration*	*On the Migration of Abraham*
– *Moses*	*On the Life of Moses*
– *Names*	*On the Change of Names*
– *Posterity*	*On the Posterity of Cain*
– *Prelim. Studies*	*On Mating with Preliminary Studies*
– *Providence*	*On Providence*
– *QE*	*Questions and Answers on Exodus*
– *QG*	*Questions and Answers on Genesis*
– *Sacrifices*	*On the Sacrifices of Cain and Abel*
– *Spec. Laws*	*On the Special Laws*
– *Worse*	*That the Worse Attacks the Better*
Pirqe R. El.	*Pirqe Rabbi Eliezer*
PL	J.P. Migne, *Patrologiae Latinae*
Plato, *Rep.*	*Republic*
– *Tim.*	*Timaeus*
– *Theaet.*	*Theaetetus*
Plotinus, *Enn.*	*Enneads*
Proclus of Constantinople, *Or.*	*Orations*
Ps.	Psalms
Pseudo-Jonathan	*Targum Pseudo-Jonathan*

Pseudo-Philo, *Bibl. Ant.*	*Book of Biblical Antiquities*
Rev.	Revelation
Rom.	Romans
Rufinus, *Apol.*	*Apology*
– *Apol. Anast.*	*Apology to Anastasius*
– *Pref. Gaud.*	*Preface to To Gaudentius*
– *Pref. Her.*	*Preface to To Heraclius*
– *Pref. Princ.*	*Preface to On First Principles*
Ruth Rab.	*Ruth Rabbah*
Sed. Eli. Rab.	*Seder Eliyahu Rabbah*
Sifra Lev.	*Sifra Leviticus*
Sifre Deut.	*Sifre Deuteronomy*
Sifre Num.	*Sifre Numbers*
Sir.	Sirach / Ecclesiasticus
Song Rab.	*Song of Songs Rabbah*
Soranus, *Gyn.*	*Gynecology*
t. Hag.	*Tosefta, Hagigah*
T. Levi	*Testament of Levi*
T. Mos.	*Testament of Moses*
Tanh. B	*Tanhuma B Yelammedenu*
Tertullian, *Ag. Jews*	*Against the Jews*
– *Ag. Herm.*	*Against Hermogenes*
– *Ag. Marc.*	*Against Marcion*
– *Ag. Prax.*	*Against Praxeas*
– *Ag. Val.*	*Against the Valentinians*
– *Apol.*	*Apology*
– *Resurrection*	*On the Resurrection of the Dead / Flesh*
– *Soul*	*On the Soul*
Theophilus of Antioch, *Aut.*	*To Autolycus*
Wis.	Wisdom of Solomon
y. Hag.	*Yerushalmi* (Palestinian Talmud), *Hagigah*
y. Peah	*Yerushalmi, Peah*
Zech.	Zechariah

THE CHRISTIAN MOSES

I

Introduction

Moses, Vision, and Human Limits

Our wise men, Moses who was the most ancient and the prophets who suc-
ceeded him, were the first to understand that "the highest good cannot at
all be expressed in words," when, seeing that God manifests himself to those
who are worthy and ready to receive him, they wrote that God appeared to
Abraham, for instance, or to Isaac, or to Jacob. But who it was that
appeared, and what sort of a person, and in what way, and to which of those
among us, are questions which they have left for the examination of *people
who can show themselves to be like the men to whom he appeared.* (Origen,
Against Celsus 6.4)[1]

Thus it is that the historian of the mystics, summoned, as they are, to say
the other, repeats their experience in studying it: an exercise of absence
defines at once the operation by which he produces his text and that which
constructed theirs. (Michel de Certeau, *The Mystic Fable*, 1:11)[2]

MOSES AND THE LIMITS OF HUMANITY

In this book, I offer an outrageous argument. I will contend that
Moses was more important in enabling emergent Christians to think
through what it means to be human than was Jesus. While Jesus
would be considered fully human and fully divine at the Council of
Chalcedon (451 CE), with some notable exceptions,[3] Jesus was considered humanity both embodied and transcended. Moses, however,
who encountered God on the mountaintop (whether Sinai, Horeb, or
Nebo) represented the possibilities and the limits of those who are
fully human in the overwhelming face of divinity, no matter how

transformative that encounter was thought to be.[4] I hope the strange-
ness of this argument will help us see early Christians with new eyes,
while delving into a much broader question at the heart of the liberal-
arts tradition: what does it mean to be human?

The study of what it means to be human has been revived in several sectors of academe. In particular, "post-humanism" has challenged
the category of human as *sui generis* or undermined humanity's singularity compared to other forms of existence, particularly animals.
Most of these studies have taken as their cue the posthumously published books by Jacques Derrida, *The Animal That Therefore I Am* and
the two-volume *Beast and the Sovereign*, all of which undermine Carte-
sian duality between mind and body and humans and animals.[5]
Nonetheless, as with all forms of "post-," its challenge has revived that
which is contested. By critiquing the category of human in general,
one is thrust back once again into thinking deeply about the human
and, more importantly, about human*s*.

The broader question of what it means to be and not to be human
is not limited to religion, philosophy, or the humanities more generally; it is part and parcel of modern knowledge production and affects
all sectors of scholarly investigation. One may be a biologist examining
the place of humans among other animal species, or investigating the
increasingly manifold and complicated boundaries between humans
and machines in evolving biotechnologies. Questions of what it means
to be human in the study of human consciousness have become
entwined with the accelerating technologies of artificial intelligence.

These sectors of investigation interrogate human uniqueness, but
this questioning is nothing new. It is not only a modern or even
medieval phenomenon. Those limits guarding humanity's uniqueness had already become undermined, blurred, and complicated in
the mists of antiquity. Ovid's *Metamorphoses*, old tales of werewolves,
or, more to the point, transformations of humans to angelic or divine
status (or vice versa), as well as the proliferation of hybrid creatures
from the sphinx, the chimera, the cherubim, or nearly every creature
in the Apocalypse of John, all haunt the reader with the spectre of
the uncanny.[6]

These are all fascinating – even disturbing – realms of inquiry, truly
a *mysterium tremendum et fascinans*. Yet in the realm of ancient to late-
ancient religion, I will examine a different set of shifting boundaries:
how the variegated group of emergent Christians considered the fur-

thest limits of humanity in the overwhelming face of divinity, in what may seem an unlikely, but ultimately one of the most fruitful, places: Christian readings of Moses on the mountaintop.

THE CHALLENGE OF MOSES: TENSIONS, QUESTIONS, AND THE THREE-PART SOLUTION

Ancient Christian readings of Moses' experiences on the mountain pressed these questions of human limitations into ever-new formations as they grappled with older biblical tensions: Did Moses see God? If so, can anyone else? If not, why not? Who decides? Who can decide?

At the heart of these questions are two rival verses of the Bible. Here is the problem. In Exod. 33:20, after Moses requests to see God's glory, God says to Moses: "you cannot see my face; for no human shall see me [Greek: my face] and live."[7] Subsequently, God offers to show Moses his backside or hindparts – whatever that means is unclear, but early Christians had some ideas.[8] On the other hand, in Num. 12:8, God says that Moses is greater than everyone else, because, "With him I speak face to face [Greek: mouth to mouth] – clearly, not in riddles; and he beholds the form [Greek: glory] of the LORD." How does one reconcile these two apparently opposing statements? How did ancient Jews and Christians do it?

While there have been many important studies on Moses, ranging from major edited volumes,[9] studies of Moses in particular books of biblical (including canonical and extracanonical) literature,[10] and some thematic studies,[11] these works rarely ever intersect with the concerns of this current study. On the contrary, most scholarship that approaches this theme does so obliquely, at occasional intersections, or while focusing on later medieval Jewish and Christian attempts to resolve this issue.

Nonetheless, scholars have occasionally considered this biblical tension in writing. Speaking directly of the materials in Exod. 33:20 and Num. 12:8, A. Gelin writes in 1954, "These anthropomorphisms and these theologoumena – or expressions by which one represents God manifesting himself – are the fruit of an fledgling theology: the face of Yahweh, his glory, his name, his hand, his back, so many manifestations more or less partial of the Inapproachable, but with whom Moses, however, has contact."[12] Gelin's discussion is sandwiched in between two quotes: Exod. 33:20 before it and Num. 12:8 after it. He interestingly notes that, at his most unapproachable and glorious, God is exceedingly anthropomorphic. He further observes the paradox that God is inapproachable, but Moses nonetheless has contact, even if conceding a potentially partial manifestation of the divine.

While Gelin would call this theological reflection between Exod. 33:20 and Num. 12:8 "fledgling" (*balbutiante*), most scholars would speak of it as surprising, or even stunning. Speaking of ancient Jewish ascent apocalypses that featured heroes, such as Moses, Enoch, Abraham, Levi, and Isaiah, who ascended to heaven and had a vision of the enthroned Glory of God,[13] Alan Segal writes, "In view of the clear polemic against such claims to firsthand knowledge of God together with the biblical statement that no man can see God and live (Exod. 33:20), it is rather surprising that so many ascension and ecstatic journeys are reported in intertestamental literature."[14] Similarly, New Testament scholar Charles Gieschen, focusing on the sources of early Christology, writes concerning these passages, "These epiphanies, especially of God as a man, are fundamental to later conceptions of the figure upon the divine throne in Jewish apocalyptic and mystical literature. It is amazing that these startling epiphanic depictions exist alongside the prominent textual traditions that one cannot see God and live."[15] Scholarly responses to these passages follow similar lines: they are surprised, amazed, startled. Indeed, these juxtaposed statements are amazing, fascinating even, even if emerging or fledgling. How does one explain it though? How did ancient Jews and Christians explain it? How do we explain their explanations? Such frequent scholarly astonishment should lead to inquiry.[16]

This is, indeed, where Elliot Wolfson begins his exceptional analysis of Jewish mysticism in his book *Through a Speculum That Shines*:

> The apparently contradictory beliefs about God's visibility (and hence corporeality) in the Bible should be viewed typologically and not chronologically. Indeed, even with respect to those examples of textual discrepancies to which source method applies, if one adopts a more organic approach, viewing the Bible hermeneutically from the perspective of canon in its completed form, the problem is raised to a secondary level: Given the final redaction of the sources, how can the two be reconciled? How can both assertions be simultaneously maintained? How can the two statements inhabit the same corpus? Yet it is precisely because both points of

view, so strikingly different, inhabit the same corpus that the history of Jewish attitudes toward the visual imaging of God unfolded in the dialectical way it did.[17]

Wolfson, here, rejects the way out of source criticism, which assigns Exod. 33:20 to J and Num. 12:8 to P, despite J's otherwise nonchalant anthropomorphic appearances of the LORD in the Pentateuch.[18] Wolfson points out that the history of Jewish representation of the divine is not a straight or progressive line. Later authors often take up much earlier views. Even while source critical theory is important for the history of the development of tradition in ancient Israel and Yehud, the problem remains for later interpreters who did not get to resort to source criticism: both views – God cannot be seen and God is seen – can be found in the same corpus of sacred literature.[19] These opposing verses created a productive hermeneutical tension for later Jews, particularly for Wolfson's analysis the Rabbis, Hekhalot mystics, Haside Ashkenaz, and medieval Kabbalists.[20] As he writes concerning specifically the Merkavah mystics, "The full force of the paradox is appreciated when one acknowledges that the God seen by the mystic is the invisible God."[21] What is more, Moses will repeatedly be represented as the prototypical and greatest of such visionaries.[22]

Early Christians in the first four centuries CE, too, made use of these duelling verses, finding in them a productive tension with hermeneutical potential. So, the questions that guide this study are not why these two "striking" sets of positions can be found in the Bible, but what early Christians did with them and why it matters. Why might one seek to affirm that Moses saw God or God's form/glory (Num. 12:8) or deny that he saw God or God's face (Exod. 33:20)? What's at stake? *Cui bono?*

Let me illustrate by quickly looking at the first century and then turning briefly to the late fourth. We will find much has, indeed, changed; the world of Jesus is not the world of post-Nicene Christianity. In the New Testament, with a couple of important exceptions, Moses has not seen God – nor has anyone else for that matter – since God is invisible; only the Son, who has come from the Father can see and know the Father or make the Father known. Instead, Moses saw angels – and the plural is significant here – and the pattern of the tabernacle (see Chapter 3). If one turns, however, to the *Apost. Const.* 8.5.46, which comes into its present form in the late fourth century (c. 380 CE), it actually quotes Num. 12:8 to illustrate that Moses had unmediated, direct contact with God, even to the exclusion of angelic mediators. It does so in order to undergird the current structure of authority of the Church, which, it says, God directly revealed to Moses in the ancient configuration of Israelite priestly authority – and that one must obey that structure (see Chapter 10). Clearly much had changed from the first century, when Moses did not see God, but only angels, to the fourth century, when Moses saw God directly without any angelic interference.

What happened in the middle? The path from denying Moses' visions to affirming them nearly wholeheartedly is a tortuous – and therefore interesting – one. As this study works through figures like Justin Martyr, Theophilus of Antioch, Irenaeus of Lyons, Clement of Alexandria, Tertullian, Origen, Basil of Caesarea, Gregory of Nazianzus, Gregory of Nyssa, and Augustine of Hippo, we will find three basic, overlapping solutions to this problem, all with important social contexts: (1) the status of the seeing subject (or who gets to see); (2) the modes or types of seeing (how one sees); and (3) the object seen (what is seen). The first indicates status. Certain types of people cannot see God; certain – purer – types of people can. Sometimes, however, the purity necessary is not fully obtainable in this life, and so must be accomplished in the next life; that is, if one cannot see God and live, one can die and see God. Other times, however, very rare figures achieve it in this life, and Moses is typically the prototype, often paired with Paul, due to 2 Corinthians 12.[23] The second solution suggests many types of seeing and, following philosophical orientations, indicates that physically seeing God is impossible (even for the Son), because God is by nature invisible. Therefore, "seeing" is intellectual activity; it is contemplative seeing with the eye of the mind. The third, and most popular, solution distinguishes between what is seen. That is, Moses saw something. What was it? Sometimes angels, but most second- and third-century Christians following Justin Martyr would say that he saw Christ, though they would disagree on *how* he saw Christ. As noted, these are not mutually exclusive, and some may say that a prophet who saw the Son in this life will see the Father in the next life. Sometimes later generations often return to earlier formulations in new contexts where they no longer fit; sometimes they will reject earlier solutions as heretical! They all, moreover, especially the second- and third-century materials, tend to appear in apologetic and polemical literature. One must, therefore, pay attention to each writer's rivals.

This tripartite matrix arose out of my analysis of each author and text. This study will, especially when looking at the early Christian materials, work through each author's arguments, rhetoric, and exegeses on their own terms, while also noting how they fit in with or sometimes modify this tripartite matrix. While each of these strategies is well-known to those who study these texts, their juxtaposition and combination in a clear framework of subject, verb, and object provides a new analytical grid. This syntax of seeing will receive direct attention in the conclusions of each chapter and be drawn together at the conclusion of the book. The result provides the reader with a useful and ready framework or matrix to study any account of ancient Jewish, Christian, Greek, Roman, or even later Muslim visions; that is, any groups or individuals who believed such a vision was supposed to be impossible, yet had authoritative accounts of such visions.

WHY MOSES?

Why Moses instead of Abraham, Sarah, Jacob, Joseph, Isaiah, Ezekiel, or Jeremiah? Or, for that matter, Hagar, Gideon, or Samson's parents? Why not Adam and Eve? Firstly, Moses is the model for many of these other figures. As Dale Allison points out in his study on Moses typology in the Gospel of Matthew, several other figures are modelled on Moses in the Bible and in later Jewish and Christian tradition: Joshua, Gideon, Samuel, David, Elijah, Josiah, Ezekiel, Jeremiah, Ezra, Baruch, the Suffering Servant, Hillel, the Messiah, Jesus, Peter, Paul, Gregory the Wonderworker, Anthony of Thebes, Constantine, Ephrem the Syrian, Basil of Caesarea, Theodoret's monks of Syria, and Benedict of Nursia.[24] Allison's list is hardly exhaustive. Clearly Moses was an important – if not the most pre-eminent – figure upon which both Jews and Christians modelled their heroes and themselves.[25]

Moreover, with Moses the stakes become especially high for several reasons. He is also being invoked by late-antique Jews to establish and extend new forms of interpretive authority with the Rabbis. Moreover, he is the seer of seers. That is, while Abraham and especially Jacob also had visions, by this period it was assumed that Moses had written the five books of the Torah. He, therefore, had to be vouchsafed their visions as well as his own. For some Rabbis, his prophecies also contained all *later* prophecies (*Exod. Rab.* 42.8).[26] Turning to the Christian side, moreover, Justin Martyr refers to him as the "first prophet," whether chronologically or in pre-eminence.

As such, Moses is an extreme case of our humanity; he is as good as it can get. While for some ancient Jews, such as Ezekiel the Tragedian and Philo of Alexandria, Moses becomes so exalted that no other human could compare, for the ancient Christians studied here, that unique role belongs to Jesus, and Moses becomes the limiting case. When Moses cannot see God; neither can you – only Jesus can (and even then, maybe even Jesus cannot). If Moses can, certain – elite – people can too, usually bishops, philosophers, and mystics, who all use Moses as a model to follow, and who, indeed, see themselves *as* Moses. When Christians disagree upon what Moses saw, they are debating what is possible for humanity. Moses is the prototype of the possible.

SEEING AND AUTHORITY: SOCIAL CONTEXTS OF VISION

These human limitations do not simply approach a line in the sand but confront a place where ancient ontologies are in conflict, where the edges of the eternal and the temporal approach yet stand apart from one another. While there exists an abyss of difference between creator and created,[27] early Christians drew these edges differently at different times as they responded to social pressures. In short, the boundary-marking by means of divine vision is multiple; the different ways early Christians used the boundary between God and humanity was a means to draw boundaries between social groups and within social groups. As Michel de Certeau writes in his posthumously published second volume of the *Mystic Fable*, "The documentation holds many other surprises for the visitor who sets out in search of mystic fields of knowledge and gradually discovers the system of intersections between the politics of order and the social 'passions' that they express, regulate, and repress without knowing them."[28] The entanglement with such social elements is so dense that he argues, "What it is difficult to discern in these products of time is not the 'social' element (it is everywhere), but the 'mystic' one."[29]

As this study works through several authors and passages, we will discover that deciding whether, how, and what Moses saw was and is no neutral exercise. When an early Christian decided whether or how Moses saw God, it was not mere speculation. It was a statement that established the interpreter's authority to determine what was possible in divine-human relations; that is, what is the nature and limits of the human condition as it seeks visual contact with the divine? It also established the interpreter's position within that realm of possibilities; that is, it determined the interpreter's relationship to others in society. Speaking of a different set of documents, but similarly true for the study of ancient Christian debates about Moses' visions, de Certeau further writes, "The fact is that these works were granted the status of 'mystical' and selected by institutions (a church, a sect, a publisher). They were 'brought to light' and defended by pressure groups during guerrilla warfare between organized trends."[30] The selection of particular models and texts, preferences for certain figures and passages over others, marked different interpreters and interpretive traditions ("organized trends") against others.

As the opening quotation from Origen illustrates, some of these interpreters saw themselves as being in *the same position as the original prophets,* like Moses. The interpreters of scripture stand between God and the people, just as Moses did. Their theology becomes an anthropology, a theory of the human, that has a social context of competition to establish, maintain, and extend authority against rival groups and within one's own group. These dynamics will unfold incrementally throughout this study in each chapter and especially in the conclusion. However, at this point, I want to consider broader social factors of vision that mirror and intersect the more concrete agonistic elements I will delineate chapter by chapter.

Seeing is a social thing. While, in the wake of William James, modern people tend to think of religious experiences as intensely private, once one takes a step back, the social dimensions of claims to such experiences come into focus. As so many feminist analyses of the male gaze have pointed out (and critiqued), visions, gazes, and spectacles are all implicated in unequal social relationships.[31] To determine who sees and what that person can see is an act of power and authority. To see can also be a transaction of power.[32] Likewise, determining who can see and whose seeing is legitimate and illegitimate, especially in terms of divine vision, is an exercise of authority.

In the wake of Michel de Certeau's first volume of *The Mystic Fable,* which traces in genealogical fashion the development of early-modern *la mystique* and its co-evolution of a new eroticism, psychoanalytic theory, historiography, and the "fable,"[33] several scholars have traced the social implications and power relations involved in calling someone a mystic or denying someone that label.[34]

For example, Grace Jantzen has laid out the power struggles of mystical experience in medieval Europe in terms of gender. While she rarely refers to de Certeau's work, she also relies upon and critiques a Foucauldian genealogical method, tracing the terminology of "mystic," "mystical," and "mysticism," and illustrates how their definitions have been entangled in power relations that have excluded or devalued the contributions of women.[35] If female mystics – particularly visionaries – were recognized by ecclesiastical authorities, then they counted as mystics; if not, they were silenced, censured, designated a heretic or a witch. For example, Marguerite Porete (1250–1310), a medieval beguine, was burned at the stake for heresy for her book *Mirror of Simple Souls*, which lays out a spiritual progression that St John of the Cross would stake out two hundred years later. She was a heretic; he was a saint, though one who was persecuted and imprisoned, nonetheless. Of course, Porete also challenged the church, charging it with hypocrisy.

In the process, Jantzen takes issue with William James' account of mystical experience in his *Varieties of Religious Experience*, where, after his famous four criteria of ineffability, noetic quality, transiency, and passivity, he stated that any mystical experience should have authority for the person having it, but it should not have authority for anyone else.[36] The first quality of ineffability and the last statement of non-transferability of authority makes mystical experience in James' account private and unconnected to social structures of authority. While one can find experiences throughout the world that meet one, some, or all of his four marks, the last element, that it ought to be private and unauthoritative for others, is descriptively false in the face of historical evidence. This is masked in James' own method, where, like many in the late-nineteenth and early-twentieth centuries, he sought phenomenological parallels without regard to context; the loss of context marked a loss of understanding of the power dynamics involved in claims and counterclaims to mystical experiential authority.

Closer to the material of this study, Laura Nasrallah has also discussed the agonistic intersections of claims to prophecy, authority, and gender in early Christianity.[37] Also drawing on Foucault, her work engages primarily the discourse of madness and rationality in the rhetoric of texts of 1 Corinthians, Tertullian's *On the Soul*, and part of Epiphanius' *Panarion*. Nasrallah demonstrates how claims to prophetic authority clashed with those of others, who, in turn, asserted that those who claimed such visions or prophetic authority were mad, demonic, or charlatans. Claims to special revelation, therefore, can be a flashpoint for the formation of group identities and jockeying for authority in the early Christian movement.[38]

Both Jantzen's and Nasrallah's approaches are genealogical in the Foucauldian sense. They trace terminology (mystic, mystical, and mysticism; reason and madness) through their source material and consider their discursive relations to power relations.[39] My method, however, varies from this terminological genealogical approach, but takes its social critique seriously:[40] my method is a complex form of the history of interpretation, yet one that does not take a single passage, but a constellation of interrelated and contradictory passages that clearly concerned ancient Jewish and Christian interpreters, tracing the tangled web of interpretive trajectories within the intersecting social fields of philosophers, teachers, biblical interpreters, preachers, presbyters, monks, and bishops.[41] Instead of a genealogy of discourse or terminology, it is one of patterns of reading, interpretation, and commentary.

Critical theories that resort solely to discourse, however, may not seem a suitable fit for what I am doing in this book. Indeed, in this study, the authority of the visionary is rarely in question – Moses was considered a great prophet by most figures analyzed. Nonetheless, power relations, rivalries, and some surprising commonalities among opponents, emerge in these histories of interpretations, as they do in the genealogical studies mentioned above. Instead of a genealogy of words, one finds a genealogy of passages and reading. Through this, Moses still becomes a means to jockey for power between and among Jews and Christians grappling over the skill and authority to interpret Moses. Moses visions – what he saw, how he saw, and when he saw it – become the means to justify particular social arrangements, relations, and identities. These rival interpretations differentiatiated oneself from a created "other" (Jew or heretic), excluded that other, and justified internal ecclesiastical graded authority.

There are some critical hermeneutical reflections that relate commentary to shifting social conditions, rivalries, co-operative endeavours, and power relations that are worth considering for a work of history of interpretation. Hermeneutical theory sometimes looks at commentary, as it does translation, as a rewriting, a re-saying, or a speaking of a new text. The task of interpretation and translation can be creative, but it disciplines or tames the original text, aligning it with its own historical situation, social arrangement, and cultural assumptions.[42]

Even though several critics have made forays into the realm of commentary, Frederic Jameson's "Metacommentary" may provide a more fruitful restarting point on the relationship for reinterpretation and social context.[43] Writing in the early 1970s in response to Susan Sontag's *Against Interpretation* and the rise of Structuralist – especially Claude Levi-Strauss' – readings, he develops some principles of what he calls "metacommentary." He notes commentary and interpretation should not only seek to resolve a problem within a work, but also provide "a commentary on the very conditions of existence of the problem itself."[44] In other words, the interpretive act is not or not only about a good, proper, or precise interpretation of the text, but an explanation of the conditions that give rise to the need or impulse to interpret to begin with.[45] Throughout his essay, he primarily considers the situation of contemporary interpreters, whom he calls not only to interpret a text, but to explain why they feel the need to interpret the text; nonetheless, he also reaches back into past occasions of the impulse to interpretation:

> Thus genuine interpretation directs attention back to history itself, and to the historical situation of the commentator as well as of the work. In this light, it becomes clear how the great traditional systems of hermeneutic – the Talmudic and the Alexandrian, the medieval and the abortive Romantic effort – sprang from cultural need and from the desperate attempt of the society in question to assimilate monuments of other times and places, whose original impulses were quite foreign to them, and which required a kind of rewriting – through elaborate commentary, and by means of the theory of figures – to take their place in a new scheme of things.[46]

In this case, there is a dissonance in the received text and the context of the interpreter, heightened in the case of Homer and the Bible by a community of readers according the received text with some official, authoritative sanction, sacred status, or canonicity. Dissonance of cultural distance and relapsed time between text and interpreter – in this case, often centuries – leads to the need to "rewrite" the work, updating it to resolve such discrepancy of perspectives from the time and place it was written to its later readings.[47] Yet "dissonance" is fairly generic. One must consider what kind of dissonance was occurring: what types of changes had occurred that gave rise to this dissonance.[48]

In the case of ancient readings of Moses' visions, moreover, there is the additionally perceived dissonance within the sacred text, a contradiction to be sorted out.[49] By how it is sorted out and why it is sorted out the way it is returns us, as Jameson says, to historicity: the conditions that call for interpretation in the first place. The dissatisfaction with the original and, therefore, the need to "rewrite" it, or as Derrida might say, displace it,[50] with commentary and interpretation reflects historical situations and, in fact, a dissatisfaction with, if not outright hostility towards, rival interpretations.

This calls for an interpretive intervention in Jameson's metacommentary: when turning to great systems like the Talmudic or Alexandrian or ancient readings in general, one must explain not only the social conditions and cultural dissonance that give rise to the need to interpret in the first place, but why already existing and contemporary alternative interpretations within one's own time and place do not satisfy other interpreters. Rival interpretations of passages at the same time or over time express shifting social and cultural conditions, tensions between groups and within groups. Along with much of critical discourse of interpretation, I am not only interested in the original meaning of the biblical passages under consideration, but, along with Jameson, concerned with the conditions that gave rise to the need to continually reinterpret these passages.

Such socially inflected histories of interpretation are nothing new, though they have become more sophisticated.[51] Other scholars have employed a history of interpretation method alongside social analysis, showing not just how Jews and Christians have interpreted a passage over time, but why. Alan Segal's first book, *Two Powers in Heaven*, traced the history of rival interpretations of a constellation of verses related to the "two powers" controversy in rabbinic texts, and looked at how these verses intersected various Jewish and Christian readings.[52]

More recently, Elizabeth Clark has traced the reading patterns (*Wirkungsgeschichte*) of ancient Christian ascetics in terms of their social contexts, inflecting her analysis with inspiration from Barthes, Derrida, Foucault, and Jameson. Along with her, "I hope here to demonstrate how the interpretation of Biblical texts intersected with the lives of these early Christians and their communities."[53] Annette Reed's first solo-authored book, too, uses reception history or the *Nachleben* ("afterlife") of a text – this time of the tradition of fallen angels, whose teachings corrupted humanity, as found in *1 Enoch* – as a lens to discuss ancient Jewish-Christian relations, examining how

Jews and Christians selected and employed this story of the origins of evil to create social boundaries.[54] Beth Berkowitz's book *Defining Jewish Difference* integrates the history of interpretation with social and cultural history, examining the construction of collective identities and social boundaries through how Jews have repeatedly returned to Lev. 18:3.[55] Her work ranges much more widely than mine, winding from ancient to modern usages of Lev. 18:3, whereas mine is more concentratedly situated in the ancient world, not venturing past Augustine of Hippo. Along with Berkowitz, I would say, "I hesitate to call this book a reception history ... This book is as much a history of some people who read the verse as it is a history of the verse itself ... The problems with the genre notwithstanding – its tendency to examine the read*ing* at the expense of the read*er* and to sacrifice depth for breadth – reception histories enable us to see shared features of reading communities that we might not otherwise see, as well as to define what is distinctive to each reader."[56] Karl Shuve has also examined a socially inflected history of interpretation by looking at how ancient Latin Christians interpreted the Song of Songs according to particular, and often very local, ecclesiastic issues with an eye to the insights and limits of works such as Foucault and Jameson. In his reading of these ancient readers, "Over the course of the third and fourth centuries, the Song became a crucial resource in defining the nature of the church and conduct required of her members."[57] It became a resource to think with. Likewise the visions of Moses.

ASSUMING ANCIENT OPTICS AND DIVINE VISIONS

Finally, before delving into the ancient Jewish and Christian materials, many of the writers in the following chapters make several overlapping assumptions on how ancient optics operated and how this relates or fails to relate to divine visions that are not shared by modern readers. Ancient optics included at least two basic directional elements. One was projective or emissive: light was emitted from the eyes and met the object seen. The other was receptive: what is seen is imprinted on one's mind or soul and becomes a part of you.

Receptive vision, also called "intromission," can be found in philosophical, medical, and legendary materials, including at least one story in the Bible. Through intromission, one becomes what one sees, and can even pass along what one sees to one's progeny. Intromission, therefore, has the greatest potential for transformation of the soul. For example, the ancient physician, Soranus, reports that whatever a woman looks at during intercourse will imprint an image onto her soul, which will be passed on physically to her offspring. He gives stories of women who looked at monkeys during intercourse giving birth to children who looked like monkeys; women would intentionally look at well-proportioned statues to give birth to good-looking children. Moreover, a woman should not have drunken intercourse, since her altered vision will lead to misshapen offspring.[58] A similar assumption seemingly lies behind the story of Jacob and Laban's sheep in Gen. 30:25–43. In this story, Laban gives Jacob every spotted or speckled lamb and goat, while keeping the rest for himself. The trickster-hero Jacob then takes poplar, almond, and plane branches, peels white streaks in them, and puts them in front of the flocks when they drink, leading to them giving birth to spotty lambs and kids.[59]

The more generalized idea that "you are what you see" permeates ancient literature beyond the physical. Both 2 Cor. 3:18 and 1 John 3:2 in the New Testament assume that you become what you see; in this case, the Lord and God. In the *Gospel of Philip*, it is matched by the idea of "only like can see like," and so, in order to see a supernal being, you must become like that being:

> People cannot see anything in the realm unless they become it. In the realm of truth, it is not as human beings in the world, who see the sun without being the sun, and see the sky and the earth and so forth without being them. Rather, if you have seen any things there, you have become those things: if you have seen the spirit, you have become the spirit; if you have seen the anointed (Christ), you have become the anointed (Christ); if you have seen the [father, you] will become the father. Thus [here] (in the world), you see everything and do not [see] your own self. But there, you see yourself; for you shall [become] what you see. (*Gos. Phil.* 61.20–34; trans. Layton)

While the *Gospel of Philip* denies the physical transformative element found in medical literature, it follows the same underlying logic: you are what you see; however, the *Gospel of Philip* only grants such a principle in the realms beyond this material world.[60] Other Christian writers discussed, such as Irenaeus or Clement, would assume or argue that a vision of God led to the attainment of God-like qualities.

The other type of vision is projective. It was developed by ancient philosophers and physicians, supposedly beginning with Empodocles, and was taken up by Plato (e.g., *Timaeus* 46a-c) in the fifth century BCE. In what has become known as emission or extramission theory, rays of light emit from the eyes and interact with the rays of the sun to touch the object of vision and, thereby, create vision. Nonetheless, even this more "active" vision is a two-way street: what is seen still imprints itself on the soul of the viewer. Thereby, "the ray theory of vision specifically insisted on the connection and essential unity and essential continuity of viewer and object in the act of vision."[61] As such, vision is a form of touch.[62]

Augustine of Hippo, following the extramission camp, writes, "I see in myself a body and a soul, one external, the other internal. Which of these should I have questioned about my God, for whom I had already searched through the physical order of things from earth to heaven, as far as I could send the rays of my eyes as messengers" (*Conf.* 10.9; cf. *City of God* 22.29; *Trinity* 9.3.3; 11.2.4–5).[63] In his *Confessions*, Augustine casually assumes that his eyes project "rays." In this, Augustine echoes a sentiment that by the early fifth century CE was already nearly a millennium old and would survive into the early modern period. In this passage, the rays of the eyes are messengers; they are feelers. As Margaret Miles points out, the rays of the eye for Augustine, like others who followed extramission optical theory, ultimately create a kind of touch, connecting seer and seen.[64]

Most of the ancient writers in the following chapters do not directly interact with these theories in their discussions of divine vision, but they do often assume them. Nonetheless, they more often directly address, accept, or reject the philosophical language of contemplation and the Greek mystery language of vision. Most of these writers either explicitly or implicitly accept or reject the Platonic distinction between physical vision and intellectual contemplation. If God is invisible, one cannot see God with the eyes of the body; if God, or a part of God, is mind or intellect, then one must approach God with the "eyes" of the mind. This is "contemplation" (*theoria*). Entangled in the philosophical distinction between physical and intellectual vision is an older type of vision of the divine mysteries. In these, as in the Eleusinian mysteries, one, upon initiation, has a revelatory vision (*epopteia*) of the divine or divine things hidden to the uninitiated. Combined with the philosophical contemplation, this vision could be intellectual, creating a combination of active intellectual striving for vision (*theoria*) and passive reception of it (*epopteia*).[65]

Ancient educated readers, whether Christian or not, in the first five centuries CE would discuss, debate, and often assume these views of optics, philosophical contemplation, and the revelation of mysteries. These cultural foundations of most ancient Christian theories of vision would, in fact, provide some of the dissonance – though also some fortuitous connections – with the biblical narrative, providing part of the impetus for reinterpretation.

ORGANIZATION OF THIS STUDY

This study has three major parts. The first part, consisting of two chapters, looks at biblical materials of the Hebrew Bible and late-antique Judaism and then the New Testament. Covering a wide range of materials, it provides the foundation of the multiple interlocking and contradicting passages that later interpreters will seek to tease out based upon their own philosophical and theological presuppositions, their received traditions, and their shifting social contexts. Nonetheless, one already finds inner biblical reflection and reinterpretation of these traditions. In the post-biblical Jewish reflections, one finds antecedents and parallels to the three strategies used by Christian writers to resolve these biblical tensions.

The second portion, consisting of six chapters and making up the bulk of the work, looks to the solutions of Justin of Neapolis, Theophilus of Antioch, Irenaeus of Lyons, Clement of Alexandria, Tertullian of Carthage, and Origen of Alexandria. This section is where the three types of variation between seer, seeing, and being seen emerge fully and clearly as these writers navigate social contexts of rival Christian groups and persecution by governing authorities.

The final main portion of the book in two chapters looks to the late-antique Christians of the Cappadocian Fathers of Basil of Caesarea, Gregory of Nazianzus, and Gregory of Nyssa, and of Augustine of Hippo, all of whom arrogate Moses' authority for themselves as ultimate mediators between God and the people, to the point of identifying themselves with Moses. Though still a complicated topic, Moses' vision is less occluded than ever before.[66] The conclusion will, after collating the various solutions to the exegetical problems offered by these various Christians, cross-examine them according to their social contexts. Throughout, we will examine the social roles of the interpreters, such as whether they are "freelance ritual experts" or have institutional ties, and the social ties of the interpretive genres used. Writers, for example, engaged external groups or individuals through apologetic and polemical works, or addressed their own community, group, or social network through biblical commentaries, homilies, and church orders. More typically, ancient interpreters employed a complex combination of the two, usually externalizing people within one's own social network – that is, relabelling someone previously thought to be orthodox as heretical – or redirecting such externalizing interpretive strategies by which one jockeys for interpretive authority against rivals toward one's own group to justify or solidify one's authority within that community. In general, second- and third-century Christians would predominantly engage in apologetic and polemical works aimed at external rivals (real or imagined), while fourth-century Christians not only engaged in polemics against other Christians, but often directed their readings toward people within their own religious community.

This study is very wide-ranging, but it also must have limits, leading to some clear omissions. Firstly, this study focuses on what E.R. Dodds calls "mystical theorists."[67] While the following chapters will discuss mystical practices where relevant, the focus is on the different ways different Christians debated the parameters of divine vision. Moreover, there are, of course, several Christian authors who discuss the nature of divine visions omitted or only briefly mentioned here (e.g., Ambrose of Milan), but the authors I have included are influential, at times critical of other views, and at times creative in their own ideas and solutions to the exegetical problems of the biblical texts. Thirdly, since my method is the history of interpretation, I do not provide a comprehensive discussion of divine vision in non-Jewish or non-Christian materials. Platonic, Plotinian, and other views of the borderlines between human and divine in Greek and Latin thought are largely scattered throughout my analysis. Fourthly, more directly related to the subject matter, I do not take up the fruitful Syrian Christian materials. I should note the study of vision has somewhat already been undertaken in a succinct monograph by Sebastian Brock, focusing on Ephrem the Syrian;[68] nonetheless, a systematic analysis, including Ephrem as well as other works, such as the *Odes of Solomon*, and especially the Pseudo-Clementines, would expand, develop, and hopefully complicate, my argument. I also do not discuss visions in monastic and martyrological materials. I think that these would be interesting avenues of discussion and hope someone else picks up the thread.[69] A penultimate omission is the Christian uses and revisions of Pseudepigraphical materials, which clearly pick up the apocalyptic tradition of Second Temple Judaism and develop its visionary tendencies. Finally, I do not work through the ancient iconographic or artistic renderings of Moses at the bush or on the mountain. These are all further avenues one could pursue – and, I hope, with a clearer framework – after reading this book.

To See God and Live in the Hebrew Bible and Ancient Judaism[1]

To see the God who is hidden – or, more precisely, the aspect of God that is hiddenness as such – is the destiny of the Jewish mystic, bestowed upon him by the name Israel, which, as some ancient authors playfully proposed, signifies the one who sees God. (Elliot Wolfson, *Through a Speculum That Shines*, ix)

Before turning to the New Testament and ancient Christian interpretation, let us dwell on the ambiguities and tensions of divine visions within the biblical texts themselves and the earliest Jewish interpretations of them. Unlike the majority of the chapters of this book, this one analyzes a multitude of sources from varying social contexts, spanning over a millennium from the Hebrew Bible to late-antique rabbinic and *hekhalot* literature. Nonetheless, we will discover that the second-temple and post-temple Jewish writers developed some of the same basic strategies Christians used: varying either the status of the seer, what was seen, or how one saw in second-temple and post-temple Judaism. Most of these will base their reflections upon the figure of Moses, though not always exclusively so. Unlike the Christian interpretations, however, some of the figures and texts analyzed here will make Moses truly exceptional and wholly unique. The limit becomes threshold, and Moses becomes humanity transcended rather than humanity exemplified. For Philo of Alexandria and perhaps Ezekiel the Tragedian, Moses uniquely stands between God and humans, a position Jesus would occupy for Christian readers.

Moreover, there is a commonplace that Judaism is a religion of hearing and not seeing, reducing the Jewish sense of God's manifest presence to the Deuteronomic emphasis on audition.[2] Did not God say to Moses that none could see God's face and live (Exod. 33:20)? This assumption, however, simplifies the biblical texts and reduces Judaism to the Hebrew Bible, ignoring the rich ambivalences of whether, how, and who can see God and live.[3]

The biblical books, while denying one can see God and live, depict various people who do so, sometimes surprisingly remarking that they have seen God and lived and sometimes mentioning it without comment, as if it were neither unlikely nor deadly. Moreover, one cannot reduce the late-antique Jewish attitudes to the biblical narrative itself. For many later interpreters, surviving a vision of God is simply impossible, following Exod. 33:20. In this case, numerous intermediary figures fill the ocular gap, allowing appearances of angels or of aspects of God – God's Memra, Shekhinah, Glory, or tefillin – establishing the strategy of differentiating between a seen representation or aspect of God and the unseen (though not always invisible) God. Others, looking more to the status of the visionary, indicate that the especially righteous and humble can endure a direct vision. Some limit this visual ability to the righteous of the distant past, such as Moses, Moses' generation, or Enoch; others see these past figures and later Jewish heroes, such as R. Akiva, R. Ishmael, and R. Nehuniah b. Ha-Kanah, as models to emulate. For all these sources, excepting Philo, a divine vision is rarely intrinsically impossible. They assume God is visible, but that God's overwhelmingly splendorous appearance is deadly.

This chapter will illustrate the vistas of optic possibilities by investigating the denial, acceptance, occurrence, and accomplishment of divine visions in biblical narrative, prophecy, and apocalypses; Hellenistic reflections by Philo of Alexandria and Josephus; how these biblical visionary stories were retold and interpreted in the *targumim* and *midrashim*; and how they provided models for late-antique Jews to ascend to and gaze upon God on his chariot throne and participate in the heavenly liturgies in the *hekhalot* literature.[4] I have notably omitted discussion of the Dead Sea Scrolls, because I have been convinced by Peter Schäfer that they lack a clear account of divine vision, even while relying upon visionary motifs in the *Thanksgiving Hymns* and the *Songs of the Sabbath Sacrifice*.[5] In the sources discussed, with maybe the exception of the prophetic literature, Moses stands at the centre of such denials and acceptances in ancient Jewish thought.[6]

Moreover, even in the greater variability of social contexts in this chapter, vision is mostly vouchsafed to Moses and others for social purposes of legitimizing their leadership of the community, legitimizing the priority of a later community in apologetics against Greek, Roman, or Egyptian claims to greater antiquity, or legitimizing the later interpreters' authority by modelling themselves on Moses, uniting the authority of the revealer of scripture and interpreter of scripture into one.

BIBLICAL VISIONS AND PROHIBITIONS

The biblical sources evince a range of seeing and not seeing the divine in the legends of the Pentateuch and Judges and the prophetic literature of 1 and 2 Kings, Isaiah, Ezekiel, and Jeremiah. These accounts delineate the possibilities and limitations of visually encountering the divine that will be reinterpreted by and provide models for later interpreters and visionaries.[7]

In the Pentateuch, God tells Moses that none can see God's face and live (Exod. 33:20), but it also includes stories of those who survive seeing the LORD or the angel of the LORD without distinguishing between them – including Moses. Sometimes the viewer comments on the unexpected survival after a vision, sometimes not. This section will explore the narration of visions by Moses and others in the Pentateuch and Judges and how they align – or fail to do so – with prophetic accounts in Isaiah, Ezekiel, and Jeremiah, starting with passages that are ambivalent toward divine vision in some way and moving toward passages that are more direct or less ambivalent about visions.

When Moses first encountered the divine presence at the burning bush, he averted his eyes, fearing to behold God (Exod. 3:6). Moses hiding out of fear implies the possibility of seeing God – all he had to do was look – and its potential inadvisability. Yet it is unclear whether Moses' fear was justified or not, whether looking is deadly presumption or a privilege. Moses' hidden face illustrates an ambivalent posture concerning whether one can or *should* see the divine.

While he hides in Exod. 3:6, in Exod. 33:20 he requests a glance of God's glory, but the LORD responds, "you cannot see my face; for no human shall see me and live."[8] When God appears, he hides; when he requests to see, God does not allow it. This prohibition does not mean that seeing God is inherently impossible, but that it is deadly. Moses cannot see the LORD's face and live, but he can survive the sight of God's "back" (אחרי; LXX: τὰ ὀπίσω) (33:23).[9] Moses could not see God's full splendour, but he did see something of God.

This prohibition has left an imprint on vision narratives through-out the Heptateuch, in which various figures are left bewildered by the fact that they have seen God and lived. Particularly in Genesis and Judges, others see God and live, but are surprised that they survived. They assume one should not see God and live while doing just that, a trope that emphasizes the exceptionality of the encounter. Nonethe-less, it is not always clear *what* they see.

Hagar is the first figure to see God and live, a rare occurrence for a foreign woman. She encounters the angel of the LORD, but when the angel departs, the passage reads: "So she called the name of the LORD who spoke to her, 'You are a God of seeing'; for she said, 'Have I really seen God and remained alive?'" (Gen. 16:13). Although 16:7–12 por-trays her interlocutor as the "angel of the LORD," 16:13–14 switches, indicating from the narrator's perspective that she had spoken to and seen the LORD.[10] This passage illustrates a slippage between seeing the LORD and the angel of the LORD.[11] According to the narration and Hagar, when she saw the angel, she saw the LORD, and, to Hagar's astonishment, she lived.

Likewise, when Jacob wrestled with a "man," he names the place "Peniel," because "I have seen God face to face,[12] and yet my life is pre-served" (Gen. 32:31).[13] While the Moses passages use "face to face" ambiguously, here it refers to a direct visual *and tactile* encounter. Jacob identifies his unnamed "man" as God;[14] like Hagar, he remarks that he has survived seeing God.

Gideon encounters the angel of the LORD (Judg. 6:11, 12, 21, 22), the LORD (6:14, 16, 23), or the angel of God (6:20). When this super-nal being disappears: "Then Gideon perceived that he was the angel of the LORD; and Gideon said, 'Alas, O Lord GOD! For now I have seen the angel of the LORD face to face.' But the LORD said to him, 'Peace be to you; do not fear, you shall not die' (Judg. 6:22–3). Gideon transfers the astonishment of seeing and living from the LORD to the angel of the LORD. Nonetheless, the LORD tells Gideon he will not die. In the rest of the passage, the LORD rather than the "angel of the LORD" or "angel of God" communicates with him (6:24; 7:2, 4, 5, 7, 9). Gideon is the only judge to whom the LORD speaks directly.[15] The LORD, unmixed with references to the angel of the LORD, occurs more frequently when a clear visual component is lacking. Even so quali-fied, the attributes of seeing the divine personage are applied to the angel of the LORD; their characteristics are indistinguishable, and the text does not fully differentiate between them.

A spectacular vision of the (angel of the) LORD occurs to Manoah and his wife (Judg. 13:2–25). The "angel of the LORD" appears first to Manoah's wife (13:3). She reports her encounter to her husband. The narrator calls the figure the "angel of the LORD," whereas Manoah's wife circumspectly refers to him as a "man of God," recalling Gen. 32:24, with the terrifying "countenance of the angel of God" (Judg. 13:6).[16] In this passage, the figure is called "angel of the LORD" (vv. 3, 13, 15, 16, 17, 18, 20, 21), the "angel of God" (vv. 9), and "God" (v. 22).[17] After the supernal being ascends back to heaven, using the altar as a transportation device (Judg. 13:20), Manoah and his wife bow down in reverence:

> And Manoah said to his wife, "We shall surely die, for we have seen God."[18] But his wife said to him, "If the LORD had meant to kill us, he would not have accepted the burnt offering and a cereal offering at our hands, or shown us all these things, or now announced to us such things as these." (13:22–4)

While previously the passage subtly differentiated between the LORD and angel of the LORD, the ending elides the difference, with them sharing the same characteristics: one should not see him and live.[19] Manoah's wife reassures Manoah that they will live, because otherwise the LORD would not have accepted the offering or given them a message.

The most remarkable prophetic vision similarly distances and deflects.[20] Ezekiel sees an extraordinary luminous vision (Ezek. 1:1–28), framed by Ezekiel stating, "I saw visions of God" (Ezek. 1:1).[21] Given its detailed description, it would set the pattern for Jewish visions of the enthroned God for centuries to come. Yet, despite giving such a visually saturated account, he backs off from saying that he saw the LORD directly; instead, he saw "the likeness as it were of a human" (דמות כמראה אדם) (1:26) and the "appearance of the likeness of the glory of the LORD" (מראה דמות כבוד-יהוה) (Ezek. 1:28). The language resembles Exod. 24:16–7 (cf. Exod. 40:34), with the pyromorphic "appearance of the glory of the LORD" on Sinai. The addition of "likeness" in Ezekiel's account results in a heightened anthropomorphism that relates the form of God to humans, referring to Gen. 1:26, where God creates the human in His image and "likeness" (דמות). As humans are in God's likeness, so God has a human likeness. "Image," "likeness," and even "Glory" indicate God's manifest presence, but also shield the visionary from a direct vision – "as it were." Even if Ezekiel directly saw God, his language circumspectly indicates that his description should be taken as analogy.[22]

God, the angel of God, the angel of the LORD, or the LORD appears to Israelite and non-Israelite, to men and women. While possible, the vision remains threatening. The prohibition by God to Moses in Exod. 33:20 does not indicate that a vision of God is impossible, but deadly. Once the recipients of the vision realize who or what they saw, they are surprised that they remain alive or need reassurance that they will not die. These stories assume the impossibility of seeing God and living, while providing exceptions to the rule. Yet who or what one sees is ambiguous; these stories elide the differences between the LORD, the angel of the LORD, God, and the angel of God by using the terms nearly interchangeably. Sometimes the narrator interchanges the designations, sometimes the narrator uses the angel language while the recipient identifies the visitor as either LORD or God, but the narration never corrects the exchange of LORD for angel of the LORD, ultimately equating them.[23] Ultimately, to see the angel of the LORD is to see the LORD.[24]

Turning to more direct visionary encounters, just before God's prohibition to Moses, one reads, "the LORD used to speak to Moses face to face as a man speaks to a friend" (Exod. 33:11).[25] These regular friendly meetings counterbalance the ominous tone of Exod. 3:6 and 33:20. "Face to face" could be a colloquialism for "directly," without clarifying the means of encounter, but it keeps the visual register within the realm of possibilities. While Moses hid his face (3:6) and one cannot see God's face (33:2), here the hidden faces of Moses and God come together – face to face (cf. Deut. 34:10–2).[26]

Num. 12:8 clearly exhibits Moses' exceptional visual perception of the divine. God does not appear to him merely in visions or dreams, but he speaks with him "mouth to mouth," and Moses "beholds the very form of the LORD (ותמנת יהוה יביט)." The Greek translation interestingly switches "form" to "glory of the Lord" and shifts to the aorist: καὶ δόξαν κυρίου εἶδεν. For the Greek vision, Moses has already seen God's glory.[27] While "face to face" has shifted to "mouth to mouth," the visual encounter has intensified. Moses beholds God more clearly than anyone else; he alone can see the "form of the LORD."[28] The passage allows the possibility of a human seeing the divine form, but limits that sight to one exceptional human: Moses. Moses is the height of humanity, but he dwells at the limit alone.

Contrasting Moses' visionary drama, Abraham and Isaac have un-ambivalent divine visions. They see God and never comment that it is extraordinary or perilous. The LORD repeatedly appears to Abraham (Gen. 15:1, 17:1, 18:1).[29] Gen. 15:1 is the most circumspect, saying that the "word of the LORD came to Abram in a vision"; mixing sight and sound, Abraham sees the LORD's "word," while the LORD's appearance in a vision rather than directly creates further distance between them (cf. Num. 12:7–8). Nonetheless, the LORD directly appears later to Abraham (17:1), promising him progeny and land. In return, Abraham circumcises himself. The LORD again appears to Abraham at Mamre (18:1).[30] Likewise, the LORD directly appears to Isaac (Gen. 26:24). When Abraham or Isaac has a divine encounter, there is little distancing; the LORD appears directly. There is no indication that this is impossible or deadly; it simply happens.

Embedded within the stories of Elijah and Elisha in the Deuteron-omistic History, better known for its emphasis on hearing God rather than seeing God, the fairly obscure tale of Micaiah b. Imlah sets the stage of the vision of God on his throne.[31] 1 Kgs 22:19 displays an archaic theology of God seeking the advice of his council. Micaiah claims, "I saw the LORD sitting on his throne, and all the host of heaven standing beside him on his right hand and on his left."[32] The prophet Micaiah sees – how is not indicated – the LORD as king on his throne among the heavenly hosts. There is no hint of inability or danger for the seer, but Micaiah is also presented as unique among the prophets in the narrative of 1 Kings 22, and even in the Deuterono-mistic History as a whole, in receiving this sight.[33]

The image of the enthroned God dominates prophetic visions.[34] Isaiah "saw the Lord sitting upon a throne, high and lifted up; and his train filled the temple" (Isa. 6:1). He emphasizes the directness of the vision, saying that he has seen God with his naked eyes: "for my eyes have seen the King, the LORD of hosts!" (Isa. 6:5). Ezekiel also sees the enthroned figure, though with more circumspection in his language. Amos sees God in the temple, standing next to the altar, rather than seated (9:1).

Turning to collective encounters with the divine, just as Moses uniquely speaks to God face to face (Deut. 34:10–2), only Israel hears God's voice (Deut. 4:32-5): "Did any people ever hear the voice of a god speaking out of the midst of the fire, as you have heard, and still live?" (Deut. 4:33). Just as one should not be able to see God and live, one cannot withstand God's voice. The Israelites en masse, however, do so. Deut. 4:4–5, however, mitigates the encounter's directness: "The LORD spoke with you face to face at the mountain out of the midst of the fire, while I stood between the LORD and you at that time, to declare to you the word of the LORD; for you were afraid because of the fire, and you did not go up into the mountain." At first this passage suggests an unmediated encounter between God and the people "face to face," yet the rest of the passage denies its directness; Moses stood between the faces. The people feared to ascend the mountain, suggesting that they otherwise could have – like Moses at the burning bush. Thus, the LORD only spoke to Moses, and Moses, in turn, to the people.

Jeremiah, who has other similarities to Deuteronomy and the Deuteronomistic History, also highlights the auditory. His call is not initiated by a vision of God on his throne, but when "the word of the LORD came to me" (Jer. 1:4). There is no suspicion of a visual aspect to the encounter until 1:9, when "the LORD put forth his hand and touched my mouth." This opens up possibilities beyond the oral and aural. This verse may or may not indicate that Jeremiah sees the LORD, but it adds a rare tactile element (cf. Isa. 6:6–7; 1 Kgs 19:5, 7).[35]

Turning to accounts of a direct, unmediated collective vision of God on the mountain, in Exodus, God states he will descend upon Sinai within sight of all the people, although it is dangerous to the one who gazes (Exod. 19:11, 21). In Exod. 24:9–11, Moses, Aaron, Nadab, Abihu, and seventy elders climb the mountain, where they saw God (vv. 10, 11), and God "did not lay his hand on the chief men of the people of Israel" (v. 11). The exceptionality of the scene is indicated by the rescinded threat – God did not, this time, lay his hand on them. Not only Moses, but also the top figures of Israel, could see God, this once, and live.

The Hebrew Bible shows a range of ocular possibilities. Although at some points it is a stated or presumed impossibility to see God and live, many people do just that. There is ambivalence surrounding the divine vision, its possibility, its exceptionality, and *what* exactly one sees, but foreigners and Israelites, men and women, and individuals and groups are vouchsafed these visions, though they are still primarily focused on male founders, leaders, or those who challenged leadership, such as some of the prophets. Already, the divine vision authorizes them to deliver God's messages and to lead people. Later Jewish interpreters took up these traditions to debate whether one can see God, how one could see God, what one saw, and who could see God, notably narrowing this last category to exclude women and non-Israelites. Whether the vision is direct or indirect, the primary image that will shape future visions is the luminous LORD on his throne.

APOCALYPTIC VISIONS OF THE ENTHRONED GLORY WITHOUT MOSES

Apocalyptic literature of the second-temple period and beyond often portrays a legendary hero beholding the enthroned God.[36] Other texts, however, show little concern with seeing God, and suggest it is dangerous or impossible, or that it is limited to these figures of the distant past.[37] Moses does not appear directly in any of these visionary texts, but his presence is regularly felt indirectly.

The earliest Jewish apocalypse, the "Book of Watchers,"[38] contains a throne vision that appropriates elements from Ezekiel 1.[39] Enoch encounters the "great glory" upon the throne (*1 En.* 14.20–2; cf. 71:10–1), yet the same passage also states that no creature can behold God's face, because no creature can endure God's overwhelming glory. Paradoxically, Enoch, though prostrate, describes his vision of it.[40] Enoch is the exception to the rule, and the only exception. Enoch states, when subsequently making a tour of revealed geography: "I, Enoch, alone saw the vision ... and no man shall see as I have seen" (*1 En.* 19.2).[41] Enoch "saw the face of the Lord" (22.1). Perhaps this is Enoch's answer to God's prohibition to Moses in Exod. 33:20: Moses could not see God, but Enoch could.[42] Or Enoch is unique, like Moses in Num. 12:8.[43]

In the second century BCE, Daniel has a dream vision in which he sees multiple thrones (Dan. 7:9), among which was the throne of the Ancient of Days with raiment like *1 Enoch*'s Great Glory. Unlike Ezekiel and Enoch, however, Daniel shows no reticence concerning the vision, except that it occurs in a dream.[44] In the much-later *Testament of Levi*, Levi sees the Most High or Great Glory upon the throne in the heavenly temple in the highest heaven (*T. Levi* 3:4; 5:1–2).

In a variation on this tradition, in the *Apocalypse of Abraham*, Abraham's mediating angel, Iaoel, takes the appearance of the Glory from Ezekiel (*Apoc. Ab.* 10–11).[45] The angel's appearance is frightening, but also temporary; his visibility will dissipate (11). Abraham eventually gazes upon the celestial throne, on which he sees an indescribable fire from which the divine voice issues forth (18–19). There is no visual anthropomorphizing; the divine glory speaks to Abraham from fire above the throne, much like Moses' experience at the burning bush (Exod. 3:1–6; cf. Deut. 4:12).[46] Yet subsequently Abraham says that above the throne was the power of invisible glory – he saw nothing except the angels *(Apoc. Ab. 19)*. God's glorious presence remains unseen not because it is overwhelming, as in earlier texts, but because it is invisible.[47] The greater emphasis, therefore, falls upon the divine voice.

There is a further apocalyptic tradition that, relying upon the tradition that one cannot see God and live, claims that upon death the righteous can see God. The Christian *Ascension of Isaiah*, which may rely upon a Jewish source, gives the righteous dead greater clout than the angels in the highest (seventh) heaven. The angels can merely glimpse God, but the righteous dead can gaze intently upon the Glory (9:37–8).

While apocalypses feature a mediating angel, who is the focus of revelation, many of them also highlight a hero's vision of the enthroned God, relying upon earlier prophetic visions. Sometimes God is so glorious that no creature can endure a vision of, or the presence of, God; sometimes the legendary adept sees the enthroned glory without danger; God's manifest presence may be visible, but indescribable; or God is invisibly present above the visible throne. All these visions are attributed to heroes and founding figures of the tradition;[48] sometimes the apocalypses denote the exceptionality of the hero and the exclusivity of their revelation of previously unknown heavenly secrets. This exceptionality may provide either a mirror or a counterpoint to the Moses traditions, or confer a special status to those Jews who recorded these revelations in the late-third and early-second centuries BCE. Other times, however, there are no such clear limitations.

THE DIVINE MOSES WHO DOES NOT SEE

Moses' visions are mostly discussed outside the visionary literature of the apocalypses.[49] He, for example, is the centre of books like *Jubilees* and the *Testament of Moses*, and of the "competitive historiography" of several authors. He is extraordinary in Ezekiel the Tragedian's *Exagoge*. He is even portrayed as divine. Nonetheless, the visionary elements, while sometimes present, are often submerged and downplayed.[50]

In much of second-temple literature, Moses is a great prophet, but his visionary elements are underplayed. Artapanus (third to second century BCE), for example, emphasizes the divine voice at the bush

(21) and at the sea (36), but not visions. The *Apocryphon of Moses* found at Qumran (4Q375 and 4Q376) is similar.

A most extraordinary vision, however, can be found in Ezekiel's *Exagoge* (third to second century BCE), an Alexandrian play written in Greek dactylic hexameter, partially preserved by Eusebius of Caesarea. In a dream vision that Moses recounts to his father-in-law, he says:

> On Sinai's peak I saw what seemed a throne
> So great in size it touched the clouds of heaven
> Upon it sat a man [φώς] of noble mien,
> Becrowned, and with a scepter in one hand
> While with the other he did beckon me.
> I made approach and stood before the throne
> He handed o'er the scepter and he bade
> Me mount his throne, and gave to me the crown;
> Then he himself withdrew from off the throne.
> I gazed upon the whole earth round about;
> Things under it, and high above the skies.
> Then at my feet a multitude of stars
> Fell down, and I their number reckoned up.
> They passed by me like armed ranks of men. (68–81)[51]

Moses has a dream vision of the divine throne and a figure on the throne. This has strong correlations with 1 Kings 22, Isaiah 6, Ezekiel 1, Daniel 7, and later *merkavah* texts. What is most striking is that the figure abdicates the throne and gives authority to Moses himself, who then does what humans are not supposed to be able to do: number the stars.[52] Moses' status is highly exalted above the angelic hosts on God's throne. Many scholars going back to P. van der Horst have argued that this indicates Moses' deification, while others see it as more symbolic.[53] What is important is that Moses is vouchsafed a striking vision of the divine figure on the throne and can count up the innumerable heavenly hosts. He has a vision of what is above and below, including God's manifest form. His father-in-law interprets the dream for Moses, saying it refers to ruling humans rather than angels, and that he will see things above, below, past, present, and future (83–9). This divine vision gives Moses a mandate to lead and makes his status unique. Others cannot do as he has done.[54]

It is a striking passage, often commented on. Less discussed, however, is the subsequent passage: the burning bush. The "divine word shines forth" to Moses (99), saying:

Take courage, son, and listen to my words;
As mortal man you cannot see my face,
Albeit you have pow'r to hear my words. (100–2)[55]

Moses cannot directly see the divine face or form, but can hear God's voice. While the dream vision was stunning, any direct waking vision is excluded. Exodus 33:20, relocated and paraphrased here, takes pride of place.

Ben Sira or Sirach (second century BCE) also transforms Moses into an exalted being, but is less reticent about his visions. Ben Sira highly praises Moses (Sir. 45:1–5). He is "beloved by God" (45:1) and God makes Moses "equal in glory to the holy ones" (ὡμοίωσεν αὐτὸν δόξῃ ἁγίων) (45:2); that is, he is angelified. His contact with God was direct and intimate: God "revealed to him his glory," "allowed him to hear his voice, and led him into the dark cloud, and gave him the commandments face to face" (45:3, 5).[56] Ben Sira focuses entirely on the positive indications of Moses' mediation, completely omitting any qualifying or conditional elements. There is no Exod. 33:20 here. Moses hears and sees God directly – by face (κατὰ πρόσωπον); it is neither presumptuous nor impossible, though nearly unique (cf. Ezekiel in Sir. 49:8);[57] it is something God allows.

In *Jubilees* (second century BCE) God and Moses converse about what will occur in the future. Yet despite the pyrotechnics of the glory of the LORD dwelling upon the mountain and the mountain being covered in a cloud, none of the language of Moses entering the cloud or seeing or even not seeing God is emphasized (*Jub.* 1.1–4). There is an interesting note that God will dwell among humans in the "ages of eternity" (1.26), indicating direct interaction between God and the righteous in the afterlife. In the rest of the book, the Angel of the Presence reveals sacred history from creation to the current point in Moses' life, the building of the sanctuary, as God fades into the background (1.29). There is less direct interaction between God and humans in *Jubilees*. God appears to Abraham in a dream (14.1–16), but appears directly to change Abram's name and to give him the command for circumcision (15.1–22), for the *Aqedah* or binding of

Isaac, and for Jacob's famous visions. The burning bush and Moses' interactions are downplayed.

According to Crispin Fletcher-Louis, 4Q374 2 II 6-8, a riff on Exod. 7:1, may be more promising.[58] It reads, "he made him like a God over the powerful ones, and a cause of reel[ing] (?) for Pharaoh ... [...] melted, and their hearts trembled, and [th]eir entrails dissolved. [But] he had pity with [...] and when he let his face shine for them for healing, they strengthened [their] hearts again."[59] Here it seems Moses becomes so elevated that people respond to him in the way that one would a vision of the deity: they die. In fact, it is the typical human response to the "divine warrior."[60] The vision of Moses, of seeing Moses rather than Moses seeing, resembles what happens to unfit "descenders to the chariot" when they enter the heavenly realm. As seeing Moses can kill, however, it can also heal, a clear reference to Moses' glorified, shining face (Exod. 34:29-35).

Most of these third-to-second-century-BCE documents, including Hellenistic historiographies, one play, and other retellings of biblical stories, highly exalt Moses, often elevating his status to the angelic, if not the divine. Moreover, even when there are elements that moderate the vision, such as Moses' father-in-law's interpretation of his dream in the *Exagoge*, these visions give Moses a mandate to lead; they are the source of his authority. Otherwise, there is no discernable pattern by genre or location, since both Alexandrian and Judean documents both emphasize and de-emphasize Moses' visions, even as they agree on his foundational leadership.

THE DIVINE MOSES WHO SEES: PHILO'S MOSES

Philo (ca. 20 BCE–50 CE) discusses Moses more extensively than any ancient Jewish author.[61] Philo grew up in a thriving Jewish community in Alexandria. He was wealthy, well-connected, and probably educated at the gymnasium.[62] In his voluminous writings we find that he was well-versed in Middle-Platonic philosophical discourse, which used a Platonic framework, yet integrated Stoic and Neo-Pythagorean elements when they were found compatible by different philosophers.[63] Yet Philo was primarily an exegete; instead of writing systematic treatises, he developed his philosophy through biblical interpretation.[64] He was proficient in the Stoic method of allegory, which was developed in Alexandria by textual critics who reinterpreted Homer, and applied these literary techniques to the Bible.[65] This project became an apologetic enterprise wherein he attempted to demonstrate that the best of Greek thought derived from Moses.[66] Considering Philo's view of Moses and the promulgation of the Torah among Greeks and "barbarians," David Winston writes, "Philo's unrestrained idealization of Moses is clearly designed to grant his legislative effort an authority of unlimited scope, and thereby secure its sacrosanct character."[67]

In addition to scattered references throughout his works, Philo wrote a two-volume work,[68] *The Life of Moses*, in which he presents Moses as the greatest and most-perfect human to ever live (*Moses* 1.1).[69] He is, to be sure, humanity at its furthest limit, but, pushing against that limit, Moses reaches a pinnacle that no other human can live up to. Moses exemplifies Plato's philosopher-king (Book 1), as lawgiver,[70] high priest,[71] and prophet (Book 2).[72] Elsewhere, Moses is the most beloved of God (*Migration* 67; *Confusion* 95–7). He is the "friend of God" (*Heir* 21). He exemplifies the heights a human can achieve in a contemplative vision. Interestingly, Philo also extensively discusses such a visionary life in scattered references to himself and in his *Contemplative Life*.[73] His autobiographical experiences and his accounts of Moses' experiences show a lot of similarities; nonetheless, Philo does not usually claim himself to be a direct channel of God's revelation as Moses was, yet his experiences inspire and authorize his interpretations of Moses' original oracles.[74] John Levison writes, "The divine spirit generates his [Philo's] ecstasy as a poet, elevates his reason as a philosopher cum biblical interpreter, and leads him to insight as an exegete."[75] As Moses was the original oracular channel of God's revelation, so Philo becomes the inspired exegete who understands Moses' oracles.

For Philo, therefore, the books of Moses have the highest authority, providing a link between God and the people in Moses' absence.[76] Though Moses is the height of humanity – and, therefore, provides much fodder for later Christian understandings of Moses – he also represents, though is not completely identified with, a divine principle, particularly the divine Logos, acquiring characteristics early Christians applied to Jesus, transcending human limitations.[77] As Schäfer notes, when discussing Philo's characterization of Moses, "Philo's language sometimes becomes exceedingly hymnic and theologically daring."[78]

Philo's practical aim in his writings is to lead humans to a divine vision.[79] As a Platonist, he differentiated between bodily and contemplative vision, speaking of the sight of the mind rather than of the

body. God is "unnamable," "unutterable," and "incomprehensible under any form" (*Dreams* 1.67).[80] God is, moreover, invisible. Even with
the eyes of the mind, God's essence is completely unknowable; one
can only know God's existence.[81] Unlike the apocalyptic tradition,
therefore, there is not so much a differentiation in *what* is seen, but in
how one sees. Just as important is *who* sees: Israel.

Philo follows a folk etymology of the name "Israel" as "the one who
sees God" (ὁρῶν θεόν) (*Abraham* 57–9);[82] it is the race that has the eyes
to see God (*Migration* 18, 54).[83] This generalizes the divine contemplative vision to all "Israel." Philo defines "Israel," in turn, as those who
have mastered their passions in obedience (*Confusion* 56). As such,
one must attain "Israel" (*Migration* 200–1).[84] Philo explains the change
of names from Jacob to Israel as a shift from the soul *hearing* God
(Jacob) to the soul *seeing* God (Israel) (*Confusion* 72; *Migration* 38–42).[85]
Only the children of those of vision, Israel rather than Jacob, therefore, can look upon God (*Confusion* 91–2).[86]

In this discussion of Israel, Philo develops a complex discussion of the
relationship between the sons of God, the sons of God's invisible image
(the holy Logos, who is the eldest image of God),[87] and "Israel" (*Confusion* 145–9). In this discussion, the Logos is the "beginning," "name of
God," "human after his image," and "he that sees" (i.e., "Israel").[88] Moses
or the high priest, of which Moses is the pre-eminent example, corre-
sponds to the Logos (*Heir* 182–5).[89] The Logos, in turn, is a high priest
– like Moses (*Migration* 102) – and the high priest is a microcosm (*Moses*
2.135).[90] Moses is also portrayed as the law-giving Logos (*Migration* 23ff;
see 28–9).[91] This is a high view of Moses, since the Logos hovers on the
border between creator and creature (*Heir* 205–6).[92]

Yet, Moses himself has a vision of the Logos, identified as the
"place" where God stands (*Confusion* 95).[93] So there is not a complete
identity between the two. A better articulation of the relationship is
that Moses, the high priest, is the microcosm and the Logos is the
macrocosm.[94] They are identified and intrinsically linked. The high
priest is identified with and represents the divine Logos (cf. *Flight*
108ff; *Giants* 52). Elsewhere, Moses is called the first-born of the Logos
(*QE* 2.44; *Heir* 205; cf. *Agriculture* 41; *Dreams* 1.215).[95] The high
priest/Logos is the soul. In short, both the Logos and the high priest,
Moses, stand between God and the people, creator and creation.

Standing in this intermediate position, the Logos/high priest/
Moses leads those who fall short of perfection (*Migration* 173). Moses,

therefore, is equated with the image of God, while the rest of humanity is the image of the image (*Heir* 230–1).⁹⁶ Moses stands one degree closer to God than the rest of humanity. Elsewhere, however, when speaking of the re-establishment of humanity after the flood, Philo equates humans with the "likeness [ἀντίμιμον] of God's power and image of His nature [εἰκὼν τῆς ἀοράτου φύσεως ἐμφανής], the visible of the Invisible, the created of the Eternal" (*Moses* 2.65). Image (εἰκών) is once removed; humans are visible image of the invisible God.⁹⁷

When discussing the intellectual vision of the Ruler of the Universe (*Migration* 76–7), even more striking correspondences are made, but ones that divide the Logos into two aspects: the Logos of understanding or mind and the Logos of utterance.⁹⁸ Interpreting Exod 7:1, in which God says that Moses will be a god to Pharaoh, Philo argues that this is Moses representing the Logos of mind (God's mind), whereas Aaron, who speaks on Moses' behalf, represents the Logos of utterance. In short, Moses is the archetypal (in all that this word can mean in a Platonic system) contemplative visionary.⁹⁹

So, how do the people of Israel attain a divine vision with Moses? The people ascend to God by God "setting before them Moses," the most beloved of God (*Confusion* 95–7). Citing Exod. 24:10, Moses is the one who leads them along the way to the "place" of the "Word."¹⁰⁰ By Moses, all who are wise may finally "behold," attaining unto "Israel," becoming the race permitted to see God (*Confusion* 91–2).

Having discussed Moses' general relation to vision, especially through or as the Logos, and his intermediate position between God and humanity, let us turn to Philo's discussions of Moses' specific visions.¹⁰¹ While Moses' ultimate vision would be the "dark cloud" and the "pattern" of the Tabernacle on the mountain, his preliminary vision was at the burning bush (*Moses* 1.65–70, esp. 66; cf. *Flight* 161–5):¹⁰²

In the midst of the flame was a form [μορφή] of the fairest beauty, unlike any visible object [τῶν ὁρατῶν ἐμφερὴς οὐδενί], an image supremely divine in appearance [θεοειδέστατον ἄγαλμα], refulgent with a light brighter than the light of fire. It might be supposed that this was the image of Him that is [εἰκόνα τοῦ ὄντος εἶναι]; but let us rather call it an angel or herald, since, with a silence that spoke more clearly than speech, it employed as it were the miracle of sight to herald future events.

Philo claims that Moses saw something astounding: "a form of the fairest beauty," "an image supremely divine in appearance." It is unlike anything else of this world. Whatever he saw, it was supernal, beyond, superlative, and "supremely divine." Did he see God? Or, since Philo reserves "God" for one of God's qualities,[103] one might ask, did Moses see "the one who is" (cf. *Moses* 1.75)? Philo cannot grant this, since, ultimately, the vision at the bush was visible, even if it was unlike other visible things, but he entertains seeing the "image" of the one who is. He grants its possibility but does not consider it the best reading. Instead, this most divine appearance is more of an angelic herald of things to come, a symbolic vision. It is not an ultimate vision of divine reality, or even the image of ultimate reality. Philo's language suggests we should put quotation marks around "angel," since it is a convenient label rather than what it substantively is. In an alternative reading of the burning bush in *Dreams* 1.231–2, Philo focuses on God's revelation to Moses, that God is "the One Who Is" (ἐγώ εἰμι ὁ ὤν). For Philo, the primary point of the revelation to Moses is that one can learn that God is, but not God's nature; one may know God's subsistence, but not essence. Nonetheless, he turns to the means of revelation:

> To the souls indeed which are incorporeal and are occupied in His worship it is likely that He should reveal Himself as He is, conversing with them as friend with friends; but to souls which are still in a body, giving Himself the likeness of angels [ἀγγέλοις εἰκοζόμενον], not altering His own nature, for He is unchangeable, but conveying to those who receive the impression of His presence a semblance in a different form, such that they take the image to be not a copy, but that original form itself.[104]

God appears as God is to incorporeal souls – angels or the dead – but to embodied souls, God puts on the appearance of an angel. It is God who speaks and God who acts, while the angel is what clothes God, revealing and concealing God at once. This is, indeed, a position close to what Tertullian would argue centuries later. Nonetheless, God – not an angel – speaks to Moses in oracles (*Moses* 1.71).[105] He and God were alone together like a pupil and master, an intimate pairing for revelation (*Moses* 1.80; cf. *Heir* 17).[106]

Before Moses enters the dark cloud to contemplate the one who is, he is invited. While rabbinic sources would speak very negatively about

Nadab, Abihu, and the seventy elders seeing God on the mountain (Exod. 24:1), Philo evaluates this episode more positively (*Migration* 168–72). He first notes the divine invitation to ascend the mountain, interpreting it as an invitation to the soul to "behold the Existent One" (169). Yet he also notes the pitfalls of ascending to such a vision, especially if one tries to ascend by one's own strength in ignorance; thus, Moses prays that God will guide him (170–1; cf. *Flight* 164). It is a general invitation, but one which few – in this case, one – will attain.

The ultimate divine vision in Philo's discussion – something developed by later Christians, such as Clement, Origen, and Gregory of Nyssa – is Moses' entrance into the dark cloud on the mountain.[107] Philo discusses Moses entering the darkness during an allegorical exegesis on Genesis 17:1–5, 15–22 (*Names*) and an exposition on Moses' life (*Moses*).[108] In the *Life of Moses*, leading into the discussion of the dark cloud and its significance, Philo primes the reader by calling Moses God's partner (1.155–6). Reminiscent of Ezekiel's *Exagoge* as God's partner, each element obeyed Moses as if Moses were the creator. As God's partner, Moses receives his title: God (1.158). As with his identification with God's Logos, Moses blurs the boundaries between human and divine:[109]

Again, was not the joy of his partnership [κοινωνίας] with the Father and Maker of all magnified also by the honor of being deemed worthy to bear the same title? For he was named god and king of the whole nation [ὠνομάσθη γὰρ ὅλος τοῦ ἔθνους θεὸς καὶ βασιλεύς], and entered, it is said, into the darkness where God was [εἴς τε τὸν γνόφον, ἔνθα ἦν ὁ θεός, εἰσελθεῖν λέγεται], that is into the unseen, invisible, incorporeal and archetypical essence of existing things [εἰς τὴν ἀειδῆ καὶ ἀόρατον καὶ ἀσώματον τῶν ὄντων παραδειγματικὴν οὐσίαν]. Thus he beheld what is hidden from the sight of mortal nature [τὰ ἀθέατα φύσει θνητῇ κατανοῶν], and, in himself and his life displayed for all to see, he has set before us, like some well-wrought picture, a piece of work beautiful and godlike, a model [παράδειγμα] for those who are willing to copy it [μιμεῖσθαι]. Happy are they who imprint [ἐναπεμάξαντο], or strive to imprint, that image [τὸν τύπον] in their souls. For it were best that the mind should carry the form [τὸ εἶδος] of virtue in perfection, but, failing this, let it at least have the unflinching desire to possess that form. (1.158–9)

As noted, Moses becomes God's partner. Philo elides this into the idea that Moses was a "god" to Pharaoh (Exod. 7:1), but, in an extension of this partnership with divinity, Philo also says that Moses was a god to Israel.[110] With this prefacing and acquired identification with the divine, Moses can enter the darkness where God is.

True reality – the darkness – is unseen, invisible, incorporeal, and the archetypal essence of all things. Philo does not delineate what this "dark" essence is, whether it is God or the Logos, whether it is created or uncreated, only that it is incorporeal and invisible. It is defined mostly by what it is not; thus, all the alpha privatives. This is how he describes the "One Who Is" in *Dreams* 1.67. These negations, however, indicate that the darkness is extraordinarily transcendent; indeed, it is where God is. Nonetheless, it has a positive substructure: the "paradigm" or "archetype."

Although darkness is invisible, Moses could see it.[111] Philo does not speculate how Moses saw it, but portrays this darkness as something that, while normally hidden from humans, can be revealed. Given the proximity to Philo's discussion of Moses as God's partner who bears God's own title, it is most likely that it is as God's partner and identity as God that Moses could see what was hidden from mortal nature. As he beholds the invisible archetypal pattern (cf. Heb. 8:5), he becomes the model to emulate, for others to see and be imprinted on their own persons.

Moreover, Philo is not instructing others how to enter that darkness;[112] rather, this passage serves the didactic purpose of mimesis. Moses becomes, in turn, "a model for those who are willing to copy it" (158). He is a "paradigm" to "copy." Once "copied," others will have his image or "form" imprinted upon them. This consists of a double-movement: Moses beholds the invisible archetype, and, thereby, becomes a model to be copied and, therefore, a unique intermediary between the divine and humans. Moses' form becomes imprinted on the souls of those who behold him. One does not need to see the invisible archetypal essence, because it has been imprinted upon Moses. One attains perfection by imitating the godlike hero of the past. The archetype that was imprinted onto Moses when he entered the darkness can be imprinted onto the soul through imitating Moses (159), while Moses remains unique.[113]

Moving to allegory, near the beginning of *On the Changing of Names*, Philo, trying to understand Genesis 17:1, explains how the text could say the Lord was seen by Abraham. He cautions the reader, "do

not suppose that the vision was presented to the eyes of the body"
(*Names* 2). Instead, "it is the eye of the soul which receives the presentation of the divine vision" (3), placing the emphasis on how one sees
God. Even so, Philo reneges to state that God cannot truly be envisioned by any human; even the soul or mind cannot see God (7).[114]
But Moses attempts the impossible, to see God: "So Moses the explor-
er of nature which lies beyond our vision, Moses who, as the divine
oracles tell us, entered into the darkness, by which figure they indicate
existence invisible and incorporeal, searched everywhere and into
everything in his desire to see clearly and plainly him, the object of
our much yearning, who alone is good" (7). From here, Philo speaks
of Moses' yearning and despair when he does not attain what he seeks.
Not receiving the vision of the invisible, God says to him: "You shall
see what is behind me, but my face you shall not see." Philo interprets
God's backside to mean those things ontologically below the Existent
One, whether material or immaterial. Otherwise, one cannot apprehend God's own nature (9). In this passage, darkness indicates the
invisible and incorporeal, but not necessarily God. The passage ends
frustratingly. Moses' ascent into the darkness is fruitless in contrast to
the expository *Life of Moses*, in which he sees the underlying essence
of all things and is imprinted with that archetype and provides a pedagogical model for others to follow.[115]

In sum, Philo does not suggest that the darkness represents God,
but the invisible and incorporeal archetype that is usually unseen. It
cannot mean God's essence, since Moses was able to attain a vision of
the invisible archetype, but not of God. Philo leaves much unan-
swered about this darkness, as well as about Moses' unfulfilled desire,
but darkness is not his primary concern. Rather, in the exposition, his
concern is didactic, suggesting that people model themselves after
Moses, who in turn has the underlying existential archetype imprinted upon him by his vision of it.[116]

Like the Exodus account does (Exod. 25–31, 35–40), Philo places
great importance on the tabernacle, particularly the "pattern of the
tabernacle" (*Moses* 2.71–146). Exodus 25 in Greek translation proved
congenial to Philo's use of a Platonic framework to read the Bible in
terms of the World of Forms being impressed upon the material
world. He directly quotes the Tabernacle passage only once (*Alleg.
Interp.* 3.102). While one would expect him to quote Exod. 25:9, he
instead takes 25:40, speaking of the two makers of the Tabernacle.
Moses made the "archetypes" (τὰ ἀρχέτυπα) of the Tabernacle and its

furnishings and Bezalel made the copies (τὰ μιμήματα) of these: "For Moses has God for an instructor, as he says, 'you shall make all things according to the pattern that was shown to you on the mount,' but Bezalel is instructed by Moses." Moses, being instructed by God, makes the archetypal Tabernacle through a clear vision of the mind,[117] whereas Bezalel, being instructed by Moses, makes the sensible Tabernacle through a shadow of such a vision, which is the process of reasoning (a step removed, but still with a positive evaluation). Philo's quotation of Exod. 25:40 differs from the LXX: whereas the LXX translates "pattern" as τὸν τύπον, Philo's quotation uses the same word as in Exod. 25:9, τὸ παράδειγμα, and a more useful Platonic term for the original to be copied.

Although he directly quoted this passage only once, he paraphrased the episode in his Moses 2.71–146. Just as in the biblical account, the entire plan of the Tabernacle is divinely revealed, but Philo piles on the terminology of "pattern," "plan," and "copy" to a much greater extent. Quoting the paraphrase at length, Philo writes:

> He saw with the soul's eye the immaterial forms of the material objects about to be made, and these forms had to be reproduced in copies perceived by the senses, taken from the original draft, so to speak, and from patterns conceived in the mind. For it was fitting that the construction of the sanctuary should be committed to him who was truly high priest, in order that his performance of the rites belonging to this sacred office might be in more than full accordance and harmony with the fabric. So the shape of the model was stamped upon the mind of the prophet, a secretly painted or molded prototype, produced by immaterial and invisible forms; and then the resulting work was built in accordance with the shape by the artist impressing the stampings upon the material substances required in each case. (2.74–6)

What Moses saw is called multiple things: immaterial forms (ἀσωμάτους ἰδέας), forms (ἔδει), original draft (ἀρχετύπου γραφῆς), patterns conceived in the mind (νοητῶν παραδειγμάτων), shape of the model (ὁ τύπος τοῦ παραδείγματος), and secretly painted or moulded prototype produced by immaterial and invisible forms.[118] The constructed tabernacle that resulted has names that serve as counterparts: material objects about to be made (τῶν μελλόντων ἀποτελεῖσθαι σωμάτων), copies perceived by the senses (αἰσθητὰ μιμήματα ἀπεικονισθῆναι), and stampings upon the material substances. The Platonic framework is clear: what Moses saw was perceptible only to the mind, whereas its "copy" was impressed on perceptible matter.

The language of the Exodus passage was already set up for Philo to place it in such a Platonic framework. Indeed, he uses "paradigm" twice and "type" once – terms found in the LXX version of the instructions to build the tabernacle – yet it also explains why he placed the term from 25:9 (παράδειγμα) into 25:40 (τύπος): in Philo's usage the latter is one step removed from the former, acting as an intermediate term of what is imprinted on the mind of the prophet between the "paradigm" or "immaterial and invisible forms" and providing the subsequent model for the "stampings upon the material substances." The paradigm/forms impress the type/shape upon the mind of the prophet, which, in turn, is impressed upon the material copies.[119]

While the "tabernacle" hardly counts as a divine vision, similar terminology and the same structure of thought surrounds this passage and Moses' ascent into the divine darkness.[120] Moreover, Philo elsewhere speaks of the tabernacle as an image of divine excellence; it is the representation and copy of wisdom (Heir, esp. 112–13). It is similar to the pattern of the cosmos and found in the pattern of the human being.[121]

In summary, Moses clearly is the apogee of human achievement for Philo.[122] This is largely apologetic in his Hellenized Alexandrian environment, as he turns Moses into the ideal leader as envisioned in Plato's Republic. Even though Philo shifts on the details of how Moses relates to God, the Logos, the divine darkness, he consistently illustrates that the divine element becomes imprinted onto Moses, so that others can, subsequently, emulate, yet never equal, Moses. Moses' ascent and intellectual vision of God leads the way for others to follow. As Esther Starobinski-Safran writes, "For the prophet, who has penetrated into the dark cloud and has long been initiated into the holy mysteries, transforms into a hierophant, into a 'preceptor of divine truths.'"[123] From mystic, he becomes a mystagogue."[124] Similarly commenting on Philo's Spec. Laws 1.37–50, Peder Borgen writes, "likewise it is impossible to have a vision of God as He really is, but one should not relinquish the quest. Moses is the hierophant, the sacred guide, to the right search for God, as seen from his prayers for God to reveal himself to him (Exod 33:13–23), and God answers that He will give him a share in what is attainable (Spec. Laws 1.41–50). Thus, the true search and the reception of revelation, as far as it is possible, have Moses as guide."[125]

In turn, Philo, the contemplative exegete, whose own experiences have important similarities to and subtle differences from Moses, becomes the exegetical guide, leading the reader to the model Moses; Philo is the mystagogue to the mystagogue.[126]

MODERATING THE MIRACULOUS
IN THE FIRST CENTURY

From Ezekiel's *Exagoge* to Philo's *Life of Moses*, Jewish works from the second-temple period exalted Moses to a very high degree, exhibiting his intimacy with and visions of God, and his achievement of a higher, angelic level of existence that sometimes even bordered on the divine. Nonetheless, there are a series of first-century CE works that moderate this exalted image.

The *Testament of Moses*, dated roughly to the first century CE, is a revelation of the history of Israel from Moses to Joshua. Though Moses is such a great prophet that he lays out early Israelite history, visionary elements are lacking. Moses, moreover, reveals the roughly contemporary *Life of Adam and Eve*, but basically gets only a byline in the preface.

Pseudo-Philo's *Biblical Antiquities* is a little more promising. For Pseudo-Philo, Moses is pre-thought of by God (9.8). God appears to Amram, Moses' father, and to Miriam, his sister, in a dream (9.7–8, 10). Although Moses becomes "glorious above all other men" (9.16), the narrative skips over the burning bush. Though Moses speaks to God directly in the narrative, there is no direct vision (10–11). There is, however, a storm theophany on the mountain (11.4–5). God speaks to the people, but, as in Deuteronomy, they fear it and ask Moses to intercede: "You speak to us, but do not let God speak to us lest perhaps we die. For behold today we know that God speaks to a man face to face and that man may live. And now we have recognized that the earth has borne the voice of God with quaking" (11.14).[127] Then Moses enters the cloud where God is (11.15). While generic visionary elements are present (storm, fearing speaking face to face, and the cloud), they are toned down. Exod. 33:20 is alluded to in altered form in the surprise that God spoke to the Israelites "face to face" and they did not die. Though they did not die, they feared future encounters, and so sent Moses in their stead.

Josephus, writing in the late first century in Flavian Rome, presents Moses similarly. In his *Antiquities*, Josephus, while presenting Moses as a pre-eminent human, consistently downplays the miraculous, including visions, in his recounting of Jewish history. Louis Feldman has argued that this reticence is due to his apologetic context, living in Flavian Rome after the Jewish War.[128]

For example, at the burning bush (*Ant.* 2.264-9), instead of waxing rhapsodic about the beautiful image within the bush, as Philo had, Josephus downplays visionary elements, though allows that the flaming bush uttered a voice. Moses simply sees a flaming bush that is not consumed. Though he is astonished at the sight, the emphasis lay completely on hearing the voice (2.270). Josephus casually mentions that Moses had seen and heard God (without qualification), and, because of this, Moses requested his name (2.275).

This reticence persists throughout. When Moses goes up Sinai (3.75-101), he prepares to "converse with God" (3.75) and has difficulty ascending the mountain. For Josephus, it is a physical ascent to the mountain and not into the heavens, as in some competing traditions. When he recounts the theophany of cloud, tempest, thunder, and lightning (3.79-80), he does so with a note of apology, fearing his readers will not believe him (3.79-80). Moses then comes down "joyful" and "greatly exalted" (3.83), but he omits what Moses saw. The entire episode plays out from the perspective of people on the ground, rather than from Moses' vantage point. When Moses reveals to the people what happened, again the emphasis is on hearing God's voice: "For I have been admitted into the presence of God, and been made a hearer of his incorruptible voice; so great is his concern for your nation, and its durations" (3.88). All the people then hear the voice (3.89-90), and receive the ten commandments (3.91-2) and further explanation of them (3.93-4). Even when Moses re-ascends (3.95-101) – when, in Exodus, he enters the cloud – again, the entire episode is from the perspective of those left below. Josephus also tones down Moses' "glory," or shining face, saying only that his appearance filled the army with gladness (3.99).

Josephus lets the tradition of what Moses saw through at only one point. When explaining the cherubim upon the mercy-seat (cf. Exod. 25), he states that their appearance is unlike anything humans have seen, but that Moses said that he had seen such beings near God's throne (3.137). In this passage, Josephus obliquely refers to the tradition that Moses saw God's throne and, interestingly, adds to the vision something like Ezekiel 1, since the Exodus account does not include Moses seeing cherubim on the mountain.

As Josephus illustrates, the traditions of Moses' ascents and visions persisted in the first century CE – these writers knew these traditions – but they tended to minimize them in their own expositions. For Josephus, this was an apologetic manoeuvre for his Roman audience; for others, the reasons are less clear.

LATE-ANTIQUE READINGS:
TARGUM AND MIDRASH

Such a range of visual possibilities inherited from the Bible, apocalypses, and second-temple traditions provided the Jews and Christians reflecting on them exegetical breadth on the theoretical possibilities and dangers of seeing God. Extending into late antiquity, the *targumim*, *midrashim*, and *hekhalot* illustrate the trends in late-antique Jewish thought and practice on the topic.[129] Whereas the *hekhalot* texts tend to use Ezekiel and Isaiah, interwoven with tales of more recent Rabbis, to provide instructions on how to "descend" to the chariot, the *targumim* and *midrashim* tend to interpret the Pentateuch to address the possibility of seeing God. The translations of the *targumim* mostly deny the possibility of a vision of God in his full splendour, while providing mediating entities – God's Memra, Shekhinah, and Glory – that one can see, differentiating visions based upon the object seen. The *midrashim* are ambivalent about divine vision, yet largely allow that a particularly righteous figure, such as Moses or Abraham, could see God, or that a unique event, like the dividing of the sea or the giving of the Torah on Sinai, provided an occasion for all Israelites to see God. Yet they would develop a theory of regressive vision: God appeared more clearly to the Israelites en masse on Mount Sinai than God did to Isaiah or Ezekiel, much less even-later righteous humans.

The Palestinian *targumim* translate the biblical texts into Aramaic for a liturgical setting. The process of translation leads to shifts in wording, glosses, and lengthy additions. This section will focus on *Targum Neofiti 1* and *Targum Pseudo-Jonathan*.[130] Both tend to distance the recipient of a vision from the visual divine presence, increasing mediating terms; the Glory, Memra, and Shekhinah become the primary means of divine manifestation.[131] This tendency varies, with *Neofiti* most consistently and strongly denying that anyone saw God rather than a mediating aspect of God. The degree to which the *targumim* mitigate previously unmediated visions is a barometer of the discomfort around one's ability to see God.

The *targumim* largely deny Moses a direct vision of God. At the burning bush, *Neofiti* states that, above Mount Horeb, the "Glory of the Shekhinah of the LORD" is revealed (3:1). The angel of the Lord is in the flames, as in the Hebrew text, but the Memra of the Lord calls out. Moses hides from the Glory of the Shekhinah of the Lord (3:6). *Pseudo-Jonathan* mediates the vision differently. The Glory of the Lord is revealed on Horeb. Instead of the Memra, the angel Zagnugel speaks; nonetheless, the Lord calls to him. Then, as in *Neofiti*, Moses is afraid to look at the Glory of the Shekhinah of the Lord.

The most telling shift in language is how God speaks to Moses. In the Hebrew text, Moses and God spoke "face to face." In both *targumim* to Exodus 33:11, the Lord or the Memra of the Lord speaks to Moses "speech against speech," making their relationship completely oral (cf. LXX). For *Neofiti* 33:20, Moses cannot see the "face of the Glory of the Shekhinah," but can see the "Dibbera of the Glory of the Shekhinah." He cannot see the divine face or form, but can "see" the divine speech (Dibbera). For *Pseudo-Jonathan*, Moses can hear the Dibbera, but cannot survive seeing the splendour of its face. He still can see the tefillin of the Glory of the Shekhinah, rabbinizing the "backsides" of the manifest presence.[132]

Finally, in Exod. 24:9–11, the Hebrew text presents seventy elders who ascend the mountain and see God. In *Neofiti* they see the "Glory of the Shekhinah of the Lord," although a marginal gloss more directly states "the God of Israel." *Pseudo-Jonathan* includes a twist: only Nadab and Abihu saw the glory of the God of Israel, whereas Moses and Aaron did not (cf. *Lev. Rab.* 20:10). The alteration heightens the threat: "But, at that time, he did not send his plague against the handsome young men Nadab and Abihu. But it was reserved for them until the eighth day of ordination, when it would afflict them" (24:11). The verse takes up the theme of the dangers of seeing God, but turns it into a breach of etiquette: seeing the Glory does not automatically kill, but it is inappropriate. Death is the punishment for presumption.

The *targumim* evince a tendency to distance figures from a direct vision of God, buffering the vision with mediating figures or aspects of God: God's Memra, Shekhinah, Glory, or tefillin. While they mostly deny the possibility of a direct vision of God, there are some complicating passages or marginal glosses that retain the directness of the Hebrew text.[133] These stories mostly remain visual encounters, however. Only *what* is seen has changed.

Midrashic collections are multivocal texts, compiling biblical interpretations by different Rabbis of different times and places. Thus, they
include multiple understandings of whether and how one can see
God. While some Rabbis deny that anyone ever saw God, there are
some trends that emerge among those who allow visions under certain conditions. In an increasingly gendered and phallocentric discourse, the primary requirement to see God and live is circumcision,
excluding women and Gentiles from direct vision.[134] Abraham could
not withstand the divine presence until he was circumcised. Moses,
furthermore, exemplifies the need for humility to see God and live,
whereas presumptive glimpses of the divine lead to death. God also
uniquely appeared with exceptional clarity to all the Israelites when
God divided the sea and gave them the Torah on the mountain.

First, according to the *midrashim*, there are two occasions when all
the Israelites of Moses' generation see God: at the sea and at Sinai. At
least for the theophany at the sea, women should have been present
for the divine appearance. Moreover, according to the *Mekhilta de-
Rabbi Ishmael*, the Israelites demanded to see God on Sinai, since seeing is greater than hearing, and God allowed them (*Bahodesh* 2). But
if God appeared for such important moments, would God appear
again in the same way? This is a difficult question, since the passages
that affirm that all – not just Moses or particularly righteous individuals – saw God at the sea and on Sinai also state that they saw God
in such splendour that not even Isaiah, Ezekiel, or any later prophets encountered.

The most famous commentary on the Song at the Sea (Exod. 15:1–
18) called the *Shirta* in the *Mekhilta*, speaks of how God appeared to
all the people:[135]

> The LORD is a man of war. Why is it said, The LORD is his name?
> For at the Sea he revealed himself as a warrior making battle, as it is
> said, "The Lord is a man of war," (while) at Sinai He revealed him-
> self as an elder full of compassion, as it is said, "And they saw the
> God of Israel," etc. (Exod. 24:10). – As for the time when they were
> redeemed, what does it say? "And the like of the very heaven for
> clearness (ibid.). – and it says, "I beheld till thrones were placed, and
> One that was ancient of days did sit" (Dan. 7:9); but it also says, "A
> fiery stream," etc. (Dan. 7:10). Now, in order to give no opening to
> the Nations of the World to say, "There are two Powers," Scripture
> reads, "The Lord is a man of war, the Lord is his Name."[136]

This interpretation of Exod. 15:3 sets out to prove that the differing manifestations of God at the sea as a warrior and on the mountain as an old man are the same God, representing God's justice and mercy respectively.[137] Thus, there are not two powers in heaven (cf. *b. Hag.* 14a). Rabbi Judah uses Exod. 24:10 as a positive vision of God's compassion, while other interpreters used it as a negative instance of human presumption.[138] Nonetheless, the point remains that the polymorphic God appears in both places to the Israelites with no qualifications or restrictions on the vision.

All of Israel saw God at the sea and on Sinai (*Song Rab.* 2.9.1). Such events, however, do not open up visual potential for later Jews. These events were special. In the *Mekhilta*, all of Israel saw what even Isaiah and Ezekiel could not (*Shirta* 3). *Deut. Rab.* 7.8 further emphasizes that all were granted a greater vision than Ezekiel's spectacular vision of the "appearance of the likeness of the glory of the LORD"; even the lowliest in Moses' time saw the Divine Presence directly (cf. *Num. Rab.* 12:4). In the days of Moses, the LORD came down and appeared to them en masse (Exod. 19:11; cf. *Mek., Bahodesh* 9), and all the Israelites spoke with the Divine Presence face to face (Deut. 5:4). No one would again see as clearly.

As the Exodus generation attained a privileged visionary status compared to later generations, Moses remains privileged vis-à-vis the rest of the Israelites.[139] When discussing Moses' visions of God, the Rabbis teased out a set of contradictory verses: Exod. 3:6, where Moses hid his face; Exod. 24:9–11, where the elders, Nadab, and Abihu saw God; Exod. 33:20, where God says that no one can see God and live; and Num. 12:8, where God says that only Moses sees God's form. From the combination of verses the Rabbis create a flirtatious interplay between hiding and revealing: Moses hides and God reveals; Moses seeks and God hides; but the elders do not play this humble game of hiding and seeking and look without humility; thus, their arrogance will be punished.[140]

The Rabbis offered differing evaluations of Exod. 3:6. In *Exod. Rab.* 3.1, God wanted to reveal himself to Moses, but Moses hid. God wanted to have Moses see him, so Moses' refusal carries a negative connotation. Yet when Moses asked to see God in Exod. 33:20, God refused (cf. *b. Ber.* 7a); nonetheless, God was ultimately pleased with the request and eventually granted Moses a vision, speaking with him face to face (Num. 12:8; cf. *Sifre* 103 on Moses seeing God directly). On the other hand, the elders on the mountain in Exod. 24:9–11 looked without permission, and "did they not receive the death penalty for what they did?"

Overall, Moses' actions of hiding and seeking permission demonstrate his humility. In *Exod. Rab.* 45.5, because Moses was humble, God exalted him; because the elders, Nadab, and Abihu were presumptuous, they were punished (cf. *Lev. Rab.* 1.5). In *Pseudo-Jonathan*, looking upon God is a punishable offence; in the *midrashim*, the offence is looking without humility or permission. In another passage, the line from Exod. 24:11 that states that God did not lay his hand on the elders indicates that they deserved punishment because they looked without permission, did not cover their heads, and ate and drank with levity (*Lev. Rab.* 20.10). Moses, however, would be rewarded with a luminous face, because he hid his face. The elders' actions on Sinai did not immediately kill them, but they sealed their doom (*Num. Rab.* 2.25; 15.24).[141]

The rabbinic commentators work around the problem inherent in Moses seeing God and God telling Moses that none can see God's face by fixating on the word "face." One interpretation is that the "face" refers to the "prosperity of the wicked," and Moses cannot see the wicked prosper. Others take a step back from direct vision and say that Moses saw God "symbolically" (*Exod. Rab.* 23.15). Another explanation is that Moses had a clearer vision than any other prophet: they saw dark visions, through specula that were modified through nine panes; Moses saw through only one pane. His vision was much clearer, but still partially occluded (*Lev. Rab.* 1.14; *b. Yev.* 49b).[142] Or God condenses his glory, which stretches throughout the heavens and earth, to make it appear *as if* it were between the cherubim in the Tabernacle. Moses' ascent on the mountain, as in earlier traditions, is also an ascent to heaven to receive Torah.[143] Finally, the word "live" suggests that one can see God at death or in the afterlife (*Lev. Rab.* 1.11). Or it means that the angelic "living creatures" cannot see God, but humans can.[144]

While many of these *midrashim* indicate one cannot see God and live, most are willing to allow that at least the humble Moses – as well as Abraham, Isaac, Jacob, and David – did. Moreover, the elders on Sinai who presumptuously saw God did in fact see God, though it was inadvisable to do so. Some Rabbis stated that all of Israel saw God at the sea and on Sinai. Some traditions exclude women at Sinai (*Exod. Rab.* 46.3), while most do not make such a gendered commentary – not yet, anyway.

The *midrashim* elsewhere repeatedly deny women divine contact. *Genesis Rabbah*, for example, repeatedly states that God never spoke to a woman, except for Sarah (20.6, 45.10, 48.20, 63.7).[145] Sarah is uniquely righteous among women, but her exceptional status as the only woman to hear directly from the LORD is hardly flattering, since God spoke to her to correct her when she denied laughing at the thought of giving birth to a son at an old age. Even then, some claim God spoke through an angel (45.7). Contact with women, moreover, through the example of Moses, inhibits theophany for men as well. The Israelites at Sinai had to separate from their wives for the fiery theophany to occur. Moses, who regularly spoke to God face to face had to separate from his wife permanently (*Exod. Rab.* 46.3).[146] Interestingly, *Exodus Rabbah* is willing to grant Moses a face-to-face vision of God to emphasize his separation from his wife.

Gentiles are also excluded. Both women and foreigners can have only an indirect revelation. Explaining why God appears to Abimelech in a dream, *Gen. Rab.* 52.5 explains that God appears to Gentiles only in "half-speech," rather than a full vision or speech, whereas, in language reminiscent of God's speech concerning Moses in Num. 12:6–8, God speaks to the Israelite prophets in complete speech. He speaks to others from afar; to Israel, near. For others, he comes only in stealth, at night; for Israel God pulls the curtain back to see fully and directly (cf. *Lev. Rab.* 1.13).

The *midrashim* never clarify why God does not appear to women or Gentiles; however, the readings on how, when, and why God appears to Abraham and the Israelite men at Sinai provide a clue: a circumcised penis is necessary.[147] The excision of foreskin perfects the body and removes the membrane that separates divine and human.[148] Nonetheless, Abraham and Moses (and David) were exceptional, because God would come to them in vision and speech rather than just one or the other, while Moses, even more so than others, could endure the divine presence.[149]

Some Rabbis, noting how a "word of the LORD" comes to Abram in Genesis 15, question whether Abraham saw God or angels (*Gen. Rab.* 44.11), yet most take Gen. 18:1 to demonstrate that he had direct visions of God.[150] While Abraham was righteous, the primary requirement to endure the direct sight and sound of God is circumcision. *Gen. Rab.* 47.10 is representative:

> Abraham said: "When I was uncircumcised, travellers would visit
> me; now being circumcised, they may not visit me." The Holy
> One, blessed be he, said to him: "When you were uncircumcised,
> humans visited you; now I in my glory come and will be revealed
> to you." Thus it is written, "And the Lord appeared to him." (trans-
> lation mine)

As Wolfson and Boyarin note, this and parallel passages read a causal,
rather than sequential, relationship between Gen. 17:1–14, which
describes Abraham's circumcision, and Gen. 18:1, when the LORD
appears to him,[151] ignoring Gen. 17:1, where the LORD appears to him
before he is circumcised. Circumcision marks the difference between
human and divine visitation: when uncircumcised, Abraham received
human visitors; when circumcised, a divine guest. Similarly, interpreting Job 19:26 – "and after my skin has been thus destroyed, then from
my flesh I shall see God" – Gen. Rab. 48.2 reads the destroyed skin as
the foreskin and that circumcision, the destruction of the foreskin,
allows one to see God while still in the body:

> Abraham said, "After I circumcised myself, many proselytes came
> to cleave to this covenant – 'from my flesh I shall see God.' If I had
> not done so, why would the Holy One, blessed be He, be revealed
> to me?" And the Lord appeared to him. (translation mine)

The necessity of circumcision for divine vision recurs throughout this
section of Genesis Rabbah.[152] This passage tacitly rejects the Pauline
position that physical circumcision has been replaced by spiritual
circumcision and baptism. Furthermore, many convert because of
this sign of the covenant, through which one, in the flesh, can see
God. They are attracted to the circumcised – bare, uncovered, unmediated – vision.[153]

These passages do not indicate, however, whether all circumcised
men can see God, or whether Abraham, Isaac, Jacob, and Moses are
special cases. Some traditions indicate that Abraham was exceptional, because God would come to him in vision and speech rather than
just one or the other (Gen. Rab. 44.6; Lev. Rab. 1:4; cf. Song Rab.
1.14.3). Lev. Rab. 1.4 includes David and Moses among those who
saw and heard God directly; Moses also endured the divine speech
longer than the Israelites. Therefore, he is the greatest of all (circumcised) visionaries.

While Abraham and Moses were exceptional, there is a tradition that the circumcision-vision linkage was available to other Jewish males. A fascinating, erotic, and gender-blurring passage associates the theophany at Sinai with circumcision and the Song of Songs, identifying the circumcised male with the daughters of Zion who gaze upon the King (God) and Abraham with the female lover (*Num. Rab.* 12.8).[154] Because the male daughters were circumcised, they were able to the see the divine presence as it entered the Tabernacle. Because they had removed the blemish of foreskin and had become whole, they could endure the sight of the divine presence as Abraham did after he was circumcised (Gen. 18:1), and not fall on their faces as he did before he was circumcised.[155] The act of circumcision is necessary before seeing the King, one's lover, and before the wedding between Israel and God.

The image of the "daughters of Zion" gazing upon the King, when applied to circumcised men, eroticizes the divine vision. It feminizes the male member through circumcision, so that the man can be made whole; through cutting off the unclean portion he becomes a "daughter" and a "beloved" of the King. As before, the passage causally relates Genesis 17 and Gen. 18:1, homologizing the relationship between God and Abraham (Solomon and the Beloved) and God and the Israelites (the King and the Daughters of Zion). The feminizing circumcision removes the membrane between human and divine, allowing one to receive divine visions.

This midrash also indicates that the male body is imperfect with the blemish of the foreskin. This excision of the fleshly barrier between human and divine makes the body whole. Although women do not have the offending blemish, making them appear naturally equipped for such a vision, it is a gender-blurring moment that paradoxically can occur only with male members, to the exclusion of Israelite women. If the circumcised male body is perfect, one cannot add, detract, or alter. Feminization is a male privilege. Although women do not have to worry about this blemish, only men can be daughters.[156]

While there is some divergence over whether one can see God and live, the *midrashim* generally accept divine vision more than the *targumim*, while developing a stronger gendered element than found in the biblical materials or the *targumim*. For the *midrashim*, the primary requirement to endure a vision of God is circumcision, mostly excluding women and foreigners. God still indirectly gives revelations to women and foreigners through intermediaries or through dark visions, incomplete speech, and dreams. The other aspect that comes through is humility. Moses saw God in a playful game of hide and seek because he was humble and because he asked. Nadab, Abihu, and others presumptuously looked upon God and died. These establishing events and founding figures all belong to the remote, legendary past. They were *exceptional* figures or belonged to *exceptional* times: they are not models for the present. Instead, midrashic authority derives from interpreting the oracles rather than seeking a new vision.

HEKHALOT:
INSTRUCTING HOW TO SEE GOD AND LIVE

Peter Schäfer, in *Hidden and Manifest God*, writes, "In rabbinic literature the question of whether one can see God plays a minor role that above all is connected to the heroic past. That one is unable to see God at the present time and that God (no longer) reveals himself directly to man is more or less self-evident."[157] This chapter has also found that many *midrashim* locate divine visions in the distant past for particular foundational individuals, rechannelling their past visionary authority into current interpretive authority.

Nonetheless, there are rabbinic and para-rabbinic traditions that present the possibilities and dangers for late-antique Jews to see God, for whom figures of the heroic past – especially Moses, but also Ezekiel and Isaiah – provide a model for more-recent visionaries, such as Rabbi Akiva, though the connection between past and present vision in these texts is allusive and elusive. Nonetheless, these texts have internalized the prohibition from Exod. 33:20 to a strong degree. They, however, tend not to view God as invisible, but God and God's angels as deadly to behold. Yet a small circle of Jewish mystics seek to do so.

B. Ber. 7a recounts a story of Rabbi Ishmael, who entered the holy of holies and saw God on an exalted throne: "R. Ishmael b. Elisha said: one time I entered, in order to offer incense, the innermost place, and I saw Achathriel Yah, the LORD of hosts, who was sitting on a high and exalted throne." It is a startling and familiar passage. Its familiarity results from being modelled on Isaiah 6. Its startling aspect is that the seer is someone of the more recent past for the Rabbis who related the tale. That Ishmael saw God is casually mentioned to get to the point:

that God prays and to discuss the relationship between God's mercy and justice. Nonetheless, its casualness speaks volumes about its acceptance that R. Ishmael could see and speak to God.[158]

By contrast, commenting on the mishnaic passage on forbidden topics, *b. Hag.* 11b–16b offers several tales of Rabbis who speculate on the accounts of creation and of Ezekiel's Chariot vision, sometimes successfully and sometimes not. It is a life-threatening exegetical experience. Included in this framework is the story of the four who entered *pardes* and gazed (14b).[159] It is unclear what they saw, although in its current context it likely refers to the exposition of Ezekiel 1. Nonetheless, in the Babylonian version – and only in this version – the passage demonstrates that there is something more than biblical interpretation occurring; exegesis becomes entwined with supernal encounters.[160] The passage most importantly demonstrates perils of a divine vision: it can cause death (Ben Azzai),[161] insanity (Ben Zoma), and apostasy (Aher). Only R. Akiva entered and exited unscathed (15b).[162]

These Talmudic stories, ranging from the casual to the perilous, are a foretaste of the extensive lore, practices, and teachings pseudonymously ascribed to R. Ishmael, R. Akiva, and R. Nehuniah b. Ha-Kanah in the *hekhalot* texts. These texts rely upon the explicit model of Moses and implicit examples of Isaiah and Ezekiel, who, in turn, serve as prototypes for the merkavah mystics who attempted to "descend" to the chariot, see the enthroned God, and participate in the heavenly liturgies.[163]

There are five basic *hekhalot* texts or "macroforms":[164] *Hekhalot Rabbati, Hekhalot Zutarti, Ma'aseh Merkavah, Merkavah Rabbah,* and *3 Enoch / Sefer Hekhalot.*[165] These complex documents contain multiple types of material that cannot be reduced to any aspect,[166] but this section will focus on the ascents to heaven to gaze upon the *merkavah* (chariot) and God enthroned upon it.[167]

Moses provides a mystical model in *Hekh. Zut.* §§335–74,[168] where he is paired with R. Akiva, both of whom ascended on high to behold God and obtain the divine names needed to keep from forgetting the Torah.[169] This is Torah in the broader sense, including the Bible, Mishnah, Talmud, Halakhot, and Haggadot.[170] With these names, moreover, Moses parted the sea, piling up the waters into mountains.[171] In addition, Schäfer notes that *Hekhalot Zutarti* is the only *hekhalot* text where the question of whether one can see God is directly posed:

Who is able to explain, who is able to see?
Firstly, it is written: For man may not see me and live.
And secondly, it is written: That man may live though God has
spoken to him.
And thirdly, it is written: I beheld my Lord seated upon a high
and lofty throne. (§350)[172]

Directly in the middle of the Moses section, this double question is asked: Who can explain? Who can see? The passage juxtaposes Exod. 33:20 with Deut. 5:21–4, ending with Isa. 6:1. The progression is important: beginning with not being able to see, moving through hearing God, and ending with an affirmation of seeing God.[173]

The two questions of seeing and explaining offer the same answer: Moses and R. Akiva. They see, and they explain. The explanation of seeing is found through biblical interpretation. Indeed, as we will later discover, such as with the discussion of Origen and the Cappadocians, interpretation and vision are strongly related: the greatest exegetes are also visionaries. Moses and Akiva, who both ascend to heaven and who receive the Torah and interpret the Torah, respectively, are mystical prototypes, models for the "descender to the chariot."[174]

It remains a question, however, of whether they are prototypes of ascent, prototypes of the mystical use of the divine name, or both. Schäfer writes, "Whereas the ascent was reserved for Moses and 'Aqiva, the name is accessible to 'Aqiva's students and therewith to a circle of initiates."[175] This is especially the case in §§685–6, where Akiva ascends to heaven and has a direct vision of God. Then Metatron himself teaches Torah to Akiva, so long as he abstains from idolatry, bloodshed, and illicit sex, and finally disseminates this knowledge to his own students.[176] Moses and Akiva are the peak of humanity, either of them most likely achieving what no other human other than these two can achieve as original receiver and greatest interpreter of the Torah – or perhaps they are mystical models for others to follow.

Even when Moses shows up in other works, like *Ma'aseh Merkavah* (§§564, 574–8)[177] or *Merkavah Rabbah* (§676),[178] the emphasis is on his receipt of divine mysteries, particularly names or letters, and on him passing along those mysteries to other humans, first to Joshua and then throughout the generations (cf. *m. Avot* 1:1). He remains mediator par excellence, along with R. Akiva, being one of the few to receive the mysteries, usually of the divine name, directly from heavenly beings.[179]

Moses otherwise rarely appears in *hekhalot* texts, which mostly look to Ezekiel 1 and Isaiah 6 as models. Nonetheless, like *Hekhalot Zutarti* these works continue to address *who* can see God and *how*. A comparison between *Ma'aseh Merkavah* and *Hekhalot Rabbati* is instructive of the range of views on the dangers and possibilities of seeing God.[180] In both, the mystic attempts to ascend (or "descend") to the merkavah, have a vision of God, participate in the heavenly liturgy, and represent Israel in the divine court. Nonetheless, they show varying attitudes in the possibility of accomplishing this quest and the dangers of the ascent and of the vision itself. *Hekhalot Rabbati* shows more internal tension about seeing God than *Ma'aseh Merkavah*. The former emphasizes the patent dangers of such a quest and apparent impossibility of surviving it, while it gives examples of figures who did so; the latter, by contrast, simply tells what one should do to see God without recounting any such difficulties. Both ultimately affirm that, with the correct level of purity and righteousness and the recitation of the correct songs, one can survive the sight of God on His chariot throne and the sound of the heavenly liturgy.[181]

Ma'aseh Merkavah, one of the clearer macroforms in terms of literary organization, instructs how to attain a divine vision with little emphasis on its dangers.[182] It probably originated as liturgies,[183] but currently is a series of questions between teacher and student Rabbis about which songs are necessary to ascend to heaven and to gaze upon the merkavah, God, and all that occurs in the heavenly court. The text also emphasizes the purity, righteousness, and endurance necessary to gaze upon the King of the Universe. While Moses' ascent to heaven is assumed, since Moses is mentioned in passing as having received instruction from the princes who split the *raqia'* (§§574–8), the primary focus is on more recent mystical models of R. Ishmael and R. Akiva (the new Moses).

The text begins with a conversation between R. Ishmael and R. Akiva concerning this emphasis: "Rabbi Ishmael said: 'I asked Rabbi Akiva a prayer one prays when he ascends to the merkavah, and I asked from him the praise of RWZYY, YHWH, God of Israel – who knows which it is?' He said to me: 'Purity and holiness is in his heart, and he prays a prayer'" (§544). *Hekhalot Rabbati* commences similarly, requesting what songs one should recite to ascend to the merkavah, but, instead of recounting all the ways such a journey and a possible vision may destroyer the beholder, as *Hekhalot Rabbati* does, the text of *Ma'aseh Merkavah* swiftly moves to gazing upon God: "Rabbi Akiva said: 'When I ascended and gazed at the Power, I saw all the creatures that are in all the paths of heaven'" (§545). R. Akiva gazed upon all the creatures of heaven and the Power, which may be an epithet for God or a semi-independent entity. He makes the statement in passing, getting to the primary focus of the songs he recited to ascend and those he heard the ministering angels recite once he ascended. R. Ishmael seeks further instruction on how to find out what RWZYY YWY God of Israel does and how one can gaze upon him (§547). At one point, Akiva exclaims on how he glimpsed a knot in God's tefillin,[184] and for this glance, R. Akiva "gave praise for all my limbs" (§550).

Other descenders to the chariot make appearances with direct visions of God – not just his tefillin – modelled on prophetic calls:

> Rabbi Ishmael said: when Rabbi Nehuniah my teacher told me the secret of the chambers of the Hekhal and the Hekhal of the Merkavah ... I saw the King of the universe sitting on a high and exalted throne, and all the chambers of the holiness of His name and His power were sanctifying His name in His praise, as it is said: "They called one to another and said, Holy, Holy, Holy is YHWH of Hosts, the whole earth is full of His Glory" (Isa. 6:3). (§556)

R. Ishmael's vision incorporates the visual and auditory elements of Isaiah 6. Like his models, Nehuniah and Isaiah, he has a direct vision, seeing the King of the Universe and the angels surrounding him. The teacher discloses to his pupil the "secret" that triggers the vision.

As the passage continues, R. Akiva teaches that a man is particularly happy and blessed if he can stand with all his strength and offer a song before God, gaze at the merkavah, and see everything that occurs in the divine court, particularly the divine decrees sent forth (§557). While *Ma'aseh Merkavah* may not emphasize dangers, it indicates that one needs much strength to endure gazing upon God and his merkavah. One comes before the God of Israel and praises with all one's strength to the point of trembling in all one's limbs (§558). One needs strength, piety, purity, righteousness, and perfection.[185]

Gazing appears everywhere in *Ma'aseh Merkavah*. One gazes upon God, the radiance of the Shekhinah (§570), the Merkavah (§579), the Shekhinah, and all that occurs before the throne (§592), and, in a curious passage, above the seraphim who stand above God's head (§595).[186]

Hekhalot Rabbati is a less-organized work with greater ocular tension: a divine vision is highly dangerous – no creature, human or angelic, can look and live – and yet that is the goal of the mystic. Divine vision is not impossible, but highly deadly. One must attempt to approach God's throne and gaze upon the King of the Universe, to gain knowledge of what is going on throughout the world now and in the future. *Hekhalot Rabbati*, more so than *Ma'aseh Merkavah*, emphasizes the necessary fear in such a quest (§96). The tension created by having an impossible goal opens a terrifying vista of the immense dangers of gazing. It may be impossible for any creature to gaze upon the divine countenance and live, but particularly righteous humans still do.

As with *Ma'aseh Merkavah*, *Hekhalot Rabbati* begins with a question concerning the correct songs one should recite to ascend to and behold the merkavah (§81; cf. 94). While the question assumes that one can ascend to the chariot with the assistance of songs, the text emphasizes the dangers and impossibility of the quest. An early string of *Qedushah* hymns commences with these difficulties and concludes with the implied accomplishment of such a vision (§§100–6).[187] When the Cherubim and holy beasts see anyone entering the seventh heaven, the ascender is terrified, faints, and falls back, "for no creature is able to attain that place" (§101). Interestingly, this passage is not directed, per se, to humans, but likely to angels.[188]

Speaking of God's exceedingly glorious appearance, "the eye of no creature is able to gaze at Him, not the eyes of flesh and blood, and not the eyes of His servants, and as for the one who gazes at Him, glimpses, or sees it, his eyeballs emit and shoot forth torches of fire and these scorch him and they burn him" (§103).[189] Even if one gazes upon God's crown or glorious garment, one's eyes burst forth in fire, and that fire consumes the beholder.

Similarly, a later passage that speaks of God's majestic face concludes with the consequences of beholding it: "He who gazes at Him is at once torn into pieces, and he who glimpses his Beauty immediately pours himself out as a vessel." This too applies to angels as much as humans. In fact, God's servants cannot endure serving him but a day, because they cannot endure the splendour of the divine Beauty (§160).[190]

Paradoxically, one knows these things will happen because R. Akiva descended to the chariot and learned these songs while he was before God's throne, where God's servants sang them (§106). So, one learns songs about how a glimpse of God or even hearing the cherubim will kill any creature, heavenly or earthly, from an account of R. Akiva, who discovered this by going there himself. Clearly, he survived.[191]

Despite the death sentence for those who glimpse God, there are those like R. Akiva who can ascend and descend peacefully. R. Nehuniah b. Ha-Kanah speaks of those who are worthy to gaze upon the King and His throne and all that surrounds Him in the heavenly court. One who is worthy is like a man who has a ladder in his house; he goes up and comes down and no creature can stop him (§§198–9, 201). There are requirements to be worthy. One must be pure, never have committed idolatry, sexual sins, murder, etc. One must keep every positive and negative commandment. There cannot be any hint of impurity (§§225–7). One must be honest, upright, humble, have understanding and wisdom, be chosen, and be separated out (§92). One must master the Mishnah, midrash, *halakhot*, and *aggadoth* (§234).[192]

Being thus pure and erudite, one can learn all the songs to ascend and the secret passwords to give to the angelic guards. R. Nehuniah also recounts exactly what one should say, how many times, and to whom. In fact, his speech within *Hekhalot Rabbati* is what the entire text is doing: instructing readers how to descend to the merkavah and gaze upon God and His throne.[193]

Once one is worthy, the threat dissipates. One can ascend and descend at will. The scene from §101, where one had been blown back at trying to enter the threshold of the heavenly throne room, is directly countered in §§247–8.

> And whenever one wants to descend to the merkavah, 'Anafiel the prince opens the doors of the entrance of the seventh palace for him. This man enters and stands on the threshold of the gate of the seventh palace. The holy beasts lift up upon him 512 eyes … and that man is stricken and trembles and falls backward. And 'Anafiel the Prince supports him, and sixty-three door-keepers of the gates of the seven palaces. And all of them help him and say to him: "Fear not, son of a beloved seed, enter and see the King in His beauty, and you will not be destroyed and you will not be burned."

Instead of fainting terrified at the sight of God and the throne or having one's eyes burst into flame and body burned, one survives. One begins to faint and fall as in §101, but 'Anafiel and the doorkeepers counter the threat, saying the descender, who is of the beloved seed

Israel, will not be destroyed and not burn; he will enter and see the King in all His Beauty – the same beauty that no creature is supposed to be able to endure wears out God's servants in a day.[194] One has accomplished the impossible; one has seen God and survived.[195]

CONCLUSIONS

In his study *Through a Speculum That Shines*, Elliott Wolfson has argued that divine vision was neither absent nor peripheral for medieval Jews; the same is true for ancient Jews, especially when reflecting upon Moses. While Moses was not always overtly present, Moses' visions left an imprint on later discussions of human possibilities of divine vision. Moses sets the terms of debate with the problem of not being able to see God and live (Exod. 33:20) and yet seeing the very form of the LORD (Num. 12:8). Standing between God and Israel, biblical and post-biblical writers returned to the Moses story to parse out whether Moses saw God, what he saw, how he saw it, and whether Moses was unique in his abilities.

The interpretations of Genesis-Judges discussed the possibilities of whether, how, and who could see God. The prophetic image of the enthroned God provided models for later visionaries to re-envision what Ezekiel or Isaiah saw, with some reconfigurations along the way.[196] While the *Apocalypse of Abraham* and especially Philo present an invisible God, most of these Jewish texts indicate that God is visible, but that a vision of God's beauty and splendour is so overwhelming that it is deadly. Very few humans have and can bear it. For Philo, the emphasis on God's invisibility shifts the focus from what one sees to *how* one sees with the mind rather than the body, and *who* sees, making Moses unique in his position between God and humanity. For most other writers, however, the emphasis is on *what* one sees: God, an angel, or an aspect of God.

Many late-ancient Jews reaffirmed the biblical denial of one's ability to survive a divine vision or that such visions ever occurred, but there was a wider range of possibilities of a visual divine encounter. If one could not see God and live, then one could see God upon death or, according to the *targumim*, could see God's manifest Glory, Shekhinah, or Memra. Other Jews affirmed direct visions. Shifting to the status of the righteous and humble seer, the *midrashim* affirmed that particularly righteous men, like Abraham, Isaac, or Moses, could see God directly once they were circumcised. The circumcision requirement occurs alongside a denial that any woman or foreigner can hear or see God directly, except for Sarah. A particularly important event, like the splitting of the sea or the theophany of Sinai, allowed greater numbers to see God, and may, in fact, open the doors to a gender-inclusive vision. Sometimes later interpreters, such as the Rabbis in the *midrashim*, saw people like Moses or Enoch, or events, such as the parting of the Sea or theophany at Sinai, as unique. Sometimes, as in the *hekhalot*, they provided models for later would-be seers of God, such as R. Ishmael, R. Akiva, and R. Nehuniah b. Ha-Kanah, who could ascend and descend to and from the merkavah, gaze upon God and the merkavah, and participate in the heavenly liturgies, despite all the dangers that pertain to such a journey and sight, providing models for late-antique Jews who sought to overcome the threat of death and see God.

While this biblical and post-biblical material has been voluminous, it provides the problems and parameters of divine vision that Christians also inherited, and antecedent and parallel strategies of overcoming those problems, differentiating between the seen and unseen elements of God (e.g., *targumim*), or differentiating how one sees (e.g., Philo), or focusing on who can see (e.g., Philo, *midrashim*, and *hekhalot*).

Finally, while covering over a millennium of development – from a kaleidoscope of contexts from Babylon to Jerusalem to Rome, from the biblical books to the *hekhalot* macroforms – to some degree all of these sources have strongly focused on the status of who can see: each seer is a leader of the community and even the visions en masse establish a foundation for the community as a whole;[197] that is, Abraham, Moses, the Israelites as a whole, Isaiah, Jeremiah, Ezekiel, all the way through R. Akiva serve or reflect a social function of authorizing the authority of these figures and especially their successors. With the exception of Sarah, whose encounter with God was a scolding, their visions give them a mandate to speak or lead. Already present in the biblical stories of Moses and the prophets, this becomes especially pronounced in Ezekiel's *Exagogue*, Philo, and even Josephus: Moses' visions justify his authority, authorizing Moses as the leader of humans. Often appearing in Hellenistic and Roman contexts, these more apologetic portrayals of Moses present him as the greatest leader that Plato could imagine, yet predating Plato. In Hellenized culture and Roman society, figures from Ezekiel the Tragedian to Philo to Josephus could portray Moses as both pre-eminent and most ancient.

While often these visions were unrepeatable, with Enoch or Moses being unique, they nonetheless undergirded broader forms of cultural authority of the antiquity of Jewish revelation in contrast to Greek or Roman traditions or were redirected to the interpretive authority of the interpreter of oracles, such as Philo, the Rabbis in general, or R. Akiva in particular. Others, nonetheless, emulated Moses and stormed heaven to have a vision of God, his temple or tabernacle, and his throne, or bring back divine names that they could pass down to their students or followers to read and remember the Torah. Visions, therefore, were not and are not an end in themselves, but qualified one to lead and ultimately read the original messages of Moses and the prophets, as they would again for the Christian bishops of the fourth century.[198]

3

Moses' and Humanity's Limitations in the New Testament

Moses' status as visionary and mediator par excellence in the Hebrew Bible and second-temple Judaism played an important role in how he would be co-opted by later Jews and Christians to discuss the nature of God, revelation, and new forms of authority based upon Moses' visions or upon the denial of such visions. Moses had become in late-second-temple Jewish thought a highly exalted figure, nearly divine himself, sometimes even seated on God's throne.[1] He was even more exalted in Samaritan circles, possessing the divine name (*Memar Marqa* 4.1).[2] People like Philo and Josephus extensively wrote about how great a leader Moses was, politically and religiously, including being the ideal philosopher-king of Plato's *Republic*.[3]

Moreover, the ambivalence of the Hebrew Bible about whether Moses saw God (Num. 12:6–8) or could not see God (Exod. 33:20) provided the basis for Jewish and Christian discussions of Moses as visionary, of what he could and did see, of what he could not see, and, most importantly, whether one could see God and live. That is, Moses was an important figure for early Christians to think with. In various ways, he was juxtaposed with Christ, who, for the early Christians, was the ultimate or only mediator. There will, therefore, be competitive readings centring around Moses that exalt or downplay his visionary abilities and update the biblical text to new assumptions and theologies. He will be juxtaposed with and surpassed by Jesus and even be used as an exemplary proto-Christian, whom Christians should emulate. Some traces of these hermeneutical manoeuvrings exist in embryonic form as early as the first-century and early-second-century documents that now form the New Testament.[4]

This chapter, like the previous one, will consider several works and authors who occupy diverse localized rhetorical contexts; nonetheless, while the previous chapter covered approximately a millennium of materials, with a geographical spread from Babylon to Rome, this current chapter is relatively focused on a century's worth of materials (c. 35–120 CE) within the confines of the Roman empire. While I do not want to belittle their differences, these works largely fit within the burgeoning of a new movement within Judaism that followed Jesus, navigating between rival interpretations by other Jews, by other Jewish Christians, and by the influx of Gentile Christians. In this context, Moses serves as marker of one's position within these newly generated social and rhetorical contexts, varying between the writings of Paul and those of the authors of the different gospels, Acts, and Hebrews.

These early documents, moreover, provide an interesting test case for the theory that Moses represents the limits of the human condition in the face of divinity. Tending to follow the path of Exod. 33:20 rather than Num. 12:8, the documents now forming the New Testament will largely deny the possibility that Moses – or anyone else – has seen or can see God. Only the Son who comes from the Father can know or see God. In this case, the earliest Christian writers repeatedly exalt Jesus at the expense of Moses, yet Moses still represents what the greatest of humans can do. Jesus, indeed, has help, especially in works with higher Christologies. Nevertheless, new exceptions to this rule emerge, which later Christians will consider together with the earlier Moses passages, compounding the hermeneutical tensions for these Christian interpreters. While Moses does not appear in every passage that addresses divine vision, he shows up more frequently than any other biblical figure.

There have been numerous studies of Moses in the New Testament. Most of these focus on Mosaic imagery in a single text, which, in turn, provides part of the basis for that text's Christology, such as Matthew,[5] Luke-Acts,[6] John,[7] Hebrews,[8] Revelation,[9] and the traditions of the New Testament generally.[10] Others have attempted a topical overview of Moses in the New Testament, dividing Moses into different roles and types and looking at what different New Testament documents, in conversation with Jewish literature, contribute to such roles.[11]

This well-trod ground will provide some pathways for discussion, but this chapter will mostly focus on Moses' ability to see God and, barring that ability, query who, in fact, Moses met at the bush and on

the mountaintop, something rarely discussed in the scholarly literature. In addition, it will consider other passages that may not have a
direct relationship to Moses in the New Testament, but which Christian interpreters in the second through fourth centuries connected to
the problem of Moses' visions. This chapter is, therefore, a thematic
sketch, neither focusing on a single book nor seeking a comprehensive evaluation of Moses.[12] This chapter, moreover, mostly proceeds
topically, rather than chronologically or by text – though it does move
chronologically within each topic – for clarity of exposition, as these
passages provide additional raw material for later Christian debates
about whether, how, and who can see God.

PARAMETERS OF VISION:
NONE CAN SEE GOD

Most New Testament authors who comment on divine visions presume that no one can see God. Paul's letters, the Deutero-Paulines,
and Hebrews refer to God, God's nature, or God's powers as "unseen"
or "invisible" (ἀόρατος; Rom. 1:20; Col. 1:15; 1 Tim. 1:17; Heb. 11:27).
   Documents dating to the late-first and early-second centuries more
forthrightly state or argue that none can see God. These documents,
the Gospel of John and 1 Timothy, are clear that neither Moses nor
anyone else ever saw God.

> The law indeed was given through Moses; grace and truth came
> through Jesus Christ. No one has ever seen God [θεὸν οὐδεὶς
> ἑώρακεν πώποτε]. It is God the only Son [alt. it is the only Son],
> who is close to the Father's heart, he has made him known. (John
> 1:17–18)[13]

> To the King of ages, immortal, invisible (ἀοράτῳ),[14] the only
> God, be honour and glory for ever and ever. Amen. (1 Tim.
> 1:17)

> It is he alone who has immortality and dwells in unapproachable
> light [φῶς οἰκῶν ἀπρόσιτον], whom no one has ever seen or can
> see [ὃν εἶδεν οὐδεὶς ἀνθρώπων οὐδὲ ἰδεῖν δύναται]. (1 Tim. 6:16)

There are a few elements to consider in all three of these quotations.
Both 1 Timothy and John are fairly late documents in the New Testa-

ment, dating to the late-first or early-second centuries.[15] There, therefore, seems to be a stronger need or a greater willingness to declare the impossibility of divine vision at this period, to a degree not found in earlier documents.

A close analogue does occur, however, in the earlier "Q" passage (Matt. 11:27; Luke 10:22);[16] it is a similar – though not the same – view. In its Lukan version, it reads: "no one knows who the Son is except the Father, or who the Father is except the Son." This suggests that the Father and the Son are the only ones who know each other's identities. Nonetheless, most Christians in later centuries will prefer Matthew's redaction: "no one knows the Son except the Father, and no one knows the Father except the Son."[17] Here, knowing seems to move beyond being able to identify the Father or Son, to a more intimate mutual knowledge,[18] though the shift from γινώσκει (to know) in Luke to ἐπιγινώσκει (to recognize) in Matthew may retain something of the original sense.

This Johannine-sounding quotation from Matthew on knowing will be quoted often by second- and third-century Christians to argue that no one can see the Father, eliding knowing and seeing in a typical Platonic manner.[19] It is unlikely, however, that Matthew or the Q passage behind it uses knowing as an analogue for seeing. Moreover, most of these Christians overlook the end of the verse in both versions: "and anyone to whom the Son chooses to reveal him." That is, as is found already in Q, the Son can reveal the Father to whomever he wants, making knowledge of the Father a possibility, though not one based upon one's own human endeavours, but by the Son's discretion.[20]

Returning to the impossibility of vision, 1 Timothy makes two separate categorical statements that deny vision and further notes that God is unapproachable; 1 Timothy more greatly emphasizes the inability to see God than John does by stating both that no one *has* seen God and that no one *can* see God. These are two different statements. To state that no one *has* seen God leaves open a possible future vision; to say that no one *can* see God closes off such a possibility.

The Gospel of John couches this impossibility differently in a polemical context at Moses' expense.[21] The passage begins with comparing and contrasting the law from Moses and grace and truth from Jesus. Raymond Brown, however, has argued that the Gospel of John treats Moses honorifically throughout (1:45; 3:14; 5:45–7; 7:19), especially arguing that Moses foresaw and wrote about Jesus. Brown argues that this honorific sense begins here, and, therefore, one should accept what John 1:17 says: the law itself was a gift, though its interpretation has become a burden.[22] In what appears to be a non sequitur, the evangelist pointedly states: "No one has ever seen God." Indeed, many scholars have seen John 1:17 as an editorial intrusion, perhaps as a commentary on the last lines of 1:16.[23]

Nonetheless, this is not necessarily a non sequitur, for both statements derive from the same moment: God's revelation to Moses.[24] Moses on the mountain receives the law and John partly affirms the statement from Exod. 33:20. No human, including Moses, has seen God; only the Son has seen the Father.[25] In this sense, Jesus is the new "Israel," understood among Hellenized Jews as the "one who sees God."[26] This theme resurfaces throughout John: "Not that anyone has seen the Father except him who is from God; he has seen the Father" (John 4:46). This is reiterated in 6:46: "Not that anyone has seen the Father except the one who is from the Father; he has seen the Father" (cf. 5:37; 1 John 4:12). Only the Son, therefore, has seen the Father; no one else has, including Moses.[27]

While Moses may have, as Brown claims, an honorific role, there remains a polemic against the tradition that he ascended to heaven on the mountain to have a vision of God (3:13–15).[28] Indeed, despite the honour given to Moses, Brown notes, concerning 1:18, "Naturally it is the failure of Moses to have seen God that the author wishes to contrast with the intimate contact between Son and Father."[29] These are fighting words against those who have claimed to ascend to and/or see God, as other traditions claimed Moses had.[30] The implication may be that what these figures saw, like Moses, was none other than the Glory, identified with the Word in John 1:14, providing an antecedent for later, clearer understandings of the pre-incarnate Son being the visible manifestation of God in the Old Testament.[31]

This rejection of vision, however, is not as sweeping as in 1 Timothy; it is only partial. Verse 1:18 switches the language from the lack of possibility to a temporal distinction; instead of "no one can see" as in Exod. 33:20 or 1 Tim. 6:16, it reads "no one has ever seen" (θεὸν οὐδεὶς ἑώρακεν πώποτε) (cf. 1 John 4:12). John 6:46 is similar. Through this subtle shift, the evangelist opens the door for a future revelation, while noting that even the greatest of visionaries of yore – Moses – has not (yet?) seen God. Moreover, the statement of lack of vision in 5:37–8 is also conditional: "You have never heard his voice or seen his form [εἶδος], and you do not have his word [τὸν λόγον] abiding in you, *because* [ὅτι] you do not believe him whom he has sent" (emphasis mine). The implication is that *if* they do believe, they could hear God's voice and see God's form.[32] Interestingly, "form" is the term used in Num. 12:8, though translated into "glory" in the LXX. Such an intertext with the Gospel of John could suggest that this "form" or "glory" is the pre-incarnate Logos (see John 1:14), possibly implying that the Son is the "form/glory" that Moses sees. It is a conclusion second-century Christians would come to at the very least.

Indeed, such a crack in the door for a possible future vision is precisely what Jesus offers in the farewell discourses, except the divine vision has been displaced by Jesus himself: "From now on you do know him [the Father] and have seen him ... He who has seen me has seen the Father; how can you say, 'Show us the Father'? Do you not believe that I am in the Father and the Father in me" (John 14:7, 9–10; cf. John 1:14; 12:45). Jesus, as God's "glory" (δόξα) provides the only visual access – and only access in general – to the Father. This vision of the divine glory, a reference back to Ezekiel 1 and Exodus 24 (among other places), has been preached since the prologue (1:14).[33] Access to vision exists, but the point is that Jesus is the visual mediator – not Moses. The point is all the more saliently made in the context of Passover.[34] Only the Son can make God known and accessible. Others can see the Father in or through the Son; by seeing the Son, God's glory, they "have seen" the Father (John 14:7).[35] One cannot ascend to heaven to see God, but one sees God through his glory's descent to earth and the historical encounter with Jesus.[36]

In sum, John demotes Moses while exalting Jesus. Jesus is the only one who has seen the Father; Moses, therefore, has not.[37] Jesus' followers can see the Father only through seeing Jesus. This general orientation – except the devaluing of Moses' visions – can be found in Col. 1:15, where Jesus is the "image of the invisible God," another favourite with later Christians debating the possibilities of divine vision. Nonetheless, all these texts have laid down the gauntlet: God is completely invisible and unapproachable in 1 Timothy; no human *can* see God. No human *has* seen God, except Jesus who came from God, in John. While John opens some possibilities of current or future vision through God's glory, nonetheless, the general assumption running through several New Testament passages, that God is invisible, makes the exceptions that appear in the New Testament conspicuous.

EXCEPTION I: THE FAITHFUL MOSES

Despite these clear statements of the impossibility of anyone seeing God, there are a few important exceptions in the New Testament. The first focuses on Moses:

> He [Moses] considered abuse suffered for the sake of Christ to be greater wealth than the treasures of Egypt, for he was looking ahead to the reward. By faith he left Egypt unafraid of the king's anger, for he persevered as though [alt. because] he saw him who is invisible [τὸν γὰρ ἀόρατον ὡς ὁρῶν ἐκαρτέρησεν]. (Heb. 11:27)

Moses stands at the centre of an outlier in the highly Hellenized Letter to the Hebrews. As Mary Rose D'Angelo has demonstrated, Moses is central to the portrayal of Jesus in Hebrews.[38] Hebrews prominently features Moses in succinct, yet complex, ways that resemble the ambivalent posture toward Moses in other New Testament texts. In Hebrews one finds traces of ideas that would become more fully elaborated by Christians in subsequent centuries: Moses' privileged place as seer, his subordination to Christ, his proto-Christian status, and, moreover, his role as a figure for Christians to emulate.

The quoted passage appears in the famous "hall of faith" chapter.[39] The Moses vignette (11:23–8) receives the most "by faiths" in the chapter: four. To be fair, the first technically refers to the faith of his parents.[40] Abraham receives the second-most "by faiths," with three. The line "τὸν γὰρ ἀόρατον ὡς ὁρῶν ἐκαρτέρησεν" can be translated as "for as seeing the invisible one, he endured" or "since seeing the invisible one, he endured." "As" preserves the original ambiguity – it is unclear whether Moses paradoxically saw the invisible one or not. Does it mean "as if" or "because"? Does it qualify his vision in some way? Did Moses "in a way" or "sort of" see the invisible one, comparable to the buffering of all of the "as ifs" in Ezekiel 1? Perhaps he foresaw, as he "looked to his reward."[41]

This passage is unusual no matter how one reads it. It places Moses in a unique situation. In one reading, because of Moses' impossible vision of the invisible, he endured Pharaoh's anger; the vision gave him strength or ability to endure. If that is the case, this vision must be referring to an earlier episode, particularly the burning bush. The other reading is that he endured not Pharaoh but the rare and frightening vision of God, the very sight of which kills. A third option is that the seeing the invisible one refers immediately to the burning bush, but ultimately refers to his status as a visionary more generally.[42] Ultimately, this passage embraces rather than resolves the tensions in the biblical tradition of God telling Moses none can see his face and live (Exod. 33:20), yet elsewhere says that Moses sees God's very form or glory (Num. 12:8).

In Hebrews, therefore, Moses appears to stand uniquely among the rest of humanity, since he is the only one granted such a vision, even if "as if." While the audience is invited to enter the enduring Sabbath rest, draw near to the throne, draw near to God, enter the heavenly sanctuary, and come to the heavenly Jerusalem, in all of these exhortations visionary language is simply not used.[43] On the other hand, the location of Moses' vision of the invisible one in the "hall of faith" chapter suggests that his faith leading to his vision and endurance should be a paradigm for imitation.[44]

Moses, moreover, sees much in Hebrews: the invisible one (potentially), the "pattern of the tabernacle" (which refers to heavenly realities; 8:5),[45] and angels (see below). Visionary language is exclusively attached to Moses in Hebrews.[46] This fact is arresting given the rest of the biblical tradition that one cannot see God and live and the rest of the New Testament passages that indicate that one cannot see God at all, for God is invisible. In Hebrews, Moses' unique closeness to God from the biblical tradition stands both alongside and in tension with Moses' role as an exemplar of faith whom one should emulate; that is, Moses both uniquely sees God, the pattern of the Tabernacle, and receives the covenant. Nonetheless, these passages also indicate that Moses, and especially Moses' faith, provides a paradigm for Jesus' followers to imitate, especially as one who endures "for the sake of Christ."

In fact, Jason Whitlark has noted the similarities in the description of Moses in Heb. 11:23–7 and the community's own hardships in 10:32–9.[47] They have similarities in choosing mistreatment and imprisonment, accepting reproach (ὀνειδισμός, 10:33; 11:26) resulting in God's future reward (μισθαποδοσία, 10:35, 11:26) for ongoing faithfulness. Both did not or are encouraged not to fear the government's anger. Whitlark concludes that Egypt in the Moses passage provides a cipher for Rome for the audience of Hebrews. If so, Moses provides an ideal model for the community itself on the proper way to respond to their contemporary challenges.

There may be a further allusion to Moses' visionary abilities in Heb. 3:5. This verse is part of a complex metaphor involving Moses' and

Jesus' relative positions regarding "God's house" in Heb. 3:1–6.[48] The passage illustrates that both Jesus and Moses were faithful in God's house, while Heb. 3:5–6 illustrates a contrast between them: "Moses, on the one hand, was faithful in all his house as a servant to be a witness of things that were to be spoken of later, but Christ as a Son over his house." This line is a paraphrase of the LXX version of Num. 12:7:

> Not so my <u>servant Moses</u>; <u>in all my house</u> he is <u>faithful</u>.
> Οὐχ οὕτως ὁ <u>θεράπων μου Μωϋσῆς</u>· <u>ἐν ὅλῳ τῷ οἴκῳ μου πιστός</u> ἐστιν.
> (Num. 12:7 LXX)

> Now <u>Moses</u> was <u>faithful in all his house</u> as a <u>servant</u>.
> Καὶ <u>Μωϋσῆς</u> μὲν <u>πιστὸς ἐν [ὅλῳ] τῷ οἴκῳ αὐτοῦ</u> ὡς <u>θεράπων</u>. (Heb. 3:5)[49]

This is the only time a work in the New Testament in its current configuration refers to this passage in Numbers.[50] The passage from Numbers was originally meant to exalt Moses above all other seers; in it, God contrasts Moses to the prophets, Aaron, and Miriam, to whom God speaks in dreams: "not so with my servant Moses; he is entrusted with all my house. With him I speak mouth to mouth, clearly, and not in dark speech; and he beholds the form (glory; LXX) of the LORD." Hebrews invokes the passage that illustrates Moses' superiority due to his direct, unmediated visions of the divine, yet employs this passage to demonstrate Jesus' superiority.[51] While Moses is "in" (ἐν) the house, Jesus is "over" (ἐπί) it. The one who is in charge rules "over" the house, while a servant is "within."[52] Hebrews is explicit concerning their relative positions: "For Jesus has been deemed worthy of more glory than Moses, just as the builder of a house has more honour than it" (3:3). Clearly the author knows the context of the story in Numbers and knows the extraordinary claim made concerning Moses there, and so it is noteworthy how close the author gets to it without actually directly stating it or without explicitly invoking one of the strongest statement about Moses' visionary abilities in order to exalt Jesus higher than Moses.[53] Moses was great, perhaps unique, the pinnacle of humanity; Jesus is better.

EXCEPTION 2: THE PURE (OF HEART)

The clearest exception to the rule of one not being able to see God is Matt. 5:8, in the middle of the beatitudes in the Sermon on the

Mount, which shares some general similarities with 1 John 3:2–3. In both of these, the exception relates to purity:

> Blessed are the pure in heart, for they will see God [μακάριοι οἱ καθαροὶ τῇ καρδίᾳ, ὅτι αὐτοὶ τὸν θεὸν ὄψονται]. (Matt. 5:8)

> Beloved, we are God's children now; what we will be has not yet been revealed. What we do know is this: when he is revealed, we will be like him, *for we will see him as he is* [ὅτι ὀψόμεθα αὐτὸν καθώς ἐστιν]. And all who have this hope in him purify themselves, just as he is pure. (1 John 3:2–3; emphasis mine)

Firstly, Matthew's statement – "blessed are the pure in heart, for they will see God [ὅτι αὐτοὶ τὸν θεὸν ὄψονται]" – unapologetically claims that some people one day will see God. Bernard McGinn calls it "one of the key texts in the history of Christian mysticism."[54] It has no parallel in the Lukan beatitudes (Luke 6:20–3), and, therefore, has no basis in Q. It is unique to Matthew. It also provides no qualification to the vision itself, as the ὡς may in Hebrews. The only qualifying factor is the status of the seer: the pure in heart. It is not immediately clear what "pure in heart" would mean in Matthew.[55] In the context of the Sermon on the Mount, it could refer to those who keep the law by not getting angry, lustful or divorced; not swearing falsely; and not only loving one's neighbours, but even one's enemies (5:17–48). There is, furthermore, a temporal distinction: *will* see. It is a future event, perhaps at death or eschatological.

While Moses does not explicitly appear in this passage, one commentator has tentatively considered Moses' visions as potential background for this beatitude.[56] More securely, Mosaic traditions permeate the Sermon on the Mount.[57] Jesus gives a new declaration from a mountain, the first of five major speeches, in which he will dip into Pentateuchal traditions and offer new interpretations of them. Having a general framework of reworking Mosaic traditions to present Jesus as a new Moses, makes the statement that the pure in heart will see God all the more striking. It simply undoes Exod. 33:20; Exodus' blanket denial is turned into an affirmation. In that sense, it is not really in the tradition of Num. 12:6–8 either, since that passage attests to Moses' uniqueness; Matthew 5:8 does not offer any singular human as unique in seeing God, but rather, a general category of a pure-in-heart human.

From here, this saying would permeate the early Christian tradition, being found, for example, in the *Acts of Paul and Thecla* 5. Even the most Platonically oriented Christians, such as Origen, who believed God is invisible, will have to come to terms with Jesus' statement in the Sermon on the Mount, as second- and third-century Christians juggle competing scriptural passages. While the allusions to Moses in this verse may appear vague or tenuous to some modern readers, Christian commentators in the subsequent three centuries repeatedly returned to this verse when they considered Moses' visions, finding in it a solution to the problems set by those visions: whether, indeed, Moses saw God and whether anyone else could, and, if so, when.

Similarly, 1 John 3 unabashedly affirms divine vision. In this passage at least four things are notable. First, 1 John 3 makes a very clear statement of a future vision of God, picking up the thread left by the Gospel of John, which negated divine vision only in the past. This indicates a shift from the Gospel of John, but it is following the trajectory mapped out above: past vision never occurred, which, indeed, 1 John 4:12 reiterates; present vision through God's Glory (i.e., Jesus) has made God visible and accessible to humans; and now a future vision without qualification or intermediary is asserted. Perhaps what was left unsaid in the Gospel of John was that we will see God in the future. Second, the passage claims that we will see God as God truly is. One may read this as Jesus, Christ, or the Son, but "God" is the nearest antecedent. Third, one must be pure in order to have this vision. Purity and impurity in 1 John relates generally to one's sinfulness. One's sins are purified by confessing them, and "he who is faithful and just" then forgives one's sins and purifies one from unrighteousness (1 John 1:9). Otherwise, one obeys Christ's commandments (1:3–6; 3:22–4), loves others rather than hates (1:9–10; 3:11–24; 4:7–8), and generally abides in Christ (2:28–3:6; 4:13–16). Indeed, "no one who sins has either seen him or known him" (1 John 3:6).

In the first and third points, 1 John 3:2–3 aligns well with Matt 5:8: not only will we see God in the future, but vision is related to purity. One must become pure in order to approach the pure, just as the "pure in heart" will see God.[58] Fourth, the passage establishes a relationship between seeing and transformation. Not only is there a transformation through purity, but the vision makes you like God. It is because we will see him that we will be like him (ὅμοιοι αὐτῷ ἐσόμεθα). In summary, to prepare for the divine vision, one purifies oneself to see the pure God; when the vision occurs, one transforms, becoming like God. The use of "for" (ὅτι) suggests that the transformation occurs through vision; one becomes like God by seeing God.

WHO OR WHAT DID MOSES SEE?

If Moses did not see God on the mountain, who or what did he see? For some New Testament authors, the answer was angels. Hebrews and Acts add the "pattern" of the Tabernacle. Later Christians, following Philo, would add divine darkness.

The tradition that asserts Moses interacted with angels – rather than directly with God – is scattered throughout a few New Testament texts: Galatians, Hebrews, and especially concentrated in Stephen's speech in Acts 7.

> Why then the law? It was added because of transgressions, until the offspring would come to whom the promise had been made; and it was ordained through angels by a mediator. (Gal. 3:19)

> For if the message declared through angels [i.e., the Torah] was valid, and every transgression or disobedience received a just penalty, how can we escape if we neglect so great a salvation? (Heb. 2:2)

> Now when forty years had passed, an angel appeared to him [Moses] in the wilderness of Mount Sinai, in the flame of the burning bush. (Acts 7:30)

> He [Moses] is the one who was in the congregation in the wilderness with the angel who spoke to him at Mount Sinai, and with our ancestors; and he received living oracles to give to us. (Acts 7:38)

> You are the ones that received the law as ordained by angels, and yet you have not kept it. (Acts 7:53)

For these traditions – though, as noted, Hebrews is more complicated – Moses never saw God; he saw angels. This appears to be a downgrading of Moses' encounters; nonetheless, this tradition is pre-Christian. It is something already implied by the biblical text, when the divine speaker oscillates between the LORD and the angel of the

LORD. Second-temple works, like *Jubilees*, solidified this trend. While the Lord speaks directly with Moses for the opening portion of *Jubilees* (1.1–26), for the rest of the book, the Angel of the Presence reveals the majority of the elements of the Torah to him. Moreover, later synagogue traditions of the *targumim* would continue this distancing between humans and the divine with needs for averted glances and mediating figures, like God's Memra.[59] If these texts are, therefore, trying to minimize Moses' visions, then one must look to each one's situation; that is, they may have different reasons for downplaying Moses' visions, due to varying social and rhetorical contexts.

Turning to the earliest document, Paul writing to the Galatians, the primary point of the passage in Galatians 3:19 is to keep newly converted Gentile Christians from getting circumcised. Paul, therefore, brings up the point that Abraham was made righteous outside the law and four hundred and thirty years before the law (3:6–18). Abraham inherits God's promises; not his law. In this context, Paul makes his statement about the law, especially its origins and role. The entire passage devalues the law and what the law can and should do. It is a disciplinarian ($\pi\alpha\iota\delta\alpha\gamma\omega\gamma\acute{o}\varsigma$) (3:23–6) until Christ came; it imprisoned (3:22); it enslaved (4:1, 21–31). But now that Christ is here one can become heirs to Abraham's promise rather than Moses' law. The rest of the passage strongly devalues the law: the pluralized angels (most pre-Christian Moses traditions have him interact with a single angel, like the Angel of the Presence) and a mediator (Moses?) indicate the law's lower status to the divine – not angelic – promise to Abraham.[60] As Paul writes, "A mediator is not of one; but God is one" (Gal. 3:20; translation mine),[61] indicating that the law is not from God, or, if so, it is highly refracted.[62] Under the law, one is a slave; under Christ or the promise, one is free. Paul will soften this rhetoric in Romans. Strikingly, this is the only place in the surviving Pauline corpus in which he even alludes to Moses' role as mediator in the giving of the Torah.[63]

Heb. 2:2 also devalues the law to exalt Jesus' promises, but it softens the blow. Instead of setting the law and promise – Moses and Jesus – as binary oppositions, like Paul does, the author of Hebrews employs a *qal v'homer* (from lesser to greater) argument. The author affirms the law's (former) validity and the fact that breaking it invoked punishment; if the law, given through angels, again plural,[64] was so valid, how much more is the promise given through the Son? Both Galatians and Hebrews invoke Jesus' promise as greater than the law, but, by contrast to Galatians, Hebrews exalts Jesus by making the thing he surpasses (Moses and the Torah) also great. One is not slavery or a curse and the other freedom; Moses and the Torah give great and valid examples of faith; Jesus' faith is greater.

Finally, Stephen's speech responds to a couple of charges brought against him: blasphemy against Moses and God (Acts 6:11) and speaking against the temple and the law (6:13–24). He responds by giving a sacred history, but importantly focusing on two sacred places (the tabernacle and the temple), Moses, and the persecution of the prophets. In the process, he makes some curious points about Moses.[65] First, Stephen's speech, while sweeping in its extent, is not a full salvation history, since Moses takes up about half of the entire speech; everything that occurs after Moses' time receives very short notice.[66] While Moses sees only angels, if he sees anything at all, he nonetheless hears the voice of the Lord at the bush. Interestingly, keeping with the biblical tradition, Moses averts his eyes at the bush, so he does not even see the angel. Yet Acts 7 does not shy away from Moses directly hearing God's voice. By contrast, Stephen states that "the God of glory appeared to our father Abraham" without any qualification or explanation (7:2).[67]

While Moses' visions are downgraded in the text to some degree as a mediator who needed another mediator (angel), as noted above, such a tradition has pre-Christian Jewish roots. On the other hand, Acts 7 presents some promotions of Moses – he is beautiful before God (7:20; cf. Heb. 11:23); "beauty" (ἀστεῖος) here originally means something like "urbane," but comes to mean general attractive appearance and can signal divine favour.[68] That he is "beautiful before God" suggests a divine attribute, much like glory.[69] Moreover, one must remember the context: Stephen is charged with blaspheming against Moses (6:13–14; cf. 21:21), and he responds by giving Moses quite a bit of praise.

Stephen, nonetheless, uses Moses to subvert his contemporaries' understanding. Indeed, what Moses received from the angels and gave to the people were "living oracles" (λόγια ζῶντα), rather than the enslavement Paul suggested in Galatians.[70] Stephen consistently accuses Moses' contemporaries and his own audience of misunderstanding Moses and persecuting him, developing a leitmotif of the persecuted prophet that will dominate the rest of his speech and culminate in Jesus, the one "like Moses," about whom Moses foretold, which, in turn, catalyzes the story of Saul/Paul in Acts. Similar to Hebrews, Stephen in Acts 7 presents Moses as a great prophet in a

lineage that leads to the greatest one, Christ, in a speech that emphasizes the continuity of the pre-temple Israelite past to the Jesus-fol-
lowing present, with the only disjuncture provided by Solomon's
stationary temple structure.

In addition to the angelic mediators of the law, Moses also saw the
"pattern" of the Tabernacle, according to Hebrews 8 and, once again,
Stephen's speech in Acts 7.[71]

> These minister in a shadowy illustration [ὑποδείγματι καὶ σκιᾷ] of
> heavenly (things) [τῶν ἐπουρανίων], just as when Moses was about
> to erect the tent, he was instructed, saying, "See that you make all
> according to the pattern [τὸν τύπον] shown to you on the moun-
> tain." (Heb. 8:5)

In the Hebrew text the word תבנית – "pattern" or "construction" – appears
twice in Exod. 25:9, and again in 25:40. In the Greek translation, 25:9
becomes τὸ παράδειγμα or "paradigm," while 25:40 becomes τὸν τύπον or
"type." Quoting Exod. 25:40, Hebrews applies the language of "types,"
"antitypes," "shadows," and "patterns" to the heavenly realm, particularly
the sanctuary, and its earthly counterpart. Heb. 8:5 introduces three
terms: ὑπόδειγμα, σκιά, and τύπος. The first and second terms, translated
as a "shadowy illustration,"[72] provide the earthly counterpart of "heavenly (things)" and the "pattern" or "type." The first is the present earthly
sanctuary and its rites, the second, heavenly sanctuary and its rites.
Moses' vision of "all" covers all aspects of the heavenly "type" and the
earthly "shadow": the tent (8:5; cf. 9:24),[73] the cult (9:23),[74] and its legal
prescriptions (10:1).[75] This explains the selection of 25:40 rather than
25:9: "paradigm" is too reminiscent of the language that Hebrews
reserves for copies, while "type" refers to heavenly originals, deploying
Platonic language in un-Platonic ways.[76] Beginning in 8:5, the author of
Hebrews creates a consistent cosmological framework, making the
earthly handmade sanctuary the "antitype" to the true, heavenly "type"
Moses saw and from which he modelled his "shadowy illustration."

This language also shows up in Stephen's speech in Acts 7:44,
which paraphrases Exod. 25:40: "Our ancestors had the tent of testimony in the wilderness, as he [God] directed when he spoke to
Moses, ordering him to make it according to the pattern [τὸν τύπον]
he had seen."

Here, the point is not to compare and contrast the heavenly type
with the earthly shadow. Indeed, that it refers to a heavenly sanctuary

at all can only be inferred if one has the text of Hebrews in mind. On its own, it does not necessarily refer to a heavenly temple complex at all. Instead, the speech contrasts the divinely revealed pattern for the tabernacle (positive) with the human-planned temple (negative). It is also not an anti-sacrifice passage; indeed, Stephen notes that God complained that the Israelites *failed* to offer sacrifice at the proper tent (8:43). When the passage turns to Solomon's temple, the language turns decidedly negative: the Most High does not dwell in houses made with hands (7:48); for Stephen, the temple becomes a turning point, as the Israelites become increasingly disobedient, persecuting the prophets, and never really keeping the law (7:51–3). One must remember that the charges against Stephen are that he spoke against the "holy place" and the "law." He, in turn, praises the prototypical law-giver (Moses) and the prototypical sanctuary (the divinely revealed tent), but turns against those who failed to understand the law and who worship God in a stationary temple rather than a mobile tent.

While Paul, Hebrews, and Stephen in Acts all place Jesus at a higher level than Moses, leading to a devaluation of Moses' signature event – receiving the Torah – they do so for different ends. Paul creates the most disjuncture between Moses and Jesus, while Acts 7 and Hebrews provides greater continuity between Moses and Christ. For one, Moses and his Torah is overcome by Christ; for the other, they lead to Christ.

SEEING THE FACE IN THE MIRROR: I AND 2 CORINTHIANS

The situational context of 1 and 2 Corinthians shows greater variation than Galatians. Paul responds to a host of issues beyond circumcision, including factions that had formed within the Corinthian church partly due to rival missionaries, problems of differentiation between wealthier and poorer members of the community during table fellowship, questions of marriage and the single life, the nature of the resurrection, and spiritual gifts among many others. His letters seek to continually reassert his authority in this community, while also responding to issues or questions that members of the community send to him. Especially in 2 Corinthians, Paul appears on the verge of losing the Corinthian congregation to missionary rivals who boast of Jewish credentials (11:22), among other things.

Within this general interchange, another devaluation of Moses' visionary abilities, that additionally comes to stand for humanity's limitations more generally, occurs in Paul's discussion of Moses' glowing face in 2 Cor. 3:7–18. In this interpretation of Exod. 34:29–35, Paul engages in a *qal v'homer* (from lesser to greater) argument: "Now if the ministry of death, chiselled in letters on stone tablets, came in glory so that the people of Israel could not gaze at Moses' face because of the glory of his face, a glory now set aside, how much more will the ministry of the Spirit come in glory?" (2 Cor. 3:7). In this statement, the ministry of death, which equals the covenant with Moses, came in great glory; therefore, how much greater glory will the ministry of spirit have? The first ministry and its glory has been set aside; it has been veiled. Moses' face and Moses' revelation of scripture – the stone tablets – are almost equated. Just as Moses' face is covered with a veil, so Israel's minds have a veil when Moses' words are read (2 Cor. 3: 12–16). Significantly, this passage refers to Exodus 32–4, the second giving of the law after the golden-calf episode, Moses destroying the first tablets, and alternating episodes between Moses' and God's wrath. This context colours Paul's statements, making the ancient Israelites/Jews idolaters like the Egyptians/Gentiles.[77]

This, subsequently, provides a contrast with the current ministry of the unveiled spirit: "And all of us, with unveiled faces, seeing the glory of the Lord as though reflected in a mirror, are being transformed into the same image from one degree of glory to another; for this comes from the Lord, the Spirit" (2 Cor. 3:18).[78] The Lord's followers will be transformed gradually through unveiled vision of the glory of the Lord, a heavily loaded term in Jewish mysticism to refer to the image of the glory upon the throne (Ezek. 1:28). By looking at the glory, one becomes glory; as noted in the introduction, you are what you see.[79] If this was true for Moses' glorified face,[80] it can be again! Yet it is still one degree removed; it is not entirely direct; it is "as though reflected in a mirror."

Paul, however, continues this same imagery of veiling and the glorified face with regard to the gospel and Jesus. In 4:3, he claims that "even if our gospel is veiled, it is veiled to those who are perishing." He admits the gospel is veiled, making a comparison with the "ministry of death" of Moses' revelation most at hand. Here it becomes less the nature of the revelation, and more the nature of the audience members, whose "minds were hardened" (3:14).[81] Moreover, the "glory of Christ" is equated with "the image of God" (cf. Col. 1:15). Paul, already having made a connection between Christ and God's glory (Ezekiel 1) is thinking of the primordial human, who was made in the image of God (Gen. 1:27).[82] He is clearly working in protological terms, since he paraphrases Gen. 1:6, which speaks of light shining out of darkness, which, circling back to Moses' glorified face, is the knowledge of the glory of God in the face of Jesus (4:6). God's glory is Jesus' face. Jesus is the greater glory that has outshone Moses' glory, which has been set aside. Both glories are signified by their faces.

In addition to the transforming vision of Jesus' face, Paul also speaks in the famous "love chapter" of 1 Corinthians 13 of some parameters of vision.[83] It is a short excerpt, but one which Christians in the next several centuries will quote incessantly next to Matt. 5:8 to illustrate the temporal parameters of vision. He writes, "For now we see in a mirror, dimly [alt. in a riddle; Gk: ἐν αἰνίγματι], but then we will see face to face [τότε δὲ πρόσωπον πρὸς πρόσωπον]. Now I know only in part; then I will know fully, even as I have been fully known" (13:12). Just as with the 2 Corinthians passage, there is a degree of separation; one does not have a direct vision, but sees in a mirror. Nonetheless, this separation describes only one's present situation; in the future, one will see "face to face." While Paul does not directly cite Moses here, it is important to recall that Moses was the pre-eminent figure in the Bible to whom God spoke "face to face." Later Christians would regularly set this passage alongside the various Moses passages in which Moses speaks with God face to face (Exod. 33:11) – and, indeed, Moses is the predominant figure with whom God spoke face to face – and especially as a counterpoint to Exod. 33:20, which says one cannot see God's face and live. "Face" provides the catchword for interpretation.

Allison notes a further catchword between Paul's discussion and Moses' visions of "mirror," though this time with God's declaration that Moses sees God in Num. 12:8. The un-vocalized or "un-pointed" Hebrew of Num. 12:8 is מראה; it is usually vocalized to read as מַרְאֶה, or "openly" or "apparently." It could be pointed or vocalized differently, as מַרְאָה; that is, a word that can mean either a "vision" or a "mirror." It could maintain one sense of an open vision, but also be read as maintaining at least one degree of separation in the sense of "mirror."[84]

SEEING MOSES AND SEEING THE SON: THE MOUNT OF TRANSFIGURATION

Another passage about Moses on a mountain, while seemingly tangential, becomes entangled in the debates of divine vision and what

Moses saw on the mountain: the Mount of Transfiguration (Mark 9:2–8; Matt. 17:1–8; Luke 9:28–36).[85] In this episode, Peter, James, and John follow Jesus up a mountain (Mark and Matthew say it was a high mountain), and Jesus is transformed, his garments shining a dazzling white. Mark notes the garments are whiter than bleach. Luke changes the verb to make the garments shine like lightning (ἐξαστράπτων).[86] Matthew adds that his face shone, probably like Moses' luminescent face;[87] Luke says that his face changed. Moses and Elijah appear and speak with Jesus. Luke adds that Moses and Elijah appeared "in glory," and even tells what Jesus, Elijah, and Moses were discussing – Jesus' "exodus," referring to his death, to be accomplished at Jerusalem.[88] A cloud overshadows them (according to Matthew, a bright cloud), and then a voice issues from the cloud, saying, "This is my Son, the Beloved; listen to him!" Matthew adds, "with whom I am well pleased," making the link to the baptism revelation stronger. Luke adds that the disciples entered the cloud before the speech. Then things return to normal.

This passage has sparked a lot of questions. Was it originally here, or is it perhaps a displaced post-resurrection appearance? Or even a displaced baptism story?[89] Why white? Perhaps signifying angelic status (Mark 16:5; Matt 28:3; cf. Luke 24:4)? Perhaps martyrological status (Dan. 11:36; Rev. 3:5, 18; 4:4; 6:9–11; 7:9, 13–14)? These two, however, are not mutually exclusive. Why Moses and Elijah? Because they are great prophets who had experiences on mountaintops (Exod. 34:1–9; 1 Kgs 19:1–18)?[90] Because they are the founder and restorer of Israel? Representatives of the law and the prophets?[91] Also legends that had never died?[92] (In that case, perhaps it was originally Enoch and Elijah?)[93] Also Jesus is consistently portrayed in terms of Elijah and Moses throughout the gospels. Speaking from a cloud on a mountain recalls Moses' encounter with God in Exodus.

The point is that this is a prophetic revelation. Jesus is glorified on a mountain, much like Moses was, and this glorification is especially heightened in the Matthean version, where his face shines, directly hearkening back to Moses' beaming face (Exod. 34:29–35). In this case, Peter, James, and John act in place of the seventy elders who join Moses on the mountain, but do not go all the way (Exodus 24).[94] Jesus is the Moses-like seer insofar as he sees the cloud and hears the voice.[95]

On the other hand, Jesus is also part of the revelation; Peter, James, and John stand in place of the prophet who receives a message (Jesus) from a divine voice. Finally, Moses himself is the one seen by the three apostles, not the seer, except insofar as he and Elijah become seers of Christ. This possible reading opened up by this passage – that Moses becomes a seer of Christ on the Mount of Transfiguration – is one several ancient Christians, such as Irenaeus and Tertullian, will develop.

CONCLUSIONS

When looking at Moses as a visionary in these documents from the first century of the Christian movement within the Roman Empire, the evidence is ambivalent, due to the shifting social and rhetorical contexts of different passages and documents, situating themselves against rival interpretations by other Jews, Christian Jews, and Gentile Christians. Paul seeks to maintain authority over his community against rival missionaries, including Peter and those from James. Paul vociferously opposes the emphasis of these rivals on food laws and circumcision of new converts. He also has to navigate the internal divisions of the Corinthian community. In these cases, Paul strongly denounces these requirements of the law and paints Moses in ambivalent tones.

These issues seem to fade to the background in Acts and Hebrews. While Acts certainly also addresses food laws and circumcision in its narration of Paul's journeys, Hebrews completely omits these issues. For Stephen's speech and Hebrews, the focus is on the divinely revealed tent and persecution. They both largely extol Moses as a great exemplar who leads to Christ, rather than presenting Moses and the law in antithetical terms with Christ and the promise as Paul had done. Hebrews, especially, presents Moses as a visionary whom Christians should emulate, and whose situation mirrors the audience's own. The gospels are more difficult to pinpoint in their rhetorical and social contexts. Nonetheless, Matthew, again, tends to align with those seeing greater continuity, as Jesus is a new, yet better, Moses figure. John, however, like Paul, presents things in more antithetical terms. Moses may have some "honorific" elements throughout, but he is also largely contrasted with the Son, rather than aligned with him.

Even when taking these situational variants into consideration, some larger patterns emerge when looking at them as a whole. Some authors and their circles demote Moses, while they exalt Jesus; that is, some authors displaced Moses from his otherwise unique station as the ultimate human mediator between God and other humans, as found in previous and contemporary Jewish literature. In so doing, most of these documents will not activate questions of how Moses saw God – since according to them he simply did not, except for Hebrews – but will raise questions of what Moses saw and who (else) can see.

First, no one has ever seen God (John) or can see God (1 Timothy), because God is invisible (Romans, Colossians, Hebrews, 1 Timothy). Moses, therefore, never saw God (John). Instead, he saw angels. Of course, seeing angels is already part of the biblical and post-biblical tradition, seeing the Angel of the LORD in Exodus or seeing the Angel of the Presence in *Jubilees*. Nonetheless, there is something different happening in the New Testament writings, since only Stephen in Acts 7 indicates that he saw a single angel as per tradition; in fact, Galatians, Hebrews, and even Acts 7 at other points pluralize the revelation, saying that he saw angels. This largely draws upon the prohibition of vision in Exod. 33:20, while ignoring other passages in which Moses and others do see God.

Moses, nonetheless, remains the measure of humanity. As Moses could not see God, neither can anyone else. Instead of Moses, only the Son has seen the Father (John; cf. Matthew); others can see the Father only through the Son. Even if one accepts Moses had a glorious vision, that his revelations were valid and true (though only angelic), nonetheless, Jesus' glory is greater (Hebrews). Individually and cumulatively, these earliest documents argue for Jesus' superiority at Moses' expense, as Jesus replaces Moses as the figure who stands between God and humanity.

Nonetheless, there are outlying authors and passages. As noted, one may see God in the future, if sufficiently pure or righteous (1 John 3; Matthew 5). Hebrews, itself, gets very close to saying Moses saw God (Hebrews 3, 11); indeed, the author of Hebrews applies visionary terminology only to Moses. Moreover, Paul's discussion in 2 Corinthians 3 on Moses' glorious face clearly implies an intimate divine encounter, which he seeks to replicate with more positive results with his audience.

In the end, there is a tension surrounding Moses and his visions in these early texts. In some ways, his uniqueness is remembered, partially retained as in Hebrews, yet ultimately opposed. He cannot remain unique: these authors cede his position to Christ. When this happens, he can remain an exemplar of faith whom one should imitate. Moses was the competition, highly revered by non-Christian Jews and Samaritans, but also the model for early Christologies and for Christ's faithful followers, even while they were reinterpreting and reappraising the Torah. This mixture of remembered but not retained uniqueness, visionary experiences with some superior entity, and becoming a model for emulation of faith and endurance in the face of suffering sets up the next several centuries of authors from Justin to Augustine to consider Moses' visions as the ultimate – and potentially duplicatable – limits of humanity.

4

Justin Martyr of Flavia Neapolis
(c. 100–165 CE)

Theophany Is Christophany

Justin, as a self-proclaimed follower of Plato (*Dial.* 2.6), believed that Plato failed to accomplish his goal as it was understood in the second century: to see God (*Dial.* 2.3).[1] The philosophers' collective failure to see the divine sent Justin on a journey to those who had seen and heard: the prophets (*Dial.* 92–3). Their seeing and hearing provided the epistemological basis of their truth for Justin (*Dial.* 7.1–3). So *what* precisely did they see? *How* did they see?

Though not the most original Christian thinker of the second century, Justin of Flavia Neapolis (modern-day Nablus in the West Bank; *Apol.* 1.1; *Dial.* 120.6), became one of the most influential.[2] Appropriating and blending ideas deriving from a variety of biblical, Jewish, emergent Christian, and Greek and Roman sources, his two apologies, and especially his *Dialogue with Trypho*, are mystifying mosaics of materials that can be difficult to follow.[3] Though from Samaria in Palestine (though himself neither Jewish nor Samaritan), he eventually settled in Rome (c. 135 CE), a city that also attracted several other Christian teachers from the Eastern Roman Empire, including rival migrant Christian teachers from the east, such as Valentinus (c. 135–55 CE) and Marcion (c. 140–65 CE).[4] In fact, Justin is our only contemporary witness to Marcion.[5] He became a freelance teacher, attracting students such as Tatian from Syria. Ever conscious of his Roman context, both city and empire, he wrote apologies directed toward the Roman emperors and the Roman people, defending Christianity and asking for tolerance, as well as polemics in a lost compilation (*Syntagma*) against sects ("heresies"), which may have had a strong focus on Marcion, and in a lengthy *Dialogue with Trypho*.

His apologetic efforts failed; he died a martyr sometime between 162 and 168 CE.[6]

In this bustling set of contexts from the eastern Mediterranean to Rome, Justin forged his exegetical skill. Though never directly approaching the exegetical problem of Moses seeing and not seeing God in Numbers and Exodus respectively,[7] his programmatic interpretation on who or what Moses, the patriarchs, and the prophets saw in their visions set the tone for second- and third-century Christian thought, being nearly thoroughly absorbed by Irenaeus and Tertullian, and partially by Clement. His solution was familiar and innovative, simple and impactful: in the tripartite scheme of the seeing subject, the means of seeing, and the object seen, he, to a greater extent than any other early Christian author, focused almost exclusively and to a greater extent on dividing the object of vision between the unseen Father and the visible Son. For Justin and many after him, all theophany was Christophany: Moses and the prophets did not merely prophesy and foresee Christ's advent; they spoke to and saw Christ in preincarnate form.[8]

JUSTIN'S TRIPARTITE THEORY OF PROPHECY

Firstly, however, Justin offers a coherent – even if not elaborated – theory of prophetic inspiration. In his *Apology* (1.36–9), Justin splits scripture into three sources of prophetic inspiration: prophecies derived from either God the Father, God the Son, or a "Spirit of Prophecy." Such tripartite divisions appear to be common in first- and second-century theology.[9] For example, Philo of Alexandria also noted that there are three types of divine utterances given by Moses: oracles spoken by god in God's own person, with Moses as interpreter; oracles emerging from question and answer, when Moses asks and God responds; and oracles spoken by Moses in his own person, but while in a state of divine possession (*Moses* 2.188–91).[10] Similarly, Ptolemy in the second century twice discusses different types of prophetic inspiration. According to Irenaeus (*A.H.* 1.7.3), Ptolemy divided the sources of prophecy among the Demiurge, the Holy Spirit/Sophia/Mother, and one's own spiritual seed. Similarly, the sayings of Jesus derived from the Mother, the Demiurge, and the Saviour. Alternatively, according to the *Letter to Flora*, Ptolemy divides scripture into three sources: the Demiurge, Moses, and the Elders. He further divides up the sayings of the Demiurge into three parts: that which is fulfilled by the Saviour (love thy neighbour), that which is to be rejected (lex talionis), and that which is to be reinterpreted spiritually (the cultic legislation). The practical effect of these divisions brings Ptolemy in line with other contemporary Christian reading strategies of the Septuagint: accept some, reject some, and spiritually/allegorically read the rest. While Ptolemy offered a useful way to differentiate what is accepted, rejected, or reinterpreted, using the Sermon on the Mount as a guide, Justin never did so. He offered some examples, mostly from Isaiah, but no real clear way to differentiate the source of any given prophecy.[11]

THE SON AS FIRE, CLOUD, GLORY, ANGEL, AND MAN

Even if a prophet could receive up to three sources of prophetic inspiration for a message, a theophany could only derive from one of the three sources: the Son. For Justin, all theophany is Christophany.[12] Building upon Platonic views that God in Godself is invisible,[13] inherited first-century traditions that only the Son could see the Father (John 1:17-28; 1 Tim 1:17; 6:16; cf. Matt 11:27), and exegetical problems of who, indeed, the Lord was who spoke to Abraham, wrestled Jacob, and appeared to Moses in (or *as*) fire on Sinai, Justin formed a theory of divine manifestation that was both bold and, given these stated trends, seemingly inevitable: any time anyone claimed to see God, they saw the preincarnate Son.

Yet, this was *not* inevitable. Other second-century Christians contemporary with Justin and likewise active in both the Eastern Mediterranean and Rome, such as Valentinus or especially Marcion, would, with the same general set of assumptions and the same general strategy of differentiating based upon what one sees, would claim that the God of the Israelites who had created this world had, indeed, appeared to them, while the God of Jesus – a different, alien, unknown God – who existed beyond this world, remained invisible and unseen, only to be revealed through Jesus.[14] Looking to the trove of ancient Christian works found in Nag Hammadi, one can read these writers in their own words (e.g., *1 Apoc. Jas.* 26.6–7; *Apoc. Pet.* 70.13–72.4; cf. 73.23–75.7; 76.23–79.31). The *Second Discourse of the Great Seth* even cites Num. 12:6–8 (cf. Heb. 3:1–6) to challenge the claim that Moses could be called the true God's friend. He had instruction from angels, but not the true God; therefore, "Moses was a joke" (63.26–64.17). In Pauline-inspired language, the revealer says that Moses' law, given by lesser beings, was to enslave. While Justin's position would become influential, therefore, it was not the only option at the time. Instead, in the urban centres of the Roman Empire, especially in Rome itself, Justin and those who developed his argument and these other Christians co-evolved, and likely interacted – if not personally, then at least by reading one others' works. While their theologies had internal developments, they also shifted in response to one another.

In this context, Justin's interpretative effort, on the one hand, draws upon a broader trajectory of accommodating divine vision to the impossibility of seeing the divine in ancient Jewish and Christian sources by distinguishing between the invisible God and a visible representative of God – either an aspect of God (e.g., Logos, Wisdom, glory, Memra, etc.) or a representative of God (e.g., an angel). Justin, as already found in the Johannine literature, adapts this stream of tradition by identifying the divine Logos, which Philo had argued appeared in the various theophanies in the Bible, with the preincarnate Christ. On the other hand, Justin's interpretation also differentiates itself from rival solutions offered by Jewish and other Christian thinkers, such as Marcion.

Throughout his *First Apology* and the *Dialogue with Trypho*, Justin assumes that no one ever saw God the Father. In *Apol.* 1.62–3, Justin uses Moses as the prototypical prophet, often called the "first prophet" throughout,[15] both chronologically and in importance. He argues that one cannot maintain that Moses saw God the Father, but only God the Son, juxtaposing Exodus 3:6 – where God appears to Moses in the bush – with Matthew 11:27 – where none can know the Father but the Son. The Son is called Word (λόγος); Angel (ἄγγελος), which he uses interchangeably with "in the image of the bodiless" or "in bodiless image" (ἐν εἰκόνι ἀσωμάτῳ; 63.10, 16); and Apostle (ἀπόστολος) (62.9–10; cf. Heb. 3:1). Justin's preincarnate Christ does not appear just in the fire, but as the fire, or literally "in the image of fire from the bush" (ἐν ἰδέᾳ πυρὸς ἐκ βάτου; 62.3; 63.10) or "the form of fire" (διὰ τῆς τοῦ πυρὸς μορφῆς; 63.16);[16] he is polymorphic, appearing here as fire, elsewhere as an angel, and finally, through the incarnation, as a human (ἄνθρωπος). Justin summarizes:

And he formerly appeared through the form of fire and a bodiless image to Moses and the other prophets; but now in the times of

your reign, as, we have said, having become a human by a virgin
according to the counsel of the father on behalf of the salvation of
those who believe in him and he endured to be made nothing
and to suffer so that, dying and rising, he would defeat death.[17]
(63.16)

To tighten the connection between old and new covenants, Justin
makes Christ the proclaimer of both. This manoeuvre, however, seems
at first glance to dilute the singularity of the incarnation. If Christ has
appeared to humans repeatedly throughout history, why is his incarnation as Jesus significant? Justin anticipates this objection with his
frequent use of "bodiless image" when the Son's preincarnate appearances are at their most anthropomorphic (e.g., in the appearance as an
"angel"), emphasizing the contrast of previous bodiless theophanies
to Moses and the prophets and the decidedly bodily emphasis on the
incarnation, which leads to salvation through death and resurrection.
To safeguard the incarnation, Jesus is "docetic" in his preincarnate
appearances to Moses and the prophets.[18]

The *Dialogue with Trypho* greatly expands the dossier of preincarnate appearances of the Son. Though the idea of theophany as
Christophany is mentioned as early as *Dialogue* 3, he explains why this
is so only late in the *Dialogue*. He relies upon all the places in the Septuagint in which there is an ambiguity of divine speaker, where the
text equivocates between the Lord, the Angel of the Lord, God, and/or
even Man to indicate Jesus' preincarnate earthly activities. Justin boldly states that all of these – as well as the Lord of Hosts – are the simple expressions or names of the Son. Every time that anyone claimed
they saw God – with special reference to Abraham (at Mamre and
Sodom and Gomorrah),[19] Jacob (several places, but especially Bethel
and the wrestling scene), or Moses (at the burning bush)[20] – it was
always the appearance of the Son. He was, furthermore, the pillar of
cloud (37–8).

Justin's greatest exegetical effort occurs in *Dialogue* 56–62 (reiterated in 113, 126–8), in which he works through the divine appearances
to Abraham (56–7), Jacob (58), and Moses (59–60) to argue that the
object of divine appearances was not the maker of all things, but a
numerically differentiated being (though not differentiated in will). It
is an extensive exegetical effort, a winding tour de force, with wide-
ranging applications.

While Justin argued this in 56–62, he provides his most programmatic statement in 127. Having drawn together the fact that the Father cannot be seen and the specific places where he has argued that the Son visited Abraham, Jacob, and – most importantly – Moses (especially as the recorder of all of the stories), Justin writes:

> These and other such sayings are recorded by the lawgiver [Moses] and by the prophets; and I suppose that I have stated sufficiently, that whenever God says, "God went up from Abraham," or, "The Lord spoke to Moses," and "The Lord came down to behold the tower which the sons of men built," or when "God shut Noah into the ark," you must not imagine that the unbegotten God Himself came down or went up from any place.
>
> ...
>
> Therefore neither Abraham, nor Isaac, nor Jacob, *nor any other man*, saw the Father and ineffable Lord of all, and also of Christ, but saw Him who was according to his will his son, being God, and the Angel because he ministered to his will; whom also it pleased him to be born man by the virgin; and also was fire when he conversed with Moses from the bush.[21] (*emphasis mine*)[22]

Not just individual theophanies, therefore, were the preincarnate Son, but all were. He appears as angel, human, fire, and cloud. This section solves two problems at once. Like Philo's Logos, it explains away embarrassing anthropomorphisms, and, in this case, pyromorphisms. Secondly, it resolves the exegetical and philosophical problem of divine vision. If no one can see the Father except the Son (John 1:17–18; cf. Matt. 11:27), if the Son is the image of the invisible God (Col. 1:15), then the Lord, the angel of the Lord, God's visible – yet intense – Glory, etc., in the Old Testament was none other than Christ. Charles Gieschen writes, "The significance of this idea should not be underestimated. Justin is not merely looking for the Angel of the Lord and then interpreting this figure Christologically; he is reading all possible visible manifestations of God as the Son, who is the visible manifestation of the Father."[23] With this simple manoeuvre, Justin transformed the Jewish scriptures into a Christian revelation, in which Christ reveals to Moses and the prophets coded messages about Christ.

It is a powerful and influential interpretation, but Justin did not
come to it in a vacuum. It is something non-Christian Jews and the
Christian Marcion would reject, since both – for opposite reasons –
would argue that the Israelite scriptures had little to do with Jesus.[24]
Moreover, the general principle of the interpretive manoeuvre – to
differentiate between hidden and manifest elements of God – was
also very popular; the identity of the manifest deity, and sometimes
even the hidden deity, often varied.

ANTECEDENTS AND PARALLELS: JUSTIN'S JEWISH AND CHRISTIAN NETWORKS

Justin's meandering analysis is both breathtaking in its ambitious
extent and strangely familiar. One can locate this general strategy of
differentiating the object seen in biblical theophanies from the
unseen God in second-temple Jewish literature – including apocalyptic works and the work of Philo of Alexandria – and contemporary
and later Jewish *targumim* and *midrashim*.[25] While more proximate
parallels and antecedents to Justin's thought will come from Philo of
Alexandria, the apocalyptic literature of second-temple Judaism provides a broad background for this type of solution of differentiating
biblical passages according to what exactly the patriarchs and
prophets beheld.[26]

As noted in Chapter 2, Genesis through Judges provide excellent
fodder for this type of speculation, especially those passages that
equivocate concerning whom exactly the seer saw. Hagar, after con-
versing with the "angel of the LORD," wonders if she has seen God
and lived (Gen. 16:13–14). Jacob wrestled with a "man," but names
the place Peniel, because "I have seen God face to face, and yet my
life is preserved" (Gen. 32:30). Gideon encounters a figure alternatively called angel of the LORD (Judg. 6:11, 12, 21, 22), the LORD
(6:14, 16, 23), or angel of God (6:20). After his astonishment at seeing the "angel of the LORD" and living, the rest of the passage indicates that he speaks with the LORD (Judg. 6:24; 7:2, 4, 5, 7, 9). Moreover, the wife of Manoah encounters a figure called the "angel
of the LORD" (Judg. 13:3, 13, 15, 16, 17, 18, 20, 21), the "angel of
God" (13:9), and "God" (13:22). At the end of it all, they believe
they have seen God (13:21–2). These are but a sampling of passages,
but the interchangeability between God/LORD and the Angel of
God/LORD can be found throughout the first seven biblical books.

With such ambivalence within the biblical text itself, it is no won-der that some later interpreters began to see the theophanies as a second figure imbued with divine authority to the point of being identified with God.

The second-temple Jewish apocalypses make such a reading explicit first. Most will rely upon the identification of the enthroned "glory" in Ezekiel 1 (cf. Exodus 24) as the basis of their vision: Enoch encoun-ters the "great glory" upon the throne, which paradoxically no crea-ture, whether angelic or human, can behold (*1 En.* 14:20–2; cf. 71:10–11). Enoch is the exception to the rule (*1 En.* 19.2). Daniel has a dream vision of the Ancient of Days that is reminiscent of Enoch's vision (Daniel 7:9). In the Christianized *Testament of Levi*, Levi sees the Great Glory upon the throne in the heavenly temple (*T. Levi* 3:4; 5:1–2).

Other apocalypses turn to an angel with the name of God within him; it is this angel that the patriarchs and prophets encountered as God. In one of the more outstanding examples, the *Apocalypse of Abraham*, Abraham sees and speaks to Iaoel, who shares God's name and has the appearance of the divine glory from Ezekiel 1 (*Apoc. Abr.* 10–11), whereas the true divine presence remains invisible above indescribable fire – not unlike Moses' burning-bush scene (*Apoc. Abr.* 18–19).[27]

Even with this broad background, most scholars have argued that Philo provides the most relevant antecedent to Justin's thought. While Justin likely had general awareness of Philo's thought, his direct reliance upon Philo's exegeses of these particular passages has proven difficult to establish.[28] Nonetheless, Philo provides a useful precedent of differentiating within the divine between an ultimate invisible principle and a manifest second figure who appears to humans. For Philo, this secondary figure was the Logos.[29]

Traketellis has drawn the connections between Philo's and Justin's work most tightly, noting that Justin used Philonic exegesis of the theophanic passages, though for ultimately different purposes and problems than Philo did.[30] For Philo, the predominant concern was explaining away the embarrassing anthropomorphisms in the biblical text.[31] While Justin occasionally addressed this, his primary concern was different. He sought to establish that visions and prophecies in the Bible pointed towards or foreshadowed Jesus' advent by making Christ the revealer in addition to the revelation. He sought to strengthen the connective tissue between old and new covenants.

Concerning Justin's arguments with regard to Abraham (*Dial.* 56, 126), he notes striking similarities and important differences with Philo's *Names* 15, *Alleg. Interp.* 3.217–19, and *Moses* 1.66.[32] Justin's analysis of Jacob's visions at Haran, Peniel, Luz, and Bethel (*Dial.* 58, 125, 126) resembles Philo's *Names* 87, *Dreams* 1.70, 129, 228–30, 238–9, *Alleg. Interp.* 3.117, *Flight* 5, and *Cherubim* 3.[33] Finally, Justin's analysis of Moses at the burning bush (*Apol.* 1.62, 63; *Dial.* 59–60) may find some inspiration in Philo's *Moses* 1.66 and *QE* 37.[34]

In these passages, Philo, as other "Middle Platonists" would, situated the originally Stoic Logos as the intermediary between the One and the material world.[35] For Philo this could resolve the biblical problem of seeing the invisible God. The Logos, the "deuteros theos" or "second God" in Philo's thought, becomes the manifest side of the deity – God's "backside"[36] – while God in Godself remains invisible. The Logos is a helper in creation,[37] and the angel who appears to humans.[38] Goodenough writes, "There is hardly a function which Philo assigns to the Logos which he does not also assign to God."[39] Justin combines Philo's solution with the Gospel of John's identification of the Logos with the principle incarnated as Jesus.[40]

On the other hand, Skarsaune has demonstrated that the similarities adduced by Traketellis are not as strong as such a listing makes them out to be.[41] Skarsaune instead argues that these passages are where we can actually see Justin at his most original. He dismantles Traketellis' argument passage by passage, from Abraham and Jacob to the burning bush.[42] He does admit general similarities on the level of terminology, but under closer analysis, the parallels shrink to nearly nothing. There is no sure proof of Justin's direct dependence on Philo, but direct or indirect contact with Philonic ideas more generally cannot be excluded.[43]

Skarsaune, furthermore, argues for Justin's originality, noting firstly that Justin works directly with the LXX throughout the *Dialogue*, starting with Abraham as the linchpin of his argument. Unlike the case nearly everywhere else in Justin's work, he does not use isolated prooftexts, but illustrates exegetical mastery of several chapters, often combining chapters that are far apart. Trypho at times praises Justin's exegesis, which seems novel to him; sometimes Trypho is especially surprised at the arguments that Christ spoke to Moses at the burning bush (*Dial.* 38:1; 40:1, 3).[44]

Instead of being directly anti-Jewish, Skarsaune argues that these passages likely were originally meant to be anti-Marcionite, but were repurposed for anti-Jewish use.[45] Justin is, first, overly literal. He is not engaged in allegorical exegesis that a Marcionite would object to on principle.[46] He makes some strange anti-Marcionite remarks that are irrelevant for the conversation with a Jew like Trypho, and, moreover, makes Trypho an ally against an unnamed opponent. Proving two gods or lords as Justin does would not impress a Marcionite, per se, but identifying the second God as Jesus in the Old Testament might. Even if Justin had started with a previously existing testimony nucleus to form this exegesis, he has greatly expanded his exegetical effort to a degree not seen before and not found elsewhere in the *Dialogue*. If, therefore, Justin is working with a previous source, Skarsaune concludes it is likely his own anti-Marcionite *Syntagma*.[47] Whether or not Skarsaune has proven that he has uncovered part of Justin's *Syntagma* with this particular exegesis, and not everyone is convinced on this point,[48] he has demonstrated that Justin has developed his theophany-as-Christophany argument largely on his own.

Skarsaune concludes: "If there is any influence from Philo on Justin's treatment of the theophanies, it is at best distant, and mainly operative in some general modes of argument, rather than in concrete exegesis of texts. In the latter respect, Justin exhibits a marked independence of Philo, often directly contradicting or ignoring Philonic exegesis."[49] Justin has taken a couple of different streams in emergent Christian traditions – traditional prooftexts that the Old Testament knows of two gods or lords and the typological materials, neither of which necessarily leads to the theory of theophany suggested by Justin – into a general theory of theophanies always being Christophanies.

Skarsaune, ultimately, argues that one should not be so preoccupied with Philo that one neglects other sources; his preferred parallels are the Rabbis and the Wisdom of Solomon. Having dismantled the argument for Justin's reliance on Philo, Skarsaune joins other scholars, such as Barnard, who look to Wisdom literature, particularly the Wisdom of Solomon 10, as the most obvious precedent for Justin's thought.[50]

In the Wisdom of Solomon, Wisdom/the Spirit is a pre-existent being and is the means by which all of the patriarchs and prophets interacted with God in a manner very similar to Son/Logos, according to Justin's argument.[51] In short, Justin's attribution of all of the saving acts and appearances of God in human – particularly Israelite – history to the Logos resembles the wisdom tradition's view of

Sophia (also identified with the Spirit of God) in Wisdom of Solomon and Sirach. It is a simple and effective explanation.

Other scholars, however, have argued that there are more direct precedents in the New Testament. Hurtado and Skarsaune before him have argued that Justin's interpretive strategy is part of a broader proto-orthodox agenda that strengthens the interconnections between the Old Testament and Christ's advent.[52] It is a three-part approach that includes: (1) proof from prophecy or demonstrations that Old Testament prophecies foreshadow, are types of, or are fulfilled in Christ; (2) use of the Old Testament in homiletic ethical exhortation; and (3) demonstration of the greater antiquity of the Old Testament compared to Greek philosophers. Hurtado breaks the first down into three further categories: (1) fulfillment of prophecy in Jesus; (2) typological exegesis; and (3) Old Testament theophanies as the preincarnate Son.[53]

Hurtado lists the preincarnate creation references in the New Testament as precedent for Justin's thinking here (1 Cor. 8:4–6; Phil. 2:6–8; Col. 1:15–17; Heb. 1:1–3; John 1:1–2). He additionally cites Paul, who says that the rock from which the Israelites drank in the wilderness "was Christ" (1 Cor. 10:4), as reflecting preincarnate existence, though it could easily be read typologically.[54] Jarl Fossum also finds precedents in Jude 5 of the Lord, God, or Jesus (depending on the manuscript) rescuing the Israelites from Egypt,[55] and John 12:41, suggesting the "glory" seen by Isaiah (Isa. 6:1) was "the Lord" Jesus. Nonetheless, unlike Justin's prooftexts, most of Hurtado's passages refer to creation accounts rather than to theophanies, though both types of accounts indicate preincarnate existence for the Son; the "rock" passage is ambiguous; and the Jude and John references are at best implied.

While it is less discussed, one should also mention the book of Revelation. There, Christ appears to John of Patmos in Chapters 1 and 10 in ways reminiscent of the enthroned figure of Ezekiel 1 and the angelophany of Daniel 10. Christ acts as an *angelus interpres*, and is, therefore, the revealer. Yet part of the vision revealed is the Lamb upon the throne, and so the Son is also part of the revelation. This doubling of Christ as revealer and revelation mirrors what Justin does in his works, even though Revelation never clearly states that Christ was the Angel of the Lord who appeared to the prophets of old.[56]

While these passages that would eventually become part of the Christian canon may provide antecedents, they have not left an obvious impact on Justin's thought. Most significantly, Justin does not rely upon or refer to these passages when discussing his own exegeses. These passages instead provide a set of premises and assumptions that he would take to further conclusions than can be found in first-century emergent Christian sources.[57]

Indeed, Hurtado agrees with Skarsaune that one finds with Justin's interpretation a "widening" of Old Testament passages that feature a preincarnate Christ compared with what had been suggested by these New Testament precedents. This puts things mildly. If this trickle of first-century proposals of potential preincarnate Christophanies is a precedent, Justin's exegesis is a mighty tidal wave. Instead, the predominant attitude of first-century texts is not that these prophets saw the preincarnate Christ – though they did see Christ insofar as they foresaw Christ – but rather that they saw angels (Gal. 3:19; Heb. 2:2; Acts 7:30, 38, 53).[58]

While disagreeing on some minor details, Hurtado and others agree on the main issue: whatever his precedents, Justin did something revolutionary when he claimed that every single theophany in the Old Testament was Christ. The Old Testament is not just Christian for this second-century thinker because it points to, predicts, foreshadows, or typifies Christ, but because it is a revelation from Christ: Christ was God on Mount Sinai. Moreover, as Hurtado notes, "his programmatic finding of the preincarnate Jesus in Old Testament passages is probably one of the traditions that helped shape Iraenaeus' idea that Jesus is the full and final manifestation of the divine Logos who has been active throughout history."[59]

In addition to the antecedents of apocalyptic literature, Philo, the Wisdom of Solomon, and the New Testament, there have been occasional considerations of Justin's parallels with emergent synagogue and rabbinic sources. As noted in Chapter 2, while rabbinic sources of late antiquity would be more cautious than earlier works about one's ability to see God, they provide continuity with the tendency to distinguish between manifest and hidden parts. One can see an aspect – usually depending upon however one defines God's backside from Exodus 33 – including God's Memra, Shekhinah, and even God's Tefillin. While holding a tenuous and tense relationship with fully rabbinic texts, the *targumim*, Aramaic translations that purportedly grew out of the synagogue tradition, provide a most relevant analogue to the usage of Justin and other early Christians.[60]

Justin's relationship with the fractured and emergent movement that would coalesce into rabbinic Judaism in late antiquity is more controversial than his reliance upon Philo. While scholarship from the nineteenth and early-twentieth century had confidence in Justin's familiarity with the burgeoning rabbinic movement, recent scholars have been less optimistic. That he would have some familiarity with more Jews than the fictional "Trypho" – who may represent a caricatured type drawn from his encounters with Jews – seems likely, given his birthplace of Neapolis in Roman Palestine in the second century.[61] However, the degree to which he encountered emergent ideas found in later synagogue and rabbinic materials is difficult to establish or discern. Yet, Justin's *Dialogue* provides a more fruitful comparison with the targumic Memra than first-century works or even the prologue of John, even if direct interactions cannot be reconstructed from surviving evidence.[62]

Daniel Boyarin has provided the most extensive recent discussion of this tendency of highlighting a secondary, sometimes visible, figure next to God. In his book, *Borderlines*, he argues that the "Logos," loosely construed to include any secondary figure alongside God, is the common inheritance of Judaism and Christianity that was constructed by Christian and Jewish orthodoxies as a Shibboleth for the production of both orthodoxies. He often highlights Justin's role in this development.[63] As noted, Boyarin operates with a very loose definition of Logos theology: that between God and the world there was an additional divine entity (whether word, wisdom, etc., who mediates the material world and God).[64] He does this without necessarily accounting for the differences between Philo's Logos, the targumic Memra, the rabbinic Shekhinah, or the early Christian Logos.[65]

Late-antique Jewish texts largely negate any possibility of seeing God directly, but provide mediating figures whom one can see, hear, or more generally encounter, such as God's Memra (Word), Shekhinah (Presence), or Glory. The targumic Memra – Aramaic for "word" – seems a useful parallel. Even if it provides an environment for a generic "logos" theology to develop that Justin and other Christians could appropriate and transform, it appears that it, too, largely serves to safeguard the biblical text from embarrassing anthropomorphisms.

To give a brief example, in Genesis 18, three figures appeared to Abraham. This is an important passage for Justin, providing him the prooftext that a second figure alongside God must exist who is also divine. In it, *Targum Neofiti* claims that the "Memra of the Lord" was revealed to Abraham on the "plain of vision" or "a word of prophecy from before the Lord." In *Targum Pseudo-Jonathan*, the "Glory of the Lord" was revealed to him. Looking to the burning bush, *Neofiti* claims that above Mount Horeb, the "Glory of the Shekhinah of the LORD" is revealed (3:1). The angel of the Lord is within the flames, but the Memra calls out to Moses. In *Pseudo-Jonathan*, it is the Glory of the Lord who is revealed on Horeb, and the angel Zagnugel speaks. In both, Moses is afraid to look, as in the Hebrew text. In *Neofiti* to Exod. 33:20, Moses cannot see the "face of the Glory of the Shekhinah," but he can see the divine speech, called "Dibbera." For *Pseudo-Jonathan*, Moses can hear the "Dibbura," but cannot survive the splendour of the face. He can, however, see the tefillin of the Glory of the Shekhinah.[66]

These synagogue translations seek to distance God from the theophanies of the Bible.[67] Instead, the patriarchs and the prophets encounter the Memra, Shekhinah, Glory, or God's Tefillin. They appear to operate similarly to Philo's Logos as the manifest aspect of the invisible God, yet, unlike the case in early Christian usage, do not develop a personality. As Segal notes, the Memra and the Shekhina in *targumim* and *midrashim* are never clearly defined as independent creatures. They would be for Justin and other early Christians; a personality was in fact what they were looking for.[68] To be fair, such "personality," a sense of a different person (though united in will) only really manifests itself in the course of the incarnation event and not in the Old Testament theophanies themselves.

Such a "personality," however, might show up in a rabbinic parallel to Justin suggested by Skarsaune. *Exodus Rabbah* 32 interprets the line "Behold, I send an angel before you" (Exod. 23:20), attempting to identify this angel. In *Exod. Rab.* 32.9 an angel appears to Moses in the burning bush and identifies himself as the angel who appeared to the patriarchs, the guardian angel leading Israel, and the captain of the host appearing to Joshua (cf. *Exod. Rab.* 32.3; *Gen. Rab.* 97:3), collapsing all biblical theophanies to a single angelic figure, much as the Wisdom of Solomon does with Wisdom/Sophia, and much like Justin does with the Son.

We should note, however, as Charles Gieschen has argued, all these intermediary traditions of Wisdom, Word, Memra, Glory, Name, principle angels, and exalted humans interact with and may ultimately derive from the Angel of the LORD tradition. They nest within each other and cannot be considered fully separate, as they so often are.[69]

CONCLUSIONS:
JUSTIN, JEWS, AND MARCION
IN SECOND-CENTURY ROME

Justin Martyr developed a comprehensive, programmatic biblical interpretation that distinguished between the unseen Father and the visible Son, placing very little emphasis on the status of the seer or the means of seeing. He used most of his rhetorical, philosophical, and especially exegetical resources to make the claim that all theophany is Christophany: it was the Son who spoke to and visibly appeared to Abraham, Jacob, and Moses in a bodiless image. Justin repeatedly returns to this triumvirate of seers, yet he reserves the title of "first prophet" for Moses. Moreover, just as they could not see the Father of all, neither can any other human being. One can see only the Son, as they did, providing the limits of humanity.

It was a simple, sweeping, and influential exegetical manoeuvre. Many Christian apologists and polemicists following in Justin's wake will simply assume his argument. Nonetheless, despite a variety of piecemeal precedents, why didn't Justin simply follow the clearer first-century precedent that Moses and the prophets saw angels? Why, as Skarsaune has argued, make a largely new argument to say that every visible appearance of the deity in the Bible was Christ, rather than that they simply foresaw Christ, as, for example, the Gospel of Matthew does? Why this need to strengthen further the connections between old and new? The answer is not simple theological evolution, but a shift in social circumstances in the second century, and the key to that situation is in the genre Justin uses to make his argument: apology and polemic.

When one reads the two apologies, especially the second one, one senses the urgency of Justin's situation; he is writing in a situation where lives were at stake. He himself would die a martyr. First, Justin seeks respectability for his brand of Christianity. To do so, he has to resist the notion that Christianity is a new religion by tying it to the ancient Israelite scriptures, which, following earlier Jewish apologetics, he argues were the source for Greek philosophy. He goes so far as to claim that all who live by reason (i.e., philosophers) are Christians (*Apol.* 1.46.2–3).

At the same time, in the wake of the failure of the Bar Kokhba Revolt (132–135 CE) against Rome, Jews were suspected by the Roman state. In fact, given his timeline, he may have moved to Rome as a refugee from his war-ravaged home in Roman Palestine. As Annette Reed notes:

> Writing in the wake of the Bar Kochba Revolt, Justin was faced with the challenge of disassociating Christians from contemporary Jews, while simultaneously stressing their continuity with the respectably ancient history of Israel. If shorn of any connection to Judaism, Christianity could be dismissed as a suspiciously new superstition that deserved to suffer persecution due to its destabilizing effects on Roman society. If perceived as simply another group of Jews, however, Christians risked falling prey to the same charges of chronic rebelliousness against the Roman Empire.[70]

He also had to combat popular conceptions of Christians as being anti-social, cannibals, involved in orgies, and engaged in illegal political associations.

Walking this tightrope, Justin Martyr takes on the mantle of the philosopher, fitting into a particular social type of religion-making activity in the second century that Heidi Wendt has described as "freelance expert."[71] This is a type that many of the Christian apologists would fit. Though belonging to particular religious communities (for Justin Martyr, Rome), their authority is based upon teaching, debating in public, and gathering students. These elements, in turn, rely upon his attempts to demonstrate his authority to interpret oracular writings (i.e., the Judean scriptures).[72] He acts as a teacher, rather than a priest or bishop. His call is not to obedience, per se, as one finds when reading Ignatius' letters (also second century), but to correct thinking and living.[73]

While Justin argues in his apologies that Christians do have correct philosophy in thought and lifestyle, therefore, he also debates rival freelancers. He contends with figures like Marcion and other ancient Christians who denied the relevance of the Israelite scriptures. He debates the rhetorically constructed Jewish figure Trypho to lay claim on the antiquity of Judaism, while claiming to be its true heir (something both Marcion and non-Christian Jews would reject). While Justin and others attempt to delimit boundaries between social groups, especially since such boundaries are not yet securely established,[74] Justin also jostles against those well-positioned to call his own apologetic efforts into question, to undermine his claims – that is, against Jews and other Christians. The Jewish rivals are most explicit – the surviving polemical text is a dialogue with a Jewish interlocutor after all. He attempts to wrest exegetical authority of the Israelite scriptures from Jewish interpreters.[75]

Marcion would be just as big threat to Justin's reading. Having come to Rome from Pontus on the Black Sea, Marcion rejected the authority of Israelite scriptures for Christians, claiming they were only authoritative for Jews. Jesus, therefore, was the Son of God, though not the Jewish Messiah and not the son of the God of the Old Testament. The higher, unknown God was never made known before Jesus' advent, and therefore was not made known in the Old Testament.[76] For Marcion, there is no need to have Jesus appear to Moses. Marcion's arguments – made before Justin's own writing activity – undermine Justin's pleas. Other Christians, such as those who wrote *First Revelation of James*, *Revelation of Peter*, or *Second Treatise of the Great Seth*, also discounted and even mocked the lesser revelations of Moses and the prophets. Judith Lieu suggests that Justin repeatedly returns to these arguments of all theophany in the Israelite scriptures being Christophany against Jewish and rival Christian interpretations, because these are the places where he felt most vulnerable and threatened by those rival interpreters.[77] Justin needed to distance himself, therefore, from Marcion, lest the local Roman authorities lumped these two eastern-Mediterranean Christian migrants together.[78]

It is this apologetic/polemic aim that leads to Justin's development. To say that Abraham, Jacob, and especially Moses saw lesser beings like angels, as first-century writings say, would simply fall right into the hands of Marcion, who had no problem with the Israelite God and his angels appearing to Israelite prophets, as long as one differentiated this God from the invisible, unknown God who sent Jesus. Likewise, the author of the *Second Treatise of the Great Seth* even grants that angels spoke to Moses in order to discount the Mosaic oracles. In this case, Moses does not even interact with the lesser demiurge, but with that demiurge's angels – several steps removed from the transcendent God beyond this world. To say that they saw Christ differentiates Justin's brand of Christianity from Marcion's and contemporary forms of Judaism (as the Bar Kokhba Revolt is not too far in the back of people's minds), while laying claim to Judaism's antiquity.

Indeed, whether inspired by precedents in the apocalypses, Philo, the Wisdom of Solomon, or the New Testament or through incipient exchanges with contemporary Jews, therefore, Justin's exegesis does further work than any of these predecessors and contemporaries did. It introduces a continuity between old and new revelations against Marcionite (and perhaps gnosticizing) opponents, yet offers an apologetic against Jews by claiming that Christians have not abandoned the old revelations, but are a natural continuation of Israel.[79] Moreover, it retains philosophical respectability by having the original principle of the universe, God, remaining invisible.

Justin's solution, however, would create theological problems for later apologists. Anticipating the incarnation with preincarnation Christophanies, for example, makes the incarnation itself less novel. Within Justin's solution lurks a danger of diluting the salvific effect of the incarnation. If this has already happened, why would it need to happen again? The need then arises to stress the differences between the theophanies and the incarnation. As anticipation, they cannot be completion. For Justin, that difference is embodiment: the Old Testament theophanies as cloud, fire, and angelomorphic "man" and "angel" are ultimately asomatic, bodiless.[80] The incarnation for Justin is necessarily somatic, embodied. Ironically, considering a potential Marcionite opponent (who did not think that Jesus had naturally begotten flesh), Justin's pre-existent Christ is similarly "docetic."[81] Others drawing upon Justin would balk at his seemingly "docetic" preincarnate Christology. Ireneaus and Tertullian, while relying upon Justin's overall framework, would devise their own solutions for the differences between the Old Testament Christophanies and the incarnation.

For Justin, moreover, much of this discussion involves an inherent subordination of the Son to the Father; the *heteros theos* is a lower God (see, e.g., *Dialogue* 56).[82] The emphasis on Jesus as always the visible aspect of the invisible God, in a philosophical framework where visible must be inferior to the invisible, will strike post-Nicene (and some pre-Nicene) Christian interpreters as problematic. In fact, it is striking that later orthodox thinkers did not abandon Justin, but claimed him as a predecessor to their own thought. At that point, Justin's interpretation no longer provides a solution to the problem of seeing God in the Old Testament. His thought will have to be altered or abandoned. In what follows, we will look at Theophilus of Antioch, Irenaeus, Clement, Tertullian, and Origen, all of whom resolve the problem in different ways. They all heavily rely upon Justin, but they provide seeds for later solutions that indicate a more progressive revelation of the Logos. While following Justin in saying that the patriarchs and prophets encountered Christ, nonetheless they claim that such past seers barely glimpsed the Son, or that the Son, in his true essence, is, like the Father, also invisible. Therefore, the Son, too, would have to put on some trappings of lower orders to be seen, the truly invisible clothed in the visible.

5

Theophilus to Autolycus

The Son's Masquerade

Theophilus of Antioch, writing during the joint reigns of Marcus Aurelius and Commodus (177–80 CE; see *Aut.* 3.27), does not directly address whom Moses and the other prophets saw in the Old Testament. While he is an often-neglected second-century apologist among ancient Christians, as well as modern scholars,[1] he offers a framework for considering how and when one may see God.

Very little is known about him. According to Eusebius of Caesarea, Theophilus was the seventh bishop of the church in Antioch, being consecrated in 169 CE (*Hist. Ch.* 4.20; 4.24). His three treatises addressed to Autolycus, which are his only surviving works, have a surprisingly limited amount of Christian doctrine in them, while evincing affinities with Hellenistic Judaism and a sympathetic attitude toward the law. This is striking for someone writing a generation or two after the Bar Kochba Revolt. Antioch had had a major Jewish contingent since its founding by Seleucus Nicanor in 300 BCE, and different Christians in Antioch seem to have been both attracted to and repelled by Jews in the city.[2] While episcopal attitudes toward Jews would turn more negative by the fourth century, in John Chrysostom's series of sermons *Against the Jews*, Theophilus' apologies may reflect a more positive relationship between Jews and Christians in the late-second century.[3] Yet positive attitudes toward the law of Moses does not necessarily mean positive relations with the Jews of the community; it may reflect a response to early Marcionite missionary activity in the city.[4] Nonetheless, Theophilus seems to have little in common with Ignatius before him, who occasionally had a dismissive attitude toward Israel's scriptures (*Phil.* 8.2; cf. *Smyrn.* 5.2; 7.2), or John Chrysostom long after him. Instead, his apologetic treatises work almost as well for Hellenistic Judaism as for ancient Christianity.[5] His work, moreover, shows some similarities with the work of his contemporary, Irenaeus of Lyons, who wrote *Against Heresies* within five to ten years after his apologetic treatises, due to Irenaeus' likely reliance upon Theophilus' letters.[6]

Theophilus encapsulates all three strategies of vision: who can see, what one sees, and how one sees. He, however, makes how one sees God primary. Like nearly every other second- and third-century figure to be considered, Theophilus has absorbed the assumption that fleshly eyes can never see the high God, God the Father. It is utterly impossible. He does not couch such impossibilities in clearly philosophical language.[7] He does not even quote those scriptures that assert one cannot see God and live. While lacking these typical signposts, he offers an argument of the impossibility of seeing God in the flesh and the possibility of seeing God otherwise, representing the parameters found in the more in-depth and substantive reflections by Justin, Irenaeus, Clement, Tertullian, and others.

HOW TO SEE THE INVISIBLE AND IMMORTAL GOD

Firstly, God is invisible. Theophilus writes, "The appearance of God is ineffable and indescribable, and cannot be seen by eyes of flesh" (1.3.1).[8] Only the invisible – that is, the soul – can see the invisible. The way to God is through the inner self (1.2); one sees God through the eyes of the soul and hears God through the ears of the heart. But not just any soul can see and hear God. The soul is blinded by sin; it tarnishes the soul's eye and needs cleaning. Like Clement, Irenaeus, and especially Origen,[9] Theophilus teaches that it is only a soul pure of sin that has the ability to see God (Matt 5:8).

After considering how one sees through one's heart, Theophilus offers three stages of seeing. First, one sees God through God's effects, through his works of creation (1.5–6). Second, one can see God when one has purified one's soul: "If you perceive these things ... living chastely, and holily, and righteously, you can see God" (1.7.4).[10] Seeing God is, ultimately, a question of one's ethics.[11] Finally, as also taught by Theophilus' contemporary Irenaeus, one shall see God when resurrected at the end of time. Theophilus argues that when one is resurrected the flesh will arise immortal with the soul;[12] having become immortal, one can fully see the one who is immortal (i.e., God).[13] It is, therefore, not just the nature of God that prevents sight, but human nature. God is perceptible given the correct conditions of the seer: a purified soul and/or an immortal resurrected body and soul.[14]

When Theophilus turns to the prophets in Book 2, he speaks generically: they were generally inspired by the Holy Spirit or by God, or the Spirit spoke through the prophets (2.9, 30). There are a few places, however, that indicate that the Word or the Spirit identified as the Word spoke to the prophets. Discussing the creation account and how Moses and the prophets would be aware of such an account, Theophilus notes that the Logos was a helper in creation, being the ἀρχή (beginning / ruling principle). He, thereby, identifies the Logos with the Spirit of God and Wisdom. As such, the Logos is the one who came to the prophets and spoke to them about the creation of the world (being the only other principle other than God who was there) (2.10).[15] While Theophilus, as Irenaeus would, largely prefers auditory rather than visionary language when describing the communication of Logos with the prophets, other passages imply a visual appearance.

In fact, the distinction between the invisible God and the potentially visible Word, rather than explaining how people can and cannot see God, explains the anthropomorphisms in the Bible, much as it had for Philo. In an extended commentary on the creation stories in Genesis 1–3,[16] Theophilus attempts to explain how God could "walk" in the Garden:

> The God and Father, indeed, of all cannot be contained, and is not found in a place, for there is no place of His rest; but his Word, through whom he made all things, being his power and his wisdom, assuming the person of the Father and Lord of all, went to the garden in the person of God, and conversed with Adam. For the divine writing itself teaches us that Adam said that he had heard the voice. But what else is this voice but the Word of God, who is also his Son? (2.22.2–3)[17]

Again, the predominant language is auditory: "converse" and "voice." Nonetheless, an appearance is implied. While nearly every second- and third-century apologist in the wake of Justin will assume that all of the anthropomorphisms in the Bible refer to the preincarnate Logos, Theophilus is more unique in his language surrounding this exegetical solution. The term "person" in "the person of the Father" (τὸ πρόσωπον τοῦ πατρὸς) appears in its more ancient sense, as a mask, much as we think of putting on a "persona." The Son does not appear as Son; the Son *pretends* to be the Father. One is left to presume that any other anthropomorphism in scripture, including any place where God is seen, moves, or speaks, must also be the Word's masquerade.[18]

While Moses is treated generally in terms of the manner in which God revealed himself to the prophets in Book 2, for Theophilus' apologetic purposes in Book 3, the position of Moses as the friend and prophet of God guarantees the authority of his revelation: the law (3.9, 23, 25). Just as other Jewish and Christian apologists had, he argues that Moses' greater antiquity (than figures such as Plato) also gives him greater authority. His authority, therefore, derives from both his close, intimate relationship to God and his antiquity. Because of this, Theophilus accords the law the highest authority, arguing that the later prophets and the gospels agree with this ultimate scriptural authority (3.12).

But such a claim that the visible God of the scriptures who appeared to the prophets was the preincarnate Christ is not made explicit by Theophilus the way it was by other second-century apologists, such as Justin and Irenaeus. They, moreover, never suggested that the Son's appearance was a *persona* or performance – he did not appear as the Father, but as himself. What it means for the Son to appear, however, will be resolved in different ways. Theophilus, though, also leaves the same problems found in Justin: if the Son appeared already, why did he need to appear later? Does this solution to the problem of seeing God dilute the significance of the Word's appearance as Jesus in the first century? Does it dilute the significance of the incarnation? While Justin and Irenaeus did try to maintain the distinctiveness of the incarnation, Theophilus, interestingly enough, is largely unconcerned with these questions or implications. Indeed, famously, Theophilus never discusses Jesus' birth, life, death, and resurrection.[19]

CONCLUSIONS

Theophilus of Antioch, in his apologetic letters to Autolycus, touches upon all three strategies of explaining visions in the Bible: who sees, how one sees, and what one sees. Nonetheless, the question of how one sees drives his conclusions. He begins with the basic assumption that God is invisible and immortal. No human fleshly eyes can see God. But the patriarchs and prophets saw God. They saw God the same way Theophilus suggests a contemporary figure could: through the soul. The soul is invisible; therefore, it can "see" the invisible God.

Yet not just any soul can do this: only a pure soul or heart. One gains purity of heart through upright moral conduct. Therefore, the status of the seer has a role to play, but, more like Irenaeus and less like Clement, it does not necessarily appear to be limited to an elite group of gnostics, bishops, or mystics. Finally, one can see God with resurrected flesh, providing a partial parallel with Irenaeus and anticipating some of Augustine's arguments. Resurrected flesh is immortal; therefore, it has gained the ability to see the immortal God.

Theophilus also briefly touches upon what one sees. In addition to seeing God with one's purified soul or in the afterlife, one can see God through God's effects, that is, through creation itself. Moreover, the prophets also saw God through the preincarnate Logos. While this solution goes back to Justin in the previous generation, Theophilus gives it his own twist. First, Theophilus, like Philo, seems most preoccupied with the embarrassing anthropomorphisms in the Bible, spending a lot of time with the Garden of Eden story. Second, and more uniquely, he suggests that the Son appeared in the "person," or "persona," or "mask" of the Father.

Theophilus, therefore, deals with most of the issues raised by God's interactions with Moses, yet without much focus on Moses. Moses may not be the measure of humanity directly, as he is in the work of other writers, but Moses and all prophetic seers together – including Adam – are.

Because of the sporadic evidence of Antiochene Christianity in the second century in contrast to the much-greater evidence of later centuries, it is difficult to piece together why Theophilus developed his exegesis in this way. He was a bishop, but his work fits the mould of apologist. While he was bishop of Antioch, his works do not quite yet resemble the later "Antiochene" school. He may have had a positive relationship to the old and sizable Jewish community in Antioch, which may explain his resemblances to Hellenistic Jewish apologetic works, and he holds the Torah/law in the highest regard, perhaps because it has the greater claim to antiquity. While it is possible his positive valuation of the law was a response against Marcionite activities, his apologetic letters do not have the polemic edge of Justin, of his contemporary, Irenaeus, or even of Clement. Contemporary to Irenaeus, yet on the other side of the Mediterranean, he has so many similarities that some linkages between the two have been suggested – Irenaeus likely relied on Theophilus. Nonetheless, while Irenaeus develops his theology in polemics against other forms of Christianity,

Theophilus develops his in defence of Christianity to polytheist leaders. He was more worried about attacks on Christianity from outside, instead of defining his own brand against other forms of Christianity. But, in doing so, he does not polemicize against Judaism as other second-century Christians did. In this context, his focus on Moses, the patriarchs, and interpreting the law reflects less an anti-Marcionite edge and more an attempt to defend Christianity against the charge of novelty and superstition. In such a context, his reliance upon Jewish apologetic tropes reaching back to Artapanus or Philo, which valorized the law and its pre-eminent antiquity, makes sense. In this way, Theophilus seems more in line with Matthew than Paul.

Ireneaus of Lyons (c. 140–202 CE)

Progressive Dispensational Visions of Purification

In this fullness of knowledge of God and participation in his incorruptible life, man becomes himself a "perfect man" in the image and likeness of God, living his life and enjoying his glory. Such is eternal life, that is, the participation for the "seizure" of the incorruptible life of God in the visions of his glory.[1]

The career of Irenaeus of Lyons partially overlapped and paralleled Justin's, while, on the other side of the Mediterranean, Irenaeus was contemporaneous to Theophilus of Antioch's episcopacy and Clement of Alexandria. Irenaeus, Theophilus, and Clement were all most active in the final quarter of the second century. Tertullian and Origen would arrive on the scene soon afterwards. It was a time of intense creativity and diversity of views among even those who would eventually be labelled "orthodox."

Like Justin, Irenaeus moved from the eastern Mediterranean to the West. He likely came from Smyrna (modern Izmir on the Aegean coast of Turkey) and learned from Polycarp, who would be burned alive in the arena in Smyrna in 157 CE. Polycarp clearly had a formative influence on Irenaeus, and, through Polycarp, Irenaeus believed he had a direct link to the original apostles (*A.H.* 3.3.4). He moved westward to Rome, like Justin before him, and likely overlapped with Justin before Justin's own martyrdom. Unlike Justin and most immigrants to Rome, he kept moving westward and travelled to Gaul. He became the bishop of Lugdunum (Lyons) in either 177 or 180 CE, after the previous, very aged, bishop Pothinus died as part of a local-

ized violent persecution against Christians involving both mob violence and official execution in the amphitheatre. Somehow Irenaeus
escaped the torture and death of his fellow congregants. At the time,
Lugdunum was the largest Roman city above the Alps, and a central
crossroads for the entire region. While several immigrants would
speak Greek, including Irenaeus, it was largely a Latin city within a
Celtic region. He remained uneasy with the "barbaric tongue," by
which he may not have meant the local Celtic language, but Latin
(*A.H.* 1.pref.3).[2]

Despite his life being punctuated by persecution and the execution
of his fellow congregants, his two surviving works, the *Refutation and
Overthrow of the Knowledge Falsely So Called*, better known as *Against
Heresies* (c. 180s CE), and the *Demonstration of Apostolic Teaching* (here-
after *Demonstration*), reveal a different orientation than the apologists.
While Justin or Theophilus would write polemically against Jews and
other Christians, particularly Marcion, their primary focus was to
defend Christianity in the face of Roman opposition. Irenaeus, whose
own congregation suffered mass martyrdom in either 177 or 180 CE,
focuses most of his attention on combatting rival Christian groups in
Against Heresies, while building up his own community (or like-minded communities) in the *Demonstration*. In fact, one rival Christian figure, Marcus, settled near Irenaeus in the Rhone valley about the time of
the writing of *Against Heresies* and may have been the catalyst for Irenaeus' ire (*A.H.* 1.13–20).[3] Despite the polemics, the work of "exposure"
of these groups indicates he is writing to his own community or network of like-minded communities to recognize rival Christian groups,
because, to Irenaeus' frustration, they are very difficult to differentiate.[4]
After describing, polemicizing against, and taxonomizing the various
Christian sects and individuals he opposes in three books of *Against
Heresies*, in Book 4 he finally strikes out his own counter-vision.[5]

Unfortunately, Irenaeus appears frustratingly inconsistent in
Against Heresies 4.[6] He seems to contradict himself from chapter to
chapter, section to section, concerning *whether* Moses and the
prophets saw God or not; or, *how* they saw anything. He sometimes
says they saw the Father; sometimes that seeing the Father is impossible and that, therefore, they saw the Son; sometimes that they did not
even see the Son, but foresaw the Son, and that it was impossible for
anyone to see God (through the Son) until the Son was incarnate in
the latter days. Sometimes he says, matter-of-factly that they did see
the Son in various forms.

Though this be madness, yet there is method in it.[7] Much of this wavering can be synthesized under two overlapping frameworks that Irenaeus devises: the progressive dispensation of vision and the progressive revelation of the Word. In the first framework, history is divided up among the age of Spirit, the age of the Son, and the age of the Father. In the first, God reveals himself through the spirit prophetically; in the second, through the Son adoptively; and in the third, in the age to come, one finally "sees" God the Father paternally, which for Irenaeus means fully and directly. Thereby, while Irenaeus is one of the most pessimistic concerning past figures seeing God (even the Son), he is optimistic in one's ability to see God (even the Father) in the future Kingdom of God.

In the second framework that overlays this one, the Word revealed to the prophets (here beginning with Abraham) mostly his later advent. Much of their visions of God (via the Son) were visions of the future incarnation, rather than (or in addition to) a face-to-face encounter. Nonetheless, they did encounter the Son through *averted* visions, seeing darkly in a mirror, as Paul would say, or partly; not (yet) in full, directly, or face to face. Only at Jesus' incarnation was God made fully visible in the last days through the Son. Only in the Kingdom will God the Father, who is invisible, be seen. So, did Moses and other Hebrew prophets see God? Yes and no. Sort of. Not quite.[8]

HEARING GOD IN *AGAINST HERESIES* 3

Almost immediately, in Book 3, Irenaeus picks up on some of Justin's arguments.[9] At first in fits and glances, but in increasingly systematic fashion, Irenaeus argues that it is the Son who appeared and spoke with the figures of old. The Spirit also spoke – though could not appear – to the prophets (cf. *Dem.* 1.1.7). Irenaeus, departing from Justin however, also states that the Father could manifest to the prophets, seemingly completely undermining Justin's entire point. Yet, when analyzed more closely, Irenaeus prefers auditory rather than visual language throughout.

Early on in his magnum opus, *Against Heresies*, Irenaeus uses some of the same passages that Justin extensively exegeted to demonstrate that the Son spoke to Abraham and Moses. Instead of exegesis, however, Irenaeus largely assumes Justin's argument. Concerning Sodom and Gomorrah, Irenaeus says, "For it here points out that the Son, who had also been talking with Abraham, had received power to judge the

Sodomites for their wickedness" (*A.H.* 3.6.1).[10] Here Irenaeus encapsulates in one sentence what it took Justin chapters to demonstrate, casually remarking that the Son spoke to Abraham. Irenaeus further makes the same claim about Moses at the burning bush. Beginning with God, soon to be revealed as Son, revealing himself as "I am who I am" (*Ego sum qui sum*), Irenaeus writes:

> And again, when the Son speaks to Moses, He says, "I have come down to deliver this people." For it is he who descended and ascended for the salvation of humans. Therefore God has been declared through the Son, who is in the Father, and has the Father in himself – he who is, the Father bearing witness to the Son, and the Son announcing the Father. As also Isaiah says, "I too am a witness," he declares, "says the Lord God, and the Son whom I have chosen, that you may know, and believe, and understand that I am." (*A.H.* 3.6.2; cf. *Dem.* 1.2.40; 2.1.46)[11]

The only figure missing from Justin's account is Jacob.[12] Abraham and Moses encounter the Son; it is something Irenaeus need not argue, unlike Justin, but is something he can assume. It is nonetheless noteworthy that, so far, Irenaeus employs only speaking and auditory language rather than optical terminology.[13] Irenaeus clearly is more comfortable having past figures hear the Son than granting them a vision of the divine. It makes, however, a certain sense to hear rather than see the "Word."[14]

At times, strangely for the late-second century at least, Irenaeus also suggests that God the Father directly interacted with the prophets. In 3.10.2, referring to the *Magnificat* (esp. Luke 1:46), Irenaeus writes, "By these and such like the Gospel points out that it was God who spoke to the fathers; that it was He who, by Moses, instituted the legal dispensation, by which giving of the law we know that he speaks to the fathers. This same God, after his great goodness, poured his compassions upon us."[15] Irenaeus is trying to demonstrate that the God of the Old Testament and Father in the New Testament are the same, not different, beings. While his stated opponents throughout Book 3 are Valentinus and Marcion together, in this passage he repeatedly mocks the system of thirty aeons developed by Valentinus or his students.[16] His immediate rhetorical target is Valentinian theology. He counters this theological opponent through mockery, to be sure, but exegetically he must go so far as to contravene the New Testament texts

(Galatians, Hebrews, and Acts), where Moses received the law through angels; instead, Irenaeus argues, the Father established law and gave it directly to Moses. God in these passages clearly refers to God the Father; thus, he is not activating Justin's arguments here. His references to Jesus, Christ, and the Son, by contrast, are typified by Word/Logos throughout this passage (see further 3.12.10). God the Father also directly speaks to Moses in 3.15.3.[17]

Furthermore, in the fourth book of *Against Heresies*, the Father speaks to Abraham, gives the law, sends the prophets, and sends the Son, again demonstrating the unity of Old and New (4.41.4). In another passage, Irenaeus also states that both Christ and the Father spoke to Moses (4.5.2). Yet again, the fact that these are all speaking passages, avoiding visual language, is significant. One may be able to hear, but not necessarily see, God and live.

Throughout the context of Book 3, Irenaeus employs several deconstructive and constructive arguments. While trying to dismantle various "gnostic" systems (Books 1 and 2), he seeks to establish an ideal unity of Christianity in the face of its actual diversity in Book 3 by focusing on apostolic succession (3.3) and a common creed (3.4.2), part of which was that the God of Jesus was the God of creation and Moses (3.5). Part of this program, therefore, needed to establish the continuity between Old and New Testaments against his opponents, lumping together Valentinus, Marcion, Cerinthus, and Basilides, though most often pairing the very different figures of Valentinus and Marcion (3.2.1; 3.3.4). The arguments work in two directions: like Justin, he has the Son speak to the patriarchs and the prophets, having the Son of gospels speak in the Israelite scriptures; parallel to this, he notes that the Father was God of creation and the law of the Israelite scriptures, which both Valentinus and Marcion would devalue, and was the God who sent the Son in the Gospel of Luke.

Irenaeus, therefore, took his assumptions, inherited from Justin, and both restricted and expanded them. He restricted them, at first glance at least, by limiting them to auditory encounters. He expanded them by allowing these past figures also to have such auditory encounters with the Father and by applying these assumptions to new (and old) problems. As such, he seems to have only partially absorbed Justin's program, yet I think he has taken it a step further, adding new strategies to bind together old and new revelations of the Father and the Son, having the Father of the law appear in the Gospel, in addition to having the Son of Gospel appear in the law. Significantly, Irenaeus in Book 4 will more closely bring these inherited assumptions from Justin into dialogue with the antithetical passages of the Bible that claim that one can and one cannot see God and live, examining those passages more directly than Justin did. But it is in those passages that one begins to find an even deeper ambivalence about what Moses, in fact, saw.

FROM SEEING TO FORESEEING THE SON: AGAINST HERESIES 4.20.9 AND RELATED PASSAGES

Despite his partial inheritance from Justin's argument that says the prophets interacted with the preincarnate Logos when they saw or heard God, Irenaeus twists the dialectic of seeing and not seeing into a new shape. *Against Heresies* 4.20 is a tour de force, which lays out several interlocking elements that unfold into an ultimate progressive revelation *of* the Logos *by* the Logos. This, in turn, purifies humanity, so that humans may, in the future, do the impossible: see God.[18]

In the first piece of the puzzle, the patriarchs and prophets never really saw the Son – or, if they did, they did so only in part. Instead, they *foresaw* the Son. Uniting the theophanic appearances to Moses with those on the Mount of Transfiguration, Irenaeus writes (*A.H.* 4.20.9):

> And the Word spoke to Moses, appearing in view, "just as any one might speak to his friend." But Moses desired to see him clearly who was speaking with him, and was thus addressed: "Stand in the deep place of the rock, and with my hand I will cover you. But when my splendour shall pass by, then you shall see my back parts, but my face you shall not see: for no human sees my face and lives." Two facts are thus signified: that it is impossible for a human to see God; and that, through the wisdom of God, humanity shall see him in the last times, in the depth of a rock, that is, in his coming as a human. And for this reason did he [the Lord] confer with him face to face on the top of a mountain, Elijah being also present, as the Gospel relates, he thus making good in the end the ancient promise. (adapted from ANF)[19]

This strange passage reflects much of Irenaeus' ambivalence about whether or to what degree the prophets even saw the Son. The ambivalence is expressed in a couple of binaries: appearing in view versus seeing clearly; face versus back parts. These binaries come together through the anaphora of "human" (*homo*; *hominem*): no human (*homo*) sees God and lives; it is impossible for a human (*homo*) to see God; but the human or humanity (*homo*) shall see him; the human shall see him in his coming as a human (*hominem*). This anaphora of "human" sets the problem – humans cannot see God – and the solution – humans can see God in God's coming as a human. Like sees like; humans see the human and will see God (from Moses' perspective) in his advent as a human. This is the basic argument of Irenaeus. It sets up something else, moreover: humans will be able to see *more* of God beyond the Logos' humanity once humans transcend and transform their humanity through the Son/Logos. But it still leaves obscure what the prophets actually saw in the past.

Returning to the quoted passage, at first, following the quotation from Exod. 33:20, Irenaeus argues that it is impossible for a human to see God in this life. But Moses saw *something*. Moses saw the "Word" (*verbum*) – the Word did not just speak, but appeared in view to him (*apparens in conspectu*). Picking up the hint from Justin, the revealer to Moses was the pre-existent Son.[20] Nonetheless, Moses requests to see this figure – the Son, not the Father – clearly, indicating he had yet to receive a full vision of the *Son*. How, then, did the preincarnate Son/Logos appear to the patriarchs and the prophets according to Irenaeus?

In addition to the passages adduced above, where the Son speaks, Irenaeus often will claim that the Logos appeared to the patriarchs and the prophets, especially when trying to counter "Jewish" readings, which, Irenaeus suggests, claim that one can know the Father apart from the Son (4.7.4; 4.10.1). It is uncertain, however, to what degree Irenaeus was personally familiar with contemporary Jewish readings, especially since many of those that survive also include intermediary beings (Glory, Memra, Shekhinah) in God's manifest form rather than revealing God in God's full splendour. These, therefore, may be rhetorical Jews or inherited literary Jews, such as from Justin's *Dialogue with Trypho*.

Irenaeus, however, takes such potential rival readings seriously enough to disrupt his typical statements of the Son's *future* visibility. In contrast to these "Jewish" readings, Irenaeus says it was not the Father, but the Son or Word, who visibly appeared to Adam in paradise (*Dem.* 1.1.12), to Abraham in human form (cf. *Dem.* 1.1.24), and

to Moses as fire as in Justin; again, the Son was not just anthropomorphic, but *pyromorphic* (*A.H.* 4.7.4; 4.10.1; see further 4.33.11). As
Irenaeus writes in 4.10.1:

> the Son of God is implanted everywhere throughout his writings:
> at one time, indeed, speaking with Abraham, when about to eat
> with him; at another time with Noah, giving to him the dimen-
> sions; at another, inquiring after Adam; at another, bringing down
> judgment upon the Sodomites; and again, when He becomes visi-
> ble, and directs Jacob on his journey, and speaks with Moses from
> the bush. And it would be endless to recount [the occasions]
> upon which the Son of God is shown forth by Moses.[21]

While in many passages, Irenaeus notes only that the Son or Logos
spoke, here the preincarnate Son appears and takes visible form – he
even eats, suggesting some form of embodiment – all according to
Moses, the putative author of these passages (cf. *Dem.* 2.1.44). Clearly
the Son is the visible manifestation of the invisible Father.[22] As Irenaeus writes in a Johannine-styled passage:

> And through the Word himself who had been made visible and pal-
> pable, was the Father shown forth, although all did not equally
> believe in him; but all saw the Father in the Son; for the Father is the
> invisible of the Son, but the Son is the visible of the Father. (4.6.6)[23]

Drawing upon Col. 1:15, the Son is the manifest form of the invisible
Father, but this is not the whole story. The Son may have appeared, but
how did he appear? Indeed, in Justin's writings, how Jesus appeared in
his preincarnate Christophanies (i.e., as a bodiless form) was important. The occasional instance of eating suggests greater corporeality
than one finds in Justin, but what did Irenaeus further think?
    Returning to 4.20.9, the Word may have appeared to Moses, but
Moses still did not see him clearly. That is, the vision was not full,
direct, or complete. It was only partial. Instead of seeing God's face,
Moses saw God's backparts (*posteriora*), interpreted here allegorically
as Christ's advent, also signified by the cleft in the rock.[24] That is, the
Word (pre-existent Jesus) predicted his own coming as a human. As
Eric Osborn summarizes, "He is both the subject and object of
prophecy."[25] So Moses saw in part Christ as revealer and foresaw more
clearly Christ as a human being (see further *A.H.* 4.20.3).

Irenaeus will reiterate this point throughout Book 4, alternating between Moses and Abraham seeing or foreseeing the Son. For example, he similarly writes that Abraham did not see, but foresaw (4.5.5) the Son in a spirit of prophecy (4.7.1). Irenaeus also tends to emphasize that the Son spoke to the prophets, but became fully visible only in the "last times":

> For not alone upon Abraham's account did He say these things, but also that He might point out how all who have known God from the beginning, and have foretold the advent of Christ, have received the revelation from the Son himself; who also *in the last times* was made visible and palpable, and spoke with the human race. (4.7.2; emphasis mine)[26]

Or, Irenaeus could even further downplay the patriarchs' and prophets' visions by foreseeing *by* the Spirit instead of foreseeing *by* the Son:

> But that it was not only the prophets and many righteous men, who, foreseeing through the Holy Spirit his advent, prayed that they might attain to that period in which they should see their Lord face to face, and hear his words, the Lord has made manifest, when he says to his disciples, "Many prophets and righteous men have desired to see those things which you see, and have not seen them; and to hear those things which you hear, and have not heard them." (4.11.1)[27]

Inverting the Jewish view of regressive vision – that God made himself most visible at Sinai and only less so later on[28] – Irenaeus quotes Jesus to say the prophets wished to see the things the disciples see plainly.

In the passages surrounding 4.20.9, Irenaeus frames the discussion to clarify that God the Father cannot be seen in this life, but unfortunately makes things even more confusing about what the prophets actually saw and how. In a perplexing passage, Irenaeus tries to clarify (paradoxically) what he means by saying the prophets "saw," and, thereby, the very nature of prophecy through vision; that is, if prophecy is about future events, then prophetic visions, including theophanies, are intimations of future – not present – divine manifestations:

> Inasmuch then as the Spirit of God pointed out by the prophets things to come, *forming and adapting us beforehand for the purpose*

of our being made subject to God, but it was still a future thing that humanity [*homo*], through the good pleasure of the Holy Spirit, should see [God], it necessarily behooved those through whose instrumentality future things were announced, to see God, whom they intimated as to be seen by humans; in order that God, and the Son of God, and the Son, and the Father, should not only be prophetically announced, but that he should also be seen by all his members who are sanctified and instructed in the things of God, *that man might be disciplined beforehand and previously exercised for a reception into that glory which shall afterwards be revealed in those who love God.* For the prophets used not to prophesy in word alone, but in visions also, and in their mode of life, and in the actions which they performed, according to the suggestions of the Spirit. *According to this invisible scheme, therefore, did they see God*, as also Isaiah says, "I have seen with mine eyes the King, the Lord of hosts," *pointing out that man should behold God with his eyes and hear his voice.* According to this scheme, therefore, did they also see the Son of God as a human conversant with humans, while they prophesied what was to happen, saying that the one who was not come as yet was present; proclaiming also the impassible as subject to suffering. (4.20.8; emphasis mine)[29]

Irenaeus delights in paradox here, but there is some coherence to it if one works to discern it. The prophets saw God "according to this invisible method" (*Secundum hanc igitur rationem invisibilem*).[30] The point is that the visions were not, in fact, appearances of God to the prophets, but prophecies themselves – as are the words and actions of the prophets.[31] That is, it was not that the prophets saw God, but that they prophesied using visions to say that one *ought* to see God – in the future (cf. *Dem.* 1.1.12; 2.1.44–5).

Isaiah provides an interesting example of Irenaeus' exegesis. Isaiah claims to have seen the Lord of Hosts (in the perfect tense), yet Irenaeus twists the vision from an indication of what has happened into a signifier of what should happen. As Osborn writes, "In contrast to Justin, for whom it was important to show that there was a plurality in God before the coming of Jesus, Irenaeus treats the theophanies of the bible as symbolic representations of a future reality. The world of types points to a word who is as yet invisible and whose manifestation only takes place in the New Testament."[32] It is a future thing, Irenaeus writes, for humans to see God. Prophets are the instruments by which

God announces such a future vision and, therefore, they ought to have a vision themselves. They used the past and present tenses to intimate the future reality. Their visions of God, therefore, were meant to be visions of God's future visibility. The purpose of such prophetic visions, moreover, is pedagogical: they adapt and prepare humanity for Christ's advent, as Irenaeus writes, "forming and preparing us in order to be made subject to God" (*praeformans nos et praeaptans ad id ut subditi Deo simus*) so that humans could see God.

Irenaeus is clearer in the passage after 4.20.9, where he interprets the difference between God's "face" and "back": "The prophets, therefore, did not openly behold the actual face of God, but the dispensations and mysteries through which humanity should afterwards see God" (4.20.10).[33] That is, the prophets did not see God, but foresaw God's appearance. He adduces further evidence from Ezekiel 1: "This, too, was made still clearer by Ezekiel, that the prophets saw the dispensations of God in part, but not actually God himself."[34] Irenaeus notes that Ezekiel did not see God or even the Son, but the "image and the likeness"; his vision was not direct or face to face; it was partial. He continues:

> If, then, neither Moses, nor Elijah, nor Ezekiel, who had all many celestial visions, did see God; but if what they did see were similitudes of the splendour of the Lord, and prophecies of things to come; it is manifest that the Father is indeed invisible, of whom also the Lord said, "No man has seen God at any time." But his word, as he himself willed it, and for the benefit of those who beheld did show the Father's brightness and explained his purposes ... not in one figure, nor in one character, did he appear to those seeing him, but according to the reasons and effects aimed at in his dispensations. (4.20.11)[35]

Ireneaus further cites Daniel, the fourth figure in the fiery furnace, and John of Patmos to illustrate the Son's appearances, comparing the similitudes of the past and the full vision of the present age. John of Patmos fits in this scheme, though he is part of a different age (after Jesus' advent and exaltation). Indeed, no one can see God (whether Father or Son) and live; that is why John of Patmos falls down (Rev. 1:17), according to Irenaeus. He did die upon having his vision of the exalted and glorified Christ, and Christ resurrected him, proving Exod. 33:20 to be true: you cannot see God and live, but you can see God and die.[36]

Returning once more to 4.20.9, there is a twist ending: Elijah was
also there. How do we know? The gospels say so: when Jesus was on
the mountain, he was there with Moses and Elijah. The passage juxtaposes Moses on Sinai and Jesus on the Mount of Transfiguration.[37]
The parallel is heightened not just in the fact that they were both
mountains, but in parallel phrasing (at least in Latin), both phrases
beginning with "*in altitudine*": "in the depth of the rock / *in altitudine
petrae*" – the place from which Moses "foresaw" parallels "on the top
of the mountain / *in altitudine montis*" – the "fulfillment" of Moses'
desire to speak "face to face" occurs on the Mount of Transfiguration.

Did Moses merely foresee, and this is confirmed on the Mount of
Transfiguration? Did he and Elijah reappear at a later time, reflecting
the traditions that said they had never actually died? Were they resurrected for this event? Or did they exist in a spiritual state?[38] While
ambiguous, Jesus' transfiguration is God keeping his promise to Moses
that he would see God (a nod to Exod. 33:21–3 and perhaps Num.
12:8).[39] Moses, the greatest of the prophets, finally saw God fully
through the Son's transfiguration, promised long ago by the Son on
Mount Sinai.[40] As Eric Osborn writes,

> The prophets have glimpsed his glories at different stages of the
> divine economy. Between the adoptive vision, which his children
> now enjoy, and the eternal vision of the kingdom there is a special
> point in the transfiguration where the king is seen and the
> promise to Moses is fulfilled. There is an anticipation here of the
> final vision of divine glory promised to men [*sic*].[41]

From prefiguration (Moses and the prophets) to manifestation (incarnation), the transfiguration not only looks backward to the promise
to Moses, but forward to an everlasting vision in Irenaeus' much
broader frameworks of the progressive vision of the Logos.

SYNTHESIS: OVERARCHING FRAMEWORKS

Irenaeus has left an untidy mess. On the one hand, he reaffirms
Justin's position that Moses and the prophets saw the preincarnate
Logos, especially in rhetorical contexts in which he seems to oppose
Valentinian and Jewish claims. On the other hand, he reworks some
of the same passages to claim that Moses and the prophets did not
really see the Son, only saw the Son in a fleeting, partial manner, or

really "foresaw" the Son and, in that manner, saw God. While much of this confusion derives from the changing rhetorical contexts and slightly different opponents Irenaeus had in mind, there are some glimmers of coherence. The overall point is that there is some sort of progression to the Son's appearances: he appeared to the patriarchs and prophets sometimes manifest, visually, and aurally, sometimes as merely a prophecy of future vision, but it was always partial; it was never the full visibility as found in the full incarnation or the full glory as in the transfiguration.

Nevertheless, this foreseeing as seeing fits into two overlapping frameworks that account for most – though not all – of his evidence. These two intersecting schemata include his progressive dispensation of visions in terms of Spirit, Son, and Father and the development and purification of the human to see God upon death and achieving deification (becoming God to see God; or seeing God, one becomes God). The first takes a divine perspective; the second, humanity's perspective.[42] The first mostly looks to historical development; the second is, as Freud would say, phylogenetic and individual.

Irenaeus develops his dispensation of visions in terms of Spirit, Son, and Father. To do this, he sets up Matt. 5:8 and Exod. 33:20 in alternation: one cannot see God's face and live, but the pure in heart will see God. Or, put another way, the prophets affirm that God should be seen, which Jesus confirms in Matt. 5:8. But the Father is incomprehensible, a typical early Christian way of interpreting the line that one cannot see God and live in Exod. 33:20.[43]

So the question is not whether God can be seen: the answer is both yes and no when stated in this manner. The question is how and when. The Father can be seen prophetically through the Spirit, as by the patriarchs and prophets (4.7.1; 4.11.1; 4.20.8), adoptively through the Son, also by the patriarchs and prophets, as the preincarnate Logos, but also by apostles, etc. (4.5.5; 4.7.2; etc.), and will be seen paternally, that is, in himself, in the Kingdom of God.[44] Irenaeus explains: "the Spirit truly preparing humanity in the Son of God, and the Son leading him to the Father, while the Father, too, confers incorruption for eternal life which comes to everyone from the fact of his seeing God." (4.20.5)[45]

The benefit of seeing God is participating in God's qualities: incorruptibility and immortality.[46] Once again, you are what you see. While the Spirit and Son prepare one for these qualities, they are only ultimately conferred and confirmed upon the impossible but necessary divine vision of the Father. Irenaeus continues,

For as those who see the light are within the light, and partake of
its brilliancy; even so, those who see God are in God, and receive
of his splendour. But splendour revivifies them; those, therefore,
who see God, do receive life. And for this reason, He, beyond comprehension, and boundless and invisible, rendered himself visible,
and comprehensible, and within the capacity of those who
believe, that he might vivify those who receive and behold him
through faith. For as his greatness is past finding out, so also his
goodness is beyond expression; by which having been seen, he
bestows life upon those who see him.[47]

Commenting on this passage, Andia notes the equation of seeing,
being, and participating: the point is that to "see" God (which is necessary and impossible) is "to be in God," enabling one to participate
in God's splendour, which bestows life.[48] Andia sees this as lessening
the tension between "seeing God" and God's invisibility, by equating
"seeing" as "participating," making vision somewhat of a euphemism.
Of course, Irenaeus could be speaking euphemistically or using "seeing" as a metaphor for "participating." Yet, he explicitly uses the terminology of participation at the end of the passage; therefore, there
is no need for such a doubling. Moreover, as discussed below, Irenaeus develops a progressive purification of humanity and individual
humans, so that they may, indeed, see God at the end of time. Andia
is partly correct: to see is to participate in God's being. They are con-
joined, but seeing is the prerequisite for such participation rather
than a metaphor for it. The vision leads to vivification, resurrection
from death, and entrance into the kingdom. In short, seeing God
fully and completely seems possible, but only beyond this life, being
necessary for life in the kingdom. Seeing as a metaphor or "figure"
belongs to the past and present; non-figurative vision occurs in the
future. Note Irenaeus' use of the future tense, borrowed from Matt.
5:8 (4.20.6):

Humans therefore shall see God, that they may live, being made
immortal by that sight, and attaining even unto God; which, as I
have already said, was declared *figuratively* by the prophets, that
God should be seen by humans who bear his spirit, and do always
wait patiently for his coming ... For certain of these used to see the
prophetic spirit and his active influences poured forth for all kinds
of gifts; others, again, the advent of the lord. (emphasis mine)[49]

In the past and the present, seeing God occurs, but only through other means: through spirit or through God's influences throughout the world; that is, the effects of God. Or by foreseeing the advent of the Lord. Nonetheless, these are all intimations of a future dispensation by which people will not only see God, *but see God the Father*. In a striking twist on the traditional "no one can see God and live" line, Irenaeus suggests that such a vision is, in fact, life-giving: one must see God *in order to* live. Or, to be more accurate, a direct divine vision may be impossible in one's earthly life, but necessary for eternal life. Irenaeus, therefore, indicates that one does not see God directly in the past tense or present tense; only in the future tense.

Having looked at it from the divine perspective (who is seen and when), Irenaeus also turns to the human perspective (the development and purification of the human being so one can be ready to see God upon death). This unfolds in two ways: preparing the human race for the divine vision in the Kingdom of God (as in the ages of Spirit, Son, and Father) and the ultimate purification of a human necessary to see God upon death. In it, he develops a progressive view of vision in a *sorites* argument (*A.H.* 4.38.3):

> For the Uncreated is perfect, that is, God. Now it was necessary that the human first be created; and having been created, should grow; and having grown, should mature; and having matured, should abound; and having abounded, should hold fast; and having held fast, should be glorified; and being glorified, should see one's Master. For God is He who is *yet* to be seen, and the beholding of God is productive of immortality, but immortality renders one near to God. (emphasis mine)[50]

This passage encapsulates human development from Adam – the first human – to the end of time, from humanity's creation, growth or increasing, maturity, and strengthening and endurance. The prophetic visions nurtured this growth and maturing process, preparing humans for their ultimate glorification and perfection in the ultimate vision of God. At the same time, this maps onto an individual human's life, using a word for created that also can be used for "begotten," "being born," promising one glorification and immortality. Individually, however, this would vary depending upon which age one lived in: humanity's birth, growth, maturation, etc. In this scheme, the prophets are out of time, seeing beyond their age's stage of development, but it is their

ability to see beyond that prepared humanity for the next stage. Irenaeus, however, would have believed that he and his audience stood on
the cusp of glorification at a time of persecution, when one needs to
hold fast. Historically and individually, Irenaeus' scheme is intensely
progressive, and glorification and immortality are near.

Throughout, Irenaeus is tortured by those passages that say Moses
and the prophets cannot see God and yet saw God. His solution is that,
while he sometimes claims the prophets saw God, it was only in part.
The full vision can only come later – later in two senses: after Jesus'
advent (seeing God through the Son) and after death (paradoxically
seeing the invisible and incomprehensible Father). Just before the
quoted passage, he states that this occurs upon one's entrance to the
Kingdom of Heaven; or, to be more accurate, it is a purification process
that allows one to enter the Kingdom of Heaven, and be revivified.

God in Godself has never been seen; nonetheless, it is the *telos* – the
end, purpose, and perfection – of one's existence to see God. The
divine vision has become less occluded throughout time from hints
and glimpses afforded the patriarchs and prophets – to the incarnation, and ultimately to the Kingdom of God. One should see God, but
one has not seen God. One cannot see God in this life, however; it is
only in the next. Once one goes through several degrees of progress,
one can see God, but seeing God is transformative; that is, it makes
one like God, making one immortal. Vision is deification.

One may not be able to see God and live, but one can die and see
God and live forever in that vision.

CONCLUSIONS

Irenaeus' *Against Heresies* at first glance appears to resist my tripartite
framework of vision more than any other Christian writer of the second and third centuries. While Irenaeus discusses what one sees, how
one sees, and who one sees, he subordinates all of these to *when* one
sees. If one expands my syntactic metaphor of subject (who sees), verb
(how one sees), and direct object (what is seen), then Irenaeus is most
interested in the verb's tense.

While partially working within the inheritance of Justin's exegesis,
much of the confusion of reading Irenaeus' work derives from the fact
that Irenaeus is actually more concerned with the status of the seer.
Yet instead of a particular person or type of person (e.g., gnostic, mystic, bishop, or even prophet), it is a dispensational era of vision. Who

sees, or the status of the seer, turns to when. Human beings, as a species, have to be prepared for the divine vision. While the prophets, especially Moses, sometimes break the pattern by occasionally encountering the Son or even the Father rather than the Spirit, they are necessary for the pattern, as they are the educators of humanity, preparing humanity for the incarnation – when all could physically see the Son – and the kingdom of God, when all will be able to see the Father. The status refers to the capacity of all humans at a given time rather than an elect few, per se, in a striking contrast to Irenaeus' slightly younger contemporary, Clement of Alexandria.[51]

How one sees God additionally takes on a different shape than it would in Clement or other more philosophically oriented Christian writers. Instead of the typical distinction between physical and intellectual vision, Irenaeus focuses on the primary means of vision allowed at a particular dispensational era. Again, how is related to when: spiritually in the past, adoptively in the present through the Son (though also a bit in the past with the prophets), and paternally and fully in the future. Past and present are "figurative" – figures of the future full vision of the Father.

Irenaeus, therefore, attempts to alleviate the exegetical tension between Exod. 33:20 and all the passages in which people saw God in several ways, explicitly or implicitly, through his use of Matt. 5:8: the future tense provided by this verse resolves past ambiguities. First, throughout, the past is always partial: either emphasizing hearing rather than seeing even to the point of being able to hear the Father; or having a partial, yet strangely embodied vision of the Son, which is a step beyond Justin's bodiless image; and foreseeing as a form of seeing. Second, Moses more uniquely foresaw the Son *and* then saw fully, suggesting that Moses' presence at the Mount of Transfiguration was the fulfillment of a promised vision, such as guaranteed in Exod. 33:21–3 or Num. 12:8. Third, one can see God and die, as John of Patmos did, and then be resurrected afterward. Finally, the future is a full, direct vision that transforms the seer. The limit of humanity becomes its threshold as the seer is transformed, becoming deified.

Though he prophesied first (*Dem.* 2.1.43), Moses, however, does not quite seem to be the measure of humanity for Irenaeus in the same way he is for other writers. For others, Moses is an exceptional human who is the model for other exceptional humans (e.g., Clement). For Irenaeus, by contrast, while he and other seers rise above the general human capabilities of their own time, they see only in the past what later humans see more clearly; their exceptional visions in the past become generalized in the present and the future. Moses, therefore, can become the model for general humanity rather than for exceptional humanity. Nevertheless, in Irenaeus' scheme, later humans can see more clearly because they stand on the shoulders of Moses and the prophets.

Irenaeus breaks many patterns and establishes new ones in a fairly confusing manner. As Annette Reed has noted, this is partly due to his shifting rhetorical contexts, as he writes against Valentinus, Marcion, and Jewish readings.[52] Like Justin and Clement, Irenaeus wrote against others. He was less an apologist and more a polemicist. He did not write to convert Greeks, per se, like Clement, though he did write a pedagogical manual (*Demonstration*); he did not write public letters to the emperor, like Justin. Instead, his lengthiest work that has come down to us and the one most cited among his successors was against rival Christians. His addressees are like-minded Christians in his own community, Rome, and elsewhere, and his purpose is to expose and refute rival Christian groups. This exposure was necessary, because, to Irenaeus' annoyance, the differences between his and other groups were hard to see at first glance. Justin had written against Marcion; Clement would critique several groups and individuals, though more haphazardly. Irenaeus attacked other Christians by grouping them into various schools, though Marcus' church, which was near his own, likely catalyzed his efforts. Valentinus, Marcion, and Jews emerge most of the time as his opponents – at least in the passages analyzed here – while Basilides and Cerinthus take a second place.

These rhetorical contexts help to sort out some of his confusion: he will more greatly emphasize the prophets' abilities to hear or see God when working against the followers of Marcion, Valentinus, Basilides, or others he paints under the broad umbrella of "gnostics." He ties the Israelite scriptures and the gospels together, by partly doing what Justin did, and having the Son/Logos speak to Moses and the prophets, but also by having the Father give the law and then "pour his compassions on us," contradicting Hebrews and Acts, the latter of which he would have held as authoritative at least. Both the Father and the Son both speak to Moses and in the Gospels. The shock is partly absorbed by his preference for auditory language in these passages. Yet, when he is countering "Jewish" readings, it is always the Logos/Son who speaks to the patriarchs and the prophets, because he is trying to oppose the idea that one could know or encounter the Father without the Son.

To counter Valentinus, Marcion, and Jewish readings all at once, however, would it not have been easier simply to have the Son do all the revealing, as Justin did? To completely break his own overarching progressive scheme, which largely relegates human interaction with the Father to the future, Irenaeus must have thought he would have benefited rhetorically when arguing against his Valentinian opponents. So why have the Father and not the Son reveal the law in a rhetorical context opposing Valentinians? Valentinus referred to the primal principle of all things as Father: the creator of the world, who also gave the law, was a deficient being; he was not the Father. But this Father did send Jesus and, through him, compassion on the world. When Irenaeus has the Father reveal the law, and then have compassion on the world through the gospel, he ties together what Valentinians would differentiate. I somewhat doubt that he would score this rhetorical point directly; he is writing to his own community. The point, therefore, was to construct a counter-scheme to Valentinus to convince his own community of Valentinus' error, perhaps even trying to keep them in his own community; that is, like the "freelance ritual experts" before him, he was competing for followers, as his comments about people in his own church leaving for Marcus' suggest as a real possibility (*A.H.* 1.13–20, esp. 1.13.7).[53]

Yet, I do not think this accounts for his emphasis on time and dispensation, that is, those larger structuring, organizing categories upon which he scaffolded his theology. It accounts for his incoherence more than his coherence. His work, while highly polemical, is also constructive, building a comprehensive theological and ecclesiological edifice. His obsession with order, succession, and unity likely springs from three sources: his newfound leadership position within the Lugdunum community after its previous bishop died, the pressures from non-Christians that often burst into violence, persecution, and death within his own community in Lugdunum and elsewhere throughout the empire, and what he perceived as a disorderly variety of Christianities that he saw around him – that is, his local Christian competition.

On the one hand, the larger systematic mythopoetic theologies he encountered among his Christian opponents inspired him to create a structured theological edifice of his own. In this macroscopic level, he resembles those he verbally scourges. At the same time, his larger framing may be part of a broader historical transition in the status of Christian apologists and polemicists from "freelance experts" to bishops. In fact, Irenaeus embodies this transition, moving like earlier apologists, polemicists, and teachers to Rome from the eastern Mediterranean before, for whatever reason, continuing on to Lugdunum, where he became bishop.

Except for Theophilus, Irenaeus is the first major figure considered here who was not a "freelance expert." Though Wendt discusses him in this context, suggesting he has much more in common with the "heretics" he disparages, when placed in his original second-century Roman and Gallic environment, he nevertheless largely eludes this categorization, and Wendt herself clearly signals her discomfort with labelling him as such.[54] As a bishop, his status was no longer peripheral, though he likely saw Lugdunum as peripheral in his broader mental map of the civilized world.[55] Yet even as a bishop seeking greater communal and theological structure, he continued to interact with the "freelancers." At the same time, his rivals were also becoming more socially organized; he casts his eyes upon those groups which, like his own, had attained a certain level of organization, which Marcus and definitely Marcion's followers had with their network of churches.

As a bishop, he did not call for obedience, per se, like Ignatius had and fourth-century bishops would, but for commonality in teaching and practice across geographical divides, sometimes trying to ameliorate differences between Christian groups rather than to exacerbate them – though he did that too. As recent work on Irenaeus has illustrated, his ideal bishop was not the fourth-century figure. He was primarily a teacher, the representative head of the "school" of Christians within each city to which others could go to get the basic teaching of that school.[56] His apostolic succession was, in the words of one scholar, those who taught what the apostles taught, rather than being what the original apostles were.[57] In the words of another, he was more of a "foreign secretary," representing all the churches within a single city to the outside world and having the right to teach.[58] In this way, his episcopacy transitions between the two points of "freelance expert" and the very different fourth-century episcopacy, for whom the bishop was who the original apostles were.

He, moreover, became the bishop of Lugdunum (Lyons) under very difficult circumstances. Many in his own community were killed in mob violence and executed in the arena by the ruling authorities. The previous bishop died due to this persecution. In these circumstances of rivalry and persecution, Irenaeus sought organizational and theological structure. His leadership position, his personal connections in Rome and Smyrna, his rivalries, and his own vulnerability swirl together, encouraging his emphasis on apostolic succession, creedal clarity, and developing a canon – that is, creating a self-identified network of churches in communication with one another for mutual aid. In short, Irenaeus sought to provide an answer to the schemes that he opposed and ultimately mirrored in a sweeping superstructure of historical dispensation of progressive revelation, in which God was partially revealed, seen, or heard in the past, greater in the present, and greatest in the future, leading to the ultimate vision of God the Father that transformed the human seer into the divine.

Clement of Alexandria
(c. 150–215 CE)

Moses as the Model Gnostic Visionary

About the same time that Ireneaus became bishop of Lyons (c. 180 CE), Clement arrived in Alexandria from Athens. He was approximately thirty years old at the time, and he remained until 202 CE, a time when a series of local persecutions against Christians erupted in Egypt and North Africa. He seems to have written all his works, except the last few books of the *Miscellanies* (*Stromateis*), while residing in Alexandria. The Alexandria he dwelled in was a bustling city, where people, ideas, and religions met, melded, and clashed, yet without the previously sizable Jewish contingent of the city and with a small, yet growing, Christian community.[1] The Jewish population had been decimated by the Diaspora Revolt in 115–117 CE, while Christians began to increase in numbers.[2] Yet we find not only Christians, but many different types of Christians. This was the city that cradled Valentinus, Basilides, and, after Clement, Origen. Clement developed his thought by opposing and appropriating various elements of Valentinian and Basilidean thought, as he, like them, would use the term "Gnostic" to describe his brand of Christianity.[3] Traditionally, scholars going all the way back to Eusebius of Caesarea thought that Clement taught in the catechetical school, while, more recently, scholars have challenged this to suggest that he may have taught more independently, attracting his own students.[4]

Standing between Philo and Origen, Clement of Alexandria seems like a transitional figure.[5] In him we find the stamp of Philo's "Middle Platonic" readings of the Bible, especially the Pentateuch,[6] and the germinating seeds that would flower not only in Origen, but in more systematic form in Pseudo-Dionysius. While he resembles his fellow

Alexandrians, differentiating sensory and intellectual vision, allowing the former for at least Christ's incarnation and some of the Old Testament theophanies and preferring the latter as more proper to the Logos as God's own Mind, he also draws upon more contemporary developments found in Justin and Irenaeus. For Clement's preliminary discussions in the *Exhortation to the Greeks* (*Protrepticus*) and the *Instructor* (*Paedagogue*), he appropriates and develops Justin's insight of Old Testament theophanies being Christophanies, uniting Moses' legislation and the Gospel under a single revealing voice of the Logos. Yet in Clement's *Miscellanies* (*Stromateis*), he turns to Moses as the model gnostic,[7] who achieved the unachievable vision of the invisible and inaccessible God, locked in uninterrupted intercourse with the divine, due to a combination of purification and perfection of the heart/soul and the divine assistance of the Logos, who is the great high priest.[8] As such, Clement of Alexandria activates all three hermeneutical strategies of vision: he distinguishes between visible and invisible objects of vision, differentiates between types of seeing, and considers the status of the seer.

THE "OTHER" CLEMENT: PROPHECY AND THE CELESTIAL HIERARCHY

While much of this discussion will focus on the traditional Clementine material – *Exhortation to the Greeks* (*Protrepticus*), *Instructor* (*Paedagogue*), and *Miscellanies* (*Stromateis*) – Bogdan G. Bucur has demonstrated how one gets a different reading when focusing on the "other Clement"; that is, by reading his "lesser" treatises – the *Excerpts from Theodotus* (*Excerpta ex Theodoto*), *Selections of the Prophets* (*Eclogae Propheticae*), and the *Sketches* (*Adumbrationes*) – one finds a different view of divine vision that Bucur argues derives more directly from Jewish apocalyptic tendencies.[9] Bucur's work discusses a wide range of issues related to pneumatology, but it is his discussion of prophecy by an "angelomorphic spirit" that concerns us most immediately.

First, Bucur notes that there are two basic functions for the spirit in Clement's writings that Clement interchanges frequently with the Logos: prophetic inspiration and indwelling of Christian believers. If one simply reads the great trinity of Clementine Writings – *Exhortation*, the *Instructor*, the *Miscellanies* – one misses the means by which this works. That is, Clement has an elaborate divine "hierarchy" or vertical "spiritual taxonomy" (*Exc.* 10, 11, 27; *Ecl.* 56–7), which he claims he inherited from the "elders."[10] The hierarchy starts with the Logos, who is the "face of God" (perhaps a hint of Exod. 33:20 lies in the background),[11] then the seven *protoctists* (πρωτόκτιστοι, "first created ones"),[12] who are the seven eyes of the Lord (Zech. 4:10; Rev. 5:6), the archangels, and finally the angels.[13] Even if a prophecy derives from a vision from the Logos, that does not mean the Logos delivered it directly, but employed all of the resources of the hierarchy. Bucur quotes and translates *Ecl.* 51.1–52.1:

> The heavens proclaim the glory of God (Ps. 18:2). By "heavens" are designated in manifold ways both "the heavens" pertaining to distance and cycle, and the proximate operation of the first-created angels, which pertains to covenant. For the covenants were wrought by the visitation of angels, namely those upon Adam, Noah, Abraham, and Moses. For, moved by the Lord, the first-created angels worked in the angels that are close to the prophets, as they are telling the "glory of God," namely the covenants. But the works accomplished by the angels on earth also came about for "the glory of God," through the first-created angels. So, [the following] are called "heavens": in a primary sense, the Lord; but then also the first-created; and with them also the holy persons before the Law, as well as the patriarchs, and Moses and the prophets, and finally the apostles. (emphasis Bucur's)[14]

At first glance, this interpretation appears to be a throwback to the New Testament, where the covenant was mediated by angels (Gal. 3:19; Heb. 2:2; Acts 7:30; 7:38; 7:53), yet the understandings of "mediated" here are more complex. In his explanation of this passage, Bucur writes:

> Prophecy occurs when the Logos moves the first rank of the *protoctists*, and this movement is transmitted from one level of the angelic hierarchy down to the next. The lowest angelic rank, which is the one closest to the human world, transmits the "movement" to the prophet. Through a sort of telescoping effect, the first move – the Logos – is simultaneously far removed from the effect of prophecy and immediately present.[15]

In this telescoping effect, the prophecy is identified with the "original mover" – whether the Logos, or an archangel like Michael – even though carried out by a lower-ranking angel.[16] This is an effective way of explaining the equivocation of the Pentateuch and Judges on who is speaking to the Patriarchs, Prophets, and Judges – the Lord, the angel of the Lord, God, the angel of God, or a "man." The answer is *all of the above*. The Logos speaks *through* the mediating angel; the angel does not merely speak on the Logos' behalf.[17] This idea, however, is located clearly only in the *Selections*, though it might appear in veiled form in the *Miscellanies*.[18] As Bucur states, "In this light, it becomes clear how Clement understands the traditional statements about the Logos speaking in the prophets ἁγίῳ πνεύματι, as in *Protr* 1:5:3, quoted above: the prophet experienced the presence and message of the Logos by receiving the 'energy' by the proximate angel."[19] Or, as he notes in a different passage, whether a patriarch or prophet saw either an angel or the Logos is a false binary: he saw the "Logos in the angelic spirit."[20] It is, as Bucur would say, "mediated immediacy."

While not directly discussing Moses, Bucur's discussion of Clement's lesser-known treatises provides a comprehensive theory of prophecy that includes Moses, both indicating what is possible for the prophet and implying the prophet's status in the overall "hierarchy" or "spiritual taxonomy" of being. Moses, the patriarchs, and other prophets encountered the Logos through angels in a "telescoping effect." The "spirit" of the Logos was present in the spirit of the angel, passing the message from higher to lower being in the long chain of existence. This much is explicit. What is implied in this scheme is that the prophet is the pinnacle of humanity, as the highest level of the human hierarchy receives messages from the lowest level of the angelic hierarchy.[21] While Moses and the prophets never encounter God directly, but encounter the Logos through the angel, they still represent humanity at its pinnacle.

JUSTIN'S MODEL AS PREPARATORY: SEEING THE "FACE" OF GOD

In his major works, Clement largely assumes Justin's view of Old Testament theophanies as the preincarnate Logos, partly in the *Exhortation to the Greeks* and throughout the *Instructor*.[22] These works are preparatory; they exhort the non-Christian and educate new Christians, keeping the advanced mysteries for the *Miscellanies*.[23]

In the *Exhortation to the Greeks*, Clement cites Matt. 11:27 – a favourite verse for Origen, among other early Christians, regarding one's (in)ability to see and know God – to argue that the only way to see and know God is through Christ. Clement writes at the end of the first chapter:

> For the gates of the Word being intellectual, are opened by the key of faith. No one knows God but the Son, and he to whom the Son shall reveal Him (Matt. 11.27). And I know well that he who has opened the door hitherto shut, will afterwards reveal within; and will show that we could not have known before, had we not entered in by Christ, through whom alone God is beheld. (*Prot.* 1.10.3)[24]

Christ is the means by which one sees and knows God, the two being largely equivalent, as "seeing" is – as with most Platonists – a metaphor for knowledge and comprehension. Nonetheless, a hint of something else is dropped here: the beginning of knowledge is faith; the end of faith is knowledge. That is, the beginner starts with faith and hope and works toward *gnosis*. Nonetheless, the true gnostic is something that will be uncovered – and then only in part – only in the *Miscellanies*. This combination of faith and knowledge to map the progress of the gnostic soul is also a polemical two-edged sword. Lilla notes that the combination of faith and knowledge – *pistis* and *gnosis* – on the one hand opposes philosophers and figures like Valentinus and Basilides, who stress *gnosis* and see little of importance in faith (*pistis*). Indeed, Clement says as much in *Strom.* 5.1.[25] On the other hand, it also stands against ordinary Christians who only stress faith (*pistis*) and do not seek higher *gnosis*.[26]

Clement, moreover, makes this comment after his discussion of the pre-existence of Christ among the patriarchs and the prophets. It explains Clement's reasoning: since one can only see/know God through Christ, and the patriarchs, Moses, and the prophets saw, heard, or somehow gained knowledge of God, they must have encountered Christ. A little earlier in *Prot.* 1, Clement writes that Christ had always revealed himself through prophecies and had always exhorted humans to salvation. His salvific exhortations were the signs and wonders in Egypt by the bush and cloud. Indeed, he was the one who spoke at the burning bush (1.1). As with Justin, the preincarnate Christ often appears by non-anthropomorphic means, since he was the pillar of cloud in the desert. He was the one who spoke to Moses, Elijah, and Isaiah, and now this is the same Lord who speaks to you. The use of the second-person address to the audience is arresting and largely lacking in second-century materials, though more common in late-antique homilies; just as Christ spoke as fire and cloud to Moses, Elijah, and Isaiah, so he now speaks to *you*, Clement's purported audience being "the Greeks."[27] The theophanic moment is not just on Sinai or in the distant past; it is now and always – an interpretive manoeuvre Clement shares with as unlikely an ally as Tertullian. As one is exhorted, guided, and initiated, one can hear and, ultimately, see exactly as the prophets – and especially Moses – did.

Having exhorted, Clement then guides or teaches in the *Pedagogue* or *Instructor*. More accurately, Clement familiarizes the reader with the divine educator, who will teach what no human instructor can. The eponymous Pedagogue or Instructor is the Logos. It is here that we find Justin's influence most extensive and expanded. The Instructor provided for people in the wilderness, appeared to Abraham, and wrestled with Jacob. Regarding Jacob's vision, in which he calls the place "Face of God," Clement writes: "the face of God is the Word by whom God is manifested and made known" (*Paed*. 1.7). In turn, the Instructor teaches Moses how to become an instructor to the Israelites (Αὐτὸς γοῦν οὗτος καὶ τὸν Μωσέα διδάσκει παιδαγωγεῖν) when Moses saw God "face to face" (πρόσωπον πρὸς πρόσωπον; *Paed*. 1.7). This resembles Moses' role in Philo's depiction of him as archetypal, impressed with the divine and, thereby, providing a model for others to follow. Here, however, the stamp upon Moses is Christ. Moreover, though this could definitely make for an interesting twist in the line "no one can see my face and live" – and thus Christ is usually interpreted either as God's backside or the "rock" where Moses stood[28] – Clement focuses more on the "face-to-face" encounter between Moses and God. Christ must be that face that spoke to Moses face to face.[29]

This is a point Clement returns to in *Strom*. 5.6, where he again says that the Son is the Father's face in terms of the incarnation, "being the revealer of the Father's character to the five senses by clothing himself with flesh."[30] Yet in the preincarnate theophanies, the angel of the LORD is equated with the Word, who is Christ. Most significantly, this means that the law was not given by Moses, but by the Logos through Moses, the servant of the Logos (*Paed*. 1.7; cf. Heb. 3:5).[31] That is, not only are the law and Gospel from the same God, but from the same messenger from God or same aspect of deity: the Logos. As was also true for Irenaeus, Christ does not just fulfill the law (Matt. 5:17–20), but is the law's originator. Indeed, the same

Instructor who speaks to Ezekiel, Moses, Isaiah, Jeremiah, etc., speaks in the Gospel (*Paed.* 1.9, 11).

While much of this can be found in previous and contemporary literature – such as Justin's and Irenaeus' works – in a more novel passage, Clement uses the preincarnate Logos as the angel of the burning bush to illustrate the unity of revelation:

> For when the Almighty Lord of the universe began to legislate by the Word, and wishes His power to be manifested to Moses, a god-like vision of light that had assumed a shape was shown him in the burning bush (the bush is a thorny plant); but when the Word ended the giving of the Law and his stay with humans, the Lord was again mystically crowned with thorn. On his departure from this world to the place whence he came, he repeated the beginning of his old descent, in order that the word beheld at first in the bush, and afterwards taken up crowned by the thorn, might show the whole to be the work of one power, he himself being one, the son of the Father, who is truly one, the beginning and the end of time. (*Paed.* 2.8)[32]

The appearance of the Logos in the burning bush of thorns marks the beginning of the giving the law, which finds its completion in the bookend event with Christ crucified with a crown of thorns. Christ, therefore, is beginning and end: of law, of salvation history, of time. Yet in Clement's pedagogical Christianity, this unity of salvation and time is for instruction. Instruction is for transformation and perfection into the very image and likeness of God: that is, transformed into the Logos itself.

Indeed, this metamorphosis of the human into God's Logos appears in another transformative passage, in which Clement again invokes the pre-existing Logos to illustrate the Instructor's ultimate pedagogical purpose:

> The view I take is, that He himself formed the human of the dust, regenerated him by water; and made him grow by his Spirit; and trained him by his word to adoption and salvation, directing him by sacred precepts; in order that, transforming earth-bound man into a holy and heavenly being by his advent, he might fulfill to the utmost that divine utterance, "Let us make man in our own image and likeness." And, in truth, Christ became the perfect real-

ization of what God spoke; and the rest of humanity is conceived as being created merely in his image. (*Paed.* 1.12)[33]

At first glance, this passage strongly resembles Irenaeus', when he traced the origins, development, and perfection of humans and humanity as a whole in his sweeping account of the dispensations of vision (*A.H.* 4.38.3). Clement, however, makes a slightly different point with his pedagogical model of human growth and perfection. Firstly, the Logos is not just the legislator, but also the creator: the one who made humans out of dust. But, though they were made in the image of God, they do not share God's likeness *yet*; the only one with the image and likeness is Christ. But the transformative moment is Christ's incarnation, turning the dusty image into a heavenly being, fulfilling what Clement takes to be a prophetic utterance: "Let us make man in our own image and likeness."[34] What does it mean to be turned into God's image and likeness? How does it occur? How does vision relate to transformation into God: is it the catalyst or the result? Does the vision transform or does one have to be transformed to attain the vision? Clement provides the answers in the *Miscellanies*.

TO SEE GOD AND DIE:
MOSES AND THE UNINTERRUPTED DIVINE VISION

Clement's *Miscellanies* is a patchwork quilt of reflection for advanced Christians, whom Clement labels "gnostics."[35] It may be obfuscating, needing oral instruction to understand it fully, an oral instruction that Clement claims descends from the apostles to the few (*Strom.* 6.7).[36] Toward the beginning of the work, Clement lays down the gauntlet by citing Moses in Exodus: God cannot be seen, grasped, or known by human beings:

Whence Moses, persuaded that God is not to be known by human wisdom, said, "Show me your glory," and pressed to enter into the thick darkness where God's voice was – that is, into the inaccessible and invisible ideas respecting Existence. For God is not in darkness or in place, but above both space and time, and qualities of objects. Wherefore neither is he at any time in a part, either as containing or as contained, either by limitation or by section. (*Strom* 2.2)[37]

The dark cloud represents a tradition of radical transcendence inherited most proximately from Philo and providing the groundwork for Gregory of Nyssa and Pseudo-Dionysius, both of whom also used Moses' entrance into the dark cloud – or thick darkness – as the preeminent example of the unknowability of God and, thereby, highlighted Moses as the paradigmatic mystic.[38] Indeed, the dark cloud, where God was (Exod. 19:16–25; 24:15–18), is not exactly where God was; rather, it was where, as Clement adds, God's "voice" was. The dark cloud represents God's transcendence of space and time: God is nowhere and everywhere all at once, the dark matter of reality. Transcendent, the dark cloud represents God's inaccessibility; yet, paradoxically, Moses entered it. Darkness, furthermore, represents God's invisibility. Unknowable, transcendent, inaccessible, and invisible, the dark cloud proved a polyvalent symbol, into which Clement would fold a variety of sources to demonstrate God's ineffability and incomprehensibility. In 5.12 alone, he cites Plato, Moses, Orpheus, Paul, Plato (again), the Gospels, Psalms, Matthew, Solon, Empedocles, John, and Luke-Acts.[39] Yet Moses pressed to enter it not by human wisdom represented by all these Greek authors, but by requesting divine aid.

Having established God's radical transcendence and complete inaccessibility and unknowability through the example of Moses' entrance into inaccessible ideas, how is one to proceed? How, in other words, did Moses paradoxically enter into the inaccessible and invisible ideas? Ideas – in the Platonic sense – are key. One can, as a good Platonist, see/know only by the intellect. Clement writes, "Reason, the governing principle, remaining unmoved and guiding the soul, is called its pilot. For access to the Immutable is obtained by a truly immutable means. Thus Abraham was stationed before the Lord, and approaching spoke. And to Moses it is said, 'But do you stand there with me'" (*Strom.* 2.11).[40] Standing stands for immutability, a quality of the divine. As Abraham's and Moses' immutability attracts like, one is drawn toward God and God's immutability.

A good student, moreover, will recall one's preliminary studies from the *Exhortation* and *Instructor*: the Logos, God's Word and Reason is the key for using one's own reason. Clement reminds,

For he who hopes, as he who believes, sees intellectual objects and future things with the mind. If then we affirm that something is just, and affirm it to be good, and we also say that truth is something, yet we have never seen any of such objects with our eyes, but with our mind alone. Now the Word of God says, "I am the truth." The Word is then to be contemplated with the mind. "Do you aver," it was said, "that there are any true philosophers?" "Yes," said I, "those who love to contemplate the truth." In the *Phaedrus* also, Plato, speaking of the truth, shows it as an idea. Now an idea is a conception of God; and this the barbarians have termed the Word of God ... When the Word becomes flesh, it is so he might be seen. (*Strom* 5.3.16.1–3, 5)[41]

The Word is the idea – in the Platonic sense – of God. In biblical terms, the Logos is the image and likeness of God. If God can be seen through the Word, as noted already in the *Exhortation* and the *Instructor*, then at Christ's incarnation God became physically visible to the senses. But this is not all. While Irenaeus and Tertullian would stop here, perceiving it to be the fullest vision possible of God through the Son or Logos – at the incarnation and especially at the Transfiguration – for Clement, it is but a step. Even the Word, who is sometimes visible, whether in preincarnate theophanies or through incarnate form as Jesus, is more properly an object of contemplation with the mind than with physical eyes, as truth – as he says, "I am the truth" – is something to be grasped with the mind's vision and not the eyes of the body (cf. *Exc.* 10.5).[42]

In a dense chapter (*Strom.* 5.11), Clement brings these strands – God's incomprehensibility and inaccessibility and the Word's noetic visual assistance – together to illustrate how to negatively ascend to God.[43] In it, he draws a similar line of inquiry as Plato's *Symposium*, where Diotima teaches Socrates to abstract from material things to attain knowledge of immaterial ideas (esp. 210A–211D) and, again, provides a germ for Pseudo-Dionysius centuries later.[44] That is, Clement seeks to abstract from material things what God is not in order to transcend those things with the mind and ascend to "cast ourselves into the greatness of Christ, and thence advance into the immensity by holiness, we may reach somehow to the conception of the Almighty, knowing not what he is, but what he is not."[45] Moving beyond space, time, name, and conception, beyond even one's own intellect, one transcends oneself in a manner similar to how God transcends, as illustrated by the dark cloud.

Unfortunately, at this particular place, Clement remains evasive concerning how exactly one reaches this exalted level. Nonetheless, the context of *Strom.* 5.11 – and even Book 5 as a whole – help. The

entire passage is infused with Stoic morality. As one abstracts negatively to God, one also divests from the body, its passions, its lusts, and
its frivolities. Since humans differ from the divine in several different
ways, mostly related to human mortality and the embodied condition, one draws closer to God by denying the body and its desires,
while adorning the soul with virtues and engaging in philosophical
and scriptural investigation, the latter two often equated in Clement's
writings.[46] This, then, is a true sacrifice of the soul to God – not those
physical animal sacrifices held in temples.

Nonetheless, even this important combination of denying the body
and its passions and lusts, and cultivation of contemplation and philosophical investigation, is not enough. One still needs help. Drawing
several biblical passages together, Clement repeats Moses' request for
God to reveal God's Glory to him, "intimating most clearly that God
is not capable of being taught by man, or expressed in speech, but to
be known only by his own power."[47] As already intimated by the
Instructor, divine knowledge is beyond human learning and striving;
there must be a divine instructor who initiates.[48] Nonetheless, with
divine aid it is attainable. Continuing in *Strom.* 5.11:

> For the region of God is hard to attain; which Plato called the
> region of ideas, having learned from Moses that it was a place that
> contained all things universally. But it is seen by Abraham afar off,
> rightly, because of his being in the realms of generation, and he is
> forthwith initiated by the angel [δι' ἀγγέλου προσεχῶς
> μυσταγωγεῖται]. Thence says the apostle: "Now we see as through a
> glass, but then face to face," by those sole pure and incorporeal
> applications of the intellect. "In reasoning it is possible to divine
> respecting God [δυνατὸν δὲ κἂν τῷ διαλέγεσθαι τὸ
> καταμαντεύεσθαι τοῦ θεοῦ], if one attempt without any of the sens-
> es, by reason [διὰ τοῦ λόγου], to reach what is individual; and do
> not quit the sphere of existences, till, rising up to things which
> transcend it, he apprehends by the intellect itself that which is
> good, moving in the very confines of the world of thought,"[49]
> according to Plato ... And since the gnostic Moses does not cir-
> cumscribe within space him that cannot be circumscribed, he set
> up no image in the temple to be worshipped; showing that God
> was invisible, and incapable of being circumscribed.
> (5.11.73.3–74.2, 74.4)[50]

Beginning with the Hellenistic Jewish apologetic trope that Plato stole from Moses, which explains why figures like Philo, Theophilus, or Clement himself can claim that Moses and Plato say the same things, Clement proceeds with an observation about Abraham.[51] Abraham reminds us of our limitations. He stands "afar off" from the region of God, which Clement identifies with Plato's ideas,[52] due to being in the realm of generation; that is, he remains in this physical world, where things are born, grow old, and die.[53] Yet all is not lost, since, while in this world, Abraham received angelic aid.

While limited by this realm and needing divine aid, one again proceeds to transcend the senses; moreover, the intellectual apprehension must be pure and incorporeal. That favourite Pauline verse wherein now we see partly through a pane of glass – seeing darkly – but later face to face, which Clement will return to repeatedly, suggests something about this ability to transcend our corporeal senses through a pure intellect: it raises the question of whether one can reach such purity of mind while remaining in the body? Or when can one see God "face to face," a key phrase that combines this Pauline verse with Moses' face-to-face conversations? When will this purity be attained?

Abraham's "far-off" vision puts one in an ambiguous place: he can see, but only in a limited way, also indicated by the repeated use of Paul's "now in a glass" and "then face to face." While God can be seen only by the intellect reflecting upon the Logos, itself the intellect of God, the full vision can occur only upon one's own perfection – a process of purification one undergoes one's entire life, completed upon one's death (*Strom.* 5.1):

> For bound in this earthly body we apprehend the objects of sense by means of the body; but we grasp intellectual objects by means of the logical faculty itself. But if one expect to apprehend all things by the senses, he has fallen far from the truth. Spiritually, therefore, the apostle writes respecting the knowledge of God, "For now we see as through a glass, but then face to face." For the vision of the truth is given but to few. Accordingly, Plato says in the *Epinomis*, "I do not say that it is possible for all to be blessed and happy; only a few. While we live, I pronounce this to be the case. But there is a good hope that after death I shall attain all." To the same effect is what we find in Moses: "No man shall see my face and live." For it is evident that no one during the period of life has

been able to apprehend God clearly. But "the pure in heart shall
see God," when they arrive at the final perfection. (5.1.7.4–7) [54]

First, as one would expect, Clement contrasts forms of apprehension
between sensory and logical, based upon the type of object: physical
and intellectual. Second, the quotation from Paul of now darkly and
then face to face, which he cites again in *Strom* 5.11, sets up a dichotomy between current and future abilities. It is a comment he drops
momentarily, only to pick up again at the end of the quotation, where
he cites Matt. 5:8. The point is that, if Paul could not yet see clearly,
Clement will definitely not say that he – or any other living human –
could in this life, yet the quotation from Matt. 5:8 indicates a future
possibility of a clear vision. Nonetheless, this subtle point is submerged for the moment to note, third, citing Plato and Moses, only a
very few have this ability to see God and none can see God *clearly*
while alive. At this point, he reiterates the difference between current
and future abilities: while living, only a few can see God (Moses, Paul,
and perhaps a few others), and even they do not see God clearly; in
the afterlife, the pure in heart will see clearly. In this compact passage,
Clement has compressed all three of the major strategies of accounting for divine vision: differentiating object seen (Logos versus Father),
how one can see (senses versus intellect), and the status of the seer (the
few who are pure of heart).

In a later chapter (*Strom* 5.12), Clement solidifies his point that
divine vision is for the few, that the pure in heart are limited in number, again using Moses' entrance into the dark cloud to do so:

"For both is it a difficult task to discover the Father and Maker of
this universe; and having found him, it is impossible to declare
him to all. For this is by no means capable of expression, like the
other subjects of instruction," says the truth-loving Plato. For he
that had heard very well that the all-wise Moses, ascending the
mount for holy contemplation [ἁγίαν θεωρίαν], to the summit of
intellectual objects [ἐπὶ τὴν κορυφὴν τῶν νοητῶν], necessarily com-
mands that the whole people do not go up with him. And when
the scripture says, "Moses entered into the thick darkness where
God was," this shows to those capable of understanding, that God
is invisible and beyond expression by words. And "the darkness" –
which is, in truth, the unbelief and ignorance of the multitude –
obstructs the gleam of truth. (5.12.78.1–3) [55]

Clement returns to the moment when Moses entered the dark cloud, but does so to express a different point. It is a place of contemplation of intellectual objects, indeed of the summit of those intellectual objects. Since the singular God transcends intelligibility, and these objects are in the plural, they are part of the realm of ideas; having reached the summit, he looks beyond such intellectual objects to that which is more difficult to express: the indescribable God.

Transfixed upon this moment of Moses' ascent, Clement performs three interpretive operations. First, he reiterates the apologetic note that Plato borrowed his ideas from Moses: in particular, that God is difficult to find, and the experience of one's divine encounter is impossible to express to another person. Second, Clement subtly substitutes the invisibility and inexpressibility of God for the summit of intellectual things; it is, indeed, beyond the intellectual objects. Finally, Clement's main point in this passage is that it is a place attained by the few, the gnostics; that is, those who have knowledge. The multitude are ignorant, and, therefore, cannot attain that place.[56] Darkness no longer represents only the incomprehensibility of God, though it still does, as he subsequently again ties this with Paul's visions (2 Corinthians 12),[57] but also the ignorance of the masses. Indeed, divine vision here is less about theology as it was in *Strom* 2.2, and more about anthropology, less about what is seen or even how one sees, and more about who can see.[58] Moses is the true gnostic, and, interestingly, the true theologian, who ascends into the thick darkness and discerns hidden truths of revelation (*Strom.* 6.15). Prophecy and the theological act of interpretation merge in the person of Moses through vision (ἐποπτεία and θεωρία).[59] As such, Moses becomes the prototype of the contemplative investigator of God, a God who expresses himself in writing (*Strom.* 5.1); that is, the theological interpreter of scripture, such as Clement himself.[60]

The quotation from Plato in *Strom* 5.1, however, has a slight ambiguity: that is, is it that only a few can attain in this life and many more can in the next, or that only a few can achieve such a vision even in the afterlife? Clement's own immediate interpretation is that, while corporeal – in this life – the vision is not fully clear, but that Matt 5:8 (the pure in heart will see God) retains a promise of future post-corporeal perfection necessary for a clear vision. Cleansing or purification of the mind is necessity for the undazzled or keen vision (*Strom.* 5.4), an image borrowed from Plato's "Allegory of the Cave" (*Rep.* 518A).[61]

Again, purification and perfection result from the mutual instantiation of faith and knowledge within the soul, which one continues to
cultivate through moral rectitude and obeying God's commandments, and through education, contemplation, and philosophical
investigation of truth; that is, of the God who speaks in writing (5.1).
This education allows one to remove the obstacles of vision, such as
passions, and develop an inclination for the good. The combination
of obedience to God's commandments, including parts of the Pentateuch, with divine contemplation – that is, contemplating the God
who gave Moses the commandments (see *Strom.* 2.10.46–7), further
differentiates Clement's gnostic from Basilides and Valentinus, for
whom the god who gave the commandments was a lower being.[62] As
a result of this purification and through the grace of the Logos, one
attains perfection, becoming equal to the angels (*Strom.* 6.13; cf. Matt.
22:5; Luke 20:36). Purification and perfection, then, allow one to
become a true gnostic.

For Clement, however, the model gnostic is none other than Moses,
who achieved such a vision in this life (*Strom.* 6.12). Largely following
Philo, Clement writes that Moses' soul was glorified due to his uninterrupted intercourse with God; his soul, stamped with the divine
through converse with the divine, in turn was stamped upon his body,
creating a radiance on his face (Exod. 34:29–35).[63] Using Moses as a
model, Clement expects a similar process for all true gnostics, whose
contemplation of God, prophetic activities, and even governance leads
to intellectual radiance and assimilation into God. Moses provides a
glimpse of human possibilities, including perfection (see Matt. 5:48),
but it is also extremely rare. Indeed, Clement continually qualifies
human/divine interactions with what is permitted by our human
nature (e.g., *Strom.* 6.12).

Moses in the dark cloud, therefore, set the problem (God's
unknowability, invisibility, and radical transcendence in *Strom* 2:2),
the solution (divine aid, purity, and perfection), and, thereby, the
model, so that one can see how one can also achieve this state. But
there is the same tension, since the Moses examples suggest he
achieved this status in this life, while Clement indicates that very few
of even those who follow his example will achieve Moses' vision in
this life; they will likely achieve this state of complete perfection and
purity of heart upon death. Or, having achieved perfect purity of
heart, a gnostic will be granted the impossible divine vision.

Subsequently in the *Miscellanies*, Clement offers a different metaphor for the path of ascent: the pattern of the tabernacle that God revealed to Moses is a cosmic map. In *Strom.* 5.6, Clement offers an elaborate interpretation of the pattern of the tabernacle that Moses saw on the mountain (Exodus 25–31) and the Day of Atonement (Leviticus 16), while exegeting Ezek. 44:9, 25–7. He depends strongly on Philo's analysis of the tabernacle, but offers his own synthesis.[64]

As Itter notes, the gnostic soul first ascends through seven spheres and reaches the ogdoad at the outer portion of the Tabernacle. The seven circuits are temporal as well as spatial or ontological – they represent the first seven days, as one moves on then to the eighth day; that is, the Lord's Day. The first seven circuits differentiate those who believe from those who do not believe. Indeed, much like the dark cloud, Clement uses the tabernacle to differentiate various levels of worthiness of proximity to God, culminating in divine vision (ἐποπτεία).

The high priest, being pure of heart (see *Strom.* 4.25), upon entering the Holy of Holies, represents the gnostic soul's ascent to heaven. At the first level, the gnostic soul ascends to the five pillars of the Tabernacle and their covering, representing the five senses and the sensory world respectively. The four colours of the covering represent the four elements. This covering keeps ordinary people back, differentiating the gnostic soul from other souls. At the second stage, the gnostic soul passes the altar of incense, representing the earth, and, at the third stage, the Menorah, which represents the seven planets. Next, the gnostic soul encounters the four pillars of the inner veil, representing the four covenants and four letters of the divine name. The veil divides the sensible and intelligible worlds; in other words, at this point, one enters the intelligible world, represented itself by the ark of the covenant. Moreover, the robe of the high priest also has cosmic significance, with seven stars representing the seven branches of the Menorah, the seven planets, and the accomplished seven stages of the soul. It also represents the four elements. This is why he must take it off when he enters the holy of holies – putting on a white linen robe to move beyond these elements and planets and enter the world of ideas. The high priest's purification activities, then, allow him to see God face to face (*Strom.* 5.39).[65]

Finally, the promised ultimate vision of the pure in heart comes up again in *Strom* 7.3, a counterpart to *Strom* 5.1 and Clement's ultimate statement of the furthest potentialities of the gnostic soul:

But I affirm that gnostic souls, that surpass in the grandeur of contemplation [τῇ μεγαλοπρεπείᾳ τῆς θεωρίας] the mode of life of each of the holy ranks, among whom the blessed abodes of the gods are allotted by distribution, reckoned holy among the holy, transferred entire from among the entire, reaching places better than the better places, embracing the divine vision (τὴν θεωρίαν ἀσπαζομένας τὴν θείαν) not in mirrors or by means of mirrors, but in the transcendently clear and absolutely pure insatiable vision which is the privilege of intensely loving souls, holding festival through endless ages, remain honoured with the identity of all excellence. Such is the vision (θεωρία) attainable by the "pure in heart." This is the function of the gnostic, who has been perfected, to have converse with God through the great high priest, being made like the Lord, up to the measure of his capacity, in the whole service to God, which tends to the salvation of humans, through care of the beneficence which has us for its object; and on the other side through worship, through teaching and through beneficence in deeds. The gnostic even creates and crafts himself; and besides also, he, like to God, adorns those who hear him; assimilating as far as possible the moderation which, arising from practices, tends to impassibility, to him who by nature possesses impassibility; and especially having "uninterrupted" converse and fellowship with the lord. Mildness, I think, and philanthropy, and eminent piety, are the rules of gnostic assimilation. I affirm that these virtues "are a sacrifice acceptable in the sight of God"; scripture alleging that "the humble heart with right knowledge is the holocaust to God"; each human who is admitted to holiness being illuminated in order to indissoluble union.[66] (7.3.13.1–14.1; translation adapted from ANF)

The series of superlatives in this passage indicate the heights the gnostic soul can achieve: the first set suggests that the state of perfection in which one becomes equal to the angels can be surpassed, surpassing the holy ranks, becoming holy among the holy.[67]

As Bogdan Bucur's work on the celestial "hierarchy" in Clement has demonstrated, this is no passing statement; it has significant content. As noted above, the hierarchy of existence starts with the Face of God (Logos), the seven first-created ones, then the archangels, and finally the angels. Bucur argues that Clement has interiorized this celestial hierarchy, likely inherited from the Jewish tradition via earlier Christians. That is, while it explains the movement of divine energies to explain prophetic inspiration, it also provides the means to ascend back to God through the purification and perfection of the soul. Looking mostly to the *Selections of the Prophets*, he argues that this interiorization of the process of ascent and divine encounter within and through the gnostic soul allows one to ascend the hierarchy.

This occurs, in good Clementine fashion, through education. The true believer is instructed by angels, leading to angelification, completed after a "millennial" cycle, at which point they become angels and their instructors become archangels. It is unclear how precisely this occurs, but the content of instruction would include the reforming of the soul in terms of moderation, mildness, philanthropy, and piety, while divesting oneself of the passions associated with embodied existence. Therefore, millennia after millennia, the gnostic soul becomes first equal with the angels, then the archangels, finally achieving equal status with the first-created beings, thence ever gazing upon the face of God, the Logos (*Ecl.* 57.5; cf. Matt. 18:10).[68] Even the first-created ones can achieve a higher status, transcending their traditional ministerial role in the hierarchy so they can rest and contemplate God alone (*Ecl.* 56.5). The first-created ones are the very models of perfected souls (*Exc.* 10:6; 11:1).[69] Yet, obviously, this must occur post-mortem, since the process takes thousands of years.

Even without Bucur's reconstruction, Clement gives a few clues in the passage that this is a post-mortem vision. First, Clement had indicated earlier that a vision in this life, exemplified by Moses and Paul and the rare gnostic visionary, was not fully clear. Returning once more to *Strom.* 7.3, however, after discussing the angelification that occurs when one reaches the highest places among the highest angels, the passage turns to the level of vision achieved: direct and unobstructed. In this festal gathering of endless ages (cf. Heb. 12:22), one finally achieves a clear vision without the encumbrance of a body. In another allusion to the Pauline passage of seeing now as through a glass/mirror and then face to face, the text makes clear that one has achieved the face-to-face vision (cf. *Strom.* 7.10). There is no aversion, no turning away, no indirection by mirrors or glass: it is "transcendently clear and absolutely pure insatiable vision."

One does not leave the Son behind to see the Father, however. It is still through the "great high priest" (see Heb. 4:14–16) and his beneficence toward gnostic humans that the pure in heart can achieve such an "insatiable" vision; that is, it is a gracious vision.[70] Clement repeats the association of purity of heart and unmediated vision of the face of God in *Strom.* 7.10. As the purified and perfected gnostic soul sees God, it becomes like God. The gnostic self-creates and self-crafts (κτίζει καὶ δημιουργεῖ) – a divine function if there ever was one, incorporating Stoic ideas of moderation.[71] These practices turn toward the present preparations for this vision: beneficence in deeds, mildness, philanthropy, moderation, piety, and humility, so the gnostic can assimilate – that is, assimilate into the deity itself.[72] Moderation forms one as impassible, and, as like attracts like, as one becomes impassible, one is drawn to the impassible God.[73] This is no longer just angelification. One achieves deification to the point that one creates oneself (*Strom.* 7.3.13).[74] Then one achieves in the next life what the gnostic Moses achieved in this one: *uninterrupted* converse.[75]

CONCLUSIONS

Compared to the apologies and polemics of earlier Christian authors, Clement of Alexandria's pedagogical writings clearly have a different quality and tone to them. Clement utilized all three strategies that explain how one can and cannot see God at the same time: like Justin, he distinguished between visible and invisible elements of God, mostly in the *Exhortation* and the *Instruction*, claiming that the Logos appeared to the patriarchs and the prophets; like Philo (and Plato), he differentiated between seeing God physically versus intellectually, using Moses as the pre-eminent example of an intellectual seer; finally, he strongly emphasizes the status of the seer: only the pure in heart and those given grace by the Instructor/Logos will or can see God as Moses did.

Moses and the dark cloud provide the floating polyvalent symbol for much of Clement's discussion. The divine darkness presents the problem of God's transcendence, inaccessibility, unknowability, and invisibility. It, however, also offers the solution of purification, perfection, and grace. It differentiates the worthy from the unworthy, the faithful from the faithless, and the knowers ("gnostics") from the ignorant. Moses, the model gnostic, entered it.

Moses becomes the pre-eminent model throughout. In the lesser writings, he, with the other prophets, forms the pinnacle of humanity in the great spiritual communication chain of being that starts with the Logos, and passes through the first-created ones, the archangels, the angels, and then the prophets. Moreover, as Logos had spoken to the prophets, Clement says, now he speaks to you. In this scheme, there are some Philonic holdovers of the Logos instructing Moses, and Moses, in turn, instructing everyone else.

Yet the model begins to shift in the three major treatises, especially the *Miscellanies*. Here the gnostic attempts to attain the level of Moses, receiving instruction from the Logos directly. In both these examples, Moses continues to define the limit of humanity. Nonetheless, there are hints in Clement's writings that the limit becomes threshold,[76] as one assimilates the Logos and even becomes the Logos oneself, becoming impassible and self-creating, moving from being simply the image of God to becoming the image and likeness of God, as the Logos is.

The late-second-century Alexandrian context marks these formulations that Moses is the archetypal gnostic seer, whom true gnostics must emulate in order to become worthy to ascend to and see God, transforming oneself into God's image and likeness. It does so in terms of the overtures to Greek philosophical content, the use of Greek mystery terminology, the combination of faith and knowledge, and the terminology of "gnostic" itself.

First, Alexandria had already become an important city for the continued development of Greek philosophy, especially the Middle Platonist framework that included Plato, often Stoic concepts (including the Logos itself) and Stoic morals, and Pythagorean number theory. In this context, Moses almost always appears next to a quotation, allusion, or citation of the "truth-loving Plato" and often Paul. This allows Clement to align the Bible with the best of Greek learning, which is found on nearly every page, claiming, following Philo and Jewish Alexandrians before him, that Plato borrowed his ideas from Moses. Moses is the font of wisdom. Clement's constant praise of Plato and other Greek thinkers, his constant attempt to show Moses anticipated all of their best concepts, in addition to his frequent use of Greek mystery language – including "mysteries" and his word for divine vision (ἐποπτεία) – all come together for his apologetic purposes.[77] But he did not write apologies or polemical treatises, as Justin and Irenaeus did. He wrote educational treatises, making Christian ideas intelligible and palatable to Greek intellectuals; the ordering of his treatises helps those educated in elite Greek culture to transition to elite Christian society.

Clement's pairing of Moses and Paul and the application of the title "gnostic" to Moses simultaneously mirror and distance him from rival

Alexandrian Christian teachers like Valentinus and Basilides. They would not so easily equate the messages of Moses and Paul, nor would they give Moses the title of "gnostic," since for them the revelations of the Israelite prophets would have come mostly from the lower-ranking, largely ignorant demiurge, rather than the high God. For Clement, by contrast, Moses is not merely some mouthpiece of the demiurge, but the highest "gnostic" seer, who incorporated the highest ideals of Basilides and Valentinus – as well as Platonic thinkers, following in the wake of Philo. The emphasis on the combination of faith and knowledge (*gnosis*), and that faith is the key that leads to the door of knowledge, is also significant in this context. In the home-town of Valentinus and Basilides, who would be labelled by others and perhaps self-described as gnostics, "knowers" of God, Clement adopts the same label, but uses it differently and makes the differential quite clear (*Strom.* 5.1). He emphasizes the necessity of faith – and, therefore, the use of one's free will – against Basilides and Valentinus, who claim one can be saved and achieve knowledge by one's innate nature (*Strom.* 5.1).[78]

Yet for Clement the mutual instantiation of faith and knowledge operates another way as well. It also opposes those Christians who think faith is enough; instead, one completes and perfects faith by *gnosis*. Unlike Justin, Clement places a much stronger emphasis on the limited number of those who can see God, whether partly in this life or fully in the next. The mystery language, the imagery of the dark cloud, and the allegory of the tabernacle used throughout Clement's work also serve this function: to mark boundaries between those with only faith and those with faith and knowledge.[79] It is an exclusivity also found in Philo, though not in Irenaeus. It is for the elite; not for the masses. Clement presents his gnosis as a secret doctrine passed down orally (*Strom.* 6.7), which may explain why his *Miscellanies* are so difficult to read; one needs an instructor. That instructor is the Logos, but also Clement himself for his immediate students. This exclusivity will persist from here on out, with some interesting exceptions, yet who counts as the elite – teacher on the periphery of church structures versus the contemplative bishop at the centre – will shift over time.

Ultimately, Clement presents himself as a teacher, attempting to attract and instruct a coterie of students. He, therefore, differentiates himself from rival teachers and their schools, though often borrows their terminology. His writings, more than those of Justin or Irenaeus, give us glimpses into the curriculum, with biblical content and models supplied by Moses and a template resembling Greek philosophical education and mysteries, as he makes his branding of Christianity accessible to the Greek educated elite, hoping to turn them into a Christian elite. The gnostic Moses, therefore, by representing the limits and threshold of our humanity, also delineates the differences between Clement and rival teachers, as well as between advanced and average Christians.

Tertullian of Carthage (c. 160–220 CE)

Theophany as Incarnation Training

Although several decades ago Auguste Luneau noted that the Latin
Christian writers had little interest in the "physiognomy" of the life of
Moses, Tertullian and, later, Augustine would nonetheless make much
use of his visions in their apologetic, polemical, and exegetical works.[1]
Tertullian, the first great theologian of Latin Christianity,[2] was born
around the time of Justin's martyrdom, and was a young man in his
late teens or early twenties when Irenaeus wrote his *Against Heresies*.
He is the first writer under discussion who had Latin as his first language and who lived in the southwest quadrant of the Roman Empire
in Carthage. While he would have his own religious journey, in terms
of his geography, he stayed home. Unlike the mobility of most of the
people discussed – like Justin, Irenaeus, Clement, Origen, or Augustine
– there is little evidence that Tertullian spent much time outside North
Africa. Therefore, while Wendt considers Tertullian to mark a persistence of the "freelance ritual expert" into the third century, he does not
fully fit the typology.[3] Carthage, already long destroyed and rebuilt by
Rome, was a bustling city of the Western Mediterranean, but, for Christians of the second and third centuries, it was a place of repeated persecutions, including a few localized ones in Tertullian's lifetime.[4]

In the midst of these pressures, Tertullian developed rhetorical skills
to challenge other brands of Christianity, but also to defend his own. He
had come to believe that the Spirit who inspired and the Lord who
appeared to the prophets continued to inspire and appear to women
and men, citing Perpetua, a woman in his own church, and Joel 1:3.
While this is called his "Montanist phase," Tertullian did not see his interest in contemporary prophecy as a break with the universal church –
though he was put on the defensive for it – as he rhetorically aligned
himself with predecessors like Justin and Irenaeus, and fought against

"heresies" old and new.[5] Indeed, some of the "heretics" he fights, like Simon the Samaritan, had been long dead, and he brings them up either out of heresiological tradition or as proofs of his own orthodoxy, finding a common enemy between himself and emergent orthodoxy. In various tracts and treatises, he argues against heretics in general, Hermogenes (who believed in the eternity of Matter), Valentinians, Marcion, Jews (mirroring his anti-Marcionite tract), pagan practices (especially games), Greek (Platonist) philosophy, as well as a newer opponent in Praxeas, all the while asking for tolerance from the Roman government in his *Apology*.[6] Unlike other authors surveyed so far, Tertullian is the first to leave a wealth of extant writings. All of these rivalries, polemics, and apologetics provided the crucible in which he forged his own theory of vision.

If one turns to Tertullian's interest in Moses and the prophets, at first glance he simply assumes and reiterates much of Justin's argument from the *Dialogue with Trypho*. *Against Praxeas* 5–16, for example, often reworks much of Justin's central theophanic sections.[7] Moreover, in *Against Praxeas*, Tertullian would develop Irenaeus' progressive vision, yet he would do so more clearly and succinctly than Irenaeus did.[8] Tertullian follows Irenaeus' assertion that no one – not even Moses – saw the preincarnate son fully, but only partially, yet afterwards, during his incarnation on the Mount of Transfiguration, Moses finally saw God/Jesus fully (esp. *Against Praxeas* 14–16).

Nonetheless, while developing these arguments inherited from Justin and Irenaeus on three polemical fronts – against Jews, against Marcion, and against Praxeas (Patripassianism) – he reaches some distinctive and often startling views: the soul is corporeal; the Son is by nature invisible (shared with Origen); the Son's preincarnate appearances were *fleshly*; and the Son's Old Testament appearances were rehearsals for the incarnation. That is, unlike many other ancient Christian writers, from Irenaeus and Clement onwards, who thought that Christ's preincarnation appearances only taught and prepared humans for Christ's eventual incarnation, for Tertullian they also taught Christ how to be human.[9]

THE PROBLEM OF GOD'S INVISIBILITY: WHAT KIND OF INVISIBILITY?

Tertullian addresses the problem of seeing God more clearly than any other ancient author in *Against Praxeas* 14–16, which is his most extensive treatment of it. He will occasionally remark on it in his multivolume work *Against Marcion*, in his *Apology*, and in *Against the Jews*, an incomplete work that often mirrors verbatim *Against Marcion*.[10] In *Against Praxeas* 14, he begins by noting the difficulty that God is invisible and that whoever sees God will die (Exod 33:20), yet there have been many people in the Bible who claimed to see God and did not die.

Praxeas, for Tertullian, represents a Trinitarian formulation that originated with a figure named Sabellius, and which states that the Father, Son, and Holy Spirit are three different modes of the divine as perceived by human beings rather than three distinct persons. This is an early Trinitarian attempt to accommodate the divinity of the Son and Holy Spirit within the framework of monotheism. In the eastern part of the Roman Empire, it was called Sabellianism after Sabellius; in the West, it was called Patripassianism, because it suggests that the same figure who suffers and dies in one mode is the same who is the Father in another mode; thus, the "father suffers."[11] While Marcion may have divided the God of the Israelite scriptures and the Son too much from Tertullian's perspective, Sabellius and Praxeas unite them so closely that there is no clear differentiation between them; they are one and the same figure. Tertullian, therefore, will navigate the Scylla and Charybdis of these two positions, using the Son's preincarnate appearances as his ship.[12]

Preliminarily suggesting that perhaps people saw God according to human faculties rather than God's full glory, he, unsatisfied, reiterates and intensifies the problem: the patriarchs (Abraham and Jacob) and prophets (Isaiah and Ezekiel) saw God and did not die. Therefore, they should have died, or scripture is proven false: "either way, the Scripture deceives, when it makes God invisible and when it produces him to our sight" (*Ag. Prax.* 14.2).[13] With this statement, Tertullian has laid down a gauntlet by pointing out what seems to be inevitable divine mendacity; with rhetorical and exegetical cleverness, he will find a way out.

But what does it mean for God to be invisible? Tertullian rejects the typical Platonic split between body and mind, while accepting the Pauline difference between flesh and spirit. The question is not whether they are different, but what *kind* of difference they represent. On this last point, he remarks, "He is invisible, though he is seen."[14] Or, as the Robert and Donaldson translation puts it, "The eye cannot see Him, though He is (spiritually) visible" (*Apol.* 17.2; ANF). While they add a lot to the plainest translation of the sentence, they hint at something deeper in Tertullian's theology, expressed throughout his vast corpus of writings. Tertullian can write that God is carnally invisible, yet spiritually visible – a position Augustine would later develop from these earlier musings – but for Tertullian this does not indicate as strong a split between physical and spiritual as is found in figures like Clement or Origen. Instead, Tertullian follows the Stoic position, stemming from Zeno, that everything is corporeal and material, but that spiritual things are composed of a subtler body – subtler than ether.[15]

When looking at Tertullian's *On the Soul*, which is largely an anti-Platonist treatise, he argues that incorporeal things cannot have sympathy with corporeal things, yet the soul clearly suffers with the body; therefore, the soul has something in common with the physical body, and that affinity is corporeality.[16] The soul has a spiritual source, because it is from the breath of God; that is, each soul is God-breathed, just as Adam's was; nonetheless, it is a body (*Soul* 3, 5, 22, 26; cf. *Resurrection* 17).[17] Filling the physical body and taking on its shape, the soul's body becomes the animating source behind the physical senses of vision, hearing, smelling, tasting, and touching (*Soul* 6, 9, 17; cf. *Resurrection* 7). "Spirit" and "mind" are activities or functions of the soul, rather than separate essences or substances (*Soul* 11–12). He garners proofs for his argument of the soul's corporeality from three sources: Zeno, the Stoic philosopher (5), the Gospel of Luke 16,[18] using Lazarus and the rich man in the afterlife (7), and the visions that an unnamed woman in his own congregation in North Africa had of angels and the Lord himself in embodied human form (9).[19]

When looking at his *On the Soul* 8, he argues that flesh and soul are not two types of things, but different degrees of corporeality. Speaking on how different types of creatures have different seeing abilities, he locates the difference in ability to see not simply in the object seen, as Justin does, but also in the eye of the beholder:

> So true is it, therefore, that to one eye an object is invisible, which may be quite plainly seen by another, without implying any incorporeality in that which is not endued with an equally strong power (of vision) ... There is the selfsame difference in respect of the soul's corporeality, which is (perhaps) invisible to the flesh, but perfectly visible to the spirit. (*Soul* 8.5)[20]

Here, the soul's vision and seeing is not metaphorical, as one finds in Platonically oriented works like Clement's and Origen's, but is meant literally. While the soul provides the basis for the physical senses, it has its own eyes and ears. As he argues: "The soul has eyes that can see more subtle substances – though non-fleshly – realities of spirit. This is how Paul saw the Lord and how John saw the souls of martyrs" (9; cf. 2 Corinthians 12; Rev. 1:10).[21]

While God is invisible to the flesh, therefore, he can and will be manifest: "Never shall God be hidden, never shall God be wanting. Always shall He be understood, always be heard, *nay even seen*, however he wishes" (*Ag. Marc.* 1.10.4; emphasis mine).[22] Put another way, God cannot be limited by God's own invisibility and incomprehensibility; God can be made manifest and known if and in the way God so chooses, evidenced by the patriarchs, Moses, the prophets, and the woman in Tertullian's own congregation in Carthage, who all saw and heard. Moreover, they saw and heard something *corporeal*.

REVISITING JUSTIN: VISIBLE OR INVISIBLE IMAGE OF THE INVISIBLE GOD?

Returning to *Against Praxeas* 14–16, Tertullian does not immediately invoke the status of the seer (human faculties rather than divine), but he begins with Justin's solution: "Now, then, he must be a different being who was seen, because of one who was seen it could not be predicated that he is invisible. It will therefore follow that by him who is invisible we must understand the Father in the fullness of his majesty while we recognize the Son as visible by reason of the dispensation of his derived mode" (14.3).[23] Similarly, in his unfinished *Against the Jews*, Tertullian simply assumes and asserts Justin's point without much argument: "For the one who spoke to Moses was the Son of God himself, who, too, was always seen. For God the Father none ever saw and lived. And, accordingly, it is agreed that the Son of God himself spoke to Moses" (9.22–3).[24] As the next line indicates, therefore, it was the Son who spoke with Moses, and the "angel" sent before him is identified with Joshua, who, in turn, foreshadows Jesus, since they have the same name.[25] Just like Justin had, Tertullian can redirect arguments against one opponent – Marcion – against a diametrically opposite group, such as Jews, since both would agree that Jesus has nothing to do with the Israelite scriptures.

These arguments in *Against Praxeas* and *Against the Jews*, however, apparently contradict much of what Tertullian writes in *Against Marcion*, where he equates the Son's invisibility with the Father's invisibility. Being visible by "derived mode" (*pro modulo deriuationis*) in *Against*

Praxeas suggests a natural visibility rather than a natural invisibility. Indeed, with Tertullian's direct reliance on Justin's thought in these places, Justin's subordinationist Christology appears to re-emerge.[26]

In *Against Marcion*, by contrast, Tertullian argues that one should not assume that, just because the Son is the image of the invisible Father, by implication, the Son is always visible – something that the line from Colossians, Justin, and other early Christians appears to assume. Instead, Tertullian argues, the Son shares in the Father's invisibility, but becomes visible. This, indeed, will be an important distinction that is taken up to a much greater extent by Augustine of Hippo.[27] Note particularly *Ag. Marc.* 5.19.3–4:

> He [Paul] calls Christ "the image of the invisible God." We in like manner say that the Father of Christ is invisible, for we know that it was the Son who was seen in ancient times (whenever any appearance was vouchsafed to men in the name of God) as the image of (the Father) himself. He must not be regarded, however, as making any difference between a visible and an invisible God; because long before he wrote this we find a description of our God to this effect: "No man can see the Lord, and live."[28]

Starting with Justin's main point – that whenever anyone saw God, they saw the Son – he, using a catena of quotations from the New Testament, beginning with Col. 1:15, rebuts the idea that there is a difference between a visible and invisible God, as Marcion, and perhaps even Justin, would argue. Instead, Tertullian argues that God the Son and the God of the Old Testament (God the Father) are equally invisible. Jesus is not *by nature* visible, though he can make himself visible. So, the question must be asked: why would Tertullian continue to employ Justin's solution of turning all theophanies into Christophanies? If the Son is by nature invisible, as the Father is, then the solution no longer does the theological work it did for Justin.

REVISITING IRENAEUS: FROM MOUNT SINAI TO THE MOUNT OF TRANSFIGURATION

In *Against Praxeas*, however, Tertullian has a different opponent: Patripassianism, the belief that the Father, Son, and Holy Spirit are different modes of the divine Monad as perceived by humans, rather than separate persons. Therefore, as he tried to draw Father (Old Testament God) and Son together against Marcion, he tries to differentiate them against Praxeas, saying scripture differentiates between Father and Son by differentiating between visible (Son) and invisible (Father). One could attribute the difference in Tertullian to either development in his thought or, more likely, the fact that he is a good rhetorician, who can argue both ways.

But Tertullian here is a bit subtler in his language and shows some consistency of thought.[29] He is not wholly inconsistent between his treatises; that is, he still seeks to avoid making the Son *naturally* visible – it would, indeed, indicate the Son's subordination, as his statement on the Son's "derived existence" also suggests.[30] Thus, he argues something else: not that the Son *must* be visible, but simply that he was. Using the varying theophanies to Moses throughout as a means to make his argument, he writes:

> We declare, however, that the Son, also, considered in Himself (as Son) is invisible, in that he is God, and word and the Spirit of God; but that he was visible before the days of his flesh, in the way that he says to Aaron and Miriam, "And if there shall be a prophet amongst you, I will make myself known to him in a vision, and will speak to him in a dream; not as with Moses, with whom I shall speak mouth to mouth, even apparently, that is to say, in truth, and not enigmatically," that is to say, not in an image; as the apostle also expresses it, "Now we see through a mirror in an enigma, but then face to face." Since, therefore, he reserves to some future time His presence and speech face to face with Moses – a promise which was afterwards fulfilled in the retirement of the mount, when as we read in the Gospel, "Moses appeared talking with Jesus" – it is evident that in early times it was always in a glass (as it were), and an enigma, in vision and dream, that God, I mean the Son of God, appeared – to the prophets and patriarchs, and also to Moses indeed himself. And even if the Lord did possibly speak with him face to face, yet it was not as a human that he could behold his face, unless indeed it was in a glass, as it were, and by enigma. Besides if the Lord so spoke with Moses, that Moses actually discerned his face, how comes it to pass that immediately afterwards, on the same occasion, he desires to see his face, which he ought not to have desired because he had already seen it? (14.6–8)[31]

Both the problem and the solution of the Son's nature – and, therefore, what the prophets saw – derive from Moses' life. Tertullian tries to have it both ways: the Son is invisible and visible. The Son as Son shares in God's invisibility, but the Son qua humans becomes visible. This exegesis is, in some ways, traditional, relying upon catchwords, tying the statement that God speaks to Moses directly and not in an enigma in Numbers 12 with Paul's statement in 1 Corinthians 13 that we see in an enigma now, but later clearly. This is how the Mount of Transfiguration gets pulled in: conflating the two statements from Moses and Paul (a common combination) of now/enigmatically and later/clearly, Tertullian overlays the Mount of Transfiguration as Moses' moment of later/clearly.

Additionally, one must note the cleverness of Tertullian's exegesis. He seems to anticipate an objection: if Moses saw clearly and not enigmatically, why make his clear vision in Moses' future (from the perspective of Numbers) rather than in the past? Tertullian astutely observes, as Augustine would after him, that Moses requests to see God's face (Exod. 33:20) just *after* he spoke with him face to face (Exod. 33:11), indicating that Moses recognized that, in the face-to-face encounter, he still had not seen God fully – God in this case being the preincarnate Son.

Tertullian might have lifted this section from Irenaeus' *A.H.* 4.20.9. Moses – and by implication all the patriarchs and prophets – though they saw the Son, never *fully* saw the Son. A full vision had yet to occur. Irenaeus and Tertullian both note that God promises to show something of himself to Moses, and Tertullian more explicitly than Irenaeus finds such a promise in Num. 12:8 – where Moses sees the very form of God, and not in riddles, enigmas, and dreams as others do. But in early times – in the olden days – the Son always appeared in riddles, enigmas, dreams, or in a glass darkly. The solution, again strongly resembling Irenaeus' *Against Heresies*, is the Mount of Transfiguration. There, seeing the incarnate Christ in full glory, Moses finally sees the Son's (i.e., God's) face.[32]

Tertullian repeats this Irenaean trope in *Ag. Marc.* 4.22.13–16, once more presenting the Transfiguration as the fulfillment of the promise to Moses:

And if we would make mention of the promise to Moses, we shall find it accomplished here. For when Moses desired to see the Lord, saying, "If therefore I have found grace in your sight, mani-

fest yourself to me, that I may see you distinctly." The sight which
he desired to have was of that condition which he was to assume
as a human, and which as a prophet he knew was to occur.
Respecting the face of God, however, he had already heard, "No
human shall see me, and live." "This thing," said He, "which you
have spoken, will I do unto you." Then Moses said, "Show me your
glory." And the Lord, with like reference to the future, replied, "I
will pass before you in my glory," etc. Then at the last he says, "And
then you though shall see my back [*posteriora*]." Not loins, or
calves of the legs, did he want to behold, but the glory which was
to be revealed in the latter days [*posterioribus*]. He had promised
that He would make himself thus face to face visible to him, when
He said to Aaron, "If there shall be a prophet among you, I will
make myself known to him by vision, and by vision will I speak
with him; but not so is my manner to Moses; with him will I
speak mouth to mouth, even apparently" (that is to say, in the
human form which he was to assume), "and not in dark speeches."
Now, although Marcion has denied that he is here represented as
speaking with the Lord, but only as standing, yet, inasmuch as he
stood "mouth to mouth," he must have also stood "face to face"
with him, to use his words, not far from him, in his very glory –
not to say, in his presence.[33]

It has almost become a trope to combine the rejection of vision in Exod.
33:20 and its subsequent passage along with Num. 12:8 as a prophecy
and promise to Moses that is fulfilled on the Mount of Transfiguration.
Tertullian places special stress on the future tense of God's/Son's speech
to Moses that he "will" see God's backside. Similar to Irenaeus' argument, the future tense and backside refers to the apparent – that is, fully
visible – glory of the "latter times." Tertullian tightens the connection
between God's "backside" and the "latter times" with a play on words of
posteriora and *posterioribus temporibus*. Indeed, for Tertullian, Jesus' incarnation, and especially the incarnate glory beaming from the mountain,
is the fullest divine vision possible.[34]

One finds a parallel action in *Against Praxeas*. There, Tertullian proceeds to discuss New Testament passages that also express the Son's
visibility in contrast to the Father's invisibility (*Against Praxeas* 15),
hitting some typical passages (John 1:18; 1 Tim. 6.16). He reiterates
nonetheless, "How, I repeat, can all this be, unless it be that He is one,
who anciently was visible only in mystery and enigma, and became

more clearly visible by his incarnation, even the Word who was also made flesh; while he is another whom no man has seen at any time, being none else than the father, even him to whom the Word belongs?" (15.4).[35] The incarnate Son, moreover, is not only seen and heard, but also handled and touched, proving very fleshly.[36] Revelation, as in Irenaeus, is progressive, not regressive. Divine vision is also progressive; it is an ongoing unfolding of the vision of God that had its first great unveiling on Mount Sinai but reached its fullest expression on the Mount of Transfiguration.

Finally, at the end of *Against Praxeas* 15, Tertullian, reiterating the line from Exod. 33:20, writes,

> This being the case, it is evident that he was always seen from the beginning who became visible in the end; and that he (on the contrary), was not seen in the end who had never been visible in the beginning; and that accordingly there are two – the visible and the invisible. It was the Son, therefore, who was always seen, and the Son who always conversed with men, and the Son who was always worked by the authority and will of the Father ... For the Father acts by mind and thought; while the Son, who is in the Father's mind and thought, gives effect and form to what he sees. (15.9)[37]

While Christ is the visible form of the invisible God; his visibility is not part of his nature or essential; it is, however, necessary for the economy of salvation. Father and Son are, thereby, divided functionally, as the Son puts into effect the Father's thought. But this is not the only aspect of his preincarnate appearances: other than noting that they were enigmatic, he has not yet addressed their nature; other than noting that they were preparatory for Moses and the prophets to predict Christ's coming as a human, he has only partially disclosed their purpose.

THEOPHANY AS TRAINING FOR THE INCARNATION

Other than "enigmatically," how, then, exactly did the preincarnate Son appear to Moses and others? Justin had argued that the means of appearance was bodiless, but did not add much to this. Irenaeus adapted this to say that the son appeared only partly, and even ate – something with which Tertullian agrees. And then to what end did he appear? This is something that Irenaeus and Clement had previously mentioned: to predict and prepare humanity for Christ's advent. And, while Tertullian also believed this, he turns it on its head: it is to prepare Christ for his own humanity.

Against Praxeas 16 provides examples of the Son's manifestation in the Old Testament that were "rehearsals" of his incarnation. In a litany that one finds paralleled in Clement, the Son created the world, destroyed the tower of Babel, flooded the earth, and rained fire upon Sodom and Gomorrah (as "the Lord from the Lord" – Justin's key line). He spoke with Adam, patriarchs, and prophets in visions, dreams, mirrors, and dark sayings – as noted above; that is, in part and not fully; darkly and not clearly – laying a foundation for his latter dispensations.

One finds a similar view in *Against Marcion*. To rebut docetic views based upon God's messengers in the Old Testament, Tertullian argues that they – whether angels or the Son – appeared in the flesh, even though they were not by nature fleshly beings.[38] Looking to the story of Abraham and the three angels – one of Justin's favourites as well – the angels not only appeared to him but *ate* with him, something a mere bodiless spectre could not accomplish. Tertullian argues that the God who made the world out of nothing could give to angelic beings whatever material he wanted to allow them to appear to human beings; so he made them human flesh, but this is not flesh that is born, differentiating it from the incarnation proper. Jesus' flesh, because he was born, regenerated human birth, and, therefore, his death dissolved our death. But, Jesus' preincarnate unborn fleshly appearances were trial runs for the incarnation; they were incarnation practice: "Therefore on that occasion He did Himself appear with the angels to Abraham in the verity of the flesh, which had not as yet undergone birth, because it was not yet going to die, although it was even now learning to hold intercourse among men" (*Ag. Marc.* 3.9.6).[39] The angels with him also took on flesh, and, in a flourish typical of Tertullian, he notes that "He has promised that he will one day form humans into angels, who once formed angels into humans" (*Ag. Marc.* 3.9.7).[40] In short, Jesus' preincarnate appearances did not (or did not merely) prepare humans for Christ's advent, as Irenaeus and Clement would argue, but prepared the Son for it as well, as the non-fleshly being practised moving around in fleshly material. The enfleshment of angels also has a parallel inverse movement of humans becoming angels (Matt 22:30; Mark 12:25; Luke 20:34–6).[41]

Tertullian develops these learning experiences further in *Against Praxeas* 16. The Son's enfleshed preincarnate appearances were not just to put into effect the Father's thought, though they did that; they were not just to prepare humans for the incarnation, though they also did that; they allowed the Son to learn:

> Thus was he ever learning even as God to converse with men upon earth, being no other than the Word which was to be made flesh. But he was thus learning (or rehearsing), in order to level for us the way of faith, that we might the more readily believe that the Son of God had come down into the world, if we knew that in times past also something similar had been one. (16.3)[42]

Tertullian continues, reciting nearly every theophany, however great or brief, in the Old Testament, arguing that, in his manifestations, Jesus learned what it meant to be human, learning about human feelings and affections, substances, body and soul, learning about hunger and thirst, tears, birth, and death. The Son is the great participant-observer anthropologist, allowing God and humanity to become accustomed to one another. Just as humanity becomes prepared for Christ, so Christ becomes prepared for humanity.

CONCLUSIONS

Tertullian writes with a clarity that often belies the subtle thinking that occurs in *Against Praxeas*. Like Justin, Tertullian considers what the Israelite visionaries saw, especially focusing on Moses, directly addressing the problem. Due to his Stoic sensibilities, which sees spirits and souls as subtler material than bodies, Tertullian pays little attention to how one sees in its classic philosophical division between body and soul, though in *On the Soul* he addresses how the soul's body and one's fleshly body work together for physical vision while the soul also has its own corporeal eyes to see. Instead, he becomes more concerned about how Christ appeared – in what corporeal form? Again, Moses' visions set the parameters of the problem and possible solutions.

In *Against Praxeas*, often thought to be a regurgitation of the central portions of Justin's *Dialogue with Trypho*, one finds not just dependence and clarification, but, with inspiration from the ramblings of Irenaeus' *Against Heresies*, a fully worked out systematic answer to the question of how no one can see God and live, as God said to Moses, and yet people, including Moses, still claimed to see God. He states the problem baldly and boldly, putting his finger on the central question that many others danced around. Drawing inspiration from his predecessors, he created a novel set of interlocking solutions.

From Justin he drew the inspiration that all the theophanies in the Hebrew Bible were the preincarnate Son, but he expanded the explicit theophanic list further than Justin did. From Irenaeus, he realized this was not good enough; if these were indeed full manifestations, the incarnation would be redundant. Thus, he echoed Irenaeus' view of progressive revelation: even the Son was not seen in full, but only in part by the patriarchs, Moses, and the prophets; thus, again, the status of the seer is strongly correlated to human capacities within a particular age. He also borrowed from him the idea that Moses' vision of the very form of God was accomplished at the Mount of Transfiguration. As such, Moses remains the model at different eras: in the past he sees partly like other prophets; in the time of Jesus' incarnation, Moses sees the fullest glory possible. Moses' visions, again, set the problem and the solution and the limits for humanity. While Tertullian, like many others discussed, thinks such visions are still possible, unlike these other writers considered in other chapters, Tertullian does not claim that pinnacle of human possibility for himself, but for the woman in his church who has visions of angels and the Lord, just as Moses, the patriarchs, and the prophets did.

Yet there the similarities stop. Tertullian's theory of the soul – that it is corporeal – already lays down a foundation that different beings vary in degree and not kind, allowing one to move up and down on the chain of being more smoothly. He clarified that the Son in essence is invisible to physical eyes – important for later Nicene views – dampening the subordinationism often found in second- and early-third-century Christian writings, such as those of Justin, and escaping St Augustine's later censure.[43] He, perhaps most uniquely, argued that all of these appearances were, in fact, fleshly. And as the Son and his angels put on flesh, so human flesh will become angelic – though, significantly, this flesh was made and not born; only the begotten flesh can redeem human flesh. Finally, in addition to preparing humanity for Christ's advent, these appearances also taught the Son what it means to be human. His teachers were Abraham, Isaac, Jacob, Hagar, Moses, Gideon, Isaiah, Jeremiah, and Ezekiel. They instructed Christ what it means to laugh and to cry, to be born and to die, to eat and to be hungry, to be rich and to be needy, to have joy and to have sorrow. After this training, the Son can appear in the full glory of begotten flesh.

Like that of his predecessors, Tertullian's thinking acquires its definition in opposition to others: Marcion, Praxeas, and, to a lesser extent, Jews. With the exception of Praxeas, the opponents remain largely the same, but his intellectual resources to combat these opponents have shifted. In addition to his oratorical gifts and withering arguments, he also brings Stoic materiality, together with his belief in the continuation of prophecy into his own day and in his own local church. His Stoicism and recourse to contemporary prophecy, which he cites as proof next to biblical texts, provide some of Tertullian's willingness to break with more Platonist-oriented Christian predecessors. He, thereby, emphasizes the Son's preincarnate fleshliness, and the soul's corporeality and ability to see things "invisible" to the flesh.

With these elements in place, Marcionite and Jewish opponents could be challenged with the same manoeuvre, bringing the Israelite scriptures and gospel together more tightly by having the preincarnate Son appearing to figures like Moses. This pre-existing challenge persists for Tertullian, which, together with Stoic theory, may additionally account for his valuation of flesh, especially against Marcionite devaluations of fleshliness.[44] Nonetheless, he also faces a challenge from the opposite direction: instead of just needing to identify the God of Israel with the God of the gospel, he now also needed to differentiate more clearly the Father and the Son in the face of Sabellius and Praxeas, leading to both a more direct consideration of the problem of theophanies and its solution. Unlike Irenaeus, who in his writings does not always make clear who is speaking, oscillating confusedly between Father, Son, and Holy Spirit, Tertullian brings clearer distinctions.

Like his predecessors, he challenged those who could offer alternative readings – whether real or imagined – that may undermine his exegetical authority, rather than institutionalized authority. While Justin, Irenaeus, Clement, and others develop their ideas in polemical contexts, Tertullian's sharp wit, clarity of expression, and organization give his writings a focused, critical, and sometimes defensive edge. It is a focus gained by not being in a position of authority within the church – he did not have pastoral responsibilities bearing down on him like Irenaeus did – and, later in life, having to defend himself as he embraced the New Prophecy movement.[45] Therefore, he does have some characteristics of earlier apologists and polemicists, whom Wendt identifies as "freelance experts."[46]

Unlike most of those freelance experts, however, he is not a transplant from the Roman east to the west; he is native to the southern west. He is not ethnically coded, per se, neither exotic nor foreign. Unlike Irenaeus, who was a Greek speaker in a Latin-speaking city in a Celtic setting, he was a Latin speaker in a Latin-speaking land. Nonetheless, without any officially recognized institutional authority, he survived by his acid pen.

9

Origen (c. 185–254 CE)

Purifying the Eye of the Mind

Our wise men, Moses who was the most ancient and the prophets who suc-
ceeded him, were the first to understand that "the highest good cannot at
all be expressed in words," when, seeing that God manifests himself to those
who are worthy and ready to receive him, they wrote that God appeared to
Abraham, for instance, or to Isaac, or to Jacob. But who it was that appeared,
and what sort of a person, and in what way, and to which of those among
us, are questions which they have left for the examination of people who
can show themselves to be like the men to whom he appeared. For they saw
him not with the eyes of the body, but with a pure heart. In the words of
our Jesus, "blessed are the pure in heart; for they shall see God." (Origen,
Against Celsus 6.4)[1]

Persecution punctuated Origen's life.[2] In 203 CE, when Origen was
around the age of seventeen, his father, Leonidas, was beheaded as a
martyr in Alexandria, during the reign of Septimius Severus. Famously, Eusebius relates that Origen desired to die a martyr's death, and his
mother stopped him by hiding his clothes.[3] He wrote his *Exhortation
to Martyrdom* during Maximin's persecution. At the age of sixty-nine,
he, himself, would succumb to injuries inflicted by torture during
the Decian Persecution, dying as a "confessor" when he was seventy
years old.[4]

In between these moments of persecution, he was a teacher, a
philosopher,[5] a preaching presbyter, and, most like Philo of Alexandria before him, a biblical commentator.[6] He taught catechism in
Alexandria, and eventually began to focus on more-advanced pupils.
He was, as David T. Runia notes, "the last of the great teachers of

Alexandria to operate in relative independence of the Church hierarchy.[7] Yet, his independence would lead to a clash with the bishop of
Alexandria, Demetrius, causing Origen to flee around 232–234, ultimately to Caesarea, which he had visited earlier in 215. He also taught
in Athens for a time, and was eventually ordained presbyter and allowed to preach in Caesarea, much to the frustration of Demetrius
of Alexandria. His life and posthumous remembrances were marked
by persecution, conflict, or at least ambivalence with ecclesiastical
authorities,[8] and by theological brilliance.[9]

Origen, usually considered the spiritual heir to Clement in Alexandria,[10] can be puzzling to the modern scholar. Although he is, "with
Saint Augustine, the greatest genius of ancient Christianity,"[11] there
are numerous difficulties when approaching his written remains. He
was posthumously condemned, and his opponents drove many of his
works underground.[12] While he was a voluminous author, perhaps
the most prodigious author of Christian antiquity before Augustine,
many of his writings were destroyed or were simply not recopied, yet
they inspired "orthodox" and "heretic" alike, including Eusebius of
Caesarea, Gregory the Wonderworker, Basil of Caesarea, Gregory of
Nazianzus, Gregory of Nyssa, and Evagrius of Pontus, among many
others.[13] Because of this, much of Origen's work survives only in Latin
translations by Rufinus and Jerome.[14] In those rare places where one
can find a Greek version, such as in the *Philokalia*, one finds that – as
per the tendencies of ancient translation in general – the Latin translators, whether Rufinus or Jerome, took great liberties with the text:
they paraphrased, abbreviated, and, not being enslaved by the wood-
en wordiness of literal translation, they conquered the meaning of the
text, turning it into Latin.[15] Indeed, all good translators are, as one
modern translator put it, "speakers of a second text."[16] It is, therefore,
important to find patterns of thought in Origen's Greek and translated works, and not rely upon individual wording in a single passage,
especially in works that survive only in Latin.[17] Fortunately, he turned
his attention to divine vision repeatedly in multiple works surviving
in Greek and Latin and, therefore, patterns do emerge.

These patterns that spread and spindle throughout different works
and repeat within the same works read like a fugue. Like Philo of
Alexandria before him, Origen has a strong philosophical orientation,
yet he works predominantly through biblical interpretation.[18] Not
only does Origen often return to the same verses, but to the same
combination of verses, covering much of the same ground each time

he uses the combination – but usually one added twist or emphasis in each usage ultimately leads to a subtly different point being made.

In the paragraph quoted at the top of the chapter, from Origen's apologetic work *Against Celsus*, which survives in Greek, he reflects upon the nature of vision.[19] When God appeared to the wise of old – particularly Moses, who, presumably, wrote all of this down – what did that mean? Origen's questions strike to the heart of the types of ways early Christians sought to resolve how people saw an invisible God: by object seen (angel, Logos, Jesus, etc.); how one "saw" or the nature of seeing (physical, prophetic, spiritual, noetic); and the status of the seer (the pure in heart, the righteous dead). Origen provides a ready way of categorizing how early Christians thought about the possibilities and impossibilities of divine vision, using Moses' visions as a starting point. But he adds an interesting twist: only those who are equal to Moses and others to whom God spoke can take on these questions. The interpreters of scripture – including Origen himself – are seers or prophets, just as the progenitors of scripture, such as Moses, were.[20] And such inspired interpreters are rare.[21] Interpretation is vision.[22]

Of the three categories, Origen, himself, focused primarily on the question of how one sees, bringing in questions of who sees and whom or what is seen as supporting the question of the means of seeing. In this way, Origen is perhaps both the simplest and most difficult to analyze. One can encapsulate his entire visionary program in a single sentence, but elaborating on the meaning and implications would take a book. That one sentence, from the most Platonically oriented thinker discussed here, is that one cannot see God with the eyes of the body; one can only "see" – or know – God with the eyes of the mind. While nearly every other author analyzed assumes this to some degree, except maybe Tertullian, Origen makes it the centre of his discussion. While he will, at times, revert to Justin's reasoning – that one can "see" or know God only through the Son – Origen finds untenable Justin's solution of a physically visible, yet non-corporeal, manifestation of the Logos to the patriarchs and prophets. Indeed, instead of the visible image of the invisible God (Col. 1:15), the Son is the *invisible* image of the invisible God, as also found in Tertullian's writings. The Son shares in the Father's invisibility; those who saw the incarnate Jesus were, of course, blessed by the encounter, yet the greater vision is, as with Clement, one encountered invisibly and intellectually. Origen will go so far as to say that – contrary to the

Gospel of John – even the Son has never seen the Father, but, then
again, neither has the Father seen the Son. Nonetheless, he still must
account for Moses' visions and Matt 5:8 – the vision of the pure of
heart. How he does so illustrates his exegetical virtuosity.

INHERITING JUSTIN

Origen inherits the now-typical assumption among several Christian
authors leading all the way back to Justin: that the revealer to the
patriarchs and prophets was, in fact, the preincarnate Logos.[23] For
example, in his preface to Book 1 of *On First Principles*, he mentions,
citing Hebrews 11:24, that Christ was the "word of God" who was
within Moses and the prophets, enabling them to prophesy about
Christ. According to his *Hom. Num.* 27 on Numbers 2, Moses wrote
"by the word of the lord." In his *Comm. John* 2.1–7, he identifies Jesus
as Word with the "word of the Lord" that came to Hosea, Isaiah, and
Jeremiah. These cases, however, are less concerned with theophany
and more with divine inspiration radiating from within. Again, this
was a useful polemical strategy against Marcionite Christians and others who would divorce the revelation of the law and the Prophets
from that of the Gospel.[24]

In a more theophanic vein, however, Origen, picking up on some
older strands of interpretation, identifies the Angel of the LORD with
the Son. Looking at the story of the binding of Isaac, Origen writes,
"And yet it must be considered that an angel is related to have spoken these words to Abraham and subsequently this angel is clearly
shown to be the Lord. Whence I think that, just as among us humans
'he was found in appearance as a human,' so also among angels he
was found in appearance as an angel" (*Hom. Gen.* 8.8; cf. *Comm. John*
1.217–8).[25] This passage is fascinating on several accounts. First, in
this homily he articulates a theophany, much like Justin would,
whereas in his more philosophically oriented (rather than pastorally
oriented) writings, he would suggest that even the Son's true essence
is invisible.[26] Such an idea may be hiding behind the idea that the
Son can appear to angels as an angel, just as he can appear to a
human as a human. The Son is polymorphic, changing his appearance as needed.[27] Second, the rest of this section indicates that the
Son appeared as an angel to show angels how to act angelically. The
Son is a pedagogue not only to humans (as in Clement of Alexandria), but also to angels.

Origen, furthermore, writes in *Hom. Num.* 27.5 that the stages of the Israelites' wandering in the desert were symbolic for one's own ascent to God: "The ascent does have for its stages names fitted to mysteries; and it has as its guide not Moses – for he did not know where to go himself – but the pillar of fire and the cloud, that is, the Son of God and the Holy Spirit."[28] Here Christ appears as fire and the Holy Spirit as cloud (usually they are put the other way around, or Christ is both). He refers to Jesus as a metaphorical pillar of cloud, moreover, in the *Comm. John* 32.2. In his discussion of Numbers, however, Origen stops short of considering this a physical theophany; it is better read as an allegory of the ascent of one's own soul to God (cf. *Ag. Cels.* 6.23). Moses is not the leader, but a follower. Christ is the mystagogue; Moses, the initiate. More traditionally, however, Origen writes in *Against Celsus* that "Jesus is the Son of God who gave the law and the prophets" (2.6), though elsewhere he reaffirms the New Testament position that the angels gave the law.[29] Moreover, he argues that the Logos of God arranged the scripture (*Ag. Cels.* 4.71), more tightly aligning old and new revelations than even Justin did.[30] Ultimately, for Origen, scripture itself is another incarnation of the Logos in language.[31] When one encounters scripture, one encounters the Logos.[32]

SEEING GOD WITH THE PURE HEART/MIND

Though other ancient Christians, such as Justin, Clement, or Theophilus, also had written that God the Father is completely invisible and incomprehensible to the senses (and sometimes even the mind), differentiating between sensible and spiritual capacities, Origen places these issues front and centre. One can open nearly any work and find Origen making some statement about God's physical invisibility and intellectual intelligibility.

For example, in *Martyrdom* 47, he writes that the soul has a kinship to God because both are intelligible, invisible, and incorporeal. In *Ag. Cels.* 7.38–9, he emphasizes that God is mind, yet also transcends minds, is simple, invisible, incorporeal, and, therefore, must be approached by one in the image of that mind. As 7.33 already indicated, moreover, the image is not only Christ – who, as we shall see, is the invisible image of the invisible God – but the human mind itself, originally created in the image and likeness of God.[33]

Once he has established divine invisibility, Origen gives Matt. 11:27 a central place in his thinking about seeing God. Whereas earlier

Christian writers employed Matt. 11:27 to discuss how only the Son saw *and/or* knew the Father, Origen leans on the precise wording to allow one and exclude the other – only the Son *knows* the Father, but even the Son has never *seen* the Father; if the Father is invisible, then the Father is invisible to all; it is an inherent divine quality rather than something dependent upon the status of the seer. The Son, sharing the Father's qualities, however, is also essentially invisible; therefore, even the Father has never seen the Son. The same, by extension, holds true for the Holy Spirit. This, however, sets Origen apart from figures like Justin and puts him more in line with Clement and, to a lesser extent, Tertullian.[34]

The stakes are heightened, and Justin's solution falls apart. For writers for whom the Son was the visible image of the invisible God (as in Col. 1:15), Justin's answer of making the preincarnate Son the object in theophanic visions worked. When the Son is essentially invisible, this solution is unnecessary; nonetheless, with the Son's equal invisibility, the Son can become essentially the same as the Father. While Origen will, again leaning on Matt. 11:27, maintain that one still needs to know (that is, "see" in the intellect) God through the Son, because the Son is equally invisible, the entirety of the contemplative program turns to means: how one sees.

Like Justin's argument, however, Origen's has an anti-Marcionite or an anti-gnostic edge to it.[35] Origen notes that those who separate the God of Moses and of the patriarchs and the creator of this world as a distinct entity from the God of Jesus do so on the basis of vision: Origen's opponents cite John 1:18, which says no one has seen the Father, while noting that Moses and the patriarchs claimed to see God. Their solution is that the God Moses saw was not Jesus' Father (*Princ.* 2.4.3). This forces Origen to bring up Exod. 33:20 to note that the God who spoke to Moses said the same thing: he cannot be seen. As with Justin, Origen's opponents resorted to differentiating between what is seen; therefore, instead of just substituting different figures for the seen and unseen divinities as Justin did, Origen shifts strategy to lean completely on how one sees: Moses saw intellectually, and then only in part.

This tendency is especially pronounced throughout *On First Principles*.[36] In *Princ.* 1.1.8, Origen discusses how the divine nature surpasses the nature of bodies. Quoting Col. 1:15, that Christ is the "image of the invisible God," Origen argues that seeing God physically does not, in fact, rely upon the status of the seer – that is, God is not visible to one and invisible to another. Neither saint nor sinner can see God. It is not merely because of human frailty that we fail to see God. Rather, backed up by John 1:18, Origen argues that God is invisible to all because invisibility is God's nature. In this same passage, moreover, Origen speculates on the Son: the Son, too, cannot see the Father. In 1.2.6, Origen elaborates what he means by "image of the invisible God." While human beings are like a painting or sculpture and, thereby, are the "image and likeness of God,"[37] the Christ is the perfect image of God as a child is to a parent; he slips in Col. 1:15 with a significant shift: Christ is the "*invisible* image of the invisible God" (*quod invisibilis dei imago invisibilis est*).[38] Just as the Father is invisible, so is the Son. The Son is Word and Wisdom, and, therefore, is incorporeal by nature. That is, the Father has never seen the Son either.[39]

In 1.1.8, Origen parries, and then steps back on the defensive; he has to avoid sounding impious. In what appears to be a bowdlerized passage,[40] Origen explains by differentiating between seeing and knowing. Seeing and being seen are the properties of bodies; knowing and being known are attributes of intellectual existence. He writes,

> Whatever therefore is proper to bodies must not be believed either of the Father or of the Son, the relations between whom are such as pertain to the nature of deity. And finally, Christ in the gospel did not say, "No one sees the Father except the Son, nor the Son except the Father," but "no one knows the Son except the Father, nor does anyone know the Father except the Son." (*Princ.* 1.1.8, quoting Matt. 11:27)[41]

Seeing is a property of bodies; knowing is the property of intellectual beings, the greatest of which is the deity and its internal relations between Father, Son, and Holy Spirit. Therefore, Matthew does not say that only the Son *sees* the Father; rather, the gospel says that only the Son *knows* the Father.

Having so argued, however, Origen has backed into a conundrum. What about Jesus' promise in the very same gospel that the pure in heart will see God (Matt. 5:8)? Seeing and knowing are differentiated yet united. Bodily seeing finds its intellectual analogue in knowing. Origen will exploit this looser sense of intellectual "seeing" to read Matt. 5:8. Speaking of the analogues or homologies that he more fully develops in his *Commentary* and *Homilies on the Song of Songs*, Origen writes,

For the names of the organs of sense are often applied to the soul,
so that we speak of seeing with the eyes of the heart, that is, of
drawing some intellectual conclusion by means of the faculty of
intelligence. So too we speak of hearing with the ears when we
discern the deeper meaning of some statement. So too we speak
of the soul as being able to use teeth, when it eats and consumes
the bread of life who comes down from heaven. In a similar way
we speak of it as using all the other bodily organs, which are
transferred from their corporeal significance and applied to the
faculties of the soul. (*Princ*. 1.1.9).[42]

As in Origen's readings of the Song of Songs[43] – and about which
Augustine would later wax rhapsodic (*Conf.* 10.27 [38]) – Origen
relates that each of the five senses has a spiritual counterpart: the senses of the heart. His exegetical manoeuvre, however, is not so heavy-
handed as to impose the physical-noetic correspondence on a verse
that cannot bear its weight. Rather, he deftly reworks the meaning of
"pure of heart." While others, and even Origen himself, will return to
this verse to consider what it means to be pure of heart in terms of the
status of the seer, here he shifts the emphasis of "heart." Instead of the
"pure of heart" will see God, Origen reads it as the "pure heart" will
see God; that is, the heart is not just a place of purity, but additionally the means of vision.

He concludes by explaining and transferring Hebrew "heart" to the
faculties of the Greek "mind": "By this divine sense, therefore, not of
the eyes but of a pure heart, that is, the mind, God can be seen by
those who are worthy. That heart is used for the mind, that is for the
intellectual faculty, you will certainly find ever and ever again in all
the scriptures, both the new and the old. (*Prin*. 1.1.9)"[44] Interestingly,
Origen began by stating that the status of the seer was of no avail: no
one could see God, since God was invisible. Therefore, even the Son
cannot ever have seen the Father. Nonetheless, he ends with a statement of the status of the seer being central: only the pure of heart can
"see" God with their pure heart, that is, their mind.

While he redefines heart as intellect, he, unfortunately, does not
indicate what makes the heart/mind pure and worthy to see God.[45]
However, he gives some further hints and clues in a later passage on
the ascent of the saints. As they ascend through the heavens or spheres
in their post-mortem existence, they will achieve perfect knowledge of
the cosmos. As in the writings of Clement, the heavenly paradise is a

school or lecture-room for the soul. These souls will do this more quickly than others because of their pure hearts, which he now equates with the unpolluted mind and well-trained understanding, obtained through intellectual growth and contemplation. Their training begins in this life and continues with increased capacity in a bodiless condition (*Princ.* 2.11.6–7). Elsewhere, however, he resorts to moral purity: the removal of all evil thoughts, not murdering, not committing adultery, not fornicating, not stealing, not bearing false witness, not committing blasphemy, not giving the evil eye, and not committing any evil deed (*Ag. Cels.* 7.33). Attainment of divine vision is, therefore, a combination of elimination of vices – avoiding impure and evil thoughts and activities – and positive contemplation.[46]

In *On First Principles*, however, Origen does not fully indicate how one attains such purity of heart/mind and, thereby, sees God. He focuses more on the possibilities of seeing God rather than the practices necessary to do so. Nonetheless, one should know already that, however pure one gets, the Son plays a key role, since the Son is the means by which one knows the Father, and since the Son is the only one who really can know the Father. Matt. 11:27 operates in two ways for Origen: it allows him to discuss invisibility and incorporeality, but it also allows him to emphasize that the Son is the only intellectual means to the Father; that is, how the Son, through knowing, remains the only means to approach the invisible Father.[47] Yet the Son as Son is also invisible, unseen.

Indeed, Origen writes that the verse "in thy light we see light" refers to how in the Son one sees the Father (*Princ.* 1.1.1). As the image of God, whoever has seen Christ has seen the Father (*Princ.* 1.2.6, quoting John 14:9). One participates invisibly and rationally in the "image of the invisible God" in proportion to the loving affection with which one clings to him (*Princ.* 2.6.3).[48] The goal of such participation, however, may not necessarily be to see God, per se, but to see as God sees.[49]

While purity of heart is something one strives for, it is something that Origen thinks is ultimately impossible for most to attain. It is achieved very rarely by exceptional people, such as Moses, due to the human condition of embodiment. One needs help. But not everyone receives equal help: that is, Christ illuminates or enlightens in accordance with each person's ability to receive the power of God's light, which varies based upon how many distractions one has in this life and whether one comes to God for mere refreshment of the soul or for incessant instruction by the Logos (*Hom. Gen.* 1.7).

Origen illustrates this rare achievement of purity and the limits of the human condition with Moses' ascent into the divine darkness in *Ag. Cels.* 6.17, much like Philo and Clement of Alexandria did. Yet, unlike Clement, Origen contrasts the scriptures to Plato to demonstrate that Plato does not lead to piety, but to idolatry and superstition. In contrast, the Bible reveals elevated thoughts of God. Quoting Psalm 17:12, he notes, "God has made darkness his hiding place."[50] This darkness demonstrates that God is incomprehensible and unknowable. With a verbal allusion to Plato's allegory of the cave (*Rep.* 518A), Origen states that humans "cannot bear the radiance of the knowledge of Him nor can they see him."[51] God's radiance is so intense that it appears to creatures as darkness. This denigrates humans as much as it exalts God, for humans cannot see God because of the "defilement of the mind" (διὰ τὸν μιασμὸν τοῦ νοῦ) due to the mind's bondage to the "body of humiliation" (σώματι ταπεινώσεως).

Even so, some knowledge of God, albeit fragmentary, can come to a very select few through the means of revelation. For this, Origen notes that Moses *alone* could draw near to God (ἐγγιεῖ Μωϋσῆς μόνος πρὸς τὸν θεόν) and others could not. People cannot fathom the "depth of the doctrines of God,"[52] especially if they do not possess the Spirit of God, for the Spirit can know God and "searches all things, and searches even the deep things of God."[53] Likewise, the Logos has knowledge of God, which then it passes to "those whose minds are illuminated by the divine Logos."[54] Darkness, therefore, unlike invisibility and incorporeality, is not an absolute quality of God, but relative to the perspective of the observer. Consequently, illumination by the Logos is key: "By participation in him who took away from the Father what is called darkness, which made 'his hiding place,' and what is called his covering, 'the great deep,' thus revealing the Father, anyone whatever who has the capacity to know Him may do so." (*Ag. Cels.* 6.17)[55] Citing Ps. 17:12 and 103:6, Origen argues that the Logos is the illuminator that removes the dark clothing of God, so that one can know God if one is capable. Both Spirit and Logos are dual keys of the knowledge and vision of God; one must possess the Spirit, who searches all things so that one may also search the depths of God with one's mind, and one's mind must participate in the light and truth of the Logos to illuminate the deep darkness. Then one may enter the darkness where God is, as Moses did.

Origen argues, therefore, that no being whatsoever, save the Logos and Holy Spirit, has the intrinsic ability to see, know, or comprehend

God, but he provides a loophole. Knowledge can be gained by those illumined by the Logos and who possess the Holy Spirit. For those elite who can participate in the Logos, the darkness is transformed into light, unknowing into knowledge. Darkness is a point of perspective; the great deep that God uses as a garment can be stripped away by the Logos to those in, and illuminated by, the Logos.

Writing more generally – rather than focusing on Moses' visions – Origen further discusses the impossibilities of attaining through one's own efforts a pure heart by which one sees God in *Ag. Cels.* 7.33:

> But in order to know God we need no body at all. The knowledge of God is not derived from the eye of the body, but from the mind which sees that which is in the image of the Creator and by divine providence has received the power to know God. And that which sees God is a pure heart, from which evil thoughts no longer proceed, nor murders, nor adulteries, nor fornications, nor thefts, nor false witnessings, nor blasphemies, nor an evil eye, nor any other evil deed. That is why it is said: "Blessed are the pure in heart, for they shall see God." However, since our will is not sufficiently strong for us to be entirely pure in heart, and because we need God to create it entirely pure, the man who prays with understanding says, "Create in me a clean heart, O God."[56]

He reiterates the necessity to see God without the body, but rather with the mind. The mind, once again, can see God because it is in the image of God; mind sees mind. He also repeats the elision between pure of heart and the pure heart, but ends on a different note. While Origen often returns to Matt. 5:8, indicating who can see God (the pure in heart) and how (with a pure heart), he only rarely indicates how the pure heart is fully attained. One must, as noted, train one's mind and, through it, one's body, to eliminate completely evil and impure thoughts and actions; one must also positively search and contemplate God through nature and scriptures.[57] He elsewhere ties the purity of heart to "circumcision of the heart," which refers to guarding one's pure faith in sincerity of conscience (*Hom. Gen.* 3.6). Furthermore, one must purify words, deeds, and thoughts to attain purity of heart (*Hom. Exod.* 3.3). Ultimately, however, purity of heart cannot be fully attained by one's own efforts. No human being has the will to fully attain it. In addition to all this striving for purity, a pure heart must also be given. It is an act of God's grace.[58]

In the *Comm. Song* 3.12, Origen reiterates that only Christ knows the father, but the pure of heart will see God; nonetheless, "they will doubtless see Him only by Christ's revealing."[59] Indeed, while one adorns oneself with virtues and purifies oneself, the final act of vision is itself an act of grace. Interpreting the Song, Christ is the "nephew," the "roe," who sees and bestows the power of seeing on others; but he must again emphasize that seeing the Father is not in the bodily sense, but in mind and spirit. Jesus makes this clear by saying that only the Son knew the Father, rather than saw.[60]

In the same *Commentary* (4.15), Origen draws in Moses' vision from the Rock – and, as one knows from Paul, the "rock is Christ" (1 Cor. 10:4) – which allowed Moses to behold the glory of the Lord with an open face.[61] In his *Hom. Song* 2.13,[62] Origen returns to the shelter of the rock: Moses had requested to see God's face; and now – as the bride now adorned – he contemplates the glory of the Lord with an unveiled face. Interestingly, in this case, God (the Bridegroom) now requests to see the Bride's/Moses' face, so they may see face to face.[63]

Origen illustrates the role of Christ in vision perhaps most vividly in his recounting of the Mount of Transfiguration. As in his *Hom. Gen.* 8.9, in *Ag. Cels.* 2.64 the polymorphic Christ adapts himself to the capacity of the beholder, suggesting that Christ never changed on the mountain; the disciples' abilities did (cf. *Gos. Phil.* 58.8). In *Ag. Cels.* 4.15–16, he further uses the transfiguration as an illustration of the soul's ascent:

> If the immortal divine word assumes both a human body and a human soul, and by so doing appears to Celsus to be subject to change and remoulding, let him learn that the Word remains the Word in essence. He suffers nothing of the experience of the body or the soul. But sometimes he comes down to the level of him who is unable to look upon the radiance and brilliance of the Deity, and becomes as it were flesh, and is spoken of in physical terms, until he who has accepted him in this form is gradually lifted up by the Word and can look even upon, so to speak, his absolute form. (4.15)[64]

Responding to a criticism from Celsus that, embodied, the Logos would undergo change, Origen claims that Christ's true essence remains completely unchanged, even as he has the ability to transform his appearance at will. He simply, again, adapts himself to the capacity of the beholder, leading to seeing, "so to speak," the Logos in his "absolute form." Continuing into 4.16, again with allusions to Plato's allegory of the cave (*Rep.* 518A), Origen describes the deity as radiant and dazzling; Christ's role is to slowly educate humans so that they can move from the base physical and gradually increase in understanding so that they can see Christ – as God – in his true form, that is, as Absolute Form.[65] Stage by stage, one ascends from physicality to the realm of the mind to see eventually with undazzled eyes.

All of this indicates that one can see God clearly. In this section, Origen resorts throughout to the language of "open face" and "face to face," as Christ bestows the power of seeing to others. This transforms the Christian seer, divinizing them, as Moses was divinized through contemplation, illustrated by his glorified face.[66] Just as only the Son can know the Father, one *becomes* a Son in order to know the Father.[67] Indeed, Origen develops a progression from belief to knowledge and from knowledge/vision of God to union with God (*Comm. John* 19.16–25). Nonetheless, he is rather ambiguous about the length of vision. Indeed, it turns out that we are no longer dealing with one like Clement, who believed that Moses held uninterrupted intercourse with the divine. Rather, while Moses saw clearly with an open face (that is, a clear and pure mind), he still only saw God's backside.[68]

WHEN WILL THE PURE IN HEART SEE GOD?

While Origen himself claims to have had brief, yet extraordinary, experiences with the divine (*Hom. Song* 1.7),[69] he largely relegates divine vision – metaphorically speaking – to the afterlife.[70] In this life, one can, however, attain to Moses' vision in Exodus 33:23, glimpsing God's backside.

In *Princ.* 2.4.3, Origen again sets up the problem of seeing God with a few different verses. He reiterates that God is invisible, even for the Son, but adds John 14:9, which says that whoever has seen the Son has also seen the Father. Yet, again, for Origen the Son as well as the Holy Spirit are truly invisible, as the Father is, in their essences; that is, in their relations with one another; therefore, true seeing is through the mind. Moses proves a problem, since Moses claims that he, himself, as well as various patriarchs (assuming that Moses wrote the Pentateuch) did see God. Origen, therefore, illustrates his principles through Moses in Exodus 33:

It is in this manner then that we must suppose Moses to have seen God, not by looking at him with the eyes of the flesh, but by understanding him with the vision of the heart and the perception of the mind, and even this in part only. For it is well known that he, that is, the one who gave the oracles to Moses, says, "You shall not see my face, but my back" (Exod. 33:23). Certainly, this statement must be understood by the aid of that symbolism which is appropriate to the understanding of divine sayings, and those old wives' fables, which ignorant people invent on the subject of the front and back parts of God, must be utterly rejected and despised.[71]

While the modern reader may want to learn more about "those old wives' fables," Origen largely sidesteps the additional problem of anthropomorphisms in this passage and keeps his focus on how to see God in this life and the next.[72] After this passage, Origen reiterates that only bodies can see and be seen – which does not apply to the Father, Son, or Holy Spirit, even in their relations to one another – finishing up with John 14:9, which, again, suggests that Moses communicated with the preincarnate Logos – though invisibly through the mind. Different authors interpret the "back" here differently: for example, Irenaeus saw it as prophetic of the "latter days" when Jesus became incarnate. Philo saw it as an ontologically lower level of reality than God's face. Origen holds back, at least here. The immediate reference, however, suggests that, while Moses saw God through his heart (recalling Matt 5:8) and mind, this still fell short of a full vision. The "back" indeed indicates that even Moses could not see God fully and clearly, even with the mind. If Moses is Origen's primary illustration of how one sees God noetically rather than bodily, this might suggest that the attempt of any other human to see God even with the mind in this life will at best be fleeting and in part.

Origen does, however, appear to believe that one can achieve purity of mind/heart in a limited way within this life, with the assistance of the Logos, contrasting Irenaeus and Tertullian, who relegate such purity to the afterlife. Origen, however, differentiates between the pure and the perfect: those seeking purification are believing beginners, whereas those seeking perfection are advanced knowers or seers (cf. *Comm. John* 19.16–20).[73] In the prologue to his *Commentary on the Song of Songs*, for example, Origen explains how Greek branches of knowledge were stolen from Hebrew wisdom, aligning Abraham,

Isaac, and Jacob with Proverbs, Ecclesiastes, and the Song of Songs. Ecclesiastes/Isaac illustrates that all that is corporeal is fleeting and brittle, while inspective knowledge or enoptics (seeing within), associated with Jacob and the Song of Songs, is for the advanced; it is for those who are already purified, who are seeking perfection (prologue.3).[74] Such purification, therefore, must be possible, while one approaches a final perfection, which one must anticipate.

In Book 2 of the same work, he writes concerning the purified Christian. The purified Christian in purity of heart (Matt 5:8) will see God as he sits by the oak of Mambre, which means "from seeing" (2.4)[75] – using Abraham as example; the most important element here for our current purposes is the time of seeing – "midday." Well within the contemplative tradition, one should put oneself at leisure to see God.[76] Reading allegorically, Abraham sits outside – that is, he is out of his body – completely removed from carnal thoughts and desires to see God.[77]

In general, Origen employs less visual language in the homilies than in the commentary. The reason is likely that he thought only the most advanced would read his commentary, whereas his homilies were delivered orally in a church setting in Caesarea with a variety of listeners. His audience is different and a bit more differentiated in their progress to purity of heart. He spoke for the advanced and the beginner, baptized and catechumen, at once.[78] As he writes in *Ag. Cels.* 3.48: "On the contrary, let the educated, wise and sensible man come if he wishes, and none the less let anyone ignorant, stupid, uneducated, and childish, come as well. For the word promises to heal even such people if they come and makes all men worthy of God."[79] In short, Origen calls upon all, no matter what their current status, to draw near to the Logos for healing and advancement. The Logos has the power to convert all to be worthy, though, he would subsequently claim in the passage, that advanced education sure does help.

While his commentaries are directed toward advanced Christians, interestingly it is within the homilies that one finds a rare glimpse of Origen's own experiences. In his first homily on the Song of Songs, speaking of the bride (one's soul) encountering the bridegroom (Logos/Christ), after the bride has purified herself, drawing the bridegroom down by her beauty (virtue), he relates a classic – in terms of William James at least – first-hand experience that is both transient and painful: the divine presence leaves as quickly as it arrives; as soon as one sees the bridegroom, he disappears, leaving one in the pain of longing to see him again.[80] This is the third and lengthiest of three autobiographical statements Origen makes in the first homily, where he identifies with the Bride, which mirrors the repeated appearance and withdrawals of the Bridegroom in the Song of Songs itself.[81]

Why would he offer such experiences in his homilies rather than in his commentaries? Neither text nor interpreter has shifted; only the audience has. If the interpreter is an "intertext," as Celia Deutsch has recently argued, so is the audience.[82] Interestingly, while Origen identifies repeatedly with the Bride, and in the Commentary he discusses how to become the perfect Bride, in the Homilies he represents the audience with the bridesmaids, yet invites them to become the Bride.[83] On the one hand, he illustrates how one can advance from bridesmaid to bride, acting, himself, as mystagogue. His fleeting vision, moreover, authorizes his interpretation. As Bride, he has intimacy with the Word, who illuminates for him the hidden meaning of the text.[84] Thereby, "His congregation has access to the Son who is Word, he implies, through his teaching."[85] As the Bride, Origen mediates the Bridegroom (Logos) to his audience, the Bridesmaids waiting to become Brides themselves. He is both exemplar and guide of that transition.[86] Both Moses (in *Principia*) and Origen himself (*Hom. Song* 1.7) have fleeting visions of the divine.[87] Together they are the receiver and interpreter of intimate revelations – that is, the biblical text itself – of the Logos.[88] Yet, on the other hand, due to humanity's mortal frailty, these must remain brief encounters.[89]

This current human limitation illustrated by Moses and Origen himself is suggested in his earlier work *On First Principles*. Early in 1.1.5, Origen writes,

> In the same way our mind is shut up within bars of flesh and blood and rendered duller and feebler by reason of its association with such material substances; and although it is regarded as far more excellent when compared with the natural body, yet when it strains after incorporeal things and seeks to gain a sight of them it has scarcely the power of a glimmer of light or a tiny lamp. And among all intellectual, that is, incorporeal things, what is there so universally surpassing, so unspeakably and immeasurably excelling as God, whose nature certainly the vision of the human mind, however pure or clear to the very utmost that mind may be, cannot gaze at or behold?[90]

In stereotypical Platonic fashion, it is the human body that limits the mind (cf. Wis. 9:15). Matter dulls and enfeebles the mind. Note the language used: when reflecting on incorporeal things, the greatest of which is God, the mind strains for its vision and receives but a glimmer. The last line is striking in light of Matt 5:8: this is true at the mind's purest. Origen is setting up a manoeuvre similar to those of Tertullian and Clement: while we may catch a glimpse of the divine in this life, true vision is for the afterlife. He reinforces this notion later in 2.6.1: humans are weak, in that they cannot see everything with their eyes, nor can they comprehend everything with the minds, being weaker than the rational creatures who dwell in heaven.

In a different context, however, Origen more practically reserves the ultimate visions for martyrs. In *Martyrdom* 13, he combines the status of the martyr with the nature of seeing. Those who sacrifice their bodies must be the truly pure hearts. With strong allusions to Moses' claim to vision in Num. 12:6–8, Origen claims that the martyrs are the "friends" of the Father: "For friends learn not by enigmas, but by a form that is seen or by wisdom bare of words, symbols, and types; this will be possible when they attain to the nature of intelligible things and to the beauty of truth."[91]

Applying Moses' status ("friend") and his means of visions (by "form" and not in an "enigma") from Numbers 12 to all martyrs, Origen indicates that the greatest of visions will be vouchsafed to martyrs.[92] Moreover, in a telling turn of interpretation in Origen's *Comm. John* 2.210–211, he plays with the etymology of "martyr" as "witness" when discussing John the Baptist as a "witness," thereby tying together the roles of prophetic seer and martyr. Giving up one's body for God, one "witnesses" God.

Returning to *Martyrdom*, he cites Paul being caught up to the third heaven (often paired with Moses' vision).[93] Origen continues,

> you will consequently realize that you will presently know more and greater things than the unspeakable words then revealed to Paul, after which he came down from the third heaven ... For in God there are treasured up much greater visions than these, which no bodily nature can comprehend, if it is not first delivered from everything corporeal. And I am convinced that stores up and keeps by Himself much greater visions than the sun, the moon, and the chorus of the stars have seen, indeed than the holy angels have seen, whom God made wind and a flame a fire.[94]

Martyrs represent, for Origen – as they had for Tertullian – the pinnacle of Christian life. They will see greater things than Paul and even
the angels – the rational creatures mentioned above who do not share
human weakness. Martyrs, indeed, having thrown off their weakness
by throwing off their corporeal nature, come to resemble God to the
highest degree possible (*Martyrdom* 47).[95]

Nonetheless, everyone else will also see, though perhaps not as
greatly as the martyrs. As he writes in his *Comm. Song* 2.1,[96] in heavenly existence, we will finally see face to face; that is, we will see all
of God's Wisdom, whom he regularly identifies with God's Word,
the Son.

CONCLUSIONS:
INTERNAL AND EXTERNAL CONTEXTS OF VISIONS

As quotations of Matt. 11:27 (only the Son knows the Father), Col.
1:15 (the Son is image of the invisible God), John 1:17 (whoever sees
the Son sees the Father), Matt. 5:8 (the pure in heart will see God), and
Exod. 33:23 (Moses' vision of God's backside) whirl in ever-shifting
configurations, Origen's views of divine vision emerge with permu-
tating emphases. While Tertullian stated the problem of divine vision
among the patriarchs and prophets most clearly and succinctly, Origen most explicitly considers the three major possible solutions to
the problem – who sees, how one sees, or what one sees – with the
strongest emphasis on how.

In nearly every passage, Origen reiterated that God is completely
invisible because God is not a body. God the Father, Son, and Holy
Spirit are not only invisible to humans, but to one another as well.
The Son is the invisible image of the invisible God. One, therefore,
must see God with the mind, which was created in the image and
likeness of God. Origen only occasionally considers what the seers
saw. He adapts Justin's view that seers of old saw the Son, appearing
in various ways as a man, an angel, or fire. Different kinds of
humans, and even angels, see the Son only according to their capacity, and one's capacity can change, illustrated by the Mount of
Transfiguration, where the essence of the Son did not change, but
the seers' status changed, aligning to the level of Moses. Ultimately,
Origen still claims that their greatest vision of the Son is with the
mind, which is how Moses ultimately saw God. But mental exertion
is not enough.

Shifting to who has the ability to see God through the mind, Origen looks to Matt. 5:8: "the pure of heart." The heart is both the means, being equated with the mind, and relates to one's status, being pure. The pure of heart see from their pure heart, the purest of which belongs to martyrs, yet also to the prophets, especially Moses, contemplatives, and interpreters of scripture like Origen himself. For the rest, purity of heart/mind is something one strives for, but never attains by one's own efforts, because the mind is defiled, dulled, and enfeebled by its attachment to the body. To glimpse God in this life through partial glances or see more fully in the next, one needs divine aid. The Son as the means of knowing/vision purifies and then perfects one's heart/mind and is the ultimate granter of the divine vision, drawing the dazzled, darkened mind upward into the heavenly light of vision.

Origen regularly illustrates the limits and possibilities of the human condition through Moses' visions. Moses shows our human weaknesses and the limits of embodiment, allowing only a partial glimpse of God's backside. Yet Moses was purified and perfected, so that he could enter the cloud. This differentiates Moses from the masses and provides the measure for the martyrs, who become God's "friend" as Moses was, and see God's true form.

Origen presents himself, moreover, as a prophetic visionary worthy to interpret the visions of Moses; he argues that one must become like Moses to read Moses. Similarly, only one with intimacy with the Logos can interpret the Logos in its other incarnation: scripture. Origen, thereby, makes divine vision necessary for biblical interpretation and, therefore, for teaching others. His authority is that of a visionary teacher, largely independent of church structure.

He is perhaps the last "freelance" thinker analyzed here. He shows the independence of a teacher, like Clement, even to the point of annoying his own bishop in Alexandria.[97] Yet he becomes folded into an emerging church structure through his own ordination in Caesarea, preaching to mixed audiences of catechumens, baptized Christians, and perhaps others. He takes the role of elite teacher-as-mystagogue that one sees with Clement, but applies it more broadly.

Internally, within the Christian community, especially as developed in his mature thought in Caesarea, he sees both a hierarchy of Christians, yet a more equalizing element than found in someone like Clement. Firstly, his hierarchy is not based solely or even primarily upon ordination, but upon studied contemplation. He interestingly applies priestly language to ordained and non-ordained Christians, differentiating based upon the advanced wisdom of those who have purified their minds more than the majority of Christians, whom he labels "Levites."[98] Like Clement, Origen differentiates Christians between the elite and the ordinary, using the terminology of purification for beginners and perfection for advanced, but the difference is not as sharp. Put another way, he is more optimistic about ordinary Christians than Clement is in his surviving writings. This is perhaps due to genre: Origen writes to and for ordinary Christians as much as he does for advanced ones. Theoretically, for Origen, all humans could achieve the visions of Moses or Origen himself, but he is painfully aware that few ever do.

This differentiation between, yet greater continuity of, the beginner and advanced Christian is also pronounced if one compares his homilies and commentaries. While scholars often discuss the differences between his homilies and commentaries, there is a surprising amount of commonality.[99] His homilies often include technical and learned exegesis, and the commentaries inversely include pastoral edification for the faithful. Origen likely relied upon his commentaries when composing his homilies; they, therefore, interilluminate one another.

Nonetheless, differences remain. While each interpretation in the homilies has a parallel in the commentary, the focus or emphasis is often different: the homilies focus on purifying the soul before approaching the mysteries; the commentaries, on perfecting it.[100] The homilies often show a greater degree of simplification and restraint, though perhaps not as much restraint as we find in Clement of Alexandria. Origen explains things more fully. He is partly a pastor, concerned with the sins of his community.

Especially in his homilies, moreover, Origen wrote for the intellectual and the ordinary Christian at once. If one comes to the Word/Logos, the Logos will make all humans worthy of God (*Ag. Cels.* 3.48).[101] There is a clear equalizing tendency here, and Origen seems to think that one part of the difference between old and new revelations is that the new was for the popular and not limited to an elect. Through the sermons and perhaps sacraments, more people can experience what only Moses and a select few prophets could in the past.[102] This is partly why he expresses his own experiences in the homilies: he provides a model, as Moses also does, but not just for the elect or perfected of the church, but for the entire church.

The commentaries tend to be more systematic, going into greater depth, amassing more parallel passages, with a greater focus on doctrinal matters.[103] As Hanson notes, "Origen in his Homilies sincerely and carefully expounds Scripture for the ordinary man and woman in the pew, but we must not expect to find the full, the whole Origen there."[104] Despite the concern for beginning Christians, there remains a difference between purified and perfected, between catechumen, baptized Christian, and advanced contemplative. To that end, Hanson can say, "I know of no passage in Origen's works which suggests that the simple and uneducated believer can attain to the higher knowledge."[105] I may modify this: the simple and uneducated believer advances to higher knowledge through the mediation of Origen and his sermons. While Origen as Bride speaks of his relationship with the Bridegroom (the Logos) to the Bridesmaids (his audience), he still invites the members of that audience to advance to become eventually Brides of the Logos themselves. Origen, thereby, becomes a new Moses, mediating between his audience and the revelation of the Logos. Nonetheless, the intellectual will continue to outstrip the ordinary – at least in this life.

Origen's writings are also marked by external pressures: he feels pressure to respond to the cultured despisers of Christianity (*Against Celsus*), to Marcionite and Valentinian schools, and to the more occasional, yet more acute, threats of persecution and martyrdom. The philosophical orientation – yet stated anti-philosophical polemics – of his work relates to the first. In this he has absorbed the philosophical assumptions found in Philo and Clement, yet without constantly citing Plato, as Clement did. His occasional adoption of and adaptations to Justin's solution – that it was the Son who appeared and spoke to the patriarchs and the prophets – continue to have an anti-Marcionite and anti-Valentinian edge. Even when he drops Justin's solution and focuses on the essential invisibility of the Son, he still does so by demonstrating the continuity with Moses and the prophets rather than differentiating from them. In fact, he directly opposes Heracleon, a Valentinian thinker, in his *Commentary on John*.

Finally, the prospect of martyrdom clearly shines through his writings. His life was punctuated by sporadic – and, eventually, systematic – persecution, related to the reigns of Severus, Maximin, and Decius. This, again, creates another tension in his thought. Who are the true athletes of Christ? While there remains the elitist impulse of vision vouchsafed to the educated few – Moses, Origen, and other perfected souls – there is also the flattening impulse or at least a competing concept of the martyr, who becomes a new Moses, a friend of God who sees God's form. And, indeed, a non-intellectual can die as a martyr, creating a different kind of elite Christian. Origen's situation, therefore, shows a potential loosening of the elitist impulse in vision, partly due to his role as teacher of a more varied congregation and partly due to his context of intensified persecution.

Moses, Vision, and Episcopal Authority in Late-Antique Christianity

Several scholars have demonstrated how, after the rise of Constantine, bishops embodied and appropriated various forms of charismatic authority.[1] Claudia Rapp has analyzed how bishops, beginning in the fourth century, combined in their persons three different types of authority: spiritual (having received the *pneuma* of God), ascetic (which she equated with what Max Weber would call "charisma," as well as traditional *askesis*), and pragmatic (how the bishop acts as a benefactor and advocate for the community).[2] Dayna Kalleres, moreover, has perspicaciously examined the spiritual powers of a bishop to navigate and battle the demonic landscape of the late-antique city.[3]

Andrea Sterk, more to the point, has argued that fourth-century bishops, most prominently Basil of Caesarea, mobilized Moses as part of the justification of the emergent power of the bishop, particularly the model of the monk-bishop.[4] There was, indeed, a great deal of appropriation of Mosaic authority for episcopal power in the fourth century, especially among Greek authors.[5] Nonetheless, the episcopal appropriation is one among many: Moses becomes the paradigm and justification for multiple overlapping channels of access to the divine, from the institutional access of the bishop to the more psychic access of the soul of the mystic (Gregory of Nyssa), with the contemplative theologian in between (Gregory of Nazianzus). These overlapping streams of authority are all, moreover, grounded specifically in Moses' visions.

While readers will find many of the older views of Moses' visions remain from the first century (that he saw angels) and from the second and third centuries (that he saw the preincarnate Christ or foresaw the incarnate Christ),[6] here one finds a greater emphasis on the directness of his visions. This is a pattern that emerges most clearly in the fourth century, developed in some different directions by Augustine of Hippo in the Latin West, and reaches its apogee in the sixth-century work of Pseudo-Dionysius. There is an exception here, but one that illustrates the broader point: Gregory of Nazianzus will say that Moses saw the "backsides" or "averted figure" of God; nonetheless, he substitutes the first-person pronoun for Moses, putting himself on Sinai as the mediator between God and the faithful, thereby falling into the broader pattern of channelling Moses' authority to establish or justify one's own in a newly empowered episcopacy.[7]

LATE-ANTIQUE JEWISH COMPARISONS:
R. AKIVA AND MOSES

Before analyzing our predominantly Christian documentation as we continue to trace the Christian Moses, we should remember it is significant that Jews were doing the same thing: the Rabbis were deploying Moses' visions on Sinai to establish their own emergent institutionalized interpretive authority within the communities of late-antique Judaism.

In addition to the materials discussed at the end of Chapter 2, one of the most famous stories is that of Moses sitting in R. Akiva's classroom in *b. Men.* 29B. In this story, Moses ascends on high and, in a strikingly anthropomorphic exchange, sees God putting decorative crowns on the letters of the Torah. Moses inquires why God is doing such a thing. God responds, saying that one day a great teacher will arise who will expound many laws from such decorations. Moses requests to see him, and immediately God takes Moses to the future, setting him in the back row of R. Akiva's classroom. R. Akiva is expounding on the Torah, but Moses and some of the other students have trouble following R. Akiva's complicated argument. Moses is distressed by all this, but when a student finally asks where R. Akiva derived his interpretation, he simply responds that it was all revealed to Moses on Sinai. At this statement, Moses is relieved and brought back to his own time. He asks God why he is revealing the Torah to such a minor person (that is, Moses himself) rather than to such a great one (R. Akiva). God simply silences Moses, saying that he has decided it this way. Moses then asks what the reward of such a great man as R. Akiva will be. God then shows him R. Akiva's martyrdom, specifically the weighing of his flesh in the market. Moses, dumfounded, asks why God would allow one of his great teachers such a horrific death. God again silences Moses, saying that he has declared it that way.[8]

This story deals with two issues: how can the exposition of the Rabbis, especially R. Akiva, be considered revealed "Torah" and the theodicy of why the righteous, here again, R. Akiva, suffer. The answer to both is simply that God has declared it to be so. End of the discussion.

The first issue is more important for our current purposes. While *Exodus Rabbah* 42.8 claimed that God revealed to Moses all later prophecies, including those attributed to Jeremiah, Isaiah, and Ezekiel, along with those attributed to himself preserved in the Torah, this story in the Babylonian Talmud claims that Moses received all later interpretations of the Torah, whether written or oral, when God revealed the Torah "on high," conflating Sinai with heaven. What is more, God revealed these to Moses *with Moses not understanding them*. While R. Akiva's interpretation receives its authority from the fact that it was revealed to Moses on Sinai, Moses does not actually understand the interpretation. As Jeffrey Rubenstein notes, Moses' placement in the back row of the classroom puts him among the least-gifted students, who cannot follow R. Akiva's complex discussion.[9] In short, while R. Akiva receives his authority through Moses' visions on Sinai, R. Akiva displaces and supersedes Moses.

The pairing of Moses and Akiva, the lawgiver and interpreter, respectively, occurred regularly in late-antique Jewish literature. As seen in Chapter 2, the *Hekhalot* macroforms, especially *Hekhalot Zutarti*, also paired R. Akiva and Moses as being among the few to receive divine mysteries directly from the heavenly source. Moreover, the traditions surrounding Yohanan b. Zakkai and his students expounding upon the Merkavah, leading to Sinai-like phenomena appearing, legitimates rabbinic exegesis within the original Sinai event (*t. Hag.* 2:1–2; *y. Hag.* 2.1; *b. Hag.* 14b).[10] Although direct relationships are difficult to establish, late-antique Christians would utilize the traditions of Moses and Sinai in parallel ways.

THE *APOSTOLIC CONSTITUTIONS*: MOSES/BISHOP AS GOD AND SEER OF GOD

Turning to Christian sources, the *Apostolic Constitutions* are quite varied, including material from multiple periods. They were likely compiled at the end of the fourth century in Syria, and are sometimes

dated precisely to 380 CE, the year before the Council of Constantinople. This compiler or compilers relied upon earlier texts of the
Didascalia (third century), part of the *Didache* (second century), and
the *Apostolic Tradition* of Hyppolytus, with some of the prayers possibly originating in a synagogue setting,[11] making it a bridge from the
earlier materials from the second and third centuries to the late-
antique figures, such as Basil of Caesarea, Gregory of Nazianzus, and
Gregory of Nyssa.[12] The material from the *Apostolic Constitutions* preserves a more-ancient analogy between the Israelite priesthood and
the emergent Christian hierarchy, which is at least as old as *1 Clem.*
40.1–43.6 (c. 95 CE).[13] The constant calls to obey one's bishop recall
Ignatius' second-century letters. The novel approach of the redactor of
the *Apostolic Constitutions*, however, is to transform this analogy into a
divinely inspired continuation of Moses' vision on Sinai and his call
from the burning bush.[14]

Before looking specifically at visions, one should note a parallel
emphasis in these documents of one element of Moses' encounter
with the burning bush, which one also encounters in its source material in the third-century *Didascalia Apostolorum*: the bishop mirrors
Moses when God calls Moses a "god" to Pharaoh (Exod. 7:1).[15] Sometimes the bishop is, likewise, directly called god, as in the following
passage: "He is your ruler and governor; he is your king and poten-
tate; he is next after God, your earthly god, who has a right to be honored by you (*Apost. Const.* 2.4.26.4; cf. *Did. Apost.* 9.2.26).[16] The bishop is next to God; he is an "earthly god." Claudia Rapp notes that the
bishop receives this divine designation as part of the reciprocal duties
that he, in turn, owes the congregation: as the intermediary between
God and the congregation, the bishop bears the congregation's sins
before God. He is responsible for their spiritual welfare, yet has the
potential for *parrhesia* before God in heaven.[17] In short, the bishop is
God's counterpart on earth, in a theological relationship that resembles Eusebius of Caesarea's depiction of Constantine.[18] As the bishop
is like God, then the deacon is like Christ; as Christ ministers to the
Father so the deacon ministers to the bishop.[19]

The text continues with this theme of the divine bishop in
2.4.29.1–30.2 (cf. *Did. Apost.* 9.2.28–31), but here more securely
grounding it in the Exodus passage:

> For if Aaron, because he declared to Pharaoh the words of God
> from Moses, is called a prophet; and Moses himself is called a god

to Pharaoh, on account of his being at once a king and a high
priest, as God says to him, "I have made you a god to Pharaoh, and
Aaron your brother shall be your prophet;" why do you not also
esteem the mediators of the word to be prophets, and reverence
them as gods?

For now the deacon is to you Aaron, and the bishop Moses. If,
therefore, Moses was called a god by the Lord, let the bishop be
honored among you as a god, and the deacon as his prophet. For
as Christ does nothing without His Father, so neither does the
deacon do anything without his bishop and as the Son without
His Father is nothing, so is the deacon nothing without his bishop; and as the Son is subject to his father, so is every deacon subject to his bishop; and as the Son is the messenger and prophet
of the Father, so is the deacon the messenger and prophet of his
bishop.[20]

The bishop could not seek a higher title, the one Moses received from
God in Exod. 7:1.[21] Strangely, though, the *Apostolic Constitutions* takes
Moses' title of god, used in juxtaposition to Pharaoh, his enemy, and
applies it to the bishop in juxtaposition to his own community. In
other words, this document employs passages of Moses' authority and
his visions that had, in previous centuries, been employed to exclude
other groups, but, instead, will now be redirected to organizing one's
own Christian congregation. What was once directed without will
now be focused within.

Nonetheless, in addition to this exaltation of the bishop as an earthly god, the bishop's position is further guaranteed through Moses'
divine visions. While various theophanies are vaguely discussed elsewhere (*Apost. Const.* 7.2.33), in a new passage not found in the source
material, Moses' visions receive primacy of importance for the legitimation of the status of bishops in 8.5.46:

Now this we all in common do charge you, that every one remain
in that rank which is appointed him, and do not transgress his
proper bounds; for they are not ours, but God's ... We say that
Moses the servant of God ("to whom God spoke face to face, as if
a man spoke to his friend;" to whom He said, "I know you above
all men;" to whom He spoke directly, and not by obscure methods, or dreams, or angels, or riddles), this person, when he made
constitutions and divine laws, distinguished what things were to

be performed by the high priests, what by the priests, and what by
the Levites; distributing to every one his proper and suitable
office in the divine service. And those things which are allotted
for the high priests to do, those might not be meddled with by
the priests; and what things were allotted to the priests, the
Levites might not meddle with; but every one observed those
ministrations which were written down and appointed for them.
And if any would meddle beyond the tradition, death was his
punishment ... But being taught by the Lord the series of things,
we distributed the functions of the high-priesthood to the bishops, those of the priesthood to the presbyters, and the ministra-
tion under them both to the deacons; that the divine worship
might be performed in purity ... High priests, priests, and Levites
were ordained by Moses, the most beloved of God. By our Saviour
were we apostles, thirteen in number, ordained; and by the apostles James, and Clement, and others with us, were ordained, that
we may not make the catalogue of all those bishops over again.[22]

A major shift has clearly occurred since the first century. If one juxtaposes this paragraph with the passages of the New Testament, the difference is striking, especially given that this fourth-century text is
placed in the mouths of the original apostles.[23] There is a new emphasis on the direct, unmediated quality of Moses' visions and his intimacy with God. It even contradicts the New Testament to say that
Moses did not receive revelations from angels (cf. Acts 7:30; 7:38; 7:53;
Gal. 3:19; Heb. 2:2). His direct visions of God guarantee the continued
viability of God's message to Moses.[24] What is this message? It is order
and hierarchy. It is knowing where you belong. It is a warning by bishops to priests and other Christians to obey.[25] Since Ignatius in the second century, bishops have been telling laity and especially lower
orders of clergy to obey, but the reference to Moses' vision as the basis
of that authority is new; yet it fits within the Christian world of
the fourth century, as the newly imperially empowered episcopate
attempted to justify its increasing authority in society.[26] Bishops will
emphasize the directness of Moses' divine visions as the basis of
Moses' own subsequent leadership of the Israelites, and simultaneously equate themselves with Moses in order likewise to undergird
their own charismatic authority in church.[27] The manoeuvre becomes
typical in the fourth century among figures such as Gregory of
Nazianzus, Gregory of Nyssa, and Basil of Caesarea, foregrounding

Moses' direct vision of God in Num. 12:8 and pushing the prohibition of vision in Ex. 33:20 into the background.[28]

BASIL OF CAESAREA:
MOSES AS IDEAL MONK-BISHOP

When Gregory of Nazianzus,[29] together with Basil of Caesarea,[30] edited the *Philokalia* of Origen's writings (c. 358 CE), much had happened since Origen's time.[31] Constantine had issued *Edicts of Toleration* and officially sanctioned Christianity,[32] the Arian controversy had sparked more precise formulations of the relationship between the members of the Trinity, particularly the Father and the Son, and the Council of Nicea (325) had produced the *homoousian* creed.[33] Nevertheless, afterwards a succession of Arian emperors advanced their own brand of Christianity.[34] Conflicts broke out between Nicenes, Homoiousians, Homoians, and the neo-Arians, Aetius and Eunomios.[35]

Basil of Caesarea, Gregory of Nazianzus, and Gregory of Nyssa have been considered roughly together as the "Cappadocians." Their influence became widespread. Nonetheless, they activate this motif of Moses' visions in some overlapping, yet divergent, paths, even while relying upon the same basic materials.[36] Basil and Gregory of Nazianzus will, as Andrea Sterk has demonstrated, use Moses' visions to different degrees to undergird the authority of the bishop. Gregory of Nazianzus will specifically limit this to the learned theologian. Gregory of Nyssa, however, will use the same materials – with enormous borrowings from, and developments of, Philo and Origen – to use Moses as a model for the mystical life, something that Pseudo-Dionysius the Areopagite later developed to the greatest extent.[37]

According to Sterk, Basil of Caesarea was the catalyst and role model of the monk-bishop, who, highly educated, nonetheless leaves the world as a monk, only to return to it in ecclesiastical leadership. In the middle ages, this became the dominant paradigm in the Byzantine church for the episcopacy.[38] While there would be many mystical models from biblical history to exemplify this leadership (Elijah, John the Baptist, etc.), Moses would be the pre-eminent model for the contemplative visionary as a leader of people.[39]

Basil's presentation of Moses as the model leader, whether episcopal or monastic, appears across his writings, including his *Asceticon*, homilies, and letters.[40] As Andrea Sterk notes, "This Old Testament patriarch served as a paragon of self-sacrificial love, contemplation, nearness to God, and the calmness of character and freedom from passion that produces meekness."[41] Basil positively compared several bishops to Moses: Musonius, Innocent, Eusebius of Samosota,[42] and, one of Basil's heroes, Gregory the Wonderworker.[43] While in the late-fourth century, this identification between Christian leadership and Moses would become nearly exclusively applied to bishops, it is an identification of leadership that goes back to Eusebius of Caesarea's portrayal of Constantine.[44]

Combining several traditions,[45] Basil presents Moses in his *Homilies on the Hexaemeron* – that is, the "six days" of creation – as being raised by Pharaoh's daughter, receiving the best education available, disdaining the power and privileges of Egypt to suffer with the people of God, retreating for forty years of contemplation in Ethiopia, and finally receiving a vision of God.[46] After this vision, he was ready to minister to the people; that is, divine vision is a means to another end. Basil writes:

> He [Moses], finally, who, at the age of eighty, saw God, as far as it is possible for a human to see him; or rather as it had not previously been granted to others to see him, according to the testimony of God himself, "If there be a prophet among you, I the Lord will make myself known unto him in a vision, and will speak unto him in a dream. My servant Moses is not so, who is faithful in all my house, with him I will speak mouth to mouth, even apparently, and not in dark speeches." It is this one, whom God judged worthy to behold him, face to face, like the angels, who imparts to us what he has learned from God. (*Hom. Hex.* 1)[47]

Basil begins with the traditional vision dance. At first, he says simply that Moses saw God, but immediately qualifies it, "as far as it is possible for a human to see Him" (ὡς ἀνθρώπῳ ἰδεῖν δυνατὸν). Then Basil does something different. Quoting Numbers 12:8, he says that it had *previously* been impossible for humans to see God, but, by God's own testimony, Moses was the *first* deemed worthy to see God; previous to Moses none had seen God. By the end, instead of qualifying, Basil is intensifying: face to face, like the angels. For Basil, Moses' direct vision – face to face, just like the angels – both prepares him for his leadership and authoritatively undergirds the content of his revelations from God: Scripture; in this case, Genesis 1. Basil's reading, like many other contemporary Jewish traditions, also associates Moses' vision with a shift of not only worldly status (that is, worthy of leadership), but potential ontological transformation: becoming (like) an angel.[48] The model bishop, according to Basil, would do the same as Moses: be educated in secular and sacred wisdom, reject the secular wisdom for a life of secluded contemplation, and then lead the people. Moreover, as Basil notes elsewhere, even after Moses returned to a life of leadership, it was a mixed life of both active leadership and contemplation.[49]

Basil's development of the Mosaic model bishop reaches its maturity as Gregory of Nyssa – Basil's younger brother – used this comparison to characterize Basil himself.[50] In an oration given in memory of Basil, Gregory writes that Basil imitated Moses in three ways, mirroring the three stages of Moses' life that Basil himself laid out in many places, including the introduction to this *Hexaemeron*.[51] First, both received the best of pagan learning, but rejected it;[52] both retreated from city and civilization to contemplate God in solitude.[53] Gregory even says that Basil had a vision of God like the one Moses had at the burning bush. Finally, this contemplation prepared both of them for their later leadership of people. Vision and leadership are united. Gregory writes, "Often we saw him [Basil] enter into the darkness where God was. By the mystical guidance of the Spirit he understood what was invisible to others, so that he seemed to be enveloped in that darkness in which the Word of God is concealed" (*On His Brother Basil*).[54] Gregory was clear: Basil was the spiritual equal of the patriarchs, prophets, and saints of old. As in the case of R. Akiva or Origen in *Ag. Cels.* 6.4, as the interpreter of Moses in the *Hexaemeron*, Basil became, in Gregory's estimation, a new Moses, as revealer and interpreter became united in the act of interpretation.[55] For Gregory of Nyssa, true mystical knowledge is vouchsafed to one and concealed from the rest, whether Moses or his brother Basil, a bishop, who, like Moses, entered the dark cloud where God was. This is mysticism that is not focused on "experience" for its own sake, but as a means to differentiate one who is worthy from those in the community who depend upon him – Moses, or Basil, or the bishop from everyone else.

Gregory of Nazianzus likewise portrayed Basil as both Moses and Paul – combining the two visionaries, as so many would often do – while claiming for himself the roles of Aaron and Barnabas (*Or.* 43).[56] In this way, Gregory recognized Basil's leadership (Moses/Paul), while also subtly indicating his own superior speaking abilities and learning, the very learning that Basil said a true Moses-Bishop should possess and, simultaneously, spurn.[57] Nonetheless, in his autobiographical poem (*De Vita Sua* 352–5), the Nazianzene very positively portrayed Basil attaining union with God in the cloud, as Moses did on the mountain.[58]

In short, Basil attempted to overhaul the episcopate, modelling a monk-bishop paradigm, for which he found great resonance with Moses, the contemplative, yet active, leader. For Basil, the monastic bishop and Moses were the ultimate *prostates*, mediating between divine power, other state powers, and the bishop's community.[59]

GREGORY OF NAZIANZUS (329–90 CE): THE THEOLOGIAN AS MOSES

For Gregory of Nazianzus, Moses cannot be a model for all bishops – only certain ones, such as Basil and himself. Gregory has been called the greatest theologian of the fourth century, and at the Council of Chalcedon (451) he was posthumously given the title "the Theologian," an epithet he shares with only St John the Divine and St Symeon the New Theologian.[60] In the Byzantine manuscript record, Gregory's writings are second only to the Bible in number of copies. Like Basil, Gregory used Moses as the prime exemplar for Christian leadership, whether as bishop or especially as a theologian.[61] Christopher Beeley, moreover, has suggested that it was not Basil, but Gregory, who catalyzed the Moses-as-bishop model.[62]

In Gregory of Nazianzus' writings, visionary experience and true leadership combine in the figure of Moses. Since Moses could approach God in the cloud and withstand God's glory, he could lead God's people.[63] One should not, according to Gregory, accept a position of authority without having an experience of divine encounter, as Moses did. Gregory's writings on Moses, vision, and authority, moreover, reflect a clear social stratification in Gregory's mind, one that gives pre-eminence to the episcopate, to be sure, but especially to the theologian. For Gregory, therefore, most of the emphasis resides in the status of the seer, who has been purified and illuminated.[64] It is a status for which Moses is the model and the measure.

Gregory often exhibited disdain for other bishops. With his aristocratic air, he regarded the largely illiterate episcopate with scorn.[65] As John McGuckin writes, "Gregory feels that he bestows honor on the office rather than vice versa."[66] Moreover, as Sterk has noted, the Cappadocians largely thought their contemporary episcopate was problematic for its moral looseness, lack of education, or general lack of qualifications, giving rise to these new moralizing, educated, and monastically oriented bishops who modelled themselves after Moses.[67]

Much of this stems from Gregory's high level of pagan and Christian education. Gregory of Nazianzus' education in Origen's writings and the more general philosophical attitude among Platonists, Stoics, and Neo-Pythagoreans of the fourth century established a context in which the highest form of philosophical insight was the visionary experience of God.[68] McGuckin notes that this shared Neoplatonic and Christian theme for Gregory "is equally a central notion of the vision of God, and is usually set within a liturgical context: the mind's admission to the heavenly sanctum where the radiant presence of God is veiled from creaturely eyes, to protect them."[69] Later McGuckin notes that visionary experience is entirely lacking in monastic desert literature,[70] but for Gregory "it has become the supreme category of authentification."[71] In the context of discussing the *Hymn of Lament* (*Carmen Lugubre*), McGuckin credits Gregory for making this a standard element of Byzantine thought.[72]

In addition to his Origenist-Platonist education, Gregory often thought of people – especially his father and himself – in terms of biblical prototypes.[73] It is not surprising, therefore, that Moses would appear among such prototypes and, combined with Gregory's interest in divine vision, with significant focus on Moses' visions. We already saw this above with his consideration of Basil as Moses and Paul, with himself as Aaron and Barnabas. In this case, comparison to Moses could be mixed praise. Indeed, in *Or.* 18.13, he praises his own father as a new Moses by alluding to the light shining round him, as Moses' face shone after he came down from the mount. Nonetheless, for a Christian this passage could conjure Paul's critical comments in 2 Cor. 3. Moreover, as Moses was slow in speech, he needed an Aaron with eloquence, a figure provided by the more-eloquent Gregory. In fact, Gregory often liked to portray himself as a new Aaron or Samuel, while his father is the tongue-tied Moses or elderly Eli (*Or.* 16; *De Vita Sua* 371–2).[74]

More significantly, however, Moses appears squarely in the middle of Gregory's famous and influential five theological orations (*Ors.* 27–31). Gregory Nazianzen delivered his five theological orations in 380, just a year before the Council of Constantinople (381),[75] making them contemporary to the editing of the *Apostolic Constitutions*.[76] In

Oration 27, Gregory primarily contends with Eunomians, indicating that only certain people should engage in theological speculation at certain times and to particular audiences, excluding Eunomios. Eunomios claimed that one could know God's essence completely, that, in fact, we know as much about God's essence as God does, a position that Gregory recoiled from. This opposition pervades and shapes the theological orations. Gregory, therefore, expresses greater pessimism about one's ability to see God in these most influential orations (27–31) than he does elsewhere in his writings.[77]

In the remaining orations, Gregory constructs his Trinitarian theology on God (28), the Son (29–30), and the Holy Spirit (31). In Oration 28, after arguing that theology is not for just anyone to dabble in, he turns to his own role as theologian, making himself into a new Moses:

> I eagerly ascend the mount ... that I may enter the cloud and company with God (for such is God's bidding). Is any an Aaron? He shall come up with me. He shall stand hard by, should be willing to wait, if need be, outside the cloud. Is any a Nadab, an Abihu, or an elder? He too shall ascend, but further off, his place matching his purity. Is any of the crowd, unfit, as they are, for so sublime contemplation? Utterly unhallowed? – let him abide below.[78] (28.2)[79]

> I was running with a mind to see God and so it was that I ascended the mount. I penetrated the cloud, became enclosed in it, detached from matter and material things and concentrated, so far as might be, in myself. But when I directed my gaze I scarcely saw the backsides of God, and this while sheltering in the rock, God the word incarnate for us. (28.3)[80]

Gregory recounts Moses ascending the mountain and entering the cloud where God is, and does so entirely in the first person. This first-person rhetoric is bold.[81] Previous authors spoke of Moses ascending the mount, and none specifically stated that others may enter that cloud.[82] While others have sought and would continue to seek to imitate Moses, Gregory has completely displaced Moses, whom he never mentions by name. While following the tradition of resisting visions, Gregory has created the hierarchy through the account, placing himself at the top in the presence of God, while extrapolating the fourth-century hierarchy of the church based upon levels of worthiness and purity.[83] One reason he has five theological orations, moreover, may be to imitate the five books of the Torah attributed to Moses.[84]

On the one hand, he does not see God (only his "backsides," or, if one follows the Williams and Wickham translation, "the averted figure" of God), yet on the other hand, he is still the only one worthy to be in the presence of God.[85] This passage, like the works of Philo and Origen, portrays "Moses" (or Gregory) as seeking an ever-elusive God. He is placed on the rock, which is equated with the Logos (cf. Origen). Gregory's encounter in the cloud reaches or passes the limits of the material world. Unlike previous authors, he speaks of concentrating in himself, while detaching from material things. Gregory's language assumes an intellectual vision that is seen by looking into oneself, seeing God through the mirror of the soul. Even with the help of the Logos, however, God remains out of grasp; Gregory scarcely sees the "averted figure of God." But this is not the negative theology it is often taken to be; Gregory does claim to see something. When put into his larger theological writings, one finds Gregory is relatively optimistic about one's ability to see something of God in this life – just not completely. In fact, in his poetry, he claims to have been granted a vision of the light of the Trinity, even if only in dreams. And those who are purified will eventually come to know the entirety of the Trinity (*Or.* 25.17).[86]

Yet, while he seeks to see and know God's essence, as Eunomios would claim one could, this "averted figure" that Gregory-as-Moses sees is definitively not God's essence;[87] it is not even the Logos (which Gregory identifies with the rock), but the part of God that "reaches us at its furthest remove from God."[88] Indeed, as he later states (28.16), no one has ever or will ever discover what God is in God's own essence – only God can know that. Instead of God's essence, Gregory, the new Moses, ascending into the cloud and seeing God's "averted nature," can see and contemplate only "shadowy reflections of the Sun in water, reflections which display to eyes too weak, because too impotent to gaze at it, the Sun overmastering perception in the purity of its light."[89] In an inversion of Plato's *Timaeus* 28c, Gregory writes, "to tell of God is not possible ... but to know him is even less possible" (28.4).[90]

While he believes that one cannot see God's essence, he ultimately suggests failure of vision has to do with human weakness; ultimately, the status of the seer as much as the nature of the seen determines one's ability to see God. That is, one can see God, but simply not as

God sees God (see 28.18; cf. 25.17). God's nature is different than God's experienced presence (28.19).[91] In this anti-Eunomian rhetorical tour de force, this is as far as any theological speculation may go, whether one entered the cloud like Moses, ascended to the third heaven like Paul, or joined the company of the angels (28.3).[92]

Whatever its nature, through this vision Gregory divides people by levels of worthiness and purity, with himself at the top, then Aaron, Nadab, Abihu, elders, the masses, and untamed "beasts."[93] In the omitted material, Gregory directly equates this to biblical interpretation: "the law has an obvious and a hidden aspect. The obvious belongs to the crowd waiting below, the hidden to the few who attain the height" (28.2).[94] While the many who remain below at the foot of the mountain have ability to understand only the obvious aspect of scripture, those who ascend the mount like Moses and Gregory himself can access its hidden meaning. Vision is directly entangled with scriptural interpretation and theological investigation. Gregory presses further: those who stay below can only hear God; those who ascend, achieve *theoria*, contemplative vision.

This passage, therefore, focuses upon the worthiness of the individual to draw near to God – that is, the status of the person – rather than on qualities of God, per se, while tying this proximity to God to scriptural insight. Commenting on this passage, moreover, Beeley notes, "By its very nature, Christian doctrine adapts itself, as it were, to the recipient's spiritual condition, conveying radically different meanings to different people."[95] Entering the cloud and joining company with God qualifies Gregory, in contrast to Eunomios or the less-pure masses, for heightened theological speculation and biblical interpretation, delving into the hidden elements.[96]

Finally, in *Oration* 20 delivered in 381 in Constantinople, Gregory again compares himself to Moses to bolster his (faltering) authority against lower clergy and against his theological opponents at the Council of Constantinople: Moses alone encountered God in the cloud and received the mantle of leadership.[97] Likewise, Gregory seeks to go inside himself to converse with God beyond his senses. McGuckin comments, "His imagery is based on an appeal to the Moses archetype, where the prophet, on Sinai, receives a luminous revelation of God, and conveys it to the elect people as the basic constitution of the covenant."[98] Unfortunately, the vision and the radiance it causes cannot be sustained as, being human beings, we fall into lower realities too soon, a condition that will be overcome in the afterlife.[99] Overall, he is claiming his authority through divine vision gained through ascetic purification.[100] Here, as in *Oration* 28, he makes distinctions between himself (the new Moses who can see the vision) and others who stand off (Aaron and the elders) and the masses below. This is, again like *Or.* 28, to establish his authority to engage in theological activities, activities that are not for the masses, in the context of anti-Eunomian polemics and the politico-theological jostling in Constantinople in 380–381.[101]

Gregory, therefore, utilizes the imagery of ascending into the cloud to great rhetorical effect. He boldly uses the first person and equates the ascent into the cloud with the impossible task of the theologian. Yet he has left pathways for speculation: the averted figure and the shadowy reflections of a light too intense for direct apprehension. The ultimate denouement, though, is that Gregory as a theologian, much like R. Akiva in rabbinic Judaism, is the new Moses worthy to enter the divine presence and mediate, through his biblical interpretations, between God and those less worthy.[102] By putting nearly all the weight into the status of the seer, the aristocratic Gregory can extrapolate and legitimize the entire social hierarchy of the Church.[103]

GREGORY OF NYSSA: MOSES AS THE IDEAL MYSTIC

While Gregory of Nyssa's portrayal of his elder brother, Basil, as a new Moses entering the dark cloud fulfilled Basil's vision of the model bishop, it also mirrored Gregory's own mystical ideal, which he lays out in his *Life of Moses*.[104] Sterk argues that Gregory of Nyssa built upon and developed Basil's usage of Moses as the ideal leader the most fully of all three Cappadocians.[105] Gregory retains some vestiges of second- and third-century thinking,[106] while decisively rejecting the first-century idea that the one who spoke to Moses was merely an angel rather than God, or "Being."[107] The younger contemporary of Nazianzus, Gregory of Nyssa takes the tale of Moses' visions, particularly his final entrance into the dark cloud, to new mystical heights.[108] In the *Life of Moses* and the *Commentary on the Song of Songs*, both written in his later years, he used Moses as the paradigm for the mystical search for God, while illustrating his distinctive thought on the infinite progress of the soul.[109] In addition, as Origen did, Gregory would tie this theme to the "pure heart" of Matthew 5 in his *Hom. Beat.* 6.[110]

In the *Life of Moses*, Gregory first contrasts Moses' "darkness" experience with the "light" of the burning bush.[111] He reconciles them in two ways. First, he connects the light of the burning bush with the Son's incarnation via the Gospel of John.[112] Second, moreover, he makes them different stations on the spiritual path.[113] Those who initially come into contact with spiritual knowledge perceive it as light, and their former condition as darkness. Nevertheless, Gregory explains, "as the soul (νοῦς) makes progress, and by greater and more perfect concentration comes to appreciate what the knowledge of truth is, the more it approaches this vision (θεωρίᾳ), and so much the more does it see that the divine nature is invisible (ἀθεώρητον)."[114] It is invisible to the senses and the mind. Thence Gregory labels this the "darkness of incomprehensibility" (γνόφῳ τῇ ἀκαταληψίᾳ), which demonstrates that "no created intellect can attain a knowledge of God."[115] As the great Alexandrians of Philo, Clement, and Origen had already indicated, the darkness of God represents incomprehensibility and invisibility.[116] Like Origen, Gregory utilizes two senses of darkness: "bad" darkness opposed to light and "good" darkness that illustrates that no created being can know or see God.

Gregory, nevertheless, transforms the tradition. Whereas Origen merely juxtaposed the two types of darkness, Gregory uses them to illustrate progress from elementary to advanced spiritual knowledge. Gregory's most significant development is making Moses an explicit paradigm of the soul of every mystic (and ascetic) seeker.[117] Nazianzus instituted the first steps of this development by substituting himself for Moses, but, by using "I" only, he implicitly suggests that others may ascend and enter the cloud, but will usually be excluded. Nyssa uses Moses as a launching point for an exposition of the progress of the human soul.[118]

Nyssa, in his *Commentary on the Song of Songs*, further nuances the forms of darkness in conjunction with the progress of the soul. He repeats the first distinction, dualistically opposing light and darkness. In this first stage, one divests oneself of wrong ideas about God (darkness) to embrace correct views (light),[119] but then Gregory's analysis acquires greater gradation: "Next comes a closer awareness of hidden things, and by this the soul is guided through sense phenomena to invisible nature. And this awareness is a kind of cloud, which overshadows all appearances, and slowly guides and accustoms the soul to look toward what is hidden."[120] This cloud now signifies knowledge enshrouded in darkness, but then revealed. It is access to hidden things not accessible to the masses.

During the final stage, the soul enters into the divine darkness, leaving behind "all that human nature can attain."[121] This is the "secret chamber (ἀδύτων) of divine knowledge."[122] "Secret chamber" or an ἄδυτον also means "innermost sanctuary." It is the most holy place of God's manifest presence. Gregory has, therefore, subtly combined two major instances of hidden divine encounter: the dark cloud and the innermost shrine of the tabernacle or temple, both revealed to Moses on Sinai.[123] This knowledge of the deep darkness or the innermost sanctuary transcends all reason: "Now she leaves outside all that can be grasped by sense or by reason, and the only thing left for her contemplation is the invisible and the incomprehensible, where God is."[124] The proof is the scriptures' claim concerning the "lawgiver," that "Moses entered into the darkness where God was."[125] The final stage of progress reaches the darkness, contemplating invisibility and incomprehensibility, but Gregory has nuanced his previous exposition of two forms of darkness into three: initial illumination, in which darkness represents "wrong and erroneous ideas about God," a second stage, in which a nebulous cloud represents hidden things revealed, and a third stage of contemplating the invisible.[126] The stages of human progress map perfectly on the life of Moses, even when Gregory comments on the Song of Songs. Origen had utilized these forms of darkness, but Gregory has organized each of these forms of darkness into a succinct progressive order.[127]

Returning to the *Life of Moses*, Gregory again speaks of progress, but coupled with desire.[128] He delineates every stage of Moses' life – again, developing Basil's original discussion of the three-stage pattern – from his refusal to pose as an Egyptian princess's son to the burning bush, the Exodus, his entrance into darkness, his vision of the archetypal tabernacle, and the radiance of his face.[129] These advancements, though, do not suffice: "though raised to such heights, he is still restless with desire, is more and more dissatisfied, and still thirsts for that which had filled him to capacity."[130] Since Gregory is addressing a group of ascetics seeking *apatheia*, his language of desire is striking, yet this is a desire to be fulfilled by God. While Moses ascends, his desire constantly increases.[131] Gregory inherits Philo's centuries-old quandary: Moses desires to see the invisible with ever-greater intensity, but can never fully reach his goal.[132] Gregory enmeshes Philo's unresolved issue with the soul's progress; if it is a never-ending search for God, it is, nonetheless, a never-ending perfecting of the soul. The soul perpetually ascends (*epektasis*) towards God, and, therefore, never reaches God.[133] But this perpetual progress, the transformation "from glory to glory" (2 Cor. 3:18),[134] is itself the attainment of perfection.[135] With this in mind, Gregory explains of what the fulfillment of desire and a vision of the invisible consist: "for the true vision of the soul is this, that the soul that looks up to God never ceases to desire Him,"[136] and, "every desire for the Beautiful which draws us on in this ascent is intensified by the soul's very progress towards it. And this is the real meaning of seeing God: never to have this desire satisfied."[137] Paradoxically, the fulfillment of desire is the increasing of desire.[138] If fulfillment were the end, then one would no longer ascend to God, the journey would be over, and the soul would cease its progress.

Like Origen, Gregory of Nyssa connects the biblical passages of Moses' passages of visions or deflected visions with Jesus' Sermon on the Mount, particularly the sixth beatitude. Commenting in his *Hom. Beat.* 6 on the phrase, "Blessed are the pure in heart, for they shall see God," Gregory offers a poetic entrance into the vertigo of those who seek to do this. He immediately notes the problem presented by the promise to see God here and the saying that none have seen God and none can see God and live. Attempting to resolve this difficulty, he writes, "Yet to see the Lord is eternal life. On the other hand, those pillars of faith, John and Paul and Moses, declare it to be impossible. Do you realize the vertigo of the soul that is drawn to the depths contemplated in these words?"[139] He dizzyingly moves back and forth between the promise of vision and its stated impossibility. Nonetheless, he concludes that the promise is greater than the prohibitions and that, in fact, John, Paul, and Moses did not lack this beatitude of vision.[140] Even if one cannot see God in Godself – God being so transcendent and beyond all mental concept – there are many modes of seeing. One can see God through God's effects, God's stamp upon the world, so to speak. One can apprehend God's goodness and existence, though not God's essence: "For he is invisible by nature, but becomes visible in His energies, for he may be contemplated in the things that are referred to him."[141] This recourse to seeing God through God's effects and energies has a long history, going back in the Christian tradition to Theophilus of Antioch, but Nyssa, as usual, charges forward with hermeneutical novelty.

More significantly, much like later medieval mystics, he finds the image of God most clearly in one's own soul – in particular, in the polished, purified heart that becomes a reflective mirror of the divine:

I do not think that if the eye of one's soul has been purified, he is promised a direct vision of God; but perhaps this marvellous saying may suggest what the Word expressed more clearly when he says to others, "The Kingdom of God is within you" [Luke 17:21]. By this we should learn that if one's heart has been purified from every creaturely and all unruly affections, he will see the Image of the Divine Nature in his own beauty. I think that in this short saying the Word expresses some such counsel as this: There is in you, human beings, a desire to contemplate the true good. But when you hear that the divine majesty is exalted above the heavens, that its glory is inexpressible, its beauty ineffable, and its nature inaccessible, do not despair of ever beholding what you desire. It is indeed within your reach; you have within yourselves the measure by which to apprehend the divine. For he who made you did at the same time endow your nature with this wonderful quality. For God imprinted on it the likeness of the glories of his own nature, as if moulding the form of a carving into wax. But the evil that has been poured all around the nature bearing the divine image has rendered useless to you this wonderful thing, that lies hidden under vile coverings. If, therefore, you wash off by a good life the filth that has been struck on your heart like plaster, the divine beauty will again shine forth in you.[142]

While there may be a glimpse of this in Gregory of Nazianzus' writings, this is the clearest, strongest interiorization of vision we have found in our analysis so far. It is one that sounds much like the medieval developments of Christian, Jewish, and Islamic mysticism. It relies upon the statement of vision of prophets of old (e.g., Moses, John, and Paul) and the promise of vision from Jesus in Matt. 5:8. It further ties this vision not as God in God's essence, but to God in God's image – the original stamp of divinity in humanity, gesturing towards Gen. 1:28. Most significant for Gregory's ascetic audience is his reliance upon the moral purification necessary to polish and see this divine image within oneself, that is, *in this life*.

Nyssa, like many theologians before him, had less circumspection or qualification about an afterlife vision of God. Speaking of a shared eschatological vision of God, he writes, "When the King of creation shall reveal Himself to human nature, seated in splendour on the throne on high, we shall see around him the innumerable myriads of angels, and eyes of all will perceive the transcendent Kingdom of Heaven" (*Hom. Beaut.* 5).[143] Here humans join the angels and all see God – or God is revealed – and will perceive the kingdom of heaven, which, he notes in the next homily, is already within you.

Gregory of Nyssa espouses many ideas articulated by earlier authors, leaning especially heavily on Philo and Origen, alongside more contemporary figures like Basil of Caesarea and Gregory of Nazianzus, yet he does so with innovation, especially when joined with the perpetual progress and ever-increasing desire of the soul.[144] Perhaps the most important aspect of his ruminations is his explicit application of Moses' life to the life of the soul.[145] As such, Nyssa deploys the Moses paradigm not simply for the official leaders of the church, such as a bishop or theologian, but for the individual mystic seeker. Nazianzus' substitution of himself for Moses may point to such an application, but Nyssa's illustration of the progress of the soul through the life of Moses signals a change in emphasis, he shifts the focus, more than any previous author, from God to the mystic seeker seeking God within oneself, the image of God.

CONCLUSIONS:
MOSES' VISIONS OF AUTHORITY

The fourth century represents a clear shift in the representation of Moses' visions. The visions are more direct. When they are not direct, as in the case of Gregory of Nazianzus seeing God's "averted figure" or "backside," they still represent the highest one can achieve on earth. Indeed, the Nazianzene's vision of God's backside is not the Son as it would have been in the second or third century, but the very presence – though not essence – of the Trinity. To be sure, a figure like Eusebius of Caesarea may sound a bit like a mixture of Justin and Origen, but by the late-fourth century, the theological ground had shifted. Both the *Apostolic Constitutions* and Gregory of Nyssa reject the notion that Moses merely saw angels, and the *Apostolic Constitutions* and Basil of Caesarea indicate that Moses saw God directly. Basil even writes that Moses was the first to do so.

Despite the strong influences of Philo and Origen, most of these thinkers claim that one can see God directly, just not entirely. Only Gregory of Nyssa develops Philo and Origen to place a strong emphasis on how one sees through one's soul/heart in its ever-increasing desire to see God as it ascends eternally and asymptotically to God. Yet, for Nyssa, the cleansed and purified heart does not indicate only the means of vision and status of the visionary as it did for Origen; it is now also the place or seat of the vision itself as one looks upon God's image within oneself. Indeed, for all three Cappadocians, one needs purification and perfection through education, withdrawal and contemplation, and moral uprightness to see God and, finally, to lead the church. Vision is a means to leadership, rather than an end in itself.

While there is little discussion of what one sees, and some discussion of how one sees through Gregory of Nyssa, the strongest emphasis rests on who sees: the educated bishop, theologian, and mystic. For all three Cappadocians, one's visions legitimize one's scriptural interpretations. As with Origen, only a true seer can interpret the writings of seers; one must become a new Moses to interpret Moses. Moreover, there is a new emphasis in the *Apostolic Constitutions* on Moses as an earthly God who mirrors God the father, and Basil would suggest that the bishop/Moses/seer was at least angelified.

Moses' visions, therefore, validated a message that was mostly sociological: it was about internal Christian organization, elevating the episcopacy from an institution one should obey to an institution one should revere. The theologian and the mystic followed in the train of this elevation.

Earlier texts from the first to third centuries used Moses' visions largely to oppose (or create) a perceived outsider, galvanizing a group identity or monitoring boundaries. In the fourth century, there are new theological controversies between Nicenes and Arians, between the Cappadocians and Eunomians, and among the Cappadocians on the status of the Holy Spirit. Nonetheless, these authors turn these same passages internally to reaffirm and further strengthen theologically the position of the bishop – as well as the theologian and the mystic – within the community. Everything shows this shift, as they use Moses' vision at the burning bush or the vision on Sinai, especially the dark cloud, to elucidate and justify a graded communal social structure. Moreover, with the exception of the writings of Gregory of Nyssa analyzed here, Basil and Gregory of Nazianzus largely developed these innovations publicly within their congregations, that is, in sermons. They proclaimed Moses' visions and the authority of the monk-bishop and theologian from the pulpit.[146]

Andrea Sterk summarizes all these developments and their later iterations most succinctly: "The ascetic bishop had seen God ... He had purged his passions, contemplated divine truths, and ultimately, like Moses, encountered the living Lord on Mt Sinai. This vision, the fruit of the bishop's monastic vocation, was the true source of his authority in the church and the world. Whatever abuses or perversions of this ideal took place, the belief persisted in the Orthodox churches that only such an individual was suited to lead the people of God."[147]

"Show Me Yourself"

*Corporeal, Spiritual, and Intellectual Vision
in Augustine of Hippo (354–430 CE)*

Due to Augustine of Hippo's enormous literary output of polemical tractates, biblical commentaries, sermons, letters, theological reflections, and his own introspective memoirs (*Confessions*), we know a lot more about him than about most figures in antiquity.[1] He was born in Thagaste on the borderlands between Punic and Latin North Africa (modern-day Algeria), and his parents, Patricius and Monica, scraped by for him to get a good education, and eventually become a teacher of rhetoric himself. Like earlier figures analyzed, such as Justin, he journeyed both geographically and spiritually. His career took him to the city of Carthage and eventually to Rome and, from there, to Milan, where he fell under the spell of Ambrose's sermons, which read the Israelite scriptures allegorically rather than literally. Before Ambrose's teaching, Augustine had found the stories of the Bible to be crude when read literally, with a style that could not compare with the dignity of Cicero. He had tried and tested various religious philosophies, including Manicheanism, astrology, and Neo-Platonism, the last of which he saw as Christianity without Christ. Unlike earlier figures like Justin or Irenaeus, he returned home, leaving Italy for Africa, and was installed as the bishop of Hippo Regius.[2]

According to Claudia Rapp, Augustine of Hippo's life also fit the prototypical pattern put forward by Basil of Caesarea of the highly educated man who retreats from the world, only to return to it as a leader of the church: that is, a new Moses.[3] While Latin, he fits the

Greek pattern of episcopal leadership, though his initial retreat after he gave up his job as a rhetorician was quite brief by comparison.[4] As the bishop of Hippo Regius, he, like his predecessors, inhabited a crossroads between several rival religious groups, including different Christian groups. A former Manichean, he would polemicize against Manicheans. In his local context, the polemical exchanges between his own and rival Donatist churches were particularly intense. Late in life he would rail against Pelagius and his gifted disciple Julian of Eclanum. Nonetheless, as some recent reconstructions of his life indicate, he knew that, compared to other bishops, such as the see of Constantinople, his authority was slight in his own time. His enormous posthumous influence has clouded our vision of his more-modest, small-scale authority in his own congregation in Hippo Regius, an authority, interestingly enough, that relied predominantly upon his status as a reader and interpreter of scripture to his congregation.[5]

Yet, unlike the Cappadocians, he increasingly developed a popularizing tendency over time, suggesting that exegesis is not just the purview of the educated elite, but of all who actively participate in prayer and worship within the community.[6] As McCarthy notes, "Scripture became a site of common, perhaps even vulgar, belonging ... Augustine places himself with the community in which he persuades laterally rather than from on high."[7] For Augustine, to be a priest or bishop meant exercising at least three functions: attracting the attention of the ignorant faithful through preaching, administering the mysterious sacraments, and providing a pattern of life by living among the people and inviting them to imitate that life (*Conf.* 13.21). A bishop leads by example, but leads, as one may say, laterally, by being among, rather than above, the people – even while he also adjudicates disputes in his diocese (13.17). He does believe the most spiritual should have the most authority, but he also believes that the most spiritual cannot know who will know God's grace and who will not, and that even a neophyte has the ability to judge spiritually (13.23).[8] Indeed, Augustine had his first experience in *Confessions* 7 and 9 – the chapters immediately before and after his conversion.[9]

Moreover, in his writings, Augustine adopts, adapts, rejects, and synthesizes all of the earlier tributaries to his thought.[10] While he was more influenced by Plotinus than his predecessors were,[11] one can see his exegetical indebtedness to them. Famously, he had his ascent and visionary experience of the light above his light in *Conf.* 7.23 and 9.24, yet his most systematic discussions of divine visions occur through biblical interpretation, particularly the final book of his *Literal Interpretation of Genesis* (401–415 CE),[12] *Letters* 92, 147, and 148, and in scattered references throughout the *City of God against the Pagans*.[13] Although he also discusses these issues in his magnum opus, *On the Trinity*, he wrote this almost simultaneously with *Literal Genesis*, where his analysis is more clearly developed.

Firstly, he seemingly reasserts the New Testament view that when Moses saw God through his bodily eyes, he saw angels, but, more accurately, Moses saw God through angels or, better yet, God manifested himself through created matter, similar to the way in which Tertullian argued that angels and the preincarnate son put on material bodies that were made, not begotten. His solution also resembles Clement of Alexandria's "telescoping" effect of revelation, because the created matter in which God manifests himself are angels. With this analysis, however, Augustine ultimately rejects Justin's solution as heresy; indeed, distinguishing divine presences between seen and unseen along lines of Son and Father would no longer do in a post-Nicene environment, as Origen and Tertullian had foreshadowed with their assertions that the Son in substance was also invisible. Since the Nicene and Constantinopolitan Creeds make the Son equal to the Father and of the same substance as the Father, the Son must essentially be invisible, just as the Father is invisible; if the Son is essentially visible, then the Son would be subordinate to the Father and, therefore, not equal.

Moreover, Augustine, following Tertullian, notes a particularity of the Exodus account. Moses, speaking with God face to face (or mouth to mouth), indicating that he already had a vision of God, asks God to "show me yourself." Why would Moses need to be shown God if God is already shown to him? For Augustine, this indicates that Moses, indeed, saw God in one manner, but sought to see God in another, higher, manner. The low manner was corporeal, the high, intellectual; the low through the senses of the body, the high through the intellect.

Ultimately, he will argue there are three types of vision: corporeal, spiritual, and intellectual. While he speaks of these types of visions throughout his late writings, such as *On the Trinity*, and gives intimations of it in the first eleven books of his *Literal Genesis*, it is the in the twelfth book that he lays out his thoughts most systematically. Through corporeal vision one sees bodies; through spiritual, images of bodies; and intellectual transcends all images to see truth in its very essence. Of course, God is invisible and bodiless, but God can be seen through bodies; or, put another way, God can put on created bodies so people can see a material manifestation of God, though such a manifestation is not God in God's essence or substance. God speaks through created beings, such as angels. One should not think, however, that one is speaking to an angel instead of God, but that the divine presence dwells within the angel and speaks through the angel. The two lower types of visions – corporeal and spiritual – are liable to corruption and deception; the intellectual vision, which is one of pure truth, is immune to corruption. The two higher types of visions – spiritual and intellectual visions – occur in states of rapture and ecstasy; the first occurs in regular waking consciousness.

JUSTIN'S HERESY; CORPOREAL VISIONS ARE GOD MANIFEST

While Augustine could speak of generic revelations,[14] one major shift from Justin to Augustine is that Augustine does not necessarily attribute a divine manifestation in the Old Testament directly to the Son; theophany is not necessarily Christophany. Augustine, in fact, argues that those who argue as Justin did are guilty of heresy, though without directly naming Justin or others who used or assumed his line of reasoning. Instead, a divine appearance in scripture could be the Son, the Father, the Holy Spirit, or all three at once, as he thoroughly argues in Book 2 of *On the Trinity*.

In particular, in his *Literal Genesis* 8.27, considering how God spoke to Adam, Augustine lays the groundwork for his theory of vision, and specifically why Justin's own theory does not work (cf. *Trinity* 2.10.17). At first, Augustine feigns ignorance on the topic, but begins to speculate on the possible modes of communication: either God spoke through his own substance or through a creature. He speaks through his own substance on two occasions: when creating the world and illuminating spiritual and intellectual creatures, such as angels, who are able to grasp his utterance, that is, his Word. But when speaking to those unable to grasp his utterance, he speaks by means of creatures, either a spiritual creature, as in a dream or in a state of ecstasy, using the likeness of material things, or a corporeal creature, in which the bodily senses are affected by a form which appears visually and/or speaks audibly. Then Augustine lays down the gauntlet, declaring earlier interpretations heresy:

> On this point I have wished to comment more at length, because some heretics think that the substance of the Son of God was visible in itself before He assumed a body, and therefore they think that the Son of God before he took a body from the Virgin was seen by the patriarchs, on the theory that it was said only of God the Father, whom no human has seen or can see [1 Tim. 6:16]. According to them, the Son was seen in His own substance before He took on the form of a slave – an impious doctrine which a Catholic mind should put far from it. (*Literal Genesis* 8.27; cf. *Trinity* 2.8.14–19.116)[15]

While Justin does not use the technical terms of "substance" as Augustine does, a shift definitely has occurred since Justin's time. That is, Justin's solution – that all theophany is Christophany – is no longer the answer it once proved. The difference is Nicaea and the mature doctrine of the Trinity.[16] Justin's solution now carries a whiff of Arianism (cf. *Letters* 147.19; 148.10). If, indeed, one distinguishes between visible and invisible among the Son and Father respectively, but note that God in God's true essence is invisible, such a position suggests the subordination of the Son to the Father. For Nicene Christians, however, when the Son is of the same substance as the Father, then the Son is equally invisible in his own substance as the Father is, something Origen and Tertullian had anticipated (cf. *Trinity* 2.5.9ff). Justin's solution, adopted and adapted by so many in the second and third centuries, will no longer work for post-Nicene Trinitarian thought.[17] Indeed, when looking at some of the same passages favoured by Justin, such as the three angels with Abraham, Sodom and Gomorrah, and Jacob's wrestling match, in all instances Augustine flatly denied that Abraham or Jacob necessarily had a vision only of the Son (*City of God* 16.29 and *Trinity* 2.10.19–11.22 for Abraham; 16.39 for Jacob/Israel; cf. *Trinity* 2.13.23–17.31 for Moses). God did not speak to Adam, Abraham, or Moses through the Son, but God the Father spoke through "some corporeal form" (*in aliqua specie corporali*) (*Literal Genesis* 8.18).[18] In short, if the Son and Father are equally invisible and of one substance, why not God the Father (*Trinity* 2.10.17ff)?

Augustine, therefore, reverts to an older view, but in a novel way: the uncreated invisible God – whether, Father, Son, Holy Spirit, or two of them or all three at once – becomes manifest through created means (*Literal Genesis* 6.12); God puts on a creature as clothing as Tertullian suggested for the Son; or God speaks through a creature, whether an angel, fire, or cloud, as Clement had suggested (cf. *Trinity* 2.7.12–16.27).[19] Elsewhere, he argues in his analysis of Moses' vision of the burning bush that the angel within the fire was either the Son or the Holy Spirit putting on created matter for the occasion (*Trinity* 2.13.23). Indeed, speaking of God "coming down" to the Tower of Babel, Augustine notes that, since God is in all places at all times, he does not "come down," except insofar as his angels, within whom God dwells, descended (*City of God* 16.5). God can be equally present in multiple angels at the same time, as when the three angels visited Abraham. When the three were with Abraham, they were all addressed as "Lord." When they split up, one staying back with Abraham and two going on ahead, each group was still "Lord" (*City of God* 16.29).[20]

Augustine, therefore, will, without any sense of contradiction, claim that Moses spoke to an angel and spoke to God in the same circumstances, since God used the angel as an instrument to be seen and heard. God dwells within the angel. Moses, therefore, communicated with an angel at the burning bush, and that angel revealed God as He Who Is (*City of God* 8.11); likewise, the law was proclaimed by angels (*City of God* 10.13; 10.15; 10.17), as the New Testament texts claim. Nonetheless, at these events, Moses saw and spoke with God through the material medium of his created angels (*City of God* 12.3).

Augustine can, in this way, uphold the Old Testament tendency to shift the speaker from the angel of the Lord to the Lord without any problem, since the Lord dwells within the angel or speaks through the angel. For example, in the *City of God* 10.13, Augustine writes:

We ought not be disturbed by the fact that, although he is invisible, God is reported to have often shown himself in visible form to our ancestors. Just as the uttered sound which makes audible the thought that has its existence in silence of the understanding, is not the same as that thought, so the visible form in which God – who exists in his invisible substance – became visible was not identical with God himself. For all that, he was seen in that corporeal form, just as the thought is heard in the sound of the voice. And those patriarchs were well aware that they were seeing the invisible God in a corporeal form, though God himself was not bodily. For God spoke to Moses, and Moses spoke to him in reply; and yet Moses said to him, "If I have found favour in your sight, show me yourself, so that I may know you and see you."[21]

As voice is to thought – an expression of thought but not equal to it – so God is to the visible manifestation of God. How do we know there is a differentiation between God's manifest (corporeal) presence and God's essence? Moses asked to see God – "show me yourself" – after, in fact, seeing God clothed in God's created, corporeal form.

One reason we cannot see God in God's essence is that God is invisible to corruptible eyes. It is, in fact, not that God cannot be seen by physical eyes – indeed, in the resurrected state, our physical eyes will be transformed so that they can perceive immaterial, "invisible" realities – but that physical eyes in this world are in a state of corruption. Therefore, God manifests himself through unmistakable signs – as at Sinai – and speaks through created beings (*City of God* 10.15). Augustine, therefore, has combined the solutions of Clement (that the Son speaks through angels and that it is really the Son who speaks) and Tertullian (that the Son put on material forms to appear bodily), but claims that it was the Trinitarian Godhead who did all these things – not necessarily or not only the Son.

INTELLECTUAL VISION:
SEEING GOD IN GOD'S ESSENCE

While they are homologized, the intellectual vision is qualitatively different from and much greater than the corporeal vision of the senses (*Literal Genesis* 7.14).[22] It is a vision of truth in which no deception is possible (*City of God* 12.14; 12.25); it begins in faith.[23] Faith and love of neighbour cleanses the heart to make one pure of heart (cf. *Trinity* 2.17.28; 8.4.6).[24] Intellectual vision is, however, nearly impossible in this life. It is, rather, the reward of the saints at the end of time (*City of God* 16.39). It remains, as in Irenaeus, the telos of human existence. In this manner, Augustine will follow earlier thinkers, such as Clement of Alexandria, that one cannot see God and live, but one can see God and die. Or, put another way, one can die and see God. As Augustine writes in his *Confessions*, "Do not hide your face from me.

Lest I die, let me die so that I may see it" (*moriar, ne moriar, ut eam videam*) (1.5). In death there is divine vision. Therefore, the ultimate vision is post-mortem: it is in the state of the resurrection, when, as Augustine notes, the righteous will be equal to the angels. Angelic existence is one of constant intellectual vision, relying upon the gospel passage that the angels of children (our angelic counterparts) always see God before his throne (Matt. 18:10). If we will be like the angels, we too will constantly see God: "The holy angels, whose equals we shall be after the resurrection, if to the end we hold to Christ our way, always behold the face of God" (*Literal Genesis* 4.24).[25] Nonetheless, certain people – particularly Moses, Paul, and, if I read his *Confessions* correctly, Augustine himself, alongside his mother, Monica – can attain a glimpse in this life.

Again, Augustine lays out many of his ideas in the *City of God* and the *Literal Genesis*. On the one hand, our corruptible bodies weigh down our souls and distract our minds; nonetheless, he avers, even without corruption and without distraction, even if one were already equal to the angels, one still would not know God as God knows Godself (*Literal Genesis* 4.6). Nonetheless, he can equally assert, en passant, that when we become like the angels – and join the company of angels – we will see God as God is (citing 1 John 3:2 in *Literal Genesis* 4.23; 4.24; esp. *City of God* 8.25). Because angels are intellectual beings, they can perceive God, who is Intellect. When we become like the angels, our minds will be unclouded and clear; we will become intellectual beings, as angels are. In short, we cannot know God as God knows God, but we can know God as God is: Intellect. This may seem to be a distinction without a difference, but it indicates status: one attains the level of angelic knowledge (intellect) rather than purely divine knowledge (unknowable).

Once we attain the status of the angelic intelligence within the city of God (*City of God* 22.1), we will see God interiorly with the mind and potentially with transformed bodily eyes. Augustine lays this out in *City of God* 22.29, in a long chapter worthy of renewed study. In the state of the resurrection, we will have immortal and spiritual bodies. Indeed, as Paul notes in 1 Corinthians 15, we have bodies, but transformed ones. While it seems that ultimate vision is beyond intellect and the angels, one can still have a vision/understanding of God by degrees of participation in God's perfection of peace. Angels may be greater than us at the moment, and therefore participate in God's perfection to have keener vision of God, but, as noted, we will become equal to the angels.[26] While we see now darkly, we will see face to face, as the angels do now, citing Matt. 18:10: our angels perpetually behold the face of the Father.

The righteous will, however, be embodied beings when they behold the face of the Father, but, whether they will only see God intellectually, or be able to see God intellectually, spiritually, and bodily, Augustine leaves as an open question. The abilities of the resurrection body, Peter Brown notes, preoccupied Augustine in his old age.[27] Augustine speculates that if we are to have bodily eyes in the world to come, they would exist for some reason; that is, we should be able to use them.[28] He suggests that the eyes will have greater potency to see immaterial things, citing Job 42.5 and Matt. 5.8:

> For such reasons it is possible, it is indeed most probable, that we shall then see the physical bodies of the new heaven and the new earth in such a fashion as to observe God in utter clarity and distinctness, seeing him present everywhere and governing the whole material scheme of things by means of the bodies we shall then inhabit and the bodies we shall see wherever we turn our eyes. (*City of God* 22.29.6)[29]

How could bodily eyes see immaterial things? Augustine suggests that the nature of the transformed body will be such that the body will participate in the qualities of the mind; that is, our bodily eyes will also have intellectual qualities in order to perceive immaterial natures (see *Letter* 148.16). Margaret Miles suggests that this late affirmation of the resurrection body was due to his own ongoing polemics against Manichean thought; that is, as Manicheans rejected the resurrection body, he increasingly affirmed it, investing it with greater spiritual capacities.[30]

Yet there were also some internal developments; it was a view Augustine tentatively came to over time.[31] In stark contrast, previously he had directly opposed such a view of seeing God with the mind in this life and in the afterlife with transformed bodily eyes in *Letter* 92.4 (c. 408 CE). Whether in this life or the next, he had argued, one must see God interiorly and one must be pure of heart (Matt. 8:5). Both *Letters* 147 and 148, however, take on this issue directly and with greater nuance. His very lengthy letter to Paulina (147) in 413 CE directly concerns the question of whether one can see God with bodily eyes (147.1).

At first, Augustine indicates that God cannot be seen either physically or with the mind in this life (147.3), but Matt. 5:8 haunts him
(147.12), as does Matt. 18:10 ("their angels always see the face of my
Father").[32] He wants to know how it can be true, since it must be
true.[33] After a long preface on the relationship between bodily seeing and mentally knowing, and between these things and belief or
faith in a testimony, he nonetheless works through the contrary
verses of seeing and not seeing in the Bible.[34] After noting that these
passages are both contradictory, but cannot be contradictory, since
they are scripture, he grapples for a solution (147.14, 17). Quoting
at length from Ambrose's commentary on Luke when Zechariah
sees the angel in the temple, Augustine follows him to the conclusion that people cannot see God in God's fullness, but that God
appeared in multiform ways as an act of grace to figures like Moses
or Isaiah. Even in the resurrection, only the pure of heart, rather
than everyone, will see God (147.18). Noting that "see" can refer to
bodily or mental seeing, Ambrose (and Augustine) conclude that
both are negated in the claim that none can see God and live,
undermining centuries of exegesis in one stroke. As with Tertullian,
God is naturally invisible, but can do whatever he wills. God
appears to whom he wills in what manner he wills as an act of
grace, but some people, like Moses, who represents a truly devout
soul, desire to see more (147.20). God's answer, however, simply
demonstrates that no one can see God as he is, but only as God
chooses to appear. God's true nature cannot be seen by the body
nor grasped with the mind.

In short, it is not in any creature's power to see God, but it is within God's power to appear. But God gives this grace only to those who
merit the occasion; that is, evil people or even Satan will not merit the
occasion, due to their lack of the requisite purity of heart (Matt. 5:8;
cf. *Trinity* 1.13.28–31). Elsewhere, Augustine claims that purity of
heart is attained through faith and love, particularly the self-less, non-
acquisitive love of neighbour (cf. *Trinity* 2.17.28; 8.8.12).[35] Failure to
love one's neighbour negates one's ability to see God (*Trinity* 8.8.12).
Even the angels, following Ambrose here, cannot see God as God is,
but as God chooses to appear, yet Augustine hints that maybe God
has willed that some of them may see him in his nature and that, perhaps, we too will do so when we become like the angels in the afterlife (147.22). Augustine further emphasizes and clarifies that no one
has seen God in God's essence, but only in the *manner* that God

chooses to appear – not simply *that* God chooses to appear, as one could read the Ambrose passage.

He slowly inches toward a fuller resurrection vision in his repeated citation that, in the kingdom, we will see him as he is (147.26; cf. *Trinity* 14.17.24; 15.8.14). As with Origen, Augustine with Ambrose suggests a "clean heart" – that is, a purified soul – as the means of divine vision, rather than just the condition for it (e.g., 147.26). Purity of heart is the necessary qualification for vision, but the pure heart (or soul) is also the organ through which one sees God. As Gregory of Nyssa argues, moreover, it is where one sees God, rather than in any physical place: one finds God within oneself. Yet, again, this fuller vision merited by the pure of heart is largely reserved for the afterlife, but it is something greater than the physical appearances of God that God wills in the biblical accounts of God appearing to various figures. Augustine slowly develops the idea that, in this life, God appears as God wills, but not as God is; in the afterlife, God appears as God is only to the clean of heart, but not in the physical form – as God does to certain people in this life (see 147.48).

Augustine, however, begins to entertain the idea that some people may, perhaps, see God in this life and not die (147.31–2), or, rather, "die" in some manner to this life by being removed from their bodily life into an angelic existence before their final death on earth, using Moses' and Paul's experiences as a model, as he does in *Literal Genesis* 12. Indeed, Augustine clarifies, that one cannot see God and live means that the divine vision belongs to different conditions beyond this life, noting that in Num. 12:8 God had appeared to Moses in his full glory: God as God is. That is, Moses saw God in ecstasy, outside the body, and, therefore, beyond the limiting conditions of the body. In *Letter* 147, Augustine largely reiterates Tertullian: God is invisible, but can be seen if God wills it; God is not limited by himself. Nonetheless, God will be seen as he is by the pure of heart in the afterlife and by exceptional people, like Moses and Paul, in this life (see summary in 147.37).

At points and then more fully, however, he posits the question of bodily resurrected eyes seeing God (in 147.40, 46), only to back off from it (147.48), and then more fully addresses it (147.49). He clearly is tentative in his strategy, claiming that if one thinks one can see God in the resurrection with one's physical eyes because God is a body, then one is clearly in error; however, if one realizes that God is not bodily, but if the resurrected physical eyes have spiritual qualities, then perhaps God could be seen with them (147.49–51, 54).[36] With 1 Corinthians 15 fully in view, he says this position is tenable, even if it turns out to be false, while he still explicitly attempts to bring the position into line with what he said in *Letter* 92, claiming that the spiritual element, rather than the bodily element, of the resurrected person is what sees God. At the end of this letter, he claims that he has not fully answered the question of the nature of the resurrected body and its ability to see God (147.54). Interestingly, in his *Retr.* 2.41, he claims he later provided such an answer in his *City of God* 22.29.

He similarly and more succinctly comes to these ideas in his letter to Fortunatus, also in 413 CE (Letter 148). In this letter, he is put on the defensive over what it seems he had written in *Letter* 92, due to the text, "we shall see him as he is" (1 John 3:2). Here, he begins to play with the possibility of the physical eyes sharing in mental or intellectual characteristics (148.3, 16), claiming that his earlier admonition was against those who thought that if one could see God with bodily eyes, it meant that God was also a body (148.1–2). He, nonetheless, lists Christians who claim that God is invisible and cannot be seen physically, including Ambrose, Jerome, Athanasius, and Gregory of Nazianzus. Jerome, he claims, notes that, since invisibility is God's nature, even the angels cannot see God. If, therefore, humans attain the rank of angels, humans will still never see God, but, like the angels in Matt. 18:10, will see God in the resurrection through the mind, even though not in God's essential nature (148.7–9).[37] Here Jerome seems to be echoing Origen, claiming that this pertains to the entire Trinity (cf. 147.53). He, therefore, struggles in his letters to think in the terms of bodily vision of an intellectual vision, but he clearly is entertaining the idea and inching towards what he would more fully develop in *Literal Genesis* 12 and *City of God* 22.29. His primary problem is that he has not found any Greek or Latin Christian thinkers who have expounded such an idea, though Theophilus of Antioch would have provided at least one predecessor. For Augustine, this understanding of post-resurrection physical vision lacks the authority of tradition. Nonetheless, he claims he holds it as a possibility due to 1 Corinthians 15 (*Letter* 148.16).

In his *Letters*, Augustine largely plays it safe, discussing what is known from traditional authorities rather than what may be speculated, making his more-confident statements in *City of God* – that it is not just possible, but also probable – more striking. While Platonically leaning thinkers and expositors of scripture have been using "see-ing" and "vision" metaphorically to denote intellectual activity, Augus-tine, even though highly influenced by his readings of Plotinus, begins to break ranks with figures like Origen, Jerome, or even his beloved Ambrose by reincorporating Paul's "spiritual body," re-literal-izing the metaphor.[38]

He alternatively suggests in *City of God* 22.29, however, that we will be able to see God through our bodily eyes by seeing God within each other. As God dwells within angels, God dwells within us, in hearts purified by love: love of neighbour and love of God. We will become the created, bodily beings through which God can then become man-ifest. At this point, one does not just see God, but one sees as God sees.[39] This was Augustine's final word on the subject.[40]

Why this striking and self-admitted imaginative departure from tradition in *City of God* 22.29? In part, he first tests these theories through dialogue with interlocutors in his letters. Nonetheless, when one examines the context of *City of God* 22 as a whole, it is surrounded by polemics against those who deny the resurrection of the body, primarily Porphyry (*City of God* 22.25–8). After four chap-ters of breaking down Porphyry's and others' arguments that "souls in bliss can have not contact with a body," comparing them to Plato and Varro, in Chapter 28 Augustine positively reconstructs what the resurrection body would be like: a fleshly resurrection, but, as Augustine is a close reader of Paul, flesh living according to the spirit.[41]

"SHOW ME YOURSELF": SEEING GOD IN THIS LIFE

While in the *City of God*, Augustine largely, though not completely, relegates ultimate vision to the afterlife; in the *Literal Genesis* 12, espe-cially 12.27 (par. 54–5), he seeks to understand Paul's vision of 2 Corinthians 12 through Moses' multiple visions in Exodus and Num-bers, concluding that one can, indeed, attain an ultimate vision of God's substance in this life.[42]

At first, when considering Paul's ascent to Paradise in light of Moses' visions, Augustine divides how one sees God into three types of vision, introducing an intermediate mode of seeing: corporeal, spiritual, and intellectual. The difference is between the body, images of the body, and visions without any images at all (12.5). Augustine

differentiates spirit from mind based upon his reading of 1 Cor.
14:14, suggesting that one could have a vision of images and likenesses of things, which are not understood; therefore, the operations
and intuition of the mind are less involved (12.8). Once understanding takes hold, one begins to move beyond the spirit to the mind. He,
therefore, equates the new, intermediate term of spiritual vision with
the imagination, using imagination in a very literal sense: that is, it is
a vision of images of corporeal things. The highest level of vision is
intellectual. Speaking of intellectual vision as a vision without any
image, he writes, "To see an object not in an image but in itself, yet
not through the body, is to see with a vision surpassing all other
visions" (12.6).[43] This vision is no longer perceived through the eyes
of the body or through the spirit; it is perceived by the intuition of
the mind. He discusses at length the nature of spiritual vision
(12.8–9), the nature of intellectual vision (12.10), and the complex
relationship between all three types of vision (12.11). For example,
the gift of prophecy involves the vision of images of things (spiritual) and understanding of the truth that those images represent (intellectual). One may have a dream (spiritual vision), as Pharaoh did, but
not understand the dream; for its interpretation, one needs the intu-
itive understanding (intellectual vision) that Joseph had (12.9). Most
importantly, *all three* types of vision will be perfected in the resurrection (12.36).

He lays out the problem of understanding how such a bulwark of
faith as Paul could not know if he was in body or out of body in his
ecstasy in 2 Corinthians 12. Indeed, Moses clearly knew the difference
between the essence of God in itself and the visible creature through
which God was wont to manifest himself to humans when he asked
God, "Show me yourself" (*ostende mihi temet ipsum*) (12.4).[44] At first,
Augustine considers that when one has a vision (later identified as
spiritual) in ecstasy or dreams in which one sees the images of bodies,
one does not really distinguish between bodies and images of bodies
until the vision is over (12.2). Nonetheless, he will ultimately reject
the fact that Paul's vision was merely spiritual.

Whereas, earlier, Augustine had tried to differentiate between corporeal and intellectual visions, he now undertakes the more difficult
task of differentiating between two types of non-corporeal visions:
imagistic (spiritual/imaginative) and intellectual (true substance
beyond images: object being God, mind, intelligence, reason, virtues,
etc.) (12.3).

He resolves his problems in 12.26–7. In 12.26, he equates the fiery Mount Sinai theophany with a corporeal vision, whereas he considers the visions of Isaiah and John in the Apocalypse to be spiritual. As he clarifies in 12.27, the Sinai theophany, visible for all to see, was the lowest form of vision, since it was corporeal. One does not see God in God's essence. Moses, by contrast with the masses, however, was able to see God spiritually and intellectually. By contrast with the corporeal or even spiritual vision, an intellectual vision is a direct vision, "and not through a dark image [1 Cor. 12], as far as the human mind elevated by the grace of God can receive it. In such a vision God speaks face to face to him whom he has made worthy of this communion. And here we are speaking not of the face of the body but of the mind" (12.26; cf. *Letter* 47).[45] This passage relies, for its structure, on combining the imagery of Moses, who speaks to God face to face and not in riddles or an enigma, but also mediates the Sinai theophany, and Paul in 1 Corinthians 12, when he speaks of seeing through a glass darkly, or enigmatically, versus face to face.[46] When combined, Augustine begins to lay the groundwork for a powerful divine vision in this life, though winding through the typical sequence of passages seen throughout this study in earlier Christian figures.

Starting in 12.27, Augustine begins to illustrate how this direct, intellectual sense can be understood through Moses' visions. Augustine ultimately seeks to understand Moses' visionary abilities recounted in Num. 12:8 (*sicut intelligendum arbitror quod de Moyses scriptum est*), but begins his narrative unsurprisingly with the counter-passage in Exod. 33:20.

> Moses, as we read in Exodus, had yearned to see God, not as he had seen him on the mountain, nor as he saw him in the tabernacle, but in his divine essence without the medium of any bodily creature that might be presented to the senses of mortal flesh. It was his desire to see God, not by imaginary likenesses of bodies in the spirit but by a vision of the divine essence as far as this can be attained by a rational and intellectual creature when withdrawn from all bodily senses and from all obscure symbols of the spirit.[47]

This passage illustrates Moses' desire to see God as God truly is and his dissatisfaction with both corporeal and spiritual visions, since he no longer wanted to see God through a bodily creature or through the likenesses of bodies in the imagination.[48] He wants a vision *beyond* the mountaintop experience. Augustine continues:

> For, according to Holy Scripture, Moses said, "If, therefore, I have found favour in your sight, show me yourself, that I may see you clearly." Now just before this we read, "And the Lord spoke to Moses face to face as a man speaks to his friend." He realized, therefore, what he saw, and he longed for what he did not see. For shortly after this, God said to him, "For you have found grace in my sight, and I have known you before all." And he replied, "Show me your brightness." And then, indeed, an answer clothed in a figure, which it would be tedious now to explain, was given him by the Lord, who said to him, "You cannot see my face and live; for a human shall not see my face and live." And then God continued, "Behold there is a place with me and you shall stand upon the rock."[49]

Again, Moses' desire to see God after speaking with him face to face indicates that Moses recognized different levels of vision and sought a higher vision (cf. *Trinity* 2.16.27). The "answer clothed in a figure" ends up being a prophetic reference to the emergence of the church. In *Trinity* 2.16.27, interestingly, Augustine claims that this is as far as Moses – and anyone else – could go; that Moses' request to see God as God is was never granted to Moses or anyone else in this life (cf. *Trinity* 2.17.28). Augustine, however, changed his mind when he reached his final book of *Literal Genesis*. While God rejects Moses' plea in Exodus, Augustine claims that God did allow Moses to see God in God's true essence, because of Num. 12:8:

> This, indeed, is not be understood as referring to a bodily substance made present to the senses of the flesh. For certainly God spoke thus to Moses face to face, the one in the presence of the other; but on that occasion said Moses to God, "Show me yourself." And now also, addressing those whom he reprimanded, above whom he thus exalted the merits of Moses, God spoke in this way through a corporeal creature, present to the senses of the body. In that other manner, then, in his own divine essence, he speaks in an incomparably more intimate and inward manner, in an unutterable converse, where no man beholds him while living

this mortal life in the senses of the body. This vision is granted only to him *who in some way dies to this life*, whether he quits the body entirely or is turned away and carried out of the bodily senses, so that he really knows not (to use the words of St. Paul) whether he is in the body or out of the body when he is carried off to this vision. (emphasis mine)[50]

In this last segment, Augustine solves two riddles at once: how did Moses see God and live (Num. 12:8) when no one can see God and live (Exod 33:20) and how might Paul not know whether his vision was in the body or not? The highest form of vision is entirely interior, but one must die to the things of this world in order to obtain it, either physically or symbolically, divesting oneself of the body in the state of ecstasy (cf. *Trinity* 2.17.28). Due to this symbolic death to oneself, by removing oneself from material things and desires, one may not be fully aware of bodily or non-bodily visions, as Paul was not (cf. *Literal Genesis* 8.25). Paul, then, achieved the highest form of vision when he was caught up to the third heaven; the third heaven is the third type of vision (12.28). Citing Matt. 5:8, Augustine concludes that Paul saw God not through symbol in corporeal or spiritual manner; he did not see through a mirror in a riddle, but face to face, as Moses did.

Considering Exod. 33:11, Exod 33:20, and Num 12:8 together, Augustine notes, as Tertullian did before him, that Moses requests to see God's face after speaking to God face to face, indicating that, having received a higher vision than the people, he realized he still had not attained a full vision. Moses requests to see God as God truly is, beyond the body and the spirit, the latter of which Augustine equates with the imagination – again, an intermediate vision of the images and likenesses of corporeal things without necessarily understanding the ultimate truth that animates them. Only the mind purified of all images can achieve an intellectual vision.

Augustine illustrates this elsewhere with his own experiences in the *Confessions*. While meditating on sensory things, one moves beyond them and withdraws from the senses, turning inward into oneself. From there, one observes and then withdraws from the "obscure symbols of the spirit" (*Literal Genesis* 12.27). Moving beyond all images, in a very Platonic-style ascent, one intensely concentrates on God as truth and especially love, and, thereby, achieves a glimpse of the One

Who Is. Augustine then proceeds to Numbers to prove that Moses did, indeed, attain such a vision in his own lifetime, and that was the vision Paul later had: such a vision is the highest a human can achieve in this lifetime.

Augustine describes something very similar to this vision in *Confessions* 7 and 9,[51] following the tendency of post-Nicene bishops to equate themselves with Moses. Yet, even so, he indicates that non-elite and non-bishops – even non-clergy – can achieve such a vision. In his own accounting, he first proceeds in a Platonic fashion, beginning by examining bodies, proceeding to the soul that adjudicates bodies, to his rational faculty, which he finds too mutable, due to the ruts of habitual thinking. At that stage he is at the imagination, and finally he "in the flash of a trembling glance it attained to that which is ... But I did not possess the strength to keep my vision fixed" (7.23). This first attempt, moreover, occurred even before his full conversion to Christianity. Similarly, in Book 9, together with his mother, Monica, and others at Ostia, he moves beyond corporeal objects and by internal reflection and dialogue entered into his own mind, when "we touched it [the eternal] in some small degree by a moment of total concentration of the heart," but returned to the "noise of our human speech" (9.24).[52] In this case, his experience occurred after he converted, but before his ordination. One may read it as something that gave him the right to lead upon his return to Africa; nonetheless, he included his mother in this experience, though she died not long afterwards. Indeed, like God's warning to Moses, she had a divine encounter and died soon afterwards. Moreover, like Origen's experience, it lasts but a moment and they come crashing back to the physical world after a mere glimpse. Augustine claims that such visions are rare; they provide a transient foreshadowing of the everlasting resurrection gaze (*Trinity* 12.14.23).[53]

CONCLUSIONS

Augustine was clearly the great systematizer of visions. By developing up to three forms of vision in a progressive fashion using the visions of Moses as a guide, he could locate different prophetic encounters as corporeal, spiritual, or intellectual. While this may seem a simple addition of a type of seeing to the earlier bipartite division between physical and intellectual vision best exemplified by Origen, it does more. Origen – and others – would often claim that physical vision is impossible, but intellectual vision is possible. For Augustine, one can see God – at least partly – in all three ways, which Moses had, in fact, done, but intellectual vision is preferred. In this way, the questions of *what* is seen and *who* sees become subordinated to *how* one sees.

While reliant upon several older streams of thought, including Clement, having the same objections as Origen, and most proximately related to Tertullian, Augustine would reject the influential interpretation stemming from Justin that all theophany was Christophany as nothing short of heresy. He does not mince words on this score. So *what* did the prophets see? In terms of corporal or physical visions, Augustine developed Tertullian's solution that Christ used fleshly means to appear to people. However, he simply rejected that it was necessarily the Son that was seen and made it God – why does it need to be solely Christ and not the entire Trinity if they are all coequal anyway? People did see God, but the crudeness of the anthropomorphism is blunted by the means of corporeal vision: God puts on created clothes or speaks through created means. The angels are not heralds; they have God's voice speaking through them.

God can also appear spiritually or imaginatively, such as in dream or even in waking visions – like those experienced by many prophets, such as Isaiah or John at Patmos. Most importantly, people can see God intellectually, but this is God in God's true essence, and it is nearly impossible to see God in this manner in this life. Most of the righteous would see God in this way only upon death. But the "nearly" is important; it lets a crack of light into the edifice, opening the door to considerations of the status of the seer: who can see God in this life? It allows exceptionally righteous human beings a glimpse of the ultimate reality in this life, after a symbolic death, who through their mode of life "die" to themselves. Moses did it; Paul did it; and Augustine thinks he had a momentary glimpse himself. Nonetheless, all three types of vision become perfected and, according to the *City of God*, collapse in the afterlife, where one will be able to see God spiritually and intellectually through one's physical eyes, as our physical bodies take on spiritual and intellectual properties.

Several shifts from earlier tradition and his own earlier writings occur in Augustine's late writings. In fact, he explicitly rejected the belief in the physical vision of God in the afterlife in his earlier writings, while he argues for such a belief – though tentatively – in his later writings. So what accounts for the several shifts from earlier Christian writers and even within his own writings? Though Augustine regularly engaged in polemical writings, unlike Justin, Irenaeus, and Tertullian before him, his developments concerning divine visions does not occur in his most overtly polemical writings against the Manicheans and the Donatists, or against Pelagius and Pelagius' gifted defender, Julian of Eclanum.

Moreover, while he develops a Moses model, and resembles that model himself, he does not use it in the same way as the Cappadocians. He does not couple it with calls to obedience within his sermons, limit the right to exegesis to himself or one of his status, or claim that the bishop should be treated as an earthly god – and, even though he believes that the most-spiritual people should lead, he also indicates that even a new convert could have such spiritual discernment. His episcopal office does have authority, but he emphasizes more its responsibility to preach, administer the sacraments, and provide an exemplar for the community to emulate. That is, if Moses is the model for the bishop, the bishop is, in turn, a model for the congregation. If, moreover, Augustine gains authority through his ability to read and interpret the biblical text, he, at points, says he is himself the biblical "text" for his own congregation to "read." It is a localized positionality of authority, to be sure, but one that leads from among the congregation and community rather than from above it. He, therefore, exercises a powerful role as a bishop, but his authority is more tenuous than usually recognized, and mediated in localized ways that are now difficult to track, despite his voluminous literary remains.

If these developments are not always obviously polemical or necessarily used to appropriate Moses' visions to authorize his own position – and, moreover, it is significant that the greatest experience he claims is just after his conversion, before his ordination, and was shared with his (assumedly) illiterate, yet charismatically gifted, mother, Monica – what is going on with Augustine's understanding of Moses' visions and, through them, divine vision in general?[54] It is not always as obvious as in Gregory of Nazianzus' *Orations* or the *Apostolic Constitutions*.

In fact, part of it seems to be an exegetical puzzle. That is, at least, the impression one gets while reading *Literal Genesis*. He returned several times to the interpretation of Genesis, reading it more typically allegorically in his earlier writings, especially against Manicheans,[55] and later in a more literal manner, yet he does not have the polemical edge here as he does in his earlier readings of Genesis. He does note that all Christians assume that the narrative must at least be taken figuratively, and so he must defend the literal sense (*Literal Genesis* 1.1).

Nonetheless, in addition to his curiosity, puzzling out potential tensions and problems in the biblical text, he subtly and indirectly defends his position against outsiders – or, at the very least, makes it intellectually respectable to insiders. Augustine can only approach this puzzle due to his assumption that the biblical account must be entirely correct and, given his context, it does not appear to be correct in its historical sense, even according to many insiders. By rejecting the way out of figurative reading that had come to dominate biblical exegesis, he escapes some of the censure of earlier critics of Christianity (and Judaism), such as Celsus. Even so, as with the earlier figurative readings, he manages to align it with the intellectual currents of his day – not just Neo-Platonism, but astronomical and biological observation – making it respectable even in its literal sense. He considers what can be known by reason and observation when deciding multiple options of how one could read a line in Genesis (*Literal Genesis* 1.19; cf. *Teaching* 2.27.38), so that Christians should not be shown to be ignorant to outsiders. This seems to be less the case in Book 12, however, where he defends Paul's visions through Moses' visions. Nonetheless, there he illustrates the unity of scripture, old and new, while also mapping a progressive visionary schema that resembles the ascent to truth from his earlier experiments and studies with Platonic and Neo-Platonic writings, including Plotinus.

Sometimes the cultured despisers of Christianity are more clearly in view. In *City of God*, Augustine develops his non-traditional view of the resurrection while defending the resurrection of the body and flesh against Porphyry's criticisms. This, if anything, is an enormous synthesis of biblical and Greek and Roman history, literature, and philosophy, shaped into an apology of Christianity in the wake of the sack of Rome.

Finally, his repudiation of anything that resembles Justin's solution to the anthropomorphisms and divine visions in the Bible has a clear trajectory and context. It had already begun to recede from view in the fourth century, though held on to by Eusebius of Caesarea. But for those who ascribed to the Nicene and then Niceno-Constantinopolitan creeds, the turning of all Theophany into Christophany, the claim that one does not see the Father but sees the Son, subordinates the

Son too much. Origen and Tertullian had already begun to back off this position in the third century, arguing the Son is essentially invisible yet, in Tertullian's version, made himself visible by putting on flesh. Augustine simply takes this argument to the next step. Once an essentially invisible entity can will to become visible by putting on created matter, then it does not matter if it is the Son or Father or Holy Spirit or all three at once.

12

Conclusion

The Agonies and the Ecstasies of Moses' Visions

Only the dead see God. Men's gaze will, at that time, be opened onto the eternity of the invisible even as their eyes, finally glazed over, are closed by those still living. They gaze at something that cannot appear to them, of course. They cannot perceive what it is. This is true for the sun: the gaze will gain no understanding of its "ti estin" and only a little of its "oion estin." (Luce Irigaray)[1]

The mountaintop was a place of liminality, the potential point of contact between earthly and heavenly realms, humans and the divine. For ancient Christians, as for ancient Jewish precedents and contemporaries, the figure of Moses focalized the tensions, ambivalences, possibilities, dangers, and limitations of such a meeting of the apex of humanity and the manifest, yet paradoxically hidden, God.

Biblical sources already evinced an ambivalence about the human potential to directly engage in visual and audible communion with God. The potential tension between Moses and no human being able to see God's face and live (Exod. 33:20) and Moses seeing the very form (or glory) of the LORD heightens the potentially discomforting juxtaposition of the prohibitions of divine contact and the various figures who saw God and lived. Israelite, Jewish, and Christian writers developed many strategies to explain these apparent scriptural dissonances. This book has sought to trace the history of those strategies, turning not only to how various Jewish and Christian writers sought to resolve the paradoxical surviving the vision of God that kills – or, to put an even finer point on the paradox, having a vision of the invisible God – but also why they chose to resolve it in the way they did. As how turns to why, the means of seeing returns the gaze to ends, and ancient reading strategies bleed into their social contexts, which, while varied, often overlapped, as writers read the works of others, which were criss-crossing the ancient Mediterranean littoral.

In these concluding thoughts, I will first collate the strategies of interpreting, using the three-part hermeneutical syntax of who sees, how one sees, and what one sees. This is a crisp overarching analytic framework whose utility depends partly upon its flexibility and partly on its clarity. As flexibility pulls against its clarity, it will admit some further subdivision, as various ancient readers adapted one, two, or all three of these strategies to new circumstances. Second, I will turn to social conditions that gave rise to new interpretations, the persistence and adaptation of old readings in new circumstances, and the eventual jettisoning of old readings. For this, the kind of writings that survive play a key role; that is, an apologetic or polemical work that looks outward may have a different role than a biblical commentary or a sermon that looks inward. Even among inward-looking documents, a commentary that assumes an elite readership will likely differ from a sermon that assumes a mixed audience of old and new Christians, educated and uneducated, advanced and catechumens. I will also look at the role of the interpreters as various forms of freelance experts – self-styled philosophers, teachers, public apologists, and polemicists – and more institutionally connected priests, presbyters, bishops, mystics, and theologians.

Finally, in terms of why, there is something that could not really be discussed until the conclusion; that is the genealogical relationship between interpreters. What I mean by this is: who is reading whom and when? Despite the differences between Lugdunum, Rome, Carthage, Alexandria, Caesarea, and various sites in Asia Minor, whether or not our writers travelled the Roman Mediterranean – and most of them did – their writings did travel, and often at a swift pace, for Irenaeus in Lugdunum to read Theophilus writing in Antioch not long after Theophilus wrote, or for Clement in Alexandria to read Irenaeus very shortly after Irenaeus finished his magnum opus. They were participating in and solidifying, thereby, social networks that often served the purpose of creating a shared identity. Reading – and accepting, more or less, the interpretations of others' writings – against other Christians' interpretations created a fledgling Mediterranean-wide network of like-minded people in a paper-war against other Christian networks in the intramural name-calling contest differentiating "us" and "them."

Therefore, it is interesting, to this writer anyway, that most of the evidence discussed chronologically "clumps" or comes in waves at the end of the first century and beginning of the second, at the end of the second and beginning of the third, and finally in the second half of the fourth century. There are important outliers to this clumping that provide some sort of continuity – for example, Justin provides the transition between the first two waves, and Augustine after the third. Moreover, figures not discussed or fully analyzed, such as Eusebius of Caesarea, Ambrose, or Jerome, would provide other lines of continuity between Origen's death, the Cappadocians, and Augustine. Nonetheless, we should note that the concern with reinterpretation – or as Frederic Jameson would note, the dissatisfaction with earlier readings – came in waves rather than in a direct line. Shifting social and political circumstances likely account for some of the impetus for reinterpretation, as would these seemingly emergent networks of readership.

STRATEGIES OF SEEING:
WHO, HOW, AND WHAT?

Especially starting in the second century onward, Christian writers ranging from Justin to Augustine were troubled by the discrepancy between the position that it was impossible to see God, due to Exod. 33:20, alongside inherited philosophical assumptions and all the sacred texts in which people saw God, especially, but not limited to, Num. 12:8. Did they really see God? If not, what did they see? If so, how? If we know how, who else can do it too? Why would one prefer one interpretation over another? Who gets to decide?

Justin, Theophilus, Irenaeus, Clement, Tertullian, Origen, Basil, Gregory of Nazianzus, Gregory of Nyssa, and Augustine drafted answers to these questions in apologies, polemical treatises against rival Christians and Jews, at least one dialogue, biblical commentaries, homilies, letters, church orders, and the occasional systematic theological treatise. They drew upon their Jewish and Christian predecessors and contemporaries, including one another, for inspiration and opposition, as they returned to these old questions in ever new ways. Dissatisfaction would develop with old and opposing interpretations, as rivals, real and imagined, proliferated and new theological orthodoxies emerged. There are worlds of difference between the New Testament, Justin and those in his wake, and, finally, the Cappadocians and Augustine. Later readers read not only the biblical text, but earlier and contemporary readings, adopting, adapting, and opposing these other options as their social position, network, and historical moment led to dissatisfaction with earlier and competing readings.

According to writers of the first century and early-second centuries of the fledgling Christian movement, no one – including Moses – could see God, except the Son, though Hebrews is more ambiguous on this score. Instead, Moses saw angels at the burning bush and on the mountain; nonetheless, the pure and pure of heart will one day see God. According to Christians in the second and third centuries, Moses and other prophets predominantly saw or foresaw the Son; nonetheless, Moses becomes increasingly the model for human possibilities and limits, already foreshadowed in Hebrews 11. At this time, there is also a heightened emphasis on how one sees God through the mind, again using Moses' visions as the model. Finally, according to fourth-century Christians, Moses saw God directly. There have been fits, spurts, and overlaps; once an idea is tried out in one century – for example, that Moses saw angels – it gets repeated in later centuries, though in new ways, as seen with Clement and Augustine.

For most of our post–New Testament authors, Moses' place was emblematic of the prophets more generally, being the greatest among them. Some authors, like Clement or especially the late-antique Cappadocian figures of Basil of Caesarea, Gregory of Nazianzus, and Gregory of Nyssa, would use Moses as an explicit model for their own spiritual authority as a gnostic, bishop, theologian, or mystic. Although for pre-Christian authors, such as Philo, Moses was truly exceptional, transcending human limitations, for all the Christian authors surveyed, Moses represented the limits of humanity, sometimes unique to himself, sometimes representative of others who, like him, could see God and live.

THE SYNTAX OF SEEING

Having sifted through many examples of ancient Christian as well as ancient Jewish attempts to set the parameters of vision through their attempts to resolve the tensions between Exod. 33:20 and Num. 12:8 and related verses, we now have a three-part matrix or framework that one can apply to any of these works, as well as other visionary texts. This is the "syntax of seeing."

One can categorize the solutions to this problem in the grammatical terms of the syntax of subject, verb, and object: the seeing subject, how one sees, and the object seen. These are the three major variables that early Christians – and other ancient peoples who shared some of their assumptions – had available to them. Some figures may manipulate only one variable at a time, whereas others will manipulate two or all three at once. For example, Justin mostly focused on the object of vision. While Origen entertains all of these, he nonetheless spends little time on what one sees, focusing instead on how one sees and who can see. Clement of Alexandria considered all three elements at once. Irenaeus, too, considered all three elements, but subordinated all three to his progressive dispensation of vision: what one saw, who or what one saw, and who can see, all correlated with when one saw: the distant past, the post-incarnation present, or the eschatological future. Each of these categories has Jewish precedents or contemporary analogues; nonetheless, each Christian thinker analyzed here contributed his own distinctive twist.

The Status of the Seeing Subject

Nearly every person or document analyzed for this study would agree that not just anyone, if anyone at all, at any time, can see God. If one can see God, such a person usually must attain a special status. The status of the seer was already important in the Hebrew Bible and in post-biblical Judaism. Great visions were attributed to heroes living in the mists of the past, such as Abraham, Jacob, and Moses, or even entire foundational communal events, such as the parting of the sea or the Sinai theophany. According to the Rabbis, the rank-and-file Israelites at Sinai saw God more clearly than even Isaiah or Ezekiel. In the late-antique Jewish *midrashim*, status related to Israelite maleness: only a circumcised male could see God. Such a circumcised visionary, moreover, could see God without occlusion, at least in *Genesis Rabbah*. Reinterpreting the Torah's portrayal of divine appearances to Sarah and Hagar, women and non-Jews were excluded.

For many of the texts and authors surveyed, faith and righteousness were the bare minimum requirements for seeing God. But something else must also be in play. For most of these interpreters, these requirements become entwined with Jesus' saying in Matt. 5:8 that the pure in heart will see God; these same Christians would additionally argue that the Son or Logos would, through grace, complete or perfect the

seeking seer who strove for such purity. Already in the late-first- and
early-second-century texts of Matt. 5:8 and 1 John 3:2, the exceptions
to the prohibition on or the impossibility of seeing God are the pure
in heart or the pure. Interestingly, the exceptions in Matt. 5:8 and 1
John 3:2 both use the future tense, suggesting either an eschatological
or post-mortem vision. Hebrews may allow an additional exception
for Moses. The evidence is ambiguous, but Hebrews recalls Moses' status as a visionary, seeing angels, the pattern of the heavenly tabernacle, and perhaps God.

Otherwise, one of the easiest ways around the exegetical problem
posed by one not being able to see God and live and the promise and
occasions of people in the Bible seeing God is that one can see God
and die, or, flipping the sequence, one can die and see God. One can
see this in pre-Christian and Christianized Jewish works, such as
Ascen. Isa. 9:37–8. Perhaps it also appears in *Jub.* 1.26. One can also
find it in rabbinic arguments (*Sifra Lev.* 2:18; *Sifre Deut.* 357, 431;
Midr. Ps. 22:32, 99a).[2]

Turning to our Christian evidence, Theophilus would succinctly
argue that only when the flesh arises immortal could it see the
immortal. While Irenaeus would be frustratingly inconsistent, he generally thought that a full vision of the divine – even of the Father –
occurred upon death, but gave hints of a this-life vision in his inconsistent discussions of seeing, hearing, and foreseeing the Son and
Father. Nonetheless, for Irenaeus, past preincarnation visions were
always partial. In his dispensation of vision, the status of the seer
loomed large, dependent upon when one saw. What one saw and how
one saw was connected to what human capacity was at the time. Past
preincarnate and present post-incarnation visions lead to the final
eschatological vision of the father that transforms one, giving life to
the dead, and assimilating one into the divine.

Clement of Alexandria repeatedly indicated that one is educated
through the Logos in this life for an undistracted, uninterrupted
divine vision in the afterlife, using Moses has his model "gnostic."
While Clement often retains a residue of Philo, in that the Logos
instructed Moses, who, in turn, instructs everyone else, once one
reaches the *Stromateis*, Clement indicates that the gnostic should
achieve the level of Moses, being instructed by the Logos directly as
he was: the gnostic soul becomes a new Moses. Oddly though, he uses
Moses' this-life uninterrupted intercourse with God for a post-life
goal, though with some hints of pre-mortem glances.

Augustine of Hippo, while taking a long time to come to this conclusion given his Plotinian roots, eventually decides, based upon 1 Corinthians 15, that once the pure in heart arise in a spiritual body, the fleshly will take part in the intellectual, and one will be able to see intellectual beings with fleshly eyes. This resembles Theophilus' position from centuries before with greater exegetical precision.

Another way death and vision interrelate is not only through the final death or eschatological vision that one finds in these and so many other sources, but also through a symbolic death, or perhaps death and resuscitation. One may note that in second-temple Jewish ascent apocalypses there is a stereotypical reaction of falling and prostration (e.g., *1 En.* 14.20–2; 71:10–11; cf. *2 En.* 22.4–5; 21.2–4; Ezek. 1:28). At some points, this prostration may indicate symbolic death (*2 En.* 21.2–4; *Apoc. Abr.* 10.1–4).[3] This is something one can also find in late-antique and early-medieval Jewish sources. For example, Merkavah mystics fainted at the threshold of the divine throne room, only to be revived before entering, having a vision of the Merkavah, and participating in the heavenly liturgy (*Hekh. Rab.* §§247–8; cf. §101).[4]

Among the Christian authors surveyed, Irenaeus indicated that John of Patmos, when he swooned, died in some way, so that he could receive the divine visions that followed. Augustine, too, would speak of this-life possibilities for Moses' visions, claiming that he – and others like him, such as Paul and likely Augustine himself – died in some way to this life to attain their visions of God without reaching a final death.

As noted, the most common passage that became entangled in the status of the seer in these overlapping discourses was Matt. 5:8, "Blessed are the pure in heart, for they will see God." Part of the emphasis of some authors lay on the future tense – that this was an eschatological vision. For others, the emphasis lay on the first part, the nature of one's heart. Theophilus, for example, claims that only a pure heart/soul that is chaste and righteous shall see God. Irenaeus, too, employs the future tense in Matt. 5:8 to resolve the problems of seeing and not seeing God: one did not see God clearly in the past, but will clearly do so in the future. For Clement, the pure in heart, instructed by the Logos, will see God as Moses did. For Origen, the pure heart was the condition and the means by which one saw God. It was obtained through effort, but also divine aid. The condition was purity, but the place was the heart, which he equated with one's mind. Again, for Origen, Moses illustrates the limits of the human condition (embodiment) in the face of a divine vision, but also represents the purification and perfection necessary to attain the vision when he enters the dark cloud. While Moses provides a model, Origen, whose life was framed by persecution, sees the martyrs as the ultimate exemplars of the seers of God. Gregory of Nyssa also indicates that a pure heart is necessary to see God. Like Origen, the pure heart is not only the condition for vision, but the means of vision. Beyond Origen's formulation, however, Nyssa indicates that it is the place of vision; it is where one sees God. Augustine, too, would reiterate that anyone who sees God must have purity of heart, meaning that one should not seriously think that Satan (in Job 1) or demons could actually see God.

When one reaches the fourth century, social status clearly marks the discussions of divine vision, focusing most strongly on who, indeed, can see God. In Jewish and Christian materials, status becomes emphasized often, to the exclusion of the prohibition of vision altogether. That is, the prohibition in Exod. 33:20 is often ignored; Num. 12:8 attains primacy. Again, in the *midrashim*, a circumcised Israelite has the capacity for divine vision; the stories of the *hekhalot* mystics do acknowledge that a vision of God on his heavenly throne should be deadly, but recount figures like Rabbi Akiva, who had attained it.

Similarly, there is a loosening of the prohibition in Christian sources of the fourth century and later that focus on the status of the seer. Basil, or perhaps Gregory of Nazianzus, established the Moses-as-model-bishop, who is educated in the best of society, rejects that for contemplation, and then returns to society to lead. The combination of high education, contemplation, and then leadership clearly indicates that Basil thinks that this model is for elite leadership only – and not just for any leader or bishop. What is more, however, the contemplative vision justifies such elite leadership, and the theologian's interpretation of scripture. As with Philo, Clement, and especially Origen, one must be a new Moses to interpret Moses. In this time period, except for the complications that one finds in Gregory of Nazianzus seeing the divine backsides and Gregory of Nyssa claiming that the desire for vision can never be fulfilled, the dominant attitude is that Moses saw God clearly and without intermediary. Moreover, the bishop, mystic, or theologian who has had a similar vision now stands in Moses' place. They, furthermore, emphasize the godlike role of Moses and the bishops. The *Apostolic Constitutions* even contradict the New Testament to say Moses did not see through angels. Instead, Moses saw God and enacted a hierarchy of the priesthood in his time, which mirrors the current hierarchy, with the bishops at the top. In a slightly different vein, Augustine would claim that a vision of the divine in this life was possible for exceptional figures: Moses, Paul, and, it seems, himself – and, interestingly, his mother.

The Means of Seeing

Most ancient-Israelite and post-biblical Jewish works from the Pentateuch to the *hekhalot* mystics read the prohibition in Exod. 33:20 as saying that the splendour of God is so overwhelming that it is deadly; nonetheless, many of the New Testament writers and others who were more philosophically oriented read it as God's essential invisibility. While some, like Justin, then turned to what they saw – what was visible if God was invisible? – others of a more middle-Platonic orientation turned to the act of seeing, asking what "seeing" signifies. The primarily middle-Platonically influenced solution – and who among all these figures is not even a little touched by this assumption, except maybe Tertullian – is that "seeing" is a metaphor. There are two types of seeing: seeing God physically, which is impossible, and seeing God spiritually or noetically, which is extremely difficult, perhaps nearly impossible, but not completely impossible for exceptional human beings. Of course, the philosopher-exegete Philo of Alexandria provides a Jewish precedent for this view, but it also may be present in the non-Platonizing *Apocalypse of Abraham*.

The idea that God is invisible is already assumed by several New Testament texts (Rom. 1:20; Col. 1:15; 1 Tim. 1:17; 6:16). While for New Testament authors, this involved a shift to what else Moses could have seen, such as angels, for others, such as Clement and Origen, it shifted the discussion to how one sees. Before them, Theophilus stated that fleshly eyes cannot see God, but the pure, holy, and righteous soul can. Nonetheless, in the resurrection, one's immortalized flesh will be able to behold God, who is immortal. It is, therefore, humanity's sinful and mortal nature that keeps one from being able to see the invisible and immortal God. While Clement also looked at what these figures saw in his *Exhortation* and *Instructor*, he also – following Philo – differentiated between seeing physically and intellectually, using Moses as the pre-eminent example. Following in Philo's foot-steps, for Clement the dark cloud Moses entered packs several concepts: God's invisibility and the exclusivity of those humans who could enter it; that is, Moses and the gnostic soul he represents.

Origen focuses most of his energies here. As Christological assumptions shifted, for Tertullian, Origen, and Augustine after them, Justin's interpretation no longer works fully. Not only did a gap between the contexts of the text and the reader widen, as Jameson would note, but so did a gap between alternative readings emerge, because for Origen, as for Tertullian and Augustine, the Son is the invisible image of the invisible God. In Origen's writings, even the Son has not physically seen the Father, nor has the Father physically seen the Son. For Origen, moreover, the means of seeing is the pure heart or mind, most significantly exemplified by Moses and the Christian martyrs. The mind and God are intelligible, invisible, and incorporeal. One approaches God through the image and restored likeness of God, that is, the mind. While embodiment holds us back, Origen, too, claims transitory divine experiences in this life, indicating that a glimpse of the divine was, indeed, possible.

Augustine of Hippo, who draws upon this differentiation between modes of seeing, is quite exceptional here. He believes God, at least in some way, can be seen in three different ways: physically (corporeally), spiritually (imaginatively), and, ultimately, intellectually, using Moses' differing visions to illustrate all three types. The difference between Augustine's tripartite differentiation and the work of his predecessors, who differentiated between physical and intellectual visions, is not just additive; it has a different evaluation. For the second- and third-century writers surveyed, the physical vision was impossible, whereas the intellectual was possible, even if extremely difficult and rare. For Augustine, all three were possible, though not equal. In this way, who sees and what one sees become subordinated to how one sees. Moreover, unlike many others, he was willing to say that one could see God in God's essence, though not fully as God knows God. Finally, in the resurrection, our physical eyes will be transformed, participating in intellectual qualities so that we may physically see God with transformed eyes. Again, he came to this last position after much reflection and earlier tentativeness, given that he could not find it in the traditional authorities of the Church, though it evinces some resemblance to Theophilus.

The Object Seen

Differentiating between a visible and invisible object was one of the earliest solutions to the problem. While there were already some traces of it within second-temple Judaism, in Christian circles this solution reached its strongest articulation in the second century CE with Justin. Nonetheless, it began to trail off again by the fourth century.

Justin had precedent. Drawing on the ambiguities in some biblical passages between the LORD and the angel of the LORD, many second-temple Jewish apocalypses and reworkings of biblical narratives would emphasize the angelic mediator. Philo regularly employed the Logos for this role, while the Wisdom of Solomon placed Wisdom (Sophia) as God's revealer; *Exod. Rab.* 32 collapsed all angelic mediators into a single figure. Other later-Jewish works, such as the *targumim*, would substitute God's Memra, Shekhinah, or, taking a page from Ezekiel, God's Glory. At some points, one sees God's Tefillin. As Charles Gieschen argues, most of these traditions have the angel of the LORD as their root.

That is what makes the New Testament re-articulations of Moses' visions so striking: it is not *the* angel of the LORD or angel of the Presence (*Jubilees*), but either *an* angel of the Lord in Acts 7 or multiple angels in Galatians and Hebrews, as well as other parts of Acts 7. The multiplication may be elevation – the more the merrier – but more likely precludes Moses encountering the high angel, or at least suggests that he primarily interacted with lower-level angels, especially in the Hellenistic preference of one over the many.

Whatever Justin's inspiration was, his sweeping formulation, that every single theophany in the Hebrew Bible was a Christophany and that the Son was the visible image of the invisible Father, was most influential. He singularly focused on what one sees, largely ignoring how one sees or the status of the seer. Like Abraham, Jacob, and Moses, no one can see the Father; one can only see the Son. Most second- and third-century figures appropriated and developed Justin's theory, though no one really adopted it wholesale. They assumed it, but they modified it in small and great ways. Some were outright uncomfortable with it. Theophilus of Antioch's idea that the Son or Logos masqueraded as the Father, putting on a persona or mask, would not really be developed, even though his terminology of *prosopon*, or persona, would reappear in later Trinitarian discussions. Clement was able in his "lesser" writings to maintain the position that

God and an angel spoke to the past patriarchs and prophets, because, in a telescoping effect, God was present in and speaking through the instrument of the angel. Otherwise, in his better-known works, Clement followed Justin closely in his *Exhortation* and *Instructor*, emphasizing that it was the Logos who spoke to the prophets and now speaks to you; just as the Logos spoke to Moses, so you can learn directly from the Logos.

This solution, of simply having the Son appear to everyone in the Bible, would develop into several variations, because Justin's solution, while it had an impact, did pose some problems. First, it potentially diluted the uniqueness of the incarnation event; thus, Justin himself emphasized that Christ or the Son appeared in polymorphous bodiless visions, strikingly like the "docetic" view of Christ's gospel appearances attributed to Marcion and others.

Yet there is a trajectory of increasing preincarnate embodiment, as other Christians balked at this seemingly "docetic" preincarnate Christ. For Irenaeus, this is implied. When he recounts the Son's visible preincarnate appearances, he even suggests that the Son ate with Abraham. Nevertheless, for Irenaeus such past visions remain partial. He, therefore, further adapts Justin's solution, claiming that Moses saw and foresaw Christ at the same time, equating the two, introducing the Mount of Transfiguration as the fulfillment of the promise that Moses would see God.

Tertullian, due to his Stoic materialism, likewise mostly focused on how precisely the Son appeared, rather than how one sees. In the process, he adapted both Justin and Irenaeus. For Tertullian, this is extraordinarily straightforward: the Son was not just embodied, but fleshly, in his preincarnate appearances. Again, this threatens to undermine the uniqueness of the incarnation event; therefore, Tertullian emphasizes that the flesh of the preincarnate appearances was "made" and just put on and off like clothes, whereas the flesh of the incarnation was "begotten," and, thereby, effectively provides salvation. As with Irenaeus before him, Tertullian states that Moses received a higher vision on the Mount of Transfiguration, indicating that his earlier visions were incomplete. But this trajectory stops short after Tertullian, especially as fourth-century authors begin to reaffirm that Moses saw God the Father or God in totality (as the Trinity as a whole).

The other problem was that, if the Son was visible and the Father invisible – and there is a philosophical assumption that whatever is visible is ontologically lower than whatever is invisible – then the Son was subordinated to the Father. This would not only become a problem after Nicaea, but Tertullian and Origen would already express discomfort with it in the third century. Despite their extraordinary differences, both Tertullian and Origen would claim that the Son is the *invisible* image of the invisible God. For Tertullian, however, God's invisibility is more about human weakness than an essential element; that is, God is spirit, but spirit, following Stoic thought here, is itself a corporeal thing. Fleshly eyes, however, are simply too weak to see it. One needs spiritual eyes of the more-subtle substance of the spirit. He largely avoids the typically Stoic terminology of matter and materiality, likely to avoid the position attributed to Hermogenes that Matter is eternal and uncreated. The Son is spiritual, but the Son did appear visibly to the patriarchs and prophets of old, not because he was necessarily or essentially visible to the flesh, but because he could put on visibility or visible flesh like a garment as he chose. While Origen would occasionally mirror Justin's descriptions of the Son's polymorphic preincarnate appearances in his homilies, he more frequently and extensively argues that the Son is essentially invisible, just as the Father is essentially invisible. Therefore, Justin's solution simply does not work in any form for him. Since it was no longer doing the work it was intended to do, Origen, as noted, shifted the question from what one sees to how one sees.

In the fourth century, the focus on the object seen that dominated the second and third centuries, fades to the background, rejecting Justin's solution and even the New Testament's emphasis on seeing angels. While Eusebius of Caesarea would retain the position that the patriarchs and prophets saw the Son to some degree, others would discreetly drop it, while Augustine would simply declare such a position as heresy, resembling Arian thought. Moreover, both the *Apostolic Constitutions* and Gregory of Nyssa would reject the idea that Moses saw angels instead of God directly. Basil, moreover, indicates that Moses was the first human who saw so clearly. For Gregory of Nazianzus, his vision of God's backside – as he displaces Moses in his homily – is not the Son, as it was according to earlier interpreters, but the entire Trinity. Beginning in the fourth century, Christian writers would claim that Moses did – and others, like themselves, could – see God directly, though not entirely.

Augustine developed Tertullian's idea that God can put on clothes of created matter and combined it with Clement's idea that God speaks through angels as an instrument to claim that the material element that God puts on is the angel itself. Indeed, it is God who spoke and not the angel. Angels are now simply garments that God can put on and off at will in order to interact with humans. Moreover, he rejects the idea that this must be the Son. If God goes around masquerading as an angel, then the prophets speak to God and angel at the same time. Moreover, if the Son has the same qualities as the Father, it could be any element of the Trinity or the entire Trinity who speaks. Having rejected Justin's solution, he can affirm the biblical texts' equivocation between the Lord and the angel of the Lord (it would not matter in this solution), and can affirm that people saw God physically (dressed up as an angelic being) or non-physically (spiritually and intellectually), using Moses to illustrate all three.

There is also a trajectory of education. Irenaeus and Clement both claim that the preincarnate appearances were meant to educate and prepare humans for the incarnation event. However, they distinguish themselves from Justin in that Christ does not simply predict the incarnation, but points to the eschatological vision, offering a progressive view of visions in history. Tertullian takes this the furthest, but flips the relationship. Not only does the preincarnate appearances of Christ prepare humanity for the incarnation, but they prepare Christ for his humanity, as he learns what it means to be human.

AGONISTIC SOCIAL CONTEXTS OF MOSES' ECSTASIES

Now the difficult question: why these individual and collective shifts? Nearly all these interpretations have informative social situations. They tend to be agonistic rather than progressive. As De Certeau, Jantzen, and Nasrallah, among many others, have maintained, when people are quarrelling over whose vision is legitimate, who can have a vision, how, and when, they are discussing authority. Whenever Christians argued about what Moses saw, they were debating what it was possible for a human to see and, therefore, who can and who cannot see the divine. Through these disputes, the interpreter established his own authority against rival Christian and Jewish groups and within his – all of these authors have been male – own community.[5] Even though these considerations appear to be most strongly related to the previous discussion of the status of the seer, I hope to have highlighted how different authors would activate all three basic strategies in accordance to their social situations, historical moments, and shifting theological assumptions.

More directly relevant, Heidi Wendt's work highlights the role and struggle for status through the social role that she calls the "freelance ritual expert." She has created a useful typology of independent readers of sacred texts competing with similarly positioned experts. With such a typology in place, it is interesting to see what happens as one moves to the edges of her typology, to those doing the same thing but with stronger institutional connections, such as Irenaeus or Tertullian.

Reading Patterns:
Creating a Multi-generational Trans-local Social Network

These discussions, therefore, have local, overlapping, and interconnected social contexts – and, moreover, social consequences. There are, in fact, several interconnections among readers, as different authors read not only the authoritative texts that would eventually form the biblical canon, various Greek philosophical and medical writings, and Hellenistic Jewish works, especially the works of Philo, but they were reading each other. We, therefore, need to consider the genealogical relations among readers as they accept, modify, and reject one another's' interpretations.

Valentinus, Marcion, and Justin, among many others, travelled from different parts of the eastern Mediterranean to Rome, bringing their own understandings of Christ with them. Justin – at some point – began to oppose Marcion and Jewish understandings of the Israelite oracle. Irenaeus, in turn, came to Rome later than Justin, but overlapped with him briefly. Their chronologies show that Irenaeus would have been quite young (about twenty) and Justin quite old (about sixty) at any point of overlap. There is, interestingly, a huge generational gap between Justin and Irenaeus that does not open up again in this network of readership until after Origen's death. Irenaeus may have met Justin or even studied under him before moving on to Lugdunum, though there is no way to be sure. He did read his works, however; he also read his exact contemporary, Theophilus of Antioch, who, it seems, had a very small readership.

Just as Irenaeus attained the episcopacy at Lugdunum, Clement, about ten years his junior, arrived in Alexandria from Athens. Irenaeus did not leave a strong stamp on Clement's thought – not as much as Plato or Philo – but Clement did read him. He began to read Irenaeus' *Against Heresies* not long after Irenaeus wrote it, as he arrived in the city that gave birth to Valentinus and Basilides. Approximately ten years younger than Clement, Tertullian, living in North Africa, cited both Justin and Irenaeus, especially in his polemical works against Valentinians. Origen was about twenty-five years younger than Tertullian, but, nonetheless, his writing activities overlap chronologically with him. Origen would have been about seventeen when Clement fled Alexandria during the local persecution that claimed Origen's father. While Origen does not acknowledge his debt, he was clearly influenced by his Alexandrian predecessor, Clement – as well as by Philo. He, furthermore, set the pattern of readership for many people not discussed much in this book – including Pamphilius, Gregory the Wonderworker, Eusebius of Caesarea, as well as Ambrose, Jerome, and Rufinus – as well as those who are discussed, such as Eusebius of Caesarea, Basil of Caesarea, Gregory of Nazianzus, and Gregory of Nyssa. The Cappadocians obviously read each other's works, and in turn Augustine cites Gregory of Nazianzus, clearly knows the readings by Tertullian – though he is careful in his use of Tertullian, due to his "Montanist phase" – as well as a dense network of other Christian writers.

While Origen is a special case – since he was posthumously condemned, though he was influential among "orthodox" and "heretic" alike – most of these writers cite each other to create a network of like-minded people – the kind of network Irenaeus himself had envisioned – often in the context of excluding others through polemical works, but also in treatises and commentaries. Networks of reading created a multi-generational and trans-local shared identity, as they read, accepted, sometimes discarded, or reframed one another's own scriptural interpretations to their own localized contexts. In the case of Tertullian, it may have been a defensive citation practice, to prove he was part of "us" and not "them" as he sought a common identity against figures like Valentinus, Marcion, Praxeas, and Hermogenes while defending his own orthodoxy in his participation in the New Prophecy movement, or "Montanism."

Finally, while interconnected, there are distinct clumps or waves of discussion, rather than a linear development. The first one hundred years after Jesus' death initiated the discussion that denied visions to Moses and other humans (c. 30–130 CE). Nonetheless, there was a new cresting interest in the late-second and early-third centuries (c. 180–250 CE). The new interpretations of Moses' visions explode after approximately 180 CE, when Theophilus, Irenaeus, and subsequently Clement began their work. Clement continued until just after the turn of the century, when the work of Tertullian and, just after him, Origen, picked up. Justin provides a connector between these two waves, as his life overlaps with the latest New Testament writings and briefly with Irenaeus. After Origen's death (254 CE), there is not much in the way of new interpretations until well after Constantine takes the throne and after the Council of Nicaea, about a generation later (c. 350–430). It is in the mid-to-late fourth century that the Cappadocians were active, while Augustine picks up the baton as they fade into the background (end of the fourth to early fifth centuries), though through the intermediate figure of Ambrose.

Why are there all these crests and falls? The crests were periods of bursting reading and interpretive activity in which various Christian authors sought to differentiate themselves from rivals. During the first crest, the primary rival Jewish interpretations provided the primary opposition. For the second, in addition to challenging Jewish readings, Christian authors challenged rival Christian readings, spurred by a growing recognition of the pluralities of Christian belief and practice alongside intense local persecutions of Christians leading to, by the time of Decius, systematic persecutions. Finally, for the third, in addition to challenging rival Christian readings, Christian interpreters redirected earlier reading strategies inward to the congregation. There is not much of a gap to explain between the first two waves, but there is nearly a century between Origen's death and the Cappadocians' rereadings of Moses. While they had a line of teachers connecting them through Gregory the Wonderworker, most readings until the mid-fourth century largely reiterated Origen's and preceding readings rather than developing them. I would speculate that the gap in innovation was due, paradoxically, to the rapid changes occurring in the late-third and early-fourth centuries: increasingly intense persecutions of Christians, especially in the eastern Mediterranean; the reorganization of the empire under Diocletian, with the four-emperor system; the eastward shift of the imperial presence under Diocletian; the quick rise of Constantine and his concentration of power back to a single emperor, now stationed in Constantinople; and, with this rise, the toleration of and preference for Christians, and all the legal and fiscal benefits accruing to bishops. It was only when the dust began to settle with the effects of toleration, the empowerment of bishops, and the repeated defences of Nicaea that theological innovation and scriptural reinterpretation could take place.

Intersections of Interpretive Strategies, Social Roles, and Shifting Contexts

Social statuses and roles are already operative in the stories within the Hebrew Bible and post-biblical Judaism. Foundational figures like Abraham, Jacob, Moses, and even Rabbi Akiva achieve visions of the divine, as do foundational communal events, like the parting of the sea and the theophany on Sinai. In fact, the entwinement of Moses' visions and social status is already present in the context of Num. 12:6–8, where Moses' clearer visions of the divine give him greater authority than the visions of Aaron, Miriam, and other prophets, which are more occluded. This greater exceptionality of Moses' visions also give him a mandate to lead according to Ezekiel's *Exagoge*, Philo's *Life of Moses*, and even Josephus' *Antiquities of the Jews*. For these authors, the status they give to Moses serves as a proxy to establish the greater antiquity of Jewish traditions than especially Greek legal and philosophical traditions; it is apologetic and polemical. Nonetheless, Philo's self-descriptions of his own experiences strongly resemble – but as Jack Levinson has noted, are still partly demarcated from – his description of the truly exceptional Moses. For rabbinic Jews, R. Akiva's greater interpretive authority – beyond what even Moses can understand – nonetheless derives from Moses' visions, while for the merkavah mystics, R. Akiva and Moses are often twinned or paired, imbuing R. Akiva with Mosaic authority.

The New Testament documents seem ambiguous about Moses and his visions when considered together. In general, there was a demotion of Moses compared to Jesus. While Moses was generally considered a great mediator of the past, giving the law and having an intimate relationship with God, he remains as deficient as others in his ability to see God: none can see or know God except the Son. Moses, therefore, saw angels, as noted. In short, the first- and early-second-century documents of the New Testament tend to emphasize the attitude of Exod. 33:20, noting the impossibility of seeing God rather than emphasizing those exceptional figures who did see God. Thereby, they make unique the Son's position as the only entity who has or can see God.

This emergent Christian Jewish apologetic argument both mirrors and contrasts many non-Christian forms of Judaism, particularly those forms of Judaism that thought that Moses was the ultimate mediator, who had ascended to heaven and was angelified or even deified. With this position now occupied by Jesus in Christian writings, Moses' role has diminished. Yet his intimacy with the divine is partially remembered, and his faith is imitable. The seeds for the argument that he was the limit of humanity are being planted, but the strongest statements about Moses in Galatians, Hebrews, and John clearly subordinate him to Jesus, although in different ways.

The social situations in which these documents came into being are hotly debated, but where they are clearer, such as in Paul's writings, one sees a strong polemic against rival Christian Jewish missionaries, who retain higher valuations of the practices of the Torah, including circumcision and a modicum of food laws. As most of the emphasis on Moses' visions and greater authority occurred in second-temple Jewish discussions of Torah interpretation, most of the devaluations of Moses' visions in the first century of emergent Christian writings come in discussions of the Torah and its interpretation. Moses, therefore, represented the competition, but he was also the model for Christology and for Christ-followers. While Hebrews 11, at least, indicates that Moses' faith is something to emulate, his unique position found in previous and contemporary traditions becomes ceded to Christ, allowing Moses to become the model of humanity for later Christianity.

In the second and third centuries, why not simply maintain the New Testament emphasis that Moses saw angels? Why shift the object of his visions to the Son? Why would angels no longer work? What new gaps and dissonances arose between text and the new hermeneutical context? And why are these new generations of writers dissatisfied with previous and alternative contemporary Christian readings? Of course, some, like Clement, did retain the angels, though in a rather sophisticated manner, claiming the Son, or Logos, spoke through the angels and was present in the angels, in a telescoping effect. Likewise, Augustine would return to an angelic interpretation from time to time. Nonetheless, the answers to these questions are difficult to delineate, because motives are not always laid bare and are not always as clear as, for example, many of the fourth-century documents. Nonetheless, it is helpful to see who develops these arguments and in what kind of literature in the second and third centuries.

First, most of these figures are what Heidi Wendt has recently described as freelance experts in the Roman empire, purveying the new – yet, they would argue, old – Christian cult among the panoply of other religious experts from various parts of the Roman empire and beyond, including rival Christian experts. This, in fact, is how Wendt analyzes Paul's activities. Paul's itinerant pattern does appear to survive into the next few centuries in modified form. For figures like Justin or Clement, their knowledge of sacred texts and traditions, and their ability to interpret them convincingly to others, is the basis of their authority. These figures tended to be peripheral to developing institutional powers, with the exception of Irenaeus and Theophilus, who were bishops. Nonetheless, as noted in the chapter dedicated to Irenaeus, the role of the bishop was as the community's authoritative teacher; it is almost an institutionalization of the freelance expert. The role of the bishop, therefore, was different than in the fourth-century accounts. Irenaeus, moreover, continued to follow the itinerant lifestyle, moving from Asia Minor to Rome to Gaul. Tertullian retains the apologetic and mostly polemical style of these earlier interpreters, yet he loses the itinerant, foreign status, largely staying home in his native Carthage.

In general, the authority of most of these figures operates to attract students, and repel rival interpretations, including those of Marcion, Valentinus, Basilides – and, for Tertullian, also Hermogenes and Praxeas. Justin, Clement, and Origen are most remembered as being great teachers, though Origen was later ordained to preach in Caesarea – to the annoyance of the bishop of Alexandria. While Clement and Origen develop their arguments often in non-polemical literature – in treatises and sermons meant for insiders or those transitioning to become insiders – their authority is still based upon their ability to interpret and teach. When Christian authority shifts into a stronger institutional setting, the strategies developed by these earlier freelance experts persist as Irenaeus tries to keep people in his own church and prevent them from going over to Marcus.[5]

At the same time, given their precarious places on the fringes of Roman society around the Mediterranean littoral – and for the mobile teachers, the suspicion often incurred by travellers would heighten their perilous situations[6] – they also had to address themselves outwardly to make their obscure and, frankly, strange religion intelligible to governing authorities, who saw Christians as superstitious, and perhaps a dangerous novelty. As such, their polemics against those who could undermine their claims to authority and antiquity, who read or rejected the same scriptures – for example, Jews and Marcion – were of a piece with the public apologetics offered to various emperors.

As such, one finds most of the arguments developing in polemical and apologetic literature, which, not incidentally, is one of the most predominant forms of literature to survive from this period.[7] The polemics of vision were less often discussed explicitly in martyrdom texts, letters, and extra-canonical gospels and acts even as works like the *Martyrdom of Perpetua* included visions that Tertullian employed for such purposes. Instead, these polemics appear to be an effective way of defining oneself against one's real or imagined adversaries in what Laura Nasrallah has called "intramural name-calling":[8] here, defining oneself against Jews, Marcion, perhaps Valentinus and his followers, like Marcus, and defending oneself against contemporary Greeks and Romans who saw this new Christian cult as primitive, unsophisticated, and lacking tradition.

In summary, the second- and third-century context is one of intensified polemics, in which different interpreters attempted to define themselves against rival interpreters. One set of interpreters tried to co-opt Israelite scriptures to claim antiquity in the face of Roman opposition, while contending with those who had rival claims on the Israelite scriptures (Jews) or those Christians who rejected them (e.g., Marcion, Valentinus, and Basilides).

Against Marcion, Valentinus, and Basilides, early Christians who thought the Hebrew Bible or Old Testament consisted largely of defective revelations of an equally defective creator, claiming that the Torah was revealed to Moses by lesser beings, like angels, would no longer work. It would simply fall right into their hands. What Justin's simple manoeuvre did was unite the old and new revelations even tighter than even the Gospel of Matthew did by making them issue from a single revealer. Furthermore, this manoeuvre fits the anti-Jewish polemic by not only making the true meaning of the law and the Prophets Christian, which had been occurring since the first century, but made Christ the one revealing it: Christ is both revealer and revealed, messenger and message. This fits both anti-Marcionite and anti-Jewish polemics by saying the same thing, creating greater continuity of revelation between Old and New Testaments, between Israelite and Christian.

For philosophically oriented Greek and Roman objections, making all theophanies Christophanies would help to explain away all of those embarrassing anthropomorphisms in the Old Testament. How can the invisible, ineffable God walk in the Garden, and visually encounter various figures? The answer is that he did not; his visible image, Jesus, did. While problematic for later interpreters, it worked in its time. Not long afterward, Theophilus adopted it, while others like Irenaeus, Clement, and Tertullian would adopt this solution, but dissolve some of its premises. It was still doing some work as late as Eusebius of Caesarea, who in the early-fourth century CE adopted it with some minor modifications.

Marcion and the Valentinians used largely the same manoeuvre: they distinguished between a visible deity seen in the Israelite scriptures and the invisible God. Indeed, all the figures discussed and their opponents often mirrored one another in reading strategy, terminology, and even social location, since Justin, Marcion, and Valentinus were all from different parts of the eastern Mediterranean living in Rome. Moreover, as Elizabeth Clark has noted, "there was no distinctively 'heretical' or 'orthodox' mode of reading."[9] For them, however, the demiurge – the creator of this world – was the God of the Old Testament, and he was the one bumbling around for people to see, whereas the hidden God, the Father, was the invisible God who sent Christ. Did Justin borrow this strategy from Marcion and Valentinus and use it against them? Or was it the other way around?

Late-second- and early-third-century writers had largely the same opponents – real or imagined – in view, but nonetheless slowly modified Justin's solution. These modifications have already been discussed, as holes and drawbacks in Justin's argument, especially his subordinationism, became more apparent in the generations of writers that followed him. Some of these modifications, however, reflect different elements of their polemical adversaries.

Irenaeus shows greater ambivalence toward what the patriarchs and prophets saw and heard, yet there is a heightening of the stakes. Through the first three books of *Against Heresies*, Irenaeus describes, exaggerates, and mocks some of the first exemplars of attempted systematic reflection in the Christian world – especially that of Valentinus' mythopoetic systematic theology, cosmology, and anthropology. With such an edifice to demolish, Irenaeus turns to building one of his own, in the process developing his own progressive vision of the Logos. While he had the same basic opponents, he developed a more systematic internal view, though one that is still fledgling.

There are two immediate social catalysts that shape Irenaeus' thought, especially his system building and his attempt to develop a network of interconnected communities: Marcus' church (and network) following a Valentinian Christian system and the persecution and execution of many in his own community, including the previous bishop, the defining event that precipitated his own rise to the epis-

copacy. His ecclesiological and theological edifice set out to differentiate his church from its entwinements and overlapping membership
with Marcus' and provide an inter-communal network as a defensive
bulwark in the face of potential and likely persecution.

Tertullian's theology develops, like iron sharpening iron, through
debate, opposition, and competition. He faces a combination of old
and new opponents: Jews, Marcion, and Valentinians on the one
hand, and Praxeas and Hermogenes on the other. His theory of vision
becomes subtler and more precise as he adopts the strategies of both
Justin and Irenaeus, and then applies them to these adversaries. He
provides novelty, however, in his stronger anti-Platonic dependence
on Stoic materialism – though differentiated from Hermogenes'
views of matter – and his recourse to contemporary, female prophets.
This allows an increased evaluation of physical embodiment and
fleshliness, even before the actual incarnation, providing a stronger
denunciation of Marcion's and, to a lesser extent, Valentinian opposition to Jesus' enfleshment. While old opponents explain Tertullian's
continued tying together of old and new revelations, uniting them
into one figure, and his philosophical leanings allow him to increase
the fleshliness of even the pre-existent Christ, it was his relatively
novel opponent Praxeas who made him address the problem of seeing
and not seeing more directly than any previous writer, and more clearly differentiate the Father and the Son in these preincarnate theophanies as well. Unlike Clement, Origen, or Gregory of Nazianzus later
on, Tertullian does not – to my knowledge – claim such experiences
for himself. He claims them for charismatic women in his church in
Carthage, who have seen angels and even the Lord in physical form.
It is they – not himself – who stand between God and humans as the
past prophets did; therefore, their experiences can be authoritative
next to received scriptures. His authoritative role, however, is to interpret these varied and inspired sources.

In terms of the apologetic face of most of these writings of the
first three centuries of Christianity, there are various confrontations
with Greek and Roman thought, culture, and politics, both positive
and negative. Indeed, the stakes were often high: they had to differentiate themselves from the dominant culture, yet often relied heavily upon it. They explained Christianity in philosophical terms,
while disparaging Greek and Roman gods and myths, presenting
Christianity as the religion of Reason (Logos), and identifying that
Reason with Christ.

Justin already presented himself – including his manner of dress –
as a philosopher, seeking to display Christianity in reasonable terms
to the philosopher-emperor Marcus Aurelius. For Justin and Clement,
Plato was a stepping stone to Christianity. Nonetheless, in the adaptation of Platonic though to Christian biblical reading, Clement and
Origen, and, through Origen, the fourth-century figures like Basil,
Gregory of Nazianzus, and especially Gregory of Nyssa, especially
shine. Through this same lineage of Platonically oriented Christian
thinkers emerged the notion that the interpreter of scripture must
have the same experience as the original prophet, that one must
become a new Moses to interpret Moses' writings. The same Spirit
inspired both the originator and interpreter of scripture. This view of
inspired reading was about as strong a statement about the status of
the interpreter against rival readers within and without the community as one could make.

For Clement, Justin's position that it was Christ who spoke to
Moses and the prophets proves preliminary, serviceable enough to
encourage novices to come into the fold. Clement's discussion dizzyingly cites Plato and other Greek authorities, alongside biblical passages, as he lays out a contemplative program that clearly relies upon
Philo, yet also offers a mirrored alternative to Valentinus and Basilides, appropriating terminology associated with them and applying it
to Moses, presenting Moses as the perfect "gnostic."

Tertullian, though anti-Platonic, was not anti-philosophical, incorporating Stoic thought, Heraclitus, and even Greek medical knowledge when it suited his rhetorical purposes. Origen, too, disparages
Greek philosophy, as Tertullian does, even though he clearly relies
upon it more. Origen, moreover, shifts away from Justin not only in
his more systematic theology *On First Principles* in which he asserts
that the Son must be essentially invisible – a statement he shares with
anti-Platonic Tertullian – but in his immediate conflicts with his
own bishop in Alexandria and ultimately persecution as a child and
as an old man, the latter Decian persecution leaving him with
injuries that would eventually kill him. When Origen claims that the
interpreter of scripture must have the same experience as the original
prophet, alongside some brief, scattered personal accounts of such
experiences and his voluminous output, he clearly seeks an independence no longer found; the time of the "freelance" expert has begun
to fade, and the expert bristles under new leadership. He positions
his own authority not only against outsiders, but against those who

have higher authority than him in the church. Yet martyrs also punctuate his life, allowing him to rethink the question of who can see God and how.

While all of these writers sought to differentiate themselves from competing Jewish and Christian readings of Moses – yet claiming to be an old tradition by appropriating the Israelite scriptures – the stakes were high, as the prospect of martyrdom loomed. These Christians sought to counter accusations of atheism, cannibalism, and incest – or, a charge perhaps more likely to stick, forming a forbidden political association – begging for tolerance from governing authorities.[10] They faced potential persecution and death, at first sporadic but increasingly systematic by the end of the third century. Justin, who wrote apologies to Roman emperors, still died a martyr. Irenaeus' community in southern Gaul experienced local persecutions, though he survived it. Origen's father died a martyr, and Origen, as mentioned, would eventually succumb to injuries sustained when he was tortured in the Decian persecution. The spectre of martyrdom and death opened up a rethinking of the parameters of vision; indeed, if one gives up one's life for God, the thought that one cannot see God and live dissolves as a prohibition and a threat and transforms into a reward: the highest visions become vouchsafed to martyrs, upon, just before, and after death. In short, engaging and praising Greek and Roman intellectual culture, demonizing Greek and Roman religion, maintaining continuity and yet distance with Jewish traditions, these authors, especially Origen, engaged in an apologetic balancing act that shaped their ideas of divine vision and access to such a vision.

Why the shift in the fourth century? Why weren't bishops and mystics satisfied with Moses seeing only the Son or Logos? Why were they now proclaiming that Moses saw God directly and clearly, or nearly so? There, indeed, was a widening gap between interpreter and alternative previous solutions due to social situations shifting away from persecution to toleration and even preference and theological developments from the Arian and Eunomian debates of the fourth century. Although, to be sure, Eusebius of Caesarea, writing history, resorted to the earlier solutions with some modification leading back to Justin – surprisingly so, given his Origenist leanings. Moreover, there was again a shift in the social roles of the participants and in the genres used. Basil, Gregory of Nazianzus, Gregory of Nyssa, and Augustine of Hippo were all bishops. The Arian and anti-Nicene *Apostolic Constitutions*, written around 380 CE, again mostly concerns itself

with the bishop's authority and the graded order of the church structure. All these writers were in the middle of church politics of the late-
fourth and early-fifth centuries; they were central to the emerging
power of the episcopate after Constantine's accession to the throne.
There is nothing "freelance" about them. Nonetheless, they still had
institutional and interpretive rivalries, sometimes among each other.
Moreover, while these writers would still be writing against rival
Christian groups, such as Arians (and the *Apostolic Constitutions* is, in
fact, an Arian document), Eunomians, and, leading to the Council of
Constantinople, even each other, many of the developments occur in
biblical commentary, sermons, treatises, and church orders addressed
to highly educated insiders.

Basil highlights Moses' vision and pattern of life of education, withdrawal and contemplation, and reintegration and leadership in letters
and sermons, such as in his *Homilies on the Hexaemeron*. Here he suggests that Moses was the first human to see God directly. Moses is a
model for bishops to follow; Basil employs him for internal authority, rather than in polemics against outsiders. Gregory of Nazianzus
uses Moses as a model bishop and, indeed, claims himself to be a new
Moses in his sermons to his parishioners. He combines these claims
to internal authority with a polemic against a rival theologian, Eunomius. Gregory of Nyssa similarly uses Moses as the model mystic for
insiders in his work *The Life of Moses* and in his homilies. The *Apostolic
Constitutions* are church orders directed at the clergy.

They proclaimed their authority as being equal to Moses to their
congregations, in letters to each other, in eulogies in each other's honour, and in biblical commentary directed toward the theological elite.
Even Augustine's reflections largely occur in his *Literal Commentary
on Genesis* and letters to other Christians, though they are also scattered through his massive apologetic tome the *City of God* and his
greatest theological speculative work, *On the Trinity*. We can more
accurately trace his development of thought as he responds to questions and reconsiders his own positions through his intricate social
network of interlocutors – though, similar to Tertullian's, Augustine's
development of thought opens up these experiences to non-elites as
well, including his own uneducated mother, Monica. She reaches the
same heights of insight as he does in *Confessions* 9.

While keeping an eye on rival Christian leaders, these fourth-century and early-fifth-century authors are all directed toward insiders,
for the already initiated. Just as Moses stood between God and Israel,

so the bishop stands between Christ and the Church. These writers are no longer jockeying primarily against rival Christians groups – though, of course, this persists (e.g., with Arians, Eunomians, Pneumatomachians, etc.) – but they are now establishing internal order and authority within a newly empowered episcopacy after the rise of Constantine. Scriptural passages previously used to establish authority against outsiders – real or perceived – are now turned inward to one's own community. The boost in Moses' authority within the Christian community mirrors and justifies their own increased authority in a post-Constintinian empire. Augustine's own use of Moses' visions seems to operate differently. As noted, he opens up the vision to non-elite Christians. Instead, as Origen had before him in *Against Celsus*, Augustine seems to be engaged in apologetics against the cultured despisers of Christianity, such as Porphyry, while maintaining the unity of scripture, the beauty so old and so new.

Why does this interpretive shift happen, however, in the *late* fourth century? Why did it not happen earlier, around the time of Nicaea with Eusebius? Partly, there may simply be a generational component; that is, the theologians convening at Nicaea were trained during a time of disempowerment. The new generation of theologians, including the Cappadocians, but perhaps to some extent Athanasius, who arose more prominently after Nicaea, trained during a time of greater empowerment. One should not exaggerate this empowerment, which was due to shifting whims of pro-Arian versus pro-Nicene emperors in the wake of Constantine and the interlude of Julian's experiments with reviving and transforming ancient pre-Christian customs. Intramural polemics between Nicenes and Arians, and more precisely between the Cappadocians and Eunomians, erupted. Gregory of Nazianzus' sermons that justify his ability to interpret Moses as a new Moses himself, having had a mountaintop experience like Moses, form an anti-Eunomian tract. Nonetheless, the shift from persecution of Christians to preference clearly marked the new generation of thinkers.

There is also a shift from thinking through martyrdom – though this cannot be exaggerated, as different Christian groups violently turned on one another, as in the case in North Africa – to a greater focus on monasticism. Basil sought to reform the episcopate by appointing monks, advocating the repackaging of Moses as an ideal active contemplative. This fusion of episcopal authority, theological correctness, and monastic charismatic authority is paralleled in Athanasius' *Life of Antony*, written in the mid-fourth century.

MOSES, THE MEASURE OF HUMANITY, AND TRAVERSING HUMAN LIMITS

Moses' visions became the central means through which to develop, maintain, and alter individual and social boundaries between groups and within groups. Moses became a model for the biblical interpreter, the true gnostic, the theologian, the bishop, and the mystic to follow, who used Moses' visions to fight off competing readers while also seeking to establish, maintain, and justify their own positions of leadership. They regularly appropriated these visions, claiming a similar situation for themselves or, in the North African cases of Tertullian and Augustine, for charismatic women.

There were, however, a few places where Moses was not quite the measure of humanity. For Philo – though not Christian, read thoroughly by Christians – Moses exceeded humanity to a degree that no one could ever live up to. He is not humanity's limit, but humanity transcended, occupying a structural position Jesus would hold in early Christian thought. For Irenaeus, due to his overarching schema of the progressive dispensations of vision, Moses does not quite seem to reach humanity at its limit, but actually falls a bit short. Moses, to be sure, sees beyond what others in his time can, but he merely sees what later visionaries would see more clearly. His exceptional visions in the past become generalized in later dispensations; in this sense, instead of becoming a model for humanity at its limit, as he does for others, he becomes a model for humanity at its centre. For Irenaeus, the prophecies of the past provide the means for the increasingly available visions in the present and the full vision in the future.

Nonetheless, aside from these exceptions, Christian readings of Moses' visions are meditations of the boundaries of the human condition, boundaries that can be approached, stretched, and sometimes even crossed over. When Moses could not see God in the New Testament documents, neither could any other human; only the Son could. When Moses saw God only through the mind, so could others, as Origen and Augustine claim they did. When Moses could see God in the fourth-century documents, other humans could, such as a bishop, theologian, or mystic. These meeting places between humans and the divine are boundaries; once one reaches them, they also have the occasional potential to become thresholds that may or may not be crossable.[11]

As one reaches one's human limits, one reaches a state of liminality, of potential transformation. In all these texts, the greatest transforma-

tion occurs mostly in the afterlife, once all our usual mortal boundaries have been shuffled off; nonetheless, occasionally, select figures
cross over in this life (*1 En.* 71.11; *2 En.* 28.11; *3 En.* 15.48C).

When one looks at these moments of transformation, crossing the
limit of the human condition usually means transforming into or
taking upon oneself the status of an angel. Enoch, Isaiah, and Zephan-
iah become angelified in Jewish apocalyptic texts.[12] Philo's transformation of Moses at the end of Moses' life turns him into a completely noetic (that is, angelic) being: "Afterwards the time came when he
had to make his pilgrimage from earth to heaven, and leave this mortal life for immortality, summoned thither by the father who resolves
his twofold nature of soul and body into a single unity, transforming
his whole being into mind, pure as the sunlight" (*Moses* 2.288). Or as
Tertullian wrote, "He has promised that He will one day form
humans into angels, who once formed angels into humans" (*Ag. Marc.*
3.9.7). Basil reaffirmed the angelic status of Moses and the bishop-
contemplative-seer. For Augustine, we shall become equal to the angels
who always behold the face of God.

Yet some authors did not stop there; for some, Moses provided a
model of deification. Moses' identification with the Logos in Philo
provided a model for this transcendent self. There may also be a hint
of this in Ezekiel the Tragedian's presentation of Moses' dream. For
Irenaeus, when reaching the final vision of the Father, the limit
becomes threshold and, following ancient optical assumptions, one is
deified, as one becomes what one sees. Clement, moreover, suggests
that, as one assimilates the Logos, one becomes the Logos, moving
from being merely the image of God to the image and likeness, as the
Logos is. As one becomes a true gnostic, moreover, one attains divine
functions, such as impassibility and self-creation.

Who could see God? What precisely did such people see? How did
they see? Who determined who could see what and how and even
when? Why did they answer these questions the way they did? What
changes in local and broader social and historical circumstances, theological presuppositions, rivalries within and without one's social networks were in play? All these questions were about limits: between
God and humans; boundary-creation and boundary-maintenance
between Christians and other groups; among rival Christians; and
among Christians in the same groups. Some of these limits marked
abysses of difference between Creator and created, while others were
semi-permeable membranes. Beneath the surface, the limit was an

ever-shifting line in the sand as the winds of theological and social boundary-making changed.

There are many limits of the human and among humans that one can study. One may be a biologist looking at the place of humans among other animal species; or one may investigate the boundaries between humans and machines in ever-evolving bio-technology. In the realm of religion, and especially ancient histories of interpretation, however, I have examined a different boundary. I have considered how one particular tradition has considered the furthest limits of humanity in the overwhelming face of divinity in what seemed an unlikely but ultimately fruitful place: Moses on the mountaintop.

Notes

1 Trans. Chadwick, *Contra Celsum*. Emphasis mine.
2 de Certeau, *The Mystic Fable*, 1:11.
3 These exceptions will be discussed throughout, especially those who did not think that Jesus was fully embodied or at least en-fleshed – a position attributed to Marcion among others.
4 On Moses' transformation, see for example, *Sir.* 45:2; *1 En.* 89:36; Philo, *Moses* 2.272, 280; b. *Yoma* 4a–b; Basil of Caesarea, *Hom. Hex.* 1; Gregory of Nyssa, *Moses* 2.217. On "the man Moses," see von Rad, *Moses*, 5–6.
5 Derrida, *Animal That Therefore I Am*, 29–31. Nonetheless, Derrida's work has retained a sense of heterogeneity between self and other, and humans and animals. It has not blurred the boundaries as much as it has complicated them. The first part of this very long lecture is interesting for religious studies, since it includes a series of interactions with Genesis 1–3. Moreover, while the title and much of the content of this essay is a reference to and a critique of Descartes' "cogito ergo sum," it is also a reference to the "I am" of Exodus 3:14. Less relevant for this study is Derrida's two-volume *The Beast and the Sovereign*. For the impact of these works on biblical studies, see, e.g., Koosed, ed., *Bible and Posthumanism*; Moore, *Untold Tales from the Book of Revelation*, 201–23. More recently, Stephen Moore (*Gospel Jesuses and Other Nonhumans*) has turned to "non-humanism," which strikes me as having a stronger materialist focus that is less relevant for this study. It is something of a "post-post-humanism." In his non-human theory, Moore not only interacts with Derrida's posthumous works, but also affect theory, especially turning to the works of Gilles Deleuze and Félix Guattari. In his "non-

humanist" readings, he moves from merely the limits between humans and animals to humans and all non-human elements, including plants, rocks, as well as animals; therefore, it is a theoretical model that melds well with "new materialism" and ecological interests. George Aichele (*Tales of Posthumanity*) also develops his discussion of posthumanism in conversation with the works of Deleuze and Guattari, more so than Derrida.

6 For a historical study of such phenomena from a medieval perspective, see Bynum, *Metamorphosis and Identity*; otherwise, see Freud, "The Uncanny," 121–62. The "uncanny" as discussed by Freud is something that is both "at home" and "not at home" at the same time; that is, it is both familiar and strange. It is the familiar that is unfamiliar, or the unfamiliar that is strangely familiar. A typical example is the return of something familiar – something repressed either individually or socially – in a new setting (e.g., ghost stories in an age of scientific knowledge); it can be the flash of recognition of something familiar that is unexpectedly out of place, creating a sudden defamiliarization. This can lead – like a lot of mystical discussions of God – to a simultaneous awe and fear, a simultaneous attraction and repulsion. See Derrida, *Beast and the Sovereign*, 1: 246, 266, for a similar sense with a discussion of a snake. This also resembles Rudolf Otto's *Idea of the Holy* as a *mysterium tremendum et fascinans*. Indeed, Otto's "holy" and Freud's "uncanny" have some striking resemblances: both inviting terror and attraction.

7 All biblical translations are by the author, unless otherwise noted, but were done consulting several other translations, including especially the New Revised Standard Version (NRSV).

8 Oddly, this conversation comes just after Moses has been speaking to God "face to face" (Exod. 33:11), which itself will begin to give Christian interpreters pause for contemplation, especially Tertullian and Augustine of Hippo.

9 Perhaps the most important is the special issue of *Cahiers Sionens* 8 (1954); the edition I used was H. Cazelles, et al., *Moïse: L'Homme de l'alliance*, including contributions by pre-eminent scholars covering ancient Israelite to Islamic representations of Moses. For such a wide-ranging set of essays, only those focused on the medieval Latin, Byzantine, and Sufi views of Moses really discuss the issues considered here: Châtillon ("Moïse Figure du Christ," 305–14) directly addresses the issues considered here in works from Augustine of Hippo to Thomas Aquinas; Blanc ("La Fête de Moïse dans le rite byzantin," 345–53) does not really discuss issues of Moses' vision as much as present liturgical works that feature his visions; Gardet, "L'Expérience intérieure du prophète Mûsâ (Moïse) selon quelques traditions sûfies," 393–402. Other essays may indicate Moses' role as mediator or even his "intimacy" with God, but not really his visions, per se. See, e.g., Cazelles,

"Moïse devant l'histoire," 22; Gelin, "Moïse dans l'Ancien Testament," 29, 43–4. Another edited volume by Martin-Achard, et al., *La Figure de Moïse*, had fewer entries, but still ranged from the Bible to Freud. In that volume, there was a strong emphasis on Moses' role as intermediary; nonetheless, only the chapter on Philo by Starobinski-Safran ("La Prophétie de Moïse et sa portée d'après Philon," 67–80) directly approached the issues of Moses' visions. The contribution by Junod ("Moïse exemple de la perfection selon Grégoire de Nysse," 81–98) also touched upon these issues.

10 These are mostly focused on New Testament and related literatures. They will mostly be cited as relevant, since they are much more voluminous, but one should note the landmark studies of Moses in the Hebrew Bible by von Rad, *Moses*; and the important study of Moses in "pagan" literature by Gager, *Moses in Greco-Roman Paganism*.

11 The most important being Meeks, *The Prophet-King*, which, while focusing on a problem in John, ranges quite widely over a great swath of literature.

12 Gelin, "Moïse dans l'Ancien Testament," 44 (translation mine). Original French: "Ces anthropomorphisms et ces théologoumena – ou expressions par lesquelle on se représentait Dieu en train de se manifester – sont le fruit d'une théologie balbutiante; la face de Yahweh, sa gloire, son nom, sa main, son dos, autant de manifestations plus ou moins partielles de l'Inapprochable, avec qui Moïse, pourtant, a contact."

13 Some of these ascent apocalypses will be discussed in Chapter 2, since not all of them will unabashedly feature a direct vision of God; instead, many will qualify such a vision in different ways, expressing the tension between seeing God and the prohibition of seeing God.

14 Segal, "Heavenly Ascent," 207. For extensive references to these ascents, see 207n5.

15 Gieschen, *Angelomorphic Christology*, 68.

16 See the discussion of astonishment and historical inquiry in de Certeau, *Mystic Fable*, 2: 2–3.

17 Wolfson, *Speculum*, 28.

18 Wolfson (*Speculum*, 27) notes that Exod. 33:20 is J. Others assign it differently. For example, Friedman (*Who Wrote the Bible?* 251) assigns it to E. Given the current state of Pentateuchal criticism, other scholars would likely assign it to JE, non-P, or L. For Wolfson's point, though, source criticism does not provide a way out for traditional Jewish readers of the Middle Ages. Likewise, for this study, it does not provide a way out for ancient Jewish and Christian readers.

19 Cf. the similar comments – though in a different context – by Clark, *Reading Renunciation*, 4; cf. McGinn, *Foundations*, 4–5.

20 He analyzes this tension in a historicizing phenomenology; that is, he picks
     different points in time, contextualizing the groups, but also resorts to phe-
     nomenological analysis in a way reminiscent of and developing on Henry
     Corbin; see, e.g., Corbin, *Creative Imagination* and *Spiritual Body and Celes-
     tial Earth*.

21 Wolfson, *Speculum*, 107.

22 This occurs repeatedly throughout Wolfson's analysis, but see particularly
     Speculum, 305–6, 351–5, 386–7, the last passage where Wolfson calls Moses
     "the prototype of the mystics."

23 Something also noted by McGinn, *Foundations*, 4, 70–1, 170, 206, 255.

24 Allison, *New Moses*, 11–134.

25 McGinn (*Foundations*, 4, 69–70, 170, 175, 255) regularly notes Moses as one
     of, if not the pre-eminent, paradigmatic mystical model, though he only
     occasionally indicates how this is the case.

26 See discussion in Meeks, *Prophet-King*, 198–9, 206–7. This positioning of
     Moses as receiver of all prophecy, including the prophecies of other
     prophets, appears to be loosely developed upon Deut. 34:10, which states,
     "There has not arisen since in Israel a prophet like Moses." Building upon
     this idea, the Rabbis will also indicate that Moses received all the canonical
     books, the Mishnah, Talmud, the haggada, and all the answers to all the
     questions a pupil may ask; that is, all rabbinic discourse was revealed to
     Moses when he ascended to heaven via Sinai to receive the Torah (*y. Peah*
     2.4; *b. Meg.* 19b; *Eccl. Rab.* 1.9).

27 This seems strangely close to Bauckham, *God Crucified*; see critique by
     McGrath, *Only True God*.

28 Michel de Certeau, *Mystic Fable*, 2:7.

29 Ibid., 2:8.

30 Ibid., 2:7.

31 The "male gaze" or just "the gaze" has been discussed and critiqued exten-
     sively, originating from Laura Mulvey's essay, "Visual Pleasure in Narrative
     Cinema." See an extensive discussion in Irigaray, *Speculum of the Other
     Woman*, esp. 47–8, 147–9. She furthermore discusses mystery and mysticism
     in 191–202. See a further discussion of the phallic gaze in the context of
     Jewish mysticism in Wolfson, *Through a Speculum* and *Language, Eros, Being*.

32 As Debord (*Society of the Spectacle*, §23) writes, "The oldest social specializa-
     tion, the specialization of power, is at the root of the spectacle. The specta-
     cle is thus a specialized activity which speaks for all the others. It is the
     diplomatic representation of hierarchic society to itself, where all other
     expression is banned." And further down (§25): "*Separation* is the alpha and
     omega of the spectacle. The institutionalization of the social division of

labor, the formation of classes, had given rise to a first sacred contemplation, the mythical order with which every power shrouds itself from the
beginning. The sacred has justified the cosmic and ontological order which
corresponded to the interests of the masters; it has explained and embell-
ished that which society *could not do*" (emphasis original).

33 De Certeau, *The Mystic Fable*, vol. 1. The plural form, "mystics," is how Smith
translates *la mystique*, paralleling other pluralized fields (e.g., physics).

34 Much of the relevant material in de Certeau's work concentrates toward the
beginning of *The Mystic Fable* (esp. 1:14–26), where he discusses socio-eco-
nomic and gender issues that give rise to the modern *mystics*, and later
(75–150) where he traces the early modern genealogy of the terminology of
and surrounding *mystics*. See further in the second volume, *Mystic Fable*,
2:1–22.

35 Jantzen, "Feminists, Philosophers, and Mystics" and *Power, Gender, and Christian Mysticism*. Jantzen's work is much clearer in its delineations of the terminology and its social implications than is de Certeau's.

36 James, *The Varieties of Religious Experience*.

37 Nasrallah, *An Ecstasy of Folly*.

38 For a recent critique of the agonistic model of relations between religious
groups – and even a questioning of whether religious affiliation would have
been the primary identifying marker for many Christian, Jewish, and polytheist philosophers – see Marx-Wolf, *Spiritual Taxonomies and Ritual Authority*, 4–5, 13–37. She notes, in particular, that polytheists and Christians were
often in agreement with one another, even while polytheists could disagree
among one another. She therefore reconstructs a situation of both co-opera-
tion and competition. She, for example, sets up agonistic contexts in a later
chapter (100–25) between philosophers and local priests as mediators of
the divine.

39 For a successful usage of the genealogical method for the fraught, yet related, category of "magic" in antiquity, see the perspicacious work by Stratton,
Naming the Witch.

40 Yet, Foucault's own geneaological approach was itself, in many ways, strikingly traditional, relying upon a Nietschean modification of the tools of
philology.

41 The method of this study is the history of interpretation that plays one
verse of the Bible off another and looks at how different authors resolved
the contradiction and why they did so. It differs from the method of James
L. Kugel, who tends to take a history of interpretation of each element in a
biblical passage (see *In Potiphar's House*; *Ladder of Jacob*; *How to Read the
Bible*). My method of the history of interpretation of duelling passages

more resembles that of Michael Fishbane's method in *The Kiss of God*, though my selection is not nearly as wide ranging as the sources he uses. For the use of a related method of reception history of a tradition, see Reed, *Fallen Angels*. See further a fusion of genealogy and history of interpretation with queer theory in Carden, *Sodomy*.

42 For interpretation and commentary, see Foucault, "The Order of Discourse," 52–64; Jameson, "Metacommentary," 9–18; for translators as "speakers of a second text," see *Why Translation Matters* by Grossman, whose own translation of Don Quixote is quickly becoming a classic. For a brief discussion of ancient and modern translation, see my essay "Translation and Transformation," 255–75.

43 See discussion by Clark, *Reading Renunciation*, 5–11.

44 Jameson, "Metacommentary," 10.

45 Ibid.

46 Ibid.

47 Cf. Spivak's preface to Derrida, *Of Grammatology*, lxxiv.

48 Clark, *Reading Renunciation*, 10–11, 177.

49 Spivak's preface to Derrida, *Of Grammatology*, lxxiv.

50 See the discussion by Clark, *Reading Renunciation*, 6–8.

51 See also the method of Margaret Miles in her article, "Sex and the City (of God)." In it, she follows a post-Freudian feminist analysis of Augustine's writings, but does so by tracing 1 Cor. 13:12 across Augustine's writings.

52 Daniel Boyarin's *Borderlines* follows similar conceptual operations, but with a different method.

53 Clark, *Reading Renunciation*, 5.

54 Reed, *Fallen Angels*. However, her social concerns are quite different, focusing on establishing fairly fluid literary and oral channels of transmission among Jewish and Christian groups.

55 Berkowitz, *Defining Jewish Difference*.

56 Ibid., 16–17; emphasis original.

57 Shuve, *Song of Songs*, 211.

58 Soranus, *Gyn.* 1.39.

59 Such stories and beliefs persist at least as late as Michel de Montaigne, who, in his essay "On the Power of the Imagination," speaks of the "ejaculative power" of the eyes, including the evil eye and women passing on what they see to their children, citing, among many other things, the story of Jacob's sheep. Also found in René Descartes' *La Dioptrique*. See Irigaray, *Speculum of the Other Woman*, 180–90; de Certeau, *Mystic Fable*, 2:42–3, 240nn67–8.

60 Cf. the logic among the Haside Ashkenaz's discussion of the appearance of angels in Wolfson, *Speculum*, 212–14.

61 Miles, "Vision," 127.

62 Plotinus (*Enn.* 4.5.7.24; 5.5.7.24) on the one hand follows the idea of an inner light that can be seen in a flash by the Intellect. Otherwise, he believes that the sun gleaming off a physical mass is how one sees, largely rejecting much of extramission theory, because he does not think the soul to be so impressionable; see comment by Miles, "Vision," 130n15.

63 Trans. Chadwick, *Confessions*, 184.

64 Miles, "Sex and the City (of God)," 323. More generally, see Miles, "Vision: The Eye of the Body and the Eye of the Mind," 125–42, and also her first book, *Augustine on the Body*, 9–39.

65 See the discussion in McGinn, *Foundations*, 24–35, 41–61.

66 In this way, this study eschews the sociological view founded by Max Weber, who argued that religious movements begin around charismatic figures, such as Jesus or Muhammad, that eventually rigidify into institutions, such as the Church or the Ummah, over time. Instead, one finds in the late-antique Christian materials that interrelated institutional actors co-opted and redirected charisma for themselves. Marx-Wolf (*Spiritual Taxonomies and Ritual Authority*, 127–9) makes a similar point using different evidence, as does Kalleres, *City of Demons*, 12, 14–21, and Rapp, *Holy Bishops in Late Antiquity*, 16–17, 23–4.

67 Dodds, *Pagan and Christian*, 70.

68 Brock, *Luminous Eye*, though his use of the term "vision" is more wide-ranging, including also "theological vision" or an "artist's vision"; for an especially lucid introduction to visions of God in Syriac Christianity, often noting the role Moses plays as a mystical model, see Todd French, "Seeing the God in the Syriac Tradition." Tonneau, "Moïse dans la tradition syrienne," discusses Moses more generally without reference to his visions.

69 Perpetua's and Saturnus' visions in the *Martyrdom of Perpetua and Felicitas* are especially striking in their content and expression. The literature on this account is voluminous, but see Castelli, "I Will Make Mary Male," 29–49, esp. 33–43; Castelli, *Memory and Martyrdom*, 85–92; Shaw, "Passion of Perpetua."

CHAPTER TWO

1 This is an updated and expanded version of a previously published essay, "To See God and Live in Late Antique Judaism."

2 See, e.g., Robin Lane Fox, *Pagans and Christians*, 112, 377, 394. For a discussion, see Wolfson, *Speculum*, 13–16.

3 Scholars of ancient and medieval Judaism have offered ample evidence of the importance of divine vision. See, e.g., Wolfson, *Speculum*; Boyarin, "The

Eye in the Torah." Boyarin argues that it is only under Hellenic influence that Jewish cultures evince anxiety about God's corporeality and visibility, affecting the Hebrew Bible and Rabbinic Judaism less. Stern ("Imitatio Hominis," 153) argues that anthropomorphic depictions of God become a problem in Jewish thought in the Middle Ages, particularly with the Aristotelian-influenced philosophers, Saadiah Gaon and Maimonides, setting the framework within which scholars unto the present day would continue to look back to earlier expressions of Judaism; he argues that rabbinic literature actually heightens anthropomorphic representations of God found in biblical works. See further Gottstein, "The Body as Image of God in Rabbinic Literature"; Aaron, "Shedding Light on God's Body in Rabbinic Midrashim"; Marmorstein, *Essays in Anthropomorphism*. I am less concerned with the elusive descriptions of God's appearance than the occasions and theoretical possibilities of seeing God.

4 I have limited the essay to these sources due to space. One omission is the late-antique speculation on God's body, the *Shi'ur Qomah*. For a general discussion of ancient Jewish mystical activity, see Schäfer, *Origins of Jewish Mysticism*. Our focuses overlap, but he discusses Ezekiel, the apocalypses, Philo, Qumran, limited rabbinic literature, and the *hekhalot* texts, whereas I include more biblical accounts and use different rabbinic passages. His discussion ranges more generally, whereas mine focuses on visions of God.

5 Schäfer, *Origins*, 152. The *Songs of the Sabbath Sacrifice* and the *Thanksgiving Hymns* (*Hodayot*) can be read in terms of the development of Jewish mysticism, including ascents to heaven; nonetheless, there is no clear development of *visionary* mysticism in these texts. Even though there are evocations of the heavenly realm and God's throne, there is no discussion of what one sees of the divine, how one sees it, or who can see it. There are some interesting parallels between Enoch's heavenly tour in *1 Enoch* and some descriptions in *Thanksgiving Hymns*, but nothing that explicitly invokes Moses' visions, except a couple of fragments that I discuss later in this chapter. While the Teacher of Righteousness is unique in the scrolls – and, therefore, may occupy a similar position as Moses – recent studies on the mystical texts typically related to the Teacher of Righteousness (the *Thanksgiving Hymns*) see this as a communal mysticism rather than a unique experience, therefore, as something several members of the community had experienced. See the excellent monograph by Harkins, *Reading with an "I" to the Heavens*; and, furthermore, Alexander, *Mystical Texts*.

6 For more general discussions of Moses in the Bible, which, only incidentally discuss some of the issues raised here, see Cazelles, "Moïse devant l'histoire"; Gelin, "Moïse dans l'Ancien Testament." See also Martin-Achard, "Moïse,

figure du médiateur selon l'Ancien Testament." Martin-Achard investigates
Moses' role as intermediary between God and the people, but places little
emphasis on his visions.

7 In general, see Barr, "Theophany and Anthropomorphism."

8 לֹא תוּכַל לִרְאֹת אֶת-פָּנָי כִּי לֹא-יִרְאַנִי הָאָדָם וָחָי; compare the Greek, which shifts "me"
to "my face": οὐ δυνήσῃ ἰδεῖν μου τὸ πρόσωπον· οὐ γὰρ μὴ ἴδῃ ἄνθρωπος τὸ
πρόσωπον μου καὶ ζήσεται.

9 See the observations by Gelin, "Moïse dans l'Ancien Testament," 43–4, noting that, even during this prohibition, God is extraordinarily anthropomorphic and glorious, yet allows Moses to approach this glory in Num. 12:8.

10 The phrase "have I really seen God and remained alive" corrects the
Masoretic Text, which reads, "Have I indeed seen after he sees me?" The LXX
largely agrees with the Masoretic text on this point. The corrected reading
aligns with the name of the well: "the well of one who sees and lives." Cf.
Booij, "Hagar's Words in Genesis XVI 13b."

11 For a discussion of the phenomenon of this slippage, see Gieschen, Angelomorphic Christology, 51–69.

12 רָאִיתִי אֱלֹהִים פָּנִים אֶל-פָּנִים.

13 Greek: εἶδον γὰρ θεὸν πρόσωπον πρὸς πρόσωπον, καὶ ἐσώθη μου ἡ ψυχή.

14 Von Rad (Moses, 21) even says, "The story leaves us in no doubt that it is
with the Lord God himself that Jacob is dealing, as he wrestles with this
nightly visitor."

15 An observation I owe to Allison, New Moses, 29n57.

16 Another similarity with Genesis 32 concerns the angel's name. When Jacob
requested the "man's" name, he refused; likewise, when they ask this "man"
in Judges, he also refuses, since his name is wonderful (Judg. 13:18).

17 There is a differentiation between "LORD" and "angel of the LORD" in the
passage. For example, Manoah prays to the "LORD" for the "LORD" to resend
his messenger, the "man." Manoah also offers food to the "angel of the
LORD," who refuses but says that he can offer a sacrifice to the "LORD."

18 מוֹת נָמוּת כִּי אֱלֹהִים רָאִינוּ. Greek: Θανάτῳ ἀποθανούμεθα, ὅτι θεὸν ἑωράκαμεν
(alt. εἴδομεν).

19 Von Rad (Moses, 19) interestingly elides the difference even more between
the LORD and the LORD's angel, saying, "God had appeared to the wife of
Manoah in the form of 'the angel of the LORD,'" which sounds a bit more
like what Clement (Chapter 5), Tertullian (Chapter 8), or Augustine (Chapter 11) would say.

20 The prophetic call narratives in the Hebrew Bible offer prime accounts of
divine encounters. They generally follow a similar pattern: God calls the
prophet, the prophet resists, indicating with his mouth that he is unworthy

or unable (speech problems, unclean lips, too young to speak), God reassures the prophet, and gives the prophet the message. The prophet or his vision tends to be related to the priesthood or the temple, the sacred locus of the divine presence. Despite the generic form, the calls of Isaiah, Jeremiah, and Ezekiel demonstrate varying understandings of what the prophet sees, from a direct divine vision to distancing language to a non-visual auditory focus.

21 ‏וארא מראות אלהים‎.

22 Segal, *Rebecca's Children*, 14; cf. Wolfson, *Speculum*, 22, 68–9, 120–1. Schäfer (*Origins*, 43–8) uses Ezekiel 1 as the counterpoint to Exodus 33, situating the unrequested vision against the denied request. His account, however, ignores the biblical narratives in which Moses sees God and does not consider the buffering effect of Ezekiel's language, although he does account for the spatial distancing of Ezekiel remaining on earth but seeing into heaven. In fact, one could argue that the increased description is due to his circumspect language that potentially removes him and the reader from a direct visualization of the divine. The language, however, directly recalls Exod. 24:16–17, where Moses encounters the "appearance of the Glory of the LORD" as a devouring fire on the mountain just after seeing the anthropomorphic figure along with the elders in 24:9–11. The glory of the LORD was pyromorphic in Exod. 24:16–17, but that does not mean that the vision was less divine or direct. Even in Ezekiel's vision, God's body may be humanoid, "but its essence is fire" (Schäfer, *Origins*, 47). Both saw the fiery glory of the LORD. The form the fiery glory takes is significant, but not in terms of whether or not they saw it.

23 This equation is set up in Judges 2, when the "angel of the LORD" speaks to the Israelites, saying, "I brought you up from Egypt ... I said, 'I will never break my covenant with you.'" (2:1, 2). The angel of the LORD says "I" regarding events in sacred history ascribed to the LORD, including the key element of establishing the covenant.

24 On this point, see Barr, "Theophany and Anthropomorphism," 33–4.

25 Greek: ἐνώπιος ἐνωπίῳ.

26 *Pace* Schäfer (*Origins*, 46), who states that, in Exod. 33:11, "the text makes it absolutely clear that Moses does not actually see God." To the contrary, the text is ambivalent. Schäfer discusses the passages that deny that one can see God (and live), but ignores those that claim that Moses or his contemporaries saw God (43–5).

27 See Allison (*New Moses*, 221), who suggests that the LXX translator is hinting that Moses did see God in Exodus 33–4, where the terminology of glory is also used. *Targum Pseudo-Jonathan*'s translation of Num. 12:8 as Moses see-

ing the "back of the Shekhinah" also supports this conjecture. One could also postulate Exod. 24:15–18 as a possibility.

28 Cf. Barr, "Theophany and Anthropomorphism," 33.

29 See Barr, "Theophany and Anthropomorphism," 32.

30 This passage has the complicating factor that the "LORD" appears and Abraham sees "three men." On the one hand, they are identified with one another, but in 18:22, the "men" go towards Sodom, but Abraham still speaks to the LORD. In 19:1, two angels appear in Sodom. In 18:1–15, there is no clear distinction between the LORD and the three figures, whereas the end of the chapter and Chapter 19 imply that the LORD was one of the three figures while the other two were angels.

31 This story occurs within the Elijah-Elisha cycle. Famously, when the LORD passed by Elijah, He was not in the wind, an earthquake, or a fire, but in the "still small voice" or "sound of sheer silence," negating the typical visual theophanic signs, such as fire, and even largely negating the auditory (1 Kgs. 19:11–13). Elsewhere in the Deuteronomistic History, excluding the stories in Judges already discussed, God predominantly communicates through audible and non-visible means: e.g., to Samuel (1 Samuel 3). Elsewhere the "word of the LORD" comes to Elijah and speaks to him (1 Kgs. 17:2, 8; 18:1; 19:9; 21:17, 28; cf. 2 Kgs. 10:17), though he is touched by an angel of the LORD (1 Kgs. 19:5, 7). Interestingly, this turn of phrase is not used for Elisha.

32 This story implicates God in a deception to kill off Ahab. The LORD wants to entice Ahab to go to battle, so that Ahab will fail and die. A spirit in God's council suggests that he will go down and deceive the prophets, so that they will give a favourable oracle to Ahab. This story has a parallel in Greek literature in *Iliad* 2, where Zeus sends a false dream to Agamemnon, telling him that, if he goes into battle, he will succeed – in order for him to engage in battle and lose. The difference is Agamemnon does not die in battle.

33 As noted, a lying spirit from God's council deceives the other prophets present; Micaiah, therefore, is the only prophet in the story not deceived by this spirit. As noted above, God communicates to Samuel and Elijah through speech. While there are ambivalent visionary elements in Judges discussed above, 1 Kings 22 is the only text in the Deuteronomistic History with an unambiguous vision – and throne vision at that – of God.

34 See Wolfson, *Speculum*, 16–24.

35 This has a parallel with the seraph touching Isaiah's lips with a coal from the altar in Isa. 6:6–7; nonetheless, there an angel touches the prophet, while here, the LORD does.

36 Other apocalypses, such as 4 Ezra and 2 Baruch lack visions of the enthroned God.

37 For apocalyptic visions, see Rowland, "The Visions of God" and *Open Heaven*; Collins, *Apocalyptic Imagination*; Himmelfarb, *Ascent to Heaven*.

38 It likely dates from the late-third to early-second century BCE and would eventually form part of *1 Enoch*; see Nickelsburg and VanderKam, *1 Enoch*, 3.

39 For a comparison between *1 Enoch* 14, Ezekiel 1, and Isaiah 6, see Rowland, "Visions of God," 140–2.

40 See Rowland, *Open Heaven*, 222; Wolfson, *Speculum*, 30.

41 For a discussion of the context of this statement in the pericope of *1 Enoch* 17–19 as a whole, see Bautch, *Geography of 1 Enoch 17–19*. For Enoch's uniqueness, see further, Reed, *Fallen Angels*, 49.

42 This is how Schäfer (*Origins of Jewish Mysticism*, 79–81) reads it; for a discussion on Moses and *1 Enoch*, see a more positive evaluation of Moses in the Enochic corpus by Bautch, *Geography of 1 Enoch 17–19*, 295–7.

43 In *2 En.* 20:3; 22:1–4; 39:1–6, Enoch sees the indescribable face of God, emphasizing "face" to counter Exod. 33:20. The vision leads to Enoch's transformation into an angelic being and the unique privilege of standing before God's face forever (22:5, 8–10). Upon angelification, Enoch's own face becomes so luminous that no human can look at it, acquiring this divine characteristic (37:2), also similar to Moses' face.

44 Barr ("Theophany and Anthropomorphism," 33) argues that dreams do not necessarily mitigate the directness of the divine appearance.

45 Cf. *Apoc. Zeph.* 6:11–13.

46 The Christian Testament takes up this imagery, including Jesus within the reference frame provided by the prophetic and apocalyptic descriptions. During Stephen's martyrdom, "he, full of the Holy Spirit, gazed into heaven and saw the glory of God, and Jesus standing at the right hand of God" (Acts 7:55). More extensively, the visions of John of Patmos reshape the prophetic/apocalyptic visionary tradition of the enthroned God (Rev. 4–5; cf. 22:1). See Rowland, "Visions of God," 145–8.

47 Rowland, "Visions of God," 150–2, emphasizes invisibility, but does not discuss the indescribable fire. See, however, Wolfson, *Speculum*, 32–3.

48 The Revelation of John in the New Testament is an exception.

49 For a discussion of Moses in second-temple literature more generally, see Vermes, "La Figure de Moïse."

50 On Moses in Hellenistic Jewish literature, see, for example, Alan Segal, *Paul the Convert*, 43–5, 89–90.

51 Trans. Robertson, "Ezekiel the Tragedian," 811–12.

52 See Gen. 15:5; 22:17; Deut. 1:10; Ps. 147:4; Is. 40:26; *1 En.* 93:14; *Apoc. Abr.* 20.1–5; Pseudo-Philo, *Bibl. Ant.* 21:2; *b. San.* 39a; Allison, *New Moses*, 224.

53 van der Horst, "Moses' Throne Vision," 25. See Segal, *Paul the Convert*, 44; Gieschen, *Angelomorphic Christology*, 163–5; DeConick, *Voices of the Mystics*, 54. On the other side, there are those who see it as symbolic, particularly with reference to the interpretation of the dream. Richard Bauckham has been the primary proponent of this view lately; see *Jesus and the God of Israel*, 166–9. See the more-balanced remarks by Hurtado, *One God, One Lord*, 57–9. See the discussion in Allison, *New Moses*, 177–8, who looks at the episode as a possible background for Matt. 5:1–2; Lierman, *The New Testament Moses*, 90–102. On possible allusions to Moses' enthronement in rabbinic literature, see Halperin, *Faces of the Chariot*, 321, 423.

54 Bauckham (*Jesus and the God of Israel*, 168) also links the vision to Moses' sovereignty – though not to divinity.

55 Trans. Robertson, "Ezekiel the Tragedian," 813.

56 ἔδειξεν αὐτῷ τῆς δόξης αὐτοῦ...ἠκούτισεν αὐτὸν τῆς φωνῆς αὐτοῦ καὶ εἰσήγαγεν αὐτὸν εἰς τὸν γνόφον καὶ ἔδωκεν αὐτῷ κατὰ πρόσωπον ἐντολάς.

57 Sir. 49:8: "It was Ezekiel who saw the vision of glory, which he [God] showed him above the chariot of the cherubim" (Ιεζεκιηλ ὃς εἶδεν ὅρασιν δόξης, ἣν ὑπέδειξεν αὐτῷ ἐπὶ ἅρματος χερούβιν).

58 Fletcher-Louis, "4Q374."

59 Martínez and Tigchelaar, *Dead Sea Scrolls*, 2:741.

60 Fletcher-Louis, "4Q374," 237.

61 For an introduction to Moses as visionary and prophet in Philo's writings, see Starabinksi-Safran, "La Prophétie de Moïse," 67–80, esp. 77–8. I relied upon the Greek text provided by Colson and Whitaker, *Philo*, vols. 1, 4, and 5; and Colson, *Philo*, vol. 6.

62 Dillon (*Middle Platonists*, 139) refers to him as "one of the most remarkable literary phenomena of the Hellenistic world."

63 See the description by Dillon, *The Middle Platonists*. He further notes (140) Philo's preferences for Plato's *Timaeus* and *Phaedrus*, though he uses several other treatises.

64 Borgen, *Philo of Alexandria*; Birnbaum, *Place of Judaism*, 16. For Philo's method of exegesis, his particular allegory, and his "revisionist" aims, see David Dawson, *Allegorical Readers*, 73–126. See also Schäfer, *Origins of Jewish Mysticism*, 154–74.

65 Dillon, *Middle Platonists*, 141–3.

66 Philo's *Alleg. Interp.* 1.108; *QG* 4.152; *Heir* 214; *Good Person* 57; *Eternity* 18–19; *Providence* 2.48; and Dillon, *Middle Platonists*, 143.

67 Winston, "Mosaic Prophecy according to Philo," 59.

68 The preface to the second volume (2.1) indicates that Philo originally wrote it in two parts, rather than that it was separated into two parts by later editors.

69 For a summary of the contents of the *Life of Moses* and its place in the Philonic corpus, see Geljon, *Philonic Exegesis*, 7–46. According to Runia (*Philo in Early Christian Literature*, 337), this was Philo's most popular work among early Christians. On perfection, see further *Abraham* 26.

70 He is a superior lawgiver to Plato (*Moses* 2.49ff).

71 *Moses* 2.66ff.

72 *Moses* 2.187ff for Moses as prophet. See *Moses* 1.334; 2.2–7 for references to Plato's *Republic*. The four roles are repeated in *Moses* 2.187; 2.292. Dillon (*Middle Platonists*, 119) alternatively suggests that various accounts written about the life of Pythagoras inspired Philo's *Life of Moses*.

73 Philo speaks of rapture and experiences in scattered sections throughout his writings. He speaks mostly of rapture, such as Moses' archetypal heaven-sent rapture (*Moses* 2.67). He even gives a glimpse into his own experiences of corybantic frenzy (*Migration* 34–5). The soul experiences a divine frenzy and sees spiritual things (*Migration* 189–91; cf. 249, 258–66). This is the same frenzy the prophets experience (*Heir* 69–70). Philo speaks of stages of spiritual ascent in *Migration* 187–94. He also says he hears a voice in his soul (*Cherubim* 27–9). He also discusses his own ascents in *Spec. Laws* 3:1–6. For the political context of Philo's own ascents, see Borgen, *Philo of Alexandria*, 171–5. Cf. the "legitimate" ascents of the people of Israel, where, again, Moses is pre-eminent, and the "illegitimate" ascents of the Emperor Gaius discussed in Borgen, *Philo of Alexandria*, 194–205; on visions in the Contemplative Life, see Deutsch, "Therapeutae," 287–311.

74 See especially the work of Levison, "Inspiration and the Divine Spirit," 280–308, 319–20; further, Deutsch, "Visions, Mysteries, and the Interpretive Task," 87–94; Afterman, "From Philo to Plotinus," 177–96.

75 Levison, "Inspiration and the Divine Spirit," 308.

76 Runia, *Philo in Early Christian Literature*, 38.

77 On Philo's portrayal of Moses as divine, see Himmelfarb, *Ascent to Heaven*, 48–9, 70–1; Borgen, "Moses, Jesus, and the Roman Emperor"; Segal, *Paul the Convert*, 44–5. Though Segal does not discuss the passages where Moses is or represents the divine Logos, focusing instead on the passages in which he encounters the divine Logos (e.g., *Flight* 164ff.) and others' encounters with the Logos (*Dreams* 1.157; *Names* 87, 126; *Migration* 158; *Alleg. Interp.* 3.177; *Heir* 205). For a more general discussion of the Logos in Philo's thought, see Segal, *Two Powers in Heaven*, 159–81. In both works, Segal emphasizes that Philo uses the Logos to explain away the embarrassing anthropomorphisms in the Bible. Nonetheless, there is more going on with the Moses passages that often link or identify Moses, the high priest, and the Logos. For a competing view, see Runia, "God and Man."

78 Schäfer, *Origins of Jewish Mysticism*, 165 (see 164–74).

79 To paraphrase Borgen (*Philo of Alexandria*, 3) who, in turn, is discussing E.R. Goodenough's extensive work on Philo, but especially *By Light, Light*.

80 Dillon (*Middle Platonists*, 155–7) notes that Philo was the first to use these terms with regard to the supreme principle.

81 Deutsch, "Visions, Mysteries, and the Interpretive Task," 87.

82 See further, e.g., *Prelim. Studies* 51; *Dreams* 2.173; *Rewards* 44. For an extensive discussion of this, see Birnbaum, *Place of Judaism*, esp. 1–127.

83 Balaam, therefore, cursed the "man of vision" (*Confusion* 159).

84 Birnbaum (*Place of Judaism*, 30) writes, "By understanding 'Israel' as an entity that sees God, Philo assigns the term a meaning that has nothing to do with birth and origin, but rather with spiritual capacity."

85 Compare the different levels of seeing with Abraham (*Names* 6–19); Segal, *Two Powers*, 177–8. In *Decalogue* 32–5, Philo does emphasize the "invisible" divine voice that makes no sound. Interestingly, here, for the giving of the ten commandments, Philo does not at all emphasize vision – only hearing.

86 The language here is stunning, "Behold ... the eye of the soul, so translucent and pure, so keen of vision, the eye of which alone is permitted to look upon God, the eye whose name is Israel" (*Confusion* 92). See Segal, *Two Powers*, 167.

87 See the now-classic work, Winston, *Logos and Mystical Theology*. He calls Philo's Logos, "the linchpin of Philo's religious thought" (11).

88 See further, Winston, *Logos and Mystical Theology*, 16–17. For a synopsis of some basic Logos-theology in Philo's works, especially in terms of Philo's own discussions of heavenly ascent, see Segal, "Heavenly Ascent," 208–13.

89 In this passage, Philo begins by speaking of the distribution of sacrificial blood by the "high priest Moses" (ὁ ἀρχιερεὺς Μωυσῆς) and ends with equivalent activity by the "holy Word" (ὁ ἱερὸς λόγος).

90 Borgen, *Philo of Alexandria*, 79.

91 Θεσμοθέτῃ λόγῳ Μωυσῇ. Many of these linkages between Moses and the Logos or Logos and high priest are downplayed in the translation by C.D. Yonge, *The Works of Philo: Complete and Unabridged*, New Updated Edition (Hendrickson, 1993). For closer readings in these portions at least, see Colson and Whitaker, *Philo*, vols. 1, 4, and 5; Colson, *Philo*, vol. 6.

92 Philo develops the concept of the Logos from Stoic thought, which had, by this time, merged with the Platonic World Soul and Demiurge, something that may have originated with Antiochus of Ascalon. See Dillon, *Middle Platonists*, 46, 83; Winston, *Logos and Mystical Theology*, 15.

93 See Segal, *Two Powers*, 167–8.

94 See discussion in Borgen, *Philo of Alexandria*, 218–23, esp. 219.

95 Segal, *Two Powers*, 171n31.

96 See also Fletcher-Louis, "4Q374," 242, who cites further *Sacrifices* 8–10; *Moses* 1.155–8; *Alleg. Interp.* 1.40; *Worse* 161–2; *Migration* 85; *Names* 19; *Dreams* 2.188. Most of these are texts that combine Exod. 7:1 with Moses' ascent on Sinai. Cf. *Tanh. B* 4.51–2. See also Winston, *Logos and Mystical Theology*, 30. Cf. Segal, *Two Powers*, 163.

97 Cf. the Pauline concept that Christ is the visible image of the invisible God (Col. 1:15).

98 Winston, *Logos and Mystical Theology*, 17–18.

99 See further *Moses* 2.127–9, discussing the mercy-seat, which Philo also calls the "reason-seat" (logion), where the archetypal and invisible ideas that also reside within humans are one part of the rational principle (logos), and the visible objects that are copies and likenesses of those ideas are the other part, the utterance. For Philo's enthusiastic embrace of "divine" language around Moses, see Borgen, *Philo of Alexandria*, 145.

100 On the importance of "place," see Segal, *Two Powers in Heaven*, 161–70. "Place," a circumlocution in the LXX to distance direct visions, is the logos, the visible (through the mind or soul) aspect of God. Winston (*Logos and Mystical Theology*, 25), furthermore, writes, "For Philo, it is through the Logos and the Logos alone that man is capable of participating in the Divine."

101 Cf. the similar material covered in Geljon, *Philonic Exegesis*, 61–2.

102 While most people would point to the burning bush as Moses' "initiation" to the prophetic office, Philo places his initiation earlier. When he saves the young women watering their flocks at the well, Moses "grew inspired and was transfigured into a prophet [μεταμορφούμενος εἰς προφήτην]" (*Moses* 1.57).

103 "God" is the divine creative potency, whereas "Lord" is the principle of justice (*Moses* 2.99; *Abraham* 121); Winston, *Logos and Mystical Theology*, 21–2.

104 Trans. Colson and Whitaker.

105 For the types of oracles, see *Moses* 2.188–91; Starobinksi-Safran, "La prophétie de Moïse," 72.

106 Cf. later in the same text, where he says one cannot even look upon the angel who led them out of Egypt in the pillar of fire/cloud with bodily eyes (*Moses* 1.166; cf. 1.273).

107 See DeConick, *Voices of the Mystics*, 57.

108 For the importance of genre and genre's audience in Philo's writings, see Birnbaum, *Judaism in Philo's Thought*, 15–21. Birnbaum argues that Philo's expository and allegorical writings are written to different, though overlapping, audiences. His allegory assumes much knowledge of both scripture

and philosophy, and, therefore, presumes a highly educated Jewish audience. Philo's expository writings, such as his treatise on Moses, do not assume great familiarity with scripture or philosophy and would be accessible to both Jews and non-Jews alike.

109 For Philo's reading of Exod. 20:21 (LXX) in *Moses* 1:158, *Posterity* 14, *Giants* 54, and *QE* 2:28, see Borgen, 194–205, who places this within a political context of legitimate and illegitimate "ascents" – the latter by Gaius, combined with Exod. 33:13 in *Posterity* 14 and *Names* 7; cf. *Spec. Laws* 1:41–50. Borgen comments especially on the role of divinization, entering into the cloud, and becoming a living embodiment of the law, a paradigm to be emulated with regard to *Life of Moses* and *Questions and Answers on Exodus*, the latter of which has several parallels with early Jewish apocalyptic and later *hekhalot*; while *Life of Moses* is highly Platonizing, *Questions and Answers on Exodus* is more like a traditional ascent narrative. See further, Borgen, *Philo of Alexandria*, 235–42, commenting on *Creation* 69–71, *Spec. Laws* 1.37–50, Borgen notes that Moses is a seer and mystagogue of the impossible quest; that is, seeing God as God is impossible, but one should strive to do so anyway; see further *Spec. Laws* 2.164–6. See further Schäfer's comments on *Spec. Laws* 1.32ff (*Origins of Jewish Mysticism*, 156–7).

110 Cf. the discussion of the *Apostolic Constitutions* in Chap. 10.

111 "He beheld what is hidden from the sight of mortal nature" (158).

112 While Philo often uses the patriarchs as archetypes of the soul, he does not here.

113 "Happy are they who imprint, or strive to imprint, that image in their souls. For it were best that the mind should carry the form of virtue in perfection, but, failing, this, let it at least have the unflinching desire to possess that form" (Colson trans.; *Moses* 159).

114 "Do not however suppose that the Existent which truly exists is apprehended by any man; for we have in us no organ by which we can envision it, neither in sense, for it is not perceptible by sense, nor yet in mind" (7). That "yet" may indicate the future potential of the mind – unencumbered by the body – to perceive God.

115 On the other hand, the things under God, represented by God's backside, could be equivalent to the archetype from the exposition. See Segal, *Two Powers in Heaven*, 162.

116 Things are also complicated by the fact that Philo often seems to mean different things by "seeing God": that God is; having an ecstatic experience; an ability or achievement one seeks to attain. As Birnbaum further notes, "Accordingly, people may strive to develop their capacity to see Him, may attain different kinds of vision, and may achieve vision of Him in different

ways. Occasionally, however, Philo also emphasizes that no one can see God without His help" (Birnbaum, *Place of Judaism*, 212).

117 On "clear vision," see DeConick, *Voices of the Mystics*, 74.

118 Note the continued use of the plural "patterns" (παραδείγματα) here and in *Moses* 2.141.

119 Elsewhere Philo often speaks of two corresponding temples, but does not as strongly employ the language found here. In the *Dreams* 1.215, Philo argues that one temple is the cosmos itself, for which the high priest is the Logos, while the other is the rational soul, which correspond to one another. In this regard, he alludes to the high-priestly garment as being a representation of the cosmos. In *Spec. Laws* 1.66ff, he also speaks of two temples: the highest and truest temple is the cosmos, while the other is the one "made with hands." He then lays out the ordinances of the temple, festivals, and sacrifices. Again, he points out that the high-priestly garments represent the cosmos (84, 95). Cf. *QE* 2.91–2. Josephus, like Philo, would also claim that the temple imitated the cosmos (*Ant.* 3.123; cf. *War* 5.212ff); however, in his recounting of Moses and the Tabernacle from Exodus, he completely omits God's instructions and only recounts the actual construction of the Tabernacle (*Ant.* 3.102ff).

120 Cf. his more specific discussion of the original pattern versus the copy of the candlestick (*Prelim. Studies* 8).

121 Tabernacle as cosmos includes the curtains as the four elements (*Moses* 2.88; *Prelim. Studies* 117), cosmic symbolism of the vestments (*Moses* 2.117ff; cf. *Spec. Laws* 1.85–95), and other general cosmic comments (*Moses* 2.101–5). General structures of forms and patterns in cosmos and in humans (2.127–30): "In the universe [τὸ πᾶν] we find it in one form dealing with the incorporeal and archetypal ideas [τῶν ἀσωμάτων καὶ παραδειγματικῶν ἰδεῶν] from which the intelligible world [ὁ νοητὸς ἐπάγη κόσμος] was framed, and in another with the visible objects [τῶν ὁρατῶν] which are copies [μιμήματα] and likenesses [ἀπεικονίσματα] of those ideas [τῶν ἰδεῶν ἐκείνων] and out of which this sensible world [ὁ αἰσθητὸς] was produced. With man in one form it resides within, in the other it passes out from him in utterance. The former is like a spring, and is the source from which the latter, the spoken, flows. The inward is located in the dominant mind, the outward in the tongue and mouth and the rest of the vocal organism." Reason has two forms: "the outward of utterance and inward of thought." Wearing such symbolic garb, the high priest wears the "type" of the universe (in terms of "copy" rather than "original"; 2.133). The "pattern" (paradigm) is enshrined in his heart, transforming him from a mere human to the world itself, a mini-world, a microcosm (2.135).

122 Winston ("Mosaic Prophecy according to Philo," 61) notes, "The Mosaic summit of spirituality is thus marked by a state of absolutely serene joy, inferior only to that of the deity itself."

123 *Giants* 54.

124 "Car le prophète, qui a pénétré dans la nuée obscure et s'est longuement initié aux saints mystères, se transforme en hiérophante, en 'précepteur des vérités divines.' De myste, il devient mystagogue." Starobinksi-Safran, "La prophétie de Moïse," 78.

125 Borgen, *Philo of Alexandria*, 239.

126 Deutsch, "Visions, Mysteries, and the Interpretive Task," 87–94.

127 Trans. Harrington, "Pseudo-Philo."

128 Feldman, "Josephus' Portrait of Moses"; "Josephus' Portrait of Moses: Part Two"; and "Josephus' Portrait of Moses: Part Three."

129 While this literature derives from late antiquity, it was reshaped well into the Middle Ages, thereby disallowing a strict periodization between late-antique and early-medieval. For a discussion of some aspects of rabbinic reflection on Moses, see Renée Bloch, "Moïse dans la tradition rabbinique."

130 *Targum Neofiti 1* may originate as early as the fourth century CE; *Targum Pseudo-Jonathan* is likely from the ninth century CE. McNamara, *Targum Neofiti 1: Genesis*, 44–5; Maher, *Targum Pseudo-Jonathan: Genesis*, 11–2. The earliest known *targumim* from the Dead Sea Scrolls (*11QtargJob* and *4Qtarg-Lev*) date to the second century BCE. Translations of *Neofiti* are by McNamara; *Pseudo-Jonathan*, Maher.

131 Urbach, *Sages*, 37–79, argued that such concepts as the Shekhinah aided late-antique Jews in balancing God's transcendence and immanence. See also Wolfson, *Speculum*, 41–51.

132 Cf. *b. Ber.* 6a, 7a; *Ma'as. Merk.* §550; Stern, "Imitatio Hominis," 152.

133 Cf. Wolfson, *Speculum*, 42–3. This tendency to deny direct vision extends throughout both *targumim*. Both Hagar and Jacob, for example, exclaimed that they saw God and lived, yet the *targumim* alter what they saw and Hagar's exclamation. Taking up the "seeing" language of the Hebrew text of Genesis 16, *Pseudo-Jonathan* denies that God can be seen; God is the unseen seer, whether being invisible, hidden, or unendurable is not explained. Unlike Hagar, the targumim partially retain Jacob's exclamation that he has remained alive; like Hagar, however, they alter what he saw. In *Neofiti* to Gen. 32:30, Jacob wrestles not with a "man" or God, but with the angel Sariel. Jacob then exclaims that he has seen angels from before the Lord face to face and lived. *Pseudo-Jonathan* does not name the angel, but agrees it was an anthropoid angel. He similarly exclaims that he has seen "angels of the Lord face-to-face." Both transfer the "seeing God and living" motif to angels, as the Hebrew text

had done with Gideon. Strangely, *Neofiti* and *Pseudo-Jonathan* agree that Isaac saw the Lord. *Neofiti* to Gen. 26:24 reads "and the Lord was revealed to him that night." This is bold for *Neofiti*, which usually places the vision at a remove, and in fact a marginal gloss alters the text to "Memra of the Lord." *Pseudo-Jonathan* reads similarly. Moreover, Hagar's epithet for God in *Pseudo-Jonathan* as the unseen seer is repeated in the *Pseudo-Jonathan* to Gen. 24:62, which relates that Isaac was heading towards the well of seeing and living (*Beer-lahai-roi*), where "the Living and Enduring One, who sees but is not seen, was revealed to him." See also *Pseudo-Jonathan* Gen. 25:11; also *y. Peah* 9, 21b and *b. Hag.* 6b for similar language of the unseen seer. In the Hebrew text, Hagar had her vision at this well, but the targum redirects the revelation to Isaac. Isaac has a revelation of the Living and Enduring One – not the Memra or Shekhinah or Glory. The directness is uncharacteristic for the *targumim* and the sentence paradoxical: the unseen one is revealed.

134 Wolfson (*Speculum*, 5) argues, following Luce Irigaray, that an ocular focus already indicates a "phallomorphic culture."

135 See the translation and discussion in Goldin, *Song at the Sea*.

136 *Mek., Shirta* 4; trans. Judah Goldin, *Song at the Sea*, 124, 126–9. *Mek., Bahodesh* 5, is nearly identical. Cf. *Mekhilta de R. Simeon b. Yohai, Shirta* 30.1.2 (Nelson edition); *Pesiq. Rab.* 21 100b–1a; 33, 155b. See Alan F. Segal, *Two Powers in Heaven*, 33–57; Wolfson, *Speculum*, 33–41; cf. E.E. Urbach, *Sages*, 396–407.

137 Cf. *Apoc. John* 2.4–8.

138 The *Mekhilta de Rabbi Ishmael* earlier uses the same verse to claim that the Shekhinah was enslaved and exiled with Israel, the bricks under the feet representing the bricks made in Egypt, but the clear sky as freedom from enslavement (*Mek., Pisha* 14).

139 Cf. *Exod. Rab.* 23.15; Wolfson, *Speculum*, 48.

140 For flirtation and eroticism in divine visions, see Boyarin, "This We Know to Be Carnal Israel," 485, 493–4. Wolfson, "Circumcision, Vision of God, and Textual Interpretation," places the motif of circumcision in the context of Kabbalistic eroticism.

141 Cf. *Mek., Pisha*, 11.61–4 (Lauterbach, 60), which claims that the angel and God's presence do not distinguish between good or evil; their presence kills automatically, citing Exod. 33:22.

142 Wolfson, *Speculum*, 26–7.

143 *Lev. Rab.* 1.15; *Abot R. Nat.* 2.3; *Exod. Rab.* 47.5; *b. Shab.* 88b, 89a; *b. Sanh.* 111a; *b. B. Metz.* 86b; *b. Yoma* 4a; *Exod. Rab.* 28.1 (end). See also Meeks, *Prophet-King*, 195, on *Pes. Rab Kah.*, *piska* 32, which portrays ascent of Moses to heaven in rabbinic tradition (cf. *Mid. Ps.* 90.1, 90.5); *Deut. Rab.* 11.4.

144 E.g., *Sifra Lev.* 2.18; see Boyarin, "Eye in the Torah," 544–5; Wolfson, *Speculum*, 44–6.

145 Other instances where it seems God spoke to a woman, it was really an angel, such as with Hagar (Gen. 16:7–14) and Rebekah (Gen. 25:23). The use of the angel for Hagar is understandable, since it has a basis in the text itself; but the LORD speaks to Rebekah, telling her that two nations are in her womb. This repeated midrash flatly denies that Hagar "saw God and lived" or that the LORD spoke to Rebekah. While only Sarah hears God, others could see an angel (e.g., *Gen. Rab.* 45.10). Hagar regularly received revelations from angels, seeing multiple angels at once (*Gen. Rab.* 45.7). This is presented as proof of how earlier generations are greater than later, since she saw five angels at once and was unafraid, whereas Manoah was afraid and said to his wife, "we shall surely die, for we have seen God" (Judg. 13:22). The Judges passage is supposed to show how much greater Hagar was; however, the Rabbis, in this case R. Hiyya, do not explicitly deny that Manoah and his wife saw God. *Num. Rab.* 10.5, however, states that Manoah's wife saw an angel, who visited her due to her righteousness.

146 On the portrayal of women in *aggadic* midrash more generally, see Baskin, *Midrashic Women*.

147 It may be fruitful to analyze these midrashic traditions alongside the Christian traditions upholding Enoch as an uncircumcised righteous person who ascended to heaven; see Justin, *Dial.* 19, 23, 43, 45, 92; Irenaeus, *A.H.* 1.27.3, 5.5.1, 4.16.2; Tertullian, *Ag. Jews*, 4; discussion in Reed, *Fallen Angels*, 157–9.

148 Wolfson, "Circumcision, Vision of God, and Textual Interpretation" and *Speculum*, 104, 249 n., 330, 342, 357, 397; Boyarin, "This We Know to Be the Carnal Israel," 485–8, 491–7.

149 *Gen. Rab.* 44.6; *Lev. Rab.* 1.4; cf. *Song Rab.* 1.14.3.

150 Nonetheless, *Mek., Beshallah* 1, seems to read Genesis 18 as referring to the ministering angels, but does not directly comment on Gen. 18:1.

151 Wolfson, "Circumcision, Vision of God, and Textual Interpetation," 192–3; Boyarin, "This We Know to Be the Carnal Israel," 492.

152 See, e.g., *Gen. Rab.* 48.1, 3, 4, 5, 6, 7; cf. 42.8, 49.9.

153 Wolfson, "Circumcision, Vision of God, and Textual Interpretation," 193–4; Boyarin, "This We Know to Be the Carnal Israel," 493. This explains why Abraham sits when God appears to him – he is still sore (*Gen. Rab.* 48.1, 7). Moreover, *Num. Rab.* 11.2 and *Song Rab.* 2.9.2 claim that, due to Abraham's circumcised vision, God now visits all the synagogues and study houses. Mark, "Crossing the Gender Divine," xiii, draws attention to *Gen. Rab.* 49:2, where God literally gives Abraham a helping hand in circumcising him, making Abraham's penis the locus of human-divine encounter.

154 See Wolfson, "Circumcision, Vision of God, and Textual Interpretation,"
     196–7; Boyarin, "This We Know to Be the Carnal Israel," 493–4.

155 Gen. 17:3; cf. *Pseudo-Jonathan* Gen. 17:3; *Gen. Rab.* 46.6, 47.3; *Tanh., Lekh
     Lekha* 20; *Pirqe R. El.* Chap. 29.

156 Boyarin ("This We Know to Be the Carnal Israel," 493–5) argues that, since
     women do not have the "blemish," they are naturally equipped for such a
     vision, as are males born circumcised. He suggests that the passages in
     which God appeared to the Israelites at the sea would imply that both men
     and women saw God. I agree that the sea passages open up this possibility,
     but the repeated rabbinic statements that no woman has ever heard the
     divine voice and that, at Sinai, one had to remove oneself from women in
     order to receive the theophany militate against his reading. Moreover, *Num.
     Rab.* 12:8, which Boyarin discusses at length, also indicates that once the
     blemish of foreskin is removed, the body with a circumcised penis is per-
     fect; that is, uncircumcised is too much penis (blemish), but no penis is not
     enough (imperfect). It would be useful to see what the rabbis say about
     eunuchs and divine visions, since they, too, would not have the offending
     blemish. For further discussion of circumcision and vision in medieval Kab-
     balah, see Wolfson, "Circumcision, Vision of God, and Textual Interpreta-
     tion," 198–215.

157 Schäfer, *Hidden and Manifest God*, 162.

158 See Wolfson, *Speculum*, 19n37.

159 Cf. *t. Hag.* 2:3f; *y. Hag.* 2:1,15f, fol. 77b; See especially Halperin, *Merkabah in
     Rabbinic Literature*; Schäfer, *Origins*, 196–203.

160 In another context, the exposition of the chariot may re-enact the revelation
     of Sinai; see Wolfson, *Speculum*, 326–92; Halperin, *Faces of the Chariot*,
     16–19; Halperin, *Merkabah in Rabbinic Literature*, 107–40; Schäfer, *Origins of
     Jewish Mysticism*, 186–94.

161 In the passage it is the death of the pious; therefore, it is a reward rather
     than a punishment. See Schäfer, *Origins*, 199.

162 For a full discussion of the exposition of the merkavah – as an exegetical
     rather than visionary endeavour – see Halperin, *Merkabah in Rabbinic Litera-
     ture*; Schäfer, *Origins*, 175–242. Schäfer, however, admits that the *bavli*
     demonstrates some influence of merkavah mystical ascent, while also offer-
     ing a polemic against it.

163 For a survey of divine visions in *hekhalot* literature, see Chernus, "Visions of
     God in Merkabah Mysticism." On the curious terminology of "descending"
     to the chariot, there are several theories. See Halperin, *Faces of the Chariot*,
     227; Segal, *Paul the Convert*, 55–6; Wolfson, "Yeridah la-Merkavah," 13–44, and
     Speculum, 83; Morray-Jones, "The Temple Within," 170–7.

164 Peter Schäfer developed the terminology of "macroforms" and "micro-forms" in multiple publications. The most readable is his *Hidden and Manifest God*. Microforms are autonomous units that comprise the larger macro-forms, which provide an overarching framework. Yet the macroforms are quite fluid from manuscript to manuscript, with microforms often appearing in different macroforms.

165 This is the chronological sequence proposed by Schäfer (*Hidden and Manifest God*, 7) but their social location, date, and provenance are difficult to determine. Some elements may have originated as early as the second to the fourth century CE and continued to develop until the Middle Ages. The macroforms were most likely para- or post-Talmudic, with continued redaction until the Hasidei Ashkenaz. See Scholem, *Major Trends in Jewish Mysticism*, 1–79; Arbel, *Beholders of Divine Secrets*, 9–11, 142–6; Wolfson, *Speculum*, 74–81.

166 They include liturgies, ascents to heaven, *Sar Torah* (adjuration to cause an angel to give you knowledge of the Torah), apocalypses, *Shiur Qomah* (the measuring and naming of God's body), and tales of different rabbinic heroes. I agree with Schäfer (*Origins*, 32) that this complex literature cannot be reduced to the ascents and visions of the enthroned God, but I would go a step further and state that this highly complex literature cannot be reduced to any of its particular components, which I suspect is Schäfer's point. Due to its provocative anthropomorphism, the *Shi'ur Qomah* is relevant, but I have omitted it due to considerations of space. Most commentators, however, note that the massive measurements of God's body are so great that they preclude the possibility of vision (e.g., Scholem, *Major Trends*, 63–7; Schäfer, *Hidden and Manifest God*, 149–50). Cf. Wolfson, *Speculum*, 91. See Cohen, *Shi'ur Qomah: Liturgy and Theurgy* and *Shi'ur Qomah: Texts and Recensions*. For a discussion of the adjuration texts, see Lesses, *Ritual Practices to Gain Power*.

167 The primary image of God is the enthroned King of the Universe, sovereign over all things above and below and past, present, and future (e.g., *Hekh. Rab.* §§82–3, 107–20, 161–4). The section numbers derive from Schäfer, *Synopse zur Hekhalot*.

168 Cf. §388, where Metatron has to help Moses remember the Torah, which shows up only in MS. New York 8128 Moreover, in a riff on *m. Avot* 1:1, Moses passes down the great name to Joshua, the elders, the prophets, the great assembly, Ezra, and Hillel (§397). Moreover, in §§498–517, Moses utters the divine name, and, because of this, the Lord passes before him, using the divine name clearly as an adjuration. Moreover, the angels have to ask Moses for God's name. All of this material appears only in MS. New York 8128. See Schäfer, *Origins of Jewish Mysticism*, 296–7, 305–6.

169 Schäfer, *Origins of Jewish Mysticism*, 285–91.

170 §§336, 340.

171 See Schäfer, *Hidden and Manifest God*, 56–7; Arbel, *Beholders of the Divine Secrets*, 17–18.

172 Following translation in Schäfer, *Hidden and Manifest God*, 57–8.

173 Schäfer, *Hidden and Manifest God*, 58, and *Origins of Jewish Mysticism*, 288–9.

174 See Schäfer *Hidden and Manifest God*, 67, 145.

175 Ibid., 69.

176 Halperin, *Faces of the Chariot*, 381–2.

177 §§574–8 appears only in manuscript N8128. The three letters/names revealed to Moses that Moses in turn reveals also show up in §§566–8; see Schäfer, *Hidden and Manifest God*, 92–4; Janowitz, *Poetics of Ascent*, 46–7, 49–50.

178 Janowitz, *Poetics of Ascent*, 120; Swartz, *Mystical Prayer in Ancient Judaism*, 108–9.

179 For a discussion of the efficacy of the receipt of divine names, see Janowitz, *Poetics of Ascent*, 83–99.

180 These two texts most frequently speak of humans seeing God; Chernus, "Visions of God," 127. *Hekh. Zut.* §§350–2, however, directly addresses the question. It cites Deut. 33:20 and 5:21–4, and Isa. 6:1, which state that God spoke to Moses face to face, focuses on the divine voice, and gives a direct vision of the enthroned God. They represent three views of the possibilities of a human-divine encounter, with the final position being that of the merkavah mystic. Schäfer, *Hidden and Manifest God*, 57–60, and *Origins*, 288–9; Wolfson, *Speculum*, 45–6.

181 Idel, *Ascensions on High*, 31. Cf. Schäfer, *Hidden and Manifest God*, 104; Gruenwald, *Apocalyptic and Merkavah Mysticism*, 93–7.

182 Although, when discussing this macroform, Schäfer discusses the divine fiery appearance, he does not discuss the issue of gazing as he does when he discusses other macroforms; see *Hidden and Manifest God*, 77–88.

183 Swartz, *Mystical Prayer in Ancient Judaism*; Janowitz, *Poetics of Ascent*. Scholem (*Major Trends*, 60) says the *hekhalot* liturgies attempt "to catch a glimpse of God's majesty and to preserve it in hymnic form."

184 Cf. *Pseudo-Jonathan* Exod. 33:20; *b. Ber.* 6a, 7a.

185 The greatest dangers appear in the Sar Torah section of *Ma'aseh Merkavah* (§562).

186 What can be seen there is not stated; just that R. Ishmael accomplished this rare feat.

187 Chernus, "Visions of God," 127–9.

188 Cf. §§184, 189; Schäfer, *Hidden and Manifest God*, 17.

189 Schäfer, *Hidden and Manifest God*, 19.

190 On the divine Beauty, so powerful and luminous that it destroys, see Schäfer, *Hidden and Manifest God*, 15–17. He focuses on §§159, 102, 104, 356. Wolfson, *Speculum*, 85–6. One also cannot withstand the voices of the cherubim, ophanim, and holy beasts. There are six voices that increase in intensity; they force one to prostrate oneself and cry out, confuse, create convulsions and death, break all the bones in one's body, dissolve you into blood, and internal combustion (104). This is if you survive the attacks of all the angels in the lower heavens who come at you with iron rods and swords (219–24).

191 *Hekh. Zut.* §421 also speaks of how God is hidden, yet paradoxically revealed to R. Akiva (cf. §§61, 384, 514, 598, 639). See Scholem, *Major Trends*, 63, 364n80. See further, Schäfer, *Hidden and Manifest God*, 19–20, 25; Arbel, *Beholders*, 122; cf. Wolfson, *Speculum*, 87–98.

192 Arbel, *Beholders*, 34.

193 Cf. §258, which differentiates between one fit and one unfit to enter.

194 Cf. Schäfer (*Origins*, 280–1), who claims this promise remains unfulfilled for the reader in this section, moving rather to the participation in the heavenly liturgy. I agree that the climax of the ascent (or descent) is the participation in the heavenly liturgy and what he calls *unio liturgica* rather than *unio mystica*, but I do not think this excludes the vision of the enthroned God for the mystic. Instead, when the merkavah mystic enters opposite the throne of Glory (§250), just after being promised a sight of the King in his Beauty, the sequence indicates the King is on his throne during the liturgy, though not physically described – an anticlimax for the reader perhaps, but not for the mystic. Schäfer elsewhere affirms divine vision for other portions of the macroform (247–9, 255, 262–3, 268). In his concluding comments, he asserts that he does not think these texts deny the divine vision or that the mystic does not see God, but that his primary point is that the editorial strategy that persistently denies the conveying of the contents of the vision of God to the reader (341–2), a nuanced position on literary strategy with which I agree, and which his detractors often misinterpret as denying divine vision completely.

195 Arbel (*Beholders*, 37–40) discusses the mystic's characteristic fainting at the threshold of the divine court as a symbolic death and the angelic assistance as a ritual initiation into the secret practices and knowledge of the divine realm, being restored and transformed into a being who can endure the vision.

196 There are differences between the prophetic, apocalyptic, and merkavah visions. For the first, it happens to the prophet on earth. For the second, it still occurs to the visionary, but the visionary is brought to heaven. For the

third, the mystic attempts on his own initiative to enter heaven and see the throne. Cf. Arbel, *Beholders*, 24, 48.

197 A point brought out through correspondence between the author and Celia Deutsch.

198 This final paragraph emerged out of conversation with Celia Deutsch.

CHAPTER THREE

1 Ezekiel the Tragedian, *Exag.* 68–9; *Sir.* 45:1–5; *T. Mos.* 1:15; Philo, *Moses* 1.149–62; *Sacrifices* 9; *Posterity* 27–31; *Giants* 49. In addition to the previous chapter, see Meeks, *Prophet-King*; see further Borgen, "Moses, Jesus, and the Roman Emperor"; DeConick, "How We Talk about Christology Matters," 7–8.

2 Gieschen, *Angelomorphic Christology*, 77–8; Fossum, *Name of God*, 87–94.

3 In addition to Meeks, *Prophet-King*, see a summary of Moses' "glorification" in McGuckin, *Transfiguration of Christ*, 46–8.

4 Allison (*New Moses*, 106, 275) warns that explicit parallels between Jesus and Moses may not always entail criticism of Moses; indeed, imitation is flattery. Nonetheless, in some of the passages in the New Testament, the subordination of Moses to Jesus is made very clear.

5 Allison, *New Moses*; more tangentially, see Powell, "Do and Keep What Moses Says."

6 See Bovon, "La figure de Moïse dans l'œvrede Luc"; Moessner, "Luke 9:1–50." See further, Croatto, "Jesus, Prophet Like Elijah, and Prophet-Teacher Like Moses in Luke-Acts."

7 Meeks, *Prophet-King*; Martyn, *History and Theology in the Fourth Gospel*, 101–43; Harstine (*Moses as a Character in the Fourth Gospel*), however, does not look at Moses as a typology for Jesus in the Gospel of John; instead, he looks at Moses' role as a character in the narration of John.

8 D'Angelo, *Moses in the Letter to the Hebrews*.

9 Borgen, "Moses, Jesus, and the Roman Emperor," 145–59, though he argues that both Philo's divine Moses and Revelation's divine Jesus rely upon modelling off the traditions of the divine emperor rather than the portrayal of Jesus directly relying upon Moses traditions.

10 For a brief discussion, see Allen, "Jesus and Moses in the New Testament," 104–6; DeConick, "How We Talk about Christology Matters," 7–8.

11 Lierman, *New Testament Moses*; see also the older treatments of Deschamps, "Moïse dans les Évangiles et dans la tradition apostolique"; and Démann, "Moïse et la loi dans la pensée de Saint Paul," which is mostly about Paul's relationship with the Torah.

12 While one might expect that much of this material would appear in John

Lierman's chapter on Moses as prophet (*New Testament Moses*, 32–64), that chapter focuses on Moses having the title of prophet in various sources rather than on investigating Moses' interactions or encounters with the divine or angels. He focuses, instead, on the performance of miraculous signs and wonders by Moses.

13 For the Greek text of the New Testament, I have consulted Aland, Aland, Kavidopoulos, Martini, and Metzger, *Greek New Testament*; Holmes, *Greek New Testament* and *Novum Testamentum Graece*. As with the Hebrew Bible, I have tried to keep my translations close to the NRSV, since it is widely available, but necessarily have to regularly diverge from it to illustrate some elements of the underlying Greek.

14 Though ἀοράτῳ is occasionally, though very rarely, omitted in some readings (see Aland et al., *Greek New Testament*, 715n5).

15 Brown, *John I–XII*, lxxx–lxxxvi.

16 For an extensive discussion of Matt. 11:25–30, see Deutsch, *Hidden Wisdom*.

17 Deutsch (*Hidden Wisdom*, 36) argues that Matthew's version retains the more original wording.

18 Deutsch has pointed out, in the LXX and the New Testament, both terms are used interchangeably to mean "perceive" or "know," yet she suggests the shift in Matthew to "recognize" has theological content, indicating election and authorization. Moreover, several early Christian readers, including Justin, Irenaeus, Clement, and Origen, quote in the aorist (ἔγνων) rather than the present tense; Deutsch, *Hidden Wisdom*, 34–6. She writes, "the object of knowledge in Matthew's Gospel is not the identity of the Father and the Son, but the Father and the Son themselves" (35).

19 On its often-noted Johannine style, see Deutsch (*Hidden Wisdom*, 13, 38), where she furthermore argues that the identification with John, especially John 10:15, is tenuous.

20 On the themes of revelation, concealment, and disclosure in this *pericope* and in its Matthean context, see Deutsch, *Hidden Wisdom*, 23–5.

21 See Gieschen, *Angelomorphic Christology*, 285–6.

22 Brown, *John I–XII*, 16. Though there are points where Jesus distances himself from Moses and the law, calling it "your" law in 10:34, though not in all manuscripts; see DeConick, *Gnostic New Age*, 145.

23 Brown, *John I–XII*, 16, 35–6.

24 See Harstine, *Moses as a Character in the Fourth Gospel*, 47–8.

25 Wolfson, *Through a Speculum*, 26–7n69.

26 Thompson, "Jesus: 'The One Who Sees God.'"

27 Brown (*John I–XII*, 271) notes that Moses is probably in mind here, as in 1:17–18.

28 For the tension of treating Moses as a type and foreseer of Christ and polemics against Moses traditions, see Martyn, *History and Theology*, 101–43. Noting points of contact and conflict, he writes, "he [the author of John] stands strongly opposed to affirmations of ascent, the granting of heavenly visions, and divine commissioning for anyone except Jesus" (103). See further Meeks, *Prophet-King*, 295–301, 308; DeConick, *Voices of the Mystics*, 25–6.

29 Brown, *John I–XII*, 36.

30 For a summary of the scholarly discussion of the polemical context of John's denial of visions and evidence of knowledge of Jewish mystical traditions – partly co-opted, but also overtly rejected as it was deployed in new ways – see DeConick, *Voices of the Mystics*, 34–67, 109–13.

31 As argues Gieschen, *Angelomorphic Christology*, 273.

32 See Gieschen, *Angelomorphic Christology*, 274.

33 See Deconick, *Voices of the Mystics*, 114.

34 Brown, *John XIII–XII*, 632.

35 This line is striking, since it places the vision of the Father (via the Son) in the past tense. DeConick (*Voices of the Mystics*, 69–73) discusses John 14:3–7 at length, focusing primarily on Jesus being the only "way," and what the term "way" meant in visionary and ascent mystical circles; surprisingly, she gives no attention to the fact that the disciples "have seen" the Father by seeing the Son, God's glory. She picks up the thread, however, much later, when she discusses the visionary elements for the original disciples, who are transformed by a vision of God's Glory – the Son. This vision, however, is unavailable for later generations, who believe without seeing, and, therefore, are blessed (113–17, 125–7).

36 See further Meeks, *Prophet-King*, 295–301; see especially Ashton (*Understanding the Fourth Gospel*, 251–9), who argues that John in 3:13 melds two separate traditions of the angelic messenger who descends and ascends with the seer who ascends and descends, to make Jesus a messenger and seer, whose privileged status excludes any other company, such as – or especially – Moses and other seer and ascent traditions. See further, DeConick, *Voices of the Mystics*, 116–17.

37 Thompson, "Jesus: 'The One Who Sees God,'" 215–26.

38 D'Angelo, *Moses in the Letter to the Hebrews*.

39 See the larger discussion of this chapter by Eisenbaum, *The Jewish Heroes of Christian History*.

40 Calaway, *Sabbath and the Sanctuary*, 66–7.

41 For the problems with translating this line, see Attridge, *Hebrews*, 342–3; Johnson, *Hebrews*, 302; cf. Koester, *Hebrews*, 504.

42 See the full discussion in D'Angelo, *Moses in the Letter to the Hebrews*,

95–149; cf. Eisenbaum, *Jewish Heroes*, 170; Calaway, *Sabbath and the Sanctuary*, 70n45.

43 See Scholer, *Proleptic Priests*; Calaway, *Sabbath and the Sanctuary*, 159–62.

44 Attridge, *Hebrews*, 343; Koester, *Hebrews*, 412.

45 Calaway, *Sabbath and the Sanctuary*, 104–9.

46 Ibid., 70n45.

47 Whitlark, *Resisting Empire*, 70–4.

48 See my analysis of this passage in Calaway, *Sabbath and the Sanctuary*, 99–104.

49 For a list of potential intertexts for Heb 3:1–6 as a whole, see Gelardini, "*Verhärtet eure Herzen nicht*," 258–66.

50 Gräßer, *An die Hebräer*, 1:165; *1 Clement*, which was included in some ancient canons of the New Testament, also alludes to it; see *1 Clem.* 17:5; 43:1.

51 Cf. *Barn.* 14.4

52 Cf. D'Angelo, *Moses in the Letter to the Hebrews*, 69–93.

53 See further the Samaritan text, *Memar Marqa* 4.6.14–16, which also invokes Num. 12:6–8 in ways reminiscent of Heb. 3:1–6. For discussion, see Fossum, *Name of God*, 150–2.

54 *Foundations*, 68; cf. 101.

55 Cf. Ps. 24:4, where those with clean hands and pure hearts ascend the hill of the LORD (cf. Ps. 73:1).

56 Allison, *New Moses*, 182, 218–23.

57 See especially Allison, *New Moses*, 172–207.

58 See DeConick, *Voices of the Mystics*, 66.

59 See Calaway, "To See God and Live," 160–5.

60 Though cf. Ps. 68:17–18, which seems to blend the Red Sea and Sinai theophanies, having God show up with his heavenly armies on Sinai. Indeed, there are angels here, but the LORD also is there. The angels are not mediators in Ps. 68:17–18; they are more for an awesome display of God's majesty. There is a possibility in Josephus, *Ant.* 15.5.3 (§136), but the ἄγγελοι there are probably meant to be human prophetic messengers.

61 The Greek is relatively straightforward, yet modern translations are less so. The Greek reads: "ὁ δὲ μεσίτης ἑνὸς οὐκ ἔστιν, ὁ δὲ θεὸς εἷς." Interestingly, while the sentence is very balanced, the "one" in the first part does not match the "one" in the second. In the first clause with the mediator, it is in the genitive, indicating the mediator is not of/from "one"; while in the second clause, it is in the nominative, positively identifying God with the quality of "one."

62 See the discussion in DeConick, *Ancient New Age*, 127.

63 An observation made by Démann, "Moïse et la loi," 214.

64 For discussion of plural angels in Hebrews 2:2, see Attridge, *Hebrews*, 64–5nn27–9, though he includes a lot of citations of singular angelic intermediation, such as in *Jubilees*.

65 See Bovon, "La figure de Moïse dans l'œvrede Luc," 54–61.

66 For a discussion of how Stephen's speech fits within Hellenistic Jewish accounts of sacred history, see Sterling, "Opening the Scriptures," 199–225. Sterling's chart of the elements of Stephen's speech and how it aligns with the LXX and other Hellenistic Jewish authors is useful.

67 See Sterling, "Opening the Scriptures," 209.

68 See Attridge, *Hebrews*, 339; deSilva, *Perseverance in Gratitude*, 406; Koester, *Hebrews*, 501.

69 Moses' beauty shows up in a lot of sources, especially beginning in Hellenistic Judaism. Philo, *Moses* 1.9, 15 (see 1.5–24 in general); *Prelim. Studies*, 132; *Confusion* 106, where Philo connects it with prophetic abilities; Josephus, *Ant.* 2.210–37; *Ag. Ap.* 1.32 (279), connected with being "divine." Rabbis also include this attribute and discuss it (*Gen. Rab.* 4.6; *Exod. Rab.* 1.16, 1.20, 18.3; *Lev. Rab.* 1.3, 20.1; *Eccl. Rab.* 4.1, 9.1; *b. Sotah* 12a). On the importance of beauty in Greek and Roman biography, see Feldman, "Josephus' Portrait of Moses," 307–10. He also emphasizes, as other Hellenistic Jews would, Moses' Egyptian education; see Sterling, "Opening the Scriptures," 210.

70 Bovon, "La Figure de Moïse dans l'œvrede Luc," 52.

71 See Calaway, *Sabbath and Sanctuary*, 104–9, 121–37.

72 See Hurst, *Hebrews*, 15–17; Schenck, *Cosmology and Eschatology*, 117–21.

73 "For Christ has entered not a handmade sanctuary [οὐ γὰρ εἰς χειροποίητα εἰσῆλθεν ἅγια Χριστός], a copy of the true one [ἀντίτυπα τῶν ἀληθινῶν], but into heaven itself [ἀλλ᾽ εἰς αὐτὸν τὸν οὐρανόν], now to appear in the presence of God on our behalf" (Heb. 9:24).

74 "And so it was necessary for the copies of heavenly things [τὰ μὲν ὑποδείγματα τῶν ἐν τοῖς οὐρανοῖς] to be purified by these [rites], but the heavenly things themselves by better sacrifices than these" (Heb. 9:23).

75 "For since the law (only) has a shadow of the good things to come [Σκιὰν γὰρ ἔχων ὁ νόμος τῶν μελλόντων ἀγαθῶν], not the form itself of these realities [οὐκ αὐτὴν τὴν εἰκόνα τῶν πραγμάτων], it can never by the same sacrifices which are offered continually perfect those who draw near" (Heb. 10:1). See D'Angelo, *Moses in the Letter to the Hebrews*, 208–14. Cf. Schenck, *Cosmology and Eschatology*, 171–3.

76 The use of ὑπόδειγμα for "copy" or "illustration" is significant when juxtaposed with Exod 25:40, since in Exod 25:9 Moses saw the παράδειγμα. Both Plato and Philo preferred παράδειγμα to ὑπόδειγμα and used it to mean "pat-

tern" or "model" of a thing to be executed, a precedent (e.g, *Tim*. 29B). But it also can be derivative, such as a copy or model of an already-existing thing, as ὑπόδειγμα is used in Hebrews. The Greek τύπος mostly means an "imprint" or "impress" of something – Philo uses it to refer to the impression made by the paradigmatic, immaterial form upon the mind of Moses (e.g., *Alleg. Interp.* 3.95–6; *Moses* 2.76) – an intermediate position between the ideal form and the Platonic "shadow" (*Rep.* 7.514–17). Thus, the specific choice of the verse with "type" rather than "paradigm" may be significant, particularly since, in Hebrews, type is associated with the original and the paradigm/hypodigm the derivative. Yet the language is relational: the copy of one thing can be the model for something else. See D'Angelo, *Moses in the Letter to the Hebrews*, 219–20, 224–5. Koester, *Hebrews*, 98ff is helpful.

77 See Marquis, *Transient Apostle*, 104–9; DeConick, *Ancient New Age*, 120.

78 See the remarks by Démann, "Moïse et la loi," 194–5.

79 See the discussion by Segal, *Paul the Convert*, 59–61, 151–8. Segal writes, "Paul explicitly compares Moses' experience with his own and that of Christian believers. The experiences are similar, but the Christian transformation is greater and more permanent ... His point is that some Christian believers also make such an ascent and that its effects are more permanent than the vision that Moses received" (60). Segal also speaks of the importance of transformation language in Paul (*Paul the Convert*, 22–5). See also the brief but helpful remarks by DeConick, *Voices of the Mystics*, 64–6. She indicates that other Pauline transformation language, particularly that of being transformed into Christ or the image of Christ, should be brought into conversation with this verse (cf. Gal. 4:19; Rom. 8:29; 12:2; Phil. 2:5; 3:20–1; 1 Cor. 15:49; 2 Cor. 5:17; and Col. 3:9–10). See further 1 John 3:2.

80 See Marquis (*Transient Apostle*, 105–6), who notes that *katargein* has been mistranslated throughout as "fading," whereas its more basic meaning is "to nullify, to render inoperative." In that sense, Moses' glorified face did not fade – and, indeed, most traditions indicate that it actually increased in glory over time – but that its effects were nullified due to the veil; that is, Moses' face had become so glorified that it would kill those who gazed upon the reflection of God's glory in his face. It protects the Israelites who, due to their sinfulness, cannot endure Moses' glorious face.

81 Cf. Rom. 9:18, 11:7, 25.

82 See, in general, Segal, *Paul the Convert*, 34–71.

83 For the rhetorical context and strategies of this passage, see Nasrallah, *An Ecstasy of Folly*, 61–94.

84 Allison, *A New Moses*, 227.

85 For extensive commentary on this *pericope*, using redaction criticism, and its

history of interpretation, see McGuckin, *Transfiguration*. He points out several allusions to the Sinai theophany throughout. See also Allison, *New Moses*, 243–8; Harstine, *Moses as a Character in the Fourth Gospel*, 84–9.

86   This is an observation I owe to a paper given by Pettis, "Fiery Twins: James, John, and the Sons of Zeus."

87   See Allison, *New Moses*, 246.

88   On the significance of this addition and how it mirrors Moses in Deut. 10:11; 1:7, see Moessner, "Luke 9:1–50," 595.

89   As in the lost *Gospel to the Hebrews*, where Jesus is carried up Mount Tabor just after baptism, which may be why the two stories in the synoptic gospels have similar language; see DeConick, *Holy Misogyny*, 13–21.

90   Also noted by Proclos of Constantinople, *Or.* 8.1.

91   This became the traditional Christian interpretation; see Origen, *Ag. Cel.* 6.68; *Comm. Matt.* 12.38; Cyril of Alexandria, *Hom. Div.* 9; Proclos of Constantinople, *Or.* 8.1; Anastasius I of Antioch, *Hom. Transf.* 5; John of Damascus, *Or. Transf.* 17; Ambrose of Milan, *Expos. Luke* 7.10; Augustine, *Hom.* 28.2, 4–5; Leo I, *Hom.* 51.4; McGuckin, *Transfiguration*, 52.

92   See McGuckin, *Transfiguration*, 16. By contrast, John of Damascus, *Or. Transf.* 3, 17, indicates that it was meant to be a dead witness (Moses) and a living witness (Elijah) or that Jesus was the Lord of the living and the dead. Cf. Tertullian, *Resurrection* 55. Jerome, *Comm. Matt.* 3.17.3, by contrast, argues that it is a witness of heaven and Hades; Elijah descending from heaven, since he had ascended to heaven, and Moses coming up from Hades, since he is dead.

93   As is often the pair outside the New Testament; see McGuckin, *Transfiguration*, 52.

94   Though Croatto ("Prophet-Teacher Like Moses in Luke-Acts," 461) argues that Luke's version of the Transfiguration – and perhaps the *pericope* in all versions – is much indebted to Deuteronomy 18.

95   A point made by Celia Deutsch (private correspondence with the author).

CHAPTER FOUR

1   Cf. Plato, *Theaet.* 176B; Allert, *Revelation, Truth, Canon, and Interpretation*, 67–9; Dodds, *Pagan and Christian*, 92; Goodenough, *Theology of Justin Martyr*, 20–1; Malherbe, "Apologetic and Philosophy in the Second Century," 785. On Justin's understanding of second-century philosophy, see Malherbe, "Justin and Crescens," 883–94. See further, Lampe, *From Paul to Valentinus*, 262–5.

2   I have used the critical editions of Justin's writings from Marcovich, ed.,

Apologiae pro Christianis and *Dialogos cum Tryphone*. All translations are my own unless otherwise noted.

3 Of all the works attributed to Justin, only the *1 Apology*, *2 Apology*, and the *Dialogue with Trypho* have broad acceptance as being authentically his. Justin's rambling style is further complicated by the fact that his works – whether authentic or forged – survive in virtually only one manuscript, Parisinus gr. 450 (dated 11 September 6872 = 1363 CE), which itself has many text-critical problems. This is a striking paucity of manuscript evidence for such an influential figure in early Christianity. For a discussion of textual critical issues of the manuscript tradition, see Marcovich, *Apologiae pro Christianis*, vii–viii, 1–8, and *Dialogos cum Tryphone*, vii–ix, 1–22. Even Leslie Barnard, a strong defender of Justin, says about Justin's thought: "Justin was not a clear thinker, if he is judged by the side of Tertullian, Origen or St Augustine. In spite of his varied contacts with leading philosophies, it cannot be said that he had fully mastered contemporary philosophy and culture" (*Justin Martyr*, 5). Cf. Erwin R. Goodenough's portrayal of Justin as a superficial dabbler in philosophy (*Theology of Justin Martyr*, 31). For an ancient appreciation of Justin, see Eusebius of Caesarea, *Hist. Ch.*, 4.16–18.

4 Wendt (*At the Temple Gates*, 203) lists Marcion, Apelles, Syneros, Lucanus, Valentinus, Ptolemy, Marcus, Hegessipus, Justin, Tatian, and Irenaeus as all vying as rivals in second-century Rome, though some are students of others and some do not fully overlap chronologically with others in this list. For dates of Marcion and Valentinus, see Wilson, "Marcion and Boundaries," 212.

5 See Moll ("Justin and the Pontic Wolf," 145), who suggests that they likely knew each other; Lieu (*Marcion and the Making of a Heretic*, 15–25) more carefully argues that Justin's portrayal of Marcion already has several layers of caricature and rhetorical construction.

6 For Justin's social background and education, see Lampe, *From Paul to Valentinus*, 257–91.

7 As Traketellis (*The Pre-Existence of Christ in Justin Martyr*, 54) notes, citing *Dial*. 56.11: "Justin does not seem to be interested in the problem of the theophanies themselves. If he introduces them in his writings he does so in order to prove his thesis that Scripture speaks about another God next to the Father of all."

8 Similarly, though not as important for this chapter, the Logos Spermatikos was the source of pagan wisdom, especially of Socrates and Heraclitus (*Ap* 1.46; *Ap* 2.13.3); see the brief discussion in Chadwick, "Gospel a Republication of Natural Religion in Justin Martyr," 237–47.

9   The attempt to try to figure out the source of any given prophecy is called
    "prosopological exegesis"; see Presley, "Irenaeus and the Exegetical Roots of
    Trinitarian Theology," 165–71.

10 ἐπιθειάσαντος καὶ ἐξ αὐτοῦ κατασχεθέντος. This is discussed extensively by
    David Winston, "Two Types of Mosaic Prophecy according to Philo," 49–67;
    see also Levison, "Inspiration and the Divine Spirit in the Writings of Philo
    Judaeus"; Starobinksi-Safran, "La prophétie de Moïse et sa portée d'après
    Philon," 72.

11 See the note by Le Boulluec, Alexandrie antique et chrétienne, 233–4.

12 See Traketellis, Pre-Existence of Christ in Justin Martyr, 53–92.

13 On Justin's social background and philosophical education, see Lampe,
    From Paul to Valentinus, 257–84; on the impossibility of seeing God the
    father, see Goodenough, Theology of Justin Martyr, 126–7.

14 The classic discussion of Marcion is von Harnack, Marcion; see further,
    Lampe (From Paul to Valentinus, 241–56) who makes a lot of Marcion's
    social status as a ship merchant; Moll, "Justin and the Pontic Wolf," 145–51;
    Lieu, Marcion and the Making of a Heretic; and Wilson, "Marcion and Bound-
    aries," 200–20.

15 On this designation of "first prophet" rather than the typical "lawgiver," see
    Lieu, Image and Reality, 179–80. Moll ("Justin and the Pontic Wolf," 150) dis-
    cusses the reasons for shying away from Moses' role as lawgiver. Cf. the rab-
    binic designation of Moses as the "father of the prophets"; Abot R. Nat. B,
    1.3; Sifre Num. 134; Sifre Deut. 306; Sed. Eli. Rab. 5, 6, 13; Mid. Prov. 25.97.
    See further discussion, Meeks, Prophet-King, 198–9. Meeks identifies the basis
    of these designations in Deut. 34:10, which says, "there has not arisen since
    in Israel a prophet like Moses." This is related to Deut. 18:15, which speaks
    of a prophet like Moses, who will arise, which is the underlying basis of the
    "prophet-like-Moses" imagery surrounding Jesus in the New Testament,
    especially Matthew and John, but also parts of Luke.

16 On "image" and "form," cf. Barnard, Justin Martyr, 94–5.

17 Καὶ πρότερον <δὴ> διὰ τῆς τοῦ πυρὸς μορφῆς καὶ εἰκόνος ἀσωμάτου τῷ
    Μωσεῖ καὶ τοῖς ἑτέροις προφήταις ἐφάνη. νῦν δ' ἐν χρόνοις τῆς ὑμετέρας
    ἀρχῆς, ὡς προείπομεν, διὰ παρθένου ἄνθρωπος γενόμενος κατὰ τὴν τοῦ
    πατρὸς βουλὴν ὑπὲρ σωτερίας τῶν πιστευόντων αὐτῷ καὶ ἐξουθενηθῆναι καὶ
    παθεῖν ὑπέμεινεν, ἵνα ἀποθανὼν καὶ ἀναστὰς νικήσῃ τὸν θάνατον.

18 Interestingly, Wolfson (Speculum) repeatedly emphasizes the "docetic"
    nature of divine disclosure in late-antique and medieval Jewish sources.

19 Gen. 19:24 – "The Lord rained upon Sodom brimstone and fire from the
    Lord out of heaven" – is especially important for Justin's exegesis, since it
    appears to postulate two different Lords (Dial. 56–67). Interestingly, b. Sanh.

38b refers to *minim* who use this verse. R. Ishmael opposes the exegesis of Gen 19:24, which derived a second power in heaven from the destruction of Sodom (as Justin did) (Segal, *Two Powers in Heaven*, 162; cf. 118). See discussion in Skarsaune, "Justin and His Bible," 61–3. This may or may not indicate contacts between Justin and the Rabbis, since, after Justin, this passage would be taken up repeatedly by other Christians. Though, see further, Chilton, "Justin and Israelite Prophecy," 77–87, who tries to establish Justin's familiarity not only with biblical tropes, but with contemporary Jewish interpretation. Skarsaune further notes the anti-Marcionite tone of this section of the *Dialogue*.

20 Skarsaune (*Proof from Prophecy*, 47–50) makes some interesting observations about the doubling of burning-bush theophany in *Apol* 1.62.3–63.17 and *Dial*. 127.4. (1) The quotations in *Apol*. 1.63 show accordance with one another against the LXX. In this reading (and not LXX), it is the angel of God who speaks to Moses and presents himself as the God of Abraham. In the LXX, by contrast, there is, first, the Angel of the Lord in verse 2, while afterward it is the Lord who speaks and presents himself as God of Abraham. Thus, in Justin's non-LXX source, he says Jews are mistaken to say God spoke to Moses, when it is clearly the Angel (who is the Son). In the LXX, however, the argument would be different. *Dial* 59–60 is more complex: First, he repeats the idea that Angel is God, but the LXX text is different, and Justin seems to be working from the LXX this time – so he puts into Trypho's mouth the objection that there was both an Angel and God in the bush. The Jewish interpretation in *1 Apology* is to identify the angel with the father; in this case, it is to say there were two beings, an angel and father. Trypho is careful to avoid the identification of angel with the father. Justin has to turn to philosophical assumptions to argue against the wording of the LXX text: that is, the God who appeared to Abraham was not the Father (as he already demonstrated), and (2) the God of the universe cannot appear on a small part of it. Justin, then, begins to identify the two speakers as one, eliding earlier interpretation with the new wording of LXX. Skarsaune writes, "One gets the impression that Justin in *Dial*. 59f is adjusting an earlier exegesis, based on a non-LXX text, to match the full LXX text. Notice the Jewish exegesis also changes with the text. It seems that Justin in *Dial*. 59f – with his fuller acquaintance with the LXX – has become aware that the Jewish counter-argument to his own exegesis would run somewhat different from what he assumed in *1 Apol*. 63" (Skarsaune, *Proof from Prophecy*, 49).

21 Justin concludes this passage by returning to his favourite passage of Abraham and Sodom, where the Lord calls upon the Lord to bring down fire

from heaven, and other passages that suggest more than one "Lord" or
"God" (e.g., Psalm 110 [109 LXX]).

22 Καὶ τὰ ἄλλα δὲ τοιαῦτά ἐστιν εἰρημένα τῷ νομοθέτῃ καὶ τοῖς προφήταις. Καὶ
    ἱκανῶς εἰρῆσθαί μοι ὑπολαμβάνω ὅπως, ὅταν μου ὁ θεὸς λέγῃ· Ἀνέβη ὁ θεὸς
    ἀπὸ Ἀβραάμ, ἢ Ἐλάλησε κύριος πρὸς Μωσῆν, ἢ Κατέβη κύριος τὸν πύργον
    ἰδεῖν, ὃν ᾠκοδόμησαν οἱ υἱοὶ τῶν ἀνθρώπων, ἢ ὅτε Ἔκλεισεν ὁ θεὸς τὴν
    κιβωτὸν Νῶε ἔξωθεν, μὴ ἡγῆσθε αὐτὸν τὸν ἀγέννητον θεὸν καταβεβηκέναι ἢ
    ἀναβεβηκέναι ποθέν ...
        Οὔτε οὖν Ἀβραὰμ οὔτε Ἰσαὰκ οὔτε Ἰακὼβ οὔτε ἄλλος ἀνθρώπων εἶδε τὸν
    πατέρα καὶ ἄρρητον κύριον τῶν πάντων ἁπλῶς αὐτοῦ τοῦ Χριστοῦ, ἀλλ᾽
    ἐκεῖνον τὸν κατὰ βουλὴν τὴν ἐκείνου καὶ θεόν, υἱὸν ὄντα αὐτου, καὶ ἄγγελον
    ἐκ τοῦ ὑπερετεῖν τῇ γνώμῃ αὐτοῦ· ὃν καὶ ἄνθρωπον γεννηθῆναι διὰ τῆς
    παρθένου βεβούληται, ὃς καὶ πῦρ ποτε γέγονε τῇ πρὸς Μωσέα ὁμιλίᾳ τῇ ἀπὸ
    τῆς βάτου.

23 Gieschen, *Angelomorphic Christology*, 189–90.

24 See some helpful comments in Judith Lieu, *Image and Reality*, 103–53, esp.
    124–9. Cf. Frederiksen, *Augustine and the Jews*, 68–70.

25 Nonetheless, as discussed below, Skarsaune, whose own work has painstak-
    ingly sought to reconstruct the sources of Justin's thought, has argued that
    this is Justin's own distinctive contribution; it is his most original exegesis.

26 For a fuller discussion, see Calaway, "To See God and Live," 148–60.

27 See further the *Apoc. Zeph.* 6:11–13.

28 For his summary of the arguments, without coming necessarily to a firm
    conclusion himself, see Runia, *Philo in Early Christian Literature*, 97–105.
    Goodenough, *Theology of Justin Martyr*, compares Justin's thought to Philo
    throughout, but see esp. 113–17, 139–75, arguing that Justin appropriated,
    sometimes misunderstood, and ultimately adapted Philo to Christian usage,
    employing similar arguments for different ends. He ultimately used Greek
    Jewish arguments to come to conclusions with which Greek Jews them-
    selves would have been uncomfortable and would have found unjustified
    (see esp. 145). Barnard, *Justin Martyr*, 82–3, 92–6, denies any significant
    Philonic influence, arguing that any similarities in thought-patterns result
    from both Philo and Justin engaging in biblical exegesis with philosophical
    training in the eclectic philosophical environment that now we loosely call
    "Middle Platonism." Segal (*Two Powers*, 223) safely indicates that both Philo
    and Justin likely reflect the same Hellenistic traditions without necessarily
    claiming any direct dependence or appropriation. On controversial aspects
    of the arguments surrounding Justin's appropriation of Philo's work, see
    Judith Lieu, *Image and Reality*, 111. For the fuller discussions by Traketellis
    (*Pre-Existence of Christ*) and Skarsaune (*Proof from Prophecy*), see below.

29 Quite helpful is Segal, *Two Powers*, 159–81; see also Hurtado, *Lord Jesus Christ*, 575, and *One God, One Lord*, 44–8; see Fossum, "Kyrios Jesus," 41–71, for other references.

30 See esp. Traketellis, *Pre-Existence of Christ*, 53–92.

31 Philo seeks to ameliorate this concern in several works, but he extensively addresses the issue in *Dreams* 1.234–7 on the Bethel revelation. See Segal, *Two Powers*, 159–61. Segal writes, "Thus God can actually appear to men as a man or angel. Any Jew or gentile would be able to call God's angels divine, or a 'second God,' as Philo himself does, while only the most trained would be able to see that this title does not compromise monotheism" (161).

32 Traketellis, *Pre-Existence of Christ*, 60–8.

33 Ibid., 68–73.

34 Traketellis, *Pre-Existence of Christ*, 73–80. Segal (*Two Powers*, 169) writes concerning Philo's exegesis of the burning bush (*Moses* 1.66), "Philo wants the logos, the goal of the mystical vision of God, to serve as a simple explanation for all the angelic and human manifestations of the divine in the Old Testament. Thus Philo hints that, at the burning bush, Moses saw the image of Being, but elsewhere calls it an angel as scripture requires."

35 For the concept of "Middle Platonism," the classic text is Dillon, *Middle Platonists*; see also the discussion by Geljon, *Philonic Exegesis*, 56–8.

36 Explicitly defined as such in Philo *Flight* 164–5; *Names* 8–10; see Segal, *Two Powers*, 162.

37 See Goodenough, *Theology of Justin Martyr*, 47; Segal, *Two Powers*, 114–15.

38 *Cherubim* 3, 35; *Flight* 5; *Unchangeable* 182.

39 *Theology of Justin Martyr*, 50.

40 Though, interestingly, it is very difficult to find a quotation or direct allusion to the Gospel of John in any of Justin's writings. See Barnard, *Justin Martyr*, 60–2; Skarsaune, *Proof from Prophecy*, 105–6; this may reflect the Gospel's tentative status at the time, rather than Justin's lack of familiarity.

41 Skarsaune, *Proof from Prophecy*, 409ff.

42 Ibid., 410–18.

43 Ibid., 415–16.

44 *Proof from Prophecy*, 208–13, 409–24; see Barnard, *Justin Martyr*, 41.

45 Skarsaune, *Proof from Prophecy*, 210; see also Le Boulluec (*Alexandrie antique et chrétienne*, 235), who largely accepts Skarsaune's analysis.

46 On Marcion's literalness with regard to the Old Testament, see von Harnack, *Marcion*, 15, 46–7, 58–9, 65; Lampe, *From Paul to Valentinus*, 249. Nonetheless, Marcion seemed to accept allegorical reading procedure in other ways, especially looking at Jesus' parables (Wilson, "Marcion and Boundaries," 214–15).

47 On his *Syntagma* (*Compilation*), which Irenaeus says was directed toward
   Marcion (*A.H.* 4.6.2), see Lampe, *From Paul to Valentinus*, 250–1; Lieu, *Marcion and the Making of a Heretic*, 18–23.

48 E.g., Lieu, *Marcion and the Making of a Heretic*, 23–5, 184.

49 *Proof from Prophecy*, 423–4.

50 Barnard, *Justin Martyr*, 82.

51 Skarsaune, *Proof from Prophecy*, 423.

52 Hurtado, *Lord Jesus Christ*, 566.

53 Ibid., 564–78.

54 Ibid., 576–7.

55 Fossum, "Kyrios Jesus," 41–71. See further DeConick, "How We Talk about
   Christology Matters," 8–15, who widens the early evidence to include several
   New Testament passages and heresiological references to Ebionite Christology. In her "Jerusalem paradigm," Jesus *becomes* the angel of the LORD in the
   New Testament. In other words, the "angel of the LORD" is not a consistent
   figure from the Old to New Testaments, but something more like an office
   or title Jesus attained. She suggests, however, that Antiochene Christians –
   as early as Paul – had developed this Christology to mean that there was a
   consistent figure – not just office – between old and new angels of the
   LORD; that is, that Jesus was present in the Old Testament as the angel of
   the LORD. She develops this with hints and fragments, but nothing as clear
   as Justin's sweeping exegesis. Indeed, she notes that Justin, himself, was the
   person who incorporated all the elements from this paradigm shift from
   Jerusalemite to Antiochene Christology (14). See also the comments in Ashton, *Understanding the Fourth Gospel*, 281–301.

56 See Gieschen, *Angelomorphic Christology*, 245–69.

57 On Justin and the New Testament, see Trakatellis, *Pre-Existence of Christ*,
   55–8, who largely argues that Justin does not build upon New Testament
   passages for these particular arguments (and that some of these passages
   would be damaging to his argument).

58 The repeated usage of the plural "angels" in New Testament texts dampens
   the idea of a singular "angel of the LORD," even reconceived as Jesus.

59 Hurtado, *Lord Jesus Christ*, 577.

60 For what follows, see Calaway, "To See God and Live," 160–75.

61 Goodenough sees Trypho as basically a straw man pieced together out of
   many encounters Justin may have had with Jews (*Theology of Justin Martyr*,
   90–5); Barnard has a much higher confidence that Trypho actually existed
   and debated Justin (*Justin Martyr*, 21). The truth is that "Trypho" was likely
   partly historical and partly fictional, but he was no "straw man." As Traketellis ("Justin Martyr's Trypho," 287–97) has argued, his objections and argu-

ments are sometimes formidable, and often Justin cannot resolve them. Goodenough, however, has debunked the late-nineteenth-, early-twentieth-century theory that Trypho was, in fact, R. Tarphon. Boyarin ("Justin Martyr Invents Judaism," 427–61, and *Border Lines*) largely sees the question of whether Trypho was real or not as moot: the important question is that the type of Judaism he represents was close to second-century reality for at least some Jews. A similar point was already made by Traketellis, "Justin Martyr's Trypho."

62 On this point, see Bruce Chilton, "Justin and Israelite Prophecy," 85. Marc Hirschman greatly doubts that Justin had much direct knowledge of Rabbis, rabbinic arguments, etc., but that later rabbinic works – especially *Mekilta de Rabbi Ishmael* and *Genesis Rabbah* preserve very early anti-pagan polemical materials that were likely reworked to counter criticism such as Justin makes in the *Dialogue*. See Hirschman, "Polemic Literary Units" and *Rivalry of Genius*, 31–41, 55–66.

63 Boyarin, *Borderlines*, 28–9, 37–73. For an earlier discussion of how Justin relates to the emergence of the "two powers" heresy in rabbinic Judaism, see Segal, *Two Powers*, 221–5.

64 Boyarin, *Borderlines*, 30–1.

65 Boyarin, *Borderlines*, 112–27, is a fascinating chapter, in which Boyarin takes on the views of Larry Hurtado. On the relationship between Philo's Logos and the rabbinic Shekhinah, see Segal, *Two Powers*, 161–2.

66 Cf. *b. Ber.* 6a, 7a; *Ma'as. Merk.* §550. Boyarin (*Borderlines*, 131) notes that, in the most rabbinized *targumim* (Onkelos and Pseudo-Jonathan), the Memra starts to drop out (or is suppressed). In rabbinic literature (midrash, etc.) it disappears entirely, suggesting different forms of piety in synagogue and the house of study (131).

67 For the general discomfort of the Rabbis with Moses' vision, see Segal, *Two Powers*, 41–2, 50–1.

68 Segal, *Two Powers*, 182. On this point, see also Goodenough, *Theology of Justin Martyr*, 34–5.

69 Gieschen, *Angelomorphic Christology*, esp. 51–183, and stated most emphatically in 350–1.

70 Reed, *Fallen Angels*, 161.

71 Wendt, *At the Temple Gates*; also Lieu, *Marcion and the Making of a Heretic*, 303–4.

72 See Wendt, *At the Temple Gates*, 195–7, where she directly applies her criteria to Justin.

73 Despite the difference in social location between Justin and Ignatius, however, both would die as martyrs.

74 Lieu, *Marcion and the Making of a Heretic*, 1, 300.

75 See Wendt, *At the Temple Gates*, 196–7; Lieu, *Marcion and the Making of a Heretic*, 315–16.

76 A point made by von Harnack, *Marcion*, 22–3.

77 Lieu, *Marcion and the Making of a Heretic*, 24–5; cf. 184.

78 For how Marcion's arguments were often not so different from contemporary Christians and even how Justin himself may have found some of his views congenial, see Moll, "Justin and the Pontic Wolf," 150; speaking more generally about Marcion's distinctiveness and often surprising lack thereof, see Wilson, "Marcion and Boundaries," 200–20.

79 Traketellis, *Pre-Existence of Christ in Justin Martyr*, 181.

80 See discussion of the ambiguities of embodiment and bodilessness in Jesus' appearances both before the incarnation and after the resurrection by Lieu, *Marcion and the Making of a Heretic*, 376.

81 Von Harnack (*Marcion*, 83–4), however, gives a more complex account of Marcion's views of Jesus' flesh, which could interact with this world, but remain untouched by it; it is made, not begotten.

82 Goodenough, *Theology of Justin Martyr*, 155; See Fredriksen, *Augustine and Jews*, 69; Bucur, *Angelomorphic Pneumatology*, 140; see also Lyman, *Christology and Cosmology*, 22–4.

CHAPTER FIVE

1 Robert M. Grant has written most substantively on Theophilus, beginning with his dissertation and in several articles, including: "Theophilus of Antioch to Autolycus"; "Bible of Theophilus of Antioch"; "Problem of Theophilus"; "Textual Tradition of Theophilus of Antioch," which addresses the reception and knowledge of Theophilus' writings and reputation; and "Scripture, Rhetoric, and Theology in Theophilus." For a brief ancient sketch, see Eusebius of Caesarea, *Hist. Ch.* 4.24

2 On this ambivalence, see also Meeks and Wilken, *Jews and Christians in Antioch*, 2.

3 Grant, "Bible of Theophilus of Antioch," 173–96. Throughout most of his articles, Grant would argue that Theophilus reflects a Jewish Christianity of a more Semitic stamp, while providing a groundwork or at least a forerunner for the later Antiochene style of more literalist biblical interpretation ("Theophilus of Antioch," 235). On the other hand, his student, Schoedel ("Theophilus of Antioch"), would dismantle the assumptions of this argument, arguing, rather, that Theophilus most closely reflects Hellenistic Jewish strains similar to those found in Philo and, to a lesser extent, in Jose-

phus. For some of Grant's own hesitancies over identifying Theophilus with being Jewish, see "Problem of Theophilus," 193. For the robust religious "pluralism" of Antioch before the time of Theophilus, including polytheist and Jewish communities, see Zetterholm, *Formation of Christianity in Antioch*. See also Meeks and Wilken, *Jews and Christians in Antioch*, 1–52.

4 Meeks and Wilken, *Jews and Christians in Antioch*, 21.

5 See Runia, *Philo in Early Christian Literature*, 110–11.

6 Schoedel, "Theophilus of Antioch," 291–4; Steenberg, "Tracing the Irenaean Legacy," 202–3.

7 Grant refers to Book 1 especially as a "confused rationalism" ("Theophilus of Antioch," 229; cf. "Problem of Theophilus," 184).

8 Τὸ μὲν εἶδος τοῦ θεοῦ ἄρρητον καὶ ἀνέκφραστόν ἐστιν, μὴ δυνάμενον ὀφθαλμοῖς σαρκίκοις ὁραθῆναι. Greek text edited by Miroslav Marcovich, *Theophili Antiocheni ad Autolycum*. See the brief remarks on this passage in Grant, "Theophilus of Antioch," 229–30.

9 See Chapters 6 (Irenaeus), 7 (Clement), and 9 (Origen).

10 Εἰ ταῦτα νοεῖς, ἄνθρωπε, ἀγνῶς καὶ ὁσίως καὶ δικαίως ζῶν, δύνασαι ὁρᾶν τὸν θεόν.

11 Sinners cannot see God; for a list of vices and sins that precludes one from seeing God, see Grant, "Scripture, Rhetoric, and Theology," 43–4.

12 This anticipates Augustine's argument centuries later based upon his reading of 1 Corinthians 15; see discussion in Chapter 11.

13 Grant ("Theophilus of Antioch," 232) sees this statement as perhaps relying upon a combination of New Testament passages: 1 John 3:3 in light of 1 Cor. 15:53f.

14 The progression of humanity into perfection is shared between the contemporaries Theophilus and Ireaneus. For Theophilus, this is based on his reading of Adam as maturing and reaching divine status (see *Aut.* 2.24–5), relying upon readings of Luke. See the informative discussion in Schoedel, "Theophilus of Antioch," 291–4. On this issue, Schoedel argues that Irenaeus relies directly on Theophilus (*A.H.* 4.37–9). In general, there appears to be some sort of relationship between Theophilus and Irenaeus, who are roughly contemporary. See Grant, "Theophilus of Antioch," 227–9; "Textual Tradition," 147.

15 See the discussion by Grant, "Theophilus of Antioch," 245–9 (on the Logos) and 250–2 (on Spirit and Sophia); Grant, "Scripture, Rhetoric, and Theology," 37–43; Curry, "The Theogony of Theophilus." Curry compares Theophilus' discussion especially of the Logos to Hesiod's *Theogony* and later Stoic adaptations of Hesiod. See some notes on the "hands" of God – the Logos and Sophia – and the garden in Schoedel, "Theophilus of Antioch," 283.

16 Theophilus, in his exegesis of the creation stories, shows thematic similarities to Philo of Alexandria, yet very little literary resemblance. See the discussion in Runia, *Philo in Early Christian Literature*, 110–16.

17 ὁ μὲν θεὸς καὶ πατὴρ τῶν ὅλων ἀχώρητός ἐστιν καὶ ἐν τόπῳ οὐχ εὑρίσκεται· οὐ γάρ ἐστιν τόπος καταπαύσεως αὐτοῦ. ὁ δὲ Λόγος αὐτοῦ, δι' οὗ τὰ πάντα πεποίηκεν, δύναμις ὢν καὶ σοφία αὐτοῦ, ἀναλαμβάνων τὸ πρόσωπον τοῦ πατρὸς καὶ κυρίου τῶν ὅλων, οὗτος παρεγίνετο εἰς τὸν παράδεισον ἐν προσώπῳ τοῦ θεοῦ καὶ ὡμίλει τῷ Ἀδάμ. Καὶ γὰρ αὐτὴ ἡ θεία γραφὴ διδάσκει ἡμᾶς τὸν Ἀδὰμ λέγοντα τῆς φωνῆς ἀκηκοέναι. Φωνὴ δὲ τί ἄλλο ἐστὶν ἀλλ' ἢ ὁ Λόγος ὁ τοῦ θεοῦ, ὅς ἐστιν καὶ υἱὸς αὐτοῦ.

18 Grant ("Problem of Theophilus," 189) notes the contrast between Justin and Theophilus further in their purpose of identifying Jesus with a preincarnate Logos who speaks to the prophets: "For Justin, the prophets remind the people of God ... and predict the coming of Christ and the end of the law. For Theophilus, the prophets remind the people of the Law (III 11); the temple was built by the will of God (III 25), and the priests, who always stayed in the temple by the command of God (III 21), could 'heal every disease' (Matt. 4:23, etc., of Jesus), including leprosy! And all these priests, rather than Jesus alone (Hebrews 7:11), were successors of Melchizedek (II 31)." See further Schoedel, "Theophilus of Antioch," 288; McVey, "The Use of Stoic Cosmogony in Theophilus of Antioch's Hexaemeron."

19 See Curry, "Theogony of Theophilus," 320.

CHAPTER SIX

1 de Andia, *Homo Vivens*, 332 (translation mine). Original French: "Dans cette plénitude de connaissance de Dieu et de participation à sa vie incorruptible, l'homme devient lui-même 'homme parfait' à l'image et à la resemblance de Dieu, vivant de sa vie et jouissant de sa gloire. Telle est la vie éternelle, c'est-à-dire la participation pour la 'saisie' de la vie incorruptible de Dieu dans la visions de sa gloire."

2 For a nice summary of Irenaeus and his social context, see Parvis, "Who Was Irenaeus?" 13–25. For the suggestion that Irenaeus may have learned from Justin directly, and that he thought Latin was barbaric, see the discussion in Secord, "The Cultural Geography of a Greek Christian," 25–33.

3 See the accessible discussion by DeConick, *Ancient New Age*, 247–52.

4 Lieu, *Marcion and the Making of a Heretic*, 28.

5 There are several problems with *Against Heresies*, especially in its later books, likely due to his millenarian views expressed in Book 5, regularly bowdlerized in Latin manuscripts and only fully surviving in Armenian.

6 For this chapter, I have consulted the critical editions by Norbert Brox, *Irenäus von Lyon III*; *Irenäus von Lyon IV*. I have also consulted and sometimes adapted the translations in ANF.

7 As Eric Osborn writes, "The apparent confusions in his thought (*doctor confusus*) may be overcome by conceptual stamina or poetic imagination" (*Irenaeus of Lyons*, 251). Or, as Annette Reed notes, "much of the difficulty in understanding *Adversus haereses* roots in the fact that it is an extremely complex work, interweaving a variety of arguments and rhetorical stances" ("ΕΥΕΙΓΓΕΛΙΟΝ," 23). See further Schoedel, "Philosophy and Rhetoric," 28–31.

8 The most relevant secondary literature for this topic in Irenaeus is Andia, *Homo Vivens*.

9 Speaking more generally, Le Boulluec (*Alexandrie antique et chrétienne*, 236n33) notes, "Les œvres de Justin tiennent une place de premier plan marmi les sources d'Irénée." Cf. Hanson, *Allegory and Event*, 110–12. Some have even suggested that Irenaeus would have known and perhaps studied under Justin in Rome; see, e.g., Slusser, "How Much Did Irenaeus Learn from Justin?" 515–20; Secord, "Cultural Geography of a Greek Christian," 30. By contrast, Lieu (*Marcion and the Making of a Heretic*, 19) notes that Ireanaeus only explicitly refers to Justin twice.

10 Filium enim hic significat, qui et Abraham collocutus sit, a patre accepisse potestatem adiudicandi Sodomitas propter iniquitatem eorum.

11 Et iterum, filio loquente ad Moysen: "Descendi," inquit, "eripere populum hunc." Ipse est enim qui descendit et ascendit propter salute hominum. Per filium itaque qui est in patre et habet in se patrem, is qui est manifestatus est Deus, patre testimonium perhibente filio et filio adnuntiante patrem. Quemadmodum et Esaias ait: "Et ego," inquit, "testis, dicit dominus Deus, et puer quem elegi, uti cognoscatis et credatis et intellegatis quoniam ego sum."

12 See Justin Martyr, *Apol.* 1.62–3; *Dial.* 3, 56–62, 127. See discussion in Chap. 4.

13 See further 4.29.2, where the Word speaks from the bush.

14 Moses likewise hears the "Word" when he receives instructions on the pattern of the Tabernacle (*Dem.* 1.1.9).

15 Per haec igitur et tanta monstrat evangelium quoniam qui locutus est patribus Deus, hoc est qui per Moysen legisdationem fecit, per quam legisdationem cognovimus quoniam patribus locutus est, hic idem Deus secundum magnam bonitatem suam effudit misericordiam in nos.

16 He often pairs Valentinus and Marcion; see Lieu, *Marcion and the Making of a Heretic*, 31–3.

17 Note the point of this passage in Book 3 is as a demonstration against gnostic thought. He seeks to demonstrate that the God of the Bible, who is also

the creator of the world (for gnostics, the demiurge) is also God the Father, and that outside the Father and the Son there are no other gods. Moreover, by placing the Son as the revealing divine agent in the Old Testament, he connects Old and New revelations – as Justin did – but against a formidable opponent.

18 Drawing heavily on Matt. 11:27, which Justin also found interesting, Irenaeus also argues that to know God is impossible (*A.H.* 4.20.1, 6–7).

19 Et verbum quidem loquebatur Moysi apparens in conspectu, quemadmodum si quis loquatur ad amicum suum. Moyses vero cupivit manifeste videre eum qui secum loqueretur, et dictum est ei: "Sta in loco alto petrae, et manu mea contegam super te. Quando vero transierit claritas mea, tunc videbis quae sunt posteriora mea; facies autem mea non videbitur tibi: non enim videt homo faciem meam et vivet," utraque significans, quoniam et impossibilis est homo videre Deum, et quoniam per sapientiam Dei in novissimis temporibus videbit eum homo in altitudine petrae, hoc est in eo qui est secundum hominem eius adventu. Et proper hoc facie ad faciem confabulatus est cum eo in altitudine montis, assistente etiam Helia, quemadmodum evangelium retulit, restituens in fine pristinam repromissionem.

20 For a discussion of this and related passages, see McGuckin, *Transfiguration*, 100–1, 146–9.

21 scilicet quod inseminatus est ubique in scripturis eius filius Dei, aliquando quidem cum Abraham loquens, aliquando cum Noe, dans ei mensuras, aliquando autem quaerens Adam, aliquando autem Sodomitis inducens iudicium, et rursus cum videtur, et in viam dirigit Iacob, et de rubo loquitur cum Moyse. Et non est numerum dicere in quibus a Moyse ostenditur filius Dei.

22 See Andia, *Homo Vivens*, 58.

23 Et per ipsum verbum visibilem et palpabilem factum pater ostendebatur; etiamsi non omnes similiter credebant ei, sed omnes viderunt in filio patrem: invisibile etenim filii pater, visibile autem patris filius.

Though, as Andia (*Homo Vivens*, 71) points out, this does not necessarily mean that the Word is visible *by nature* in Irenaeus – in fact, likely the opposite, since the earliest visions can only be partial.

24 "Rock" is a typical early Christian typology of Christ, due to Paul's statement interpreting another verse in Num. 20:11 that "the rock was Christ" (1 Cor. 10:4). For other early Christians who interpreted the "hindparts" as Christ's incarnation, see Methodius, *Or. Simeon and Anna* 6.

25 Osborn, *Irenaeus of Lyons*, 88.

26 Non enim tantum propter Abraham haec dixit, sed ut ostenderet quoniam

omnes qui ab initio cognitum habuerunt Deum et adventum Christi
prophetaverunt revelationem acceperunt ab ipso filio, qui et in novissimis temporibus visibilis et palpabilis factus est et cum humano genere
locutus est.

27 Quoniam autem non solum prophetae sed et iusti multi, praescientes per
Spiritum adventum eius, oraverunt in illud tempus venire in quo facie ad
faciem viderent dominum suum et sermones audirent eius, dominus fecit
manifestum, dicens discipulis: "Multi prophetae et iusti cupierunt videre
quae videtis et non viderunt, et audire quae aditus et non audierunt."

28 *Mek.*, *Shirta*, 3; *Deut. Rab.* 7.8; cf. *Num. Rab.* 12.4; see Calaway, "To See God
and Live," 171–5; also Chapter 2 of this book.

29 Quoniam ergo Spiritus Dei per prophetas futura significavit, *praeformans
nos et praeaptans ad id ut subditi Deo simus*, futurum autem erat ut homo per
sancti Spiritus beneplacitum videret <Deum>, necessario oportebat eos per
quos futura praedicabantur videre Deum, quem ipsi hominibus videndum
intimabant, uti non solum dicatur prophetice Deus et Dei filius et filius et
pater, sed et ut videatur omnibus membris sanctificatis et edoctis ea quae
sunt Dei, *ut praeformaretur et praemeditaretur homo applicari in eam gloriam
quae postea revelabitur his qui diligunt Deum*. Non enim solum sermone
prophetabant prophetae, sed et visione et conversatione et actibus quos
faciebant secundum id quod suggerabat spiritus. *Secundum hanc igitur
rationem invisibilem videbant Deum*, quemadmodem Esaias ait: "regem
dominum Sabaoth vidi oculis meis," significans quoniam videbit oculis
Deum homo et vocem eius audiet. Secundum hanc igitur rationem et filium Dei hominem videbant conversatum cum hominibus, id quod futurum
erat prophetantes, eum qui nondum aderat adesse dicentes, et impassi-
biliem passibilem annuntiantes. (emphasis mine).

30 *Ratio/Rationem* has so much more flexibility in Latin than can be translated, ranging from an account, calculation, reason, or rational faculty to transaction, affair, etc. The cluster of meanings around "method," "order," "rule,"
or "scheme" seems most appropriate in this context.

31 For actions of prophets as a type of vision of God, see 4.20.12

32 Osborn, *Irenaeus of Lyons*, 112.

33 Non igitur manifeste ipsam faciem Dei videbant prophetae, sed dispositiones et mysteria per quae inciperet homo videre Deum.

34 Manifestius autem adhuc et per Ezechiel factum est quoniam "ex parte" dispositiones Dei, sed non ipsum videbant prophetae proprie Deum.

35 Igitur si neque Moyses vidit Deum neque Helias neque Ezechiel, qui multa
de caelestibus viderunt, quae autem ab his videbantur errant "similitudines
claritatis domini" et prophetiae futurorum, manifestum est quoniam pater

quidem invisibilis, de quo et dominus dixit: "Deum nemo vidit unquam,"
verbum autem eius, quemadmodum volebat ipse et ad utilitatem viden-
tium, claritatem monstrabat patris et dispositiones exponebat ... non in una
figura neque in uno charactere videbatur videntibus eum, sed secundum
dispensationum eius causas sive efficaciam ...

36 See Osborn, *Irenaeus of Lyons*, 206. Irenaeus' discussion of John of Patmos
has some general similarities with classic accounts of Shamanism, in which
the Shaman would have some sort of initiatory death (whether symbolic,
illness, etc.) before becoming a mediator between the physical world and
the spirit world. See, e.g., Eliade, *Shamanism*; Neihardt, *Black Elk Speaks*.

37 On the significance of the Mount of Transfiguration among ancient and
medieval Christians (particularly of the Byzantine tradition), see McGuckin,
Transfiguration of Christ. For this point in particular – the transfiguration
as the fulfillment of God's promise to Moses that he would see his glory,
see 100–1.

38 For many early Christian writers, the Mount of Transfiguration and the
existence of Moses and Elijah in it demonstrate or prove the state of resurrection, however that state is interpreted as a physical or spiritual reality.
See, e.g., Methodius, *Resurrection* 13; *Treatise on the Resurrection* (NHC I,4).

39 Irenaeus more directly refers to Num. 12:7 through the lens of Heb. 3:14 in
A.H. 2.2.5 and 3.6.5; Bingham, "Irenaeus and Hebrews," 71.

40 See McGuckin, *Transfiguration*, 101, for some keen insights on this passage.

41 Osborn, *Irenaeus of Lyons*, 208. See further Andia, *Homo Vivens*, 329, who discusses this passage's Trinitarian implications.

42 See Andia, *Homo Vivens*, 321–2, especially 321–3.

43 See generally Andia, *Homo Vivens*, 127–45.

44 Cf. Osborn, *Irenaeus of Lyons*, 168, 202–5.

45 Spiritu quidem praeparaente hominem in filium Dei, filio autem addu-
cente ad patrem, patre autem incorruptelam donante in aeternam vitam,
quae unicuique evenit ex eo quod videat Deum.

46 These issues, immortality and incorruptibility lost and regained, permeate
Irenaeus' writings, touching upon nearly every aspect of his thought. See
Andia, *Homo Vivens* in its entirety. Andia's work culminates in a final chap-
ter on how the vision of the Father bestows these qualities.

47 Ὥσπερ οἱ βλέποντες τὸ φῶς ἐντός εἰσι τοῦ φωτὸς καὶ τῆς λαμπρότητος αὐτοῦ
μετέχουσιν, οὕτως οἱ βλέποντες τὸν Θεὸν ἐντός εἰσι τοῦ Θεοῦ, μετέχοντες
αὐτοῦ τῆς λαμπρότητος· ζωῆς οὖν μετέξουσιν οἱ ὁρῶντες Θεόν. Καὶ διὰ τοῦτο
ὁ ἀχώρητος καὶ ἀκατάληπτος καὶ ἀόρατος ὁρώμενον ἑαυτὸν καὶ
καταλαμβανόμενον καὶ χορούμενον τοῖς πιστοῖς παρέσχεν, ἵνα ζωοποιήσῃ

τοὺς χωροῦντας καὶ βλέποντας αὐτὸν διὰ πίστεως. Ὡς γὰρ τὸ μέγεθος αὐτοῦ ἀνεξιχνίαστον, οὕτως καὶ ἡ ἀγαθότης αὐτοῦ ἀνεξήγητος, δι᾿ἧς βλεπόμενος ζωὴν ἐνδίδωσι τοῖς ὁρῶσιν αὐτόν. The Greek fragment is preserved by John of Damascus (fr. 10); Brox, *Irenäus von Lyon*, 162–3. The Latin reads: Quemadmodum enim videntes lumen intra lumen sunt et claritatem eius percipiunt, sic et qui vident Deum intra Deum sunt, percipients eius claritatem. Vivificat autem Dei claritas: percipiunt ergo vitam qui vident Deum. Et propter hoc incapabilis et incomprehensibilis <et invisibilis> visibilem se et comprehensibilem et capacem hominibus praestat, ut vivificet percipients et videntes se. Quemadmodum enim magnitudo eius investigabilis, sic et benignitas eius inenarrabilis, per quam visus vitam praestat his qui vident eum.

48 Andia, *Homo Vivens*, 324–5.

49 Homines igitur videbunt Deum ut vivant, per visionem immortales facti et pertingentes usque in Deum. Quod, sicut praedixi, per prophetas *figuraliter* manifestabatur quoniam videbitur Deus ab hominibus qui portant spiritum eius et semper adventum eius sustinent ... Quidam enim eorum videbant spiritum·propheticum et operationes eius in omnia genera charismatum effusa; alii vero adventum domini.

50 Translation mine, based upon the Greek: Τέλος γὰρ ὁ ἀγένητος, οὗτος δέ ἐστι Θεός. Ἔδει δὲ τὸν ἄνθρωπον πρῶτον γενέσθαι, καὶ γενόμενον αὐξῆσαι, καὶ αὐξήσαντα ἀνδρωθῆναι, καί ἀνδρωθέντα πληθηνθῆναι, καὶ πληθυνθέντα ἐνισχῦσαι, ἐνισχύσαντα δὲ δοξασθῆναι, καὶ δοξασθέντα ἰδεῖν τὸν ἑαυτοῦ Δεσπότην· Θεὸς γὰρ ὁ μέλλων ὁρᾶσθαι, ὅρασις δὲ Θεοῦ περποιητικὴ ἀφθαρσίας, "ἀφθαρσία δὲ ἐγγὺς εἶναι ποιεῖ Θεοῦ." Greek supplied by John of Damascus, Fr. 25; Brox, *Irenäus von Lyon*, 339–40. Latin translation: perfectus enim est infectus, hic autem est Deus. Oportuerat autem hominem primo fieri, et factum augeri, et auctum corroborari, et corroboratum muliplicari, et muliplicatum convalescere, convalescentem vero glorificari, et glorificatum videre suum dominum: Deus enim est qui habet videri, visio autem Dei efficax est incorruptelae, "incorruptela vero proximum facit esse Deo."

51 On this democratizing tendency in Irenaeus' theology, see Slusser, "The Heart of Irenaeus's Theology," 134, 138.

52 Reed, "ΕΥΕΙΓΓΕΛΙΟΝ," 23.

53 Secord ("Cultural Geography of a Greek Christian," 32) suggests his expertise led to his rise to the episcopacy of Lyons.

54 Wendt, *At the Temple Gates*, 207–9.

55 Ibid., 217. On Irenaeus' mental map, see Secord, "Cultural Geography of a Greek Christian," 25–33.

56 Brent, "How Irenaeus Has Misled the Archaeologists," 35–52.
57 Parvis, "Who Was Irenaeus?" 14.
58 Brent, "How Irenaeus Has Misled the Archaeologists," 40–6.

CHAPTER SEVEN

1 For studies on Clement in Alexandria or on Alexandria in general, see Le Boulluec, *Alexandrie antique et chrétienne*. For a beautiful, yet enormous, photographic engagement with ancient Alexandria, see Charles Méla and Frédéric Möri, eds., in collaboration with Sydney H. Aufrère, Gilles Dorival, and Alain le Boulluec, *Alexandrie la divine*. For a readable summary, see Hägg, *Clement of Alexandria*, 15–70.

2 On the Diaspora Revolt in 115–17, see the extensive analysis by Horbury, *Jewish War under Trajan and Hadrian*, who discusses it, together with the Bar Kokhba Revolt of 132–135 CE. For some briefer sketches, see Cohen, *From the Maccabees to the Mishnah*, 32–4; Schäfer, *Jews in the Greco-Roman World*, 141–2. On the lack of flesh-and-blood Jews in Clement's work, as opposed to references to Jewish writers to which Clement makes ample reference, see Le Boulluec, *Alexandrie antique et chrétienne*, 49–50. Le Boulluec suggests that any Christians of Hebrew origin in Alexandria were likely recent transplants from Palestine. On the Palestinian Jewish character – in addition to the heritage of Alexandrian Jewish writings – of Alexandrian Christianity, see the discussion in Hägg, *Clement of Alexandria*, 44–50.

3 While concepts of "gnosticism" and, to a lesser degree, "gnostic" are modern concepts, the term "gnosis" was quite common. The term *"gnostikos"* was by contrast rather rare, though Clement uses it quite often. For critiques of the terminology of "gnostic" and "gnosticism," see Smith, "The History of the Term 'Gnostikos'"; Williams, *Rethinking "Gnosticism"*; King, *What Is Gnosticism?*; for a defence of the terminology, see Pearson, *Gnosticism and Christianity in Roman and Coptic Egypt*, 201–23. See also DeConick, *Ancient New Age*. Others, like Bentley Layton (*Gnostic Scriptures*, xv–xxiii) and Brakke (*Gnostics*) limit the term "gnostic" to what is typically thought of as Sethian Gnosis.

4 For discussion, see especially van den Hoek, "'Catechetical' School of Early Alexandria," who, while not adhering to the official account by Eusebius of Caesarea (see, e.g., *Hist. Ch.* 5.11, 6.6), argues for some sort of a school using Clement's literary sources. Dawson (*Allegorical Readers*, 220–2) by contrast adheres to a view that Clement was one of many independent teachers hovering around the margins of the emerging church of Alexandria. See also Le Boulluec, *Alexandrie antique et chrétienne*, 13–57; Itter, *Esoteric Teaching*, 7–15; Hägg (*Clement of Alexandria*, 55–60) largely follows van den Hoek.

5 There are many works on Clement's use of Philo. See especially the excellent monograph by van den Hoek, *Clement of Alexandria and His Use of Philo*. See also Runia, *Philo in Early Christian Literature*, 132–56; Harding, "Christ as Greater than Moses," 397–400; Osborn, *Clement of Alexandria*, 81–110; Dawson, *Allegorical Readers*, 183–234.

6 Clement's philosophical inclinations have been long observed, and the literature is voluminous. See, e.g., Butterworth, "Clement of Alexandria's *Proptrepticus*," 198–205; Casey, "Clement of Alexandria and the Beginnings of Christian Platonism," 39–101. For a lengthier, more recent, and more systematic discussion, see Lilla, *Clement of Alexandria*. For Clement's philosophical context, also see Hägg, *Clement of Alexandria*, 71–133.

7 For Clement's use of Philo's *Life of Moses*, see van den Hoek, *Clement of Alexandria*, 48–68. She notes that these borrowings tend to stand in an apologetic context meant to illustrate that Moses' wisdom predates Plato's and that Plato relied upon Moses and/or Jewish law; see further Geljon, *Philonic Exegesis*, 13–14. On "gnostic perfection," see Le Boulluec, *Stromate VII*, 16–18.

8 I have relied upon the following critical editions of Clement's writings: Marcovich, *Clementis Alexandrini: Protreptricus*; Marcovich, *Clementis Alexandrini: Paedagogus*; Stählin, *Clemens Alexandrinus*, vol. 3; Otto Stählin, Ludwig Früchtel, and Ursula Treu, *Clemens Alexandrinus*, vol. 2; Alain le Boulluec, *Stromate V*; idem., *Stromate VII*. I also consulted Butterworth, *Clement of Alexandria*.

9 These may be portions of his lost *Hypotyposes*. Bucur, "The Other Clement," "Revisiting Christian Oeyen," and *Angelomorphic Pneumatology*, 3–71. Contrast Stroumsa (*Hidden Wisdom*, 111–17), who, like everyone else, focuses on the major treatises and sees a "rather slim interest in the Jewish inheritance of Christianity" (111), especially as compared to Origen. See also the note on the *Hypotyposes* in Le Boulluec, *Alexandrie antique et chrétienne*, 125–6, 133–8. Cf. the list of Clement's writings by Eusebius of Caesarea, *Hist. Ch.* 6.11, which includes the three major writings, as well as *Who Is the Rich Man Who Shall be Saved?*, the *Easter Festival*, *On Fasting*, *On Slander*, *To the Newly Baptized*, and the *Canon of the Church*. Interestingly, Eusebius' list omits the three treatises Bucur analyzes.

10 Cf. *Strom.* 6.7, where "gnosis" is derived from the oral teachings of the apostles. Bucur, "The Other Clement," in its entirety; "Revisiting Christian Oeyen," 395–9. For a discussion on how interest in such hierarchies or vertical "spiritual taxonomies" developed among third-century Christians and polytheists, see Marx-Wolf, *Spiritual Taxonomies and Ritual Authority*.

11 See Hägg, *Clement of Alexandria*, 204–5.

12 Cf. van den Hoek, *Clement of Alexandria*, 203.
13 Cf. *Strom.* 7.2.5.1–6; 7.2.9.1–4.
14 "Οἱ οὐρανοὶ διηγοῦνται δόξαν θεοῦ." οἱ οὐρανοὶ λέγονται πολλαχῶς, καὶ οἱ κατὰ διάστημα καὶ περίοδον καὶ ἡ κατὰ διαθήκην τῶν πρωτοκτίστων ἀγγέλων ἐνέργεια προσεχής· κυριωτέρᾳ γὰρ παρουσίᾳ ἀγγέλων αἱ διαθῆκαι ἐνηργήθησαν ἡ ἐπὶ Ἀδάμ, ἡ ἐπὶ Νῶε, ἡ ἐπὶ Ἀβραάμ, ἡ ἐπὶ Μωυσέως. Διὰ γὰρ τοῦ κυρίου κινηθέντες <οἱ> πρωτόκτιστοι ἄγγελοι ἐνήργουν εἰς τοὺς προσεχεῖς τοῖς προφήταις ἀγγέλους <δι>ηγούμενοι "δόξαν θεοῦ," τὰς διαθήκας. ἀλλὰ καὶ τὰ ἔργα τὰ κατὰ τὴν γῆν γενόμενα ὑπ' ἀγγέλων διὰ τῶν πρωτοκτίστων ἀγγέλων ἐγένοντο εἰς "δόξαν θεοῦ." Καλοῦνται δὲ οὐρανοὶ κυρίως μὲν ὁ κύριος, ἔπειτα δὲ καὶ οἱ πρωτόκτιστοι, μεθ' οὓς καὶ οἱ ἅγιοι πρ ὸ νόμου ἄνθρωποι, ὡς οἱ πατριάρχαι, καὶ Μωυσῆς καὶ οἱ προφῆται, εἶτα καὶ οἱ ἀπόστολοι.
15 Bucur, "Revisiting Christian Oeyen," 401; cf. Bucur, *Angelomorphic Pneumatology*, 52–4.
16 This hierarchical framework of revelation somewhat resembles Songs 6 and 8 of the *Songs of the Sabbath Sacrifice* at Qumran. See Davila, *Liturgical Works*, 115–22, 132–6.
17 Cf. *Adum.* in 1 Pet 2:3; 4:14; Bucur, "Revisiting Christian Oeyen," 402–3.
18 *Strom.* 5.6.35; 6.6.34; cf. *Adum.* in 1 Pet. 2:3; Bucur, "Revisiting Christian Oeyen," 401–2n74, 410.
19 Bucur, "Revisiting Christian Oeyen," 402.
20 Ibid., 403.
21 Bucur ("Revisiting Christian Oeyen," 401n71) makes a similar observation, while also noting that, by the time one gets to the Pseudo-Dionysius the Areopagite, this position will be inhabited by the bishop – a position which, we will see, is quite typical of post-Nicene Christianity as a whole. See also Bucur, *Angelomorphic Pneumatology*, 36.
22 On Clement's familiarity with Justin's writings, see Dawson, *Allegorical Readers*, 187; Lilla, *Clement of Alexandria*, 18.
23 On the use of mystery language, see Deutsch, "Visions, Mysteries, and the Interpretive Task," 95–8.
24 Λογικαὶ γὰρ αἱ τοῦ λόγου πύλαι, πίστεως ἀνοιγνύμεναι κλειδί· "θεὸν οὐδεὶς ἔγνω, εἰ μὴ ὁ υἱὸς καὶ ᾧ ἂν ὁ υἱὸς ἀποκαλύψῃ." Θύραν δὲ εὖ οἶδ' ὅτι τὴν ἀποκεκλεισμένην τέως ὁ ἀνοιγνὺς ὕστερον ἀποκαλύπτει τἄνδον καὶ δείκνυσιν ἃ μηδὲ γνῶναι οἷόν τε ἦν πρότερον, εἰ μὴ διὰ Χριστοῦ πεπορευμένοις, δι' οὗ μόνου θεὸς ἐποπτεύεται.
25 See a similar discussion of the *Excerpts from Theodotus* in McGinn, *Foundations*, 102–3.
26 See *Strom.* 2.6.28.2–3; 5.1.1.1–6; 5.13.85.2–3; 7.2.5.1; 7.10.55.1–7. Lilla,

Clement of Alexandria, 118–226; see further Osborn, *Clement of Alexandria*, 188–9; Hägg, *Clement of Alexandria*, 150–2, 210–11.

27 Considering that Clement himself was born in Athens, and likely "Greek" in that sense, Clement himself divides the world ethnically in terms of Jews, Greeks, and Christians. "Greeks," therefore, stands for any non-Jewish and non-Christian polytheist. See *Strom.* 6.5.41.6; for fuller discussion of ethnicity in the writings of Clement and other early Christians, see Buell, *Why This New Race?*; see further Deutsch, "Visions, Mysteries, and the Interpretive Task," 95–6.

28 See, e.g., Irenaeus, *A.H.* 4.20.9.

29 Osborn, *Clement of Alexandria*, 258.

30 ἐντεῦθεν πρόσωπον εἴρηται τοῦ πατρὸς ὁ υἱός, αἰσθήσεων πεντάδι σαρκοφόνος γενόμενος, ὁ λόγος ὁ τοῦ πατρῴου μηνυτὴς ἰδιώματος.

31 Διὸ καί φησιν ἡ γραφή· "ὁ νόμος διὰ Μωσέως ἐδόθη," οὐχὶ ὑπὸ Μωσέως, ἀλλὰ ὑπὸ μὲν τοῦ λόγου, διὰ Μωσέως δὲ τοῦ θεράποντος αὐτοῦ.

32 ἐπεὶ γὰρ ὁ παγκρατὴς κύριος τῶν ὅλων, ὁπηνίκα νομοθετεῖν ἤρχετο τῷ λόγῳ, [καὶ] τῷ Μωσεῖ καταφανῆ ἐβούλετο γενέσθαι τὴν αὐτοῦ δύναμιν, ὄψις αὐτῷ δείκνυται θεοειδὴς φωτὸς μεμορφωμένου ἐπὶ φλεγομένῳ βάτῳ· τὸ δὲ ἀκανθῶδες φυτόν ἐστιν, ὁ βάτος· ἐπειδὴ <δὲ> ἐπαύσατο τῆς νομοθεσίας καὶ τῆς εἰς ἀνθρώπους ἐπιδημίας ὁ λόγος, ὁ κύριος μυστικῶς αὖθις ἀναστέφεται ἀκάνθῃ, ἐνθένδε ἀπιὼν ἐκεῖσε ὅθεν κατῆλθεν, ἀνακεφαλαιούμενος τὴν ἀρχὴν τῆς | καθόδου τῆς παλαιᾶς, ὅπως ὁ διὰ βάτου τὸ πρῶτον ὀφθείς, ὁ λόγος, διὰ τῆς ἀκάνθης ὕστερον ἀναληφθεὶς μιᾶς ἔργον τὰ πάντα δείξῃ δυνάμεως, εἷς ὢν ἑνὸς ὄντος τοῦ πατρός, ἀρχὴ καὶ τέλος αἰῶνος.

33 Καί μοι δοκεῖ αὐτὸς οὗτος πλάσαι μὲν τὸν ἄνθρωπον ἐκ χοός, ἀναγεννῆσαι δὲ ὕδατι, αὐξῆσαι δὲ πνεύματι, παιδαγωγῆσαι δὲ ῥήματι, εἰς υἱοθεσίαν καὶ σωτερίαν ἁγίαις ἐντολαῖς κατευθύνων, ἵνα δὴ τὸν γηγενῆ εἰς ἅγιον καὶ ἐπουράνιον μεταπλάσας ἐκ προσβάσεως ἄνθρωπον, ἐκείνην τὴν θεϊκὴν μάλιστα πληρώσῃ φωνήν· "Ποιήσωμεν ἄνθρωπον κατ' εἰκόνα καὶ καθ' ὁμοίωσιν ἡμῶν." Καὶ δὴ γέγονεν ὁ Χριστὸς τοῦτο πλῆρες ὅπερ εἴρηκεν ὁ θεός, ὁ δὲ ἄλλος ἄνθρωπος κατὰ μόνην νοεῖται τὴν εἰκόνα.

34 Osborn, *Clement of Alexandria*, 256.

35 See Clement's reflections about the *Miscellanies* in *Strom.* 7.18.111.1–4. Casey ("Clement of Alexandria," 70) amusingly says of it, "From a literary point of view the *Stromateis* is the weakest of all Clement's works, but in its thought it is the most important one … the *Stromateis* is easily his master-piece of rambling obscurity." For a discussion of the place of the *Stromateis* in Clement's corpus of writings, see Itter, *Esoteric Teaching*, 15–32. For the purported audience of the *Stromateis*, see Kovacs, "Concealment and Gnostic Exegesis"; Ridings, "Intended Audience of the *Stromateis*," 517–21. Kovacs

argues that the audience consists of advanced "gnostic" Christians, whereas Ridings reads it more as a document used to ease Greco-Roman converts into their new faith. Hägg (*Clement of Alexandria*, 69–70) follows Ridings, but thinks it would have been useful for more-educated Christians in Clement's own community as well. For a basic introduction to the *Stromateis*, see Le Boulluec, *Alexandrie antique et chrétienne*, 111–23.

36 See Hanson, *Origen's Doctrine of Tradition*, 63–4.

37 ὁ Μωσῆς οὔποτε ἀνθρωπίνῃ σοφίᾳ γνωσθήσεσθαι τὸν θεὸν πεπεισμένος, "ἐμφάνισόν μοι σεαυτόν," οὗ ἦν ἡ φωνὴ τοῦ θεοῦ, εἰσελθεῖν βιάζεται, τουτέστιν εἰς τὰς ἀδύτους καὶ ἀειδεῖς περὶ τοῦ ὄντος ἐννοίας· οὐ γὰρ ἐν γνόφῳ ἢ τόπῳ ὁ θεός, ἀλλ᾿ ὑπεράνω καὶ τόπου καὶ χρόνου καὶ τῆς τῶν γεγονότων ἰδιότητος. Διὸ οὐδ᾿ ἐν μέρει καταγίνεταί ποτε ἅτε περιέχων οὐ ππεριεχόμενος ἢ κατὰ ὁρισμόν τινα ἢ κατὰ ἀποτομήν. Cf. Philo, *Posterity* 14–16.

38 Clement adopts much of the language of Philo, *Moses* 158–9; *Posterity* 13–15; cf. *Names* 2–9; Osborn, *Clement of Alexandria*, 87. For a study of God's unknowability in Clement's work, see Hägg, *Clement of Alexandria*. He discusses some of the passages mentioned below on pages 160–1 and the history of interpretation of the dark cloud on pages 256–60. Hägg tends to emphasize that most allusions to the thick darkness of God are to Exodus 19, though I tend to think Exodus 24 makes a better fit. For divine darkness in the works of Pseudo-Dionysius, see Turner, *Darkness of God*, 11–49.

39 Clement can rein in these disparate sources because he believes that the Logos of God has implanted Gnosis to varying degrees among the Greeks (the philosophers and especially Plato) and the Jews (the prophets and particularly Moses), and then incarnated and imparted Gnosis directly as Jesus. He writes, "There is only one river of truth, but a lot of streams disgorge their waters into it" (*Strom.* 1.29). Cf. Justin's concept of the spermatic Logos (*Apol.* 2.10.8; see further *Apol.* 1.5, 44, 46; 2.10). For parallels between Justin and Clement on this point, see Lilla, *Clement of Alexandria*, 21–7. For Clement's general doctrine of the Logos, see Lilla, *Clement of Alexandria*, 199–212.

40 ὁ λογισμὸς καὶ τὸ ἡγεμονικὸν ἄπταιστον μένον καὶ καθηγούμενον τῆς ψυχῆς κυβερνήτης αὐτῆς εἴρηται· ὄντως γὰρ ἀτρέπτῳ πρὸς τὸ ἄτρεπτον ἡ προσαγωγή. Οὕτως "Ἀβραὰμ ἑστὼς ἦν· ἀπέναντι κυρίου καὶ ἐγγίσας εἶπεν·" καὶ τῷ Μωυσεῖ λέγεται 'σὺ δὲ αὐτοῦ στῆθι μετ᾿ ἐμοῦ.'

41 Ἐπεὶ καὶ ὁ ἐλπίζων, καθάπερ ὁ πιστεύων, τῷ νῷ ὁρᾷ τὰ νοητὰ καὶ τὰ μέλλοντα. Εἰ τοίνυν φαμέν τι εἶναι δίκαιον, φαμὲν δὲ καὶ καλόν, ἀλλὰ καὶ ἀλήθειάν τι λέγομεν, οὐδὲν δὲ πώποτε τῶν τοιούτων τοῖς ὀφθαλμοῖς εἴδομεν ἀλλ᾿ ἢ μόνῳ τῷ νῷ, ὁ δὲ λόγος τοῦ θεοῦ "ἐγώ" φησιν "εἰμὶ ἡ ἀλήθεια" νῷ ἄρα

θεωρητὸς ὁ λόγος. "τοὺς δὲ ἀληθινούς," ἔφη, "φιλοσόφους τίνας λέγεις;" "Τοὺς τῆς ἀληθείας," ἦν δ᾿ ἐγώ, "φιλοθεάμονας." ἐν δὲ τῷ Φαίδρῳ περὶ ἀληθείας ὡς ἰδέας λέγων ὁ Πλάτων δηλώσει. Ἡ δὲ ἰδέα ἐννόημα τοῦ θεοῦ, ὅπερ οἱ βάρβαροι λόγον εἰρήκασι τοῦ θεοῦ ... ὅταν ὁ λόγος σὰρξ γένηται, ἵνα καὶ θεαθῇ.

42 See Osborn, *Clement of Alexandria*, 128–9; on the role of "contemplation" in Clement's works, see McGinn, *Foundations*, 104–5.

43 On apophatic theology in Clement's writings, see Trigg, "Receiving the Alpha," 540–5; for a short discussion on this chapter, see Osborn, *Clement of Alexandria*, 88–9. For a discussion of this passage, see Itter, *Esoteric Teaching*, 167–8.

44 See especially *On Mystical Theology* (PG Migne 997A–B, 1000C–1001A), but also *On Divine Names*, *Celestial Hierarchy*, *Ecclesiastical Hierarchy*, and *Letters*. Cf. other "Middle Platonic" thinkers who also used the *via negativa*: Albinus (Alcinous), Celsus, and Numenius; see Osborn, *Clement of Alexandria*, 121.

45 ἐπιρρίψαιμεν ἑαυτοὺς εἰς τὸ μέγεθος τοῦ Χριστοῦ κἀκεῖθεν εἰς τὸ ἀχανὲς ἁγιότητι προΐοιμεν, τῇ νοήσει τοῦ παντοκράτορος ἀμῇ γέ πῃ προσάγοιμεν <ἄν>, οὐκ ὅ ἐστιν, ὃ δὲ μή ἐστι γνορίσαντες. (5.11.71.3)

46 See Deutsch, "Visions, Mysteries, and the Interpretive Task," 96.

47 ἐναργέστατα αἰνισσόμενος μὴ εἶναι διδακτὸν πρὸς ἀνθρώπων μηδὲ ῥητὸν τὸν θεόν, ἀλλ᾿ ἢ μόνῃ τῇ παρ᾿ αὐτοῦ δυνάμει γνωστόν. (5.11.71.5)

48 See the summary statement by Lilla, *Clement of Alexandria*, 117.

49 Plato, *Rep.* 7.532 AB.

50 Δυσάλωτος γὰρ ἡ χώρα τοῦ θεοῦ, ὃν χώραν ἰδεῶν ὁ Πλάτων κέκληκεν, παρὰ Μωυσέως λαβὼν τόπον εἶναι αὐτόν, ὡς τῶν ἁπάντων καὶ τῶν ὅλων περιεκτικόν. ἀτὰρ εἰκότως πόρρωθεν ὁρᾶται τῷ Ἀβραὰμ διὰ τὸ ἐν γενέσει εἶναι, καὶ δι᾿ ἀγγέλου προσεχῶς μυσταγωγεῖται. ἐντεῦθεν ὁ ἀπόστολος, "βλέπομεν νῦν ὡς δι᾿ ἐσόπτρου" φησί "τότε δὲ πρόσωπον πρὸς πρόσωπον," κατὰ μόνας ἐκείνας τὰς ἀκραιφνεῖς καὶ ἀσωμάτους τῆς διανοίας ἐπιβολάς. "δυνατὸν δὲ κἂν τῷ διαλέγεσθαι τὸ καταμαντεύεσθαι τοῦ θεοῦ, ἐὰν ἐπιχειρῇ τις ἄνευ πασῶν τῶν αἰσθήσεων διὰ τοῦ λόγου ἐπ᾿ αὐτὸ ὅ ἐστιν ἕκαστον ὁρμᾶν καὶ μὴ ἀκοστατεῖν τῶν ὄντων, πρὶν <ἄν>, ἐπαναβαίνων ἐπὶ τὰ ὑπερκείμενα, αὐτὸ ὅ ἐστιν ἀγαθὸν αὐτῇ νοήσει λάβῃ, ἐπ᾿ αὐτῷ γινόμενος τῷ τοῦ νοητοῦ τέλει" κατὰ Πλάτωνα ... Καὶ ὅτι οὐ περιλαμβάνει τόπῳ τὸ ἀπερίληπτον ὁ γνωστικὸς Μωυσῆς, ἀφίδρυμα οὐδὲν ἀνέθηκεν εἰς τὸν νεὼν σεβάσμιον, ἀόρατον καὶ ἀπερίγραφον δηλῶν εἶναι τὸν θεον. Cf. Philo, *Posterity* 14–20; *Dreams* 1.61–71. While this study is most interested in how Clement plays Moses off Paul here, Abraham is important to the passage, especially to interpret what the "region" or "place" is at the beginning of it. For Clement's reading of Abraham and how it adopts and adapts much of

Philo's readings, see Choufrine, *Gnosis, Theophany, Theosis*, 77–158.

51 For Clement's reliance on Philo here, see van den Hoek, *Clement of Alexandria*, 168–76. For the Hellenistic Jewish tendency to claim that Moses – and other figures of Israelite heritage – were the great founders of culture, see, e.g., Collins, *Between Athens and Jerusalem*, 37–54.

52 For a brief sketch on the world of ideas among Middle Platonic philosophers, see Dillon, *Middle Platonists*, 47–9.

53 See Runia, *Philo in Early Christian Literature*, 147.

54 ἐνδεδεμένοι γὰρ τῷ γεώδει σώματι τῶν μὲν αἰσθητῶν διὰ σώματος ἀντιλαμβανόμεθα, τῶν δὲ νοητῶν δι' αὐτῆς τῆς λογικῆς ἐφαπτόμεθα δυνάμεως. Ἐὰν δέ τις αἰσθητῶς τὰ πάντα καταλήψεσθαι προσδοκήσῃ, πόρρωθεν τῆς ἀληθείας πέπτωκεν· πνευματικῶς γοῦν ὁ ἀπόστολος ἐπὶ τῆς γνώσεως τοῦ θεοῦ γράφει· "βλέπομεν γὰρ νῦν ὡς δι' ἐσόπτρου, τότε δὲ πρόσωπον πρὸς πρόσωπον." Ὀλίγοις γὰρ ἡ τῆς ἀληθείας θέα δέδοται. Λέγει γοῦν καὶ Πλάτων ἐν τῇ Ἐπινομίδι· "Οὔ φημι δυνατὸν εἶναι πᾶσιν ἀνθρώποις μακαρίοις τε καὶ εὐδαίμοσι γίνεσθαι πλὴν ὀλίγων· μέχρι περ ἂν ζῶμεν, τοῦτο διορίζομαι· καλὴ δὲ ἐλπὶς τελευτήσαντι τυχεῖν ἁπάντων." τὰ ἴσα τούτοις βούλεται τὰ παρὰ Μωυσεῖ· "οὐδεὶς ὄψεταί μου τὸ πρόσωπον καὶ ζήσεται·" δῆλον γὰρ μηδένα ποτὲ δύνασθαι παρὰ τὸν τῆς ζωῆς κρόνον τὸν θεὸν ἐναργῶς καταλαβέσθαι·"οἱ καθαροὶ δὲ τῇ καρδίᾳ τὸν θεὸν ὄψονται," ἐπὰν εἰς τὴν ἐσχάτην ἀφίκωνται τελείωσιν.

55 "τὸν γὰρ πατέρα καὶ ποιητὴν τοῦδε τοῦ παντὸς εὑρεῖν τε ἔργον καὶ εὑρόντα εἰς πάντας ἐξειπεῖν ἀδύνατον. ῥητὸν γὰρ οὐδαμῶς ἐστιν ὡς τἄλλα μαθήματα," ὁ φιλαλήθης λέγει Πλάτων. Ἀκήκοεν γὰρ εὖ μάλα ὡς ὁ πάνσοφος Μωυσῆς εἰς τὸ ὄρος ἀνιὼν (διὰ τὴν ἁγίαν θεωρίαν ἐπὶ τὴν κορυφὴν τῶν νοητῶν) ἀναγκαίως διαστέλλεται μὴ τὸν πάντα λαὸν συναναβαίνειν ἑαυτῷ· καὶ ὅταν λέγῃ ἡ γραφὴ "εἰσῆλθεν δὲ Μωυσῆς εἰς τὸν γνόφον οὗ ἦν ὁ θεός," τοῦτο δηλοῖ τοῖς συνιέναι δυναμένοις, ὡς ὁ θεὸς ἀόρατός ἐστι καὶ ἄρρητος, γνόφος δὲ ὡς ἀληθῶς ἡ τῶν πολλῶν ἀπιστία τε καὶ ἄγνοια τῇ αὐγῇ τῆς ἀληθείας ἐπίπροσθε φέρεται.

56 See also Itter, *Esoteric Teaching*, 46.

57 The subsequent section (5.12.79.1–4) pairs Moses' vision with Paul's in 2 Corinthians 12, a very common juxtaposition in ancient Christian thought, in order to indicate that the vision or experience was unutterable by human powers.

58 As noted in Chapter 2, Philo used this passage to indicate that it was a "vision" attained only by Moses and, as the invisible archetypal essence was imprinted onto Moses when Moses entered the cloud, it, in turn, will be imprinted upon others as they imitate Moses by following his legislation (*Moses* 158–9; cf. *Names* 2–9). He attains the invisible archetype, but it does

not seem that Moses actually sees God; instead he sees God's "backside" (that is, those things ontologically below the existent one, but still invisible and immaterial). Much later, Gregory of Nazianzus (*Or.* 28.2–3) would use the same moment anthropologically to delineate the degrees of worthiness between Moses, Aaron, Nadab, and Abihu, the elders, the masses, and the "untamed beasts," and himself in the place of Moses.

59 Van den Hoek (*Clement of Alexandria*, 50, 58, 60–2, 64) notes that Clement, when borrowing from Philo's characterization of Moses, omits the title of high priest, reserving it for Christ or the Logos, and adds the title of theologian, which he equates with being both a prophet and an interpreter of sacred laws. In fact, he equates theology with spiritual vision, being the first surviving author to use the term ἐποπτεία in a Jewish or Christian context. See also Itter, *Esoteric Teaching*, 166. Itter writes, "To learn how to be a gnostic with Christ in the light of his eternal cosmogonic act, the initiate has to become a theologian like Moses" (172).

60 Deutsch ("Visions, Mysteries, and the Interpretive Task," 96) writes, "Clement understands the sacred text as the guiding 'eye' to contemplation."

61 Cf. the dazzling in Origen, *Ag. Cels.* 6.17, where he writes that God's radiance is so overwhelming it appears as darkness due to the defilements of the mind (again suggesting the need of purification); cf. also other "Middle Platonic" thinkers who emphasized the necessity of a "purified" mind: Maximus of Tyre, Celsus, and Numenius; Osborn, *Clement of Alexandria*, 121.

62 On the relationship between purification, perfection, ascetical practice, moral rectitude, and education for a divine vision in Clement, see Deutsch, "Visions, Mysteries, and the Interpretive Task," 101–2; on the regular pairing of obedience to God's commandments and contemplation in *Strom.* 2.10.46–7, see Berkowitz, *Defining Jewish Difference*, 62–5.

63 Cf. Philo, *Moses* 158–9.

64 For discussion, see Lilla, *Clement of Alexandria*, 173–81; Itter, *Esoteric Teaching*, 39–47, 156–7. Itter thinks Clement shows familiarity here with post-biblical non-Philonic Jewish traditions, particularly with the practices of the Days of Penitence. For Clement's reliance on Philo in this passage, see van den Hoek, *Clement of Alexandria*, 116–47. For the language of the mysteries that can be found in this passage, see Deutsch, "Visions, Mysteries, and the Interpretive Task," 96–7.

65 Lilla, *Clement of Alexandria*, 175; Itter (*Esoteric Teaching*, 52, 77) also attempts to map the major writings of Clement onto this schematic.

66 Πλὴν ἐκείνας φημὶ τὰς γνωστικὰς ψυχάς, τῇ μεγαλοπρεπείᾳ τῆς θεωρίας ὑπερβαινούσας ἑκάστης ἁγίας τάξεως τὴν πολιτείαν, καθ᾿ ἃς αἱ μακάριαι θεῶν οἰκήσεις διωρισμέναι διακεκλήρωνται, ἁγίας ἐν ἁγίοις λογισθείσας καὶ

μετακομισθείσας ὅλας ἐξ ὅλων, εἰς ἀμείνους ἀμεινόνων τόπων τόπους
ἀφικομένας, οὐκ ἐν κατόπτροις ἢ διὰ κατόπτρων ἔτι τὴν θεωρίαν ἀσπαζομένας
τὴν θείαν, ἐναργῆ δὲ ὡς ἔνι μάλιστα καὶ ἀκριβῶς εἰλικρινῆ τὴν ἀκόρεστον
ὑπερφυῶς ἀγαπώσαις ψυχαῖς ἑστιωμένας θέαν, ἀϊδίως ἀΐδιον εὐφροσύνην
[ἀκόρεστον] καρπουμένας εἰς τοὺς ἀτελευτήτους αἰῶνας, ταυτότητι τῆς
ὑπεροχῆς ἁπάσης τετιμημένας διαμένειν. Αὕτη τῶν καθαρῶν τῇ καρδίᾳ ἡ
καταληπτικὴ θεωρία. Αὕτη τοίνυν ἡ ἐνέργεια τοῦ τελειωθέντος γνωστικοῦ,
προσομιλεῖν τῷ θεῷ διὰ τοῦ μεγάλου ἀρχιερέως, ἐξομοιούμενον εἰς δύναμιν
τῷ κυρίῳ διὰ πάσης τῆς εἰς τὸν θεὸν θεραπείας, ἥτις εἰς τὴν τῶν ἀνθρώπων
διατείνει σωτηρίαν κατὰ κηδεμονίαν τῆς εἰς ἡμᾶς εὐεργεσίας κατά τε αὖ τὴν
λειτουργίαν κατά τε τὴν διδασκαλίαν κατά τε τὴν δι' ἔργων εὐποιίαν. Ναὶ μὴν
ἑαυτὸν κτίζει καὶ δημιουργεῖ, πρὸς δὲ καὶ τοὺς ἐπαΐοντας αὐτοῦ κοσμεῖ
ἐξομοιούμενος θεῷ ὁ γνωστικός, τῷ φύσει τὸ ἀπαθὲς κεκτημένῳ τὸ ἐξ
ἀσκήσεως εἰς ἀπάθειαν συνεσταλμένον ὡς ἔνι μάλιστα ἐξομοιῶν, καὶ ταῦτα
"ἀπερισπάστως" προσομιλῶν τε καὶ συνὼν τῷ κυρίῳ. Ἡμερότης δ', οἶμαι, καὶ
φιλανθρωπία καὶ μεγαλοπρεπὴς θεοσέβεια γνωστικῆς ἐξομοιώσεως κανόνες.
Ταύτας φημὶ τὰς ἀρετὰς "θυσίαν δεκτὴν" εἶναι παρὰ θεῷ, τὴν ἄτυφον καρδίαν
μετ' ἐπιστήμης ὀρθῆς "ὁλοκάρπωμα τοῦ θεοῦ" λεγούσης τῆς γραφῆς,
ἐκφωτιζομένου εἰς ἕνωσιν ἀδιάκριτον παντὸς τοῦ ἀναληφθέντος εἰς ἁγιωσύ
νην ἀνθρώπου·

67 Cf. *Strom*. 7.1.4; 7.10.57.1–4; 7.12.78.3–6; cf. Boulluec, *Stromate VII*, 16–18.
68 Bucur, *Angelomorphic Pneumatology*, 41–51. See Lilla, *Clement of Alexandria*,
    181–6.
69 Bucur, "The Other Clement," 257.
70 See Osborn, *Clement of Alexandria*, 141.
71 See also Bucur, *Angelomorphic Pneumatology*, 45; Itter (*Esoteric Teaching*,
    204–7), who has more confidence that Clement thought such a deification
    would occur in this life.
72 Boulluec, *Stromate VII*, 158n1.
73 Cf. *Strom*. 7.7.45.4–46.6.
74 Lilla (*Clement of Alexandria*, 142) writes, "In Clement's conception of *gnosis*
    it is possible to distinguish two different stages. *Gnosis* can already be
    attained by man to some extent during his stay on earth; but it reaches its
    climax after the death of the body, when the soul of the γνωστικός is
    allowed to fly back to its original place where, after becoming a god, it can
    enjoy, in a complete and perpetual rest, the contemplation of the highest
    divinity 'face to face,' together with the other θεοί." See also his comments
    on deification in *Clement of Alexandra*, 181–9. See also Bucur, "The Other
    Clement," 262–4. Deification is, indeed, the ultimate goal of all faith and
    knowledge for Clement; see especially *Strom*. 7.10.56–7, which has many

parallels to the above quoted passage, such as the importance of purity of heart to see God face to face and attain equality with the angels; cf. Strom. 4.5.40; 4.23.149; 6.14.114; 6.16.146; 7.13.82; 7.16.95; Guilea, "'Demonstrations' from the First Principle," 211–12. On the nature of deification and how it contrasts with, for example, Irenaeus' concepts of deification, see Choufrine, *Gnosis, Theophany, Theosis*, 10–12, 159–97. Choufrine argues that for Clement "deification" signifies asymptotically drawing nearer to God as an "unending end" and assimilating to or participating in the divine.

75 Hägg (*Clement of Alexandria*, 259–60) notes that this differs from Origen, who allowed some momentary glimpses in this life, and seems more in line with the Cappadocians. He cites Gregory of Nazianzus, though Gregory of Nyssa is a very strong fit as well on this point of perpetual progress of the soul towards God.

76 On limit versus threshold, see Deleuze and Guattari, *A Thousand Plateaus*, 438–40; Derrida, *Beast and the Sovereign*, 1:300–13.

77 See Deutsch, "Visions, Mysteries, and the Interpretive Task," 95–8; Dillon (*Middle Platonists*, 398) notes other philosophers relating philosophical contemplation with the language of the mysteries.

78 On the polemic against Valentinus and Basilides throughout Clement's works, but especially the *Miscellanies*, see Lilla, *Clement of Alexandria*, 144–13; Kovacs, "Concealment and Gnostic Exegesis," 418–20; see further Deutsch, "Visions, Mysteries, and the Interpretive Task," 97–8.

79 Deutsch, "Visions, Mysteries, and the Interpretive Task," 97.

CHAPTER EIGHT

1 Luneau, "Moïse et les pères latins," esp. 295–6, where he briefly discusses Moses' visions in Latin Christian literature more generally, especially in Tertullian, Cyprian, and Augustine.

2 For a general discussion of Tertullian, see Osborn, *Tertullian*. For an older primer on Tertullian's Carthage, see Enslin, "Puritan of Carthage." For a discussion of Tertullian's rhetorical strategies in an agonistic context of the discussion of the nature of prophecy in his *On the Soul*, see Laura Nasrallah, *An Ecstasy of Folly*, 95–154.

3 Wendt, *At the Temple Gates*, 201. Like such a specialist, he relies upon his own knowledge of scriptures, which to the outside world may seem exotic, in order to establish and defend his status; nonetheless, he himself is not as mobile as those in Wendt's typology. If he is, then the typology is adapting to different social situations: as, for example, in Irenaeus' case with someone who has institutional authority; in this case, with someone who stayed home.

4 The most famous being the one in 202–203, leading to the martyrdom of
  Perpetua, Saturus, and Felicity; see *Martyrdom of Perpetua*. After Tertullian's
  time, Cyprian died a martyr in Carthage in 258 CE, during the reign
  of Valerian.

5 Osborn, *Tertullian*, 164, 176–7.

6 Osborn (*Tertullian*, 246) writes, "Most thinkers write under the stimulus of
  controversy, and Tertullian was fortunate to have many opponents to make
  him think."

7 Trakatellis, *Pre-Existence of Christ in Justin Martyr*, 91.

8 Both Irenaeus and Tertullian reiterate Justin's arguments in better-orga-
  nized form than Justin did (see Skarsaune, *Proof from Prophecy*, 4); likewise,
  Tertullian often more succinctly reiterates points made by Irenaeus.

9 For critical editions of the Latin text of Tertullian's writings, I have relied
  upon the Corpus Christianorum Series Latina volumes: Dekkers, et al., *Tertullianus: Opera I*; Gerlo, et al., *Tertullianus: Opera II*. All translations are
  adaptations of the widely available ANF series.

10 See Lieu, *Marcion and the Making of a Heretic*, 53–4, 58–9, 78–9.

11 For some borderline cases of this phenomenon among those usually considered "orthodox," see Lieu, *Marcion and the Making of a Heretic*, 378–9.

12 Cf. Osborn (*Tertullian*, 117), who writes, "Tertullian's trinitarian ideas may
   be best understood as third in a logic of apologetic, where his answer to the
   Jews made it necessary to argue with Marcion, while the answer to Marcion
   made it necessary to argue with Praxeas, who had identified father and son.
   It is difficult to win one argument without starting another."

13 Haud scriptura mentitur, neque cum inuisum neque cum uisum Deum
   profert. All translations are adaptations of the *Ante-Nicene Fathers* series
   unless otherwise noted.

14 Inuisibilis est, etsi uideatur.

15 I would note, however, that Tertullian largely avoids the Stoic formulation
   that everything is *material* or a mixture of God and matter. Instead, he
   prefers the language of corporeality, substances, and bodies; note especially
   his phrasing in *Soul* 21, 22. This is also why he occasionally cites Lucretius
   positively. See Miles, *Augustine on the Body*, 12–13. On the Stoic views of
   matter and corporeality, see, e.g., Dillon, *Middle Platonists*, 83–4; Long, "Soul
   and Body in Stoicism." In general, Tertullian displays an antipathy toward
   Platonic thinking, preferring Stoic development stemming from Zeno; see
   Nasrallah, *An Ecstasy of Folly*, 101–11. One should note, however, how this
   spiritual materiality can also be found among various "Middle Platonic"
   and "Neo-Platonic" philosophers who brought together various strands of
   Platonist, Pythagorean, and Stoic thought. Antiochus of Ascalon may have

believed that the World Soul and the mind were both material. Otherwise, these Middle Platonic philosophers tended to focus on intermediate spirits, or *daimons*, rather than the highest beings in their taxonomies; or, put another way, the material spirits are differentiated from the immaterial highest being. In Porphyry, for example, the soul acquires *pneuma* ("spirit") as it descends from the celestial realms to this world. The *pneuma* is a vehicle for the soul that becomes thicker and heavier as it descends through the sublunary regions. In this case, "spirit" is an intermediate state between the soul and matter. In short, to have a pneumatic vessel is to be embodied, but to attract different types of materiality to it depending where one is in the cosmos. Nonetheless, the Platonists, such as Numenius or Albinus (Alcinous), would still maintain a dualism between the soul and matter, though in different ways (Hägg, *Clement of Alexandria*, 94). Galen, moreover, relates *pneuma* to blood. For Christians, such as Origen, non-human sublunary spirits are demons. While Clement of Alexandria could speak of a πνεῦμα σαρκικόν (fleshly spirit), for him it denoted the animal sensations, appetites, and passions in humans, that is, the irrational part of the soul; instead, he explicitly denounced Stoic materialism of the spirit and divine realm and Stoic fate (Lilla, *Clement of Alexandria*, 48–51, 85–7). See a recent discussion by Marx-Wolf, *Spiritual Taxonomies and Ritual Authority*, 6, 17–18, 24–8, 39–40, 65–8, 111; Kalleres (*City of Demons*, 29, 74, 163) focuses on the materiality of demons as well as Stoic theories of tactile vision through intromission and extramission. See also the relevant discussion by Martin, *Corinthian Body*, 3–37.

16 See Miles, *Augustine on the Body*, 12–13.

17 In these sections, he brings up his treatise *Against Hermogenes*, in which he claims he does not believe in "matter," by which he does not seem to mean physical things, but an eternal primal matter out of which everything is made. Instead, God creates from nothing rather than from such a primal matter, and Adam from the earth rather than undifferentiated "matter." See also *Resurrection* 11. For further discussion of the relationship between the flesh and soul, see *Resurrection* 5–7, where he further differentiates between original substance of the flesh (clay or earth) and its refined product (flesh), which will be further refined in the resurrection. He discusses other interactions between flesh and soul in *Resurrection* 8, 15.

18 Cf. his use of Luke 16 also in *Soul* 57 in his discussion of the afterlife.

19 He also cites Perpetua's visions to justify his view of the afterlife – in this case, that martyrs directly go to Paradise when they die, while everyone else goes to Hades, a "good" part of Hades for the good and a punitive part of Hades for everyone else. After the judgment, when everyone receives their

flesh back, then the Christians in the good part of Hades and the martyrs in Paradise may enter the Kingdom of Heaven. See *Soul* 55; on his further support of visions, citing Joel 1:3, see *Soul* 47; cf. *Martyrdom of Perpetua* 1, 4, 11–12. See further *Resurrection* 11, where he cites the prophetess Prisca as an authority.

20 Est adeo alteri quid inuisibile, alteri non, quod non ideo incorporale sit, quia non ex aequo uis ualet ... Tantundem et animae corpus inuisibile carni, si forte, spiritui uero uisibile est.

21 See further Bynum, "Images of the Resurrection Body," 223–5.

22 Numquam deus latebit, numquam deus deerit, semper intellegetur, semper audietur, etiam uidebitur, quomodo uolet.

23 Iam ergo alius erit qui uidebatur, quia non potest idem inuisibilis definiri, qui uidebatur, et consequens erit ut inuisibilem Patrem intellegamus pro plenitudine maiestatis, uisibilem uero Filium agnoscamus pro modula deriuationis.

24 Nam qui ad Moysen loquebatur, ipse erat dei filius, qui et semper uidebatur; 'deum enim patrem nemo umquam uidit et uixit.' Et ideo <si> constat ipsum dei filium Moyseo esse locutum.

25 Slightly more elaborated in *Ag. Marc.* 3.16, where Christ is also equated with the Spirit of the Creator; further *Ag. Marc.* 4.29; cf. *Ag. Prax.* 22.

26 Tertullian occasionally supports the Son's subordination when it suits his argument, arguing in *Ag. Herm.* 3, 18, for example, that there was when the Son was not; cf. Osborn, *Tertullian*, 133–6.

27 See Chapter 11. As Osborn (*Tertullian*, 52) notes, Tertullian "seems to have provided Augustine with some of his best lines."

28 Inuisibilis dei imaginem ait Christum. Sed nos enim inuisibilem dicimus patrem Christi, scientes filium semper retro uisum, si quibus uisus est, in dei nomine, ut imaginem ipsius; ne quam et hinc differentiam scindat dei uisibilis et inuisibilis, cum olim dei nostri sit definitio: dominum nemo uidebit et uiuet. See further the rest of the passage: "If Christ is not 'the first-begotten before every creature,' as that 'word of God by whom all things were made, and without whom nothing was made'; if 'all things were' not 'in Him created, whether in heaven or on earth, visible or invisible, whether they be thrones or dominions, or principalities, or powers'; if 'all things were' not 'created by him and for him' (for these truths Marcion ought not to allow concerning him), then the apostle could not have so positively laid it down, that 'he is before all.'" (Si non est Christus primogenitus conditionis, ut sermo creatoris, per quem omnia facta sunt uniuersa in caelis et in terris, uisibilia et inuisibilia, siue throni siue dominationes siue principatus siue potestates, si non cuncta per illum et in illo sunt con-

dita, – haec enim Marcioni displicere oportebant – non utique tam nude posuisset apostolus: et ipse est ante omnes.)

29 On other subtle consistencies, see Osborn, "The Subtlety of Tertullian," 361–70.

30 Cf. his subordinationism in *Ag. Herm.* 3, 18.

31 Dicimus enim et Filium suo nomine eatenus inuisibilem, qua sermo et Spiritus Dei, ex substantiae condicione iam nunc, et quia Deus, ut sermo et spiritus Dei, uisibilem autem fuisse ante carnem eo modo quo dicit ad Aaron et Mariam: Et si fuerit prophetes in uobis, in uisione cognoscar illis et in somnio loquar illi, non quomodo Moysi: Os ad os loquar illi, in specie, id est in ueritate, et non in aenigmate, id est non in imagine, sicut et apostolus: Nunc uidemus tan quam per speculum in aenigmate, tunc autem facie ad faciem. Igitur cum Moysi seruat conspectum suum et collo-quium facie ad faciem in futurum, – nam hoc postea adimpletum est in montis secessu, sicut legimus in euangelio uisum cum illo Moysen collo-quentem – apparet retro semper in speculo et aenigmate et uisione et som-nio Deum, id est Filium Dei, uisum tam prophetis et patriarchis quam et ipsi adhuc Moysi. Et ipse quidem Dominus, si forte coram ad faciem loque-batur, non tamen ut est, homo faciem euis uideret, nisi forte in speculo, in aenigmate. Denique si sic Moysi locutus esset Dominus ut et Moyses faciem eius cominus sciret, quomodo statim atque ibidem desiderat faciem eius uidere quam, quia uiderat, non desideraret?

32 While I have not seen a study comparing Tertullian's argument in *Against Praxeas* with Irenaeus' *Against Heresies*, Tertullian had definitely read at least portions of it, since he cites it in *Ag. Val.* 5, where he also cites Justin; see Steenberg, "Tracing the Irenaeus Legacy," 204.

33 Et si commemoremur promissionis Moysi, hic inuenietur expuncta. Cum enim desiderasset conspectum domini Moyses dicens: si ergo inueni grati-am coram te, manifesta mihi te, ut cognoscenter uideam te, eum conspec-tum desiderans, in quo hominem esset acturus, quod propheta sciebat, – ceterum dei faciem, iam audierat, nemo homo uidebit et uiuet – et hunc, inquit, sermonem, quem dixisti, faciam tibi. Et rursus Moyses: ostende mihi gloriam tuam. Et dominus similiter de future: ego praecedam gloria mea, et reliqua. Et in nouissimo: et tunc uidebis posteriora mea, non lumbos nec suras, sed quam disderauerat gloriam in posterioribus temporibus reue-landam, in qua facie ad faciem uisibilem se ei repromiserat, eteiam ad Aaronem dicens: et si fuerit prophetes in uobis, in uisione cognoscar illi et in uisione loquar ad eum, non quomodo ad Moysen; os ad os loquar ad eum, in specie – utique hominis, quam erat gestaturus – non in aenigmate. Nam et si Marcion noluit eum conloquentem domino ostensum, sed stan-

tem, tamen et stans os ad os stabat et faciem ad faciem, – cum illo, inquit, non "extra illum" – in gloria ipsius, nedum in conspectu.

34 Tertullian will also use the Transfiguration as evidence of the continuation of bodily state in the resurrection, since Moses and Elijah – clearly in post-mortem existence, remain embodied (*Resurrection* 55; cf. the Valentinian *Treatise on the Resurrection*, which, similarly, uses the existence of Moses and Elijah in the Mount of Transfiguration as evidence of a rather different type of resurrection state). For a discussion of Tertullian among other late-antique thinkers concerning resurrection, see Bynum, "Images of the Resurrection Body," 215–37. She notes the increased emphasis not only in *bodily* resurrection but *fleshly* resurrection seen in figures like Tertullian offered a rebuff to docetic doctrines, such as those found among Marcionites.

35 Atquin si idem ante carnem inuisibilis, quomodo uisus etiam retro inueni-tur ante carnem? Aeque si idem post carnem uisibilis, quomodo et nunc inuisibilis pronuntiatur ab apostolis, nisi quia alius, quem, et retro uisum in aenigmate, plenius uisibilem caro effecit, sermo scilicet qui et caro factus est, alius quem nunquam quisquam uidit, [nisi] pater scilicet cuius est sermo?

36 See Bynum, "Images of the Resurrection Body," 217.

37 Si haec ita sunt, constat eum semper uisum ab initio qui uisus fuerit in fine et eum nec in fine uisum qui nec ab initio fuit uisus et ita duos esse, uisum et inuisum. Filius ergo uisus est semper et Filius conuersatus est semper et Filius operatus est semper ex auctoriate Patris et uoluntate quia ... Pater enim sensu agit, Filius uero quod in Patris sensu est uidens perficit.

38 Osborn, *Tertullian*, 57.

39 Ideoque et ipse cum angelis tunc apud Abraham in ueritate quidem carnis apparuit, sed nondum natae, quia nondum moriturae, sed ediscentis iam inter homines conuersari.

40 Eius esse promissum homines in angelos reformandi quandoque, qui ange-los in homines formarit aliquando.

41 Cf. *Resurrection* 42. Cf. Philo, *Dreams* 1.232–9, in which he argues that the "angels" of the Pentateuch were visions of God who appeared as an angel in order to be apprehended by mortals, whereas to angels God can appear as Godself; in short, God appears as one ontological level higher than the per-son to whom God appears. The end of this section suggests that this "image" was his "halo," "ray," or "angel word"; see also Goodenough, *Theology of Justin Martyr*, 192.

42 Ita semper ediscebat et Deus in terries cum hominibus conuersari, non alius quam sermo qui caro erat futurus. Ediscebat autem ut nobis fidem sterneret ut facilius crederemus Filium Dei descendisse in saeculum <si> et retro tale quid gestum cognosceremus.

43 Though his position often has much in common with Arius as much as Nicene Christians; see his statements in *Ag. Herm.* 3, 18. On Augustine's censure of earlier Christians, see Chapter 11.

44 Bynum, "Images of the Resurrection Body," 215–37. Bynum argues that this also accounts for Tertullian's stronger emphasis on the fleshliness of the resurrection.

45 Osborn, *Tertullian*, xiv.

46 Wendt, *At the Temple Gates*, 201.

CHAPTER NINE

1 All translations of *Against Celsus* come from Chadwick, trans., *Origen: Contra Celsum*. Greek text is Marcovich, *Origenes: Contra Celsum: Libri VIII.*
Πρῶτοι δὲ ἡμῶν σοφοί, Μωϋσῆς ὁ ἀρχαιότατος καὶ οἱ ἑξῆς αὐτῷ προφῆται, "οὐδαμῶς ῥητὸν" ἐπιστάμενοι τὸ πρῶτον ἀγαθὸν ἔγραψαν μέν, ὡς θεοῦ ἑαυτὸν ἐμφανίζοντος τοῖς ἀξίοις καὶ ἐπιτηδείοις, ὅτι "ὤφθη" ὁ θεὸς φέρ᾽εἰπεῖν τῷ Ἀβραὰμ ἢ τῷ Ἰσαὰκ ἢ τῷ Ἰακώβ· τίς δὲ ὢν ὤφθη καὶ ποταπὸς καὶ τίνα τρόπον καὶ τίνι τῶν ἐν ἡμῖν, καταλελοίπασιν ἐξετάζειν τοῖς δυναμένοις ἑαυτοὺς ἐμπαρέχειν παραπλησίους ἐκείνοις οἷς ὤφθη ὁ θεός· ὀφθεὶς <δ᾽> αὐτῶν οὐ τοῖς τοῦ σώματος ὀφθαλμοῖς, ἀλλὰ τῇ καθαρᾷ καρδίᾳ. Καὶ γὰρ κατὰ τὸν Ἰησοῦν ἡμῶν "Μακάριοι οἱ καθαροὶ τῇ καρδίᾳ, ὅτι αὐτοὶ τὸν θεὸν ὄψονται."

2 As Daniélou (*Origène*, 22) writes, it was a "constant" in his life.

3 See Eusebius, *Hist. Ch.* 6.1–2. Though this contradicts Origen's own writings, such as in *Comm. John* 28.193–5, where he suggests avoiding martyrdom if possible, though to stand firm if caught; see Heine, *Commentary on John 13–32*, 11.

4 For a brief discussion, see Kolbet, "Torture and Origen's Hermeneutics of Nonviolence."

5 Even though highly indebted to especially Plato, he regularly downplayed and denounced Greek philosophy in much stronger terms than, for example, Clement of Alexandria; for his philosophical milieu, see Daniélou, *Origène*, 85–108.

6 On Philo in Origen's writings, see Runia, *Philo in Early Christian Literature*, 157–83.

7 Runia, *Philo in Early Christian Literature*, 157.

8 Lyman (*Christology and Cosmology*, 40–1) notes that, "As an ascetic intellectual in Alexandria, Origen's relationship to the Christian community lay in the independence of the *didaskalos* rather than in the ordered ecclesiastical hierarchy."

9 Eusebius of Caesarea, a theological grandchild of Origen through Pamphilus, dedicates nearly a whole book to Origen and those directly connected to him in his *History of the Church* 6. For modern reconstructions of Origen's life and times, see Daniélou, *Origène*, 19–40; Hanson, *Origen's Doctrine of Tradition*, 1–30.

10 Runia, *Philo in Early Christian Literature*, 157.

11 Daniélou, *Origène*, 7: "Origène est, avec saint Augustin, le plus grand genie du christianisme antique."

12 For an especially lucid social account of the Origenist controversy, see Clark, *Origenist Controversy*.

13 Daniélou, *Origène*, 7–8, 287–8.

14 For a list of principle works in Greek or in Latin translation, and works circulating under others' names, see Daniélou, *Origène*, 12–14; see further Crouzel, *Théologie de l'image de Dieu*, 11–13. For the dating and order of his works, see also Hanson, *Origen's Doctrine of Tradition*, 8–30. See also the list of commentaries in Eusebius, *Hist. Ch.* 6.24–25, 32, which Eusebius largely uses to reconstruct canonical issues.

15 Rufinus and Jerome tend to discuss the importance of translating the sense rather than word for word in the prefaces of their translations, including, but not limited to, their translation work on Origen, and, for Jerome, the prefaces to his translations of biblical books. See, e.g., Rufinus, *Pref. Princ.* 1.2–3; *Pref. Her.*; *Apol.* 2.40; *Apol. Anast.* 7; *Praf. Gaud.*; Jerome, *Ep.* 57.5. For Rufinus, see the discussion in Heine, *Homilies on Genesis and Exodus*, 27–39. As Jerome reflected on his translation of Samuel and Kings: "Read, then, my Samuel and Kings; mine, I say, mine. For whatever by diligent translation and careful emendation we have mastered and made our own, is ours" (quoted in Arrowsmith, "Jerome on Translation," 267). See further Jerome defending his own and attacking Rufinus' translation methods in his letter to Pammachius (*De optimo genere interpretandi* 5–6). Overall, however, Jerome appears to be a more accurate translator than Rufinus when we can compare the Greek and Latin versions side by side. See further my own comments about translation as conquering in antiquity in my essay, "Translation and Transformation," 255–75; see further Marx-Wolf, *Spiritual Taxonomies and Ritual Authority*, 149n17; see also the discussion of the relative reliability of Origen's translators by Hanson, *Origen's Doctrine of Tradition*, 40–7; Torjesen, *Hermeneutical Procedure*, 14–18.

16 Grossman, *Why Translation Matters*, 10.

17 See Heine, *Commentary on John 13–32*, 20.

18 Crouzel, *L'image de Dieu*, 46; Daniélou (*Origène*, 137) writes, "L'écriture est le centre de sa vie." See also Heine, *Commentary on John 1–10*, 3. On Origen

and Philo, see Geljon, *Philonic Exegesis*, 14; Runia, *Philo in Early Christian Literature*, 157–83.

19 For a bibliography, sometimes annotated, of recent scholarship on *Against Celsus*, see Boulluec, *Alexandrie antique et chrétienne*, 335–53.

20 And, in an interesting twist, Origen claims that Moses saw all the allegorical meanings of scripture in his mind when they were revealed to him (*Comm. John* 6.22); interpretation is already embedded in the original revelation; cf. the story of Moses and Rabbi Akiva in *b. Men.* 29b. Cox ("Origen and the Bestial Soul," 119–20) notes that this also applies to interpreting nature; the world is a text to interpret as well as scripture.

21 See *Comm. Ps.* 119.85; Hanson, *Origen's Doctrine of Tradition*, 106.

22 See Heine, *Commentary on John 1–10*, 13; Cf. Wolfson, *Speculum*, 326–92. While Wolfson mostly discusses Kabbalah, he looks at earlier Rabbinic works in which the act of interpretation of especially the Torah leads to a re-experiencing of the Sinai theophany (*Song Rab.* 1:10; *Lev. Rab.* 16:4). As such, the hermeneut is a new prophet and, most significantly, a new Moses. Halperin, *Merkabah in Rabbinic Literature*, 107–40; Halperin (*Faces of the Chariot*, 16–19), from a different perspective, offers some similar observations, also discussing *y. Hag.* 2:1, 77b (and parallels) as well as, interestingly, Acts 2:3–4. Both are relying upon an old article, Urbach, "Traditions about Merkabah Mysticism." See also the discussion in Schäfer, *Origins of Jewish Mysticism*, 186–94.

23 See Hanson, *Allegory and Event*, 200–3. For a discussion of the further potential influence of Irenaeus of Lyons on *On First Principles*, see Le Boulluec, *Alexandrie antique et chrétienne*, 265–73; cf. Daniélou (*Origène*, 125–6, 130–1), who speaks of Irenaeus' influence in other parts of Origen's writings.

24 See, e.g., Martens, *Origen and Scripture*, 128, 201–5, 217. In short, the one Jesus Christ, the Word, both inspired and interpreted the Scriptures.

25 Et tamen considerandum est, quia angelus haec refertur ad Abraham locutus, et quia in consequentibus evidenter hic angelus Dominus ostenditur. Unde puto quod sicut inter nos homines habitu repertus est ut homo, ita et inter angelos habitu est repertus ut angelus. PG 12.208 83A. Trans. Heine, *Homilies on Genesis and Exodus*, 143–4.

26 In this homily, Origen's predominant method is what we would call typology, something he very occasionally does, whereas in the very next one (*Hom. Gen.* 9), he turned to more characteristic allegorical readings. Origen, however, did not make much of a distinction between the two. He, himself, claimed to have a tripartite reading strategy of literal, moral, and anagogical, mirroring the body, soul, and spirit, based upon a reading of Prov.

22:20–1 (*Princ.* 4.2.4). In practice, however, he only occasionally proceeded in this threefold manner, mostly dividing things between their literal and spiritual senses, absorbing the moral and typological senses into a broader spiritual or "anagogical" sense, which "lifts the soul up." See Heine (*Commentary on John 1–10*, 11–2, 14–15), who notes that, contrary to one's expectations, Origen will often expound at great length on the historical or literal meaning, with few considerations of the spiritual meaning, in his *Commentary on John*, often resorting to the spiritual or allegorical mode when hermeneutical problems cannot be adequately resolved at the literal level. For a balanced literal and anagogical reading, see, e.g., *Comm. John* 13.101, 173–5. In fact, he will criticize Heracleon for failing to fully understand the literal sense of a passage (*Comm. John* 10.261); Cf. Daniélou, *Origène*, 164. For a thorough and somewhat distancing analysis of Origen's method of reading, see Hanson, *Allegory and Event*, especially 235–58. See especially Torjesen, *Hermeneutical Procedure*, 39–43, 135, 144. For a more contemporary analysis of Origen's hermeneutical methods, using his readings of the Song of Songs as a test case, see King, *Song of Songs as the Spirit of Scripture*, esp. 38–76. More generally, see Clark, *Reading Renunciation*, 70–103, 170–4. She, moreover, identifies up to eleven methods of ancient Christian reading strategies in *Reading Renunciation*, 104–52.

27 Cf. *Gos. Phil.* 57, 28–58,10.

28 Habet nomina mansionum mystic is aptata vocabulis, habet et deducentem se non Moysen, et ipse cuim quo iret ignorabat; sed columnam ignis et nubem; Filium scilicet Dei, et Spiritum sanctum. PG 12.785–786 377A. For a discussion of the journey of the soul in Origen's exegesis, see Torjesen, *Hermeneutical Procedure*, 70–107.

29 ἔστιν οὖν υἱὸς τοῦ δόντος τὸν νόμον καὶ τοὺς προφήτας θεοῦ ὁ Ἰησοῦς· For law given by angels, see *Comm. Song* 2.8; *Comm. John* 13.329, though here the focus is on divine and angelic cooperation; see also Torjesen, *Hermeneutical Procedure*, 108–9. I have relied upon PG Migne for the Latin translation of the *Commentary and Homilies on the Song of Songs*. I have consulted and used the English translation by Lawson, *Song of Songs*. This passage shows up on p. 148.

30 In a passage defending the Bible from Celsus' critique of its anthropopathisms, Origen mentions this in passing, "οὕτως ἔοικεν ὁ τοῦ θεοῦ λόγος ᾠκονομηκέναι τὰ ἀναγεγραμμένα." This might also be related to the lingering influence of Marcionite Christians, while also, in the process, diluting the significance of the new revelation; see the remarks by Hanson, *Allegory and Event*, 204–5.

31 Interpreting 2 Cor. 3:15–17, referring to the veil over the hearts when Moses is read, Origen writes, "But if we turn to the Lord, where also the Word of God is, and where the Holy Spirit reveals spiritual knowledge, the veil will be taken away, and we shall then with unveiled face behold in the holy scriptures the glory of the Lord" (*Princ.* 1.1.2); see Torjesen, *Hermeneutical Procedure*, 120. See also the discussion by Miller, "Pleasure of the Text, Text of Pleasure."

32 For other discussions of Old Testament theophanies not analyzed here, see *Comm. Matt.* 12.43, 25.32; *Frag. Gen.* 12.128; *Hom. 2 Sam.* 1.5; *Hom. Jer.* 9.1.

33 See further his *Hom. Gen.* 1.13; *Comm. John* 1.103–4. For a classic and extensive discussion of the theology of the "image" in Origen's writings, see Crouzel, *Théologie de l'image*; Daniélou, *Origène*, 290.

34 As noted in the discussion of Tertullian, for Tertullian, the Son is *essentially* invisible, but can become visible. That is, the Son is not necessarily visible; he just sometimes is. See Chapter 8.

35 See Hanson, *Allegory and Event*, 139.

36 On the journey of the soul, vision, and divine knowledge in *On First Principles*, see Torjesen, *Hermeneutical Procedure*, 70–84.

37 See Origen's extensive discussion of humans as being made according to the image (that is, Christ) in his *Hom. Gen.* 1.13.

38 For *On First Principles*, I have relied upon the text edited by Gorgemanns and Karpp, *Origenes: Vier Bücher von den Prinzipien*. I have consulted and largely relied upon the translation by Butterworth, *On First Principles*.

39 For a longer discussion of the Son being the invisible image of the invisible God, see Crouzel, *L'image de Dieu*, 75–83.

40 Butterworth, trans., *On First Principles*, 440n4.

41 Quicquid ergo proprium corporum est, hoc nec de patre nec de filio sentiendum est; quod vero ad naturam pertinent deitatis, hoc inter patrem et filium constat. Denique etiam ipse in evangelio non dixit quia "nemo vidi patrem nisi filius neque filium nisi pater," sed aid: "Nemo novit filium nisi pater, neque patrem quis novit nisi filius."

42 Frequenter namque sensibilium membrorum nomina ad animam referuntur ita, ut "oculus cordis" videre dicatur, id est virtute intellegentiae aliquid intellectuale conicere. Sic et audire auribus dicitur, cum sensum intellegentiae profundioris advertit. Sic et uti eam posse dentibus dicimus, cum mandit et comedit panem vitae, qui de caelo descendit. Similiter et ceteris uti membrorum officiis dicitur, quae ex corporali appellatione translata virtutibus animae coaptantur.

43 He discusses this directly in the *Comm. Song* Prologue.2, but his uses of the

"spiritual senses" extend throughout the *Commentary* and *Homilies*; Cox ("Origen and the Bestial Soul," 115–40) notes how this analogizing of the senses and spirituality endows nature with spiritual significance.

44 Hoc ergo sensu divino non oculorum, sed "cordis mundi," quae est mens, deus videri ab his, qui digni sunt, potest. Cor sane pro mente, id est pro intellectuali virtute nominari in omnibus scripturis novis ac veteribus abundanter invenies.

45 This status likely has some relation to becoming equal to the angels (Luke 20:36), but I have not found as strong a correlation as, for example, Clement has; see, however, Origen's *Comm. John* 2.140.

46 On role and terminology of contemplation in Origen's writings, see McGinn, *Foundations*, 128.

47 Or, as Crouzel states, the Son is the "intermediary image" (*L'image de Dieu*, 122–7). Moreover, Crouzel further argues (*L'image de Dieu*, 129–42, 147–79) that this participation in the Son's knowledge/vision works because the human heart – including the incarnate Jesus' human heart – is the image of the image of God, which is identified as the Son, since God created humans or the human heart according to the image of God. Therefore, the Son is the image, and God creates humans according to that image. Origen further distinguishes between the "image" and the "likeness"; see Crouzel, *L'image de Dieu*, 217–45.

48 For the language of participation in the image of God versus the image of the devil, see Crouzel, *L'image de Dieu*, 181–215.

49 A point brought up by Cox, "Origen and the Bestial Soul," 120.

50 ἔθετο σκότος ἀποκρυφὴν <αὐτοῦ> ὁ θεός.

51 Μὴ φέρουσι τὰς τῆς γνώσεως αὐτοῦ μαρμαρυγὰς μηδὲ δυναμένοις αὐτὸν ὁρᾶν.

52 τὸ βάθος ... τῶν περὶ θεοῦ δογμάτων.

53 πνεῦμα τὸ πάντ' ἐρευνῶν, ἐρευνῶν δὲ καὶ τὰ βάθη τοῦ θεοῦ.

54 τοῖς ἐλλαμπομενοις τὸ ἡγεμονικὸν ὑπ' τοῦ λόγου καὶ θεοῦ.

55 Οὗ μετοχῇ, περιαιροῦντος ἀπὸ τοῦ πατρὸς τὸ λεγόμενον "σκότος," ὃ "ἔθετο ἀποκρυφὴν αὐτοῦ," καὶ τὸ λεγόμενον "περιβόλαιον" αὐτοῦ, "τὴν ἄβυσσον," καὶ ἀποκαλύπτοντος οὕτω τὸν πατέρα, ὅστις ποτ' ἂν χωρῇ γινώσκειν αὐτὸν γινώσκει. Cf. *Ag. Cels.* 2.55, where Origen responds to Celsus' arguments that he had purportedly derived from a Jewish informer against Christianity. This Jewish opponent oddly cites extensive miracle stories from Greek sources in order to show that the Jesus stories are not unique. In order to respond to an allegedly "Jewish" argument, Origen responds by reference to Moses, a Jewish authority. By doing so, Origen charges the "Jewish" source with disbelief in Moses. Origen argues that this "Jewish" argument

would be more plausible for an Egyptian, who does not believe the miracles of Moses, to quote the instance of Rhampsinitus; for he would say that the story that he descended to Hades and played dice with Demeter and carried off a golden napkin from her, showing it as a sign for what had happened in Hades, and that he had returned from there, was far more convincing than that of Moses when he writes that he entered "the darkness where God was," and that he alone drew nearer to God than the rest. For he wrote as follows: "And Moses alone shall come near unto God, but the others shall not come near." Accordingly, we who are disciples of Jesus will say to the Jew when he says this: Defend yourself now, you who attack us for our faith in Jesus, and say what you would reply to the Egyptian and the Greeks if the charges which you have brought against our Jesus had first been brought against Moses. And even if you strive energetically to defend Moses, seeing that the narratives about him are also capable of a striking and clear vindication, in your defense of Moses you will in spite of yourself establish that Jesus is more divine than Moses.

In this polemic, the descent of Demeter to Hades mirrors Moses' ascent to Mt Sinai. By using Moses, Origen turns the "Jewish" opponent's argument on its head, since his arguments against Jesus' miracles could just as easily have been launched against Moses. Although there is no discussion of darkness representing God's incorporeality or invisibility, the episode demonstrates that Moses drew closer to God "than the rest," a division between Moses and the masses found in both Philo and Clement. This is followed with the quotation from Exod. 24:2, which states that only Moses may come near to God and others may not draw near. Interestingly, though, if this Jewish source seeks to vindicate Moses against such Greek and Egyptian oppositions, he will thereby, with such arguments, not only vindicate the miraculous stories surrounding Jesus' life, but also demonstrate Jesus' superiority to Moses. Therefore, although Moses alone was allowed to enter the thick darkness and draw near to God, Jesus remains superior to him, since "no one knows the father except for the Son" (Matt. 11:27; *Comm. Eph.* 1:3). This is because, when Moses sought to see God (Exod. 33:22), Moses has to stand on a rock near God and see only God's backside. Origen interprets elsewhere the rock by which Moses could see the hindparts of God to be Christ (see *Hom. Jer.* 8:9; *Hom. Ps.* 36.4.1). See Heine, "God," 112.

56 ἀλλ' εἰς γνῶσίν γε θεοῦ σώματος οὐδαμῶς χρήζομεν. Τὸ γὰρ γινῶσκον θεὸν οὐκ ὀφθαλμός ἐστι σώματος, ἀλλὰ νοῦς, ὁρῶν τὸ κατ' εἰκόνα τοῦ κτίσαντος καὶ τὸ δυνάμενον γινώσκειν θεὸν προνοίᾳ θεοῦ ἀνειληφώς. Καὶ τὸ ὁρῶν δὲ θεὸν καθαρά ἐστι καρδία, ἀφ' ἧς οὐκέτι ἐξέρχονται διαλογισμοὶ πονηροί, οὐ

φόνοι, οὐ μοιχεῖα, οὐ πορνεῖα, οὐ κλοπαί, οὐ ψευδομαρτυρίαι, οὐ βλασφημίαι, οὐκ ὀφθαλμὸς πονηρὸς οὐδ᾿ ἄλλο τι τῶν ἀτόπων·δι᾿ ἃ λέγεται· "μακάριοι οἱ καθαροὶ τῇ καρδίᾳ, ὅτι αὐτοὶ τὸν θεὸν ὄψονται." ἐπεὶ δ᾿ οὐκ αὐτάρκης ἡ ἡμετέρα προαίρεσις πρὸς τὸ πάντῃ καταρὰν ἔχειν τὴν καρδίαν, ἀλλὰ θεοῦ ἡμῖν δεῖ, κτίζοντος αὐτὴν τοιαύτην, διὰ τοῦτο λέγεται ὑπὸ τοῦ ἐπιστημόνως εὐχομένου· "καρδιάν καθαρὰν κτίσον ἐν ἐμοί, ὁ θεός."

57 On nature as scriptural text, see Cox, "Origen and the Bestial Soul," 119–20.

58 He further connects this pure heart with "building the tabernacle," which he doubly interprets as the cosmos and as the body (*Hom. Exod.* 9.3–4). On the combination of human and divine action for vision, see Crouzel, *L'image de Dieu*, 239–44. Daniélou (*Origène*, 72–3) also notes how such visionary language relates to the sacraments, especially baptism (see Origen's *Comm. Matt.* 25.23; *Comm. Luke* 24).

59 videbunt ipso sine dubio revelante. PG 13, 177D.

60 PG 13, 177C–178A.

61 PG 13, 189C–191B.

62 PG 13, 58B–D.

63 See also Origen's comparison of Moses' glory and Jesus' glory with other references to glory in the Bible in *Comm. John* 32.331–44, where he again connects Moses' mind with the purity needed to have an intimate knowledge/vision of God; cf. *Comm. John* 13.47; also see Hanson, *Allegory and Event*, 210–11, 219.

64 Εἰ δὲ καὶ σῶμα θνητὸν καὶ ψυχὴν ἀνθρωπίνην ἀναλαβὼν ὁ ἀθάνατος θεὸς λόγος δοκεῖ τῷ Κέλσῳ ἀλλάττεσθαι καὶ μεταπλάττεσθαι, μανθανέτω ὅτι ὁ λόγος τῇ οὐσίᾳ μένων λόγος οὐδὲν μὲν πάσχει ὧν πάσχει τὸ σῶμα ἢ ἡ ψυχή, συγκαταβαίνων δ᾿ ἔσθ᾿ ὅτε τῷ μὴ δυναμένῳ αὐτοῦ τὰς μαρμαρυγὰς καὶ τὴν λαμπρότητα τῆς θειότητας βλέπειν οἱονεὶ σὰρξ γίνεται, σωματικῶς λαλούμενος, ἕως ὁ τοιοῦτον αὐτὸν παραδεξάμενος κατὰ βραχὺ ὑπὸ τοῦ λόγου μετεωριζόμενος δυνηθῇ αὐτοῦ καὶ τήν, ἵν᾿ οὕτως ὀνομάσω, προηγουμένην μορφὴν θεάσασθαι.

65 Cf. Torjesen, *Hermeneutical Procedure*, 84.

66 See ibid., 85; Origen discusses Moses' divinization in terms of his glorious face; or, his glorious face indicated his divinized mind; see *Comm. John* 32.339.

67 Torjesen, *Hermeneutical Procedure*, 122–3.

68 Cf. *Hom. Exod.* 3.2, where he juxtaposes – but does not fully discuss – Moses on Sinai and the Mount of Transfiguration.

69 PG 13, 45B–C.

70 See Martens, *Origen and Scripture*, 229–30, and especially 234–42, who grounds this eschatological vision in the activity of scriptural interpretation.

In other words, exegesis was the means by which to glimpse God's backside in this life and prepare one to see/contemplate God in the next. Scripture is a curriculum of divine vision.

71 Hoc ergo modo etiam Moyses deum vidisse putandus est, non oculis eum carnalibus intuens, sed visu cordis ac sensu mentis intellegens, et hoc ex parte aliqua. Manifestum est enim quia "Faciem" inquit "meum non vidibis" (is scilicet, qui Moysi response praebebat), "sed posterior mea." Quae utique cum eo sunt intellegenda sacramento, quo intellegi convenit dicta divina, abiectis profecto illis et spretis anilibus fabulis, quae de anterioribus dei ab imperitis posterioribusque finguntur.

72 Elsewhere he identifies the rock and the hindparts as Christ or, at the very least, prophecies about the last times; see *Hom. Jer.* 8:9; *Hom. Ps.* 36.4.1. See Heine, "God," 112; Runia, *Philo in Early Christian Literature*, 170.

73 Cf. the differentiation between "Levites" and "priests" in his *Hom. Lev.*; discussion by McGuckin, "Origen's Doctrine of the Priesthood."

74 PG 13, 73A–74C, 75D.

75 PG 13, 122A–B.

76 Though see Miller ("Pleasure of the Text," 244), who argues that Origen's concept of contemplation is more active.

77 Cf. Origen's extensive interpretation of Abraham's vision at Mambre in *Hom. Gen.* 4, where, again, he connects it to Abraham's pure heart.

78 *Hom. Song* 2.7 acknowledges the presence of catechumens. Curious Jews, rival Christians, and polytheists may also have been present for the homilies; only baptized Christians would be able to remain for the celebration of the Eucharist. For a brief discussion of the audience of the homilies, especially on the Song of Songs, see Deutsch, "Interpreter as Intertext," 224.

79 Ἀλλὰ προσίτω μὲν πεπαιδευμένος καὶ σοφὸς καὶ φρόνιμος ὁ βουλόμενος· οὐδὲν δ᾽ ἧττον προσίτω καὶ εἴ τις ἀμαθὴς καὶ ἀνόητος καὶ ἀπαίδευτος καὶ νήπιος. Καὶ γὰρ τοὺς τοιούτους προσελθόντας ἐπαγγέλλεται θεραπεύειν ὁ λόγος, πάντας ἀξίους κατασκευάζων τοῦ θεοῦ.

80 PG 13, 45B–C. King (*Origen on the Song of Songs*, 16–18) notes that this experience is bound up inextricably in the process of biblical interpretation itself, writing, "True, Origen is describing an experience of textual interpretation here. Yet, it is only an impoverished attitude towards texts and their reading that would construe the hermeneutical process as necessarily counter- or sub-affective." Deutsch ("Interpreter as Intertext," 223) also notes:
     In the First Homily on the Canticle of Canticles, Origen uses his own experience as an intertext with the biblical text, and invites his hearers/readers to enter that process. That is, at various places, where the Bride speaks in the first person singular, Origen writes himself into the text of the Song of

Songs, appropriating the Bride's voice as his own and making autobiographical statements about his experience of the presence and absence,
approach and withdrawal of Christ the Bridegroom. Origen thus uses personal experience as a narrative to illuminate the biblical text, but that usage
also shows ways in which the text illuminates Origen's experience.
See also Torjesen, *Hermeneutical Procedure*, 108–47.

81 For a discussion of all three, see Deutsch, "Interpreter as Intertext," 221–54.

82 A point she also grants on the final page of her essay: Deutsch, "Interpreter
as Intertext," 254.

83 See, e.g., *Hom. Song* 1.1; Torjesen, *Hermeneutical Procedure*, 87.

84 See *Comm. Song* 1.1.11; Deutsch, "Interpreter as Intertext," 228.

85 Deutsch, "Interpreter as Intertext," 241; see also 249.

86 Deutsch ("Interpreter as Intertext," 249–54) also suggests that his interpretation served to create a communal boundary between his group and rival
Christians, such as Valentinians, and rival Jewish interpretations of the
Song. The latter is well established, but the former, while certainly a possibility, is less sure for Caesarea than it was for Alexandria, where Origen previously lived.

87 Crouzel (*L'image de Dieu*, 44) compares this to Plotinus' vision of the One;
see further Dodds, *Pagan and Christian*, 97–8.

88 Deutsch, "Interpreter as Intertext," 248–9.

89 See discussion by Deutsch, "Interpreter as Intertext," 234–9.

90 Ita mens nostra cum intra carnis et sanguinis claustra concluditur et pro
talis materiae participation hebetior atque obtunsior redditur, licet ad com-
parationem naturae corporeae longe praecellens habeatur, tamen cum ad
incorporea nititur atque eorum rimatur intuitum, tunc scintillae alicuius
aut lucernae vix obtinet locum. Quid autem in omnibus intellectualibus, id
est incorporeis, tam praestans omnibus, tam ineffabiliter atque
inaestimabiliter praecellens quam deus? Cuius utuque natura acie humanae
mentis intendi atque intueri, quamvis ea sit purissima mens ac
limpidissima, non potest.

91 Οἱ γὰρ φίλοι ἐν εἴδει καὶ οὐ δι' αἰνιγμάτων μανθάνουσιν ἢ γυμνῇ σοφίᾳ
φωνῶν καὶ λέξεων καὶ συμβόλων καὶ τύπων, προσβάλλοντες τῇ τῶν νοητῶν
φύσει καὶ τῷ τῆς ἀληθείας κάλλει. Greek text provided by von Stritzky,
Origenes: Aufforderung zum Martyrium.

92 Cf. the excerpt of a letter from Phileas to Thmutis, quoted by Eusebius of
Caesarea (*Hist. Ch.* 8.10), concerning martyrs in Alexandria, "The blessed
martyrs among us did not hesitate, but directing the eye of the soul with all
earnestness towards the Almighty, and resolved to die for their faith, they
clung firmly to their vocation." (Trans. Williamson).

93 See, e.g., Augustine, *Literal Genesis* 12.

94 ἀκολούθως εἴσεσθε ὅτι τῶν τότε Παύλῳ ἀποκαλυφθέντων ῥημάτων ἀρρήτων, μεθ' ἃ καταβέβηκεν ἀπὸ τοῦ τρίτου οὐρανοῦ ... ἔστι γὰρ ἐν τῷ θεῷ ἐναποτεθησαυρισμένα πολλῷ μείζονα τούτων θεάματα, ἅτινα οὐδεμία φύσις τῶν ἐν σώματι μὴ πρότερον ἀπολλαγεῖσα παντὸς σώματος χωρπῆσαι δύναται. Πέπεισμαι γὰρ ὅτι ὧν εἶδεν ἥλιος καὶ σελήνη καὶ ὁ τῶν ἀστέρων χορὸς ἀλλὰ καὶ ἀγγέλων ἁγίων, οὓς ἐποίησεν ὁ θεὸς πνεῦμα καὶ πυρὸς φλόγα.

95 Crouzel, *L'image de Dieu*, 147.

96 PG 13, 106D.

97 On Origen's authority as a teacher, independent of church structure, see Runia, *Philo in Early Christian Literature*, 157; Lyman, *Christology and Cosmology*, 40–1.

98 McGuckin, "Origen's Doctrine of Priesthood," 277–86.

99 Hanson, *Allegory and Event*, 183–6.

100 Torjesen, *Hermeneutical Procedure*, 60–2.

101 Cf. *Philocalia* 18.19; Hanson, *Allegory and Event*, 213.

102 Daniélou, *Origène*, 72–4.

103 Torjesen, *Hermeneutical Procedure*, 59–62.

104 Hanson, *Allegory and Event*, 186.

105 Ibid., 214.

CHAPTER TEN

1 For a realpolitik examination of Constantine's interactions with various Christian bishops, see Drake, *Constantine and the Bishops*. For a classic discussion see Jones, *Constantine and the Conversion of Europe*. For a general discussion of the state and society from Diocletian to Constantine, see Treadgold, *Byzantine State and Society*, 13–51. What most of these sources share is the idea that Constantine, building upon Diocletian, refounded the Roman Empire.

2 Rapp, *Holy Bishops in Late Antiquity*, 23–152. See also her review of scholarship that notes the combination of political and spiritual forms of authority, especially the merging of the figure of the bishop and the holy man (13–16, 250). Drake (*Constantine and the Bishops*, 103–9) argues that it was the pragmatic authority, especially the ability to organize one's own community in communication with other communities criss-crossing the Mediterranean, that turned Christianity, and especially Christian bishops, into political players in the late-antique empire, but he also notes (104), in a more Weberian fashion, how spiritual – which he identifies with charismatic – authority and more pragmatic authority can be at odds. For him, the Spirit or spiritual

authority is anarchy, the centrifugal force of Christianity; the bishop is order, the centripetal force that counteracts the Spirit. See, for example, his line, "Ignatius, Cyprian, and others were equally steadfast in their support of the primacy of the bishop, paradoxically asserting the role of the Spirit to do so" (108). It is only a paradox if one thinks the bishop and the Spirit are at odds. Nonetheless, Rapp's and Kalleres' books show this to be a false dichotomy, how the episcopacy tied together different forms of authority, including institutional and spiritual authorities. The truth, however, may lie somewhere between these two positions.

3 Kalleres, *City of Demons*.

4 Sterk, *Renouncing the World* and "On Basil, Moses, and the Model Bishop"; she is followed by Rapp (*Holy Bishops in Late Antiquity*, 20, 125–52), who, moreover, argues that Moses fit the tripartite scheme of spiritual, ascetic, and pragmatic authority – or was perceived to do so by bishops in late antiquity.

5 A point made by Rapp, *Holy Bishops in Late Antiquity*, 125, 131. She notes that, among Latin authors, the predominant identification was with Aaron (131–2).

6 This is especially the case in Eusebius of Caesarea's writings. Relying upon Matt. 11:27, as Origen had done, he noted, as Justin did, that every theophany in the Old Testament was Christ (*Hist. Ch.* 1.2; cf. 1.4), stating that Moses and Abraham before him, "recognized Him in vision seen with the pure eyes of the mind, and paid due honor to him as God's Son." Trans. Williamson, *Eusebius: The History of the Church*, 4. One can discern Origen's emphasis of seeing with the mind's eye rather than physically; nonetheless, Eusebius usually reverts to earlier reading strategies leading back to Justin. Eusebius, much like Justin had, works through the stories of Sodom and Gomorrah and Jacob, Joshua, and Moses, additionally identifying Christ with Wisdom in Proverbs. Moreover, he argues, much like Clement of Alexandria did, that the preincarnate Logos had a pedagogical function. In a break from previous tradition, however, Eusebius emphasizes that Christ could appear only in human form, whereas Justin and others following him often associated Christ with non-anthropomorphic theophanies, such as fire and cloud. For a discussion of Eusebius as "old-fashioned" in his own context, see Lyman, *Christology and Cosmology*, 82–90. See also the note by Runia, *Philo in Early Christian Literature*, 224–5.

7 As Drake (*Constantine and the Bishops*, 11) notes, Constantine diverted massive amounts of state resources into the hands of the bishops, and gave them unprecedented legal and juridical privileges.

8 See the translation and introduction by Rubenstein, *Rabbinic Stories*,

215–17. For a discussion of R. Akiva's martyrdom in other rabbinic passages, see Boyarin, *Dying for God*, 94–126.

9 Rubenstein, *Talmudic Stories*, 271, and *Culture of the Babylonian Talmud*, 19.

10 Halperin, *Merkabah in Rabbinic Literature*, 118, 128–40; Halperin, *Faces of the Chariot*, 16–19; Deutsch, *Hidden Wisdom*, 94–6; see further Wolfson, *Speculum*, 326–92; Schäfer, *Origins of Jewish Mysticism*, 186–94. See the earlier foundational article by Urbach, "Traditions about Merkabah Mysticism."

11 See Fiensky, *Prayers Alleged to be Jewish*, 19–27, and "Redaction History and the Apostolic Constitutions"; Metzger, *Constitutions Apostoliques*, 14–33, 55–60; Mueller, *L'Ancien Testament dans l'ecclésiologie des pères*, 36–57, 86–92. Mueller (117–26) argues that this Syrian church order is also anti-imperial, especially against the Niceno-Constantinopolitan formulation.

12 While such a bridge may seem strange given the likely Arian or semi-Arian tendencies of the *Apostolic Constitutions*, the relationship between Moses' visions and episcopal authority in the document shows that this is not just a preoccupation of the defenders of Nicea, but a broader concern of the fourth-century episcopate. On the alleged Arian theology of the *Constitutions*, see Fiensky, *Prayers Alleged to Be Jewish*, 26; Metzger, *Constitutions apostolique*, vol. 1, 59. See the fuller discussion in Mueller, *L'Ancien Testament dans l'ecclésiologie des pères*, 86–110.

13 Give or take a decade; see Holmes, *Apostolic Fathers*, 35–6.

14 As Fiensky notes (*Prayers Alleged to be Jewish*, 20, 165), sometimes the compiler is an editor, but sometimes an author. See also Metzger, *Constitutions apostoliques*, vol. 1, 18–19, 30–3. *1 Clem.* 43.1–6 also relates the authority of the bishop to Moses' prophetic abilities, and even paraphrases Num. 12:7 and Heb. 3:5, that Moses was faithful in all God's house, but emphasizes the episode of Aaron's blossoming rod (Numbers 17) rather than Moses' visions to justify priestly authority, both Israelite and emergent Christian.

15 A history of the interpretation of Exod. 7:1 would be a rich area of research. The biblical text in both Hebrew and Greek is very direct: "I will make you God to Pharaoh." Often modern translations will add "as" or "like" to lessen the directness of the biblical text. The Aramaic *targumim*, however, downgrade this to "ruler" or "Lord" (*Neofiti*) or actually do add the "as" or "like" (*Pseudo-Jonathan*). Cf. *Exod. Rab.* 8.2. Although, as Chapter 1 illustrates, Philo and perhaps Ezekiel the Tragedian's *Exagoge* exalt Moses to godlike status, when Philo turns directly to this verse, he allegorizes it to mean that godlike intellect (Moses) should govern speech (Aaron) or speaks of the relationship between sophistry and true reason (*Alleg. Interp.* 1.13.40; *Sacrifices* 1.9; *Worse* 12.38; *Migration* 15.82–5; *Names* 22.125–9; *Dreams* 28.188–9). The Rabbis were clearly troubled by this passage, whether concerned about

Moses' speech abilities or about the designation of God, often downgrading Moses to "judge" or "angel" (*Mek.*, *Pisha*, 1.11; *Mek. R. Shim. b. Yoh.* Sanya II:V 1.A. *Num. Rab.* 14.6 clarifies that Moses shall be god to Pharaoh alone and no other, and will only maintain this status if he keeps the God of Israel above himself (cf. *Ruth Rab.* Proem 1). Later on, Exod. 7:1 is given as proof that God gives a portion of God's glory to those who fear him (*Num. Rab.* 15.13). *Lev. Rab.* 26.7 identifies the *elohim* of 2 Samuel 28 – when Saul has a medium call up Samuel from the dead – with Moses. See further *Exod. Rab.* 8.1; *Deut. Rab.* 2.2; *Mek. R. Shim. b. Yoh.* III.I E.

16 Οὗτος ἄρχων καὶ ἡγούμενος ὑμῶν, οὗτος ὑμῶν βασιλεὺς καὶ δυνάστης· οὗτος ὑμῶν ἐπίγειος θεὸς μετὰ θεόν, ὃς ὀφείλει τῆς παρ᾽ ὑμῶν τιμῆς ἀπολαύειν. Following the reading by Metzger, *Constitutions apostoliques*, vol. 1, 238. Cf. PG 1, 668A.

17 Rapp (*Holy Bishops in Late Antiquity*, 31–2, 73–99). She, however, omits to discuss the designation of "God" in this passage, focusing on the bishop as a father-figure.

18 Drake, *Constantine and the Bishops*, 384; Geljon (*Philonic Exegesis*, 15–16, 75) suggests that Eusebius might have picked up this relationship from Philo's *Life of Moses* as does Runia, *Philo in Early Christian Literature*, 222. See even earlier Chesnut, *First Christian Histories*, 154–5.

19 This reflects the work's theological subordinationism. See Mueller, *L'Ancien Testament dans l'ecclésiologie des pères*, 92–101, 465–8. Mueller also notes the extensive parallels between ecclesiastical hierarchy of church offices and the theological hierarchy of the Trinity (e.g., 554–5).

20 Εἰ γὰρ Ἀαρών, ἐπειδὴ ἤγγελλεν τῷ Φαραὼ παρὰ Μωϋσέως τοὺς λόγους, προφήτης εἴρηται, Μωϋσῆς δὲ θεὸς τοῦ Φαραώ, ὡς βασιλεὺς [ὁμου] καὶ ἀρχιερεύς, ὥς φησιν ὁ Θεὸς πρὸς αὐτόν· "Θεὸν τέθεικά σε τῷ Φαραώ, καὶ Ἀαρὼν ὁ ἀδελφός σου ἔσται σου προφήτης·" διατί μὴ καὶ ὑμεῖς τοὺς μεσίτης ὑμῶν τοῦ λόγου, προφήτας εἶναι νομίσητε, καὶ ὡς θεοὺς σαβασθήσεσθε;

Νῦν γὰρ ὑμῖν μὲν ἐστιν Ἀαρὼν ὁ διάκονος, Μωϋσῆς δὲ ὁ ἐπίσκοπος· εἰ οὖν ἐρρέθη Μωϋσῆς ὑπὸ κυρίου θεός, καὶ ὑμῖν ὁ ἐπίσκοπος εἰς θεὸν τετιμήσθω, καὶ ὁ διάκονος ὡς προφήτης αὐτοῦ. Ὡς γὰρ ὁ Χριστὸς ἄνευ τοῦ Πατρὸς οὐδὲν ποιεῖ, οὕτως οὐδὲ ὁ διάκονος ἄνευ τοῦ ἐπισκόπου· καὶ ὥσπερ Υἱὸς ἄνευ τοῦ Πατρὸς οὐκ ἔστιν, οὕτως οὐδὲ διάκονος ἄνευ τοῦ ἐπισκόπου· καὶ ὥσπερ ὑπόχρεως Υἱὸς Πατρί, οὕτω καὶ πᾶς διάκονος ἐπισκόπῳ· καὶ ὥσπερ ὁ Υἱὸς ἄγγελός ἐστι καὶ προφήτης τοῦ Πατρός, οὕτως καὶ ὁ διάκονος ἄγγελος καὶ προφήτης ἐστὶ τοῦ ἐπισκόπου. Following Metzger, *Constitutions apostoliques*, vol. 1, 248. See his textual notes on the same page. Cf. PG 1, 676C–677B.

21 Interestingly, Rapp (*Holy Bishops in Late Antiquity*, 131) uses this passage to explain the equation of Moses with the emperor Constantine.

22 ἐκεῖνο δὲ κοινῇ πάντες παραγγέλλομεν, ἕκαστον ἐμμένειν τάξει τῇ δοθείσῃ
αὐτῷ, καὶ μὴ ὑπερβαίνειν τοὺς ὅρους· οὐ γάρ εἰσιν ἡμέτεροι, ἀλλὰ τοῦ Θεοῦ
... Λέγομεν ὡς Μωσῆς, ὁ τοῦ Θεοῦ θεράπων, ᾧ ὁ Θεὸς ἐνώπιος ἐνωπίῳ
ὡμίλει, ὡς εἴ τις λαλήσῃ πρὸς ἑαυτοῦ φίλον, ᾧ εἶπεν· "Οἶδά σε παρὰ πάντας·"
ᾧ κατὰ πρόσωπον ὡμίλει καὶ οὐ δι' ἀδήλων, ἢ ἐνυπνίων, ἢ ἀγγέλων, ἢ
αἰνιγμάτων· οὗτος ἡνίκα τὴν θείαν νομοθεσίαν διετάσσετο διεῖλε τίνα μὲν χρὴ
ὑπὸ τῶν ἀρχιερέων ἐπιτελεῖσθαι, τίνα δὲ ὑπὸ τῶν ἱερῶν, τίνα δὲ ὑπὸ τῶν
λευιτῶν, ἑκάστῳ τὴν οἰκείαν καὶ ἀνήκουσαν τῇ λειτουργίᾳ θρησκείαν
ἀπονείμας, καὶ ἅπερ μὲν τοῖς ἀρχιερεῦσι προστέτακτο ἐπιτελεῖν, τούτοις τοὺς
ἱερέας οὐ θεμιτὸν ἦν προσιέναι· ἅπερ δὲ τοῖς ἱερεῦσιν ὥριπτο, τούτοις οἱ
λευῖται οὐ προσίεσαν· ἀλλ' ἕκαστοι ἅπερ παρειλήφεισαν ὑπερεσίας
περιγεγραμμένας, ἐφύλαττον· εἰ δέ τις πέρα τῆς παραδόσεως προσιέναι
ἐβούλετο, θάνατος ἦν τὸ ἐπιτίμιον ... Ὑπὸ Μωσέως μὲν γὰρ τοῦ
θεοφιλεστάτου ἀρχιερεῖς κατεστάθησαν, καὶ ἱερεῖς, καὶ λευῖται, ὑπὸ δὲ τοῦ
Σωτῆρος ἡμῶν ἡμεῖς, οἱ δεκατρεῖς ἀπόστολοι· ὑπὸ δὲ τῶν ἐγὼ Ἰάκωβος· καὶ
ἐγὼ Κλήμης, καὶ σὺν ἡμῖν ἕτεροι· ἵνα μὴ πάντας πάλιν καταλέγωμεν. PG 1,
1149C, 1152B–C, 1153B.

23 For a discussion of this section of the *Apostolic Constitutions*, see Mueller,
L'Ancien Testament dans l'ecclésiologie des pères, 294–8.

24 Mueller (*L'Ancien Testament dans l'ecclésiologie des pères*, 470) also notes the role
of Samuel as foundational for the *Apostolic Constitutions*, alongside Moses.

25 Cf. *Apost. Const.* 2.27.1–6. For a parallel exegetic manoeuvre throughout the
Apostolic Constitutions to use of the tabernacle revealed to Moses to justify
ecclesiastical hierarchy, see Mueller, *L'Ancien Testament dans l'ecclésiologie des
pères*, 185–7, 227–33, 291–8.

26 As Mueller (*L'Ancien Testament dans l'ecclésiologie des pères*, 110) writes, "Une
chose est claire. Les CA suivent la tendance de l'ecclésiologie de leur siècle
en faisant remonter cette tradition des institutions ecclésiale jusqu'à l'Ancien Testament." He proceeds to note that this procedure resembles those of
both Basil of Caesarea and John Chrysostom. See also 256, 411–77, 492.
Also see Metzger, *Constitutions apostolique*, vol. 1, 45–6.

27 For the anti-Weberian formulation of the church as a "charismatic structure"
in the *Apostolic Constitutions*, especially Book 8, yet a term that will fit the
discussions of most fourth-century Christian leaders, see Mueller, *L'Ancien
Testament dans l'ecclésiologie des pères*, 447–50.

28 Cf. the use of Num. 12:6-8 in *Apost. Const.* 2.32.1–2.

29 For an introduction to Gregory and his thought, see McGuckin, *Saint Gregory of Nazianzus*.

30 For an introduction to Basil and his formation as a bishop, see Rousseau,
Basil of Caesarea.

31 On Origen and Gregory of Nazianzus in particular, see Beeley, *Gregory of Nazianzus*, 271–8.

32 Constantine himself had converted to, or adapted to his own use, some form of Christianity. He seems to have combined, in his own practice, Christianity with the worship of other deities, including Mars, Hercules, and the Unconquered Sun (*Sol Invictus*). See the classic study by Jones, *Constantine and the Conversion of Europe*, esp. 83–9. See the notes on the edict in Drake, *Constantine and the Bishops*, 194.

33 See the succinct account by Jones, *Constantine and the Conversion of Europe*, 129–43.

34 In the end, Constantine himself was baptized by an Arian bishop, Eusebius of Nicomedia; Jones, *Constantine and the Conversion of Europe*, 195–200.

35 Gregory of Nazianzus, Basil of Caesarea, and Gregory of Nyssa, together referred to as the "Cappadocians," championed the Nicene position. There were, however, disagreements among the three, particularly at the Council of Constantinople (381), on the doctrine of the Holy Spirit.

36 Warnings not to lump them together have become commonplace among any scholars who have devoted extensive study to their theology, biography, or social networks. Note, for example, the warnings by John McGuckin not to quickly lump the three together and to respect their many differences (*Saint Gregory of Nazianzus*, xxi–xxii). Rousseau (*Basil of Caesarea*, xviii) largely thinks it a mistake to consider Basil only in relationship to his friend, Gregory of Nazianzus, and younger brother, Gregory of Nyssa, both of whose theology and style often overshadow the influential activity of Basil. See also Beeley, *Gregory of Nazianzus*, viii.

37 See, for example, Turner, *Darkness of God*, 11–49.

38 While Basil would provide the model for future monk-bishops, he was fairly idiosyncratic in his own time; see Philip Rousseau, *Basil of Caesarea*, esp. xiii–xvii. In general, for the importance of both passivity and activity for the bishop, see Rapp, *Holy Bishops in Late Antiquity*, 56–7.

39 In general, see Sterk, *Renouncing the World*, 13–92.

40 This paragraph relies heavily on Sterk, *Renouncing the World*, 62–3; for a discussion of Basil's ascetic writings, see Rousseau, *Basil of Caesarea*, 190–232, 354–9.

41 *Renouncing the World*, 62.

42 See Rousseau, *Basil of Caesarea*, 254–8.

43 Gregory of Nyssa, Basil's younger brother, would also compare Gregory the Wonderworker with Moses in his oration in honour of Gregory the Wonderworker's feast day (Sterk, *Renouncing the World*, 106–8). Gregory of Nyssa writes, "Both Moses and Gregory left the turbulence and bustle of life, each

in his own time living alone until out of the vision of God the benefit of a pure life was made manifest to both … Therefore they both had the same end in view, for the goal of both men in withdrawing from the crowds was to contemplate the divine mysteries with the pure eye of the soul" (*Thaum.*; quoted in Sterk, *Renouncing the World*, 107). The Cappodocians would continue to use Moses as the standard for contemporary bishops. In the next generation, John Chrysostom would continue the trend, comparing Flavian of Antioch with Abraham and especially Moses. He also referred to himself in terms of Moses. Palladius, in turn, would compare John to Moses as well. Likewise, Athanasius and Theophilus of Alexandria referred to themselves as Moses or a new Moses (Sterk, *Renouncing the World*, 153, 156; cf. 203, 223, for some later appropriation of this theme of Moses-as-model-bishop; Rapp, *Holy Bishops in Late Antiquity*, 128–30).

44 For Constantine as a new Moses see Eusebius of Caesarea's *Hist. Ch.* 9.9.4–8 and *Life of Constantine* 1.12, 38; 2.11, 12; 12.14; see Drake, *Constantine and the Bishops*, 376–7, 391; Rapp, *Holy Bishops in Late Antiquity*, 128–9. While Constantine preferred Paul, Eusebius insistently compared him to Moses, who not only ruled, but passed on his rule to the priests.

45 Including Philo's own *Life of Moses*; see Geljon, *Philonic Exegesis*, 49; Runia, *Philo in Early Christian Litearture*, 235–41.

46 Basil relied heavily on Philo's *Creation* for his homilies and, more to the point, his portrayal of Moses within them; see Lim, "Politics of Interpretation," 352. For a broader discussion of Basil's *Hexaemeron*, see Rousseau, *Basil of Caesarea*, 318–49.

47 ὅς, ὀγδοηκοστὸν ἤδη γεγονὼς ἔτος, εἶδε Θεὸν ὡς ἀνθρώπῳ ἰδεῖν δυνατόν, μᾶλλον δὲ ὡς οὐδενὶ τῶν ἄλλων ὑπῆρξε κατὰ τὴν μαρτυρίαν αὐτὴν τοῦ Θεοῦ, ὅτι ἐὰν γένηται προφήτης ὑμῶν τῷ Κυρίῳ, ἐν ὁράματι αὐτῷ γνωσθήσομαι, καὶ ἐν ὕπνῳ λαλήσω αὐτῷ. Οὐκ οὕτως, ὡς ὁ θεράπων Μωϋσῆς, ἐν ὅλῳ τῷ οἴκῳ μου πιστός εστι· στόμα κατὰ στόμα λαλήσω αὐτῷ, ἐν εἴδει, καὶ οὐ δι' αἰνιγμάτων. Οὗτος τοίνυν ὁ τῆς αὐτοπροσώπου θέας τοῦ Θεοῦ ἐξίσου τοῖς ἀγγέλοις ἀξιωθείς, ἐξ ὧν ἤκουσε παρὰ τοῦ Θεοῦ διαλέγεται ἡμῖν. PG 29, 5B–C.

48 This is an old tradition, but I am thinking particularly of *b. Yoma* 4a–b: "Moses went up in the cloud, and was covered by the cloud and was sanctified by the cloud in order that he might receive the Torah for Israel in sanctity … R. Nathan says: the purpose of scripture was that he might be purged of all food and drink in his bowels so as to make him like the ministering angels."

49 *Adol.* 2; PG 31, 568 C; see Sterk, *Renouncing the World*, 63; Rapp, *Holy Bishops*, 132–6. For a lengthier discussion of *To Adolescents*, see Rousseau, *Basil of Caesarea*, 48–57.

50 *On His Brother Basil*; PG 46.788–817.

51 In the same oration, he also compares Basil to Paul, John the Baptist, Elijah, and Samuel, but, moving in reverse chronological order, he culminates the series of *synkriseis* with Moses, the longest comparison in the oration.

52 Nonetheless, as Sterk (*Renouncing the World*, 37–9) notes, the Greek *paideia* of the day, which he would have received in Athens, would have reinforced Basil's proclivities for contemplation and *ascesis*. See the discussion of Basil's education in Rousseau, *Basil of Caesarea*, 27–60.

53 For a more complex account of Basil's retreat, see Rousseau, *Basil of Caesarea*, 61–92.

54 Πολλάκις ἔγνωμεν αὐτὸν καὶ ἐντὸς τοῦ γνόφου γενόμενον, οὗ ἦν ὁ Θεός. Τὸ γὰρ τοῖς ἄλλοις ἀθεώρητον, ἐκείνῳ ληπτὸν ἐποίει ἡ μυσταγωγία τοῦ Πνεύματος, ὡς δοκεῖν ἐντὸς τῆς περιοχῆς εἶναι τοῦ γνόφου, ᾧ ὁ περὶ τοῦ Θεοῦ λόγος ἐναποκρύπτεται. PG 46, 812C. Translation found in Daniélou, *From Glory to Glory*, 28. I have also relied in this paragraph on the analysis by Sterk, *Renouncing the World*, 103–4.

55 *Hom. Hex.*, PG 44, 61A–64B; Sterk, *Renouncing the World*, 98.

56 See discussion in Sterk, *Renouncing the World*, 136–8. Nazianzus makes a contrast, however, between Basil and Moses in *Or.* 43.35; see Rousseau, *Basil of Caesarea*, 137.

57 *Ors.* 9.2, 9.5, 11.2, and 12.2. On Gregory of Nazianzus' doubled use of biblical figures – that is, using the same figure to both praise and perhaps critique someone at the same time – see McGuckin, *Saint Gregory of Nazianzus*, 144; cf. Sterk, *Renouncing the World*, 127. On Gregory of Nazianzus' complicated relationship to Basil's theology, see Beeley, *Gregory of Nazianzus*, 292–303.

58 This three-part pattern culminating in a religious vision would persist into later centuries, as Christian leaders read the works of Basil, Gregory of Nyssa, and Gregory of Nazianzus, such as in Eustratius' *Life of Eutychius*. Eustratius, though, interestingly claims that Eutychius was both a new Basil and a new Moses, indicating how much the Moses model had become attached to the Cappadocian (Sterk, *Renouncing the World*, 215–17).

59 For how late-antique concepts of patronage (*prostasia*) informed Basil's views and practices, see Sterk, *Renouncing the World*, 66–76. Sterk even writes, "One could also say that Basil fused the divine authority of a holy ascetic with the civic clout of a post-Constantinian bishop. Knowing his reputation as a monk and holy man, leaders as influential as the prefect and the emperor allegedly hoped to escape or to benefit from his mediation of divine power" (*Renouncing the World*, 71). For Basil's own practices and the emerging role of the bishop as a broker in the patronage system, alongside

the blending of, competition between, or complex interrelationships between the "secular" patronage of a state official and the religious patronage through the increasing authority of the bishop, especially as clergy take over benefactions typically associated with governors, see also Rousseau, *Basil of Caesarea*, 158–82. For how the "holy man" became a new form of patron in late antiquity, especially in small villages in Syria and Asia Minor, see Brown, "Rise and Function of the Holy Man in Late Antiquity." See also the shorter synopsis in Brown, "Town, Village, and Holy Man."

60 Beeley, *Gregory of Nazianzus*, vii, 319–23.

61 For an exceptional treatment of Gregory of Nazianzus' theology, see Beeley, *Gregory of Nazianzus*.

62 Beeley, *Gregory of Nazianzus*, 65n6, 251n61.

63 In addition to the passages discussed below, see *Or.* 2.92, 32.16–17 (for the episcopacy); and 7.2, 11.2, 18.14, 21.3, and 43.72 (for general leadership); see also Sterk, *Renouncing the World*, 124–5; Rapp, *Holy Bishops in Late Antiquity*, 42–4.

64 See Beeley, *Gregory of Nazianzus*, 63–113.

65 Rapp, *Holy Bishops in Late Antiquity*, 174, 199. She notes that Basil of Caesarea shared this scorn, and that increasingly it became easier for men of wealth than for those of modest means to become bishop.

66 McGuckin, *St Gregory of Nazianzus*, 4. Cf. Basil of Caesarea's note to Eusebius of Samosota that when he ordained Gregory of Nazianzus as the bishop of Sasima, Gregory refused to serve. At that point, Basil writes that Gregory was meant for greater things, but since those things were not forthcoming, he would bestow his own greatness upon lesser things. He writes, "let him [Gregory] be a bishop not deriving honor from his see, but honoring his see by himself. For it is the mark of a really great man not only to be sufficient for great things, but also to make small things great by his own power" (*Letter* 98.2; quoted in Sterk, *Renouncing the World*, 82).

67 Sterk, *Renouncing the World*, 46–65, esp. 46–8, 96, 119, 122–3, 128–9, 132, 136.

68 McGuckin, *St Gregory of Nazianzus*, 35–83. In Gregory's early experiences of initiation into mysteries of Eleusis, he wrote a poem in his *Hymn of Lament* (*Carmen Lugubre*), connecting the Eleusinian rites to Christian baptism:

> God governs all men of good will
> But keeps the heights of his wisdom still hidden
> And opaque darkness lies between our race and God
> Which few can ever penetrate
> With farseeing eyes, acutely discerning beyond this life:
> The pure who attain to pure wisdom.

For discussion, see McGuckin, *St Gregory of Nazianzus*, 67–76.

69 McGuckin, *St Gregory of Nazianzus*, 67n159; see further, Sterk, *Renouncing the World*, 135.

70 This is especially the case if one sees the *Apothagemnata Patrum* as the pre-eminent desert monastic literature; nonetheless, there may be a hint in the more Origenist desert monks, including Antony himself. Antony, in *Letter* 5.8, for example, says either that one cannot see God or cannot inherit God without sanctity. It is difficult to know which term – see or inherit – was Antony's original meaning. *Letter* 6.54, however, seems to assume that God is unseen and hidden, while we dwell in this "heaviness." See Rubenson, *Letters of St Antony*, 212n9, 219–20.

71 McGuckin, *St Gregory of Nazianzus*, 220.

72 Ibid., 220.

73 See McGuckin, *St Gregory of Nazianzus*, 1–34; for Gregory as a second Samuel, and, therefore, his mother as a new Hannah, see *De Vita Sua* 68–92; *Or.* 18.11; Beeley, *Gregory of Nazianzus*, 6.

74 McGuckin, *St Gregory of Nazianzus*, 13–15; cf. Rapp, *Holy Bishops in Late Antiquity*, 131.

75 To see how the theology of the five theological orations fits within Gregory's overarching theological program, see Beeley, *Gregory of Nazianzus*.

76 The spring of 380 to the spring of 381 was, as Beeley notes, "the most concentrated period of theological productivity of Gregory's life" (*Gregory of Nazianzus*, 37). For the social context of this writing, see Beeley, *Gregory of Nazianzus*, 37–43.

77 For the idiosyncrasies of the theological orations in comparison to Gregory's other writings, due to their anti-Eunomian overtones, see Beeley, *Gregory of Nazianzus*, 40, 67, 90–3.

78 Ἀνιότι δέ μοι προθύμως ἐπὶ τὸ ὄρος ... ἵνα τῆς νεφέλης εἴσω γένωμαι, καὶ Θεῷ συγγένωμαι (τοῦτο γὰρ κελεύει Θεός)· εἰ μέν τις Ἀαρών, συνανίτω, καὶ στηκέτω πλησίον, κἂν ἔξω μένειν τῆς νεφέλης δέῃ, τοῦτο δεχόμενος. Εἰ δέ τις Ναδὰβ, ἢ Ἀβιοὺδ, ἢ τῆς γερουσίας, ἀνίτω μὲν, ἀλλὰ στηκέτω πόρρωθεν, κατὰ τὴν ἀξίαν τῆς καθάρσεως. Εἰ δέ τις τῶν πολλῶν καὶ ἀναξίων ὕψους τοιούτου καὶ θεωρίας, εἰ μὲν ἄναγνος πάντη, μηδὲ προσίτω, οὐ γὰρ ἀσφαλές· εἰ δὲ πρόσκαιρα γοῦν ἡγνισμένος, κάτω μενέτω. PG 36, 28A–B.

79 Note that, in the omitted material, he relates this to biblical interpretation: that is, the many who must remain below at the foot of the mountain have ability to understand only the obvious aspect of scripture; those who ascend the mount like Moses and Gregory himself can access its hidden aspect. Those who stay below can only hear God; those who ascend, achieve *theoria*, contemplation.

80 ἔτρεχον μὲν, ὡς Θεὸν καταληψόμενος, καὶ οὕτως ἀνῆλθον ἐπὶ τὸ ὄρος, καὶ τὴν

νεφέλην διέσχον, εἴσω γενόμενος ἀπὸ τῆς ὕλης καὶ τῶν ὑλικῶν, καὶ εἰς ἐμουτὸν, ὡς οἷόν τε, συστραφείς. Ἐπεὶ δὲ προσέβλεψα, μόλις εἶδον Θεοῦ τὰ ὀπίσθια· καὶ τοῦτο, τῇ πέτρᾳ σκεπασθεὶς, τῷ σαρκωθέντι δι᾽ ἡμᾶς Λόγῳ. PG 36, 29A. Translation adapted from Williams and Wickham, trans., On God and Christ, 37–9.

81 This startling first-person usage can be seen elsewhere (Or. 12.1), where he portrays himself qua bishop as mystagogue:

> I opened my mouth and drew in the spirit [LXX Ps. 118:131]. To that spirit I dedicate my entirety, and my very self: all my deeds, my discourse, my contemplation and my silence. Only let him have me, and lead me and move me – hand, mind, and voice. Take them wherever he wishes, wherever is right, and stop them moving wherever is unfitting. I am the divine instrument, a rational instrument, tuned and played by that master musician the spirit. Yesterday he worked a silence in me. My philosophy was not to speak. Today he plays the instrument of my mind – let the word be heard. My philosophy shall be to speak. I am not so talkative as to desire to speak when he is moved to silence, or so taciturn and stupid as to "set a watch before my lips" [Ps. 140:3] when it is time to speak out. I shall open and close the door of my self to that Supreme Mind, to the Word, and to the Spirit, who are all of one nature and Godhead. (translation quoted in McGuckin, St Gregory of Nazianzus, 204)

He did, moreover, write an autobiography in verse (De Vita Sua) – and may have been the first person to do so.

82 The closest is Origen's notion that, by participation in the Logos, the darkness is, in a sense, dispelled.

83 See Beeley, Gregory of Nazianzus, 66.

84 For an extensive discussion of this passage in terms of purification and illumination, using Moses as the ideal, see Beeley, Gregory of Nazianzus, 63–113.

85 Though see his statement in Oration 27, where he challenges Eunomius, whom he mockingly asks if he is like a second Moses, being worthy to see God (27.9).

86 See Beeley, Gregory of Nazianzus, 8–9, 101–2.

87 It is not "nature prime, inviolate, self-apprehended (by 'self' I mean the Trinity)."

88 ἀλλ᾽ ὅση τελευταία καὶ εἰς ἡμᾶς φθάνουσα.

89 ὥσπερ αἱ καθ᾽ ὑδάτων ἡλίου σκιαὶ καὶ εἰκόνες ταῖς σαθραῖς ὄψεσι παραδεικνῦσαι τὸν ἥλιον, ἐπεὶ μὴ αὐτὸν προσβλέπειν οἷόν τε, τῷ ἀκραιφνεῖ τοῦ φωτὸς νικῶντα τὴν αἴσθησιν.

90 ἀλλὰ φράσει μὲν, ἀδύνατον, ὡς ὁ ἐμὸς λόγος· νοῆσαι δὲ, ἀδυνατώτερον. See Beeley, Gregory of Nazianzus, 99.

91 He interestingly turns to compare Moses to Paul in the third heaven, as had so many people before him and Augustine of Hippo after him (see further *Or.* 28.20).

92 See especially Beeley, *Gregory of Nazianzus*, 93, 96–7, 251–2.

93 For comparison, see the discussion of the seventy elders in the *Apost. Const.* 8.16.3–5 in Mueller, *L'Ancien Testament dans l'ecclésiologie des pères*, 308–14.

94 διά τε τὸ φαινόμενον τοῦ νόμου, καὶ τὸ κρυπτόμενον· τὸ μὲν τοῖς πολλοῖς καὶ κάτω μένουσι, τὸ δὲ τοῖς ὀλίγοις καὶ ἄνω φθάνουσιν.

95 Beeley, *Gregory of Nazianzus*, 89.

96 Beeley (*Gregory of Nazianzus*, 66, 87–8), moreover, notes that this is not a one-time purification, but, much like Gregory of Nyssa, an ongoing increase in purity and holiness.

97 Cf. *Or.* 2; see discussion in Sterk, *Renouncing the World*, 128–9.

98 McGuckin, *St Gregory of Nazianzus*, 245.

99 Beeley, *Gregory of Nazianzus*, 105.

100 See ibid., 65–90.

101 McGuckin, *St Gregory of Nazianzus*, 245–6.

102 In another context (*Or.* 1.6) the priest and bishop is even a new Christ in this role; Beeley, *Gregory of Nazianzus*, 239–40.

103 See further McGuckin, *St Gregory of Nazianzus*, 284–5. Interestingly, Nicetas David the Paphlagonian would, in the late-ninth or early-tenth century, write an *Encomium of Gregory Nazianzen*, strongly comparing Gregory to Moses. He writes, "Gregory, if any man, saw the Invisible One. And looking with unveiled face upon the glory of the Lord as in a mirror, he was filled with contemplation and power and was sent off to this pleasure-loving Egypt of ours" (20.60–75; quoted in Sterk, *Renouncing the World*, 229).

104 For the relationship between this work and Philo's own *Life of Moses*, see Geljon, *Philonic Exegesis*. See Gregory's use of Philo more generally in Runia, *Philo in Early Christian Literature*, 243–61. Gregory of Nyssa's *Life of Moses* also clearly builds upon Origen.

105 Sterk, *Renouncing the World*, 95–118, esp. 97.

106 In Gregory of Nyssa's homilies on the Beatitudes, for example, he notes the Word vouchsafing knowledge to Moses almost as an aside (*Hom. Beat.* 3; PG 44, 1229B).

107 Partly because this was the position of Eunomios; see Gregory of Nyssa's *Ag. Eun.* 3.9.22–41, esp. 32–4; Geljon, *Philonic Exegesis*, 55.

108 Jean Daniélou has synthesized and analyzed Gregory's writings, including those on darkness, in *Platonisme et theologie mystique*. He has also selected an anthology of Gregory's mystical theological texts, including all of those that I will be discussing, in his *From Glory to Glory*. See especially his comments

on 23–33. The introduction to this latter collection (3–78) provides a nice introduction to some of the outlines of Gregory of Nyssa's thought for an English-speaking audience. For a shorter discussion, also see Daniélou, "Moïse, exemple et figure chez Grégoire de Nysse." Unfortunately, he does not discuss the "allegorical Moses" in this essay, which contains much material of interest for this chapter. See also Junod, "Moïse, exemple de la perfection selon Grégoire de Nysse."

109 For Moses as initiate and mystagogue, see Daniélou, "Moïse, exemple et figure," 275; for Moses as exemplar and model, see Geljon, *Philonic Exegesis*, 66–8, 126–7.

110 Daniélou, "Moïse, exemple et figure," 269–70, also draws attention to these themes in Gregory's *Inscr. Ps.* 44 on Psalm 89.

111 PG 46, 376C–377A. Cf. rabbinic juxtapositions of Moses' unwillingness to look upon the burning bush, God's refusal to be seen in Exodus 33, and God's full revelation in Numbers 12, as discussed in the chapter on Moses' visions in Jewish literature. For some basic information on the *Life of Moses*, see Geljon, *Philonic Exegesis*, 63–70.

112 Especially John 1:9, 8:12, and 14:16; see Geljon, *Philonic Exegesis*, 94.

113 See the discussion in Elliot R. Wolfson, *Language, Eros, Being*, 215–17; Geljon, *Philonic Exegesis*, 93–9.

114 Προϊὼν δὲ ὁ νοῦς, καὶ διὰ μείζονος ἀεὶ καὶ τελειοτέρας προσοχῆς ἐν περινοίᾳ γινόμενος τῆς ὄντως κατανοήσεως, ὅσῳ προσεγγίζει μᾶλλον τῇ θεωρίᾳ, τοσούτῳ πλέον ὁρᾷ τὸ τῆς θείας φύσεως ἀθεώρητον. PG 46, 376D.

115 πάσῃ νοητῇ φύσει τῆς θείας οὐσίας τὴν γνῶσιν ἀνέφικτον εἶναι. PG 46, 377A.

116 This is one place where Gregory of Nyssa clearly agrees with Philo and Clement of Alexandria; see Geljon, *Philonic Exegesis*, 58–62, 128–31. Geljon (59) also notes that the incomprehensibility element comes within the context of anti-Eunomian polemics; see *Against Eunomios* 2.85–105.

117 Gregory wrote this text for primarily an ascetic audience. See the discussion of Gregory's views of virginity and sexuality in Smith, "Body of Paradise," 208–9, 224–8.

118 Afterwards, Gregory of Nyssa continues to reminisce on Moses' darkness experience. Not long after initially speaking of Moses' spiritual advancement from light and darkness to darkness, Gregory informs his readers that, when Moses entered this darkness, he did see something. Although God was there and was completely incomprehensible and invisible, Moses sees the heavenly tabernacle (of which he made a material imitation) (*Moses*, PG 44, 377 C–385 A); on the relationship between Gregory of Nazianzus' *Or.* 28 and Gregory of Nyssa's portrayal of Moses in the darkness, see Geljon, *Philonic Exegesis*, 133–4.

119 "Our initial withdrawal from wrong and erroneous ideas of God is a transition from darkness to light" (ἡ πρώτη ἀπὸ τῶν ψευδῶν καὶ πεπλανημένων περὶ Θεοῦ ὑπολήψεων ἀναχώρησις, ἡ ἀπὸ τοῦ σκότους εἰς φῶς ἐστι μετάστασις) (Comm. Song; PG 44, 1000D).

120 Ἡ δὲ προσεχεστέρα τῶν κρυπτῶν κατανόησις, ἡ διὰ τῶν φαινομένων χειραγωγοῦσα τὴν ψυχὴν πρὸς τὴν ἀόρατον φύσιν, οἷον τις νεφέλη γίνεται, τὸ φαινόμενον μὲν ἅπαν ἐπισκιάζουσα πρὸς δὲ τὸ κρύφιον βλέπειν τὴν ψυχὴν χειραγωγοῦσα καὶ συνεθίζουσα. PG 44, 1000D.

121 ὅσον ἐφικτόν ἐστι τῇ ἀνθρωπίνῃ φύσει, τὰ κάτω καταλιποῦσα. PG 44, 1000D.

122 ἐντὸς τῶν ἀδύτων τῆς θεγνωσίας γίνεται.

123 For Gregory's discussion of the revelation of the tabernacle to Moses on Sinai in Life of Moses, see PG 44, 377C–385A.

124 ἐν ᾧ τοῦ φαινομένου τε καὶ καταλαμβανομένου παντὸς ἔξω καταλεφθέντος, μόνον ὑπολείπεται τῇ θεωρίᾳ τῆς ψυχῆς τὸ ἀόρατόν τε καὶ ἀκατάληπτον, ἐν ᾧ ἐστιν ὁ Θεὸς (PG 44, 1000D–1001A).

125 ὅτι εἰσῆλθε δὲ Μωϋσῆς εἰς τὸν γνόφον οὗ ἦν ὁ Θεός. PG 44, 1001A.

126 The second category, either the cloud at Sinai or, more likely, the pillar of cloud that led the Israelites by day, "slowly guides and accustoms the soul to look towards what is hidden" (οἷόν τις νεφέλη γίνεται, τὸ φαινόμενον μὲν ἅπαν ἐπισκιάζουσα· πρὸς δὲ τὸ κρύφιον βλέπειν τὴν ψυχὴν χειραγωγοῦσα καὶ συνεθίζουσα) (PG 44, 1000D).

127 Gregory also brings up darkness in On his Brother Basil 129.5–9; Inscr. Ps. 44.18–19; Thaum. 10.10–14.

128 PG 44, 397D–405A.

129 For discussion of the series of "ascents," see Geljon, Philonic Exegesis, 125–40.

130 καὶ διὰ τοσοῦτον ἐπαρθεὶς ὑψωμάτων, ἔτι σφριγᾷ τῇ ἐπιθυμίᾳ, καὶ ἀκορέστως ἔχει τοῦ πλείονος, καὶ οὐ διὰ παντὸς κατ' ἐξουσίαν ἐνεφορεῖτο, ἔτι διψῇ. PG 44, 401C–D.

131 Gregory writes, "this hope constantly inflamed his desire to see what was hidden because of all that he had attained at each stage" (ἥν ἀεὶ ἡ ἐλπὶς ἀπὸ τοῦ ὀφθέντος καλοῦ πρὸς τὸ ὑπερκείμενον ἐπεσπάσατο, διὰ τοῦ πάντοτε καταλαμβανομένου, πρὸς τὸ κεκρυμμένον αἰεὶ τὴν ἐπιθυμίαν ἐκκαίουσα). In words reminiscent of Philo, Moses "wants to be filled with the very impression of the archetype" (αὐτοῦ τοῦ χαρακτῆρος τοῦ ἀρχετύπου ἐμφορηθῆναι ποθεῖ). (PG 44, 401D)

132 See Geljon, Philonic Exegesis, 62.

133 The darkness of God provides "an infinite abyss of contemplation" (ἀμέτρητόν τινα βυθὸν νοημάτων παραδεικνύουσα) (PG 44, 404A). See the discussion in Geljon, Philonic Exegesis, 142–5.

134 On transformation, especially of Moses-as-ideal-mystic, see Junod, "Moïse, exemple de la perfection selon Grégoire de Nysse," 92–3.

135 As Gregory writes elsewhere, "perfection consists in our never stopping in our growth in good, never circumscribing our perfection by any limitation" (αὐτίκα γὰρ ἐστιν ὡς ἀληθῶς τελειότης τὸ μηδέποτε στῆναι πρὸς τὸ κρεῖττον αὐξανόμενον, μηδέ τινι πέρατι περιορίσαι τὴν τελειότητα) (On Perfection, PG 46, 285D). This stands directly against the Platonic notion that everything mutable is corrupted, while simultaneously relying upon it. On Moses as the model of perfection, see Junod, "Moïse, exemple de la perfection selon Grégoire de Nysse," 94–7.

136 ὡς ἐν τούτῳ ὄντος τοῦ ἀληθῶς ἰδεῖν τὸν Θεόν, ἐν τῷ μὴ λῆξαί ποτε τῆς ἐπιθυμίας τὸν πρὸς αὐτὸν ἀναβλέποντα (PG 44, 404A).

137 ἀλλὰ πᾶσα πρὸς τὸ καλὸν ἡ ἐπιθυμία ἡ πρὸς τὴν ἄνοδον ἐκείνην ἐφελκομένη, ἀεὶ τῷ δρόμῳ τῷ πρὸς τὸ καλὸν ἱεμένῳ συνεπιτείνεται. Καὶ τοῦτό ἐστιν ὄντως τὸ ἰδεῖν τὸν Θεόν, τὸ μηδέποτε τῆς ἐπιθυμίας κόρον εὑρεῖν (PG 44, 404D). See discussion in Junod, "Moïse, exemple de la perfection selon Grégoire de Nysse," 93.

138 Put another way, Gregory writes, "Moses' desire is filled by the very fact that it remains unfulfilled." (οὔτε οὖν πληροῦται τῷ Μωϋσεῖ τὸ ποθούμενον, δι' ὧν ἀπλήρωτος ἡ ἐπιθυμία μένει) (PG 44, 404B).

139 ἀλλὰ μὴν αἰώνιος ζωὴ τὸ ἰδεῖν ἐστι τὸν Θεόν. Τοῦτο δὲ ἀμήχανον οἱ στύλοι τῆς πίστεως, Ἰωάννης καὶ Παῦλος καὶ Μωσῆς διορίζονται. Ὁρᾷς τὸν ἵλιγγον, ᾧ ψυχὴ πρὸς τὸ βάθος τῶν ἐν τῷ λόγῳ θεωρουμένων συνέλκεται; (PG 44, 1264D); for translations of Gregory's Homiles on the Beatitudes, I have largely used, with some modifications, the work by Graef, trans., St Gregory of Nyssa.

140 On Moses with Paul in Gregory of Nyssa's Life of Moses and other writings, see Geljon, Philonic Exegesis, 66–7.

141 ὁ γὰρ τῇ φύσει ἀόρατος, ὁρατὸς ταῖς ἐνεργείαις γίνεται, ἔν τισι τοῖς περὶ αὐτὸν καθορώμενος (PG 44, 1269A). For a discussion of existence versus essence, see Geljon, Philonic Exegesis, 128–9.

142 οὐ γὰρ μοι δοκεῖ ὡς ἀντιπρόσωπόν τι θέαμα τὸν Θεὸν προτιθέναι τῷ κεκαυαρμένῳ τὸν τῆς ψυχῆς ὀφθαλμόν· ἀλλὰ τοῦτο τάχα ἡ τοῦ ῥητοῦ μεγαλοφυΐα ἡμῖν ὑποτίθεται, ὃ καὶ πρὸς ἑτέρους ὁ λόγος γυμνότερον παρίστησιν, ἐντὸς ὑμῶν εἶναι τὴν βασιλείαν τοῦ Θεοῦ εἰπών· ἵνα διδαχθῶμεν, ὅτι ὁ πάσης τῆς κτίσεως καὶ ἐμπαθοῦς διαθέσεως τὴν ἑαυτοῦ καρδίαν ἀποκαθήρας· ἐν τῷ ἰδίῳ κάλλει τῆς θείας φύσεως καθορᾷ τὴν εἰκόνα. Καὶ μοι δοκεῖ δι' ὀλίγων ὧν εἶπεν, τοιαύτην συμβουλὴν περιέχειν ὁ Λόγος· ὅτι, Ὦ ἄνθρωποι, ὅσοις ἐστί τις ἐπιθυμία τῆς τοῦ ὄντως ἀγαθοῦ θεωρίας, ἐπειδὰν

ἀκούσητε ὑπὲρ τοὺς οὐρανοὺς ἐπῆρθαι τὴν θείαν μεγαλοπρέπειαν, καὶ τὴν δόξαν αὐτῆς ἀνερμήνεθτον εἶναι, καὶ τὸ κάλλος ἄφραστον, καὶ τὴν φύσιν ἀχώρητον· μὴ ἐκπίπτετε εἰς ἀνελπιστίαν τοῦ μὴ δύνασθαι κατιδεῖν τὸ ποθούμενον. Τὸ γὰρ σοι χωρητὸν, τῆς τοῦ Θεοῦ κατανοήσεως μέτρον ἐν σοί ἐστιν. Οὕτω τοῦ πλάσαντός σε τὸ τοιοῦτον ἀγαθὸν εὐθὺς τῇ φύσει κατουσιώσαντος. Τῶν γὰρ τῆς ἰδίας φύσεως ἀγαθῶν ὁ Θεὸς ἐνετύμωσε τῇ σῇ κατασκευῇ τὰ μιμήματα, οἷόν τινα κηρὸν σκήματα γλυφῆς προτυπώσας. Ἀλλ' ἡ κακία τῷ θεοειδεῖ χαρακτῆρι περιχυθεῖσα ἄχρηστον ἐποίησέ σοι τὸ ἀγαθὸν ὑποκεκρυμμένον τοῖς αἰσχροῖς προκαλύμμασιν. Εἰ οὖν ἀπακλύσειας πάλιν δι' ἐπιμελείας βίου τὸν ἐπιπλασθέντα τῇ καρδίᾳ σου ῥύπον, ἀναλάμψει σοι τὸ θεοειδὲς κάλλος (PG 44, 1269C–1272A).

143 ὅταν ὁ βασιλεύων τῆς κτίσεως ἑαυτὸν ἀνακαλύψῃ τῇ ἀνθρωπίνῃ φύσει, ἐπὶ τοῦ ὑψηλοῦ θρόνου μεγαλοπρεπῶς προκαθήμενος, ὅταν ὀφθῶσι περὶ αὐτὸν αἱ ἀναρίθμητοι μυριάδες τῶν ἀγγέλων, καὶ δὴ ὅταν ἐν ὀφθαλμοῖς γένηται πάντων ἀπόρρητος τῶν οὐρανῶν βασιλεία. PG 44, 1261B.

144 For example, on the differences between Philo's and Gregory of Nyssa's presentations of Moses, see Geljon, *Philonic Exegesis*, 157–8, 171–2

145 While Philo often used biblical figures, such as Abraham, to describe the life of the soul, he conspicuously does not do so in the texts referring to Moses entering the dark cloud, whether in the exposition or in the allegory, likely because for Philo Moses' experience is unique. One can imitate Moses, but one cannot become equal to Moses. See, in general, Geljon, *Philonic Exegesis*, 7–46, esp. 37–8 and 131.

146 These meditations of Moses' visions from Basil, Gregory of Nazianzus, and Gregory of Nyssa subsequently provided the platform for later development that finds its apogee in Pseudo-Dionysius' *Mystical Theology*, which would then resound throughout medieval Latin and Greek Christianity. The Moses-as-Monk-Bishop theme would also continue to resound in Slavic Christianity. Serbian hagiographers used the Moses-as-seer (*bogovidac*) model for the various lives of St Sava. Hagiographers even suggested St Sava was greater than Moses (Sterk, *Renouncing the World*, 235–7). On the other hand, through St Symeon the New Theologian, the divine vision would potentially challenge the hierarchy, since, for him, the divine vision is unrelated to ecclesiastical rank: the lowest of monks could receive the greatest of visions, though he, himself, was an ordained priest and his greatest vision occurred while consecrating the eucharist. Nonetheless, highly influenced by Gregory Nazianzus, he claimed that a divine vision was necessary for church leadership, again echoing Moses as an example (*Eth* XV, 68–73; Sterk, *Renouncing the World*, 239–40).

147 Sterk, *Renouncing the World*, 244.

CHAPTER ELEVEN

1   This includes roughly eight hundred surviving homilies and nearly four hundred letters, many of them quite lengthy.

2   This paragraph largely summarizes the first nine books of the *Confessions*. For a classic account of Augustine's life, see Brown, *Augustine of Hippo*.

3   Rapp, *Holy Bishops in Late Antiquity*, 135, 186–7. His initial retreat from the world, however, was fairly short. At times, he would also express the incompatibility of the monastic and the episcopal life, though he tried to maintain both; see Brown, *Augustine*, 155.

4   Rapp (*Holy Bishops in Late Antiquity*, 131–2) notes that, among Latin authors, the predominant identification was with Aaron.

5   Brown, *Augustine of Hippo*, 31–2.

6   *Conf.* 8.7.18. See the complex relations set out by McCarthy, "We Are Your Books," esp. 332–3. His analysis focuses on Augustine's sermons, especially on the Psalms, which would have been sung in liturgy, and is inflected by Foucault, to be sure, but perhaps more strongly by Bakhtin. Also Brown, *Augustine*, 100.

7   McCarthy, "We Are Your Books," 333.

8   Cf. McGinn, *Foundations*, 237–8.

9   For a discussion of Augustine's view of episcopal leadership, see Miles, *Desire and Delight*, 116–20.

10 See some comments by Luneau, "Moïse et les Pères latins," 295–6, and occasional references in Châtillon, "Moïse figure du Christ et modèle de la vie parfaite," who focuses mostly on medieval Latin literature, but with a healthy dose of Augustine and Pseudo-Dionysius (see esp. 311–13, where he looks first at Augustine's usage of 2 Cor. 12:2 next to Num. 12:8 and unwinds a constellation of interrelated verses discussed by Augustine and those after him in terms of Moses' visions and intimacy with God).

11 Cary (*Augustine's Invention of Inner Self*) works through a lot of the Platonic, particularly the Plotinian sources that Augustine relied upon, but also heavily adapted. See esp. 39. Also see Brown, *Augustine*, 86.

12 He wrote this largely simultaneously while writing his magnum opus, *On the Trinity*, which he worked on from 400 to 416 CE.

13 For editions and translations of Augustine of Hippo, I have consulted the following works. For *Confessions*, I have consulted the LCL editions, William Watts, *St. Augustine's Confessions*. For an English translation, I have relied upon Chadwick, *Saint Augustine: Confessions*. For the Latin of *City of God*, I have used the LCL editions, especially Wiesen, *Saint Augustine: The City of God*, vol. 3; Sanford and Green, *Saint Augustine: The City of God*, vol. 5; and Green,

Saint Augustine: The City of God, vol. 7. For English translation of the City of God, I have relied primarily on Bettenson, *St. Augustine: City of God*, alongside the LCL editions with some minor adaptations. For *Literal Interpretation of Genesis*, I have relied primarily on the Migne's Patrologia Latina, volume 34; for English translation, I have consulted Taylor, *St. Augustine: Literal Genesis*.

14 *Teaching*, preface, 15; *Conf.* 12.9

15 Ad hoc enim et aliquanto latius de hac re disserere volui, quia nonnulli haeretici putant substantiam Filii Dei nullo assumpto corpore per seipsam esse visibilem, et ideo atequam ex Virgine corpus acciperet, ipsum visum esse Patribus opinantur, tanquam de solo Deo Patre dictum sit, Quem nemo hominum vidit, nec videre poteat; quia Filius visus sit ante acceptam servi formani, etiam per ipsam substantiam suam: quae impietas procul a catholicis mentibus repellenda est (PL 34, 392–3).

16 Similar questions are raised in terms of God speaking to Adam in the Garden (*Literal Genesis* 11.33): was it through an interior means of the intellect (as God speaks to the angels) or through a creature in ecstasy in spirit with corporeal images or through bodily senses (just as God is accustomed to be seen or heard in a cloud through the ministry of angels). If visible, it must be through a creature, since "we cannot suppose that the substance of the Father, the Son, and the Holy Spirit, which is invisible and everywhere present in its totality, appeared to the sense of the body, moving through space and time" (ne substantia illa invisibilis et ubique tota, quae Patris et Filii est et Spiritus sancti, corporabalibus eorum sensibus locali et temporali motu apparuisse credatur) (PL 34, 417).

17 He does shift his stance at one point to say that the same mediator spoke in former times through the prophets, later through his own mouth, and afterward through the apostles (*City of God* 11.3), suggesting a position much closer to Justin and those in Justin's wake.

18 PL 34, 387.

19 In Book 3 of *On the Trinity*, Augustine explores whether God used a preexisting creature, adapting it for the manifestation, or created a new creature in an ad hoc manner.

20 In *City of God* 16.29: "It is, to be sure, within the capacity of divine and invisible power, of incorporeal and immutable nature to appear to mortal sight, without any change in itself, not appearing in its own being, but by means of something subordinate to itself – and what is not subordinate?" (Est quidem divinae potestatis et invisibilis, incorporalis inmutabilisque naturae, sine ulla sui mutatione etiam mortalibus aspectibus apparere, non per id quod est, sed per aliquid quod sibi subditum est; quid autem illi subditum non est?) PL 41, 508 reads *incommutibilis* instead of *immutabilis*.

21 Nec movere debet quod, cum sit invisibilis, saepe visibiliter patribus apparuisse memoratur. Sicut enim sonus quo auditur sententia in silentio intellegentiae constituta non est hoc quod ipsa, ita et species qua visus est Deus in natura invisibili constitutus non erat quod ipse. Verum tamen ipse in eadam specie corporali videbatur, sicut illa sentential ipsa in sono vocis auditor; nec illi ignorabant invisibilem Deum in specie corporali, quod ipse non erat, se videre. Nam et loquebatur cum loquente Moyses et ei tamen dicebat: Si inveni gratiam ante te, ostende mihi temetipsum, scienter ut videam te.

22 Though for an account of their intricate continuities, see Miles, "Vision," 125–42.

23 Cary, *Augustine's Invention of the Inner Self*, 41, 160–1n43.

24 Miles, "Vision," 130–1.

25 Quapropter cum sancti Angeli, quibus post resurrectionem coaequabimur, si viam (quod nobis Christus factus est) usque in finem tenuerimus, semper videant faciem Dei (PL 34, 313).

26 While in *Letter* 92 (to Italica), Augustine largely keeps to the idea that God can be seen only through the mind, he nonetheless writes something similar, "We shall therefore see him according to the measure in which we shall be like him" (92.3).

27 Brown, *Augustine of Hippo*, 366; see the extensive discussion by Miles, *Augustine on the Body*, 99–125.

28 This contrasts with *Letter* 92 (dated to 408 CE), where he explicitly denies that bodily eyes will be able to see God, either now or in the afterlife. Instead, he writes that only the purified mind could see.

29 Quam ob rem fieri potest valdeque credibile est sic nos visuros mundana tunc corpora caeli novi et terrae novae ut Deum ubique praesentem et universa etiam corporalia gubernantem per corpora quae gestabimus et quae conspiciemus, quaqua versum oculos duxerimus, clarissima perspecuitate videamus.

30 Miles, *Augustine on the Body*, 111–12.

31 For a discussion of this development, see Miles, "Sex and the City (of God)," 314–21; see also Miles, "Vision," 141–2.

32 For a discussion of the ancient Christian interpretation of Matt. 18:10 – though not discussing Augustine directly – see Bucur, *Angelomorphic Pneumatology*, 62–7, 169–72, 185–6.

33 Much of his discussion of the nature of the mind here strongly resembles his reflections on memory in *Confessions* 10.

34 E.g., in 147:13 alone; Matt. 5:8 and 1 John 3:2 – "we shall see him as he is"; 1 John 1:18; Gen. 32:30; Exod. 33:11; and Isa. 6:1.

35 Miles, "Vision," 130–8.
36 On Augustine's tentativeness here and elsewhere – as well as all of his disclaimers – see Miles, "Sex and the City (of God)," 315.
37 Jerome, *Comm. Isa.* 1.10.
38 It remains a surprising turn in this evolution toward a transformative physicalized intellectual vision in *City of God*. Given this trajectory, I must slightly disagree with Carey, when he writes, "This metaphor [vision] in turn becomes fundamental for the next thousand years of Western Christianity, as theologians came to define ultimate human happiness as beatific vision – seeing God with the eye of the soul. But the metaphor is not without its problems. It does not really explain intelligibility but only compares it with visibility – that is, it likens intelligibility to precisely what it is not. From the *Phaedo* to the *Confessions*, Platonism insisted that seeing with the eye of the body is a hindrance to seeing with the eye of the mind, and that it is of the utmost importance to know the difference between the two. But the difference is precisely what a metaphor that likens them cannot elucidate" (*Augustine's Invention of the Inner Self*, 19). On the contrast between Ambrose and Augustine, especially Ambrose's greater debt to earlier Greek Chrsitian thought, see Brown, *Augustine*, 105, 147.
39 See Miles, *Desire and Delight*, 128.
40 Miles, "Vision," 141–2.
41 On the polemical situatedness of Augustine's bodily resurrection against Porphyry, see Miles, "Sex and the City (of God)," 314.
42 Cf. *Letter* 147.31. On *Literal Genesis* 12, see Kenney, *Mysticism of St. Augustine*, 130–4, who also discusses the related literature of *Letter* 147 to Paulina; *Confessions* 7 and 9; cf. *Hom. Ps.* 41.
43 quod autem non imaginaliter, sed proprie videtur, et non per corpus vidatur, hoc ea visione videtur, quae omnes ceteras superat.
44 Cf. Jerome's translation in the *Vulgate*: ostende mihi viam tuam.
45 Non per aenigmata, quantum eam capere mens humana potest, secundum assumentis Dei gratiam, ut os ad os loquatur ei quem dignum tali Deus colloquio fecerit; non os corporis, sed mentis.
46 Contrast *Conf.* 10.7.
47 Concupiverat enim, sicut in Exodo legimus, videre Deum; non utique sicut viderat in monte, nec sicut videbat in tabernaculo, sed in ea substantia qua Deus est, nulla assumpta corporali creatura, quae mortalis carnis sensibus praesentetur: neque in spiritu figuratis similitudinibus corporum; sed per speciem suam, quantum eam capere creatura rationalis et intellectualis potest, sevocata ab omni corporis sensu, et ab omni significativo aenigmate spiritus.

48 On the role of desire and longing for vision in Augustine's writings, see Miles, "Vision," 134.

49 Sic enim scriptum est, Si ergo inveni gratiam in conspectu tuo, ostende mihi temetipsum manifeste, ut videam te; cum paulo superius legatur locutus Dominus ad Moysen facie ad faciem, sicut quis loquitur ad amicum suum. Sentiebat ergo quid videbat, et quod non videbat disderabat. Nam et paulo post, cum dixisset ei Deus, invenisti enim gratiam in conspectu meo, et scio te pro omnibus; respondit ei, ostende mihi claritatem tuam. Et tunc quidem responsum accepit a Domino figuratum, de quo nunc longum est disputare, quando ei dixit: non poteris videre faciem meam, et vivere. Non enim videbit homo faciem meam, et vivet. Deinde subiecit et ait illi: ecce locus penes me, et stabis super petram.

50 Neque enim hoc secundum substantiam corporis, quae carnis sensibus praesentatur, intelligendum est; nam utique sic loquebatur ad Moysen facie ad faciem, contra in contra, quando tamen dixit ei, ostende mihi temetipsum; et nunc etiam ad ipsos quos obiurgabat, et quibus Moysi meritum ita praeferabat, sic loquebatur per creaturam corporalem praesentatam sensibus carnis. Illo ergo modo, in illa specie qua Deus est, longe ineffabiliter secretius et praesentius loquitur locutione ineffabili, ubi eum nemo videns vivet vita ista, qua mortaliter vivitur in istis sensibus corporis: sed nisi ab hac vita quisque quodammodo moriatur, sive omnino exiens de corpore, sive ita aversus et alienatus a carnalibus sensibus, ut merito nesciat, sicut Apostolus ait, utrum in corpore an extra corpus sit, cum in illam rapitur et subvehitur visionem.

51 Note Kenney, *Mysticism of St. Augustine*, 73–86, 130–4; Carey, *Augustine's Invention of Inner Self*, 63–76.

52 Cf. Plotinus, *Enn.* 4.8.1; McGinn, *Foundations*, 44–5; Turner, *Darkness of God*, 78–9.

53 On the glimpse in this life versus the gaze in the afterlife, see Miles, "Vision," 133–8.

54 On Monica's charisma and reliance upon dreams, see Brown, *Augustine of Hippo*, 21.

55 *On Genesis against the Manicheans in Two Books*, which he wrote very early in 388, just after he returned to North Africa from Italy. Technically, he sought the literal meaning of a passage first, and then resorted to allegory when he was unable to do so.

CHAPTER TWELVE

1 Irigaray, *Speculum of the Other Woman*, 306.

2 Discussed in Wolfson, *Speculum*, 44–6. One variation that Wolfson discusses

is that Isaac's blindness is caused by seeing God – a form of symbolic death (*Pirqe R. El.* 32, 73B; cf. *Deut. Rab.* 11:3).

3 For the pattern of fear, horror, prostration, or falling, see Schäfer, *Origins of Jewish Mysticism*, 332–3.

4 See Arbel, *Beholders*, 37–40.

5 Though notably some of them used their interpretive authority to attribute charismatic authority to women in their community, especially the North African writers Tertullian and Augustine.

6 Horden and Purcell, *Corrupting Sea*, 342, 378; Marquis (*Transient Apostle*) traces ancient evaluations of travel from outright hostility to hospitality.

7 Of course, there are many forms of literature that survive: martyrdom texts, letters, apocryphal Christian texts, etc.

8 Nasrallah, *An Ecstasy of Folly*, 130.

9 Clark, *Reading Renunciation*, 11.

10 Malherbe, "Apologetic and Philosophy," 782–90.

11 See the notes of Derrida, *Beast and the Sovereign*, 1:308–13. While thresholds are and appear to be indivisible, they also presuppose a means – however difficult – of crossing or even invading, such as a key or secret code: "We love the threshold, both crossing it and not crossing it" (311). See further Deleuze and Guattari, *A Thousand Plateaus*, 438–40.

12 See Schäfer, *Origins of Jewish Mysticism*, 333–4.

Bibliography

Aaron, David H. "Shedding Light on God's Body in Rabbinic Midrashim: Reflections on the Theory of a Luminous Adam." *Harvard Theological Review* 90, no. 3 (1997): 299–314.

Afterman, Adam. "From Philo to Plotinus: The Emergence of Mystical Union." *Journal of Religion* 93, no. 2 (April 2013): 177–96.

Aichele, George. *Tales of Posthumanity: The Bible and Contemporary Popular Culture*. Sheffield: Sheffield Phoenix Press, 2014.

Aland, Barbara, et al. *The Greek New Testament*. 4th rev. ed. D–Stuttgart: United Bible Societies, 1983.

– *Nestle-Aland: Novum Testamentum Graeca*. 27th rev. ed. Regensburg: Deutsche Bibelgesellschaft, 2004.

Alexander, Philip. *Mystical Texts: Songs of the Sabbath Sacrifice and Related Manuscripts*. T&T Clark, 2006.

Allen, E.L. "Jesus and Moses in the New Testament." *Expository Times* 67 (1955–56): 104–6.

Allert, Craig D. *Revelation, Truth, Canon, and Interpretation: Studies in Justin Martyr's Dialogue with Trypho*. Leiden: Brill, 2002.

Allison, Dale. *The New Moses: A Matthean Typology*. Minneapolis: Fortress Press, 1993.

Arbel, Daphna. *Beholders of Divine Secrets: Mystics and Myth in the Hekhalot and Merkavah Literature*. Albany, NY: SUNY Press, 2003.

Arrowsmith, William, trans. "Jerome on Translation: A Breviary." *Arion* 2, no. 3 (1975): 358–67.

Ashton, John. *Understanding the Fourth Gospel*, 2nd ed. Oxford: Oxford University Press, 2007. First edition, 1991.

Attridge, Harold W. *The Epistle to the Hebrews: A Commentary on the Epistle to the Hebrews*. Philadelphia: Fortress Press, 1989.

Barnard, Leslie. *Justin Martyr: His Life and Thought*. Cambridge: Cambridge University Press, 1967.

Barr, James. "Theophany and Anthropomorphism in the Old Testament." In *Congress Volume: Oxford 1959* (Vetus Testamentum Supplements 7; Leiden: Brill, 1960): 31–8

Baskin, Judith R. *Midrashic Women: Formations of the Feminine in Rabbinic Literature*. Hanover, NH: Brandeis University Press, 2002.

Bauckham, Richard. *God Crucified: Monotheism and Christology in the New Testament*. Grand Rapids, MI: Eerdmans, 1998.

– *Jesus and the God of Israel: God Crucified and Other Studies on the New Testament's Christology of Divine Identity*. Grand Rapids, MI: Eerdmans, 2008.

Bautch, Kelley Coblenz. *A Study of the Geography of 1 Enoch 17–19: "No One Has Seen What I Have Seen."* Leiden: Brill, 2003.

Beeley, Christopher A. *Gregory of Nazianzus on the Trinity and the Knowledge of God: In Your Light We See Light*. Oxford Studies in Historical Theology. Oxford University Press, 2008.

Berkowitz, Beth A. *Defining Jewish Difference: From Antiquity to the Present*. Cambridge University Press, 2012.

Bettenson, Henry, trans. *St. Augustine: Concerning the City of God against the Pagans*. London: Penguin, 2003.

Birnbaum, Ellen. *The Place of Judaism in Philo's Thought: Israel, Jews, and Proselytes*. Brown Judaic Studies 290, Studia Philonica Monographs 2. Atlanta, GA: Scholars Press, 1996.

Bingham, D. Jeffrey. "Irenaeus and Hebrews." In *Irenaeus: Life, Scripture, Legacy*, edited by Paul Foster and Sara Parvis, 65–79. Minneapolis: Fortress Press, 2012.

Blanc, J. "La fête de Moïse dans le rite byzantin." In *Moïse: L'Homme de l'alliance*, edited by H. Cazelles, et al., 345–53. Paris: Desclée & Co., 1955.

Bloch, Renée. "Quelques aspects de la figure de Moïse dans la tradition rabbinique." In *Moïse: L'Homme de l'alliance*, edited by H. Cazelles, et al., 93–167. Paris: Desclée & Co., 1955.

Booij, Th. "Hagar's Words in Genesis XVI 13b." *Vetus Testamentum* 30, no. 1 (1980): 1–7.

Borgen, Peder. "Moses, Jesus, and the Roman Emperor: Observations in Philo's Writings and the Revelation of John." *Novum Testamentum* 38, no. 2 (Apr. 1996): 145–59.

– *Philo of Alexandria: An Exegete for His Time*. Atlanta: Society of Biblical Literature, 1997.

Bovon, François. "La figure de Moïse dans l'œvrede Luc." In *La figure de Moïse*, edited by Robert Martin-Achard, 47–65. Geneva: Labor et Fides, 1978.

Boyarin, Daniel. *Borderlines: The Partition of Judaeo-Christianity*. Philadelphia: University of Pennsylvania Press, 2004.

– *Dying for God: Martyrdom and the Making of Christianity and Judaism*. Stanford, CA: Stanford University Press, 1999.

– "The Eye in the Torah: Ocular Desire in Midrashic Hermeneutic." *Critical Inquiry* 16, no. 3 (Spring 1990): 532–50.

– "Justin Martyr Invents Judaism," *Church History* 70, no. 3 (Sept. 2001): 427–61.

– "'This We Know to Be the Carnal Israel': Circumcision and the Erotic Life of God and Israel." *Critical Inquiry* 18 (1992): 474–505.

Brakke, David. *The Gnostics: Myth, Ritual, and Diversity in Early Christianity*. Cambridge: Harvard University Press, 2010.

Brent, Allen. "How Irenaeus Has Misled the Archaeologists." In *Irenaeus: Life, Scripture, Legacy*, edited by Paul Foster and Sara Parvis, 35–52. Minneapolis: Fortress Press, 2012.

Brock, Sebastian. *The Luminous Eye: The Spiritual World Vision of Saint Ephrem*. Kalamazoo, MI: Cistercian Publications, 1992.

Brown, Peter. *Augustine of Hippo: A Biography*. New edition with an epilogue. Berkeley: University of California Press, 2000 [1967].

– "The Rise and Function of the Holy Man in Late Antiquity." *Journal of Roman Studies* 61 (1971): 80–101. Reprinted in *Society and the Holy in Late Antiquity*, 103–52. University of California Press, 1982.

– "Town, Village and Holy Man: The Case of Syria." In Brown, *Society and the Holy in Late Antiquity*, 153–65. University of California Press, 1982.

Brown, Raymond E. *The Gospel According to John I–XII*. Anchor Bible 29. New York: Doubleday, 1966.

– *The Gospel According to John XIII–XII*. Anchor Bible 29A. Garden City, NY: Doubleday, 1970.

Brox, Norbert. *Irenäus von Lyon: Adversus Haereses: Gegen die Häresien III*. Frieburg: Herder, 1995.

– *Irenäus von Lyon: Adversus Haereses: Gegen die Häresien IV*. Frieburg: Herder, 1997.

Buell, Denise K. *Why This New Race? Ethnic Reasoning in Early Christianity*. New York: Columbia University Press, 2005.

Bucur, Bogdan Gabriel. *Angelomorphic Pneumatology: Clement of Alexandria and Other Early Christian Witnesses*. Leiden: Brill, 2009.

– "The Other Clement of Alexandria: Cosmic Hierarchy and Interiorized Apocalypticism." *Vigiliae Christianae* 60, no. 3 (2006): 251–68.

– "Revisiting Christian Oeyen: 'The Other Clement' on Father, Son, and Angelomorphic Spirit." *Vigiliae Christianae* 61, no. 4 (2007): 381–413.

Butterworth, G.W. *Clement of Alexandria: Exhortation to the Greeks, The Rich Man's Salvation, To the Newly Baptized*. Loeb Classical Library 92. Cambridge, MA: Harvard University Press, 1999. First published in 1919.

– "Clement of Alexandria's Proptrepticus and the Phaedrus of Plato." *Classical Quarterly* 10, no. 4 (1916): 198–205

– *Origen: On First Principles*. Notre Dame, IN: Ave Maria Press, 2013.

Bynum, Caroline Walker. "Images of the Resurrection Body in the Theology of Late Antiquity." *Catholic Historical Review* 80, no. 2 (Apr. 1994): 215–37.

– *Metamorphosis and Identity*. New York: Zone Books, 2001.

Calaway, Jared C. *The Sabbath and the Sanctuary: Access to God in the Letter to the Hebrews and Its Priestly Context*. WUNT 2, 349. Tübingen: Mohr Siebeck, 2013.

– "To See God and Live in Late Antique Judaism." In *Seeing the God: Ways of Envisioning the Divine in Ancient Mediterranean Religion*, edited by Jeff B. Pettis, 147–88. Piscataway, NJ: Gorgias Press, 2013.

– "Translation and Transformation: The Coptic Soundscapes of *The Thunder: Perfect Mind*." In *Crossing Boundaries in Early Judaism and Christianity: Ambiguities, Complexities, and Half-Forgotten Adversaries: Essays in Honor of Alan F. Segal*, edited by Kimberly B. Stratton and Andrea Lieber, 255–75. Leiden: Brill, 2016.

Carden, Michael. *Sodomy: A History of a Christian Biblical Myth*. London: Equinox, 2004.

Cary, Phillip. *Augustine's Invention of Inner Self: The Legacy of a Christian Platonist*. Oxford: Oxford University Press, 2000.

Casey, Robert P. "Clement of Alexandria and the Beginnings of Christian Platonism." *Harvard Theological Review* 18, no. 1 (1925): 39–101.

Castelli, Elizabeth. "'I Will Make Mary Male': Pieties of the Body and Gender Transformation in Late Antiquity." In *Body Guards: The Cultural Politics of Gender Ambiguity*, edited by Julia Epstein and Kristina Straub, 29–49. New York: Routledge, 1991.

– *Memory and Martyrdom: Early Christian Culture Making*. New York: Columbia University Press, 2004.

Cazelles, H. "Moïse devant l'histoire." In *Moïse: L'homme de l'alliance*, edited by H. Cazelles, et al., 11–27. Paris: Desclée & Co., 1955.

Cazelles, H., et al. *Moïse: L'homme de l'alliance*. Paris: Desclée & Co, 1955.

Chadwick, Henry, trans. *Augustine: Confessions*. Oxford: Oxford University Press, 1991.

– "The Gospel a Republication of Natural Religion in Justin Martyr." *Illinois Classical Studies* 18 (1993): 237–47.

– *Origen: Contra Celsum*. Cambridge: Cambridge University Press, 1953.

Châtillon, J. "Moïse figure du Christ et modèle de la vie parfaite." In *Moïse: L'homme de l'alliance*, edited by H. Cazelles et al., 305–14. Paris: Desclée & Co., 1955.

Chernus, Ira. "Visions of God in Merkabah Mysticism." *Journal for the Study of Judaism* 13 (1982): 123–46.

Chesnut, Glenn F. *The First Christian Histories: Eusebius, Socrates, Sozomen, Theodoret, and Evagrius*. Paris: Beauchesne, 1977.

Chilton, Bruce. "Justin and Israelite Prophecy." In *Justin Martyr and His Worlds*, edited by Sara Parvis and Paul Foster, 77–87. Minneapolis: Fortress Press, 2007.

Choufrine, Arkadi. *Gnosis, Theophany, Theosis: Studies in Clement of Alexandria's Appropriation of His Background*. Patristic Studies 5. New York: Peter Lang, 2002.

Clark, Elizabeth A. *The Origenist Controversy: The Cultural Construction of an Early Christian Debate*. Princeton: Princeton University Press, 1992.

– *Reading Renunciation: Asceticism and Scripture in Early Christianity*. Princeton: Princeton University Press, 1999.

Cohen, Martin. *The Shi'ur Qomah: Liturgy and Theurgy in Pre-Kabbalistic Jewish Mysticism*. Lanham, MD: University Press of America, 1983.

– *The Shi'ur Qomah: Texts and Recensions*. Tübingen: Mohr/Siebeck, 1985.

Cohen, Shaye J.D. *From the Maccabees to the Mishnah*. Philadelphia: Westminster Press, 1987.

Collins, John J. *The Apocalyptic Imagination: An Introduction to Apocalyptic Literature*. Grand Rapids, MI: Eerdmans, 1998.

– *Between Athens and Jerusalem: Jewish Identity in the Hellenistic Diaspora*. 2nd ed. Grand Rapids, MI: Eerdmans, 2000.

Colson, F.H. *Philo*. Vol. 6. Loeb Classical Library 289. Harvard University Press, 1935.

Colson, F.H., and G.H. Whitaker. *Philo*. Vols. 1, 4, and 5. Loeb Classical Library 226, 261, 275. Harvard University Press, 1929, 1932, 1934.

Corbin, Henry. *Creative Imagination in the Sufism of Ibn 'Arabi*. Translated by Ralph Manheim. Princeton: Princeton University Press, 1969.

– *Spiritual Body and Celestial Earth: From Mazdean Iran to Shi'ite Iran*. Translated by Nancy Pearson. Princeton: Princeton University Press, 1977.

Cox, Patricia. "Origen and the Bestial Soul: A Poetics of Nature." *Vigiliae Christianae* 36 (1982): 115–40.

Croatto, J. Severino. "Jesus, Prophet Like Elijah, and Prophet-Teacher Like Moses in Luke-Acts." *Journal of Biblical Literature* 124, no. 3 (Fall 2005): 451–65.

Crouzel, Henri. *Théologie de l'image de Dieu chez Origène*. Aubier: Éditions Montaigne, 1956.

Curry, Carl. "The Theogony of Theophilus." *Vigiliae Christianae* 42, no. 4 (December 1988): 318–26.

D'Angelo, Mary Rose. *Moses in the Letter to the Hebrews*. Missoula, MT: Scholars Press, 1979.

Daniélou, Jean, ed. *From Glory to Glory: Texts from Gregory of Nyssa's Mystical Writings*. Translated by Herbert Musurillo, SJ. Crestwood, NY: St Vladimir's Seminary Press, 2001.

– "Moïse, exemple et figure chez Grégoire de Nysse." In *Moïse: L'homme de l'alliance*, edited by H. Cazelles, et al., 267–82. Paris: Desclée & Co., 1955.

– *Origène*. Paris: La Table Ronde, 1948.

– *Platonisme et théologie mystique: Essai sur la doctrine spirituelle de Saint Grégoire de Nysse*. Paris: Aubier, 1944.

Davila, James R. *Liturgical Works*. Grand Rapids, MI: Eerdmans, 2000.

Dawson, David. *Allegorical Readers and Cultural Revision in Ancient Alexandria*. Berkeley: University of California Press, 1992.

de Andia, Ysabel. *Homo vivens: Incorruptibilité et divinisation de l'homme selon Irénée de Lyon*. Paris: Études Augustiniennes, 1986.

de Certeau, Michel. *The Mystic Fable*, Vol. 1: *The Sixteenth and Seventeenth Centuries*. Translated by Michael B. Smith. Chicago: University of Chicago Press, 1992.

– *The Mystic Fable*, Vol. 2: *The Sixteenth and Seventeenth Centuries*. Edited by Luce Giard. Translated by Michael B. Smith. Chicago: University of Chicago Press, 2015.

DeConick, April D. *The Gnostic New Age: How a Countercultural Spirituality Revolutionized Religion from Antiquity to Today*. New York: Columbia University Press, 2016.

– *Holy Misogyny: Why the Sex and Gender Conflicts in the Early Church Still Matter*. London: Continuum, 2011.

– "How We Talk about Christology Matters." In *Israel's God and Rebecca's Children: Christology and Community in Early Judaism and Christianity: Essays in Honor of Larry W. Hurtado and Alan F. Segal*, edited by David B. Capes, April D. DeConick, Helen K. Bond, and Troy A. Miller, 1–23. Waco, TX: Baylor University Press, 2007.

– *Voices of the Mystics: Early Christian Discourse in the Gospels of John and Thomas and Other Ancient Christian Literature*. JSNTSS 157. Sheffield: Sheffield Academic Press, 2001.

Debord, Guy. *Society of the Spectacle*. Detroit: Black & Red, 1983.

Dekkers, E., et al. *Tertullianus: Opera I: Opera Catholica. Adversus Marcionem*. CCSL 1. Brepols, 1954.

Deleuze, Gilles, and Félix Guattari. *A Thousand Plateaus: Capitalism and*

Schizophrenia. Translated by Brian Massumi. Minneapolis: University of Minnesota Press, 1987.

Démann, Paul. "Moïse et la loi dans la pensée de Saint Paul." In *Moïse: L'Homme de l'alliance*, edited by H. Cazelles., et al., 189–242. Paris: Desclée & Co., 1955.

Derrida, Jacques. *The Animal That Therefore I Am*. Edited by Marie-Louise Mallet. Translated by David Wills. Perspectives in Continental Philosophy. New York: Fordham University Press, 2008.

– *The Beast & the Sovereign*. 2 vols. Translated by Geoffrey Bennington. Chicago: University of Chicago Press, 2009, 2011.

– *Of Grammatology*. Translated by Gayatri Chakravorti Spivak. Baltimore: Johns Hopkins University Press, 1976.

Deschamps, Albert. "Moïse dans les évangiles et dans la tradition apostolique." In *Moïse: L'homme de l'alliance*, edited by H. Cazelles, et al., 171–87. Paris: Desclée & Co., 1955.

deSilva, David A. *Perseverance in Gratitude: A Socio-rhetorical Commentary on the Epistle "To the Hebrews."* Grand Rapids, MI: Eerdmans, 2000.

Deutsch, Celia. *Hidden Wisdom and the Easy Yoke: Wisdom, Torah, and Discipleship in Matthew 11.25–30*. JSNTSS 18. Sheffield: JSOT Press, 1987.

– "The Interpreter as Intertext: Origen's First Homily on the Canticle of Canticles." In *Crossing Boundaries in Early Judaism and Christianity: Ambiguities, Complexities, and Half-Forgotten Adversaries: Essays in Honor of Alan F. Segal*, edited by Kimberly B. Stratton and Andrea Lieber, 221–54. Leiden: Brill, 2016.

– "The Therapeutae, Text Work, Ritual, and Mystical Experience." In *Paradise Now: Essays on Early Jewish and Christian Mysticism*, edited by April D. DeConick, 287–311. Atlanta: Society of Biblical Literature, 2006.

– "Visions, Mysteries, and the Interpretive Task: Text Work and Religious Experience in Philo and Clement." In *Experientia*, Vol. 1: *Inquiry into Religious Experience in Early Judaism and Early Christianity*, edited by Frances Flannery, Colleen Shantz, and Rodney A. Werline, 83–108. Atlanta: Society of Biblical Literature, 2008.

Dillon, John. *The Middle Platonists: 80 BC to AD 220*. Ithaca, NY: Cornell University Press, 1977.

Dodds, E.R. *Pagan and Christian in an Age of Anxiety: Some Aspects of Religious Experience from Marcus Aurelius to Constantine*. New York: Norton, 1970, First published by Cambridge University Press, 1965.

Drake, H.A. *Constantine and the Bishops: The Politics of Intolerance*. Baltimore, MD: Johns Hopkins University Press, 2000.

Eisenbaum, Pamela Michelle. *The Jewish Heroes of Christian History: Hebrews 11 in Literary Context*. Atlanta, GA: Scholars Press, 1997.

Eliade, Mircea. *Shamanism: Archaic Techniques of Ecstasy*. Translated by Willard R. Trask. Bollingen Series 76. Princeton: Princeton University Press, 1964.

Enslin, Morton S. "Puritan of Carthage." *Journal of Religion* 27, no. 3 (July 1947): 197–212.

Feldman, Louis H. "Josephus' Portrait of Moses." *Jewish Quarterly Review* 82, nos. 3–4 (January–April 1992): 285–328.

– "Josephus' Portrait of Moses: Part Two." *Jewish Quarterly Review* 83, nos. 1–2 (July–October 1992): 7–50.

– "Josephus' Portrait of Moses: Part Three." *Jewish Quarterly Review* 83, nos. 3–4 (January–April 1993): 301–30

Fiensky, David A. *Prayers Alleged to be Jewish: An Examination of the Constitutiones Apostolorum*. Chico, CA: Scholars Press, 1985.

– "Redaction History and the Apostolic Constitutions." *Jewish Quarterly Review* 72, no. 4 (April 1982): 293–302.

Fishbane, Michael. *The Kiss of God: Spiritual and Mystical Death in Judaism*. Seattle: University of Washington Press, 1994.

Fletcher-Louis, Crispin. "4Q374: A Discourse on the Sinai Tradition: The Deification of Moses and Early Christology." *Dead Sea Discoveries* 3, no. 3 (Dec. 1996): 236–54.

Fossum, Jarl E. "Kyrios Jesus: Angel Christology in Jude." In *The Image of the Invisible God: Essays on the Influence of Jewish Mysticism on Early Christology*, 41–71. Göttingen: Vandenhoeck & Ruprecht, 1995.

– *The Name of God and the Angel of the Lord: Samaritan and Jewish Concepts of Intermediation and the Origin of Gnosticism*. WUNT 1, 36. Tübingen: Mohr Siebeck, 1985.

Foucault, Michel. "The Order of Discourse." In *Untying the Text: A Poststructuralist Reader*, edited by Robert Young and translated by Ian McLeod, 52–64. Boston: Routledge 1981.

Fox, Robin Lane. *Pagans and Christians*. New York: Knopf, 1987.

Frederiksen, Paula. *Augustine and the Jews: A Christian Defense of Jews and Judaism*. New York: Doubleday, 2008.

French, Todd. "Seeing the God in the Syriac Tradition." In *Seeing the God: Ways of Envisioning the Divine in Ancient Mediterranean Religion*, edited by Jeff B. Pettis, 187–221. Piscataway, NJ: Gorgias Press, 2013.

Freud, Sigmund "The Uncanny." In *The Uncanny*, translated by David McLintock, 121–62. New York: Penguin, 2003.

Friedman, Richard Elliott. *Who Wrote the Bible?* San Francisco: HarperSanFrancisco, 1987.

Gager, John G. *Moses in Greco-Roman Paganism*. Atlanta: Society of Biblical Literature, 1989. First published by Abingdon Press, 1972.

Gardet, L. "L'expérience intérieure du prophète Mûsâ (Moïse) selon quelques traditions sûfies." In *Moïse: L'homme de l'alliance*, edited by H. Cazelles, et al., 393–402. Paris: Desclée & Co., 1955.

Gelardini, Gabriella. *"Verhärtet eure Herzen nicht": Der Hebräer, eine Synagogenhomilie zu Tischa be-Aw*. Leiden: Brill, 2007.

Gelin, A. "Moïse dans l'Ancien Testament." In *Moïse: L'homme de l'alliance*, edited by H. Cazelles, et al., 29–52. Paris: Desclée & Co., 1955.

Geljon, Albert C. *Philonic Exegesis in Gregory of Nyssa's "De Vita Moysis."* Providence: Brown Judaic Series, 2002.

Gerlo, A., et al. *Tertullianus*. Opera 2: *Opera Montanistica*. CCSL 2. Brepols, 1954.

Gieschen, Charles. *Angelomorphic Christology: Antecedents and Early Evidence*. Library of Early Christolology. Waco, TX: Baylor University Press, 2017. First published by E.J. Brill, 1998.

Goldin, Judah. *Song at the Sea: Being a Commentary on a Commentary in Two Parts*. Philadelphia: Jewish Publication Society, 1990.

Goodenough, E.R. *By Light, Light: The Mystic Gospel of Hellenistic Judaism*. New Haven: Yale University Press, 1935.

– *The Theology of Justin Martyr: An Investigation into the Conceptions of Early Christian Literature and Its Hellenistic and Judaistic Influences*. Amsterdam: Philo Press, 1968.

Gorgemanns, Herwig, and Heinrich Karpp, eds. *Origenes: Vier Bücher von den Prinzipien*. Darmstadt: Wissenschaftliche Buchgesellschaft, 1976.

Gottstein, Alon Goshen. "The Body as Image of God in Rabbinic Literature." *Harvard Theological Review* 87, no. 2 (1994): 171–95.

Graef, Hilda C., trans. *St. Gregory of Nyssa: The Lord's Prayer: The Beatitudes*. Ancient Christian Writers 18. Mahwah, NJ: Paulist Press, 1954.

Grant, Robert M. "The Bible of Theophilus of Antioch." *Journal of Biblical Literature* 66, no. 2 (June 1947): 173–96.

– "The Problem of Theophilus." *Harvard Theological Review* 43, no. 3 (July 1950): 179–96.

– "Scripture, Rhetoric and Theology in Theophilus." *Vigiliae Christianae* 13, no. 1 (Apr. 1959): 33–45.

– "The Textual Tradition of Theophilus of Antioch." *Vigiliae Christianae* 6, no. 3 (July 1952): 146–59.

– "Theophilus of Antioch to Autolycus." *Harvard Theological Review* 40, no. 4 (Oct. 1947): 227–56.

Gräßer, Erich. *An die Hebräer*. 3 vols. Zurick: Benziger, 1990–97.

Green, William M. *Saint Augustine: The City of God against the Pagans*. Vol. 7. Loeb Classical Library. Cambridge: Harvard University Press, 1972.

Grossman, Edith. *Why Translation Matters*. New Haven: Yale University Press, 2010.

Gruenwald, Ithamar. *Apocalyptic and Merkavah Mysticism*. Leiden: Brill, 1980.

Guilea, Dragos Andrei. "'Demonstrations' from the First Principle: Clement of Alexandria's Phenomenology of Faith." *Journal of Religion* 89, no. 2 (2009): 187–213.

Hägg, Henny Fiskå. *Clement of Alexandria and the Beginnings of Christian Apophaticism*. Oxford: Oxford University Press, 2006.

Halperin, David J. *Faces of the Chariot: Early Jewish Responses to Ezekiel's Vision*. Tübingen: Mohr Siebeck, 1988.

– *The Merkabah in Rabbinic Literature*. New Haven, CT: American Oriental Society, 1980.

Hanson, R.P.C. *Allegory and Event: A Study of the Sources and Significance of Origen's Interpretation of Scripture*. London: SCM Press, 1959.

– *Origen's Doctrine of Tradition*. London: SPCK Publishing, 1954.

Harding, Sara Fletcher. "Christ as Greater than Moses in Clement of Alexandria's Stromateis I–II," *Studia Patristica* 31 (1995): 397–400.

Harkins, Angela Kim. *Reading with an "I" to the Heavens: Looking at the Qumran Hodayot through the Lens of Visionary Traditions*. Berlin: De Gruyter, 2012.

Harrington, D.J., trans. "Pseudo-Philo." in *Old Testament Pseudepigrapha*, vol. 2, edited by James H. Charlesworth, 297–377. New York: Doubleday, 1985.

Harstine, Stan. *Moses as a Character in the Fourth Gospel: A Study of Ancient Reading Techniques*. JSNTSS 229. Sheffield: Sheffield Academic Press, 2002.

Heine, Ronald E. trans. *Origen: Commentary on the Gospel according to John, Books 1–10*. Washington, DC: Catholic University of America Press, 1989.

– *Origen: Commentary on the Gospel according to John, Books 13–32*. Washington, DC: Catholic University of America, 1993.

– *Origen: Homilies on Genesis and Exodus*. Washington, DC: Catholic University of America Press, 1982.

Himmelfarb, Martha. *Ascent to Heaven in Jewish and Christian Apocalypses*. New York: Oxford University Press, 1993.

Hirschman, Marc. "Polemic Literary Units in the Classical Midrashim and Justin Martyr's 'Dialogue with Trypho.'" *Jewish Quarterly Review* 83, nos. 3–4 (Jan.–Apr. 1993): 369–84.

– *Rivalry of Genius: Jewish and Christian Biblical Interpretation in Late Antiquity*. Trans. by Batya Stein. Albany: SUNY Press, 1996.

Holmes, Michael W., ed. *The Apostolic Fathers*. 3rd ed. Grand Rapids, MI: Baker Academic, 2007.

- *The Greek New Testament: SBL Edition*. Atlanta: Society of Biblical Literature, 2010.

Horbury, William. *Jewish War under Trajan and Hadrian*. Cambridge University Press, 2014.

Horden, Peregrine, and Nicholas Purcell. *The Corrupting Sea: A Study of Mediterranean History*. Oxford: Blackwell Publishing, 2000.

Hurst, L.D. *The Epistle to the Hebrews: Its Background of Thought*. Cambridge: Cambridge University Press, 1990.

Hurtado, Larry W. *Lord Jesus Christ: Devotion to Jesus in Earliest Christianity*. Grand Rapids, MI: Eerdmans, 2003.

- *One God, One Lord: Early Christian Devotion and Ancient Jewish Monotheism*. 2nd ed. London: T&T Clark, 1998. First published by Augsburg Fortress, 1988.

Idel, Moshe. *Ascensions on High in Jewish Mysticism: Pillars, Lines, Ladders*. New York: Central European University Press, 2005.

Irigaray, Luce. *Speculum of the Other Woman*. Trans. by Gillian C. Gill. Ithaca, NY: Cornell University Press, 1985.

Itter, Andrew C. *Esoteric Teaching in the* Stromateis *of Clement of Alexandria*. Leiden: Brill, 2009.

James, William. *The Varieties of Religious Experience: A Study in Human Nature: Being the Gifford Lectures on Natural Religion Delivered at Edinburgh in 1901–1902*. New York: Modern Library, 1999.

Jameson, Frederic. "Metacommentary." *PMLA* 86, no. 1 (Jan. 1971): 9–18.

Janowitz, Naomi. *The Poetics of Ascent: Theories of Language in a Rabbinic Ascent Text*. Albany, NY: State University of New York Press, 1989.

Jantzen, Grace. "Feminists, Philosophers, and Mystics." *Feminist Philosophy of Religion* 9, no. 4 (Autumn 1994): 186–206.

- *Power, Gender, and Christian Mysticism*. Cambridge, UK: Cambridge University Press, 1995.

Johnson, Luke Timothy. *Hebrews: A Commentary*. Louisville, KY: Westminster John Knox Press, 2006.

Jones, A.H.M. *Constantine and the Conversion of Europe*. Toronto: University of Toronto Press, 1978. First published by Macmillan, 1948.

Junod, Eric. "Moïse, exemple de la perfection selon Grégoire de Nysse." In *La figure de Moïse: ecriture et relectures*, edited by Robert Martin-Achard, 81–98. Geneva: Labor et Fides, 1978.

Kalleres, Dayna S. *City of Demons: Violence, Ritual, and Christian Power in Late Antiquity*. Berkeley: University of California Press, 2015.

Kenney, John Peter. *The Mysticism of St. Augustine: Rereading the Confessions.* New York: Routledge, 2005.

King, J. Christopher. *Origen on the Song of Songs as the Spirit of Scripture: The Bridegroom's Perfect Marriage-Song.* Oxford: Oxford University Press, 2005.

King, Karen L. *What Is Gnosticism?* Cambridge, MA: Belknapp Press of Harvard University Press, 2003.

Koester, Craig R. *Hebrews.* Anchor Bible 36. New York: Doubleday, 2001.

Kolbet, Paul R. "Torture and Origen's Hermeneutics of Nonviolence." *Journal of the American Academy of Religion* 76, no. 3 (Sept. 2008): 545–72.

Koosed, Jennifer L. ed. *The Bible and Posthumanism.* Atlanta: Society of Biblical Literature Press, 2014.

Kovacs, Judith L. "Concealment and Gnostic Exegesis: Clement of Alexandria's Interpretation of the Tabernacle." *Studia Patristica* 31 (1995): 414–37.

Kugel, James L. *How to Read the Bible: A Guide to Scripture, Then and Now.* New York: Free Press, 2007.

– *In Potiphar's House: The Interpretive Life of Biblical Texts.* Boston: Harvard University Press, 1994.

– *The Ladder of Jacob: Ancient Interpretations of the Biblical Story of Jacob and His Children.* Princeton: Princeton University Press, 2006.

Lampe, Peter. *From Paul to Valentinus: Christians at Rome in the First Two Centuries.* Minneapolis, MN: Fortress Press, 2003.

Lawson, R.P. *Origen: The Song of Songs: Commentary and Homilies.* Ancient Christian Writers 26. Newman Press, 1957.

Layton, Bentley. *The Gnostic Scriptures.* New York: Doubleday, 1987.

Le Boulluec, Alain. *Alexandrie antique et chrétienne: Clément et Origène.* Revised 2nd ed. Paris: Institut d'Études Augustiniennes, 2012.

– *Clément d'Alexandrie: Les Stromates: Stromate V.* Sources Chrétiennes 278. Paris: Cerf, 2006.

– *Clément d'Alexandrie: Les Stromates: Stromate VII.* Sources Chrétiennes 428. Paris: Cerf, 1997.

Lesses, Rebecca Macy. *Ritual Practices to Gain Power: Angels, Incantations, and Revelation in Early Jewish Mysticism.* Harrisburg, PA: Trinity Press International, 1998.

Levison, John R. "Inspiration and the Divine Spirit in the Writings of Philo Judaeus." *Journal for the Study of Judaism* 26, no. 3 (1995): 271–323.

Lierman, John. *The New Testament Moses: Christian Perceptions of Moses and Israel in the Setting of Jewish Religion.* Tübingen: Mohr Siebeck, 2004.

Lieu, Judith. *Image and Reality: The Jews in the World of the Christians in the Second Century.* London: T&T Clark, 1996.

– *Marcion and the Making of a Heretic: God and Scripture in the Second Century*. Cambridge, UK: Cambridge University Press, 2015.

Lilla, Salvatore R.C. *Clement of Alexandria: A Study in Christian Platonism and Gnosticism*. Oxford: Oxford University Press, 1971.

Lim, Richard. "The Politics of Interpretation in Basil of Caesarea's 'Hexaemeron.'" *Vigiliae Christianae* 44, no. 4 (Dec. 1990): 351–70.

Long, A.A. "Soul and Body in Stoicism." *Phronesis* 27, no. 1 (1982): 34–57.

Luneau, Auguste. "Moïse et les pères latins" In *Moïse: L'homme de l'alliance*, edited by H. Cazelles, et al., 283–303. Paris: Desclée & Co., 1955.

Lyman, J. Rebecca. *Christology and Cosmology: Models of Divine Activity in Origen, Eusebius, and Athanasius*. Oxford: Clarendon Press, 1993.

Maher, Michael. *Targum Pseudo-Jonathan: Genesis: Translated, with Introduction and Notes*. The Aramaic Bible, Vol. 1B. Collegeville, MI: Liturgical Press, 1992.

Malherbe, Abraham J. "Apologetic and Philosophy in the Second Century." In *Light from the Gentiles: Hellenistic Philosophy and Early Christianity: Collected Essays, 1959–2012, by Abraham Malherbe*, Vol. 2, edited by Carl R. Holladay, John T. Fitzgerald, Gregory E. Sterling, and James W. Thompson, 782–90. Leiden: Brill, 2014.

– "Justin and Crescens." In *Light from the Gentiles: Hellenistic Philosophy and Early Christianity: Collected Essays, 1959–2012, by Abraham Malherbe*, Vol. 2, edited by Carl R. Holladay, John T. Fitzgerald, Gregory E. Sterling, James W. Thompson, 883–94. Leiden: Brill, 2014.

Marcovich, Miroslav. *Clementis Alexandrini: Paedagogus*. Supplements to Vigiliae Christianae 61. Leiden: Brill, 2002.

– *Clementis Alexandrini: Protreptricus*. Supplements to Vigiliae Christianae 34. Leiden: Brill, 1995.

– *Iustini Martyris: Apologiae pro Christianis*. Berlin: Walter de Gruyter, 1994.

– *Iustini Martyris: Dialogos cum Tryphone*. Berlin: Walter de Gruyter, 1997.

– *Origenes: Contra Celsum: Libri VIII*. Leiden: Brill, 2001.

– *Theophili Antiocheni ad Autolycum*. Berlin: De Gruyter, 1995.

Mark, Elizabeth Wyner. "Crossing the Gender Divide: Public Ceremonies, Private Parts, Mixed Feelings." In *The Covenant of Circumcision: New Perspectives on an Ancient Jewish Rite*, edited by Elizabeth Wyner Mark, xii–xxvi. Brandeis Series on Jewish Women. Lebanon, NH: Brandeis University Press, 2003.

Marmorstein, Arthur. *The Old Rabbinic Doctrine of God*. Vol. 2: *Essays in Anthropomorphism*. London: Oxford, 1937.

Marquis, Timothy Lukhritz. *Transient Apostle: Paul, Travel, and the Rhetoric of Empire*. New Haven: Yale University Press, 2013.

Martens, Peter W. *Origen and Scripture: The Contours of an Exegetical Life*. Oxford: Oxford University Press, 2012.

Martin, Dale B. *The Corinthian Body*. New Haven: Yale University Press, 1995.

Martin-Achard, Robert, et al. *La figure de Moïse: ecriture et relectures*. Geneva: Labor et Fides, 1978.

– "Moïse, figure du médiateur selon l'Ancien Testament." In *La figure de Moïse*, edited by Robert Martin-Achard, 9–30. Geneva: Labor et Fides, 1978.

Martínez, Florentino García, and Eibert J.C. Tigchelaar. *The Dead Sea Scrolls: Study Edition*, Vol. 2. Leiden: Brill; Grand Rapids, MI: Eerdmans, 1998.

Martyn, J. Louis. *History and Theology in the Fourth Gospel*. 3rd ed. Louisville, KY: Westminster John Knox, 2003.

Marx-Wolf, Heidi. *Spiritual Taxonomies and Ritual Authority: Platonists, Priests, and Gnostics in the Third Century CE*. Philadelphia: University of Pennsylvania Press, 2016.

McCarthy, Michael C. "'We Are Your Books': Augustine, the Bible, and the Practice of Authority." *Journal of the American Academy of Religion* 75, no. 2 (June 2007): 324–52.

McGinn, Bernard. *The Presence of God: A History of Western Mysticism*. Vol. 1: *The Foundations of Mysticism*. New York: Crossroad, 1991.

McGrath, James F. *The Only True God: Early Christian Monotheism in Its Jewish Context*. Urbana, IL: University of Illinois Press, 2009.

McGuckin, John A. "Origen's Doctrine of the Priesthood: I." *Clergy Review* 70 (1985): 277–86.

– *St Gregory of Nazianzus: An Intellectual Biography*. Crestwood, New York: St Vladimir's Seminary Press, 2001.

– *The Transfiguration of Christ in Scripture and Tradition*. Studies in the Bible and Early Christianity 9. Lewiston/Queenston: Edwin Mellen Press, 1986.

McNamara, Martin. *Targum Neofiti 1: Genesis: Translated, with Apparatus and Notes*. The Aramaic Bible, Volume 1A. Collegeville, MI: Liturgical Press, 1992.

McVey, Kathleen E. "The Use of Stoic Cosmogony in Theophilus of Antioch's *Hexaemeron*." In *Biblical Hermeneutics in Historical Perspective: Studies in Honor of Karlfried Froehlich on his Sixtieth Birthday*, edited by M.S. Burrows and P. Rorem, 32–58. Grand Rapids, MI: Eerdmans, 1991.

Meeks, Wayne. "Moses as God and King." In *Religions in Antiquity: Essays in Memory of Erwin Ramsdell Goodenough*, edited by Jacob Neusner, 354–71. Leiden: Brill, 1968.

– *The Prophet-King: Moses Traditions and the Johannine Christology*. Leiden: Brill, 1967.

Meeks, Wayne, and Robert L. Wilken. *Jews and Christians in Antioch: In the First Four Centuries of the Common Era*. SBL Sources for Biblical Study 13. Missoula, MT: Scholars Press, 1978.

Méla, Charles, and Frédéric Möri, eds., in collaboration with Sydney H. Aufrère, Gilles Dorival, and Alain le Boulluec. *Alexandrie la divine*. 2 Vols. Geneva: LaBaconnière, 2014.

Metzger, Marcel. *Les Constitutions apostoliques*. Vol. 1, Books 1 and 2. Sources Chrétiennes 320. Paris: Latour-Maubourg, 1985.

Miles, Margaret. *Augustine on the Body*. Eugene, OR: Wipf & Stock, 2009. First published by American Academy of Religion, 1979.

– *Desire and Delight: A New Reading of Augustine's Confessions*. New York: Crossroads, 1992.

– "Sex and the City (of God): Is Sex Forfeited or Fulfilled in Augustine's Resurrection of Body?" *Journal of the American Academy of Religion* 73, no. 2 (2005): 307–27.

– "Vision: The Eye of the Body and the Eye of the Mind in Saint Augustine's 'De Trinitate' and 'Confessions.'" *Journal of Religion* 63, no. 2 (April 1983): 125–42.

Miller, Patricia Cox. "'Pleasure of the Text, Text of Pleasure': Eros and Language in Origen's Commentary on the Song of Songs." *Journal of the American Academy of Religion* 54, no. 2 (1986): 241–53.

Moessner, David P. "Luke 9:1–50: Luke's Preview of the Journey of the Prophet Like Moses of Deuteronomy." *Journal of Biblical Literature* 102, no. 4 (Dec. 1983): 575–605.

Moll, Sebastian. "Justin and the Pontic Wolf." In *Justin Martyr and His Worlds*, edited by Sara Parvis and Paul Foster, 145–51. Minneapolis, MI: Fortress Press, 2007.

Moore, Stephen D. *Gospel Jesuses and Other Nonhumans: Biblical Criticism Post-poststructualism*. Atlanta, GA: SBL Press, 2017.

– *Untold Tales from the Book of Revelation: Sex and Gender, Empire and Ecology*. Atlanta, GA: SBL Press, 2014.

Morray-Jones, Christopher R.A. "The Temple Within." In *Paradise Now: Essays on Early Jewish and Christian Mysticism*, edited by April D. DeConick, 145–78. SBL Symposium Series 11. Atlanta: Society of Biblical Literature, 2006.

Mueller, Joseph G. *L'Ancien Testament dans l'ecclésiologie des pères: une lecture des constitutions apostoliques*. Brepols, 2004.

Mulvey, Laura. "Visual Pleasure in Narrative Cinema." *Screen* 16 (Autumn 1975): 6–18.

Nasrallah, Laura. *An Ecstasy of Folly: Prophecy and Authority in Early Chris-

tianity. Harvard Theological Studies 52. Cambridge, MA: Harvard University Press, 2003.

Neihardt, John G. *Black Elk Speaks: Being the Life Story of a Holy Man of the Oglala Sioux*. Lincoln, NE: University of Nebraska Press, 2004.

Nickelsburg, George W.E., and James C. VanderKam. *1 Enoch: A New Translation*. Minneapolis, MI: Fortress Press, 2004.

Osborn, Eric. *Clement of Alexandria*. Cambridge, UK: Cambridge University Press, 2005.

– *Irenaeus of Lyons*. Cambridge, UK: Cambridge University Press, 2001.

– "The Subtlety of Tertullian." *Vigiliae Christianae* 52, no. 4 (Nov. 1998): 361–70.

– *Tertullian: First Theologian of the West*. Cambridge, UK: Cambridge University Press, 1997.

Otto, Rudolf. *The Idea of the Holy: An Inquiry into the Non-rational Factor in the Idea of the Divine and Its Relation to the Rational*. Trans. by John W. Harvey. London: Oxford University Press, 1923.

Parvis, Paul. "Who Was Irenaeus? An Introduction to the Man and His Work." In *Irenaeus: Life, Scripture, Legacy*, edited by Paul Foster and Sara Parvis, 13–25. Minneapolis, MI: Fortress Press, 2012.

Pearson, Birger A. *Gnosticism and Christianity in Roman and Coptic Egypt*. New York: T&T Clark, 2004.

Pettis, Jeff. "Fiery Twins: James, John, and the Sons of Zeus." Paper Presented in the Mysticism, Esotericism, and Gnosticism in Antiquity Unit at the Society of Biblical Literature. Denver, Colorado, November 18, 2018.

Powell, Mark Allan. "Do and Keep What Moses Says (Matthew 23:2–7)." *Journal of Biblical Literature* 114, no. 3 (Autumn 1995): 419–35.

Presley, Stephen O. "Irenaeus and the Exegetical Roots of Trinitarian Theology." In *Irenaeus: Life, Scripture, Legacy*, edited by Paul Foster and Sara Parvis, 165–71. Minneapolis, MI: Fortress Press, 2012.

Rapp, Claudia. *Holy Bishops in Late Antiquity: The Nature of Christian Leadership in an Age of Transition*. Berkeley: University of California Press, 2013.

Reed, Annette Yoshiko. "ΕΥΕΙΓΓΕΛΙΟΝ: Orality, Textuality, and the Christian Truth in Irenaeus' *Adversus Haereses*." *Vigiliae Christianae* 56, no. 1 (Feb. 2002): 11–46.

– *Fallen Angels and the History of Judaism and Christianity: The Reception of Enochic Literature*. Cambridge, UK: Cambridge University Press, 2005.

Ridings, Daniel. "Clement of Alexandria and the Intended Audience of the *Stromateis*." *Studia Patristica* 31 (1995): 517–21.

Robertson, R.G., trans. "Ezekiel the Tragedian." In *The Old Testament Pseude-*

pigrapha, Vol. 2, edited by James H. Charlesworth, 803–19. New York: Doubleday, 1985.

Rousseau, Philip. *Basil of Caesarea*. Berkeley: University of California Press, 1994.

Rowland, Christopher. *The Open Heaven: A Study of Apocalyptic in Judaism and Early Christianity*. London: SPCK Publishing, 1982.

– "The Visions of God in Apocalyptic Literature." *Journal for the Study of Judaism in the Persian, Hellenistic, and Roman Period* 10, no. 2 (1979): 137–54.

Rubenson, Samuel. *The Letters of St. Antony: Monasticism and the Making of a Saint*. Minneapolis, MI: Fortress Press, 1995.

Rubenstein, Jeffrey L. *The Culture of the Babylonian Talmud*. Baltimore: Johns Hopkins University Press, 2003.

– *Rabbinic Stories*. Classics in Western Spirituality. New York: Paulist Press, 2002.

– *Talmudic Stories: Narrative Art, Composition, and Culture*. Baltimore: Johns Hopkins University Press, 1999.

Runia, David T. "God and Man in Philo of Alexandria." *Journal of Theological Studies*, New Series 39 (1988): 49–75.

– *Philo in Early Christian Literature: A Survey*. Minneapolis: Fortress Press, 1993.

Sanford, Eva Matthews, and William McAllen Green. *Saint Augustine: The City of God against the Pagans*. Vol. 5 of 7, Loeb Classical Library 415. Cambridge, MA: Harvard University Press, 1965.

Segal, Alan F. "Heavenly Ascent in Hellenistic Judaism, Early Christianity, and Their Environment." In *The Other Judaisms of Late Antiquity*, 179–252. 2nd ed. Waco, TX: Baylor University Press, 2017. First published in *Aufstieg und Niedergang und Römischen Welt* 23, no. 2 (Berlin: De Gruyter, 1980): 1333–94.

– *Paul the Convert: The Apostolate and Apostasy of Saul the Pharisee*. New Haven: Yale University Press, 1990.

– *Rebecca's Children: Judaism and Christianity in the Roman World*. Cambridge, MA: Harvard University Press, 1986.

– *Two Powers in Heaven: Early Rabbinic Reports about Christianity and Gnosticism*. Leiden: Brill, 1977.

Schäfer, Peter. *Hidden and Manifest God: Some Major Themes in Early Jewish Mysticism*. Trans. by A. Pomerance. Albany, NY: State University of New York Press, 1992.

– *The History of the Jews in the Greco-Roman World*. Rev. ed. London: Routledge, 2003.

– *The Origins of Jewish Mysticism*. Princeton, NJ: Princeton University Press, 2011.

Schäfer, Peter, in collaboration with M. Schlüter and H.G. von Mutius. *Synopse zur Hekhalot Literatur*. Tübingen: Mohr Siebeck, 1981.

Schenck, Kenneth L. *Cosmology and Eschatology in Hebrews: The Settings of the Sacrifice*. Cambridge, UK: Cambridge University Press, 2007.

Schoedel, William R. "Philosophy and Rhetoric in the *Adversus Haereses* of Irenaeus." *Vigiliae Christianae* 13 (1959): 22–32.

– "Theophilus of Antioch: Jewish Christian?" *Illinois Classical Studies* 18 (1993): 279–97.

Scholem, Gershom. *Major Trends in Jewish Mysticism*. New York: Schocken Books, 1995.

Scholer, John M. *Proleptic Priests: Priesthood in the Epistle to the Hebrews*. JSNTSS 49. Sheffield: JSOT Press, 1991.

Secord, Jared. "The Cultural Geography of a Greek Christian: Irenaeus from Smyrna to Lyons." In *Irenaeus: Life, Scripture, Legacy*, edited by Paul Foster and Sara Parvis, 25–33. Minneapolis, MI: Fortress Press, 2012.

Shaw, Brent D. "Passion of Perpetua." *Past and Present* 139 (1993): 3–45.

Shuve, Karl. *The Song of Songs and the Fashioning of Identity in Early Latin Christianity*. Oxford: Oxford University Press, 2016.

Skarsaune, Oskar. "Justin and His Bible." In *Justin Martyr and His Worlds*, edited by Sara Parvis and Paul Foster, 53–76. Minneapolis, MI: Fortress Press, 2007.

– *The Proof from Prophecy: A Study in Justin Martyr's Proof-Text Tradition: Text, Type, Provenance, Theological Profile*. Leiden: Brill, 1987.

Slusser, Michael. "The Heart of Irenaeus's Theology." In *Irenaeus: Life, Scripture, Legacy*, edited by Paul Foster and Sara Parvis, 133–9. Minneapolis, MI: Fortress Press, 2012.

– "How Much Did Irenaeus Learn from Justin?" *Studia Patristica* 40 (2006): 515–20.

Smith, J. Warren. "The Body of Paradise and the Body of the Resurrection: Gender and the Angelic Life in Gregory of Nyssa's 'De hominis opificio.'" *Harvard Theological Review* 99, no. 2 (Apr. 2006): 207–28.

Smith, Morton. "The History of the Term 'Gnostikos.'" In *The Rediscovery of Gnosticism II: Sethian Gnosticism: Proceedings of the International Conference on Gnosticism at Yale New Haven, Connecticut, March 28–31, 1979*, edited by Bentley Layton, 796–807. Leiden: Brill, 1981.

Stählin, Otto. *Clemens Alexandrinus*. Vol. 3. Leipzig: J.C. Hinrich's Buchhandlung, 1909.

Stählin, Otto, Ludwig Früchtel, and Ursula Treu, *Clemens Alexandrinus.* Vol. 2. Berlin: Akademie Verlag, 1985.

Starobinski-Safran, Esther. "La prophétie de Moïse et sa portée d'après Philon." In *La figure de Moïse: ecriture et relectures,* edited by Robert Martin-Achard, 67–80. Geneva: Labor et Fides, 1978.

Steenberg, Irenaeus M.C. "Tracing the Irenaean Legacy." In *Irenaeus: Life, Scripture, Legacy,* edited by Paul Foster and Sara Parvis. 199–211. Minneapolis, MI: Fortress Press, 2012.

Sterk, Andrea. "On Basil, Moses, and the Model Bishop: The Cappadocian Legacy of Leadership." *Church History* 67, no. 2 (1998): 227–53.

– *Renouncing the World, Yet Leading the Church: The Monk-Bishop of Late Antiquity.* Cambridge, MA: Harvard University Press, 2004.

Sterling, Gregory E. "'Opening the Scriptures': The Legitimation of the Jewish Diaspora and the Early Christian Mission." In *Jesus and the Heritage of Israel: Luke's Narrartive Claim upon Israel's Legacy,* edited by David P. Moessner, 199–225. Harrisburg, PA: Trinity Press International, 1999.

Stern, David. "Imitatio Hominis: Anthropomorphism and the Character(s) of God in Rabbinic Literature." *Prooftexts* 12, no. 2 (May 1992): 151–74.

Stratton, Kimberly B. *Naming the Witch: Magic, Ideology, and Stereotype in the Ancient World.* New York: Columbia University Press, 2007.

Stroumsa, Guy G. *Hidden Wisdom: Esoteric Traditions and the Roots of Christian Mysticism.* 2nd ed. Leiden: Brill, 2005.

Swartz, Michael. *Mystical Prayer in Ancient Judaism: An Analysis of Ma'aseh Merkavah.* Tübingen: Mohr Siebeck, 1992.

Taylor, John Hammond, SJ, trans. *St. Augustine: The Literal Meaning of Genesis.* 2 vols. New York: Paulist Press, 1982.

Thompson, Marianne Meye. "Jesus: 'The One Who Sees God.'" In *Israel's God and Rebecca's Children: Christology and Community in Early Judaism and Christianity: Essays in Honor of Larry W. Hurtado and Alan F. Segal,* edited by David B. Capes, April D. DeConick, Helen K. Bond, and Troy A. Miller, 215–26. Waco, TX: Baylor University Press, 2007.

Tonneau, Raymond Marie. "Moïse dans la tradition syrienne." In *Moïse: L'homme de l'alliance,* edited by H. Cazelles, et al., 245–65. Paris: Desclée & Co., 1955.

Torjesen, Karen Jo. *Hermeneutical Procedure and Theological Method in Origen's Exegesis.* Berlin: de Gruyter, 1986.

Traketellis, Demetrius C. "Justin Martyr's Trypho." *Harvard Theological Review* 59, no. 1–3 (Jan.–Jul. 1986): 287–97.

– *The Pre-Existence of Christ in Justin Martyr: An Exegetical Study with Refer-*

ence to the Humiliation and Exaltation Christology. Harvard Dissertations in Religion 6. Missoula, MT: Scholars Press, 1976.

Treadgold, Warren. *A History of the Byzantine State and Society*. Palo Alto, CA: Stanford University Press, 1997.

Trigg, Joseph W. "Receiving the Alpha: Negative Theology in Clement of Alexandria and Its Possible Implications." *Studia Patristica* 31 (1995): 540–5.

Turner, Denys. *The Darkness of God: Negativity in Christian Mysticism*. Cambridge, UK: Cambridge University Press, 1995.

Urbach, E.E. *The Sages: Their Concepts and Beliefs*. Translated by Israel Abrahams. Cambridge, MA: Harvard University Press, 1975.

– "The Traditions about Merkabah Mysticism in the Tannaitic Period." In *Studies in Mysticism and Religion Presented to Gershom Scholem* (Hebrew section), edited by Ephraim E. Urbach, R.J. Zvi Werblowsky, and Chaim Wirszubski, 1–28. Jerusalem: Magnes, 1967.

van den Hoek, Annewies. "The 'Catechetical' School of Early Alexandria and its Philonic Heritage." *Harvard Theological Review* 90, no. 1 (1997): 59–87.

– *Clement of Alexandria and His Use of Philo in the* Stromateis: *An Early Christian Reshaping of a Jewish Model*. Supplements to Vigiliae Christianae 3. Leiden: Brill, 1988.

van der Horst, P. "Moses' Throne Vision in Ezekiel the Dramatist." *Journal of Jewish Studies* 34 (1983): 21–9.

Vermes, Geza. "La figure de Moïse au tournant des deux testaments." In *Moïse: L'homme de l'alliance*, edited by H. Cazelles, et al., 63–92. Paris: Desclée & Co., 1955.

von Harnack, Adolf. *Marcion: The Gospel of the Alien God*. Translated by John E. Steely and Lyle D. Bierma. Eugene, OR: Wipf & Stock, 2007. First published by Baker Books, 1990.

von Rad, Gerhard. *Moses*. 2nd ed. Edited by K.C. Hanson. Eugene, OR: Cascade Books, 2011.

von Stritzky, Maria-Barbara. *Origenes: Aufforderung zum Martyrium*. Berlin: De Gruyter, 2010.

Watts, William. *St. Augustine's Confessions*. 2 vols. London: William Heinemann, 1912.

Wendt, Heidi. *At the Temple Gates: The Religion of Freelance Experts in the Roman Empire*. Oxford: Oxford University Press, 2016.

Wiesen, David S. *Saint Augustine: The City of God against the Pagans*. Vol. 3. Loeb Classical Library. Cambridge: Harvard University Press, 1968.

Williams, Frederick, and Lionel Wickham, trans. *St. Gregory of Nazianzus: On God and Christ: The Five Theological Orations and Two Letters to Cledonius*. Crestwood, NY: St Vladimir's Seminary Press, 2002.

Williams, Michael Allen. *Rethinking "Gnosticism": An Argument for Dismantling a Dubious Category*. Princeton, NJ: Princeton University Press, 1996.

Whitlark, Jason A. *Resisting Empire: Rethinking the Purpose of the Letter to "the Hebrews."* London: Bloomsbury/T&T Clark, 2014.

Williamson, G.A., trans. *Eusebius: The History of the Church from Christ to Constantine*. Revised and edited. London: Penguin Books, 1965, 1989.

Wilson, Stephen G. "Marcion and Boundaries." In *Crossing Boundaries in Early Judaism and Christianity: Ambiguities, Complexities, and Half-Forgotten Adversaries: Essays in Honor of Alan F. Segal*, edited by Kimberly B. Stratton and Andrea Lieber, 200–20. Leiden: Brill, 2016.

Winston, David. *Logos and Mystical Theology in Philo of Alexandria*. Cincinnati, OH: Hebrew Union College Press, 1985.

– "Two Types of Mosaic Prophecy According to Philo." *Journal for the Study of the Pseudepigrapha* 4 (1989): 49–67.

Wolfson, Elliot R. "Circumcision, Vision of God, and Textual Interpretation: From Midrashic Trope to Mystical Symbol." *History of Religions* 27 (1987): 189–215.

– *Language, Eros, Being: Kabbalistic Hermeneutics and Poetic Imagination*. New York: Fordham University Press, 2004.

– *Through a Speculum That Shines: Vision and Imagination in Medieval Mysticism*. Princeton, NJ: Princeton University Press, 1994.

– "*Yeridah la-Merkavah*: Typology of Ecstasy and Enthronement in Ancient Jewish Mysticism." In *Mystics of the Book: Themes, Topics, and Typologies*, edited by R.A. Herrera, 13–44. New York: Peter Lang, 1993.

Yonge, C.D. *The Works of Philo: Complete and Unabridged*. Updated edition. Peabody, MA: Hendrickson, 1993.

Zetterholm, Magnus. *The Formation of Christianity in Antioch: A Social-Scientific Approach to the Separation Between Judaism and Christianity*. London: Routledge, 2003.

Index

1 Clement, 339n14
1 Corinthians, 81
1 John, 74–5
1 Timothy, 66 –7
2 Corinthians, 79–81

Abraham, 28, 30–1, 33–4, 51–4, 76,
    93–4, 98–9, 113–14, 119, 140,
    142–3, 164, 172, 183, 217–18,
    275n30
Acts of the Apostles, 77–9
Adam, 107–8, 216–17, 354n16
Alexandria, 34, 132–3, 151
Allison, Dale, 9, 81, 274–5n27
Ambrose of Milan, 213, 222–3
Amos, 28
angel of the LORD, 25–7, 47, 75–6,
    90–3, 96, 99–100, 137, 172, 245,
    273n17, 273n19, 274n23, 302n55
angelification, 33, 146, 149, 164, 166,
    198–9, 220–4, 263. *See also* deifica-
    tion; transformation
anthropomorphisms, 5, 26, 91, 93,
    98, 107, 182, 192, 255
anti-Jewish polemics, 89, 94–5,
    101–3, 105, 117–18, 128–9, 155,
    158, 167, 251, 255

Antioch, 105, 109
Antiochus of Ascalon, 322–3n15
Antony, 346n70
Apocalypse of John. *See* Revelation,
    Book of
apocalypses, 6, 30–3, 93, 133, 241
apologetics: Christian, 85–6, 100–3,
    105–6, 108–10, 151, 155, 189,
    254–5, 257–9, 261; Hellenistic
    Jewish, 24, 35, 44–6, 62, 100,
    105–6, 108–10, 142–3, 145, 151,
    225, 233, 252, 332–3n55
Apostolic Constitutions, 7–8, 193–7,
    201, 243, 247
Arbel, Daphna, 289n195
Arianism, 217, 247, 339n12. *See also*
    subordinationism, Christology
Artapanus, 31–2
Ascension of Isaiah, 31
Augustine of Hippo, 18, 213–34,
    241–2, 244, 247–8, 253, 260, 263,
    354n16, 354nn19–20

Bar Kokhba Revolt, 101–2
Barnard, Leslie, 300n28, 302–3n61
Basil of Caesarea, 191, 197–200, 205,
    213, 242–3, 247, 260, 263, 345n66

Basilides, 132, 136, 146, 151–2, 255
Beeley, Christopher, 200, 204
Berkowitz, Beth, 16
Borgen, Peder, 43
Boyarin, Daniel, 98, 272n3, 286n156, 302–3n61
Brock, Sebastian, 20
Brown, Peter, 221
Brown, Raymond, 67–8
Bucur, Bogdan, 133–5, 148–9

Carthage, 154
Chalcedon, Council of, 3, 200
Choufrine, Arkadi, 320–1n74
Clark, Elizabeth, 15, 256
Clement of Alexandria, 128, 132–53, 189, 215, 219, 240–1, 243–6, 248–50, 253–4, 258, 263, 316n39, 319n59, 320–1n74, 322–3n15
Constantine, 191, 194, 197–8, 261, 338n7
Constantinople, Council of, 194, 201, 204–5
Crouzel, Henri, 332n47

D'Angelo, Mary Rose, 70
Daniel, 30, 93
Daniélou, Jean, 170
de Certeau, Michel, 10–11
Dead Sea Scrolls, 23, 32, 34, 272n5
Debord, Guy, 268–9n32
DeConick, April, 292n35, 302n55
deification, 32, 34–5, 39–40, 64, 74–5, 123–7, 138–9, 148–51, 181, 263, 320–1n74
Derrida, Jacques, 4
Deuteronomistic History, 28, 275nn31–3
Deuteronomy, 28–9
Deutsch, Celia, 184, 335–6n80

Diaspora Revolt, 132
Drake, H.A., 337–8n2, 338n7

Eleusinian mysteries, 18, 345n68
Elijah, 82–3, 116, 122, 275n31
Enoch, 30, 93, 276n43
episcopal authority, 101, 105, 111–12, 129–30, 170, 191–212, 213–14, 242–3, 254, 259–61, 337–8n2, 338n7
Eunomius/Eunomians, 201–5, 261
Eusebius of Caesarea, 105, 132, 169, 194, 198, 247, 338n6
Ezekiel, 26–7, 57, 121, 274n22
Ezekiel the Tragedian, 32–3

faith. See *pistis*
Fletcher-Louis, Crispin, 34
Fossum, Jarl, 96
freelance ritual experts, 86, 101, 129–30, 152–3, 154, 168–9, 187, 249, 253–4, 258, 321n3. *See also* Wendt, Heidi
Freud, Sigmund, 266n6

Galatians, Epistle to, 76, 293n61
Galen, 322–3n15
Gelin, A., 5–6
genealogical method, 11–13
Gideon, 25, 92
Gieschen, Charles, 6, 91, 99–100, 245
glory of the LORD, 26–7, 30–1, 68–9, 74, 80–1, 93, 96, 162, 222, 274n22, 274–5n27, 292n35
gnosis/gnostic, 133, 136, 139, 145–53, 240, 243, 258, 263, 316n39, 320–1n74. *See also* Clement of Alexandria
God: angel, appearing as, 38,

215–19, 231, 247–8, 253, 326n4;
angels, speaking through, 133–5,
246, 253; backsides of, 5, 24, 41,
94, 97, 116–18, 121, 162, 181–2,
187, 192, 202–3, 205, 210,
318–19n58, 332–3n55; image of,
36–7, 80–1, 91, 111, 118, 121,
138–9, 151, 159, 173–9, 208–11,
244, 263, 332n47; invisibility of,
36–7, 41, 61, 66–9, 70–1, 84, 88,
103, 106, 108, 140, 142, 145–6,
150, 156–63, 171–82, 186, 189,
206–8, 215–19, 222–4, 235–6, 243,
246–7, 291n14, 354n20; name of,
55–6, 287n168; throne of, 28,
30–2, 45, 54–5, 58, 60, 289n194.
See also seeing God
Goodenough, Erwin R., 94, 300n28,
302–3n61
Gospel of Philip, 17
Grant, Robert, 306n18
Gregory of Nazianzus, 192, 197,
199–206, 242, 247, 260–1,
318–19n58, 345n66, 345n68,
346n79, 347n81
Gregory of Nyssa, 140, 197, 199,
205–11, 242, 247, 260, 342–3n43,
349n118, 350n126, 350n131
Gregory the Wonderworker,
342–3n43
Grossman, Edith, 170

Hagar, 25, 92, 283–4n133, 285n145
Hanson, R.P.C., 189
Hebrews, Epistle of, 70–2, 76–8,
240
Heine, Ronald E., 329–30n26
hekhalot, 54–61, 241–2, 287nn167–8
Hermogenes, 247, 323n17
Hurtado, Larry, 96–7

Ignatius, 101, 105, 130, 196
Iliad, 275n32
incarnation, 90, 103, 113, 116–19,
137, 139, 141, 155, 162–5, 173,
202, 206, 246
interpretation: ancient methods of,
329–30n26; history of, 13–16,
269n41
interpreter as visionary like Moses,
11, 24, 35, 43, 56, 62–3, 145, 152,
169, 171, 183–4, 188–9, 192–3,
199, 204–5, 242, 252, 258, 261,
318–19nn58–9, 329n20, 334n70,
335–6n80, 346n79
Irenaeus of Lyons, 106, 111–31, 133,
139, 155, 158–63, 166, 182, 241,
246, 248–9, 254, 256–7, 262–3
Isaac, 28, 283–4n133
Isaiah, 28, 54–8, 119, 227
Israel: as "one who sees God," 36–7,
279n86
Itter, Andrew C., 147, 319n59

Jacob, 17, 25, 92, 94, 137, 217,
283–4n133
James, William, 11–12, 183–4
Jameson, Frederic, 14–15, 237
Jantzen, Grace, 11–12
Jeremiah, 29
Jerome, 170, 224
John, Gospel of, 66–9
John Chrysostom, 105, 342–3n43
John of Patmos, 121, 127, 158, 208,
227, 241. *See also* Revelation,
Book of
Josephus, 44–6, 282n119
Jubilees, 33–4, 76
Justin Martyr, 86–104, 111, 113–16,
128, 133, 135, 155, 158–9, 163,
166, 172–4, 189, 215–17, 231, 245,

249, 256, 258, 299n20, 306n18, 338n6

Kalleres, Dayna S., 191
King, J. Christopher, 335n80

Levinson, John, 252
Lieu, Judith, 102
Life of Adam and Eve, 44
Lilla, Salvatore, 320–1n74
Logos: as face of God, 134, 137, 148–9; as high priest, 36, 133, 148, 319n59; and Moses, 36–7; as scripture, 173, 331n31; and Stoicism, 94, 151
love of neighbour, 219, 222, 225
Luneau, August, 154
Lyons/Lugdunum, 111–12, 129–30

Manicheans, 221, 232–3
Manoah and his wife, 26, 92, 273n17
Marcion and Marcionites, 86, 88, 92, 94–5, 101–3, 105, 114–15, 128–30, 155–6, 158–60, 162, 167, 172, 174, 189, 255–7
Marcus, 112, 128, 130, 256–7
Martens, Peter W., 334n70
martyrs/martyrdom, 86–7, 111–12, 129–30, 154, 169, 185–6, 189–90, 192–3, 250, 256–9, 323–4n19
McCarthy, Michael C., 214
McGinn, Bernard, 73
McGuckin, John Anthony, 200–1, 204
Micaiah b. Imlah, 28, 275nn32–3
midrashim, 46, 48–54, 99, 239, 242, 245, 339–40n15
Miles, Margaret, 18, 221
Moses: and angels, 7, 71, 75–8, 84, 97, 102, 114–15, 134, 173, 195–6,

203, 215, 218–19, 238, 245, 247, 299n20; ascent of, 45, 55–7, 178, 193, 332–3n55; and burning bush, 24, 31–3, 37–8, 45, 47, 49–50, 70–1, 75, 89, 91, 99, 114, 136, 138, 194, 199, 206, 218, 299n20; and dark cloud, 39–41, 44, 139–41, 144–5, 150, 152, 178–9, 199–200, 202–7, 242, 244, 318–19n58, 332–3n55, 349n118, 352n145; and the elders, 29, 38–9, 47, 49–50, 82, 202, 204, 318–19n58; as first and greatest prophet, 9, 72, 89, 100, 122; glorified/luminous face of, 34, 50, 79–82, 146, 201, 207, 331n31; as god on earth, 194–5, 242–3, 339–40n15; as human limit/model, 3–5, 7, 9–10, 22, 35, 40–1, 43–4, 56, 61, 64, 71–2, 79–80, 84–5, 100, 127–8, 135, 137, 140, 146, 150–1, 153, 166, 184–6, 188–90, 191, 194–212, 235, 238, 242, 248, 252–3, 262–4, 342–3n43; and Jesus, comparisons with, 64–5, 67–9, 71–3, 76–84, 252–3; and Paul, 8, 142–5, 149, 151–2, 160–1, 180, 185–6, 199, 201, 204, 208, 222, 225–30, 241; as Platonic philosopher-king, 35, 43; as proto-Christian, 64, 70; on Sinai, 45, 75, 192–3; and tabernacle, pattern of, 7, 41–3, 71, 78–9, 147, 152, 207, 282n121, 349n118. *See also* seeing God
Mount of Transfiguration, 81–3, 116, 122, 127, 141, 155, 160–2, 166, 180, 186, 246, 326n3

Nag Hammadi codices, 88–9, 102

Nasrallah, Laura, 12–13, 255
Nicaea, Council of, 197, 215, 217, 233–4, 250

Origen, 3, 169–90, 201, 206, 230–1, 241–2, 244, 247, 250, 254, 258–9, 329n20, 329–30n26, 331n31, 332–3n55
Osborn, Eric, 118, 120, 122

Patripassianism. *See* Praxeas
perfection, 125–6, 133, 138, 143–50, 182–3, 187–9, 208, 211, 239–40, 242
Perpetua, 154, 323–4n19
Philo of Alexandria, 34–44, 87, 89, 169, 182, 243, 252, 262–3, 318–19n58, 339–40n15, 352n145; Christian reception of, 93–5, 137, 146, 150–1, 207, 300n28, 319n59; religious experiences of, 35, 44, 252, 278n73
pistis, 136, 146, 151–2, 219, 222, 320–1n74
Plato/Platonism, 18, 41–3, 78, 86, 140–5, 151, 156, 178, 181, 201, 203, 229–30, 258; allegory of the cave, 145, 178, 181; Middle Platonism, 34, 94, 132–3, 151, 243, 322–3n15; philosopher-king, 35, 43, 64; world of forms, 41, 78, 140–5. *See also* Philo of Alexandria
Plotinus, 214, 233, 271n62
Polycarp, 111
Porphyry, 225, 233, 261, 322–3n15
posthumanism, 4
Praxeas, 155–6, 159–60, 167, 257
preincarnate Christophany, 8, 68, 86–104, 107–8, 113–14, 135–9,
150, 155, 158–66, 172–3, 186, 189, 215–19, 245–8, 255, 306n18, 338n6; as auditory, 113–14; as bodiless, 89–90, 100, 103, 153, 246; criticisms of, 215–19, 231; as embodied, 118, 127, 163, 246; as fleshly, 155, 164–7, 246; as foreseeing, 116–22; as mask, 107–8; origins of, 68–9, 92–100; as pedagogical, 120–1, 127, 137–9, 155, 163–7, 172, 246, 248, 338n6; as polymorphic, 89–91, 103, 117–18, 136–7, 172–3, 180, 186, 246
prophecy: theories of, 87–8, 133–5; practice of, 154, 157, 167, 323–4n19
prosopological exegesis. *See* prophecy
Pseudo-Dionysius, 140–1, 197
Pseudo-Philo, 44
Ptolemy, 87–8
purity/purity of heart, 72–5, 106, 109, 116, 123–7, 133, 143–50, 169, 172–89, 200, 202–5, 208–9, 211, 219, 221–5, 238–42, 320–1n74

Qumran. *See* Dead Sea Scrolls

R. Akiva, 54–5, 59–60, 242; and Moses, 9, 55–8, 192–3, 252
R. Ishmael, 54–5, 57–8
R. Nehuniah b. Ha-Kanah, 58, 60
Rapp, Claudia, 191, 194, 213, 337n2
reading networks, 236–7, 249–51
Rebekah, 285n145
reception history. *See* interpretation: history of
Reed, Annette, 15–16, 101, 128
Revelation, Book of, 96–7
Rome, 65, 71, 86–7, 101–2, 249, 256

Rubenstein, Jeffrey, 193
Rufinus, 170
Runia, David T., 169–70,

Sabellianism. *See* Praxeas
sanctuary: cosmic significance of,
     43, 147, 282n119, 282n121; physi-
     cal temple, 77–80
Sarah, 51
Schäfer, Peter, 23, 54, 56, 274n22,
     289n194
Second Discourse of the Great Seth,
     88–9, 102
seeing God: in the afterlife/
     resurrection, 31, 33, 38, 73, 106–7,
     113, 124–6, 144–6, 149, 181,
     185–6, 204–5, 209–10, 219–26,
     230–1, 240–1, 243–4, 320–1n74;
     and circumcision, 48, 51–4, 61–2,
     239, 242, 286n156; dispensations
     of, 113, 119, 122–7, 139; and
     dying, 24, 27, 29–31, 121, 126–7,
     219, 223, 228–9, 231, 240–1,
     289n195; *epopteia*, 18, 144–5, 147,
     151–2; face to face, 5–8, 25, 27,
     29, 33, 44, 47, 49–52, 81, 116, 122,
     127, 137, 142–4, 147, 149–50,
     160–2, 180–1, 186, 195–6, 198,
     215, 221, 227–9, 320–1n74; form
     of, 5–8, 27, 61, 64, 68–9, 71–2, 81,
     88–9, 122, 127, 160–2, 185, 187,
     195–8, 222, 227–9, 235, 237–8,
     242, 252; and Gentiles, 51–4; and
     grace, 142, 149, 177–80, 182, 187,
     222, 227, 239–40; and how one
     sees, 8, 18, 174, 176, 215–16,
     219–31, 243–4; impossibility of,
     5–8, 22–4, 27, 29–30, 33, 41, 44,
     47, 50, 54, 56–7, 59–61, 64–5,
     67–9, 71, 73, 81, 84, 115–17, 121,
     123, 127, 139, 143–4, 156, 159,
     161–3, 174, 198, 208, 227–9, 235,
     237–8, 242–3, 252, 283–4n133;
     and living, 25–30, 60–1, 70, 125,
     156, 235, 238; en masse, 48–9,
     61–2, 227; moral requirements
     for, 48, 50, 57–8, 60, 73–4, 106,
     108, 141–2, 145, 148–50, 176–7,
     179, 209, 211; social dynamics of,
     10–16, 23–4, 32, 34–5, 44, 54, 56,
     62–3, 65, 71, 76, 79, 83, 86–7, 89,
     100–6, 108–10, 111–12, 114–15,
     117–18, 128–31, 136, 151–6,
     158–9, 166–7, 169–70, 172, 174,
     183–4, 187–215, 221, 225, 231–4,
     236–8, 242–3, 248–61, 268–9n32,
     337–8n2, 342–3n43; and status of
     the seer, 8, 10, 23, 62, 72–5, 106–7,
     126–7, 150, 176, 186, 191–212,
     220, 231, 239–43, 248–61; *theoria*,
     8, 18, 35–7, 41, 61, 106, 108–9,
     132–3, 141, 143–50, 169, 171,
     173–89, 202–12, 215–16, 219–31,
     242–4, 338n6, 342–3n43; and
     what one sees, 8, 23, 46–7, 61–2,
     71, 75–8, 86–104, 107–8, 150, 174,
     245–8; and women, 25, 50–4,
     61–2, 154, 157, 167, 230, 232, 239,
     257, 283–4n133, 285n145,
     286n156, 323–4n19. *See also*
     God; Moses; transformation;
     vision
Segal, Alan, 6, 15, 295n79, 300n28
Sermon on the Mount, 72–4
Shuve, Karl, 16
Sirach, 33
Skarsaune, Oskar, 94–7, 299n20
Song of Songs, 53, 183–4
Soranus, 17
source criticism, 6–7

spiritual senses, 157–8, 175–6
spiritual taxonomy, 133–5, 148–51
Starobinski-Safran, Esther, 43
Stephen, 77–9
Sterk, Andrea, 191, 197–8, 200–1, 205, 211–12
Stoicism, 258; allegorical reading, 34–5; ethics, 141–2, 150–1; materialism, 157–8, 165, 246–7. *See also* Logos
subordinationism, Christology, 103, 158–60, 166, 233–4, 246–7, 324n26. *See also* Arianism
Symeon the New Theologian, 352n146
Syriac Christianity, 20

Talmud, 54–5, 192–3
targumim, 46–7, 76, 97–9, 245, 283–4n133, 339–40n15
temple. *See* sanctuary
Tertullian of Carthage, 154–68, 219, 246–50, 257–8, 263, 322n15, 323n17, 323–4n19
Testament of Levi, 30, 93
Testament of Moses, 44
Theophius of Antioch, 105–10, 241, 243, 245, 306n18

theoria. *See* seeing God: *theoria*
Traketellis, Demetrius, 93–4, 302–3n61
transformation, 16–17, 80–1, 117, 208, 262–3, 295n79. *See also* angelification; deification
Trinity, 156, 159–60, 202–3, 210, 217, 219, 248
tripartite matrix of vision, 8–9, 126, 133, 150, 144, 171, 186, 236–48. *See also* seeing God

Valentinus/Valentinians, 86, 88, 114–15, 128–9, 132, 136, 146, 151–2, 189, 255–6
van den Hoek, Annewies, 319n59
vision: extramission, 17–18; feminist critique of, 11–13; intromission, 16–17. *See also* seeing God

Weber, Max, 191, 271n66
Wendt, Heidi, 101, 130, 154, 168–9, 249, 253–4, 321n3. *See also* freelance ritual experts
Whitlark, Jason, 71
Winston, David, 35
Wisdom of Solomon, 95–6, 245
Wolfson, Elliott, 6–7, 22